A POLITICAL AND ECONOMIC DICTIONARY OF THE MIDDLE EAST

A POLITICAL AND ECONOMIC DICTIONARY OF THE MIDDLE EAST

David Seddon

FIRST EDITION

Europa Publications
Taylor & Francis Group

LONDON AND NEW YORK

First Edition 2004
Europa Publications
Haines House, 21 John Street, London WC1N 2BP, United Kingdom
(A member of the Taylor & Francis Group)

© **David Seddon 2004**

ISBN 1 85743 212 6

Development Editor: Cathy Hartley
Copy Editor and Proof-reader: Simon Chapman

Typeset in Times New Roman 10/12

Typeset by AJS Solutions, Huddersfield • Dundee
Printed and bound by MPG Books Ltd, Bodmin, Cornwall

FOREWORD

The boundaries selected for this first *Political and Economic Dictionary of the Middle East* may appear somewhat arbitrary. It is difficult to define precisely 'the Middle East': this foreword attempts to explain the reasoning behind my selection. For the purposes of this Dictionary, the region includes six countries and one disputed territory in North Africa (Mauritania, Morocco, Algeria, Tunisia, Libya, Egypt and Western Sahara), eight countries in Western Asia (Jordan, Israel, Palestine, Lebanon, Syria, Turkey, Iraq and Iran), seven in Arabia (Saudi Arabia, Kuwait, the United Arab Emirates, Oman, Qatar, Bahrain and Yemen), five newly independent states in southern Central Asia (Kazakhstan, Kyrgyzstan, Turkmenistan, Tajikistan and Uzbekistan) and Afghanistan. It also, somewhat controversially, includes the 'Turkish Republic of Northern Cyprus'. (A full treatment of Cyprus will appear in the companion volume *A Political and Economic Dictionary of Western Europe*.)

We have chosen not to include all of the countries where Arabic is spoken, although, arguably, many of the countries of the Sahelian region just south of the Sahara (Mali, Niger, Chad, Sudan), constitute in some sense a part of the 'Arab world', as do Djibouti and Comoros. These countries appear in a companion volume, *A Political and Economic Dictionary of Africa*. We have also chosen not to include Pakistan, despite its close links with Afghanistan, seeing it as more properly treated within the context of South Asia as a whole—although it is not ignored here either. Nor have we included the Caucasus region, despite its links with the Middle East.

We have, by contrast, chosen to include the predominantly Arabic-speaking countries of western North Africa (the Maghreb), including Mauritania (which is a member of the Arab Maghreb Union) and the non-Arabic-speaking countries in the northern part of the region that are sometimes referred to as 'the northern tier'—Turkey, Iran, Afghanistan—and the relatively new independent republics in southern Central Asia, which previously constituted a part of the Union of Soviet Socialist Republics (USSR) or Soviet Union. The countries of Arabia and the Gulf constitute a distinctive yet integral part of the Middle East, while the history and location of Israel, despite its extraordinary characteristics, ensures that it remains, as it has done at least since 1948, at the centre of Middle Eastern politics.

Finally, although the majority of the population of the Middle East consists of Arabic-speaking Muslims, many are members of important ethnic, linguistic and religious minorities, with their own distinctive economic, social, cultural and political concerns, ensuring that the politics and economics of the Middle East are both complex and complicated. This should provide an important counter to any tendency to equate the region with either 'the Arab world' or 'the world of Islam'. In the world of the 21st century, particularly following the events of 11 September 2001, we need to be both more aware of, and at the same time cautious about generalizing from, the complex phenomenon which is 'political Islam'. In the same way, although for many analysts the defining feature of the region is 'the oil economy', which contributes crucially to the global geo-political significance of the region, there are major differences between not only the oil-producing and - exporting countries and those dependent on oil and energy imports within the region, but even between these categories and groupings. While there is a sense in which it is possible to identify a regional economy, in terms of the links provided by flows of capital, commodities and labour within the region, most economies in the region have more important and often arguably defining links outside the region.

It is therefore as dangerous to generalize about the Middle East as it is any region in the world. This is not only because it consists of a considerable number of different and distinct states and territories, each with its own unique history, environment, economy, society and cultural and political characteristics, but also because much depends also on which of these countries and territories is/are included in the generalizations. For example, the Arab Human Development Report, which provides a valuable up-to-date account of the economic, social and political dynamics and status of 'the Arab countries', fails to include the non-Arab countries of the Middle East and therefore cannot strictly be used to make comparisons with other aggregates, such as 'the Middle East and North Africa' or 'the Middle East' as used by other agencies including the United Nations and the World Bank.

If the Middle East is clearly—as this introductory section has attempted to demonstrate—more than the sum of its parts, a full appreciation would require a comprehensive study. That is not the purpose of this book, which is designed rather as a reference work, providing succinct and up-to-date entries for a wide range of political and economic topics, organizations, institutions, individuals, and of course for the countries which together comprise the region.

Entries are arranged alphabetically, and cross-referencing between entries is indicated by the simple and widely familiar device of using a bold typeface for those words or entities which have their own coverage.

The reader is, however, recommended as companions to this Dictionary, the very full reference books provided by, for example, *The Middle East and North Africa* and *Africa South of the Sahara*, also published by Europa Publications, and the Political and Economic Dictionaries of other regions of the world.

David Seddon, October 2004

ACKNOWLEDGEMENTS

Although the main compiler of this Dictionary, I have been assisted by several others, whose help I wish to acknowledge. Firstly, my thanks go to my son, Daniel Seddon, who was involved from the outset and devoted a good deal of his time, before going up to Cambridge to read Geography, providing valuable assistance and support. Then, many thanks to Donna Simpson, Vlad Wexler, Atle Kjosen and Pat Holtom, all of whom took my final year regional course on North African and Middle Eastern Development at the School of Development Studies, acquired an interest in the region and, in some cases (Donna and Atle), spent some time in the region (Lebanon and Egypt respectively) as a consequence. Cathy Hartley was my supportive editor at Europa Publications and Simon Chapman an invaluable copy editor, who dealt admirably with the draft text provided. Omissions and other inadequacies are my responsibility, but readers are invited to make constructive suggestions for future editions.

THE AUTHOR

David Seddon is Professor of Development Studies at the University of East Anglia (UEA).

His disciplinary focus is in politics, political economy, sociology and social anthropology, and his research interests lie in rural development, social welfare, social and popular movements, the political and social implications of macro policy, long-term change, class, race and gender. His geographical focus is Africa, North Africa and the Middle East, South Asia and Eastern Europe.

David Seddon is also the Co-ordinator of the Steering Committee of UEA's new Saharan Studies Programme, a collaboration between the Schools of Development Studies, Environmental Sciences, Medicine, and World Art and Museology.

ABBREVIATIONS

Capt.	Captain	m.	million
Co	Company	Maj.	Major
Col	Colonel	Pres.	President
Corpn	Corporation	rtd.	retired
DC	District of Columbia	Sgt	Sergeant
GDP	Gross Domestic Product	Sq	Square
Gen.	General	UK	United Kingdom
GNI	Gross National Income	UN	United Nations
Gov.	Governor	US	United States
km	kilometre(s)	USA	United States of America
Lt	Lieutenant	USS	United States Ship
Ltd	Limited	USSR	Union of Soviet Socialist
m	metre(s)		Republics

TRANSCRIPTION OF ARABIC NAMES

The Arabic language is used over a vast area. Though the written language and the script are standard throughout the Middle East, the spoken language and also the pronunciation of the written signs exhibit wide variation from place to place. This is reflected, and even exaggerated, in the different transcriptions in use in different countries. The same words, names and even letters will be pronounced differently by an Egyptian, a Lebanese, or an Iraqi—they will be heard and transcribed differently by an English person, a French person, or an Italian. There are several more or less scientific systems of transliteration in use, sponsored by learned societies and Middle Eastern governments, most of them requiring diacritical marks to indicate Arabic letters for which there are no Latin equivalents.

Arabic names occurring in the entries of this book have been rendered in the system most commonly used by British and American Orientalists, but with the omission of the diacritical signs. The system used is a transliteration—i.e. it is based on the writing, which is standard throughout the Arab world, and not on the pronunciation, which varies from place to place. In a few cases consistency has been sacrificed in order to avoid replacing a familiar and accepted form by another which, although more accurate, would be unrecognizable.

Sun- and Moon-Letters

In Arabic pronunciation, when the word to which the definite article, *al*, is attached begins with one of certain letters called 'Sun-letters', the *l* of the article changes to the initial letter in question, e.g. *al-shamsu* (the sun) is pronounced *ash-shamsu*; *al-rajulu* (the man) is pronounced *ar-rajulu*. Accordingly, in this book, where the article is attached to a word beginning with a Sun-letter, it has been rendered phonetically.

There are 14 Sun-letters in the Arabic alphabet, which are transcribed as: d, dh, n, r, s, sh, t, th, z, zh (d, s, t and z and their emphatic forms are not differentiated in this book). The remaining 15 letters in the Arabic alphabet are known as 'Moon-letters'.

A

Abbas, Ferhat

Ferhat Abbas and his followers developed a form of anti-colonial politics that accepted the constitutional framework of French rule but sought equality of civil and political rights for Muslim Algerians. He was the first President (ceremonial) of independent Algeria, when **Ahmed Ben Bella** was Prime Minister.

Abbas, Mahmoud ('Abu Mazen')

Born in Safad in northern Palestine in 1935, Abbas left as a refugee for Syria in 1948. He gained a BA in law from **Damascus** University and a Ph.D. in history from the Oriental College in Moscow, on links between the Zionist movement and the German National Socialists. He was a civil servant in Qatar in the 1960s, and there began to manage and organize Palestinian groups. He was a founding member of **al-Fatah** and was instrumental in initiating the 1965 Palestinian revolution for national independence. He has been a member of the **Palestine National Council** (PNC) since 1968 and a member of the **PLO** Executive Committee. He initiated dialogue with Jewish and pacifist movements in the 1970s, which later led to the decision by the PNC to work with them. He led negotiations with Matiyahu Peled that resulted in the announcement of 'principles of peace' based on a two-state solution in January 1977. He has headed the PLO department for national and international relations since 1980 and was elected as chairman of the portfolio on the **Occupied Territories** in 1988. He headed the Palestinian negotiating team at the secret Oslo talks and signed the **Declaration of Principles on Palestinian Self-Rule** that launched the Palestinian-Israeli **'peace process'** on 13 September 1993, on behalf of the PLO. He has been the head of the PLO negotiating affairs department since 1994 and signed the interim agreement in September 1995 on behalf of the PLO. He returned to the Occupied Territories in September 1995 after 48 years in exile. In October 1995 he drafted the controversial Framework for the Conclusion of a Final Status Agreement Between Israel and the PLO (also known as the **Abu Mazen-Beilin Plan**) together with **Yossi Beilin**. With Uri Savir he headed the first session of the Israel-**Palestinian National Authority (PNA)** final status talks in May 1996. He served as head of the Central Election Commission for the

Palestinian Legislative Council elections in January 1996 and was himself elected as the representative for Qalqilya. He was elected as secretary-general of the PLO Executive Committee in 1996. He was for long considered as **Yasser Arafat**'s deputy and likely successor. In March 2003 he was nominated as the first Prime Minister of the PNA. Internationally, he is considered a moderate, a pragmatist and a 'dove'. Arguably, the **Road Map to peace** could not have been initiated without Abbas as Prime Minister. However, his remarks about the **al-Aqsa** *intifada* (he stated that the end of the *intifada* was a prerequisite for peace and called for a halt to armed attacks on Israeli targets in both Israel proper and the Occupied Territories) at the launch of the Road Map in Aqaba, Jordan, alienated him from many ordinary **Palestinians** as well as from the militant **Hamas**, al-Jihad and the **al-Aqsa Martyrs' Brigade**. He resigned as Prime Minister in September 2003, despite strong support from the USA, to be replaced by **Ahmed Qurei.** He currently resides in **Gaza** and Ramallah. He is not a charismatic figure and has no political machine of his own. He is respected as a statesman both regionally and internationally. He has little credibility, however, on the Palestinian street. He is a member of the PLO 'Tunisians' and is widely perceived to be one of the most corrupt individuals in the PNA. Soon after the PNA was established in Gaza, the construction began of a lavish US $1.5m. villa, funded by unknown sources, in the midst of Palestinian squalor and poverty. Abbas is also deeply mistrusted by Palestinians for his authorship along with senior Israeli figures of various peace plans that they believe relinquish fundamental Palestinian rights and maintain the occupation intact albeit under another name.

Abbasi – *see* **Madani, Abbasi**

Abdel Aziz, Muhammad

President of the **Sahrawi Arab Democratic Republic (Western Sahara)** and secretary-general of the **POLISARIO Front**. Re-elected secretary-general in October 2003, he has been leader of the Front since the mid-1970s and President of the Republic since it was proclaimed in February 1976.

Abduh, Muhammad (1849–1905)

One of the great 19th century influences on the Islamic reformist movement. Born into a peasant family in Egypt, he was influenced by both **Sufism** and European liberalism. He visited Europe frequently and in 1884 joined Jamal ad-Din al-Afghani—whose pupil he had become during the 1870s while al-Afghani was in Egypt—in Paris, France, where together they published a periodical, *Al-'Urwa al-Wuthqa* (*The Strongest Link*). In 1888, after the collapse of the journal, Abduh returned to Egypt where he concentrated his efforts on **education** and legal reform. He entered the legal service and rose to become first a judge and eventually the

Mufti of Egypt. In his theology, he followed al-Afghani, trying to maintain a balance between reason and revelation. He believed that the truths of religion and science could be reconciled. His main concern was to interpret **Islam** in a manner that would release its liberating spirit, enabling Muslims to take their place scientifically and culturally alongside the nations of Europe. His miscellaneous writings and lectures were collected and published between 1897 and 1935 in the periodical *Al-Manar* (*The Lighthouse*) by his disciple Rashid Rida, who tended to emphasize the **Salafist** aspect of Abduh's thought, making it more acceptable to conservatives or fundamentalists than it would otherwise have been.

Abdul Aziz ibn Abdul Rahman as-Saud – *see* Ibn Saud

Abdul Haq, Hadij

The first Afghan *mujahidin* commander to meet Ronald Reagan and Margaret Thatcher.

Abdullah, bin Hussein, Emir (then King) of Jordan

Great-grandfather of the present King of Jordan. Established by Great Britain as ruler of the newly created territory of **Transjordan** in 1921, Abdullah was a son of the **Hashemite**, Sherif Hussein, and brother of **Faisal I**. Abdullah annexed **Jerusalem** and the **West Bank** in 1950 and renamed the country over which he ruled Jordan. He was assassinated in July 1951, and was succeeded by his son, **Talal**.

Abdullah II, King of Jordan

Abdullah ibn Hussein succeeded to the throne of Jordan after the death of his father, **Hussein**, in 1999. He formerly headed Jordan's Special Forces. He has actively promoted initiatives designed to improve Jordan's weak economic position, by establishing the Higher National Economic Consultative Council (chaired by himself) with private-sector representatives as well as ministers, and by taking Jordan into the **World Trade Organization**. He has invited Bill Gates and others to help develop Jordan's **information technology** sector and, following a USAID report on the promising job and export earnings potential of this sector, met world business leaders at the World Economic Forum in Davos, Switzerland, in February 2000. He has vigorously promoted Qualifying Industrial Zones—which qualify goods partly made in Israel and Jordan to enter the USA duty- and quota-free. On the political front, however, he has maintained strong control over political opposition, particularly from the Islamist groups, although some dialogue has been maintained with the **Muslim Brotherhood (Jordan)**. The leadership of **Hamas**, however, was expelled to Qatar in January 2000. Abdullah has also cracked down on the press and academics.

3

Abdullah ibn Abdul Aziz as-Saud, Crown Prince, Saudi Arabia (1923–)

After the illness of King **Fahd** in the mid-1990s, Crown Prince Abdullah took control of economic decision-making. In 1999 he established the **Higher Economic Council**, of which he became the chairman. It included a consultative committee of 10 private-sector representatives, as well as the key economic ministers and the governor of the central bank.

'Abu Ala'a' – *see* Qurei, Ahmed

'Abu Ali'

'Abu Ali' is the *nom de guerre* of Qaed Senyan al-Harthi, a member of **al-Qa'ida** believed to be based in Yemen. He has been associated with the bombing of *USS Cole* in Yemen in October 2000.

'Abu Ammar' – *see* Arafat, Yasser

Abu Bilal

Abu Ameenah Bilal Philips, academic and thinker. Founder of the Islamic Studies Department of Shariff Kabunsuan Islamic University in the Philippines, and of the Islamic Information Centre in the United Arab Emirates.

Abu Dhabi, Emirate of

Member of the United Arab Emirates (UAE). One of the former **Trucial states**. Largest emirate in the UAE. Located on the offshore island of the same name, the Emirate of Abu Dhabi was founded by members of the Ahl bu Falah clan of the Bani Yas tribe in 1761. Until the early 1960s the local inhabitants were dependent on pearl fishing and petty trading. The discovery and extraction of **petroleum** in the early 1960s began to transform the emirate. Agreements made in the 1970s gave the government a majority share in the Abu Dhabi National Oil Co (ADNOC), founded in 1971, which has a monopoly on distribution and is responsible for all oil installations and oil-based industries in the emirate. Oil contributes about 25% of Abu Dhabi's gross domestic product. Following the installation of Sheikh **Zayed bin Sultan an-Nahyan** as emir in 1966, ambitious plans were initiated to modernize Abu Dhabi. With the formation of a confederation of seven emirates, named the UAE in 1971, **Abu Dhabi City** was selected as interim capital. Sheikh Zayed took office as President of the UAE in December 1971 and has since been re-elected five times (most recently in December 2001).

Abu Dhabi City

Capital of the United Arab Emirates and of **Abu Dhabi** emirate. It has a population of more than 600,000.

Abu Dhabi Fund for (Arab Economic) Development

The Abu Dhabi Fund for Development is an autonomous institution established in 1971. Its purpose is to provide economic aid to Arab and other developing countries in support of their economic development, including direct loans, grants, and technical assistance. The Fund also manages development projects financed by the **Abu Dhabi** government.

Abu Dhabi TV

Modelled on **al-Jazeera**, Abu Dhabi TV has become one of the new 'breed' of **Arabic**-language television stations operating in the **Middle East**—with good news coverage and incisive reporting and analysis.

Abu Hafs al-Masri Brigade

An Islamist paramilitary group thought to be linked to **al-Qa'ida**. Claimed responsibility for bombing the UN headquarters in **Baghdad** in August 2003. Also claimed responsibility for the bombing of two synagogues in **Istanbul** in November 2003, alleging that **Mossad** agents were working at them. They declared that the bombings were in part a punishment for Turkey's 'infidel' international friendships. They believe that Turkish exceptionalism is an affront to the Muslim *ummah*.

'Abu Iyad'

Nom de guerre of Salah Khalaf, co-founder of **al-Fatah**. Active with **Yasser Arafat** and Khalil al-Wazir (**'Abu Jihad'**) in **Cairo** in the early 1950s in the Palestinian Students Union, editing a magazine—*The Voice of Palestine*—and establishing al-Fatah. Became one of Arafat's closest supporters within the leadership of the **Palestine Liberation Organization** (PLO). He was head of the intelligence and security apparatus and was responsible for the PLO's and al-Fatah's undercover and clandestine units.

'Abu Jihad' – *see* Wazir, Khalil

'Abu Mazen' – *see* Abbas, Mahmoud

Abu Mazen-Beilin Plan

The controversial Framework for the Conclusion of a Final Status Agreement Between Israel and the PLO, drafted in October 1995 by **Mahmoud Abbas** and **Yossi Beilin**.

Abu Musa Island

The island of Abu Musa, only a few sq km in area, lies in the **Persian (Arabian) Gulf** about midway between Iran and the United Arab Emirates (UAE), and was the source of a dispute between them as both regarded it as vitally important for economic, security and environmental reasons. Abu Musa and the two **Tunb Islands** constitute the strategic keys to the Straits of Hormuz. After Great Britain withdrew from the island in 1971, the sheikhdom of **Sharjah** (later part of the UAE) controlled the island. However, the Shah of Iran claimed that Abu Musa had been taken from Iran at a time when there had been no central government. In the same year the two sides agreed that Sharjah would maintain sovereignty over the island but that Iran would station military forces there, and that revenues from the oilfields surrounding the island would be shared. Iran stationed troops on Abu Musa, but also occupied the two nearby Tunb Islands. No military action in opposition to this was sanctioned either by the West or by the **Arab World**. Recently the UAE has urged Iran to refer the dispute to the International Court of Justice.

'Abu Nidal' – *see* al-Banna, Sabri

'Abu Qatada'

An influential Muslim radical who came to Britain in 1993 and is thought to have been a key **al-Qa'ida** leader in Europe. Described by the Spanish authorities as 'the spiritual head of the *mujahidin* in Britain, he is said to have had links with 'Abu Dahda', who was arrested in Spain shortly after the attacks on US targets on 11 September 2001, and to have met **Osama bin Laden** in Pakistan in 1989. Videotapes of his preaching were found in the Hamburg (Germany) flat of the 11 September suicide bombers. He claimed to have powerful spiritual influence over the Algerian community in London. 'Abu Qatada' was detained and jailed without trial in Britain in 2003 after spending 10 months 'on the run'.

'Abu Saleh'

Formerly a member of the central committee of **al-Fatah**, 'Abu Saleh' was a member of the group of al-Fatah cadres who had, since 1974, been opposed to a political solution based on a Palestinian state in the **West Bank** and **Gaza**. Unlike

'**Abu Nidal**', who split with **Arafat**, these dissidents had remained with al-Fatah. However, following the departure of the **Palestine Liberation Organization** from **Beirut**, Lebanon, in 1982, Abu Saleh—together with others—expressed his dissent from the dominant line again. They reproached Arafat for having accepted the **Fez Plan**, particularly its seventh point, which amounted to a recognition of the Jewish State. They condemned the contacts established between Jordan and Egypt and with peace forces in Israel. They also criticized al-Fatah's 'non-democratic operational procedures' as well as its **corruption**. At first the dissidents received a good deal of support, but the movement rapidly became marginal. Crisis broke out among the dissidents themselves, different groups opposed each other in armed struggle, and Abu Saleh was dismissed.

'**Abu Yasser**'

Senior leader, and one of the founders, of the **al-Aqsa Martyrs' Brigade**.

Achdut HaAvoda (Unity of Labour)

This Israeli party, founded in 1919 as the successor to **Poale Zion**, had three separate existences: first, from 1919 to 1930, when it merged with HaPoel HaTzair to form **Mapai**; second, in 1944, when its name was taken over by Siah B, a faction that split from Mapai and formed a new party—HaKibbutz HaMeuhad (United Kibbutz Movement); and, finally, from 1954 when Achdut HaAvoda was reconstructed by the HaKibbutz HaMeuhad faction after it broke away from **Mapam**. Achdut HaAvoda was aligned with Mapai from 1965 until 1968, when both were absorbed, together with **Rafi**, into the **Israel Labour Party**. Following the **Six-Day War** in 1967 many of its members, including the party's spiritual leader, Itzhak Tabenkin, supported the idea of Greater Israel—the Land of Israel (**Eretz Israel**); however, another leader, **Yigal Allon**, advocated the return of some of the administered territories, so as not to endanger Israeli's security.

Acre (Akko)

An ancient seaport and one of the oldest continuously inhabited cities in the world. Captured by Great Britain in 1918, Acre became part of the British Mandate in Palestine. In 1920 Acre became the site of the British central prison in the **Middle East**. In 1948 the Israeli army captured Acre. In the following year it was incorporated into the modern State of Israel.

Action for Change

Mauritanian political party.

Aden (South Yemen)

Aden had been Great Britain's principal naval base and military outpost protecting the sea lanes south of the **Suez Canal** and the Red Sea in the Indian Ocean since 1839. Until 1934 it was known as the Aden Protectorate and the Hadrawmawt; before the outbreak of the Second World War it was transformed into a Crown Colony. The naval base was developed. Britain refused Yemeni claims to Aden and the Hadrawmawt but placated local tribal leaders by promoting the formation of the Federation of the Emirates of the South. In 1963 Aden was permitted to join this Federation and it was renamed the **Federation of Saudi Arabia**. Nationalist movements demanding independence began to form during the early 1960s. The **Front for the Liberation of Occupied South Yemen** (FLOSY) and the more radical (Marxist-Leninist) **National Liberation Front** (NLF) of **South Yemen** began a struggle for independence. The NLF took up armed struggle and FLOSY began to lose ground to its leftist rivals. When Britain decided in 1967, after a relatively short but bloody struggle against the Yemeni nationalists, to leave the region (including the port and base of Aden itself), it left it in the hands of the NLF, and in 1970 South Yemen was officially declared the **People's Democratic Republic of Yemen**.

Aden-Abyan Islamic Army – *see* Islamic Army of Aden/Abyan

ADIA—Abu Dhabi Investment Authority

The ADIA is the largest official investor in Abu Dhabi, with an estimated portfolio of US \$300,000m.–\$350,000m. invested in fixed interest government securities, notably US Treasury bonds/bills and eurodollar deposits, as well as in real estate. Other major regional investment agencies include the Saudi Arabian Monetary Agency, the **Kuwait Investment Authority** and the Qatar Investment Office, all of which hold large external portfolios that provide annual **income** in the form of interest, profits and dividends.

Al-Adl w'al-Ihsan

Justice and Charity

Islamist organization founded by **Abdessalam Yassine** in Morocco in the 1970s. During the 1980s Yassine tried to establish the group as a political organization but the authorities refused permission. He then sought and was reportedly granted authorization for the group to operate as an Islamic charity. In December 1989 police arrived at Yassine's home and informed him that he was under house arrest. He was forbidden to receive even his lawyers or to exchange letters with them for prolonged periods. No charges were brought against him, and no copy of a detention order has ever been produced by the authorities. According to an interview Yassine gave to the foreign media, al-Adl w'al-Ihsan was dissolved in January 1990. In July 1992 his lawyer lodged an appeal against the illegal detention of his client before the Administrative Chamber of the Supreme Court. No response was ever received. In 1993 **Amnesty International** received a letter from Morocco's permanent representative in Geneva, Switzerland, which stated that al-Adl w'al-Ihsan had no right to propagate religion or carry out religious activities, first because it was registered as a charity and religious activities were outside its mandate, and, second, because **Islam** belonged to the nation and could not be appropriated by any group: 'the statutes of that association provide for activities of a general nature, whereas in practice that association makes Islam its only focus of interest. Such a practice represents a threat to public order. As Islam is by virtue of the Constitution the state religion, no group has the right to appropriate Islam as its ideology'. In December 1995 Yassine was allowed to leave his house to visit the mosque, but otherwise remained under house arrest until May 2000.

Afghan Arabs

The collective name given to the thousands of men from Arab countries who joined the *mujahidin* in Afghanistan fighting first against the Soviet troops and then, later, in support of the **Taliban** regime against the so-called **Northern Alliance**. The fighting groups under **Osama bin Laden** were basically hit-and-run guerrilla units, operating from caves or the desert. The members of the Egyptian **Islamic Jihad**, under **Ayman az-Zawahiri**, fought differently. Zawahiri knew the clandestine ways in which to set up cells, secret communications, and the basics of planning urban warfare. In 1998 the two groups merged after the war against the Soviet Union, many of the Afghan Arabs returned to their own countries, but others went on to fight elsewhere. In Yemen they reassembled under the leadership and direction of bin Laden. Later they settled back in Afghanistan under the protection of **Mullah Omar**, leader of the Taliban, where they provided a cadre in support of the Taliban.

Afghan civil war

After Soviet forces withdrew from Afghanistan in 1989, the ethnically diverse guerrilla groups and their warlords continued fighting for power. It was during this Afghan civil war that much of the capital, **Kabul**, was razed. Fighting continued during the first half of the 1990s until the rise of the **Taliban** from 1996 onwards.

Afghan Interim Authority (AIA)

The AIA was inaugurated in December 2001 and administered Afghanistan until the **Islamic Transitional Government of Afghanistan** assumed power.

Afghan Service Bureau

Maktab al-Khidmat lil Mujahidin al-Arab (MAK)

This service or organization was founded in Peshawar, Pakistan, in 1984 by **Osama bin Laden** and his mentor, Sheikh Dr **Abdullah Azzam** (a Jordanian Palestinian). It was initially established to provide support and cater for foreigners, especially Arabs, who intended to fight alongside the Afghan resistance in their ongoing war against Soviet occupation forces (1979–89). Subsequently, the Afghan Service Bureau raised significant funds and actively recruited *mujahidin* (fighters) from many parts of the world, notably the **Arab World**, to take part in the struggle against the Soviet forces and government troops in Afghanistan. It established guesthouses and training camps for these foreign fighters and also distributed some US \$200m. of funds (originating as Middle Eastern and Western—mainly US and British—**aid**) to those involved in the anti-Soviet effort in Afghanistan. It worked closely with Pakistan's **Inter-Services Intelligence** agency and maintained a presence in at least 30 US states. Towards the end of the Soviet occupation of Afghanistan, the organization evolved into 'the Base' (**al-Qa'ida**), which was a network of former *mujahidin* committed to the Islamist cause. In 1989, Azzam, by then the group's spiritual leader, was murdered in a bomb attack in Peshawar together with his two sons. This left bin Laden (who had previously split from Azzam over differences as to how the Bureau/Base should evolve—and who was suspected by some to have organized Azzam's murder) firmly in charge of al-Qa'ida, which he then proceeded to reshape according to his own vision for it.

Afghan–Soviet War—initial intervention

In December 1979 Soviet forces were deployed in Afghanistan in order to support the existing People's Democratic Party of Afghanistan (PDPA) Government. Former Prime Minister Hafizullah Amin had just ousted President Mohammed Taraki in a coup in September and was beginning to extend his political contacts with the USA and other Western powers. The Amin coup also gave impetus to the insurrection that was making directionless progress in Afghanistan and soon spokesmen for the resistance group based in Pakistan were claiming that several Afghan provinces were already under the control of the insurgents. Iran openly and Pakistan covertly were supporting the *mujahidin* fighting against the PDPA regime, which was strongly backed by the Soviet Union. Soviet President Brezhnev was concerned about the survival of the PDPA regime and ordered a military intervention. At the end of the first week of December a fully equipped Soviet airborne assault brigade was airlifted into the Bagram air base some 40 km north of **Kabul** and from there secured key points in the surrounding area to permit the unhindered invasion of Soviet ground troops and a massive airlift. Before the end of December President Amin had been killed and Babrak Karmal, leader of the Parcham faction of the PDPA, recalled hastily from exile in eastern Europe to become the new

President of Afghanistan. Karmal's remit was to unite the Khalk and Parcham factions of the PDPA, and to work to persuade the Afghan people of the benefits of a socialist regime. The USA, Pakistan and Iran were all apparently taken by surprise by the Soviet intervention, but opposition to the 'invasion' was mobilized and a UN Security Council resolution calling on the Soviet Union to withdraw was immediately prepared, only to be vetoed by the USSR itself. The Soviet military build-up proceeded steadily throughout the late winter and in April 1980 the Soviet military presence was legalized by a Status of Armed Forces Agreement catering for a 'temporary occupation' by a 'limited contingent of Soviet forces'. As the Soviet military build-up proceeded, the Afghan army dissolved to the point where its strength was only 33,000 men. By the end of 1980, after two major offensives in the spring and the autumn, the Soviet forces, supported by the Afghan army, were directly embroiled in a major war with the various Afghan 'resistance' forces, most of them belonging to different groups of *mujahidin* (*jihadi* fighters or holy warriors).

Afghan–Soviet War (1979–89)

The Afghan–Soviet War was a war in which local Islamist guerrilla forces opposed a much better equipped conventional army and air force, comprising, in fact, the combined Afghan and Soviet armies and air forces. The strength of the Limited Contingent of Soviet Forces in Afghanistan by the end of 1983 was probably around 110,000. Thereafter, it was rarely more and often less than that. The technological superiority of the government and Soviet forces proved inadequate, ultimately, to secure the military defeat of the Afghan resistance, despite adopting a variety of different tactics and strategies during the course of the war. Throughout 1982–83 neither the Afghan government and Soviet forces nor the resistance gained any significant advantage. From 1984 onwards the latter began to receive increasing support from outside. In July 1984 the US Congress approved US $50m. and in 1985 $250m. to support the **mujahidin** against the 'communists'. Pakistan also increased its support, particularly for the more radical rather than the more traditional Islamist groups. The *mujahidin* were divided among themselves. In March 1985 10 major groups (seven fundamentalist and three traditionalist) formed the United Military Command, but this soon foundered. In May the so-called Peshawar Seven formed the Islamic Unity of Afghanistan, which included both **Shi'a** and **Sunni** groups. Some of the former were under Iranian influence, most of the latter linked to Pakistan, the USA and Saudi Arabia. It was clear by now that the war would be of long duration rather than quick and decisive; all those involved prepared themselves for this. In 1986 the Soviet Union, now under President **Gorbachev**, took a hard look at its Afghan policy and decided on a combined political and military strategy in order to ease President Karmal out of power and bring in Mohammed Najibullah, a founder-member of the Parcham faction of the PDPA; and at the same time to make it clear that although a satisfactory settlement would result in a gradual Soviet withdrawal, without such a settlement the Soviet Union would maintain a strong commitment to its forces in Afghanistan. The tide began to turn against the *mujahidin*. In November 1986 Najibullah replaced Karmal as President of the PDPA Government in Afghanistan. In 1987 the increasing availability to the resistance of ground-to-air missiles (especially the *Stinger* and the *Blowpipe*) had a major impact on government and Soviet air supremacy and swung the balance of advantage towards the *mujahidin*. It was beginning to become clear that sooner or later the Soviet forces would recognize that they were not going to win this war. In June 1987 eight of the Shi'a *mujahidin* groups had come together to form the Alliance of Eight. This provoked a move among the various Sunni groups towards unification within the Islamic Unity of Afghanistan coalition. By the beginning of 1988 the Soviet military withdrawal was becoming a matter of 'when' rather than 'if'. Gorbachev had described Soviet involvement in Afghanistan as a 'bleeding wound', but planned to leave Afghanistan with a friendly government in power if at all possible.

Afghan Transit Trade Agreement (ATTA)

The ATTA was signed between Pakistan and Afghanistan in 1950 in order to give Afghanistan—a landlocked country—the right to import duty-free goods through the port of Karachi. During the **Afghan–Soviet War**, the **Inter-Services Intelligence** (ISI) and the Islamic parties took advantage of the ATTA to launch a lucrative smuggling business in duty-free goods. Duty-free goods destined for Afghanistan were loaded into sealed containers in trucks heading for **Kabul**. Some of the products were sold in Afghanistan, but the bulk of them never left the trucks; they were returned to Pakistan to be sold in the local markets there. The trucks were 'taxed' at various roadblocks by Pakistani customs officers and the transport mafia; warlords who controlled the territories they had to cross levied their own 'taxes' and even the customs officers in Kabul took their cut. Even so, ATTA duty-free goods were available in Pakistani markets at lower prices than identical products imported legitimately into the country. What made ATTA items so competitive was the exceptionally high import duties levied by the Pakistani government on imports, especially of electronic equipment from the Far East. ATTA stereos, televisions, video recorders and compact discs could be as much as 40%–50% cheaper. This form of smuggling gave Pakistan a limited supply of inexpensive duty-free foreign goods and the ISI an additional source of income. Throughout the 1980s the ATTA and illegal trade expanded, servicing most of the communist-controlled Afghan cities and generating about US $50m. annually. After 1992 contraband activities increased dramatically. ATTA duty-free goods began to reach the new Central Asian states and their emerging markets. In 1992–93 the business was worth $128m. and its growth was accelerating. By 1997 Pakistan's and Afghanistan's share alone amounted to $2,500m.—equivalent to more than one-half of Afghanistan's estimated gross domestic product. Over the same period, the figure for **Central Asia** rose to a staggering $5,000m.

Afghani

Official currency of Afghanistan. In recent times at least there have been several different banknotes in circulation, making it difficult to assess the value of the *afghani*. Until the end of 2001, in addition to the **Taliban** currency, which was worth almost four times the currency of the **Northern Alliance**, there were four different Afghan banknotes in circulation: the one issued during the rule of former King **Zahir Shah**; another by the government of **Burhanuddin Rabbani**, which had the same value; a third, printed by the Soviet authorities for **Uzbek** warlord Gen. **Rashid Dostum**, traded at about one-half the value of the first two; and a fourth, issued by the Northern Alliance, also traded at a discount. Inside Afghanistan, **gold** was the most reliable means of exchange, and *hawaladars* (*hawala* traders) used gold to balance their books. In 2001, before the war against the Taliban, one US dollar was worth 60,000 *afghani*. As the Taliban were dispersed, the value of the currency rose and the exchange rate hardened to 25,000 to the US dollar. Yet, over the same period, the price of gold remained the same.

Afghanistan, Transitional Islamic State of

Dowlat-e Eslami-ye Afghanestan

Afghanistan is a land-locked country in southern central Asia to the north-east of Iran, north-west of Pakistan and south of the five former 'Muslim' Central Asian republics of the Soviet Union. The Hindu Kush mountains that run north-east to south-west divide the northern provinces from the rest of the country. It covers some 647,500 sq km, and had an estimated population of 27,755,775 at July 2002.

The capital is **Kabul**, and the country is divided into 32 provinces (*velaya*, plural *velayat*): Badakhshan, Badghis, Baghlan, Balkh, Bamian, Farah, Faryab, Ghazni, Ghowr, Helmand, Herat, Jowzjan, Kabol, Kandahar, Kapisa, Khowst, Konar, Kondoz, Laghman, Lowgar, Nangarhar, Nimruz, Nurestan, Oruzgan, Paktia, Paktika, Parvan, Samangan, Sar-e Pol, Takhar, Vardak, and Zabol. The population is divided ethnically into **Pashtuns** (44%), **Tajiks** (25%), **Hazaras** (10%), **Uzbeks** (8%) and minor ethnic groups (Aimaks, Turkmans, Baloch, and others, 13%). The official religion is **Islam**, with the overwhelming majority (84%) being **Sunni** Muslims and a minority (15%) **Shi'a**, with other religions accounting for 1%. The official language is Pashtu (35%), but 50% of the population speak Afghan Persian (Dari), 11% Turkic languages (e.g. Uzbek and Turkmen), and 4% some 30 minor languages (primarily Baluchi and Pashai). There is much bilingualism.

Political profile

The **Bonn Agreement** called for a **Loya Jirga** (Grand Council) to be convened within 18 months of the establishment of a Transitional Authority (TA) to draft a new constitution for the country; the basis for the new constitution should be the

1963/64 Constitution. The **Afghan Interim Authority (AIA)**—comprising 30 members, headed by a chairman—was inaugurated on 22 December 2001 with a six-month mandate. After its succession, for a period of two years, by a TA, elections were to be held; the structure of the follow-on TA was announced on 10 June 2002, when the Loya Jirga (a non-elected body made up of selected notables, ex-warlords and other leading political figures) convened to establish the Transitional Islamic State of Afghanistan (TISA) which has an 18-month mandate to hold a Loya Jirga to adopt a constitution and a 24-month mandate to hold nation-wide elections. The head of state (and head of government) is President **Hamid Karzai** (since 10 June 2002). His Cabinet is the 30-member AIA.

As regards the judiciary, the Bonn Agreement called for a judicial commission to rebuild the justice system in accordance with Islamic principles, international standards, the rule of law, and Afghan legal traditions. The Bonn Agreement called for the establishment of a Supreme Court. Little progress has been made in this regard. In March 2004 elections were postponed until September, owing to insecurity and the UN's slow pace in registering voters. More than six months after the end of the six-month period allotted for voter registration, the UN had registered barely 10% of the 10.5m. estimated to be eligible. There was still no electoral law to define constituencies and no registered political parties. **Taliban** forces, resurgent in the south, threatened to disrupt attempts to hold elections. It was unlikely that elections would be held in September 2004. There has been no properly constituted legislative body since June 1993.

The Afghan political system, during and following the **Afghan–Soviet War**, had consisted of tribal warlords or ethnic/religious *mujahidin* factions and political groupings since 1992. Some of the more organized groups included: **Harakat e Enqelab e Islami**, **Hezb-e Islami**, **Hizb-i Wahdat** (Unity Party), Harakat al-Jihad al-Islami, **Jabha ye Nejat e Milli ye Afghanistan** (Afghan National Liberation Front), **Jamiat-i Islami**, Mahaz e Mill ye Islami ye Afghanistan (National Islamic Front of Afghanistan), and **Ulema Union**. This configuration was effectively disrupted by the Taliban takeover in 1996. After the US-led ouster of the Taliban and the subsequent AIA's failure to establish political normalcy, the political system largely reverted to warlordism and political conflict in most of the country, with the exception of a few urban areas. As of mid-2004, US forces continued to fight against Taliban fighters in the south of the country, and the UN maintained a presence confined largely to Kabul and surrounding areas.

History

Afghanistan's recent history is characterized by war and civil unrest. The Soviet Union invaded in 1979 but was forced to withdraw 10 years later by anti-Communist *mujahidin* forces supplied and trained by the USA, Saudi Arabia, Pakistan, and others. Fighting subsequently continued among the various *mujahidin* factions, giving rise to a state of warlordism that eventually gave rise to the Taliban. Backed by foreign sponsors, the Taliban developed as a political force and eventually seized power. The Taliban were able to capture most of the country, aside from **Northern Alliance** strongholds primarily in the north-east, until US and allied military action in support of the opposition following the 11 September 2001 terrorist attacks forced the group's downfall. In late 2001 major leaders from the Afghan opposition groups and diaspora met in Bonn, Germany, and agreed on a plan for the formulation of a new government structure that resulted in the inauguration of Hamid Karzai as chairman of the AIA on 22 December 2001. The AIA held a nation-wide Loya Jirga in June 2002, and Karzai was elected President by secret ballot of the TISA. Government control does not extend much beyond Kabul, the rest of the country being under various warlords. Since the ouster of the Taliban the grip of the warlords has tightened increasingly. In 2003 **al-Qa'ida** and Taliban forces were returning along the southern Pakistani border. Karzai is pressing for the international force of 11,000 to expand its operations beyond Kabul. In addition to occasionally violent political jockeying and ongoing military action to crush remaining *mujahidin* and Taliban supporters, the country suffers from enormous poverty, a crumbling infrastructure, and widespread landmines. Close ties with the Pashtuns in Pakistan makes the long south-eastern border difficult to control; some Pashtuns lay claim to the North West Frontier Province of Pakistan.

Afghanistan, economy

Afghanistan is an extremely poor, land-locked country, highly dependent on farming and livestock production (sheep and goats) and a **trade** in agricultural exports, which include carpets, rugs and **opium**. Economic considerations have been displaced by political and military upheavals during two decades of war, including Soviet military occupation (which ended on 15 February 1989, having lasted almost 10 years). During that conflict one-third of the population fled the country, with Pakistan and Iran sheltering a refugee population that rose to more than 6m. at its peak. Gross domestic product has fallen substantially over the past 20 years because of the loss of labour and capital and the disruption of trade and **transport**; severe drought added to the country's difficulties in 1998–2001. The majority of the population continues to suffer from insufficient food, clothing, housing, and medical care, problems exacerbated by military operations and political uncertainties. Inflation remains a serious problem.

Following the war prosecuted by the US-led coalition that led to the defeat of the **Taliban** in November 2001 and the formation of the **Afghan Interim Authority (AIA)** resulting from the December 2001 **Bonn Agreement**, international efforts to rebuild Afghanistan were initiated at the Tokyo Donors Conference for Afghan Reconstruction in January 2002, when US $4,500m. was collected for a trust fund to be administered by the **World Bank**. Priority areas for reconstruction include **education**, **health**, and sanitation facilities, enhancement of administrative capacity, the development of the agricultural sector, and the rebuilding of road, **energy**, and telecommunications links. It has been estimated that the reconstruction of

Afghanistan will cost at least $4,000m., given peaceful conditions. Although $4,500m. in **aid** has been pledged by the international community, this aid has yet to materialize, in particular that pledged by the USA. International pledges made by more than 60 countries and **international financial institutions** at the Tokyo Donors Conference amounted to $4,500m. for the period up to 2006, with $1,800m. allocated for 2002; according to a joint preliminary assessment conducted by the World Bank, the Asian Development Bank, and the **UNDP**, rebuilding Afghanistan will cost some $15,000m. over the next 10 years.

Opium production and smuggling have both escalated, with production of **heroin** estimated to have increased tenfold, since the fall of the Taliban. The amount of land used for opium cultivation rose from 1,685 ha in 2001 under the Taliban to 30,750 ha in 2002, with opium production potential amounting to 1,278 metric tons, in spite of attempts at eradication. There are many narcotics-processing laboratories throughout the country; the **drugs** trade is substantial and many local interests (including farmers and merchants) are vested in it. Afghanistan is now again the world's leading producer of opium and source of heroin. It is also a source of hashish. Some 80%–90% of the heroin consumed in Europe is derived from Afghan opium. Considerable value is thought to be involved in '**money-laundering**', possibly through the *hawala* system.

Agriculture is the largest sector, but Afghanistan has been affected by severe drought in recent years and decades of war have left the basic infrastructure in ruins. Industrial potential is limited for the time being; there is limited interest in medium- or long-term investment, although overseas assets have been unfrozen since 2002. The country is a strategic location for **gas/oil** pipelines, and has some natural deposits of gas, oil and coal. The volatile political and military situation makes national economic recovery difficult.

Aflaq (Aflak), Michel (1910–89)

Syrian intellectual and political organizer, founder of the Syrian and Iraqi **Ba'ath** parties. Born in **Damascas**, a Greek Orthodox Christian. Studied philosophy at the Sorbonne, and became active in Arab student politics. In 1940 Aflaq established a study circle in Damascus called the Movement of Arab Renaissance, which in 1947 became the Ba'ath Party, Ba'ath meaning 'resurrection' or 'renaissance'. The Party's ideology was based on Unity (Arab unity), Freedom (freedom from imperialist oppression) and **Socialism** (referring less to economics than to a way of life, and a commitment to revolution). By the mid-1950s the Ba'ath Party had become a major force in Syria. Aflaq was its secretary-general and chief ideologist. However, in 1966 he was defeated in an intra-party power struggle and left for Lebanon and then Brazil. Two years later **Saddam Hussain** and his Iraqi Ba'ath Party cadres staged a successful coup and took control of Iraq in the name of **Ba'athism**. Aflaq was invited to settle in Iraq, accepted the offer, and eventually became the leader of the National Command of the Iraqi Ba'ath Party.

African Union (AU)

The AU replaced the **Organisation of African Unity** (OAU) in July 2002. The AU aims to support unity, solidarity, and peace among African states. Members include: Algeria, Egypt, Libya, Mauritania and Tunisia. The **Sahrawi Arab Democratic Republic** (SADR) was admitted to the OAU in February 1982, but its membership was disputed by Morocco and other states. Morocco withdrew from the OAU with effect from October 1985 and has not applied to join the AU. The SADR ratified the Constitutive Act in December 2000 and is a full member of the AU. In July 2001 the OAU adopted a New African Initiative, which was subsequently renamed the New Partnership for Africa's Development (NEPAD) and was launched in October 2001. The heads of state of Algeria and Egypt have played a major role in the preparation and management of NEPAD. NEPAD is ultimately answerable to the AU Assembly.

AFTZ – *see* Arab Free Trade Zone

Aga Khan IV, His Highness Prince Karim

The spiritual leader of the Nizari **Ismailis**.

Aga Khan, Prince Sadruddin

Iranian UN official. The son of Mohammed Shah. Educated at Harvard University, he acted as a **UNESCO** consultant for Afro-Asian projects in 1958 and, from 1959—60, as an adviser to the **UNHCR**. Further UN involvement included his role as a founding member and chairman of the Independent Commission On Internal Humanitarian Issues in 1983, and head co-ordinator of economic and humanitarian programmes in Afghanistan in 1988–91. Khan also founded the Harvard Islamic Association Press.

Agriculture

The economies of the region most dependent on agriculture and livestock production are four of the former Soviet republics of **Central Asia**—Kyrgyzstan (38% of gross domestic production (GDP) derived from agriculture), Uzbekistan (35%), Tajikistan and Turkmenistan (29%). Syria and Mauritania are both also heavily reliant on the farming sector, which contributes 22% and 21%, respectively, of their GDPs. Among the countries of the region that are least dependent on agriculture are Bahrain (0.8%), Jordan (2.1%) and Oman (3.2%). The highest average annual rates of growth in agriculture recorded in 1991–2001 were in the United Arab Emirates (13.7%), Yemen (6.4%), Syria (4.7%), Mauritania (4.5%) and Oman (4.4%). During the same decade, the **Occupied Territories** of the **West Bank** and **Gaza Strip** experienced the highest average annual negative rates of growth in agriculture (-6.7%). The only other two countries to experience a decline in agricultural growth rates were Tajikistan (-4.9%) and Morocco (-2.4%). Major agricultural exporters in the region include Iran (eighth in the world among fruit exporters with 11,800m. metric tons), Turkey and Egypt (fourth and seventh in the world, respectively, as regards exports of vegetables. Turkey is also the world's 10th largest producer of wheat and one of its largest consumers, as are Egypt and Iran. Turkey is also a major exporter and consumer of tea. Uzbekistan, Turkey and Syria are among the world's largest cotton producers, ranking fifth, sixth and 10th, respectively). Iran and Turkey are the world's fifth and sixth largest producers of raw wool, and the seventh and fifth largest consumers respectively, using much of it for rug and carpet production and export.

Agudat Israel (Society or Community of Israel)

Founded in 1912 at the Congress of Orthodox Jewry in Kattowitz (then in Germany, now in Poland), the Society or Community of Israel was a political movement of ultra-Orthodox Jews. One of its objectives was to help solve the problems facing Jews world-wide. It established itself as a political party in Palestine in the early 1920s, while maintaining a global mandate (the Agudat Israel World Organization). In 1949 the party formed part of the United Religious Front. In 1959 it joined **Poale Agudat Israel** to form the Torah Religious Front. It has a Council of Torah Sages to guide its religious-political strategy. Originally, anti-Zionist and messianic, in the 1980s it still favoured a theocracy and increased state financial support for its religious institutions. In 1988 it increased the number of seats it held in the **Knesset** from five to eight. Its leaders are Avraham Shapiro and Menachem Porush. The Agudat Israel World Organization now has more than 500,000 members in 25 countries across the world. Its chairman in **Jerusalem** is Rabbi J. M. Abramowitz.

Ahali Group

Opposition group in Iraq in the 1930s, composed mainly of young men who advocated **socialism** and **democracy** and sought to carry out reform programmes. Together with another opposition group (led by Hikmat Sulayman), the Ahali Group participated in a **military** *coup d'état* in 1936. Yet, after jointly taking power, it failed to improve social conditions, with the army increasingly dominating the political scene.

Al-Ahbash

The Association of Islamic Charitable Projects (Jami'at al-Mashari' al-Khayriya al-Islamiyya), known as al-Ahbash ('the Ethiopians'), is a pan-Sufi organization, an activist expression of the Sufi (spiritualist) movement (with roots in Egypt and Lebanon). It has almost 8,000 members. One of the most controversial and interesting of contemporary Islamic groups, due to its origins, its eclectic theological roots, and its teachings, which do not fit the conventional Islamist mould. The

Ahbash devoutly follows the teachings of Sheikh 'Abdallah ibn Muhammad ibn Yusuf al-Hirari ash-Shibi al-Abdari, also known as al-Habashi, a religious thinker of Ethiopian origins. It is spiritually Islamist but not politically. By the late 1980s the Ahbash had become one of Lebanon's largest Islamic movements, having grown during the civil war from a few hundred members to its present size. The Ahbash did not create a militia of its own, nor did it engage in sectarian violence or fight Israel. Proselytizing and recruitment are its main aims, along with a commitment to moderation and political passivity. The Ahbash became a key player in Lebanese politics by offering a moderate alternative to **Islamism**, attracting a wide following among the **Sunni** urban middle class by advocating pluralism and tolerance. Its ideology makes the Ahbash politically significant, including sharp controversies with Islamist movements. While Habashi pays allegiance to the pious ancestors (*salaf*) and the **Shari'a**, his emphasis on 'the science of *hadith*' makes him suspect as being a follower of the Kalamiya (literalist) tradition of the Mu'tazila who stressed the superiority of reason over revelation. He rejects such Islamist authorities as Ibn Taymiya, Ibn 'Abd al-Wahhab, and **Sayyid Qutb**. In contrast to **Hezbollah** and the **Islamic Association**, the Ahbash opposes the establishment of an **Islamic state** on the grounds that this divides Muslims. Instead, it accepts Lebanon's confessional system (which used to over-represent Christians at the expense of Muslims, but now gives them parity). Its foreign policy orientation is equally mild, making no reference to *jihad* and directing no anger towards the West. To achieve a civilized Islamic society, it recommends that members study Western learning. The Ahbash has established branches in Australia, Canada, Denmark, France, Sweden, Switzerland, Ukraine, and the USA (with headquarters in Philadelphia). It enjoys excellent relations with most Arab states, particularly Syria. In rivalry with the Islamic Association for dominance of the Sunni community, it contested the Lebanese parliamentary elections of 1992 and won one seat in **Beirut**, though it lost it in 1996.

AHC – *see* **Arab Higher Commission/Committee for Palestine**

Al-Ahd

Pledge

Jordanian political party. First achieved representation in the general elections of November 1993.

Ahmed, Hocine Aït

Born in 1919. A key Algerian nationalist leader, who founded the **Front de libération nationale** (National Liberation Front) and began the eight-year war of independence against France. After Algeria achieved independence in 1962, he strongly opposed the ruling faction of **Ahmed Ben Bella**. Having been sentenced to death for opposition activities, Hocine was subsequently pardoned and escaped to France. In 1999 he stood as a presidential candidate in Algeria, but later withdrew his candidacy in opposition to political fraud.

Ahoti – *see* Sista-Ahoti

Ahvaz

Ancient city on the banks of the Karun river (Iran). Named Suq al-Ahvaz by Arab conquerors in AD 637 (Ahvaz being the plural of Huzi/Khuzi, the local **tribe**), Ahvaz is today the capital of the Iranian province of Kuzistan. Boosted by the discovery of petroleum in the region in 1908, Ahvaz grew to become a prosperous city with a population of around 725,000 (1991). Today it is the sixth largest urban centre in Iran. As one of the centres of the **oil** industry, it played a crucial role in the revolutionary movement that toppled the Shah in 1979. During the **Iran–Iraq War** of 1980–88 it became a front-line city and suffered considerable damage.

AIA – *see* Afghan Interim Authority

Aid

Official overseas development assistance is the major form of aid provided (and received) by countries in the region. Saudi Arabia is a major aid donor (ranked 17th in the world, distributing some US \$490m., equivalent to 0.35% of its gross domestic product (GDP), as is the United Arab Emirates (ranked 24th for \$127m., equivalent to 0.23% of its GDP). Kuwait donates 0.27% of its GDP in aid. The largest recipient of aid in the region is Egypt (\$1,250m., the seventh largest in the world), while the **West Bank** and **Gaza Strip** receive \$865m. and together constitute the 15th largest recipient in the world. The West Bank and Gaza together receive more aid per head than any other territory or country (apart from New Caledonia, French Polynesia and the Netherlands Antilles). Mauritania is the 10th largest recipient of aid per head in the world, Jordan is the 13th largest and Lebanon the 17th largest. Morocco, Jordan, Yemen, Afghanistan and Tunisia all rank (in that order) among the world's largest recipients of aid in overall value.

AIS—Armée islamique du salut (Algeria)—*Islamic Salvation Army*

The AIS was established in mid-1994 as the armed wing of the banned Front islamique du salut (**FIS**, Islamic Salvation Front). Its precise numerical strength is unknown, but in 1995 it was estimated at approximately 6,000. The exact relationship with the FIS was not always clear, but AIS leaders evidently acted with a degree of autonomy and were not directly controlled by the FIS. The AIS merged with the Armed Islamic Movement. Its main leader was Medani Mezrag. Following a cease-fire in October 1997, the AIS declared a definitive end to its guerrilla operations and armed struggle against the state on 6 June 1999. The AIS took advantage of the amnesty provided by the Civil Concord Law and disbanded in January 2000. Some of its members were integrated into the army in operations against the **GIA—Groupe islamique armé** (Armed Islamic Group). In February 1998 four other armed Islamist groups—the Ansar Battalion, the Mawt Battalion, the **ar-Rahman Battalion** and the **Islamic League for Call and Jihad** joined the truce announced by the AIS in October 1997.

Aix-les-Bains Conference

Took place in August 1955 to discuss the future of Morocco. The French delegation of five ministers was led by Prime Minister Edgar Faure. A key issue was the future role of the Sultan **Mohammed V**, exiled in Madagascar. **Ben Barka**, for the **Istiqlal** party, favoured a solution that avoided the return of the sultan—a position that angered the resistance movement, which aimed at the restoration of the sultan.

Akayev, Askar Airf

President of Kyrgyzstan since 1991. Akayev was born on 10 November 1944 in the village of Kyzyl-Bairak, Keminsky District, into the family of a collective-farm worker. At a Special Session of the Supreme Soviet of the Republic, held in October 1990, he was elected President of Kyrgyzstan—the only non-communist to be elected as President of a Central Asian Republic. As the President of Kyrgyzstan, he actively opposed the coup attempt of August 1991 in Russia. After the new Constitution of Kyrgyzstan was adopted in May 1993, it was decided that a referendum should be held in order to determine the level of confidence in Akayev, who had been accused of creating a cult of personality and becoming increasingly authoritarian. In January 1994 the people of Kyrgyzstan ratified the powers of the President.

Alawis or Alawites (Syria)

An Islamic sect, which believes that the **Prophet Muhammad** was merely a forerunner of 'Ali, his cousin and son-in-law, and that the latter was the incarnation of Allah. Estimated to number 1.5m.–1.8m., the Alawites live mainly in north-west Syria, in the mountains near the city of Latakia, but many also live in the cities of **Hamah** and Homs, and in recent decades there has been a migration to **Damascus**. Their name is a recent one—earlier they were known as Nusairis, Namiriya or Ansariyya. The names 'Nusairi' and 'Namiriya' derive from their first theologian, Muhammadu bin Nusairi an-Namiri; the name 'Ansariyya' refers to the mountain region in Syria where this sect lived. The Alawites are a **minority**, disproportionally prominent in positions of power. Their members have included former President

Hafiz al-Assad and his son **Bashar**, the current President of Syria. Their religious belief is similar to other Muslims, with two differences. One is their commitment to *jihad*, and the other to *waliya*—devotion to 'Ali and struggle against his enemies.

Alawite dynasty

The present king, **Mohammed VI**, is the most recent ruler of the Moroccan Alawite dynasty, which claims to be descended from 'Ali and the **Prophet Muhammad**, via the holy lineage of the Filali *shorafa* (holy men), who established themselves in the oases of Sijilmassa in the 15th century. The first Alawite sultan of Morocco was Moulay Isma'il, who came to power in the middle of the 17th century. Sultan **Mohammed V** of Morocco, who was the first king of Morocco after independence, was the grandson of Moulay Hassan (d. 1894). King Mohammed's father, Moulay Yussef (d. 1927), was the brother of both Moulay Abd al-Aziz and Moulay Hafidh, the last two sultans before the establishment of the French Protectorate.

Aleppo

City in Syria with 1.9m. inhabitants, dating back to 1000 BC. It is the commercial and cultural capital of northern Syria, known for its university, and traditional architecture. Aleppo's economy is largely based on the trading of agricultural products.

Alexandria

Al-Iskandariyah

Coastal city in northern Egypt with a population of 3.9m. Founded by Alexander the Great in 332 BC, Alexandria is a large tourist resort, as well as a commercial and economic centre, with 80% of all Egypt's imports and exports passing through the city's harbours.

ALF – *see* **Arab Liberation Front**

Algeria, People's Democratic Republic of

Al-Jumhuriyah al-Jaza'iriyah ad-Dimuqratiyah ash-Sha'biyah

Lying between Morocco and Tunisia along the **Mediterranean** coast and down into the Sahara, Algeria's southern borders are with Mauritania, Mali and Niger. Algeria is the second largest country in Africa after Sudan, with an area of 2,381,740 sq km, only 3% of which, however, is arable. The capital is **Algiers**. Algeria is divided into 48 provinces (*wilaya*, plural *wilayat*): Adrar, Ain Defla, Ain Temouchent, Alger, Annaba, Batna, Bechar, Bejaia, Biskra, Blida, Bordj Bou Arreridj, Bouira, Boumerdes, Chlef, Constantine, Djelfa, El Bayadh, El Oued, El Tarf, Ghardaia,

Guelma, Illizi, Jijel, Khenchela, Laghouat, Mascara, Medea, Mila, Mostaganem, M'Sila, Naama, Oran, Ouargla, Oum el Bouaghi, Relizane, Saida, Setif, Sidi Bel Abbes, Skikda, Souk Ahras, Tamanghasset, Tebessa, Tiaret, Tindouf, Tipaza, Tissemsilt, Tizi Ouzou, and Tlemcen. The population was estimated at 32,277,942 in July 2002, of which 75% were Arabs, 24% **Berbers**, and 1% others (mostly Europeans). The overwhelming majority of the population are **Sunni** Muslims, with about 1% belonging to other sects or faiths. The official state language is **Arabic**, with French and Berber dialects also recognized.

Political profile

Algeria is a republic, of which the President (**Abdelaziz Bouteflika** since April 1999) is head of state. The Council of Ministers is appointed by the President, as is the Prime Minister (Ali Benflis from August 2000 until April 2003, when he was dismissed by President Bouteflika). The President is elected by popular vote for a five-year term. The legislature includes the **Majlis** ech-Chaabi al-Watani (National People's Assembly) and the Council of the Nation. The members of the Assembly (whose number was raised from 380 to 389 in the 2002 elections) are elected by popular vote to serve five-year terms. Elections to the National People's Assembly were last held on 30 May 2002, and are scheduled to be held next in 2007. The Council has 144 members, one-third of whom are appointed by the President, the remainder being elected by indirect vote. Members serve six-year terms and the Constitution requires one-half of the Council to be renewed every three years. Elections to the Council of the Nation were last held on 30 December 2000, and were due to be held in 2003. The legal system is based on French law and **Islamic Law**; judicial review of legislative acts takes place in an *ad hoc* Constitutional Council composed of various public officials, including several Supreme Court justices. Algeria has not accepted compulsory International Court of Justice jurisdiction.

Until 1988 Algeria was a single party regime, with the **Front de libération nationale** (FLN, National Liberation Front) in power. During 1988–90, following economic liberalization and large-scale anti-government demonstrations, which were brutally crushed, the government allowed a degree of political liberalization. Other political parties, including Islamist groups, were recognized. In 1991 the Front islamique du salut (**FIS**, Islamic Salvation Front) was poised to win the second round of the national elections, but the army intervened to prevent the party from taking power, plunging Algeria into civil unrest, violence and a state of emergency from 1992 onwards. The **military** plays a major role in Algerian politics. A law specifically banning political parties based on religion was enacted in March 1997.

The major political groupings are:

- Algerian National Front; Leader Moussa Touati
- Democratic National Rally; Chair. Ahmed Ouyahia

- **Front islamique du salut**; Leaders **Ali Belhadj**, Dr **Abbasi Madani** (imprisoned), Rabeh Kebir (self-exiled in Germany); the Front was outlawed in April 1992
- Movement of a Peaceful Society; Chair. Mahfoud Nahnah
- National Entente Movement; Leader Ali Boukhazna
- **Front de libération nationale**; Sec.-Gen. Boualem Benhamouda
- National Reform Movement; Leader Abdallah Djaballah
- National Renewal Party
- Progressive Republican Party; Leader Khadir Driss
- Rally for Culture and Democracy; Sec.-Gen. Said Saadi
- Renaissance Movement (En Nahda Movement); Leader Lahbib Adami
- Social Liberal Party; Leader Ahmed Khelil
- Socialist Forces Front; Sec.-Gen. **Hocine Aït Ahmed** (self-exiled in Switzerland)
- Union for Democracy and Liberty; Leader Moulay Boukhalafa
- Workers Party; Leader Louisa Hanoune
- National Liberation Army
- **Groupe islamique armé**

Media

All media are subject to state control and criticism of the government is not permitted. There are some 23 daily newspapers, one state-run television station, four state-run radio stations, two internet service providers and, as of 2001, 180,000 internet users.

History

Algeria was occupied by French forces in 1830. Despite continuing local resistance for several decades, by the 1870s Algeria was a French colony characterized by a substantial French settler population. The nationalist movement began to take shape after the Second World War and in 1945 fighting broke out. The nationalists were ruthlessly suppressed and some 15,000 killed. All they demanded at this stage was autonomy in a federation with France. In 1947 France made a number of concessions and constitutional reforms, not wishing to abandon the white settlers (*colons*). In 1952 **Ahmed Ben Bella** formed the Algerian Revolutionary Committee in **Cairo**. In 1954 the nationalists formed the FLN and the Armée de Libération Nationale (ALN). In 1956 France, Great Britain and Israel collaborated to invade Egypt when **Gamal Abdel Nasser** nationalized the **Suez Canal**. After the failure of the old European imperial powers to gain control of Suez, the FLN gained support from the governments of the newly independent non-aligned countries. The war of liberation in Algeria, which resulted in the deployment of some 500,000 French troops there, contributed to the collapse of the Fourth Republic in France. Gen. Charles de Gaulle was recalled. In January 1960 the *colons* rebelled against de Gaulle. He began secret negotiations with the FLN provisional government in Cairo. **Oil** was discovered in the Sahara, leading France to consider retaining control of the oil-rich desert region while granting independence to the rest of Algeria. In 1962 Algeria became independent, with a government under the control of the FLN. For the next 27 years, until 1989, the FLN was the only political party in Algeria. The February 1989 amendments to the Constitution permitted the formation of other political associations, with some restrictions; the right to establish political parties was not guaranteed by the Constitution until November 1996. This political 'opening' in the late 1980s, however, enabled several new groupings to contest elections. The surprising success of the FIS, first in municipal elections and then, in December 1991, in the first round of the general election, led the army to intervene, cancel the subsequent elections and ban the FIS. The response from the Islamists, who established a number of militant armed groups to oppose the government and fight for an **Islamic state**, resulted in a continuing civil conflict with the secular state apparatus, which nevertheless allowed legislative elections featuring pro-government and moderate religious parties in June 1997 and elections to the Council of the Nation in December 1997 and again in December 2000. The FIS's armed wing, the **Islamic Salvation Army**, disbanded itself in January 2000 and many armed militants surrendered under an amnesty programme designed to promote national reconciliation. Nevertheless, the conflict continued well into 2004, albeit on a reduced scale, with groups such as the **Groupe islamique armé** and the **Groupe salafiste pour la prédication et le combat** remaining active. General elections to the National People's Assembly were held in May 2002 and presidential elections in April 2004. The first produced a majority for the FLN, and the second secured the re-election of President Bouteflika. In the previous presidential election, held on 15 April 1999, Bouteflika had received more than 70% of the vote. The six candidates who opposed him withdrew on the eve of the election, having alleged electoral fraud. In the elections of April 2004 Bouteflika was the army's candidate and favourite to win; his main rival was Ali Benflis, Bouteflika's campaign manager in the previous elections and Prime Minister until dismissed in 2003. Bouteflika won with an overwhelming majority, gaining some 87% of the vote in a poll in which nearly 60% of registered voters participated. Benflis secured only 8% of the vote. A 'moderate' Islamist candidate, Abdallah Djaballah, came third with 5% of the vote, and a left-wing woman candidate (and leader of the **Workers Party**), Louisa Hanoune, also stood. Major outstanding political concerns include Berber unrest in Kabylia—clashes during the April 2004 elections between Berbers and members of the security forces disrupted voting in Tizi Ouzou, Bejaia and Bouira provinces.

Algeria, economy

Gross domestic product (GDP) totals 4,222,000m. dinars (US $54,700m., equivalent to per caput GDP of $1,770). Average annual growth in GDP in 1991–2001 was only 1.7%. **Industry** and manufacturing account for more than one-half of GDP, **agriculture** for 10.5% and services for 38%. The hydrocarbons sector is the backbone of the economy, accounting for approximately 60% of budget revenues, 30% of GDP, and more than 95% of export earnings. Algeria's principal exports are petroleum and **natural gas**, together generating some $11,600m. f.o.b., with other **energy** products accounting for $9,400m. Algeria has the fifth largest reserves of natural gas in the world and is the second largest gas exporter; it ranks 14th in the world in respect of **oil** reserves. Algeria's financial and economic indicators improved during the mid-1990s, in part because of policy reforms supported by the **International Monetary Fund** and **debt** rescheduling by the Paris Club. Algeria's finances in 2000 and 2001 benefited from the temporary spike in oil prices and the Government's tight fiscal policy, leading to a large increase in the **trade** surplus, record highs in foreign exchange reserves, and reduction in foreign debt. Economic growth, which was slow in the 1990s, is now a brisk 7%, boosted by oil and gas exports. In 2001 the Government signed an Association Treaty with the **European Union** that will eventually lower tariffs and should increase trade. Political instability in the 1990s threatened many projects and led to an exodus of skilled, mostly expatriate, workers. The situation is improving, however, and although the security and human rights situation remains repressive, there are signs that the long civil war is coming to an end. The Government's continued efforts to diversify the economy by attracting foreign and domestic investment outside the energy sector have, however, had little success in reducing poverty or high (nearly 30%) unemployment or in improving the availability of housing and living standards. Agriculture remains under-funded and poorly-performing; there are often shortages in basic foodstuffs. There is a large black market. The bureaucracy remains cumbersome, inefficient and corrupt.

Algerian League for the Defence of Human Rights

A legally recognized Algerian NGO, headed by Ali Yahia Abdennour.

Algerian National Congress – *see* Congrès national algérien

Algerian National Front

Front national algérien

Algerian political grouping, founded in 1999. Led by Moussa Touati, it advocates the eradication of poverty and supports the government's domestic peace initiatives.

Algiers

El-Djezair

Capital of Algeria, with a population of some 1.5m. Port and major industrial and commercial centre.

Algiers Accord

Treaty between Iran and Iraq, signed in June 1975, concerning their dispute over borders, **water**, and navigation rights. Under the Treaty, the median course of the **Shatt al-Arab** waterway was designated as the border between the two countries and the Shah withdrew Iranian support for the Kurdish rebellion. Yet, ultimately, the Treaty was not honoured by either side, leading to the **Iran–Iraq War**.

Ali, Ahmed ibn

Member of the ruling **ath-Thani** dynasty of Qatar. Supplanted in 1972 by his cousin (and Prime Minister) Khalifa ibn Hamad, who in 1977 named his own son, Hamad ibn Khalifa, as crown prince.

Alignment Bloc-Maarach

An alliance formed between the **Israel Labour Party** and **Mapam** in 1969, after the former had been established in 1968 by **Mapai**, the dominant partner, **Achdut HaAvoda** and most of **Rafi**. Mapam and the Labour Party retained their own organizations and memberships after the Alignment, but shared a common platform in elections to the **Knesset**, the **Histadrut**, and local government offices. The Alignment lasted until 1984.

Aliya

The term *aliya* (plural *aliyat*) has two meanings in **Hebrew**. It means to 'call up' a member of congregation to read the scroll of the Jewish law during a synagogue service. It also refers to a 'wave' of Jewish immigration into Palestine. Organized Jewish immigration into Palestine began in 1882, inspired by the Zionist movement. Between 1882 and the formation of the State of Israel there were four *aliyat* into Palestine.

Allawi, Ayad

Fifty-eight-year-old British-educated neurosurgeon, and head of the **Iraqi National Accord** (INA). Allawi was appointed interim Prime Minister in Iraq towards the end of May 2004 by unanimous vote of the **Iraqi Provisional Governing Council** (IGC), in preparation for the establishment of an interim or 'caretaker' Iraqi government at the end of June 2004. Allawi, described as a 'secular liberal' from Iraq's **Shi'ite** community, is an Iraqi nationalist and former member of the **Ba'ath Party**, who left Iraq in 1971 and moved into the opposition while in exile in Britain. He survived an assassination attempt organized by **Saddam Hussain** in 1978 and during the 1980s travelled widely cultivating links with other Iraqis in exile. After the invasion of Kuwait in 1990 he set up the INA as an organization that offered itself to several sympathetic foreign agencies as a vehicle for the overthrow of

Saddam Hussain. During the 1990s and in the approach to the US-led intervention in Iraq in 2003 the INA provided intelligence for both the US **Central Intelligence Agency** and the United Kingdom's MI6 intelligence agency, was responsible for information that referred to the possibility of the deployment in 45 minutes of Iraqi **weapons of mass destruction** and provided a counterbalance to the **Iraqi National Congress** and **Ahmad Chalabi** which were favoured by the Pentagon. On his return to Iraq after the war, he was appointed by **Paul Bremer** to the IGC, of whose security committee he is chairman. He is from one of Iraq's leading **Shi'a** families: his grandfather helped negotiate Iraq's independence from Great Britain and his father was a politician as well as a doctor. He is related to Ali Allawi, Iraq's defence minister.

Allenby Bridge

The bridge between Jordan and the Occupied Territory of the **West Bank**. Named after Gen. Allenby, a British general who headed the British High Command in **Cairo** during the First World War.

Alliance nationale républicaine (ANR)

Algerian political grouping, founded in 1995. An anti-Islamist party, it is led by Redha Malek.

Allon, Yigal (1918–80)

An Israeli statesman and **military** commander. Allon was a commander and one of the founders of the Palmah crack commando unit of the **Haganah**, leading decisive operations during the **War of Independence**. After the War of Independence Allon returned to education (obtaining degrees from the Hebrew University and Oxford University), and then went into politics. From 1961 until 1968 he served as Minister of Labour and in June 1967 was a member of the inner war Cabinet that planned the **Six-Day War** strategy. In 1968 Allon became Deputy Prime Minister, and in the following year became Minister of Education and Culture, and acting Prime Minister, after **Levi Eshkol** and before **Golda Meir**. From 1974 until 1977 he was Israel's foreign minister.

Aloni, Shulamit

Israeli politician and lawyer. Born in 1929. Participated in the **War of Independence**, defending **Jerusalem**. Worked as a teacher, producer, and columnist. Joined **Mapai** in 1959. Elected as a member of the **Knesset**.

Am Ehad

One Nation

Israeli political party. Workers' and pensioners' party affiliated to the **Histadrut**, the trade union federation.

Amal

An abbreviation of Afwaj al-Muqawma al-Lubnaniya (Lebanese Resistance Detachments or Lebanese Militia); also known as the Amal ('Hope') Organization of Lebanon—the acronym means 'hope' in **Arabic**. It succeeded the **Movement for the Deprived** (Harakat al-Mahrumin), launched in 1974 by **Musa as-Sadr** who, in the following year, founded Amal as the military wing of the Movement for the Deprived. By about 1976 Amal had become more of a political organization with a **Shi'ite** Islamist character. After Sadr's disappearance in August 1978, Amal (first under Husayn al-Husayni and then under **Nabih Berri**) lost its Islamist character. Led since 1980 by Nabih Berri, who was born in Freetown, Liberia, in 1949, into a poor family that originated from Tibneen in southern Lebanon, and whose father emigrated back to Lebanon, Amal became one of the most important Muslim militias during the **Lebanese civil war**, growing strong through its close ties with the Islamic regime of Iran and the Shi'a internal **refugees** from southern Lebanon after the Israeli bombing in the early 1980s. At one point Amal had as many as 14,000 troops. Criticized by **Hezbollah** for its laicism, its compromises with Israeli forces in the south and its hostility towards the **Palestinians**, in May 1988 Amal fought with Hezbollah forces in **Beirut**. This encouraged the deployment of Syrian troops in the southern outskirts of the city. Hostilities began again during the winter of 1988–89 and again in late 1989 and 1990. Amal and the Supreme Islamic Shi'a Council (headed by Muhammad Mahdi Shams ad-Din, who is also Principal Controller of the Command Council of Amal), now propose a democratic pluralism (*at-ta'addudiya*) based on inter-sectarian consensus. Amal currently has 10 seats in Lebanon's parliament. Nabih Berri remains the leader of Amal.

AMAN

Israel's **military** external intelligence service, linked to the Directorate of Military Intelligence. Its full name is Agaf Modiin (Information Bureau). It collaborates with **Mossad**, especially in the collection of intelligence on armaments, logistics and enemy defence systems. It includes all military and other service attachés overseas, has its own press and information service and is also responsible for imposing censorship regulations concerning anything connected with the army and internal security. Every foreign correspondent in Israel has to work through this organization.

American-Egyptian Chamber of Commerce

The USA has fostered the creation of several think-tanks and business associations in Egypt, notably the American-Egyptian Chamber of Commerce, to promote the Washington Consensus.

Amin, Samir

Egyptian intellectual, writer on development issues. Author of, notably, *The Arab Nation*.

Amman

Capital of Jordan, with a population of 1.2m. inhabitants. Commercial, industrial and administrative centre lying in the west of Jordan. The city has diverse industries, but **phosphate** extraction and **petroleum** refining are the most important. Amman has a university, and has grown since the Second World War, largely due to the influx of Palestinian refugees following the **wars** in Palestine after the establishment of the State of Israel.

Amnesty International

Amnesty International is one of several international human rights organizations which have led the campaign to put pressure on governments in the **Middle East** to liberalize their repressive political systems and improve their records on human rights.

AMU – *see* Arab Maghreb Union

Amu Darya (Oxus river)

This major river originates in the Pamir plateau of **Central Asia**. It is approximately 2,500 km long and follows a course south-west between Tajikistan and Afghanistan before turning north-west between Turkmenistan and Uzbekistan, until it empties into the Aral Sea. It was established as a line of control between imperial Russian and British interests during the final decades of the 19th century. The Amu Darya was accepted by Russia as the northern boundary of Afghanistan, where Britain had given support to Emir Sher Ali, the Afghan king, in 1873. This was officially confirmed in 1887. The Bolsheviks acknowledged the Amu Darya border in 1920 and the Afghan-Soviet Treaty of 1946 again proclaimed its significance, applying the *thalweg* (middle channel) principle of international law to the boundary.

Anfal campaign

The campaign against the **Kurds** waged by the Iraqi regime in 1988, during which poison gas was used on cities, including **Halabja**. Some 100,000 civilians were killed, more than 4,000 villages were destroyed and nearly 1m. people displaced.

Anglo-American Committee

Committee formed shortly after the Second World War, following disclosure of the horrors of the Holocaust and the problem of **refugees** and displaced persons. It concluded that no country other than Palestine was ready or willing to help find homes for Jews wishing to leave Europe.

Anglo-Egyptian Treaty of 1936

Military agreement between Great Britain and Egypt, signed in 1936 in response to the Italian–Ethiopian War of 1935. Britain acquired exclusive rights to equip and train the Egyptian **military**, and hence a means of protecting its economic interests in both Egypt and the **Suez Canal**.

Anglo-French Convention of 1904

In this Convention, France agreed not to interfere with British administration in Egypt. It confirmed and legalized the multilateral convention of 1888, which guaranteed use of the **Suez Canal** to all countries at all times. The entry into force of the 1888 treaty had been delayed because France was reluctant to permit Britain to defend the Canal. France now gave Britain its support in return for acceptance of France's claim to Morocco.

Anglo-Iranian Oil Co

The discovery of **oil** in Iran in 1908 led William Knox D'Arcy to found the Anglo-Persian Oil Co, later designated the Anglo-Iranian Oil Co (AIOC). In 1914 the British government acquired an interest in the company which was to increase to 55.9% in subsequent years. In 1948 Britain offered to pay higher royalties to offset its majority share in the company, but the Iranian parliament rejected the offer and eventually, in April 1951, the **Majlis** approved the nationalization of Iran's oil company. In the following month one of the leaders of the opposition to British control of Iran's oil, Mohammed Mossadegh, became Prime Minister. The AIOC was called upon to close its operations and evacuate its personnel. The repercussions of Iran's nationalization of its oil company were far-reaching. In 1953 the Shah of Iran fled into exile, only to return after a US-engineered counter-coup removed Mossadegh from power.

Anglo-Iraqi Treaty of 1922

Protectorate treaty, signed in 1922 and ratified in 1924, giving Iraq partial independence, but leaving Great Britain with economic and military control over the country. The treaty was superseded by the **Anglo-Iraqi Treaty of 1930**.

Anglo-Iraqi Treaty of 1930

A redrafted agreement based on the **Anglo-Iraqi Treaty of 1922**, and taking into consideration the change in Iraq's importance after the discovery of **oil** in 1927. The Treaty assured independence in most fields, together with British support for Iraq's membership of the League of Nations. However, British troops would still be stationed in Iraq.

Anglo-Jordanian Treaty of 1948

A new agreement, following the **Anglo-Transjordanian Treaty of 1923**, a consequence of King **Abdullah**'s changing the name of his kingdom from Emirate **Transjordan** to the **Hashemite** Kingdom of Jordan. The main principles in the agreement involved common war and foreign policies, allowing Great Britain to station military bases in Jordan, with the promise of mutual assistance in war and an assurance of an annual subsidy of £12m. to the king. The Treaty was abrogated on the initiative of the King of Jordan in March 1957.

Anglo-Ottoman Convention of 1913

A short-lived agreement signed in July 1913 between the Ottoman Sultan Muhammad VI and Britain, giving Sheikh Mubarak I authority over the city of Kuwait. However, at the beginning of the First World War in 1914 the Convention was declared void, and Britain declared Kuwait an independent sheikhdom.

Anglo-Persian Agreement of 1919

The Agreement represented a Persian attempt to obtain assistance with its extreme post-First World War financial problems, and a British attempt to turn Persia/Iran into a weak protectorate. The Agreement's proposals met with strongly negative reactions in Persia/Iran, as well as in the USA and Russia, and it was never ratified.

Anglo-Russian Agreement of 1907

This Agreement of August 1907 divided Iran, then called Persia, into British and Russian spheres of influence. It followed the revolution of 1905–06, which led to the elaboration of Iran's first Constitution and revealed the ability of the Great Powers to subvert the sovereignty of an independent country. Russian influence remained strong until the First World War, when Iran became a battleground for Turkish, Russian and British armies.

Anglo-Transjordanian Treaty of 1923

The Treaty under which **Transjordan**, now Jordan, came to be a country. The Treaty was intended to avert conflict between **Abdullah bin Hussein** and his brother Faisal bin Hussein, King (**Faisal I**) of Iraq. Britain stationed troops on Transjordanian soil with the promise to protect the country against foreign attack

Anjoman Islamie

Iranian Islamist group. Iranian members in the USA, who were often students, were tasked to monitor US policy towards the **Middle East** in general and Iran in particular.

Ankara

Capital of Turkey. Major industrial and commercial centre in central Anatolia. Population 3,582,000 (2003).

ANO—Abu Nidal Organization

Also known as the Fatah Revolutionary Council (FRC)—and also as the Arab Revolutionary Brigades, **Black September** and the Revolutionary Organization of Socialist Muslims. The ANO/FRC emerged as a result of a split from the **Palestine Liberation Organization** (PLO) in 1974 by **Sabri al-Banna** (also known as 'Abu Nidal') after his split with **Yasser Arafat** following disagreements over the strategy and policy of the PLO. The Organization had a limited effectiveness until it joined with the **Popular Front for the Liberation of Palestine** (PFLP) in the early 1980s. The reputation of 'Abu Nidal' is very much associated with the subsequent terrorist operations of the ANO/FRC. ANO/FRC was allegedly responsible throughout its existence for attacks in 20 countries which resulted in the death or injury of almost 900 persons. It was thought to be implicated in the rue des Rosiers attack in Paris, France, in 1982; in the massacres of passengers at the desks of **El Al**, the Israeli national airline, in Rome (Italy) and Vienna (Austria) airports in 1985; in the **hijacking** of an Egyptian passenger aircraft to Malta, also in 1985; in the attack on the Neve Shalom synagogue in **Istanbul**, Turkey, and the hijacking of Pan Am Flight 73 in Karachi, Pakistan, both in September 1986. In November the group boarded a ship off **Gaza** and took hostage a French woman and her children, whom they subsequently released. It was responsible for the City of Poros day-excursion ship attack in Greece in July and for an attack on a Pan Am Boeing 747 in December 1988. The Organization had various functional committees, including political, military, and financial bodies, with a limited overseas support structure. This included support in the form of safe haven training, logistic assistance and financial aid from Iraq, Libya and Syria. During 1989 bloody internal conflicts seriously weakened the Organization. 'Abu Nidal' left Libya, where he had been based, and relocated to Iraq, although the group maintained an operational presence in

Lebanon, where it was established in several Palestinian refugee camps. Financial and internal disorganization during the 1990s reduced the group's activities and capabilities. However, it was widely suspected of assassinating PLO deputy chief '**Abu Iyad**' and PLO security chief 'Abu Hul' in **Tunis**, Tunisia, in January 1991. ANO/FRC also assassinated a Jordanian diplomat in Lebanon in January 1994 and has been linked to the killing of the PLO representative there. 'Abu Nidal' was condemned to death by the PLO, which also claimed that the group had been heavily infiltrated by the Israeli intelligence services. Operations of the ANO/FRC in Libya and Egypt were closed down by the authorities in 1999. It is unclear who assumed leadership of the group after the death of 'Abu Nidal'/al-Banna in November 2002 in **Baghdad**.

Ansar-e Hezbollah

Iranian youth movement, founded in 1995. Seeks to gain access to the political process for religious militants.

Ansar al-Islam

The name means 'the supporters of Islam' in **Arabic**. Reputed to have started life as **Jund al-Islam**, a radical offshoot of an Iranian-backed Islamist group, based in **Halabja** with a predominantly Kurdish membership. After their formation Jund seized Tawela and Biyara and declared *jihad* against the secular Kurdish authorities and the **Patriotic Union of Kurdistan** (PUK). There were, almost immediately, clashes with the PUK. In September 2001 Jund militants slit the throats and mutilated more than 20 PUK *peshmerga*. They also attempted to assassinate Barham Salih, the PUK's Prime Minister. In the winter of 2002–03 they merged with another small group called Islah ('reform') to constitute Ansar al-Islam. The group has, perhaps, 1,000 members, who seek to establish an independent **Islamic state** in northern Iraq. The group has claimed to have produced cyanide-based toxins, ricin, and aflatoxin. It is also reputed to have had links with, or even to include, **Afghan Arabs** and members of **al-Qa'ida**, but this is denied by the leadership—although Ansar's leader, **Mullah Krekar**, has described **Osama bin Laden** as 'the jewel in the crown of the Muslim nation'. Krekar, who enjoys asylum status in Norway, where his wife and four children live, left Iraq for Iran, and, subsequently, Norway, during 2002. His visits to Europe before his departure apparently enabled him to secure resources and weapons for the group (the group's treasurer and chief of propaganda/information is his brother, Khaled). Since obtaining asylum in Norway he has travelled widely in Europe (including the United Kingdom and Italy—specifically Milan) building and developing links and recruiting fighters, and has returned to Iraq periodically. Ansar al-Islam has continued to operate in northern Iraq since Krekar's official departure, mounting ambushes, attacks and assassination attempts in PUK areas. Before the **Iraq War (2003)** Ansar al-Islam was based in northern Iraq near the Iranian border. The group is thought to have scattered over the Iranian frontier after being attacked by US forces fighting alongside Kurdish *peshmerga* in the first week of the war. Since then, however, Ansar militants have regrouped into cells and have established themselves in some northern cities, such as **Mosul** and **Kirkuk**. Ansar al-Islam is thought by PUK leaders to have been responsible for a suicide bomb attack in November 2003 on the PUK headquarters in Kirkuk, which killed five and injured 40. PUK officials in Kirkuk indicated that they had increased security following threats from Ansar al-Islam, which is believed by some to have established links with **Saddam Hussain** loyalists in areas north and west of **Baghdad** to launch a number of major suicide bomb attacks across Iraq during the latter part of 2003. A statement purporting to come from Osama bin Laden, which threatened increased terrorist activity in Iraq, praised Ansar militants and named individual **Kurds** as legitimate targets. Speculation continues as to the nature of Ansar's links with the Saddam Hussain regime, and with al-Qa'ida. Investigations carried out in Norway in 2004 suggest that Krekar is actively involved with Ansar al-Islam in Iraq and that links with al-Qa'ida do exist. On the other hand, much of the negative intelligence comes from PUK sources, which are strongly influenced by US links.

Ansar al-Qa'ida

A (possibly fictional) terrorist group. A letter faxed to the Spanish newspaper *ABC* in the aftermath of the Madrid train bombing in 2004 which threatened more attacks in Spain, was signed, in the name of Ansar al-Qa'ida, by Abu Dujana al-Afghani, the name used in a videotape claiming responsibility for the Madrid bombings. They may have links with the **Moroccan Islamic Combatant Group** thought to be responsible for both the Spanish terrorist actions and the **Casablanca** bombings in May 2003.

Ansar al-'Usba al-Islamiya – *see* Supporters of the Islamic League

Ansarollah Group

Libyan opposition group, founded in 1996.

Antonius George (1891–1941)

Palestinian writer and politician, born in **Cairo**, Egypt, in 1891. Having graduated from Cambridge University, United Kingdom, in 1913, Antonius began a civil service career in Palestine in 1921. In 1930, however, he resigned from the British civil service in protest at Britain's discriminatory policies towards **Palestinians**. In 1936–37 Antonius appeared before the **Peel Commission**, and one year later he authored *The Arab Awakening*, a classic work of **Arab nationalism**. He was a member of the Palestinian delegation at the London Conference in 1939.

Aoun, Michel

Born 1935, Lebanese **military** leader and politician. President of Lebanon during the military government from September 1988 to October 1990. Born a Christian, Aoun became popular among Muslims after his military campaign against fellow Christians in 1989. The political élite in Lebanon regarded him as an uncontrollable rebel, while **Hafiz al-Assad** considered him an enemy for undermining his plans to take control in Lebanon. Aoun continued to criticize the Syrian presence in Lebanon from exile in France after 1991.

Aqaba, Gulf of

The Gulf of Aqaba is an arm of the Red Sea that runs along the Sinai to the west and the Saudi Arabian shore to the east. It terminates at a point where Israel and Jordan come together at the southernmost extent of the Negev Desert. The Israeli port of Eilat and the Jordanian port of Aqaba face each other across the Gulf. Commanding the entrance to the Gulf of Aqaba, on the south-western tip of the Sinai, is Sharm esh-Sheikh, which was occupied by Israeli forces during the war of 1956 before they withdrew when a UN peace force was interposed between them and the Egyptian forces. The Israeli army again swept through the Sinai and seized Sharm esh-Sheikh during the Arab–Israeli **Six-Day War** of 1967. Israel agreed at **Camp David** to withdraw its forces from Sinai when Egypt signed a peace treaty in 1978; Sharm esh-Sheikh and the entire Sinai was returned to Egyptian control in April 1982. By the terms of the treaty Sharm esh-Sheikh was demilitarized and the Gulf of Aqaba opened to innocent passage.

Al-Aqsa International Bank

The financial arm of **Hamas**. A 20% stake is held by **Beit al-Mal Holdings**, a public investment holding company the majority of whose shareholders are members of Hamas or Hamas supporters.

Al-Aqsa *intifada* – *see Intifada*, al-Aqsa

Al-Aqsa Martyrs' Brigade

The al-Aqsa Martyrs' Brigade comprises an unknown number of small cells of **al-Fatah**-affiliated activists that emerged at the outset of the current **al-Aqsa *intifada*** to attack Israeli targets. It operates mainly in the **West Bank** and has claimed attacks inside Israel and the **Gaza Strip**, but may also have followers in Palestinian refugee camps in southern Lebanon. It aims to remove the Israeli **military** and settlers from the West Bank, Gaza Strip and **Jerusalem** and to establish a Palestinian state. The al-Aqsa Martyrs' Brigade has carried out shootings and suicide operations against Israeli military personnel and civilians and has killed **Palestinians** who it believed were collaborating with Israel. In January 2002 the Brigade claimed responsibility for the first suicide bombing carried out by a woman. It also claimed to have been responsible for a suicide bombing in May 2003 in Israel, which killed two people outside a shopping mall in Afula, just north of **Jenin**. Some witnesses suggested that the bomber was a woman. Another Islamist group—**Islamic Jihad**—also claimed responsibility for the attack. Hours earlier a suicide bomber on a bicycle injured three Israeli soldiers in Gaza. This wave of bombings began on 17 May with an attack on a Jewish settlement in **Hebron** in which a middle-aged couple were killed. On the following day seven people were killed in the bombing of an early morning commuter bus in Jerusalem. Half an hour later another suicide bomber blew himself up in a failed attack. Al-Aqsa Martyrs' Brigade announced in June 2003 that it was prepared to declare a cease-fire if Israel lifted its siege of **Yasser Arafat**, ended 'targeted assassinations' and released more prisoners. In December 2003 al-Aqsa Martyrs' Brigade condemned the Palestinian delegation which negotiated the **Geneva Accord** as 'collaborators with Israel'.

Al-Aqsa mosque

The area of the mosque is known as al-Haram ash-Sharif (the Noble Sanctuary). At its southernmost end is al-Aqsa mosque and at its centre the celebrated **Dome of the Rock**, on the Temple Mount, located at the heart of **Jerusalem**. The entire area is regarded as a mosque and comprises nearly one-sixth of the walled city of Jerusalem. Al-Aqsa is considered the third most holy shrine in **Islam**, after **Mecca** and **Medina** in Saudi Arabia. As such, its control by Israel is a symbol of fallen grandeur for many Muslims, exploited by Islamic fundamentalists across the world.

Arab(s)

The birthplace of the Arabs was the **Arabian Peninsula**. After the advent of **Islam** on the Peninsula Arab armies embarked on a conquest of the world in the name of Islam. Gradually they assimilated, or were assimilated into, the populations they dominated—large numbers of whom converted to Islam. The term 'Arab' is used to designate a people made up of individuals who speak one of the variations of the **Arabic** language, possess an Arab identity, and consider themselves a part of the history and culture that has developed in the **Middle East** and northern Africa since the establishment of Islam in the 7th century AD. Though there are close links between the Arabs and Islam they are not synonymous; there are many Christian Arabs as well as many non-Arab Muslims. Today what is known as the **Arab World** corresponds approximately with the membership of the **Arab League**.

However, there are Arab minorities on the fringes of this area in Turkey, Africa and Israel (see **Israeli Arabs**).

Arab African International Bank

Founded in 1964 as the Arab African Bank, renamed in 1978. Shareholders are the governments of Kuwait, Egypt, Algeria, Jordan and Qatar, Bank al-Jazira (Saudi Arabia), Rafidain Bank (Iraq) and Arab individuals and institutions. Based in **Cairo**, Egypt. Deposits: US $769m.; capital: $100m.; reserves: $231m.

Arab Ba'ath Party – *see* Ba'ath Party

Arab Bank (Jordan)

Founded in 1930 in **Jerusalem** by Abdul Hameed (Abdel Hamid) Shoman, a Palestinian. In 1948 it lost three branches in **Haifa**, Jerusalem and **Jaffa**, all of which fell under Israeli control. To prove its loyalty to the Arabs of Palestine, it honoured all of the deposits in these branches. In 1967, during the **Arab–Israeli War**, the bank lost six more branches in the **West Bank** and one in **Gaza**. However, it was able to transfer most of its funds to **Amman** before Israel took control of the banking network in the **Occupied Territories**. The move to Jordan was very successful. Within two decades, the Arab Bank, acting as the financial arm of the **Palestine Liberation Organization** (PLO), had established a strong presence inside the Jordanian economy. By the mid-1980s the PLO controlled as much as 70% of Jordan's economy by virtue of its ownership of textile factories, fruit plantations, transport and construction companies. More than once the Arab Bank alleviated the financial difficulties of King **Hussein** of Jordan. It also supervised the PLO's capital outflow and investment in other countries, mostly via the Arab Bank for Economic Development. When **Yasser Arafat** withdrew funds from Lebanon at the outset of the 1982 Israeli invasion, the Arab Bank was used to disperse them across the **Middle East**, Europe and the USA. Abdul-Majeed Shoman, son of the founder, is the chairman of the **Palestine National Fund** and the man who masterminded the PLO's investment programme. The Arab Bank is the sole bank trusted by the PLO and the one that has managed the PLO's finances for the most part since its origins. At times, the Bank has acted as the central bank of Palestine. In July 1988, for example, the Jordanian Government renounced its claim to sovereignty over the West Bank, and almost immediately ceased paying the wages of 18,000 Palestinian civil servants working there. The PLO intervened to guarantee all remuneration in question, appointing the Arab Bank to disburse the US $6m. a month required. The Bank is today one of the largest financial organizations in the world, with assets in the 1980s in excess of $10,000m. and more than 400 branches and offices spread across five continents. It is the only non-**GCC** bank in the region with a truly global presence. It is active in project and trade financing and in facilitating investment flows between the Middle East and other regions. The Bank's excellent credentials stand out, reflecting experienced management, sound credit quality and advanced IT infrastructure. Despite regional problems, the Bank has built vibrant businesses over the past three decades. It has recently undergone restructuring—credit management functions were merged to improve risk control and provide enhanced branch synergy, while a separate private banking division will help to expand treasury management services.

Arab Bank for Economic Development in Africa

Established in 1973 by the **Arab League**. It provides loans and grants to African countries to finance development projects. By the end of 2001 the total value of loans and grants approved since the start of funding activities in 1975 was some US $2,200m. Subscribing countries: all of the members of the Arab League except the Comoros, Djibouti, Somalia and Yemen. Recipient countries: all countries in the **African Union** except those which are also members of the Arab League.

Arab banking (Gulf Co-operation Council)

The **energy**-rich **Gulf Co-operation Council** member states (Saudi Arabia, Kuwait, the United Arab Emirates (UAE), Bahrain, Qatar and Oman) remain at the heart of Arab banking (see **Arab Banks—top 100)** and are net 'creditors' to the international banking system. The regulatory structure of the Gulf banking industry is well developed and efficient. All six central banks ensure full compliance with the Basle Committee's Core Principles for Effective Banking Supervision. Besides a sound legal and regulatory framework, the Gulf financial system boasts 'First World' clearing, settlements and default procedures. The main banks' branches are connected to the SWIFT systems to ensure efficiency and customer convenience. The six individual banking sectors—with total financial assets of more than US $300,000m. and foreign assets of $72,000m. in March–April 2003—have proved remarkably vibrant and resilient amidst bearish global capital markets, low interest margins, the Iraq conflict and ongoing geopolitical risk aversion. Three years of greater-than-anticipated **oil** revenues have had positive multiplier effects on economic activity in the Gulf thanks to higher government expenditure and fixed investments. Stronger crude oil prices and record low interest rates have injected considerable liquidity across the Gulf, conducive to corporate earnings and an expanding economy. Arab banks benefited from falls in major western stock markets. In 2002 the average returns on equity for Saudi banks were 19.7%, for Kuwaiti banks 17.6% and for UAE banks 13.3%. The three most profitable banks were the **National Commercial Bank**, the National Bank of Kuwait and the Saudi-British Bank. Most banks reported healthy growth in assets and earnings during the first half of 2003. Even so, the Gulf banks are relatively small players in a global context—the total assets of the top 50 GCC banks in 2002 were worth $342,000m., equivalent to those of the United Kingdom's Lloyds TSB Group, with only a handful of institutions holding assets in excess of $20,000m.

Arab Banking Corporation (ABC)

The ABC (Bahrain) was the first bank to issue a credit card structured according to Islamic principles.

Arab Banks—top 100 (at 31 December 2002)

No.	Name of Bank	Country	Capital (US $m.)
1	National Commercial Bank	Saudi Arabia	2,381
2	Saudi American Bank	Saudi Arabia/USA	2,339
3	Arab Banking Corpn	Bahrain	2,195
4	Riyad Bank	Saudi Arabia	2,164
5	Arab Bank	Jordan	2,096
6	Al-Rajhi Banking & Investment Corpn	Saudi Arabia	1,826
7	National Bank of Kuwait	Kuwait	1,470
8	Qatar National Bank	Qatar	1,368
9	Gulf International Bank	Bahrain	1,270
10	Banque Saudi Fransi	Saudi Arabia/France	1,269
11	Gulf Investment Corpn	Kuwait	1,178
12	Emirates Bank International	UAE	1,177
13	National Bank of Dubai	Dubai	1,174
14	Saudi British Bank	Saudi Arabia/Britain	1,142
15	Abu Dhabi Commercial Bank	Abu Dhabi	1,112
16	Investcorp Bank	Bahrain	1,040
17	National Bank of Abu Dhabi	Abu Dhabi	980
18	Arab National Bank	Saudi Arabia	952
19	National Bank of Egypt	Egypt	948
20	Mashreqbank	UAE	862
21	Ahli United Bank	Bahrain	807

Table (cont'd)

No.	Name of Bank	Country	Capital (US $m.)
22	Kuwait Finance House	Kuwait	767
23	Commercial Bank of Syria	Syria	730
24	Gulf Bank	Kuwait	685
25	Crédit Populaire du Maroc	Morocco	648
26	Saudi Hollandi Bank	Saudi Arabia/Holland	615
27	Burgan Bank	Kuwait	587
28	Saudi Investment Bank	Saudi Arabia	577
29	Al-Ahli Bank of Kuwait	Kuwait	566
30	Commercial Bank of Kuwait	Kuwait	551
31	Banque Commerciale du Maroc	Morocco	551
32	Banque Marocaine du Commerce Extérieur	Morocco	516
33	The Arab Investment Co	Saudi Arabia	505
34	Bank of Kuwait & The Middle East	Kuwait	492
35	Banque de la Mediterranée	Lebanon	470
36	Union National Bank	UAE	462
37	Banque Misr Egypt	Egypt	455
38	Libyan Arab Foreign Bank	Libya	445
39	Commercial International Bank	Egypt	435
40	Arab International Bank	Egypt	420
41	Dubai Islamic Bank	Dubai	401
42	Blom Bank	Lebanon	401
43	The Housing Bank for Trade and Finance	Jordan	374
44	Banque Audi	Lebanon	363
45	Commercial Bank of Dubai	Dubai	359
46	Abu Dhabi Islamic Bank	Abu Dhabi	355
47	National Bank of Bahrain	Bahrain	348

Table (cont'd)

No.	Name of Bank	Country	Capital (US $m.)
48	Arab Bank for Investment & Foreign Trade	UAE	344
49	Kuwait Real Estate Bank	Kuwait	342
50	Bank Muscat	Oman	324
51	Wafa Bank	Morocco	317
52	Banque du Caire	Egypt	315
53	Banque Nationale d'Algérie	Algeria	312
54	Bank of Bahrain and Kuwait	Bahrain/Kuwait	306
55	Bank of Alexandria	Egypt	276
56	Byblos Bank	Lebanon	271
57	Oman International Bank	Oman	269
58	Sahara Bank	Libya	269
59	Banque Libano-Française	Lebanon	266
60	Banque Nationale Agricole	Tunisia	263
61	Misr International Bank	Egypt	262
62	Shamil Bank of Bahrain	Bahrain	258
63	National Bank of Oman	Oman	244
64	Fransabank	Lebanon	244
65	Société Tunisienne de Banque	Tunisia	235
66	Doha Bank	Qatar	215
67	United Gulf Bank	Bahrain	209
68	Bank al-Jazira	Saudi Arabia	201
69	Commercial Bank of Qatar	Qatar	200
70	National Bank of Sharjah	Sharjah (UAE)	182
71	Banque Internationale Arabe de Tunisie	Tunisia	178
72	Bahrain International Bank	Bahrain	176
73	National Bank of Fujairah	Fujairah (UAE)	169
74	Banque de Tunisie	Tunisia	164

Table (cont'd)

No.	Name of Bank	Country	Capital (US $m.)
75	First Gulf Bank	UAE	161
76	Suez Canal Bank	Egypt	159
77	Rakbank	UAE	158
78	Invest Bank	UAE	144
79	Arab African International Bank	Egypt	142
80	National Bank of Umm al-Qaiwain	Umm al-Qaiwain (UAE)	132
81	Crédit du Maroc	Morocco	128
82	United Arab Bank	UAE	126
83	TAIB Bank	Bahrain	125
84	National SocGen Bank	Egypt	125
85	Bank Dhofar Al-Omani Al-Fransi	Oman/France	123
86	Banque de l'Habitat	Tunisia	116
87	Bank of Sharjah	Sharjah (UAE)	114
88	Egyptian American Bank	Egypt/USA	113
89	Qatar Islamic Bank	Qatar	108
90	Delta International Bank	Egypt	108
91	Crédit Libanais	Lebanon	108
92	Oman Arab Bank	Oman	107
93	Bahrain Islamic Bank	Bahrain	102
94	Banque du Sud	Tunisia	101
95	Jordan National Bank	Jordan	98
96	National Bank for Development	Egypt	95
97	Bahraini Saudi Bank	Bahrain	88
98	Faisal Islamic Bank of Egypt	Egypt	77
99	Jordan Kuwait Bank	Jordan	76
100	Jordan Islamic Bank for Finance & Investment	Jordan	76

Source: *The Middle East*, October 2003

Arab Centre for the Study of Arid Zones and Dry Lands

Established in 1971 to conduct regional **research and development** programmes related to **water** and soil resources, plant and animal production, agro-meteorology and socio-economic studies of arid zones. The Centre also sponsors and hosts conferences and training courses and encourages the exchange of information by Arab scientists.

Arab Common Market

The implementation of an Arab Common Market by the **Council of Arab Economic Unity** (CAEU) was proposed in August 1964. This was eventually to involve all of the members of the CAEU. A meeting of the ministers of the Council in **Baghdad** in June 2001 issued 'the Baghdad Declaration' proposing a four-economy free-trade area to start with, involving Egypt, Iraq, Syria and Libya. Palestine expressed interest in joining, which delayed implementation. This initiative was regarded as a cornerstone for a **(Greater) Arab Free Trade Area** being implemented by the **Arab League**.

Arab Conference on Justice

The first such conference was held in **Beirut** in 1999. Participants included both members of judiciaries across the Arab region and non-governmental individuals, such as social scientists. The Conference addressed the state of the judiciary in the 21st century in the Arab region. A second conference was held in February 2003 in **Cairo**, with the objective of promoting independent judiciaries in Arab countries.

Arab Co-operation Council

Established 16 February 1989. The Arab Co-operation Council aims to promote economic co-operation and integration, possibly leading to an **Arab Common Market**. Its member states are Egypt, Iraq, Jordan and Yemen.

Arab Democratic Front

Jordanian political coalition, formed in September 2000. Founded by Ahmed Ubeidat and Taher al-Masri.

Arab Democratic Party

Lebanese pro-Syrian political party, otherwise known as the Red Knights. Mainly supported by **Alawites** and based in Tripoli. Its leader is Ali Eid.

Arab Deterrent Force

A 30,000-strong peace-keeping force, deployed in June 1976 by the **Arab League** to supervise successive attempts to bring an end to hostilities in Lebanon and afterwards to maintain peace. The Arab League summit in October 1976 agreed that costs were to be paid as follows: Saudi Arabia and Kuwait, 20% each; the United Arab Emirates (UAE), 15%; Qatar, 10%; other Arab states, 35%. The mandate of the force has been successively renewed. It was initially composed mostly of Syrian troops, but also included contingents from Saudi Arabia, Sudan, Libya and the UAE. Over time, the majority of troops from other Arab states have been withdrawn, leaving the force manned largely by Syria.

The Arab East

The Arab East (*mashreq*) is the term applied to the **Arabic**-speaking **Middle East** excluding North Africa (*maghreb*). It includes Egypt, Jordan, Lebanon, Syria, the **Occupied Territories** of Palestine, Iraq, Saudi Arabia, Kuwait, Oman, Yemen, Qatar and the United Arab Emirates.

Arab Economic Unity Council

Arab organization established in June 1957 by a resolution of the Arab Economic Council of the **Arab League**, consisting of Egypt, Iraq, Jordan, Kuwait, Libya, Mauritania, the **Palestine Liberation Organization** (now Palestine), Somalia, Sudan, Syria, the United Arab Emirates and Yemen. The Council's focus is regional, devoted to achieving economic integration through the framework of economic and social development.

(Greater) Arab Free Trade Area

In 1997 renewed interest was expressed in the formation of a regional trading bloc by the member states of the **Arab League**. Eighteen Arab states approved an executive programme to establish the Arab Free Trade Area (AFTA), which came into effect on 1 January 1998. The AFTA will lead to the elimination of import duties and other barriers to **trade** on goods of Arab origin over a 10-year period. These developments imply that by 2008 intra-Arab imports will enter each country of the region without encountering tariffs and tariff-like barriers. (See also **MAFTA**.)

Arab Free Trade Zone (AFTZ)

An association established in May 2003 to promote economic co-operation and **trade** between its members, when Egypt, Jordan, Tunisia and Morocco signed a declaration—the Arab Free Trade Agreement—to this effect. Officials have expressed the hope that four countries will have the zone operational by the end of 2004 and that other Arab countries will also join during the next decade. Yemen is expected to be the first new member of this association, gaining full membership in 2005. The AFTZ is regarded by some as the last means to preserve a significant role for the **Arab League**, whose reputation and effectiveness has been severely limited over the past decade. Advocates point out that external pressures and the structures afforded by the **World Trade Organization** are propelling this initiative forwards. Others, however, are sceptical. They point out that the region as a whole lacks a significant intra-regional trade base, apart from **energy** products and some agricultural commodities; that intra-Arab commerce accounts for only 8% of the overall foreign trade of the countries involved and that many Arab countries compete to sell similar goods in global markets; that any potential for regional economic co-operation will be hampered by significant territorial disputes; and that smaller-scale initiatives (the **Arab Maghreb Union** and the **Gulf Co-operation Council**) have had limited success. Finally, it is remarked that the **Euro-Mediterranean Partnership** is progressing rapidly, with the objective of creating a Euro-Med Free Trade Zone by 2010 that incorporates 27 countries, including 20 (not all Arab) that directly border the **Mediterranean**. The scale of this initiative will dwarf any attempt at a regional AFTZ.

Arab Fund for Economic and Social Development (AFESD)

Established on 16 May 1968 by the Economic Council of the **Arab League**, although it did not begin operations until 1974. Its aim is to promote economic and social development in the **Arab World**. Its member states are Algeria, Bahrain, Djibouti, Egypt (suspended 1979, but subsequently allowed to re-enter), Iraq (suspended 1993), Jordan, Kuwait, Lebanon, Libya, Mauritania, Morocco, Oman, Qatar, Saudi Arabia, Somalia (suspended 1993), Sudan, Syria, Tunisia, the United Arab Emirates, Yemen and the **Palestine Liberation Organization**. AFESD makes loans and grants for economic and social development projects in Arab (and some other) countries. It co-operates with other Arab agencies, such as the **Organization of Arab Petroleum Exporting Countries**.

Arab Fund for Technical Assistance to African Countries

Established in 1975 to provide technical assistance for development projects by providing Arab and African experts, grants for scholarships and training, and finance for technical studies.

Arab Higher Commission/Committee for Palestine

Radical group established in 1945 by the **Arab League**. It sought to represent Palestinian interests and take a firm stance in rejecting all compromise on the rights of Jews to **Eretz Israel**.

Arab Human Development Report

Sponsored by the **UNDP**'s Regional Bureau for Arab States and by the **Arab Fund for Economic and Social Development**, the Arab Human Development Report was produced by a team of Arab scholars advised by a panel of distinguished regional policy-makers to provide an overall assessment of the state of human development in the **Arab World** and guide-lines for a development strategy. Since 1990 the UNDP has published annual Human Development Reports that set out the basic social and economic indicators for the nations of the world. The Arab Human Development Report, however, is exclusively focused on the 22 Arab states. Subtitled 'Creating Opportunities for Future Generations', it makes clear how much still needs to be done to provide current and future generations with the political voice, social choices and economic opportunities that they need in order to build a better future for themselves and their families. Published in 2002, it gives special attention to issues of human rights, freedom and **democracy**, complete empowerment of Arab **women**, and better production and utilization of knowledge. It contains up-to-date statistics and analysis on a wide range of issues pertaining to economic, social and political development.

Arab Industrial Development and Mining Organization

Established in 1990 by the merger of the Arab Industrial Development Organization, the Arab Organization for Mineral Resources and the Arab Organization for Standardization and Metrology. It comprises a 13-member executive council, a high committee of **mineral** resources and a co-ordination committee for Arab Industrial Research Centres. It also has a council of ministers responsible for **industry**, which meets every two years.

Arab Industrialization Authority

Established following Arab co-operation during the **Arab–Israeli War** of 1973. In 1978, however, when Egypt signed the **Camp David Accords** with Israel, the Authority collapsed.

Arab International Bank

Founded in 1971 as the Egyptian International Bank for Foreign Trade and Investment, renamed in 1974. Owned by Egypt, Libya, the United Arab Emirates, Oman, Qatar and private Arab shareholders. Offshore bank which aims to promote **trade** and investment in shareholders' countries and other Arab states. Deposits: US $2,300m.; reserves: $143.2m.; capital: $262m.

Arab–Israeli Conflict – *see* **Arab–Israeli War, various years**

Arab–Israeli War (1948–49)

There had been increasing conflict in Palestine since the end of 1947, when the Arabs had rejected the UN Partition Plan and the implicit creation of a state for the Jews in Palestine. Until March 1948 the fighting was largely in favour of the Arabs in Palestine, who received assistance from the Arab states, but thereafter the Jewish forces began to gain the upper hand. The first of the Arab–Israeli **wars** broke out on the day after the declaration of independence of the State of Israel on 14 May 1948, when the armies of **Transjordan**, Egypt and Syria, backed by Lebanese and Iraqi contingents, invaded Palestine. Egyptian forces gained some territory in the south and Jordanian forces captured **Jerusalem**'s Old City, but the other Arab forces were soon halted. In June the UN succeeded in establishing a four-week truce. This was followed in July by significant Israeli advances before another truce. Fighting erupted again in August and continued sporadically until the end of 1948. An Israeli advance in January 1949 isolated Egyptian forces and led to a cease-fire. Protracted peace talks in February–July 1949 resulted in armistice agreements between, on the one hand, Israel and, on the other, Egypt, Syria and, later Jordan, but no formal peace. The armistice agreements ratified the enlargement, by one-third (from 14,000 sq km to almost 21,000 sq km), of the area of the Jewish state as defined by the Partition Plan. The Arab state in Palestine failed to come into being. Large numbers of Palestinian Arabs had fled, to be eventually settled in refugee camps near Israel's new border. In December 1948 the UN proclaimed their right to return, but the new Israeli leaders refused to recognize this proclamation. In April 1950 the UN recorded almost 1m. Palestinian refugees in Jordan, **Gaza**, Lebanon and Syria.

Arab–Israeli War (1956)

The second Arab–Israeli conflict, the Suez crisis, involved an attack by Britain and France, together with Israel, on Egypt, following the nationalization of the **Suez Canal** by President **Nasser** of Egypt in July 1956. Great Britain and France secretly prepared an offensive against Egypt, having provided Israel with arms and equip-ment. On 29 October war was initiated by Operation Kadesh and in no more than six days the **Israeli Defence Force** successfully occupied **Gaza** and the Sinai. On 31 October British and French forces bombed Egyptian targets and five days later, despite an appeal for a cease-fire by the UN, landed troops at Port Said and Ismailia. They were forced to leave in December, however, after intense diplomatic pressure had been exerted by the USA and the Soviet Union. Israeli forces were obliged to withdraw from Sinai and Gaza by March 1957, having gained free navigation in the **Gulf of Aqaba** and around the port of Eilat as a result of the presence at Sharm esh-Sheikh and Gaza of UN observers.

Arab–Israeli War (1967)

The third Arab–Israeli war, also known as the Six-Day War, took place in June 1967. The **Palestine Liberation Organization** (PLO) was formally established in **Jerusalem** in May 1965 and almost immediately began operations against Israel. Israel reacted with retaliatory strikes. Anxiety on the part of the Arab states regarding a build-up of Israeli forces for a possible large-scale offensive increased to reach breaking-point in mid-May 1967, when an Israeli march past in Jerusalem effectively broke the armistice agreement. Two days later the Egyptian Government had placed its troops on alert and on 18 May called for a withdrawal of the UN observers from Sharm esh-Sheikh and **Gaza**, which Egyptian troops occupied, closing the **Gulf of Aqaba**. In **Tel-Aviv** these actions, together with the subsequent rallying of Jordan (31 May) and Iraq (4 June) to the Egyptian-Syrian pact, appeared threatening. At the end of the first week of June the **Israeli Defence Force** struck on several fronts. They annihilated the Arab air force, secured Gaza and the Sinai and occupied the Jordanian **West Bank** and the Syrian **Golan Heights**, all within a week. The Israeli victory was crushing—a catastrophe (***nakhba***) from the Arab point of view. After five months of bargaining, the UN Security Council (in **UN Security Council Resolution 242**) declared the need for Israel's withdrawal from the Arab territories it had occupied in exchange for a cease-fire, the recognition of all states in the region, freedom of navigation on the **Suez Canal** and in the Gulf of Aqaba, and the creation of demilitarized zones.

Arab–Israeli War (1973)

Also known as the Yom Kippur, October, or **Ramadan** War, this was the fourth Arab–Israeli military conflict. It arose out of a growing sense of frustration, in Egypt in particular, at the failure of numerous UN resolutions and initiatives by various different parties to secure the withdrawal of Israel from the territories it had occupied in 1967 during the third Arab–Israeli War. As early as 1971 the new President of Egypt, **Anwar es-Sadat**, had announced that 'there being no longer any hope of a peaceful solution, our decision is to fight'. Nearly two years later, on 6 October 1973, the date that year of the Jewish holiday of Yom Kippur, Egyptian tanks crossed the **Suez Canal** and entered the Sinai, while Syrian troops advanced into the **Golan Heights**. After this initial show of strength, the Arab offensive halted for a week, giving Israel, which had been caught by surprise, a chance to regain the initiative. On 17 October Gen. **Ariel Sharon**, who had moved his forces into the Sinai, engaged the Egyptian forces in a major tank battle. On the same day the decision was taken in Kuwait to initiate an **oil** embargo. Five days later **UN Security Council Resolution 338** was accepted by both Egypt and Israel, although the latter continued its counter-offensive on the ground. The USA and the Soviet Union both applied intense diplomatic pressure and a cease-fire was agreed.

Arab Israelis—Israeli Arabs

There are some 800,000 Arab citizens of Israel, representing about 20% of the total Israeli population. They carry Israeli identity cards and have Israeli citizenship, but their national identity, according to the identity cards issued to them, is 'Arab' not 'Jew'.

Arab Labour Organization

The equivalent, within the **Arab League**, to the International Labour Organization. Established in 1965 to promote co-operation between member states in labour issues, unification of labour legislation and general conditions of work, research, technical assistance, social insurance, training, etc. It has a tripartite structure, with government, employer and union representation.

Arab League (League of Arab States)

The League of Arab States was created on 22 March 1945, in **Alexandria**, Egypt. Its founding members were Egypt, Iraq, Lebanon, Saudi Arabia, Syria, **Transjordan** and Yemen (North). As other Arab states gained independence, the League was enlarged and now numbers 22 members, having admitted the United Arab Emirates, Bahrain, Tunisia, Algeria, Djibouti, Sudan, Somalia, Oman, Palestine, Qatar, Comoros, Kuwait, Libya, Morocco and Mauritania. The League's headquarters is located in **Cairo**. Its aim is to promote economic, social, political, and **military** co-operation.

Arab League Council Resolution

The **Arab League** Council, meeting in **Baghdad** in March 1979, agreed to expel Egypt from the League, following the conclusion of a **Peace Treaty between Egypt and Israel**.

Arab (League) Educational, Cultural and Scientific Organization (ALECSO)

Organization of the **Arab League**. Established in 1970 to promote and co-ordinate educational, cultural and scientific activities in the **Arab World**.

Arab Liberation Front (ALF)

Founded in 1968. Iraqi-backed Palestinian political group. Its leader is Mahmoud Ismail.

Arab Maghreb Union (AMU)

Established on 17 February 1989, the AMU aims to promote co-operation and integration among the Arab states of northern Africa. Its member states are Algeria, Libya, Mauritania, Morocco and Tunisia. The AMU was envisaged initially by Col **Muammar al-Qaddafi** as an Arab super-state. It was expected to eventually function as a North African common market, although domestic economic problems and civil unrest (especially in Algeria), divisions between the member states, and external events (e.g. the sanctions applied against Libya after **Lockerbie**, and the **Euro-Mediterranean Partnership** process) have hindered and even undermined progress on the Union's joint goals. The AMU has not held a meeting since 1994, despite several attempts to convene one. A summit meeting of heads of state, intended to create a free-trade zone and planned for December 2003, was postponed, largely because of the continuing dispute between Morocco and Algeria over the **Western Sahara** 'peace process'. On this occasion, **King Mohammed VI** of Morocco refused to attend, calling for direct talks with Algeria before participating in an AMU meeting. Moreover, the Mauritanian authorities accused Libya of funding a plot to overthrow the government of Mauritania that was led by a former **military** leader now on trial. The failure to meet was a set-back for President **Bouteflika** of Algeria, who was committed to improving Algeria's image and revitalizing the *maghreb*.

Arab Monetary Fund (AMF)

Established on 27 April 1976 by the Economic Council of Arab States, the Fund commenced operations in the following year. Its member states are Algeria, Bahrain, Djibouti, Egypt, Iraq, Jordan, Kuwait, Lebanon, Libya, Mauritania, Morocco, Oman, Palestine, Qatar, Saudi Arabia, Somalia, Sudan, Syria, Tunisia, the United Arab Emirates and Yemen. Egypt was temporarily suspended from the Fund in 1979, but was subsequently readmitted. From July 1993 loans to Iraq were suspended as a result of that country's failure to repay debts. The offices of the AMF are the board of governors, the board of executive directors and the president. Its finances are computed in the Arab accounting dinar, worth three **International Monetary Fund** (IMF) Special Drawing Rights. Its objective is to assist Arab co-operation, development and economic integration in monetary and economic affairs. It makes available technical and financial assistance to client states, with particular reference to balance-of-payments problems. It supports the Arab Trade Financing Programme. It is, in effect, a regional IMF.

Arab nationalism

The belief that the Arabs constitute a unified people and a single nation, despite the existence of colonial territories and post-colonial independent states. Arab nationalism emerged in the late 19th century, but it was greatly encouraged by European promises of an independent Arab state in the **Middle East** made in the context of the **Arab Revolt** during the First World War. It was (and to some extent still is) defined in opposition to foreign rule, first by the **Ottoman Empire**/Ottoman Turkey and then by Great Britain and France. It found its clearest expression in the period after the First World War, between 1920 and 1945, when the 'betrayal' by the European powers (see the **Sykes-Picot Agreement**) and their division of the **Arab World** took place. It was during this period that **Ba'athism** was developed. *The Arab Nation*, by Samir Amin, offers a classic exposition of the concept.

Arab Nationalist Movement

Pan-Arab political party. Founded in 1952 and composed mainly of students and staff from the American University in **Beirut**. Its main slogan was 'Unity [of Arabs], Liberation [of Palestine], Revenge [against the Zionist state]'.

Arab Nationalist Movement (Kuwait)

Unofficial political grouping.

Arab Nationalist Movement (North Yemen)

Political grouping in **North Yemen (Yemen Arab Republic)**.

Arab Nationalist Movement (Saudi Arabia)

Opposition movement.

Arab Organization for Agricultural Development

Established in 1970, and based in Khartoum, Sudan, the Organization began operations in 1972 to contribute to co-operation in agricultural activities and in the development of natural and human resources for **agriculture**, to compile data, conduct studies, develop training programmes and implement a food security programme. It includes the Arab Institute of Forestry and Range, the Arab Centre for Information and Early Warning, and the Arab Centre for Agricultural Documentation.

Arab Petroleum Investment Corpn

Established in 1975 to finance investments in petroleum and petrochemicals projects and related industries in the **Arab World** and in developing countries, with priority being given to Arab joint ventures. Projects financed include **gas** liquefaction plants, petrochemicals, tankers, **oil** refineries, pipelines, exploration, detergents, fertilizers and process control instrumentation. Based in Saudi Arabia, its shareholders are: Kuwait, Saudi Arabia and the United Arab Emirates (17%

each), Libya (15%), Iraq and Qatar (10% each), Algeria (5%), and Bahrain, Egypt and Syria (3% each).

The Arab Revolt

The uprising of the Arabs against Ottoman rule, known as the Arab Revolt, began in June 1916, during the First World War (in which Turkey supported Germany). Led by Ali, the eldest son of Sherif Hussein of **Mecca**, and **Faisal**, his third son, with the support of Britain (in particular **T. E. Lawrence**, known as 'Lawrence of Arabia', who was seconded to the Arab forces), two Arab armies were formed. They operated initially against Turkish forces in the **Hejaz**, forcing the surrender of their garrisons in Mecca and other towns, except **Medina**. Then Faisal's army joined the main British **Middle East** force under Gen. Allenby. It captured a number of towns, forcing its Turkish opponents to retreat. On 1 October 1918 Faisal and the British force jointly entered **Damascus**. The remainder of Syria (including Palestine) was liberated as far as **Aleppo**, where **Mustafa Kemal** organized a successful Turkish rearguard action, which was terminated by the signing of an Anglo-Turkish armistice at Mudros. The Revolt was popularized and 'westernized' through the writings of T. E. Lawrence in *The Pillars of Wisdom*.

Arab Revolutionary Brigades – *see also* 'Abu Nidal' and ANO

In September 1983 a Gulf Air Boeing 737 flying from Karachi, Pakistan, to Dubai, United Arab Emirates (UAE), crashed a few kilometres from Abu Dhabi airport killing all passengers and crew. A defector from the Arab Revolutionary Brigades, the fictional group that claimed responsibility for the crash, confirmed that **'Abu Nidal'** and the **ANO** had masterminded the attack. A few months later, in February 1984, the UAE's ambassador to France was shot dead in Paris. In October 1984 another diplomat from the UAE was assassinated in Rome, Italy. In both cases, the Arab Revolutionary Brigades claimed responsibility. It is thought that these incidents were linked to threats made by Abu Nidal to Sheikh **Zayed** bin Sultan, the ruler of Abu Dhabi, when the latter refused a demand for money; eventually Sheikh Zayed agreed to pay Abu Nidal US $17m.

Arab Revolutionary Workers Party

Established in the mid-1960s in Iraq after the Marxist wing of the **Ba'ath Party**, led by Ali Salah Saadi, had broken away from the main Ba'athist movement.

Arab socialism

Arab socialism has tended to be, ideologically and in political practice, a form of radical authoritarian **populism**. It has little to do with the classic Marxist notion of **socialism** and has shown itself to be hostile to the various 'communist' parties and groupings which derive their political theory and practice from the Marxist-Leninist tradition. Arab socialism has emphasized above all the importance of **Arab nationalism** and of the Arab people. It has stood for radical economic and social change, and above all for 'modernization'. It has drawn heavily on the European 'national socialist' tradition and emphasized the importance of national unity, strictly controlling the extent to which different interests may be expressed (through trades unions, political parties, etc.) and often banning such organizations entirely, in favour of the 'national front' or single party representing 'the people' as a whole. Arab socialism has been predominantly secular in outlook, particularly in the **Middle East** (the *mashreq*) although attempts have been made in some cases (e.g. Mauritania and Libya) to combine it with '**Islam**'. The Arab socialist movements of the Middle East have been led generally by men from the 'new middle classes' (army officers, civil servants, school teachers, etc.) opposed to the old ruling élites, but firmly believing in the possibility of radical reform and modernization by suitably educated and/or trained cadres, rather than in Marxist-style revolution from below. The most important of these movements was the Arab Socialist Party, usually called the **Ba'ath Party**. In later years, President **Nasser** of Egypt regarded himself as espousing a form of Arab socialism, **Nasserism**. His efforts to create a **United Arab Republic** were linked to his vision of Arab socialism.

Arab Socialist Party (Syria) – *see* Ba'ath Party

Arab Socialist Union (ASU)

The ASU developed during the 1950s and was spurred on by **Gamal Abdel Nasser**'s move towards **socialism** after taking power in Egypt in 1952. Its coming to power instigated the large-scale nationalization of Egypt's financial and industrial enterprises, as well as expropriation of large landholdings and the placing of all important sectors of the economy under state control. It replaced the **National Union Movement** in 1961 and was established in 1962 as the only legal (and official mass) party in Egypt (and Syria for the lifetime of the **United Arab Republic**). During its 'Vanguard' period (1965–68) it was relatively effective as a popular movement, but for much of its existence it was more of an official organ, carrying out government policy 'in the name of the people'. It remained in existence until long after the death of Nasser. In 1976–77 other parties were granted legal recognition, and the ASU was soon reformed as the centrist **National Democratic Party**. It was maintained by President **Anwar es-Sadat** until 1978, and was formally abolished only in April 1980.

Arab Trade Financing Programme (ATFP)

Established in 1989 to develop and promote **trade** between Arab countries and to enhance the competitiveness of Arab exporters. The ATFP extends lines of credit to

Arab exporters and importers through more than 120 national agencies throughout the **Arab World**. The **Arab Monetary Fund** (AMF) provided 50% of ATFP's authorized capital of US $500m. Participation is also invited from private and official Arab financial institutions and joint Arab-foreign institutions. The ATFP administers the Inter-Arab Trade Information Network and organizes meetings to promote Arab goods. It is based at the AMF building in Abu Dhabi, United Arab Emirates.

Arab Union – *see* United Arab Republic

The Arab West

The Arab West (***maghreb***) refers to the Arab countries of North Africa: Libya, Algeria, Tunisia, Morocco and Mauritania, which all belong to the **Arab Maghreb Union**. It includes by implication the **Western Sahara**, whose status remains undetermined.

Arab Women's Solidarity Association

Preparatory meetings for the establishment of an Arab Women's Solidarity Association were held through the 1970s in Egypt, Lebanon, Kuwait, Tunisia, Syria, Jordan, Morocco, Sudan, Algeria and Yemen. In 1982 the Association was formed. It was to be international, non-profit-making and aimed to promote Arab women and Arab society in general, politically, economically, socially and culturally. It would also seek to consolidate the ties between all **women** in all Arab countries. Since then a large number of Arab women, in the **Arab World** and abroad, have joined. In 1985 it was granted consultative status as an Arab non-governmental organization with the Economic and Social Council of the UN. In the same year the Association sent a delegation to the International Conference on Women in Nairobi, Kenya. In 1986 a Conference on the Challenge Confronting Arab Women at the end of the 20th Century was held in **Cairo**. The Conference was successful, despite criticism from both the left and the right and from Islamists. The first draft resolution, adopted by the Association at the general assembly held in September 1986, called for the establishment of a publishing house and the issue of a newspaper or magazine to propagate the views of the Association. In 1987 the Association (in collaboration with Zed Books) published *Women of the Arab World*.

Arab World

A term used to refer to a cultural and geographical area grouping together peoples whose common Arab heritage and use of the **Arabic** language enables them to identify themselves as Arabs. Overlapping with more formal groupings of states (e.g. the 22 members of the **Arab League**) which may include non-Arabs (i.e. **Berbers** in the ***maghreb***) as ethnic and linguistic **minorities**, the Arab World consists broadly of all those who consider themselves Arabs and thus kinsmen to Arabs everywhere and part of the Arab nation, whether in the Sahelian countries south of the Sahara or in Iran to the east.

Arabia – *see* **Arabian Peninsula, Saudi Arabia**

Arabian-American Oil Co – *see* **ARAMCO**

Arabian Peninsula

The Arabian Peninsula is a large area of land at the junction of Africa and Asia, east of Ethiopia and northern Somalia, south of Palestine and Jordan, and south-west of Iran. It is bounded on the south-west by the Red Sea and **Gulf of Aqaba**, on the south-east by the Arabian Sea, and on the north-east by the Gulf of Oman and the **Persian (Arabian) Gulf**. It includes Saudi Arabia, Yemen, Oman, the United Arab Emirates and Qatar. Saudi Arabia is by far the largest country. Saudi Arabia and Yemen are the most populous. It constitutes the land of the Arabs where the **Arabic** language developed and **Islam** was established.

Arabic

The language of the Arabs that originated among the indigenous peoples of the **Arabian Peninsula**. The language of the **Koran** and therefore the language of **Islam**. It is spoken today by 250m. people in Arab countries, and by many of the world's approximately 1,000m. Muslims. Arabic is divided into three groups: Classical written Arabic; written Modern Standard Arabic; and spoken Arabic. Classical written Arabic is principally defined as the Arabic used in the Koran and in the earliest literature from the Arabian Peninsula. Modern Standard Arabic is a modernization of the structures of classical Arabic, and includes words for modern phenomena as well as many additions from dialects across the **Arab World**. Spoken Arabic is a mixed form, usually with a dominating influence from local languages, and it is correct to refer to different versions of Arabic as separate languages. Classical Arabic usually refers to the formal language of poetry, prose, oratory and sermons, and to the language of the Koran. The Koran is expressed in Arabic and traditionally Muslims deemed it untranslatable. Arabic is, therefore, a sacred language—it is the only language in which the Koran is believed to be fully understood, with all translations reducing the quality of the revelations of God. Arabic is the language of Islam, but is also spoken by Arab Christians, Arabs of other faiths and so-called **Oriental Jews**. Arabic is a Semitic language, closely related to the **Hebrew** language. Standard Arabic usually refers to the language as used by the press, radio and television across North Africa and the **Middle East** (from Mauritania and the **Western Sahara** to Iraq). Arabic in a wider sense— colloquial Arabic—can also refer to one of the many national or regional so-called dialects spoken across North Africa and the Middle East, which can sometimes differ enough to be mutually incomprehensible. These dialects are frequently not written.

Arabistan – *see* Khuzistan

Al-Arabiya

Arabic-language television network channel. Like **al-Jazeera**, al-Arabiya has been subject to vilification for its coverage of Middle Eastern affairs. It has been banned for weeks at a time by the **Iraqi Provisional Governing Council** for 'incitement to murder', particularly after it broadcast tapes of **Saddam Hussain**. Two of its journalists were shot dead by US forces at a US checkpoint in March 2004.

Arabiyat, Abd al-Latif

General secretary of the **Islamic Action Front**.

Arabization

The process of converting to the use of the **Arabic** language as the official or main language in a country where previously French or English (or some other language) was dominant among the educated classes and in the public sector. Controversial in some countries, particularly where substantial ethnic-linguistic **minorities** exist, which regard the process as an attack on their cultural traditions and identity (e.g. the **Berbers** in Algeria). A similar process is involved in Turkey where the Kurdish language and cultural traditions are proscribed in favour of Turkish.

Arafat, Yasser

Born 24 August 1929, Mohamed Abed Arouf Arafat went on to become president of the **Palestinian National Authority** (PNA), which controls the Palestinian territories in **Gaza** and the **West Bank**. In 1952 Arafat joined the **Muslim Brotherhood** and the Union of Palestinian Students, and four years later participated in the Suez campaign with the Egypt army. In 1957 he established **al-Fatah**, an organization that carried out attacks on Israel. Throughout the 1960s Arafat was regarded by many as a terrorist. In 1968 he was elected as chairman of the **Palestine Liberation Organization** (PLO), and embarked on changing its ideology of **Pan-Arabism** to one of Palestinian nationalism. In 1974 Arafat delivered a speech on behalf of the **Palestinians** to the UN General Assembly. In 1982 the PLO was forced to relocate its headquarters from Lebanon to Tunisia due to Israeli attacks. By the 1980s Arafat had begun to gain more support from the West, particularly in the context of unpopular Israeli actions such as the attacks on Lebanon and the massacres in the **Sabra and Chatila** refugee camps in **Beirut**. In

1988 the State of Palestine was proclaimed at a meeting in Algeria, and one year later Arafat was elected as President of Palestine by the **Palestine National Council**. In the 1990s Arafat was considered pragmatic and moderate, and fewer questioned his intentions in the **peace process**. The US-led talks in Madrid in 1991 were unsuccessful, though the **Oslo Agreements** in 1993 brought the peace process forward, based on the 'land-for-peace' principle. In the same year Arafat recognized Israel's right to existence, and a year later Israeli forces withdrew from the town of **Jericho**, handing it over to Palestinian authorities. In 1994 Arafat, together with **Itzhak Rabin** and **Shimon Peres**, was awarded the Nobel Peace Prize. In 1996 Arafat was elected as President of the PNA in public elections, gaining 88% of the vote. In 2000 Arafat declined a peace proposal by the Israeli Prime Minister, **Ehud Barak**. Later in the same year Palestine entered a period of civil unrest, known as the **al-Aqsa** *intifada*, after **Ariel Sharon** had deliberately entered the al-Aqsa area. Palestinians threw stones at Israeli soldiers, whose retaliation led to hundreds of Palestinians being killed. In 2001 dialogue between Israel and Palestine disintegrated, following numerous suicide bombings in Israel. During 2001 Arafat's position weakened and his popularity declined. Other Palestinian groups became more active and were often more representative of Palestinian public opinion. Israeli actions against Palestinian infrastructure made it difficult for Arafat to exercise much power, creating an image of him as weak and inactive even among his former supporters. There were indications that Arafat himself sympathized with radical groups and allowed them sufficient freedom to carry out attacks on Israeli targets. In 2002 Arafat was humiliated by Ariel Sharon, being placed under house arrest in Ramallah from December 2001 until April 2002. This temporarily strengthened Arafat's position, making him seem a martyr of the Palestinian cause.

Aramaic

Like **Arabic** and **Hebrew** a Semitic language, Aramaic served as the common language of the **Middle East** from around 600 BC until after the death of Jesus of Nazareth (who spoke Aramaic). Divided into two groups (West Aramaic and East Aramaic), the language is closely related to Hebrew, Syriac and Phoenician.

ARAMCO

The Arabian American Oil Co, founded in the late 1930s and registered in Delaware, became the world's largest **oil**-producing company. Effectively a consortium of American oil companies, it administered the oilfields of Saudi Arabia until 1990. It still provides technical assistance.

Arbain

The 'fortieth' day (*arbain* means 'forty' in **Arabic**) that marks the end of the 40-day period of mourning for the 8th century martyr, Imam Hussein.

Arif, Abdul Rahman

Born 1916, Iraqi **military** leader and politician, President of Iraq in April 1966–July 1968. Coming to power after the death of his brother, **Abdul Salam Arif**, Abdul Rahman sought to continue many of his policies. He was forced out of power by **Ba'ath Party** members, including former President **Ahmad Hassan al-Bakr** and **Saddam Hussain**.

Arif, Abdul Salam (Abd as-Salaam) (1920–66)

Leader of a **military** coup in Iraq in November 1963 whose objective was to replace the Ba'athist **National Council of Revolutionary Command** led by **Ahmad Hassan al-Bakr** and Arif himself. Arif's coup was made possible by the disintegration of the **Ba'ath Party** after party moderates influenced by him had been expelled and the leader of the Marxist wing of the Ba'athist movement, Ali Salah Saadi, had severed ties with the Ba'ath to form the **Arab Revolutionary Workers Party**. He became President of Iraq in November 1963. A pan-Arabist who favoured union with Egypt and Syria, Arif is remembered for enlarging the public sector and seeking solutions to facilitate coexistence with the Kurdish-dominated regions in the north. He died in a helicopter accident in April 1966. He was succeeded by his brother, **Abdul Rahman Arif**, who was President of Iraq from April 1966 until he was overthrown by a Ba'athist coup, led by former President Ahmad Hassan al-Bakr and **Saddam Hussain**, some five years later, in July 1968.

Armed forces – *see also* Defence spending

Turkey and Iran have the largest armed forces in the region, the former with 515,000 regulars and 379,000 reserves, and the latter with 513,0000 regulars and 350,000 reserves. Egypt has 443,000 regulars and 254,000 reserves; Iraq (under **Saddam Hussain**) had 424,000 regulars and 650,000 reserves. Syria has 321,000 regular troops and 354,000 reserves. Saudi Arabia has armed forces consisting of 201,000 regular troops. Morocco and Algeria have 199,000 and 124,000 regular troops respectively, and both have 150,000 reserves. Israel maintains an army of 164,000 and keeps 425,000 troops in reserve.

Armed Islamic Group – *see* GIA—Groupe islamique armé

Armée islamique du salut – *see* AIS

Armenia

Formerly a region—home of the **Armenians**—in what is now the independent state of Armenia and in the north-east of what is now Turkey.

Armenian massacres

Historical evidence suggests that the deportation of the Turkish **Armenians** from eastern Anatolia was brutally effected, with much destruction of property. Even German pressure failed to prevent the Minister of the Interior, Talaat Pasha, from carrying out this policy. The Armenian massacres remain one of the most controversial acts of any Turkish government, and are still denied officially.

Armenian Republic of Yerevan

An independent state in the region of **Armenia** for four years (1917–21) prior to its incorporation into the Soviet Union.

Armenian Revolutionary Federation (ARF)

Socialist party, established in 1890. The principal Armenian party in Lebanon. Also known as the Tashnag Party after the dominant nationalist party in the independent **Armenian Republic of Yerevan** of 1917–21 prior to its becoming part of the Soviet Union. It has a collective leadership.

Armenians

People of **Armenia**, some of whom lived in Turkish Armenia and some of whom lived in Russian Armenia. In 1915 the Ottoman Government, doubtful of the loyalty of the Armenians (whose head bishop or Catholicos, living in Russian Armenia, had declared that the Tsar was the protector of all Armenians), began a systematic deportation of Turkish Armenians from eastern Anatolia to the west or south into Syria. This 'resettlement' was, according to many historians, accompanied by massacres—see **Armenian massacres.**

Arsuzi, Zaki (1908–68)

Born in Antioch (now Turkey). Syrian politician, thinker and counsellor. Arsuzi was one of the original founders, with **Michel Aflaq** and **Salah ad-Din Bitar**, of the **Ba'ath Party**, as well as being an important counsellor to **Hafiz al-Assad.**

Arvand Rud (River) – *see* Shatt al-Arab

Asabiyya

Arabic word originally meaning 'spirit of kinship' (the *'asaba* are male relations in the male line) or 'solidarity in the family, tribe or community'. Already used in the **hadith** in which the **Prophet Muhammad** condemns *'asabiyya* as contrary to the spirit of **Islam**, the term became famous as a result of the use to which it was put by

Ibn Khaldun, who made this concept the basis of his interpretation of history and his analysis of the rise and fall of dynasties/states.

Asbat al-Ansar

Emerging in the early 1990s, Asbat al-Ansar (The League of Followers) is a Lebanon-based, **Sunni** extremist group, composed primarily of **Palestinians** and associated with **Osama bin Laden**. The group commands about 300 fighters in Lebanon and has its primary base of operations in the 'Ayn al-Hilwah Palestinian refugee camp near Sidon in southern Lebanon. Its aims include the overthrow of the Lebanese government and to thwart perceived anti-Islamic and pro-Western influences in the country. Asbat al-Ansar has carried out multiple terrorist attacks in Lebanon. The group assassinated Lebanese religious leaders and bombed nightclubs, theatres, and liquor stores in the mid-1990s. It was involved in clashes in northern Lebanon in December 1999 and carried out a rocket-propelled grenade attack on the Russian embassy in **Beirut** in January 2000. During 2000 there were two other attacks against Lebanese and international targets. In 2002 there was an increase in attacks on US targets, including bombings of US-franchised restaurants and the murder of an American missionary. The perpetrators were believed to be Sunni extremists linked to Asbat al-Ansar.

Asharq al-Awsat

Saudi Arabian newspaper (*The Middle East*) with the largest international circulation of all **Arabic**-language newspapers.

Ashkenazim

A term applied in the Middle Ages to Jews living along the Rhine in northern France and western Germany. After some Ashkenazi Jews moved to Sephardi, in Spain, a new Jewish group (the **Sephardim**) was formed. Ashkenazim came to be equated with European Jews and Sephardim with Middle Eastern or **Oriental Jews**. Ashkenazim outnumbered Sephardim, and still do today, representing 90% of world Jewry. Ashkenazim and Sephardim have developed different prayer liturgies, Torah services, **Hebrew** pronunciation and ways of life. Ashkenazim have been in the past, and remain, the political élite of Israel, and political tensions have existed and arguably grown between the two groups since the creation of the State of Israel and substantial immigration of both groups into the country.

Ashrawi, Hanan

Born 1946. University professor and Palestinian diplomat and negotiator, known for her pragmatic, Western-style negotiating skills. She was a representative of the **Palestine Liberation Organization** (PLO) and a member of the Palestinian negotiating team at the Madrid peace talks in 1991 and at other meetings until her resignation in 1993, after which she became the head of the PLO mission in Washington, DC, USA. In 1996, after a brief return to Bir Zeit University (in the post of professor of comparative literature), where she headed the Palestinian Independent Commission on Civil Rights, Ashrawi was elected to a seat on the Palestinian Council representing **East Jerusalem**. In 1998, complaining of political **corruption**, and unhappy with **Arafat**'s handling of the peace talks, she resigned, going on to found MIFTA—the Palestinian Initiative for the Promotion of Global Dialogue and Democracy. This reflected her drive to end Israeli occupation on humanitarian rather than historical or ideological grounds. Ashrawi is a member of the Palestinian parliament.

Ashura

Voluntary fast-day in **Islam**, a major religious festival that takes place on the 10th day of the lunar month of Muharram. The day is considered a celebration of different historical events, such as the day Noah left the Ark. However, it is particularly associated for **Shi'a** Muslims with the death of the Imam Hussein, grandson of the **Prophet Muhammad**, who was killed in battle against the forces of Caliph Yazid on this day, near **Karbala** in modern Iraq, more than 13 centuries ago. He was beheaded and his head taken to **Damascus**, seat of the Ummayad dynasty, to which Yazid belonged. Observed as a major holy festival in Iraq, and in other countries with sizeable Shi'a populations (including Afghanistan, Azerbaijan, Bahrain, Lebanon, Pakistan and Syria), Ashura serves as a reminder of the divisions between **Sunni** and Shi'a Muslims, which date back to disagreements over the Prophet Muhammad's succession. In early March 2004 a series of major attacks by suicide bombers killed some 170 people observing ashura at the Khadimiya/ Khazimia mosque in **Baghdad** and at the shrine of al-Abbas and the shrine of Hussein (and other sites) in the holy city of Karbala. Meanwhile, in Quetta, Pakistan, at least 41 people were killed and 150 injured when three gunmen fired on and threw grenades at a procession of Shi'a worshippers observing ashura. Responsibility for the attacks was attributed to Sunni extremists, possibly with links to **al-Qa'ida**.

Al-'Asifa – *see* **al-Fatah**

Al-Assad, Bashar

Born in 1965, Bashar al-Assad became President of Syria in 2000 following the death of his father, **Hafiz al-Assad**. He was not considered to be his father's likely successor until his brother Basil died in an accident in 1994. On coming to power Bashar instigated an anti-**corruption** campaign. He has shown himself capable of maintaining the regime in Syria and Syria's distinctive foreign policy in the face of pressure both internal and external.

Al-Assad, Hafiz

President of Syria in 1971–2000. Born in October 1930 in the small village of Qardaha in northern Syria into a rural **Alawite** (a sect of **Shi'ite** origin) family. As a student activist he joined the **Ba'ath Party** in 1946 and graduated from the Homs **Military** Academy in 1955. He trained in the Soviet Union as a fighter pilot before being sent to Egypt during the period of the **United Arab Republic** (1958–61). There, together with several other Syrian officers, he formed the Ba'athist Military Committee, which was largely instrumental in bringing the Ba'ath to power in **Damascus** in 1963. He was appointed commander-in-chief of the air force in 1965 and in the following year, together with Salah al-Jadid, helped to eliminate the regime in power. As head of the air force and Minister of Defence from 1966, he opposed the radicalization imposed by al-Jadid. He was defence minister when Syria lost the **Golan Heights** to Israel during the **Six-Day War** of 1967. Internal divisions between the ruling circle subsequently became more intense and in November 1970 a coup brought him to power. In the months that followed he was elected first as secretary-general of the Ba'ath Party and, subsequently, in February 1971, as President of the Republic. Within a few years he had consolidated his position and Alawites, although constituting no more than 12% of the Syrian population, came to occupy important positions in every sector of the state and economy. His position depended heavily on the **armed forces**, in particular the Defence Brigades, a Praetorian guard led by his brother **Rifa'at (al-Assad)**. Throughout the 1970s he effectively suppressed opposition and retained personal control over all major policy decisions, particularly those relating to Israel— including participation in the **Arab–Israeli War (1973)**, negotiations with Henry Kissinger in 1974–75, intervention in Lebanon in 1976, rejection of the **Camp David Accords** in 1978 and intervention again in Lebanon when Israel invaded that country in 1982. Assad was keen to maintain state control over the economy, thus preventing other groups in society from gaining economic or political power. Politically, he sought to build a system where the army was a symbol of Syria's power, as well as a prominent actor in controlling the country. In November 1983, after a serious heart attack kept him out of public life, a virtual 'war of succession' took place between his brother Rifa'at and the army generals. His return from illness brought an end to the discord and the President took advantage of the situation to undermine the position of his brother, eventually sending him into exile. His return to supreme power was confirmed at the eighth party congress in January 1985. Although Syria had always maintained good relations with the Soviet Union in previous decades, Assad began to turn somewhat more towards the West in the late 1980s, having seen the benefits that had accrued to Iraq during its war with Iran. He agreed to join the US-led coalition against Iraq in the **Gulf War (1991)**. He continued to regard Israel as a major regional enemy, however, and at the 1991 **Middle East** peace conference insisted on an uncompromising line on 'land for peace', demanding Israel's withdrawal from the Golan Heights. The September 1993 Israeli accord with the **Palestine Liberation Organization**, which put an end to the ***intifada*** in the **Occupied Territories** without giving the **Palestinians** any substantial gains, represented a set-back for Assad, as did the increasingly friendly relationship between Israel and Jordan. By the late 1990s Assad increasingly suffered from ill health. After his death in 2000, his son **Bashar al-Assad** became President.

Al-Assad, Rifa'at

Syrian politician, born in Qardaha, Syria, in 1930. Rifa'at was the brother of former President **Hafiz al-Assad**, and uncle of President **Bashar al-Assad**. For many years he led the Defence Brigades, a Praetorian force providing the core of support for the Syrian regime. When Hafiz al-Assad retired from politics after a heart attack in 1983, Rifa'at sought to become President. His struggle for power with the army generals was ended when his brother returned to politics, resolved the internal conflict and exiled Rifa'at.

Assembly of Experts

Following Iran's Islamic revolution in 1979, the country's new religious leader, Ayatollah **Khomeini**, looked to a group of religious experts and clerics to translate his idea of the model **Islamic State** into reality. The 73-strong group rewrote Iran's largely secular draft consitution to make it more sensitive to Islamic teachings. The Assembly is elected every eight years by popular vote. The Constitution institutio-nalized the office of the *faqih*, the country's religious leader and ultimate decision-maker. It designated Khomeini as *faqih* for his lifetime. The Assembly of Experts was formally elected by the country to choose Khomeini's successor after his death in 1989.

Assembly of the Followers of the Imam's Line

Political grouping in Iran.

Association of Islamic Charitable Projects – *see* **Al-Ahbash**

Association of Israel – *see* **Agudat Israel**

Association of Muslim Clergy

Tajammu' al-Ulama' al-Muslimin

An umbrella group led by two activist sheikhs, Mahir Hammud (a **Sunni**) and Zuhayr Kanj (a **Shi'a**), that seeks to promote Muslim unity in Lebanon. Founded by Sunni and Shi'ite leaders in response to the Israeli invasion of 1982, the Association represents a coalition of militant clerics who shared the ideals of Ayatollah

Khomeini and a determination to fight Israel and to establish an Islamic order in Lebanon. The organization has almost 200 members.

Association of Reformist Ulema

Founded in 1931 in Algeria by Sheikh **Abdelhamid Ben Badis** (1889–1940), a leading Islamist reformer. The movement had actually begun to develop at least 10 years before this date. While careful not to challenge French rule, the reformers actively challenged the idea that Algerian Muslims could become French—they espoused a form of cultural anti-**colonialism**. They were also opposed to the traditional popular forms of **Islam** practised in Algeria—including the Sufi orders and the cult of saints (**Maraboutism**). The Association promoted a reformed, scripturalist and puritan Islam and the revival of **Arabic** language and culture. The Association rallied to the **Front de libération nationale** (National Liberation Front) in 1956 and was integrated into its structures, thereby losing its autonomy.

Assyrian(s)

The term used today to refer to the settlements of Nestorian Christians living in the western parts of Azerbaijan (north-western Iran), beyond Lake Urmia. Historically, the term is used to refer to the ancient civilization in the northern area of **Mesopotamia** between the **Tigris** and **Euphrates** rivers.

Aswan High Dam (Lake Nasser)

Dam constructed in southern Egypt to control and exploit the waters of the **Nile** river. Started in 1960 and financed with help from the USSR, the construction became an expression of political tensions. Eventually, Lake Nasser grew from the construction, named after President **Gamal Abdel Nasser**. The power station at the dam has a yearly output capacity of 2.1 gigawatts.

Atatürk, Kemal

'Father of the Turks', Turkish nationalist, **military** leader and subsequently President of independent Turkey. The great Turkish modernizer. Born in 1881 in Salonica, then an Ottoman city, now in Greece. In 1893 he entered a military high school where his mathematics teacher gave him the second name Kemal (meaning perfection) in recognition of young Mustafa's superior achievement. He was thereafter known as Mustafa Kemal. In 1905 Mustafa Kemal graduated from the War Academy in **Istanbul** with the rank of staff captain. Posted in **Damascus**, he and several colleagues started a clandestine society called 'Homeland and Freedom' to fight against the Sultan's despotism. In 1908 he assisted the group of officers who toppled the Sultan. In 1915, when the Dardanelles campaign was launched, Col Mustafa Kemal became a national hero by winning successive victories and finally repelling the invaders. Promoted to the rank of general in 1916, at the age of 35, he liberated two major provinces in eastern Turkey that year. In the next two years he served as commander of several Ottoman armies in Palestine, **Aleppo**, and elsewhere, achieving another major victory by halting the enemy advance at Aleppo. On 19 May 1919 Mustafa Kemal Pasha landed in the Black Sea port of Samsun to start the War of Independence. In defiance of the Sultan's Government, he rallied a liberation army in Anatolia and convened the Congress of Erzurum and Sivas which established the basis for the new national effort under his leadership. On 23 April 1920 the Grand National Assembly was inaugurated. Mustafa Kemal Pasha was elected to its presidency. At the end of August 1922 the Turkish armies won their ultimate victory. Within a few weeks, the Turkish mainland was completely liberated, an armistice had been signed, and the rule of the Ottoman dynasty abolished. In July 1923 the national Government signed the Lausanne Treaty with Great Britain, France, Greece, Italy, and others. In mid-October **Ankara** became the capital of the new State of Turkey. On 29 October the Republic was proclaimed and Mustafa Kemal Pasha was unanimously elected as its President. The 15 years of Atatürk's presidency were characterized by modernization. He created a new political and legal system, abolished the **Caliphate**, made both government and **education** secular, gave equal rights to **women**, changed the alphabet and the attire, and advanced the arts, the sciences, **agriculture** and **industry**. In 1934 the national parliament gave him the name 'Atatürk' ('Father of the Turks'). Kemal Atatürk died on 10 November 1938. The legacy of Atatürk continues to mark Turkish society. 'Kemalism' is a distinctive political ideology and approach to political development.

Atef, Mohamed

Leading member of **al-Qa'ida**. Killed in bombing in **Kabul**, Afghanistan.

Atilim

Turkish newspaper sympathetic to the Marxist-Leninist Communist Party of Turkey.

ATTA – *see* Afghan Transit Trade Agreement

Al-Attas, Haider Abu Bakr

President of the **People's Democratic Republic of Yemen** in 1986–1990.

Attasi, Nur ad-Din

Former Prime Minister of Syria, replaced by **Hafiz al-Assad** in 1970.

Australia

Previously little involved in the region, but provided 850 military personnel for the **coalition** forces occupying Iraq in the aftermath of the **Iraq War (2003)**. The commitment to support the coalition made by Prime Minister John Howard became an issue in the federal election campaign of 2004, with the opposition Labour Party advocating the withdrawal of Australian troops by Christmas.

Avalanche – *see* Operation Avalanche

Ayatollah

Literally 'the sign of God'. Senior cleric in **Shi'a Islam** qualified to pronounce independent judgment in religious matters. Not a formal rank or position but one gained by learning, religiosity and respect or veneration by others. A Grand Ayatollah is an even greater figure of religious authority, with a major following.

Azerbaijan

A country located in south Caucasus, with a Turkic and majority Muslim population.

It gained its independence after the collapse of the Soviet Union in 1991. Azerbaijan is famed for its **oil** springs and **natural gas** resources. In 2001 it became a member of the Council of Europe, and is now attempting to build a democratic, law-governed and secular state

Azerbaijan (Iran)

Province in north-west Iran.

Azeri

Short for Azerbaijani—refers to the language and the people.

Al-Azhar University

One of the oldest and most influential—some would say one of the most conservative—centres of religious jurisprudence in the **Middle East**. The Sheikh of al-Azhar is one of **Sunni Islam**'s highest religious authorities.

Aziz, Tariq

Iraqi politician, born in 1936. Aziz was educated at the **Baghdad** College of Fine Arts, became a teacher and, later, a journalist with the *al-Jamaheer* and *ath-Thawra* newspapers. In 1974 Aziz was appointed a member of the Regional Command (the **Ba'ath Party**'s highest governing unit), becoming a member of **Saddam Hussain**'s

Revolutionary Command Council in 1977. He was the only Christian in the Iraqi leadership. Deputy Prime Minister in 1979; foreign minister in 2001, in which role he acted as diplomat and spokesman. During the **Gulf War (1991)** he was an instantly recognizable figure in the Western media. Shortly after the collapse of Saddam Hussein's regime in April 2003, Aziz surrendered himself to US forces.

Azzam, Abdullah

Author, fighter, and propagandist of **Islamic Jihad**, born in Seelet al-Hartiyeh in the **West Bank**. He was one of the first Arabs to join the Afghan *jihad* against the Soviet forces in 1979. In the early 1980s he emigrated to Pakistan and founded Bait-ul-Ansar (**Afghan Service Bureau**, or MAK) with the purpose of establishing and supporting projects of the cause, as well as training volunteers to participate in the Afghan war. He was an important influence on **Osama bin Laden** and, therefore, in the creation of **al-Qa'ida**. He wrote a number of books, including *Join the Caravan* and *Defence of Muslim Lands*. With the *jihad* movement split by rivalries and factionalism, Azzam was assassinated by his internal enemies in 1989.

B

Ba'albek

Phoenician city in Lebanon, known as Heliopolis during the Hellenistic period. It retained its religious functions during Roman times, when the sanctuary of the Heliopolitan Jupiter attracted thousands of pilgrims. Ba'albek, with its colossal structures, is one of the finest examples of Imperial Roman architecture.

Al-Ba'ath – *see* Ba'ath Party

(Arab) Ba'ath Party

The Ba'ath Party was founded in 1940 in Syria and held its first congress in **Damascus** in 1947. Regional sections were subsequently created in **Transjordan** (1948), Lebanon (1949–50) and Iraq (1950–51). In 1953 it merged with Akram Hourani's Arab Socialist Party to become the **(Arab) Ba'ath(ist) Socialist Party**. Al-Ba'ath remains a Syrian political party, but its secretary-general, Abdullah al-Amin, is based in **Beirut**.

(Arab) Ba'ath(ist) Socialist Party – *see also* Arab socialism

The Ba'ath(ist) Socialist Party adopted as its watchword: 'unity, liberation, **socialism**'. Arab unity is at the centre of the Party's doctrine and has priority over all other aims. Secular in orientation, it nevertheless accepts the role that **Islam** plays in the life and thought of the Arabs. The socialist elements of the doctrine remained vague, but similarities with the ideas of **national socialism** in Europe were evident. The mission of the Ba'athists was to bring an end to **colonialism** and promote humanitarianism. To achieve this, the Party presented itself as nationalist, populist, socialist and revolutionary. The Party rejected many concepts and theories commonly found in other 'socialist' parties, particularly the concept of class, though it did favour redistribution of land and public ownership of commons. It also initially stood for representative and constitutional form of government, freedom of speech and association. According to the Ba'ath Party, the Arabs form a single nation that is currently divided into several artificial countries or regions. The Party is therefore headed by a National Command that covers all of the **Arab World** and serves as the central executive authority. Under that there are Regional Commands in countries where the party is strong enough to justify the establishment of one. There have been or currently are Ba'ath(ist) parties in Syria, Iraq, Mauritania, Egypt, Jordan, Lebanon, **North Yemen** and **South Yemen** (now unified).

Ba'ath(ist) Socialist Party (Iraq)

Established secretly in Iraq in 1950, from 1955 the Iraqi Ba'ath Socialist Party started to co-operate with other nationalist groups. By February 1963 the Party had grown strong enough to take control of Iraq. This only lasted for a short while, until November, when a non-Ba'ath Prime Minister came to power. With co-operation from the **military**, however, the Party took full control of Iraq in July 1968, and began the process of making the state and the Ba'ath Party identical. In the 1970s a number of far-reaching measures, including the reorganization of **agriculture** (through a 'socialist' style land reform) and the establishment of a powerful bureaucracy backed by the military, supported by assistance from the Soviet Union, created a strong command economy and centralized state. By the mid-to-late1980s, however, the '**socialism**' had been filtered out of Ba'ath ideology, to leave a form of authoritarian **populism**, with some latitude given to the private sector, and **Arab nationalism** giving way to Iraqi nationalism. The **Iran–Iraq War** of the 1980s enabled the regime and the Party to establish almost complete control over the political process and a command economy, while at the same time presenting itself as a champion of the Arabs against non-Arab Iran. In 1990 the Iraqi regime under **Saddam Hussain** decided to invade Kuwait, formerly a part of Iraqi territory. The **Gulf War (1991)** followed. The Ba'ath Party remained in power throughout the next decade, despite pressures from within and from outside. In March–April 2003 much of the leadership of the Ba'ath Party was destroyed (arrested, captured or killed) by the US-led forces in the **Gulf War (2003)**. The Ba'athist President of Iraq, Saddam Hussain, was overthrown and eventually captured by US forces. The US-led **Coalition Provisional Authority** initially instituted a virtual purge of Ba'athists from positions of authority and responsibility, but was later, during 2004, obliged to bring many of them back into the political process and into public service.

Ba'ath(ist) Socialist Party (Jordan)

Founded in 1948, the Jordanian Ba'ath Party grew strong during the annexation of the **West Bank**, receiving extensive public support and establishing a nationalist-leftist alliance. The alliance became the strongest in the parliament after the 1956 elections. The alliance attracted many members from the educated classes living in cities and had strong support from students. In 1958–61, the Ba'ath Party was active in working against the **monarchy** of Jordan, receiving economic aid from Syria. As the West Bank was occupied by Israel in 1967, the Party was seriously weakened, and has not really recovered since.

Ba'ath(ist) Socialist Party (Lebanon)

The regional section of the Ba'ath(ist) Party in Lebanon was established in 1949–50. Lebanon was the location of Ba'ath Party congresses held in 1959 and 1968. The Ba'ath Party in Lebanon is a secular, pro-Syrian party with a policy of Arab union. During the **Lebanese civil war** the Party's militia was supported by economic aid from Syria. In 1987 the Ba'ath Party joined a coalition of several political parties. This group later became central in forming the government of Lebanon, in which key posts were given to Ba'ath Party members.

Ba'athist Party (Libya)

Libyan opposition party, linked to Ba'athist parties elsewhere. It has been subject to purges by the regime.

Ba'ath(ist) Socialist Party (North Yemen)

Established in 1955, but lacked importance until the Yemeni civil war in 1970. The Party never entered office, and in 1976 was merged with other parties to form the **National Democratic Front**.

Ba'ath(ist) Socialist Party (South Yemen)

Established in 1955, but did not operate freely until 1967, following the independence of South Yemen. The Party was dissolved in 1978, after the introduction of a one-party system.

Ba'ath(ist) Socialist Party (Syria)

The Syrian branch of the party was a direct continuation of the original Ba'ath movement, which was first established in Syria. The Party was suppressed from 1958 until 1961, during the union between Syria and Egypt. In 1963 it took control of Syria. Yet, in the same year, the Party split into two factions, one anti-Marxist and civilian, the other military. The latter was led by Salah al-Jadid. In 1966 tensions grew stronger, and Jadid's group forced **Michel Aflaq**, the leader of the civilian group, into exile. In 1970 a two-week party congress attempted to solve the conflict between Jadid and **Hafiz al-Assad**, but did not succeed. Soon after Assad had Jadid removed from power and jailed, taking control of the Party. There was dissent, but by 1979 Assad had removed opponents from important positions.

Ba'athism

Ba'athism, the basis of the Ba'ath(ist) movement, was conceived as an ideology of renaissance and reform for the **Arab World** (in **Arabic** *ba'ath* means 'renaissance') around the notion of Arab unity and the Arab nation. According to its creators, the Arabs form a single nation aspiring to form an Arab state and play a unique role in the world. Ba'athism was developed in **Damascus** in the 1940s by the Orthodox Christian, **Michel Aflaq**, and the **Sunni** Muslim, **Salah ad-Din Bitar**. The Ba'ath(ist) movement established the **(Arab) Ba'ath Party** at its first congress in 1947.

Ba'athists (Mauritania)

The largest and most active Arab nationalist faction in Mauritania, this group has maintained close ties with the Iraqi **Ba'ath(ist) Socialist Party**. It favours the full **Arabization** of Mauritania. Its extreme views have been considered racist by the government, and by many other political groupings, in view of the ethnic diversity of the country and the risk that ethnic divisions may be expressed violently as they sometimes have been (particularly during 1989). Scores of Ba'athist activists were arrested by security forces during **Ould Haidalla**'s presidency. The Ba'athists have also been under constant scrutiny during the long period of **Ould Taya**'s presidency. On the other hand, the government of Mauritania was broadly sympathetic during the **Gulf War (1991)** towards Iraq, and there were even rumours that members of **Saddam Hussein**'s family took refuge in Mauritania. More recently, however, in 2003, Ba'athists in Mauritania have been arrested on suspicion of plotting against the government.

Babylon

Ancient city that was located on the east side of the **Euphrates** river. It was the capital of Babylonia in the 2nd and 1st millennia BC. Its ruins are 90 km south of modern **Baghdad**.

Badr Brigade

Armed wing of the **Supreme Council for the Islamic Revolution in Iraq**.

Al-Badr, Muhammad

Born in 1926, died in 1996. Ruler (imam) of **North Yemen** in 1962, and leader of monarchist factions during the **North Yemen civil war** in 1962–70.

Badran, Mudar

Jordanian politician and civil servant, born in 1934 and educated at the University of **Damascus**. Lieutenant and legal consultant to the Jordanian **armed forces**. He became chief of the Jordanian foreign intelligence services in 1965, and progressed to become deputy chief of general intelligence in 1966. National security adviser to King **Hussein** of Jordan in 1970. Minister of Defence and Foreign Affairs 1976–79. Prime Minister 1976–79, 1980–84 and 1989–91. Former member of the executive council of the Arab National Union.

Baghdad

Capital of Iraq, the largest city in Iraq and seat of government. Ancient city located in the centre of the country, with more than 3m. inhabitants. The Kazimain/Kadhimain mosque in Baghdad is a celebrated **Shi'a** shrine, containing the tomb of Musa al-Kazim/Kadhim, the seventh Imam of the **Twelver** Shi'is.

Baghdad Pact

Agreed in 1955, the Baghdad Pact was a military alliance involving Great Britain, Pakistan, Iraq, Iran and Turkey. (See also **CENTO**.)

Baha'i

Described by **Baha'is** as 'the youngest of the world's independent religions', the Baha'i faith developed out of an Islamic reformist movement of the mid-19th century. Baha'i claims to be a universal religion, and its teachings include better social conditions for the underprivileged, mutual love, harmony between different races, sexual equality, and a universal language. It represents itself as distinct from **Judaism**, **Christianity** and **Islam**. It is committed to the goals of ending ethnic and racial strife and to world peace. It teaches that the followers of all the major religions are on valid journeys towards truth. It has an estimated 2m. and more adherents world-wide. The world centre of the faith is in **Haifa**, and Baha'is are often accused of being agents of **Zionism** or of aiding Israel, as well as other crimes and misdemeanours. The holiest Baha'i shrine in Iran, the House of the Bab in **Shiraz**, was destroyed by **Shi'a** mobs in September 1979.

Baha'is

Followers of the **Baha'i** religion, founded in 1863. There are over 2m. Baha'is in various countries around the world. In the **Middle East** the religion is most prominent in Iran, where it has as many as 500,000 followers, most of whom have faced persecution since the **Iranian Revolution** of 1979. With 300,000 remaining in Iran, despite considerable persecution and many social restrictions following the establishment of the Islamic Republic, it is also the case that around half of the 6,000 Baha'is in Britain are Iranian exiles. David Kelly, a weapons inspector in Iraq and employee of the British Ministry of Defence, who allegedly killed himself over his involvement in the controversial 'dossier' on Iraq's **weapons of mass destruction**, was a member of the Baha'i faith. The Baha'is are reviled by some Muslims as apostates from **Islam** and are not recognized as a legitimate religious group, despite their numbers. In Iran they are not mentioned in the Constitution and have no seat in parliament. Many Baha'is had posts under the Shah, although officially they were forbidden by the religion to accept political posts. After the fall of the Shah, many Baha'is lost their jobs, had their property confiscated and were imprisoned or executed when they refused to recant their faith.

Baha'is in Morocco

In December 1962 14 Baha'is were brought to trial in Morocco on charges of forming an illegal association, corrupting youth, and seeking to destroy **Islam** and the Moroccan state. After the trial had begun, King **Hassan II** described **Baha'ism** as 'a true heresy' and therefore unacceptable in Morocco. One day later the court at Nador sentenced three of the Baha'is to death and five to life imprisonment. The trial caused a national and international reaction and the verdict was appealed before the Supreme Court in Morocco which, in December 1963, dismissed the judgment of the Nador court, pointing out that the Baha'is had undertaken no criminal activities covered by the Moroccan penal code.

Bahrain, Kingdom of

Mamlakat al-Bahrayn

A small (area: 665 sq km) archipelago in the **Persian (Arabian) Gulf**, east of Saudi Arabia. The capital is **Manama**. The state is divided for administrative purposes into 12 municipalities (*mintaqah*, plural *manatiq*): Al-Hadd, Al-Manamah, Al-Mintaqah al-Gharbiyah, Al-Mintaqah al-Wusta, Al-Mintaqah ash-Shamaliyah, Al-Muharraq, Ar-Rifa' wa-al-Mintaqah al-Janubiyah, Jidd-Hafs, Madinat-Hamad, Madinat 'Isa, Juzur Hawar, and Sitrah. All municipalities are administered from Manama. Bahrainis comprise 63% of the total population of 656,397, and 'others'—including Asians (mostly Indian and Pakistani) 19%, other Arabs 10%, and Iranians 8%—37% or 228,424 (estimated at July 2002). The indigenous Bahrainis are 70% **Shi'a** and 30% **Sunni** Muslims. The main languages are **Arabic**, English, **Farsi** and Urdu.

Political profile

The **al-Khalifa family** has dominated politics since 1783 by means of an effectively autocratic system, although the Emir (ruler) has been advised since 1993 by a Consultative Council. The first elections to the unicameral National Assembly were held in December 1973. The National Assembly was dissolved on 26 August 1975. A National Action Charter created a bicameral legislature on 23 December 2000; this was approved by referendum on 14 February 2001. Bahraini **women** were permitted to hold office and vote in elections. The Supreme Council for Women was established in October 2001, with a mandate to improve the position of women. In

February 2002 Bahrain was declared a (hereditary) constitutional **monarchy**. According to the Constitution, all citizens are equal before the law. It guarantees freedom of speech, press, conscience and religious beliefs. There is compulsory free **education** and free medical **health** care. The head of state is King **Hamad bin Isa al-Khalifa** (who acceded as emir on 6 March 1999 and was proclaimed king on 14 February 2002). The Prime Minister is Sheikh **Khalifa bin Sulman al-Khalifa** (since 1971). Crown Prince Sheikh **Salman bin Hamad al-Khalifa** (son of the monarch, born 21 October 1969) is commander-in-chief of Bahraini Defence. The Prime Minister and the Cabinet are appointed by the monarch. The bicameral parliament consists of the **Majlis ash-Shura** (Consultative Council) and the House of Representatives. Both bodies have 40 members who serve four-year terms of office. The Consultative Council is appointed by the king and the members of the House of Representatives are now elected by popular vote. The most recent elections to the House of Representatives were held on 31 October 2002 (the next elections are due to be held in 2006). The first legislative session of parliament was held on 25 December 2002. Municipal elections were held in May 2002. Although Bahrain now has an elected House of Representatives, political parties are still prohibited. Independent trade unions are also illegal. However, several politically oriented NGOs and civic groups (previously in exile) now operate in the country— more than 330 NGOs are now registered. As regards the judiciary, the legal system is based on a combination of **Islamic (Shariʻa) Law** and English common law. There is a High Civil Appeals Court.

The main political groupings are:

- Arab-Islamic Wasat (Centre) Society; seeks to support the principles of the National Charter of Action and confirm the Arab and Islamic character of Bahrain
- **Democratic Progressive Forum**; leftist antecedents within the Communist Party
- National Action Charter Society
- National Democratic Gathering Society
- National Islamic Forum

A number of new groups have been established since 2001. Several small, clandestine leftist and Islamic fundamentalist groups are also active. The main dissident groups, which chose to boycott the first election to the House of Representatives, are:

- National Democratic Rally
- National Democratic Action Society; represents nationalist and Arab Baʼathist political trends; Chair. Abdul-Rahman an-Nuaimi
- Islamic Association for National Reconciliation
- Islamic National Accord Association; a Shiʻa grouping; Leader: Sheikh Ali Salman.

Prominent NGOs/advocacy groups include:

- Bahrain Human Rights Society
- Supreme Council for Bahraini Women (Shayka Saika Bint-Ibrahim al-Khalifa)
- Organization Against Normalization with Israel

Media

Bahrain is considered to have a relatively liberal press compared to other **Gulf States**. However, the regime still has considerable control over the media and some government critics have been prosecuted. Bahrain's domestic radio and television stations are state-run. A press law guarantees the right of journalists to operate independently and to publish information. However, they are liable to jail terms for offences that include insulting the king, and self-censorship is practised. There are five daily newspapers—*Akhbar al-Khaleej*, *Gulf Daily News*, *Khaleej Times*, *Bahrain Tribune*, *Al-Ayam*—and several other periodicals. The Bahrain Radio and Television Corpn is state-run and operates five terrestrial television networks. Satellite television is freely available. In 2000 there was one internet service provider, and in 2002 there were 140,200 internet users.

History

Bahrain achieved independence from Britain in 1971. Shi'a activists fomented unrest sporadically throughout the mid-1990s, demanding an elected National Assembly and an end to unemployment. In 1999 Sheikh Hamad bin Isa al-Khalifa came to the throne, first as emir and subsequently, in February 2002, as king. Beneficiaries of the King's extensive patronage form the wealthiest group in society. The largest religious community, the Shi'a Muslims, is the poorest. The new King promoted economic and political reforms, and worked to improve relations with the Shi'a community. In 2001 the State Security Law was repealed, promising an end to detention of political dissidents (mostly Shi'a opponents of the regime). In February 2001 Bahraini voters approved a referendum on the National Action Charter—the centrepiece of the King's political liberalization programme. In local elections held in May 2002 Bahraini women were allowed to vote and seek office for the first time. Bahrain's small size and central location among Persian (Arabian) Gulf countries require it to perform a delicate balancing act in foreign affairs among its larger neighbours. A dispute with Qatar over the Hawar islands was resolved in Bahrain's favour in 2001.

Bahrain, economy

Bahrain's major economic strength lies in activities associated with **oil** and **gas**. Petroleum production and refining account for about 60% of export receipts, 60% of government revenues, and 30% of gross domestic product. Bahrain is dependent on Saudi Arabia for oil revenue granted as **aid**. A large share of exports consists of petroleum products made from refining imported crude. Possessing minimal oil reserves, Bahrain has turned to petroleum processing and refining, and has transformed itself into an international banking centre. It has provided the **Arab World**'s major offshore banking centre since the 1980s. With its highly developed communications and **transport** facilities, Bahrain is home to numerous multinational firms with business in the **Gulf**. Construction proceeds on several major industrial projects. Unemployment, especially among the young, and the depletion of oil and underground **water** resources are major long-term economic problems. Economic weaknesses include Bahrain's continuing reliance on depleted oil reserves and insufficient diversification. The economy also suffers from high levels of government borrowing and of unemployment among Bahraini nationals.

Bahrain Monetary Agency (BMA)

The BMA is the regional leader in bank regulation. It has developed new supervisory mechanisms to monitor 26 Islamic banks within its jurisdiction. In the post-11 September 2001 world anti-'**money-laundering**' laws have been passed in most countries, most recently in Saudi Arabia.

Bakdash, Khalid

Leader of the Syrian **Communist Party.**

Bakhtiar, Shahpur

Born in 1917, he was the last Iranian Prime Minister under the Shah's regime, despite his opposition to the Shah. Leader of the **National Iranian Resistance Movement** formed in 1979 in exile in Paris, France. Open to the idea of a constitutional **monarchy** for Iran, but basically a social democrat.

Bakhtiaris

Bakhtiaris are a major tribal ethnic and linguistic **minority** in Iran, numbering 600,000–800,000. They are **Shi'a** and found only in Iran.

Al-Bakr, Gen. Ahmad Hassan

Born in **Tikrit**, Iraq, in 1914. He led a coup against the government of **Abdul Rahman Arif**, together with **Saddam Hussain**, in July 1968 to establish a Ba'athist regime in Iraq. After purging the top echelons of the party in the early 1970s, al-Bakr and Saddam Hussain dominated the **Revolutionary Command Council** (RCC). Additional purges in 1977 left only Saddam Hussain's close associates in the Baghdad National Command and in the RCC. Al-Bakr resigned, for reasons of health, in July 1979, after which Saddam Hussain took full control of the **Ba'ath Party**.

Balad

Israeli political grouping comprising the **National Democratic Alliance** and the Arab Movement for Renewal. Founded in 1999 as a united Arab party. Balad is led by Azmi Bishara.

Balfour Declaration (1917)

Statement issued in 1917 by the British foreign secretary, Arthur, Lord Balfour, supporting the idea of a 'homeland' for Jews in Palestine. It is often regarded as the initiation of the process that led to the establishment of the State of Israel. At the beginning of the First World War Great Britain needed the support of the world Jewry, which had been neutral, and which represented a large part of the population of Germany and Austria-Hungary. The declaration was drafted with the help of US President Woodrow Wilson, a strong Zionist. Furthermore, Britain needed to protect the sea route to India, which passed through the **Suez Canal**. Supporting **Zionism** and a homeland for the Jews in Palestine was considered a way to secure lasting British influence in the region east of the Canal.

Baluchis

A major tribal group or people in the south-east of Iran and west of Pakistan. They inhabit a desert region known historically as Baluchistan and speak a distinctive language—Baluchi. Historically, long-distance transhumants, they are now largely settled in Iran in the provinces of Sistan and Baluchistan, where they number 500,000–750,000. They also constitute a significant **minority** in Pakistan, with smaller numbers in south-west Afghanistan. Adherent for the most part to **Sunni Islam**.

Bam

Major historic town in south-eastern Iran. Subject to an earthquake measuring 6.8 on the Richter scale in December 2003, which killed an estimated 42,000 people (a figure later revised down to some 25,000 by the Iranian authorities) and rendered some 90,000 homeless. In January 2004 the UN appealed for US $31.3m. to meet the immediate and rehabilitation needs of the people of Bam. Technical and financial assistance from numerous agencies and countries (including the USA) was provided within weeks. The process of reconstruction was aided by the rapid deployment by the Iranian government of technical and human resources to the area and the provision of large numbers of prefabricated units.

Bandung Conference (1955)

The Bandung Conference was a meeting of representatives of 29 African and Asian nations, held at Bandung, Indonesia, in 1955. The aim was to promote economic and cultural co-operation and to oppose **colonialism**. Not invited to the conference were South Africa, Israel, Taiwan, South Korea, and North Korea. The conference ultimately led to the establishment of the **Non-aligned Movement** in 1961.

Bani Sadr, Abol Hassan

Elected as President of Iran in January 1980, receiving more than 75% of the vote. Clerics were barred by Ayatollah **Khomeini** from contesting the presidency in the first two presidential elections, but this rule was subsequently changed. Bani Sadr was replaced in September 1980 by President **Muhammad Ali Raja'i**.

Bank Ha'Mizrahi

The Bank Ha'Mizrahi was owned by a movement of Orthodox Jews that constitutes one of Israel's political parties until 1983, when it was effectively nationalized by being brought under direct government control, after a crash of the stock exchange caused by various major banks making use of their depositors' funds to speculate in their own shares.

Bank Ha'Poalim

The Bank Ha'Poalim was controlled by the **Histadrut**, the Israeli Labour Federation, until 1983, when, like the other private or corporate banks, it was brought under direct government control, after a crash of the stock exchange caused by various major banks making use of their depositors' funds to speculate in their own shares. In the period 1997–2000 it was reprivatized, to emerge in June 2000 as a fully privatized company controlled by a conglomerate, the Arison-Dankner Group.

Bank Leumi

The Bank Leumi was founded in the early 20th century by the Zionist movement and came under the Jewish National Fund, which continued to own it until, like the other big banks, it came under direct Israeli government ownership in 1983, following a crash of the stock exchange which itself resulted from the use made by various major banks of their depositors' funds for speculation in their own shares. As of 2000, plans to sell off the government's 43% stake in Bank Leumi (and 53% stake in Israel Discount Bank) depended on negotiations with suitable core investors.

Bank Muscat

Flagship of the Sultanate, the Bank Muscat is the best connected and largest (in terms of assets) of Omani institutions, with expanding domestic franchises in both retail and commercial banking and a solid equity base. Sultan **Qaboos ibn Said** is the major shareholder. The Bank boasts expertise in stock brokering, foreign exchange markets, and advisory and project financing services. It functions as a clearing bank for the Muscat securities market. Bank Muscat regards itself as a trendsetter. Having purchased ABN Amro's Bahrain branch, it has ambitions of regional expansion.

Bank of Credit and Commerce International (BCCI)

Founded in 1972 by Agha Hasan Abedi, a Pakistani businessman, the BCCI became the world's largest Muslim banking institution, with more than 400 branches in 73 countries. The BCCI was nominally owned by Arab capital from the **Gulf States**. Twenty per cent was controlled by Khalid bin Mahfouz, the son of the founder of the **National Commercial Bank** of Saudi Arabia, the bank used by the Saudi royal family, who received unsecured loans well in excess of his share in the Bank. Another leading shareholder was Kamal Adham, a former head of Saudi intelligence, whose business partner was the former station chief of the US **Central Intelligence Agency** (CIA) in Saudi Arabia, Raymond Close. Other shareholders included a core of 12 Arab sheikhs and Pakistani bankers. While shareholders benefited from their relationship with the Bank, the Bank also benefited. In the 1970s and 1980s, for example, Ghaith Pharaon, a Saudi tycoon, received an estimated US $500m. in unsecured loans, but the loans were used to purchase stocks in a wide range of companies, including two US banks, the National Bank of Georgia and the Independence Bank of Encino in California, for the BCCI. Pharaon acted as a smokescreen against international banking regulations and auditing; the Bank more than once hid behind him to avoid US banking investigations. The BCCI acted on behalf of Saudi interests in several covert operations. The BCCI helped **Saddam Hussain** appropriate funds from **oil** revenues and deposit them all over the world; a similar service was provided for Gen. Noriega of Panama and for UNITA in Angola. The Bank was also of service to several US institutions, including the National Security Council, which had funnelled money for the Iran-Contras arms deals, and the CIA, which regularly used BCCI accounts to fund its covert operations. The BCCI also brokered secret arms deals for a wide range of customers, including Western intelligence organizations and even Israeli secret agencies. The BCCI was a central player in the channelling of funds and arms to Pakistan and then on to the ***mujahidin*** fighting against the Soviet troops in Afghanistan. From the mid-1980s the Bank donated large sums (up to $10m.) to finance a secret laboratory run by Dr Abdul Qadeer Khan, the expert responsible for Gen. Zia's effort to develop nuclear weapons. The money originated from a tax-free foundation set up in Pakistan by the BCCI and run by Pakistan's finance minister and future President, Ghulam Ishaq Khan. In 1987 the BCCI financed the purchase of highly resistant steel on behalf of Gen. Inam ul-Haq, the man responsible for Pakistan's nuclear armaments programme. The headquarters of its 'black network' was in Karachi and from this centre, BCCI acted as a full-service bank for the CIA.

A fully integrated operation, it financed and brokered covert arms deals, shipped goods using its own fleet, insured them with its own agency and provided manpower and security *en route*. While the Bank was still in operation, the largest capital flights originated from India, Pakistan and African countries. The Bank eventually crashed, and ceased trading in 1991, but its failure was attributed by many in **Islamic banking** circles to its links with Western financial institutions rather than its own fraudulent management. Supposedly worth $20,000m. in 1991, with operations in more than 60 countries, it was already in effect bankrupt. However, only two months before regulators shut it down, the Bank of England governor, Lord Kingsdown, declared the BCCI to be 'in fairly good shape'.

Banking – *see* **Arab banking (Gulf Co-operation Council)** and **Islamic banking**

Al-Banna, Hassan (1905–49)

Egyption Islamist leader, and founder of the **Muslim Brotherhood**. Al-Banna was an active writer and produced memoirs, articles and speeches. Among his most important books is *Letter to a Muslim Student*, in which he explains the principles of his movement. The Muslim Brotherhood has established itself in many other Muslim countries. Al-Banna was assassinated by the Egyption secret service.

Al-Banna, Sabri – *see also* **ANO—Abu Nidal Organization**

Longstanding member of **al-Fatah**. 'Abu Nidal' is the *nom de guerre* of Sabri al-Banna. Born in **Jaffa** in Palestine in 1937, into a wealthy family. **Refugees** in **Gaza** after 1948 and the establishment of the State of Israel, his parents later settled in **Nablus** in the **West Bank**. In 1960 al-Banna emigrated to Saudi Arabia where he worked as a technician. He became involved in politics, first with the **Ba'ath Party** and then with the Palestinian group, al-Fatah. He was arrested and tortured and then deported. After the **Arab–Israeli War (1967)** he rejoined the Palestinian *fedayeen* in **Amman**, Jordan. He was sent to Khartoum, Sudan, in 1969 and then made representative of al-Fatah and the **Palestine Liberation Organizaton** (PLO) in **Baghdad**, Iraq, in 1970. In 1974 he came out against the 'pragmatic' policy adopted by the PLO, and declared himself in favour of an all-out armed struggle against Israel. He had also belonged to that group within al-Fatah that opposed a political solution through the establishment of a Palestinian state in the West Bank and Gaza. He now split with **Yasser Arafat** and formed the **Fatah Revolutionary Council** (FRC), which was supported by the Iraqi leadership. The influence of the FRC remained limited until it merged in the mid-1980s (following an agreement between Arafat and King **Hussein** of Jordan which proved highly controversial) with the **Palestine National Salvation Front**, a grouping of Arafat's opponents—including the **Popular Front for the Liberation of Palestine** (PFLP), the **PFLP-General**

Command, al-Fatah dissidents and Saika—based in **Damascus**, Syria, and became more active. He is held responsible for several terrorist attacks, including organizing the **hijacking** of a Pan Am flight in Karachi in 1985, and the killing of one of the PLO's highest officers, Salah Khalaf, in 1991. He died in 2002.

Banque Commerciale du Maroc (BCM)

Morocco's leading private bank. In 1987 **Omnium Nord Africain**, a leading industrial corporation, acquired a major stake in the BCM, as well as in other banks.

Banque du Crédit Populaire

Leading Moroccan public-sector bank, whose internal management problems delayed privatization.

Banque du Liban

Lebanon's central bank. In June 1982, following the Israeli invasion of Lebanon, the Bank was visited by **Israelis** wishing to investigate the bank accounts of the **Palestine Liberation Organization**. Apparently, the governor of the central bank, Michel Khoury, contacted President **Bashir Gemayel** who telephoned **Menachem Begin**, the Israeli Prime Minister, in order to remind him of the rules of confidentiality of the Lebanese banking system and of the full commitment of the Lebanese Government and the central bank to respect them.

Banque Marocaine du Commerce Extérieur (BMCE)

Morocco's leading private export bank. In 1995 Othman Benjelloun—a leading member of the wealthy Benjelloun family from Fez—acquired a core stake in this bank, which was previously a public-sector bank. It is said that his winning offer for the BMCE was so high that it indicated official (royal) patronage. It served to exclude outsider Miloud Chabbi from acquiring the Bank.

Banque Misr

Egypt's first national bank, established in May 1920, inspired by Talaat Harb, the nationalist industrialist, who published a book calling for the foundation of a national bank. The shares of the Bank were nominal and exclusively held by Egyptians, all of the Bank's dealings were in **Arabic**, and it was operated by Egyptian employees. The foremost aim of Banque Misr was to serve national economic interests.

Barak, Ehud

Born 1942, former Prime Minister of Israel, former leader of the **Israel Labour Party**, as well a Israel's most decorated soldier. Barak's Government received much criticism, and one year and a half after defeating **Binyamin Netanyahu** in the prime ministerial elections Barak resigned in December 2000. In February 2001 Barak lost the prime ministerial election to **Ariel Sharon**, and promptly resigned as leader of the Israel Labour Party. He is best remembered for his proposal that some 90% of the **West Bank** should be left in the hands of an independent Palestine. Unpopular in Israel for being too generous, the proposal was also rejected by **Yasser Arafat**.

Al-Baraka

International **Islamic banking** group. Established a joint venture with a public-sector bank in Algeria in 1988, and paved the way for other private-sector Islamic banks to gain permission to operate in Algeria after 1992. In Morocco it was able only to establish a leasing company.

Barghouti, Marwan

Palestinian leader. Architect of the cease-fire agreement with **al-Jihad** and **Hamas** (Palestine). Imprisoned by Israel in 2002.

Barzan

Kurmanji-speaking Kurdish **tribe** from the Barzan Valley in the less developed northern part of Iraqi **Kurdistan**.

Barzani, Masoud

Member of the Barzan **tribe** or family, and, since the death of his father, **Mustafa Barzani,** leader of the **Kurdish Democratic Party** (KDP) which dominates the western part of Iraqi **Kurdistan** from **Erbil**. The KDP has a fighting force of approximately 35,000 men.

Barzani, Mustafa

Member of the **Barzan tribe** or family, and leader of the Kurdish movement in Iraq from the mid-1950s until the collapse of the unified movement in March 1975 following the **Algiers Accord** between the Shah of Iran and **Saddam Hussain** (then prime Minister of Iraq). Founder and leader of the **Kurdish Democratic Party**, which fought not only against the Iraqi **Ba'ath Party** regime, but also waged a long 'civil war' with the **Patriotic Union of Kurdistan**, led by **Jalal Talabani**, of the **Talabani** tribe, over a period of some 25 years from 1975 onwards.

Basmachi

Term derived from the Russian word for 'brigand', now widely used to refer to fighters against government authority in several parts of former Soviet **Central Asia**.

Basmachi (revolt)

Anti-Red Army revolt that swept **Central Asia** following the Bolshevik revolution. An indigenous resistance movement that proved to be the last barrier to the assimilation of Central Asia into the Soviet Union. In the 1920s more than 20,000 people fought Soviet rule in Central Asia. Russia referred to them by the derogatory term **Basmachi** (which originally meant 'brigand'), and although the resistance did not apply that term to itself, it none the less entered common usage. The several Basmachi groups had conflicting agendas and seldom co-ordinated their actions. After arising in the **Fergana Valley**, the movement became a rallying ground for opponents of Russian or Bolshevik rule from all parts of the region. Peasant unrest already existed in the area because of wartime hardships and the demands of the Emir and the Soviets. The Red Army's harsh treatment of local inhabitants in 1921 drove more people into the resistance camp. However, the Basmachi movement became more divided and more conservative as it gained numerically. It achieved some unity under the leadership of Enver Pasha, a Turkish adventurer with ambitions to lead the new secular government of Turkey, but Enver was killed in battle in early 1922. Except for remote pockets of resistance, guerrilla fighting in Tajikistan ended by 1925. The defeat of the Basmachis caused as many as 200,000 people, including non-combatants, to flee eastern Bukhoro in the first half of the 1920s. A few thousand subsequently returned over the next several years. The communists used a combination of military force and conciliation to defeat the Basmachis. The military approach ultimately favored the communist side, which was much better armed. The Red Army forces included **Tatars** and Central Asians, who enabled the invading force to appear at least partly indigenous. Conciliatory measures (grants of food, tax relief, the promise of land reform, the reversal of anti-Islamic policies launched during the civil war, and the promise of an end to agricultural controls) prompted some Basmachis to reconcile themselves to the new order.

Basra

Major town in southern Iraq.

Bay'a

A term meaning 'recognition' or 'allegiance of or to a superior authority' in **Arabic**. It was current at the time when the second successor/caliph of the **Prophet Muhammad** was to be chosen. In modern times *bay'a* forms the basis of theories of Islamic **democracy**.

Bayar, Mahmum Celal

President of Turkey from 1950 until May 1960, when he was overthrown by a **military** coup.

Al-Bayoumi, Omar

Referred to in a US congressional report on the attacks of 11 September 2001, al-Bayoumi was a suspected Saudi intelligence agent who befriended and helped two of the hijackers involved in the attacks. He was reported to have visited the Saudi Arabian consulate in Los Angeles in January 2000, where it is believed he met Fahad ath-Thumairy, a member of the Islamic and cultural affairs section (who was later stripped of his diplomatic visa and barred from the USA on suspicion of having links with terrorist groups) and then went to meet two of the hijackers, Nawaf al-Hamzi and Khalid al-Midhar. Al-Bayoumi assisted the two hijackers when they moved to San Diego in February 2000, allowing them first to stay in his flat and then signing their lease and paying the first month's rent and security deposit on an apartment for them. Despite being officially a student, he had apparently unlimited access to funds. On one occasion he delivered US $400,000 to purchase a mosque in San Diego for the Saudi government. In July 2003 the Saudi authorities agreed to allow the US **Central Intelligence Agency** and the Federal Bureau of Investigation to interview al-Bayoumi.

Bayt Ashuhada (House of the Martyrs)

One of the 'guest houses' in Peshawar financed by **Osama bin Laden** in which **Afghan Arabs** and, later, members of **al-Qa'ida** were accommodated.

Bazargan, Mehdi

President of Iran, after the overthrow of the Shah, from1979 until 1980.

BDL – *see* Banque du Liban

Bedouin

Literally 'people of the countryside' (**Arabic**: *bedu*). Widely used to refer to tribal populations still living in the desert regions of the **Middle East**, particularly in southern Libya, eastern Jordan, southern Israel and the **Arabian Peninsula**.

Begin, Menachem Wolfovitch

Born in August 1913 at Brest-Litovsk in Russia, where the Zionist movement was already very active, Menachem Begin was a militant, from the age of 12, first on the left with **Hashomer** Hatzair and then on the right, with Betar, a revisionist paramilitary youth organization—an offshoot of **Zionism**, ultra-nationalist, author-itarian, not to say fascist in character—created in the 1920s by **Vladimir Jabotinsky**. He became the leader of Betar while studying law in Warsaw. When Germany invaded Poland, Begin fled to the east, but was arrested by the Soviet secret police and interned in a labour camp in the polar circle. Released after an agreement between Stalin and the Polish government, Begin enlisted in Gen. Anders' Polish army. In the spring of 1942 he emigrated to join his wife in Palestine. There he was appointed commissar of Betar and head of a secret Jewish nationalist force, the **Irgun Zvai Leumi**. In 1944 he joined forces with secessionists from **Lechi**, the **Stern Gang** (formed in 1943), to mount an armed struggle against the British. He was critical of organizations, like the **Haganah**, for their 'wait-and-see' policy; the Haganah, in return, conducted a witch-hunt of Begin supporters during 1944–45. The Irgun was responsible for a number of actions which were condemned by many at the time, including, notably, the attack in July 1946 on the King David Hotel in **Jerusalem**, seat of British headquarters in Palestine, which left 200 dead and injured, and the massacre in the village of Deir Yassin in April 1948.

After the creation of the State of Israel, Begin founded the **Herut** (Freedom) party and embarked on a career in Israeli politics. In 1949, however, the Herut party gained barely 11.5% of the vote and Begin eventually joined the **Likud** party, which, nearly 30 years later, came to power with Begin as the first non-Labour Prime Minister. Although a committed conservative, he was always determined to advance Israel's interests, and in the late 1970s he embarked on a major initiative to secure a peace treaty with Egypt. This was achieved after the meeting with **Anwar es-Sadat**, President of Egypt, at **Camp David** in the USA, under the auspices of US President **Carter**, in 1978. As a result of this he was awarded the Nobel Peace Prize in that year. While praised for establishing peace with Egypt, Begin was condemned for the invasion of Lebanon and the subsequent occupation of southern Lebanon in 1982. His term of office as Prime Minister came to an end in 1983, when he ceded his place to **Itzhak Shamir**. After that, he effectively retired from active politics.

Beilin, Yossi

Yossi Beilin was a prominent member of the **Israel Labour Party**. A former Israeli Cabinet minister and one of the Israeli architects of the 1993 **Oslo Agreements**, he has been a longstanding proponent of negotiation for peace between Israel and the **Palestinians**. Increasingly marginalized as Israeli political opinion moved to the right and a harder line towards the Palestinians was adopted during the latter part of the 1990s, in 2002 he was removed from the Labour Party's list of candidates for election to the **Knesset**, having slipped to 39th place on the Party's list, far out of range of a parliamentary seat. Beilin is a member of **Meretz**. In 2003 he was leader of a team of Israeli negotiators involved in discussions with Palestinians, including Yasser Abed Rabbo, of new peace plans which resulted in the **Geneva Accord**.

Beirut

Capital of Lebanon with 1.5m. inhabitants, situated on the sea and an important sea port. Much of present-day Beirut is destroyed due to the civil war, Israeli attacks and Syrian occupation from 1975 until 1991. Although the town centre has been rebuilt to older plans, the reconstruction process has been slow. Beirut has long been one of the most important commercial and financial centres of the **Middle East**, albeit somewhat hampered by events in recent decades. It is divided into three regions: east for Christians, west for **Sunnis** and south for **Shi'ites** and **Palestinians**. The city is a mixture of Western and Arab architecture.

Beit al-Mal Holdings

Beit al-Mal Holdings was a public investment company with offices in **East Jerusalem** fully controlled by **Hamas**. The majority of shareholders were members of Hamas or had strong links to it. Beit al-Mal Holdings carried out construction work, supported economic, social and cultural organizations run by Hamas activists and provided funds for other more directly political and paramilitary activities. Beit al-Mal Holdings also had a 20% stake in the **Al-Aqsa International Bank**, the financial arm of Hamas. In December 2001 Beit al-Mal Holdings and al-Aqsa International Bank were closed down by the authorities because they were suspected of helping Hamas recruit and train suicide bombers.

Beka'a Valley

Extending over some 4,280 sq km in the east of Lebanon, the Beka'a Valley is of major strategic importance, with Syria to the east and Israel to the south. When civil war broke out in Lebanon, the Beka'a Valley became an arena for struggles by various local warlords and the different armed militias and political movements of the region to establish their own training camps and bases. The 40,000 Syrian troops and many groups involved in the civil war used it as their gateway into Lebanon. It continues to be an area in which training camps and bases for armed militias and political groups, including **Hezbollah**, are maintained. It was also, during the 1970s and 1980s, an important location of **cannabis** production and a centre of the **drugs** trade, and through this a source of funding for various interests in the region, including the **Palestine Liberation Organization**.

Belhadj, Ali (Sheikh)

Born 1954. Deputy leader of the **FIS—Front islamique du salut** (Islamic Salvation Front), an Algerian political party. A high school teacher and the imam of the al-Sunna mosque in the popular quarter of Bab el-Oued in **Algiers**, he, together with the more moderate **Abbasi Madani**, registered the FIS as a political party in 1989. Belhadj personified the younger generation of the FIS, with a powerful appeal to the deprived and frustrated urban youth. A year later the party won a majority of votes in local elections. In 1991, however, the Algerian Government proclaimed martial law and imprisoned Belhadj and Madani. In 1994 Belhadj was transferred to house arrest.

Ben Ali, Zine el-Abidine (1936–)

President of Tunisia (1987–). Educated in France and the USA, he entered the army and became Minister of National Security (1984–86) and interior minister

(1986–87). In October 1987 he became Prime Minister under the ageing Tunisian President **Habib Bourguiba**, whom he deposed in a bloodless coup in November 1987. Ben Ali was elected as President in 1989 and then re-elected in 1994 and again in October 1999. He has had a moderating influence on the **Palestine Liberation Organization**, whose leaders were based in Tunisia for 10 years, and has been a supporter of **Yasser Arafat**'s attempts at reaching peace with Israel. Domestically, he has continued to develop a relatively secular, Westernized, and increasingly middle-class nation.

Ben Badis, Sheikh Abdelhamid (1889–1940)

Major Algerian reforming Islamist. Influenced initially by the visit to Algeria of Muhammed Abduh, Ben Badis founded the Association of Reformist Ulema in 1931, but the movement had been active for at least 10 years prior to this. Its principal purpose was to promote a reformed, scripturalist and puritan **Islam** and the revival of **Arabic** language and culture. Vigorously opposed to the political movement led by **Ferhat Abbas** on the one hand, and to the traditional popular forms of Algerian Islam on the other. He was succeeded by Sheikh Bachir el Ibrahimi (1889–1965) in 1940.

Ben Barka, Mehdi

Charismatic leader of the Moroccan left-wing **UNFP—Union nationale des forces populaires** (National Union of Popular Forces) during the late 1950s and early 1960s. During the mid- to late 1950s, divisions developed in the Moroccan nationalist party, the **Istiqlal**, of which Ben Barka was a founding member. **Allal al-Fassi** and Mehdi Ben Barka came to represent the 'old turbans' (conservatives) and the 'Young Turks' (radicals) respectively within the Istiqlal, although this characterization is too neat with regard to both politicians. Ben Barka had been associated, in the executive of the party, with the 'old guard' since 1944 and had always been a tireless organizer, ruthlessly committed to the domination of Moroccan post-independence politics by a unified Istiqlal. He was not a dogmatist nor a doctrinaire leftist, although his methods were often radical, his vocabulary characteristically Marxist and his political concepts authoritarian. However, he was responsible for setting up structures within the party, which, during 1956–58, gave him considerable political control and were designed to increase his power and influence. When a split developed between the radicals and the conservatives in mid-1958, provoked by the resignation of the Istiqlal Prime Minister, M'Barek Bekkai, Ben Barka effectively joined the radicals and was removed from his post as editor of the party newspaper, *L'Istiqlal*, which ceased publication in June 1958.

At first, the split remained within the party. In January 1959 a new body was launched in the name of the Istiqlal: the National Confederation of the Istiqlal Party. Ben Barka, who had severed all ties with the 'old turbans' in November 1958, received most of the public credit, and blame, for this. By September, however, a new party, the UNFP, had been established, with Ben Barka as its leading figure. What had begun essentially as a split within the party élite, increasingly reflected social, political and ideological divisions: the UNFP accused the Istiqlal of archaic leadership, lack of ideology and bourgeois prejudices and sought to recruit support from the 'three great forces of Morocco, the organized workers, the peasantry and the resistance'. The UNFP was supported by the Moroccan Trade Union Federation and most unions, and also significant sections of public-sector workers and students. In the first local elections, held in May 1959, the Istiqlal won about 40% of seats, and the UNFP 23%: a good showing for a party not one-year old. Its strength was clearly among urban workers, small businessmen and migrants to the cities. The UNFP successfully contested the National Assembly elections in 1962. Soon after this, however, Ben Barka was forced into exile, where he continued to represent the party. He had been in exile for three years and had twice been condemned to death in Morocco when he was kidnapped in Paris, France, in October 1965 and went missing, presumed dead. His body was never found. He had escaped previous assassination attempts, but on this occasion, according to a report published 36 years later, Ben Barka was kidnapped, then tortured and finally killed in a house south of the French capital, by the former Moroccan Minister of the Interior, director of the secret services and right-hand man of King **Hassan II**, **Mohammed Oufkir**. Also named as present during the torture was Oufkir's assistant, Ahmed Dlimi. Ben Barka's body was taken back to **Rabat** and dissolved in acid. The account, published in 2001 in the French newspaper *Le Monde*, and in the Moroccan newspaper *Le Journal* (as well as in the United Kingdom, in *The Independent*), relied on information provided by a former Moroccan secret agent, Ahmed Boukari, who kept a meticulous record of the operation.

Ben Bella, Ahmed

Born 1916, first President of Algeria from 1963 until 1965. Served in the French army in the Second World War, thereafter becoming active in the Algerian struggle for independence. Bella was one of the nine members of the revolutionary committee that developed into the **Front de libération nationale** (National Liberation Front). He was imprisoned from 1956 until 1962, when the Evian Agreement was signed, and Algeria gained independence. He became President in 1962, but lost power to **Houari Boumedienne** in 1965, and was placed under house arrest until 1980.

Ben-Gurion, David (1886–1973)

Born David Grin in Plonsk, Poland, in October 1886 and educated in Warsaw, he embraced the Zionist-socialist doctrine of the **Poale Zion** (Workers of Zion). He emigrated in 1906 to Palestine, where, after working as an agricultural labourer for four years, he joined the staff of the socialist journal *Ahdut* (Unity) and wrote his first political articles under the name of Ben-Gurion. He hoped at this time to see a

Jewish renaissance within the framework of an Ottoman Palestine. The alliance of the Turks with Germany shattered his hopes and, banished from the **Ottoman Empire**, he left for the USA. There he wrote his first book, *Eretz Yisrael* (The Land of Israel). When he heard of the **Balfour Declaration** he warned that only the Jewish people could construct a 'national home' and that it would be 'by its body and soul, by its strength and its capital'. Ben-Gurion returned at the end of 1918 to Palestine and worked to help form the **Histadrut**, the labour federation. He increased the membership of the Histadrut tenfold and widened its sphere of influence. He played a central role in forming the Israeli Workers Party, **Mapai**. When, in 1929, various small socialist parties merged, Ben-Gurion became secretary-general of Mapai. In 1934 Mapai gained 42% of the vote of the **Yishuv** (Jewish community) and one-half of the votes of the 19th Zionist World Congress in 1935. In 1939, after Britain introduced restrictions on Jewish immigration to Palestine, Ben-Gurion called for a Jewish rebellion, involving both peaceful and military actions. Shortly afterwards, he was elected president of the Zionist Executive, the highest body of international **Zionism**. He was also elected chairman of the **Jewish Agency** for Palestine, considered by the British as the representative voice of Jews in Palestine. When, in the face of rising tension between Arabs and Jews, Britain proposed the **partition** of Palestine, Ben-Gurion accepted the proposal, stating that 'a partial Hebrew state is not an end but merely a beginning', but then proceeded to lobby the US government persistently on the issue of a separate Jewish state, travelling to the USA and organizing the Biltmore Conference, which in May 1942 recommended the constitution of a 'Jewish Commonwealth'. Formulated in detail in August 1946, the partition proposal of the Executive of the Jewish Agency was the inspiration for the Partition Plan adopted by the UN in November 1947. As president of the Executive, Ben-Gurion drafted and on 14 May 1948 delivered the declaration of independence. He imposed the new state's authority on those who were opposed to the move. During the **Arab–Israeli War (1948–49)**, he was defence minister in charge of the Jewish forces. With arms reinforcements from Prague, he launched the spring counter-offensive in 1948, then created **Zahal**, the **Israeli Defence Force** (IDF), securing victory for it. His strategy was to take advantage of the Arab attack to prevent the birth of a Palestinian Arab state, extend the territory of the new Jewish state and rid it of the majority of its Arab population. In 1949 he noted that 'we have liberated a very large territory, much more than we expected. Now we shall have to work for two or three generations. As for the rest, we shall see later'. From 1949 to 1953 he applied himself as Prime Minister (and also defence minister) to the transformation of Israel. He retired in 1953, but the **Lavon** affair brought him back to public life, once again as Prime Minister. During 1955–56 he agreed Israel's support for the British and French attacks on Egypt that brought about first the occupation of Sinai and then the Suez war. However, pressure from the USA and the USSR forced the IDF to withdraw. Already an old man, 70 years of age, at the time of Suez, Ben-Gurion stayed on for several more years, but eventually retired 'for personal reasons' in 1963. After leaving prime ministerial office, Ben-Gurion broke with Mapai (in 1965) and founded two parties—**Rafi** and LaAam. He also completed two books: *Israel: A Personal History* and *The Jews in Their Land*. He criticized the leadership for taking the initiative in the **Arab–Israeli War (1967)** and recommended the return of all occupied Arab territories. During the elections of 1969 he again headed a 'State List', which gained only four seats. This set-back precipitated his definitive retirement in the following year. He died at the beginning of December 1973. Ben-Gurion was known for determination and cynicism in reaching his goals, making, despite his hero status at home, few friends in the leaderships of major states such as Britain and the USA. He was a wholehearted Zionist, believing that the Jews had a God-given right to Palestine. Yet he also believed that Israel could be re-established by human efforts. He is referred to by **Israelis** as 'father of the nation'.

Ben-Zvi, Itzhak (1884–1963)

Former President of Israel, born in Russia. Ben-Zvi emigrated to Palestine in 1907, and became one of the founders of the Bar Giora and **Hashomer** clandestine Jewish defence organizations. After a period in Turkey and the USA, he returned as a soldier in the Jewish Legion, in 1931 became president of the National Committee of Palestine Jewry, and was also a member of the first and second **Knesset**. In 1952 he was elected as the second President of Israel after the death of **Chaim Weizmann**, and was re-elected to that office in 1957 and 1962.

Berber(s)

Indigenous peoples of North Africa who were referred to by the Greeks as *barbaroi*, hence 'Berbers' (those who speak a language other than Greek). Used by all those who subsequently colonized North Africa, from the Romans to the French. In fact, the 'Berbers' speak a variety of dialects, and possibly languages, under the general rubric Tamazight. The Tuareg, who inhabit the central Sahara (southern Algeria, northern Mali and Niger), are also Berbers and speak **Tamasheq**. The Berbers today have a strong but controversial identity in Algeria, and, to a lesser extent, in Morocco, Libya, Tunisia and Mauritania. In 2003 around 300 schools in Morocco began to teach Tamazight. Education officials have stated that it will be available in all schools by 2008, a move that represents a victory for Berber rights activists. In Algeria, although Berber is widely recognized as a national language, Berber rights activists consider themselves discriminated against and have clashed with the police on several occasions in recent years.

Berri, Nabih

Born 1938, Lebanese politician, became speaker of parliament in 1992—the highest political office a **Shi'a** Muslim can occupy according to the Lebanese Constitution.

Effectively, if not formally, Berri became one of Lebanon's three heads of state, together with **Emile Lahoud** and **Rafiq Hariri**. Berri's unpopularity with many Shi'is is one of the reasons for the success of the alternative Shi'a group, **Hezbollah**.

Bet Nahrain Democratic Party

An Iraqi political group seeking the creation of an autonomous state for **Assyrians** in Bet Nahrain.

Bethlehem

City in Palestine, located on the **West Bank**, with 40,000 inhabitants, presently under **Palestinian National Authority** rule, but still the subject of Israeli military control. Bethlehem is very important to **Christianity** and **Judaism**—for the latter as the supposed place of King David's birth, and for the former as the traditional birthplace of Jesus. The tomb of Rachel, important to Christianity, Judaism and **Islam**, is just outside the town.

Bey

A Turkish title for local governor, including of a province or territory in the **Ottoman Empire**.

Beyyat al-Islam

Islamist splinter group in Turkey. Possibly linked with (overlapping membership) **Islamic Action** and with the Turkish **Hezbollah**.

Bible

Two collections of religious texts central to **Christianity** and **Judaism**. In Christianity the two texts are called the Old Testament and the New Testament.

Biltmore Programme

This was a programme approved by the Zionist Conference held at the Biltmore Hotel in New York on 11 May 1942. American Zionists offered a message of hope and encouragement to fellow Jews in the ghettos and concentration camps in Hitler-dominated Europe and sent their warmest greetings to the **Jewish Agency** Executive in **Jerusalem**, to the Va'ad Leumi, and to the whole **Yishuv** in Palestine. The Conference reaffirmed the stand previously adopted at congresses of the **World Zionist Organization**, expressing the readiness and the desire of the Jewish people for full co-operation with their Arab neighbours. It called for the fulfilment of the original purpose of the **Balfour Declaration** and the Mandate which 'recognising the historical connection of the Jewish people with Palestine' was to afford them the opportunity, as stated by US President Wilson, to found there a Jewish Commonwealth. The Conference rejected the British government's White Paper of May 1939, which, it suggested (quoting Winston Churchill), constituted a breach and repudiation of the Balfour Declaration.

Bin Laden, Osama

Notorious international terrorist and Islamic extremist. Born in 1957 into great wealth as the son of a Yemeni-born owner of a leading Saudi construction company. In 1979 bin Laden left Saudi Arabia to support the Afghan *mujahidin* against the Soviet invasion of Afghanistan. The Afghan *jihad* was financially and militarily backed by the USA and supported by Saudi Arabia and Pakistan. While in Afghanistan bin Laden helped found the **Afghan Service Bureau**, which recruited and organized fighters from around the world and imported equipment to aid the Afghan resistance against the Soviet army. Many were from the **Arab World** and came to be known as the **Afghan Arabs**. After the Soviet withdrawal in 1989 the 'Arab Afghans' (bin Laden's faction) dispersed, some returning to their own countries, others continuing to fight as Islamists in ongoing struggles elsewhere (including **Chechnya**) while the 'base' of international *mujahidin* that he had established evolved into an international Islamist network, **al-Qa'ida**. Bin Laden returned to Saudi Arabia to work in the family construction business, but was expelled in 1991 because of his anti-government activities, which stemmed from his growing antagonism to the Saudi regime, which he regarded as corrupt and deviating from its strict Islamic foundations. He spent the next five years in Sudan until US pressure prompted the Sudanese government to expel him, where-upon bin Laden returned to Afghanistan to lead the operations of al-Qa'ida. Bin Laden's ideology is strongly anti-American, anti-Western, and also anti-Israeli. It has its foundations in **Wahhabism** and leads him (and many of his followers) to consider Saudi Arabia both as the fount of **Islam** and as a betrayer of Islam's fundamental principles and values. Some believe that al-Qa'ida is therefore a 'fundamentalist' Islamic movement, operating at a global level and seeking in some way to unite Islamic forces against 'the ungodly'. Bin Laden is alleged to have financed, inspired and even directly organized various terrorist attacks. According to the US government, he was, it seems, involved in at least five major attacks. First, the 1993 **World Trade Center** bombing. Second, the killing, in 1996, of 19 US soldiers in Saudi Arabia. Third, the bombing, in 1998, of US embassies in Kenya and Tanzania which killed more than 200 people. Fourth, the bomb attack, in October 2000, on the *USS Cole* in Yemen. Fifth, in September 2001, the multiple plane **hijackings** and co-ordinated attacks on the World Trade Center and the Pentagon. The World Trade Center towers were destroyed, with a death toll of some 3,000 people. In response, the USA, with much international support, launched a war to remove the **Taliban** from power. After the collapse of the Taliban regime, which had provided a safe haven as well as training and other facilities, bin Laden went into hiding. It is thought he may still be in Afghanistan.

Bin Laden Group

A construction firm managed by members of **Osama bin Laden**'s family. One of the largest businesses in the **Middle East**, the firm was the only Arab company bidding to construct what will be the world's tallest building, the Burj Dubai tower (at a planned 705 m almost twice the height of the **World Trade Center** destroyed by associates of Osama bin Laden's **al-Qa'ida** organization in September 2001). It has been shortlisted for the construction of this American-designed building, being developed by Emaar Properties. Due for completion in 2008, the tower will be part of a complex including the world's largest shopping mall.

Bitar, Salah ad-Din (1912–80)

Syrian politician, Prime Minister 1963–66, foreign minister 1956–57. Also known for playing a central role in the formation of the **(Arab) Ba'ath Party**—in 1940 Bitar, together with **Michel Aflaq**, established a study circle which they called Movement of Arab Renaissance, from which the Ba'ath movement developed. He was assassinated in Paris, France, in 1980.

Black September

This term is used to designate both the events of September 1970 that ended in the crushing of the **Palestine Liberation Organization** (PLO) by the Jordanian army and a Palestinian organization created as a result of those events (see below for latter). The **Arab–Israeli War (1967)** led to a dramatic increase in the number of **Palestinians** living in Jordan. Its Palestinian refugee population—700,000 in 1966—grew by a further 300,000 originating from the **West Bank**. During the period following the 1967 war the Palestinian *fedayeen* (fighters) of the PLO had established their bases in Jordan, and from these they launched attacks into Israel. This created increasing tension both between the regime of King **Hussein** and the PLO, and between Palestinians and native Jordanians. Confrontations between Jordanian and Palestinian forces increased. In the summer of 1970 the **Rogers Plan** was accepted by both President **Nasser** of Egypt and King Hussein; it was rejected by the PLO. On 7 September commandos of **George Habash**'s **Popular Front for the Liberation of Palestine** (PFLP) hijacked three planes from international airlines to the town of Zarka in north Jordan. The airport was declared a liberated zone. Although the PFLP had been suspended from the PLO, on **Yasser Arafat**'s request, King Hussein took advantage of the situation to eliminate the PLO in Jordan. On 16 September he formed a military government and the army received the order to intervene. The fighting, which was extremely violent, resulted in thousands of Palestinian civilian casualties. A Syrian tank force took up positions in northern Jordan to support the *fedayeen* but was forced to retreat. Within a week Arab foreign ministers meeting in **Cairo**, Egypt, had arranged a cease-fire. The major fighting stopped before the end of September, but sporadic violence continued until Jordanian forces won a decisive victory over the *fedayeen* in July 1971, expelling them from the country.

Black September (organization)

On 28 November 1971 a Palestinian commando squad assassinated the Jordanian Prime Minister, Wasfi at-Tal. The Black September organization was born. Created by **al-Fatah** in the aftermath of the events of '**Black September**' which led to the crushing of the **Palestine Liberation Organization** in Jordan and its effective expulsion from that country, the organization was to carry out some 40 operations outside Israel, of which the most spectacular was the massacre of Israeli athletes at the Munich Olympic Games in 1972. The Black September group disappeared after the **Arab–Israeli War (1973)**. According to **'Abu Iyad'**, 'the organization acted as an auxiliary to the Resistance, at a time when the latter was no longer able to fulfil its military and political duties to the full … Its members reflected the profound feelings of frustration and anger felt by the entire Palestinian people faced with Jordan's butchery and the complicity that made it possible…'.

Blessed Relief

The Blessed Relief Foundation, whose name in **Arabic** is *Muwafaq*, is a charity supported and managed by Saudi families. Yasin al-Qadi, a Saudi magnate, has transferred millions of dollars, via the Blessed Relief Foundation, to the **al-Qa'ida network**. Al-Qadi is an international businessman involved in real estate, chemicals, banking, and consulting companies operating in Saudi Arabia, Turkey, Kazakhstan, Albania and Pakistan. He was implicated in 1998 in a '**money-laundering**' scheme for **Hamas** via the **Qur'anic Literacy Institute**, a Chicago-based charity whose founder, Mohamed Salah, was a front man for Hamas. After 11 September 2001 al-Qadi's assets and investments were frozen in several countries. In Tirana, Albania, for example, the authorities blocked works carried out by his Karavan Construction Co on two high-rise buildings.

Bloc national libanais

Established in 1943. Right-wing Lebanese political party with policy of power-sharing between Christians and Muslims and the exclusion of the **military** from politics. Its president is Selim Salhab, its secretary-general Jean Hawat.

BMA – *see* Bahrain Monetary Agency

Bojinka Plan

A plot to blow up several jumbo jets simultaneously which was aborted after a fire broke out in the flat rented by Ramzi Yousef and his associates in Manila,

Philippines. A laptop computer containing vital information relating to the plan was left in the flat, and one of the associates (Abdul Hakim Murad) was sent back to recover the computer and was arrested. According to Murad's confession, Yousef intended to hijack several commercial flights in the USA and crash the 'planes into the CIA headquarters and the Pentagon'. Data on the computer were also used to reveal links between Ramzi Yousef and **al-Qa'ida** through Riduan Isamuddin (known as Hambali), regarded by the Filipino authorities as the regional head of al- Qa'ida.

Bonn Agreement

In December 2001 a number of prominent Afghans met under UN auspices in Bonn, Germany, to decide on a plan for governing Afghanistan. Central to the process set out in the agreement was the convening of an emergency **Loya Jirga**, or traditional Afghan Grand Council. As a result, the **Afghan Interim Authority**—made up of 30 members, headed by a chairman—was inaugurated on 22 December 2001 with a six-month mandate, to be followed by the establishment of a two-year Transitional Authority (TA), after which elections were to be held. The structure of the TA was announced on 10 June 2002 when the Loya Jirga convened, establishing the Transitional Islamic State of Afghanistan with an 18-month mandate to adopt a constitution and a 24-month mandate to hold nation-wide elections.

Boudiaf, Mohammed

President of Algeria and head of the five-member High Council of State (HCS) from 1992 until 1994. One of the historical founders of the **Front de libération nationale** (National Liberation Front), Boudiaf had quit politics in 1963, but was popular and charismatic. Intended as a figurehead, he became too active, assailing **corruption** within the government and bureaucracy, and was assassinated. He—and the HCS— was replaced by Gen. (retd) **Liamine Zéroual**, who was appointed as President in January 1994.

Ould Boulkheir, Messoud

Mauritanian politican, leader of the **Action for Change** party.

Boumedienne, Houari

President of Algeria from June 1965 until December 1978. His original name was Muhammad Ibrahim Bukharruba. While studying in **Cairo**, Egypt, during the early 1950s he joined a group of expatriate Algerian nationalists that included **Ahmed Ben Bella**. Boumedienne secretly re-entered Algeria (1955) to join a group of guerrillas operating in the province of Oran. He was (1960–62) chief of staff of the exiled National Liberation Army in Tunisia and served as Algeria's Minister of Defence from the time of its independence. Boumedienne supported Ben Bella, and was his defence minister until 1965. However, after a series of disputes with Ben Bella, Boumedienne led a coup that overthrew his former ally's Government. After the coup, Boumedienne assumed the posts of President, Prime Minister, and chairman of the revolutionary council until his death in December 1978.

Bourguiba, Habib

Former President of Tunisia. The son of a low-ranking government functionary in the Sahel (southern) town of Monastir, Bourguiba rose to become the charismatic leader of the nationalist Tunisian **Neo-Destour Party**, the founding father of modern Tunisia, Prime Minister and then President. He belonged to Tunisia's first nationalist party, the **Destour Party**, which was led by members of the traditional élites. Early on it became apparent to Bourguiba and his colleagues –who were mainly bright young men from the provinces who had received an education in Franco-Arab schools, especially at Saidik College, in Tunisia, and further education in France—that the nationalist movement needed to be broader-based than the Destour. They formed a new party, which included some members of the Destour and of the traditional urban élite but reached out to the mass of the Tunisan population, including those in the rural areas.

He became Prime Minister of Tunisia in 1956 on independence and held this position until July 1957, when Tunisia formally became a republic. He then became President, holding office as head of state for 30 years, from July 1957 until November 1987, when he was deposed after a bloodless coup. He was succeeded by **Zine el-Abidine Ben Ali**. He died on 6 April 2000 at the age of 96..

Bouteflika, Abdelaziz

President of Algeria from April 1999 after winning a heavily rigged presidential election from which six of the rival presidential candidates withdrew. Bouteflika had served as Algeria's foreign minister from 1963 until 1979 after being a charter member of the **Oujda clan**. Brought out of retirement to deal with the crisis, he attempted to reduce the level of the conflict within Algeria by offering an amnesty in June 1999 to the Islamist paramilitary opposition groups. Some of these groups took advantage of this to lay down their arms. Others, however, notably the **GIA— Groupe islamique armé** (Armed Islamic Group) and the **GSPC—Groupe salafiste pour la prédication et le combat** (Salafist Group for Call and Combat), maintained the armed struggle against the state. Bouteflika was successful in the presidential elections held in April 2004, in which he won an overwhelming majority of the votes cast and significant political credibility as a consequence.

Boutros-Ghali, Boutros

Born in 1922, Egyptian statesman, and secretary-general of the UN in 1992–96. Educated in **Cairo** and Paris, France, he was professor of international relations at

Cairo University from 1949 until 1979, and was present at the Egypt-Israel **Camp David Accords** negotiations. He served as Egypt's delegate to the UN, and held the posts of Egyptian Minister of State for Foreign Affairs and Deputy Prime Minister for Foreign Affairs. Boutros-Ghali was the first African and Arab head of the UN. He sought to reorganize and streamline the UN Secretariat and strengthen the UN's peace-keeping role. In 1996, after policy disagreements mainly with the USA, he was forced from office. In 1997 he became secretary-general of La Francophonie, an organization of French-speaking nations.

Brahimi, Abdelhamid

Algerian Prime Minister from 1983.

Bread riots

Throughout the period from the mid-1970s to the mid-1990s there was a virtual epidemic of claims for social justice across the region (except in the **oil**-rich **Gulf States**) and popular protest against economic reform policies that effectively cut public expenditure, reduced subsidies and increased the price of basic goods. Widely referred to as 'bread riots', these waves of mass protest were an indication of growing opposition to the programmes of economic liberalization and structural adjustment which increased inequality and changed the relationship between the state and the ordinary mass of the people in terms of responsibility for basic welfare. Also termed 'food riots' and 'IMF riots' because of the perceived role of the **International Monetary Fund** (and the International Bank for Reconstruction and Development—**World Bank**) in orchestrating and enforcing the 'austerity measures' that accompanied the reforms, this form of more or less spontaneous mass protest has been increasingly replaced by more organized and orchestrated opposition not only to the economic reform programmes, but also to the oppressive regimes which continue to implement them. Despite this general tendency, similar incidents have also occurred in various countries in response to price rises in more recent years.

Bremer, Paul (1941–)

US envoy in Iraq. Chief civilian administrator of Iraq (2003–). Head of the **Coalition Provisional Authority (Iraq)**. Former diplomat and counter-**terrorism** expert with little experience of the **Middle East**. He replaced **Gen. Jay Garner**.

British forces in the Coalition

In the aftermath of the **Iraq War (2003)** British troops were deployed in a peace-keeping role, as part of the US-led **Coalition in Iraq**, mainly in the southern part of the country, around **Basra**. The size of the force was 8,700. As the situation deteriorated during the spring of 2004, and the USA was considering increasing the level of its forces in Iraq, the British government refused to comment in any detail on the withdrawal or augmentation of existing forces. There has, however, been some increase in the British commitment since the decision of some other members of the coalition, notably Spain, to withdraw their troops.

British forces in the Iraq War (2003)

British forces deployed in the war with Iraq in 2003 eventually amounted to about 20,000. Initial deployment was of a naval task force consisting of 3,000 marines and 2,000 sailors on board the aircraft carrier HMS *Ark Royal*, the helicopter carrier HMS *Ocean*, the destroyers HMS *Liverpool*, *Edinburgh* and *York*, the frigate HMS *Marlborough*, three landing ships, two minesweepers, a submarine and four Royal Fleet auxiliary vessels, to provide medical facilities. In addition, 1,500 reservists were called up, including medical staff, logistics officers and intelligence analysts. Later deployment of British forces after the war involved all of the services.

British Petroleum (BP)

Major **oil** 'giant' and one of the so-called 'seven sisters'. The largest British corporation and the fourth largest corporation in the world.

Broader Middle East and North Africa Initiative

This American initiative, designed to encourage regimes in the region to develop better governance and more **democracy**, was endorsed in June 2004 by the G8 (the Group of Eight rich and powerful countries) at its meeting in Savannah, Georgia. Countries in the region, however, are loath to have 'American values' imposed upon them.

Bulgaria

Previously little involved in the region, Bulgaria sent 480 soldiers to Iraq to support the coalition forces during 2003–04. They were deployed together with Polish forces in the area of **Karbala**. Bulgaria declined a request to complement the Polish-led battalion in central-southern Iraq after the anticipated withdrawal of Spanish troops in June 2004.

Bush, George

President of the USA in 1989–1993. He led a coalition of states and military forces under UN auspices first under **Operation Desert Shield** and then under **Operation Desert Storm** to force Iraq to retreat from Kuwait, which it had occupied in 1990, in what is referred to as the **Iraq War (1991)**.

Bush, George W.

Son of former US President (1989–93) **George Bush**. President of the USA (2001–). He ordered the bombing of **Taliban** forces in Afghanistan in order to bring down the Taliban government and punish them for hosting **al-Qa'ida**, the terrorist network thought to be responsible for the attacks on Washington and New York on 9 September 2001. He ordered the intervention of US forces in Afghanistan following the air bombardment of Taliban positions and of suspected al-Qa'ida training camps. In 2003 he led a coalition of military forces against the regime and forces of **Saddam Hussain** in Iraq, which resulted in the overthrow of the regime and the occupation of Iraq by the **Coalition Provisional Authority** and troops from several members of the coalition. These various interventions in the region were undertaken under the broad umbrella of the President's declared 'war on terror'.

Byzantium

Strictly the former name of **Constantinople** or **Istanbul**. In a broad sense also used to refer to the eastern Roman Empire, of which Constantinople was the capital from AD 330.

C

Cairo

Al-Qahirah

Capital of Egypt with more than 8m. inhabitants. Major industrial and commercial centre at the mouth of the **Nile** near the **Mediterranean**. Greater Cairo is inhabited by around 15m. people, and is made up of the original Cairo, the city of Giza, the islands Gezira and ar-Ruda, and parts of Qalubliyya. The area has been populated for at least 6,000 years. Cairo has more than 500 mosques, and boasts the world's first university (**al-Azhar**), which serves as the most important centre of Islamic learning for the whole **Sunni** world.

Cairo Agreement

Agreement reached in November 1969 between the Supreme Commander of the Lebanese army and the **Palestine Liberation Organization** (PLO) in an effort to regulate the relationship between the Lebanese government and the PLO, and the latter's activity in and from Lebanon.

Cairo Agreement on the Gaza Strip and Jericho

An agreement reached on 4 May 1994 between the government of Israel and the **Palestine Liberation Organization**, within the framework of the **Middle East** peace process initiated at Madrid, Spain, in October 1991, regarding the scheduled withdrawal of Israeli military forces from the **Gaza Strip**, the transfer of authority to a **Palestinian Authority** (PA), the structure and composition of the PA, its jurisdiction, powers and responsibilities, legislative powers and arrangements for security and public order. It also included articles relating to the establishment of a Palestinian Directorate of Police Force, arrangements for safe passage between the areas under the jurisdiction of the PA, relations between Israel and the PA, and other matters.

Caliph

Literally means 'successor to the Prophet'. Abu Bakr was the first caliph after the **Prophet Muhammad**. Also used more generally to refer to eminent religious and political figures in Muslim societies throughout the **Middle East**.

Caliphate

The **Islamic State** established by successors to the **Prophet Muhammad** that in the early Islamic period after his death united all Muslims under a single caliph. Who is a caliph was a major source of debate among Islamic scholars and jurists until the caliphate was officially dissolved at the time of the demise of the **Ottoman Empire** after the First World War.

Camp David

Maryland summer residence and retreat of the President of the USA. Used by successive Presidents as a place to discuss major international issues.

Camp David Accords/Camp David Agreement

Widely used to refer to the draft agreements signed by **Anwar es-Sadat** and **Menachem Begin**, President of Egypt and Prime Minister of Israel respectively, between 5–17 September 1978 during a series of meetings at **Camp David**, Maryland, USA, under the auspices of US President **Jimmy Carter**. The first involved the concluding of 'a peace treaty' between Egypt and Israel, the other the setting out of 'a framework for peace in the Middle East'. Egypt had technically been at war with Israel since the establishment of the latter in 1948. The agreements represented the culmination of a long process of negotiating a separate peace agreement between Egypt and Israel. Shortly after the **Arab–Israeli War (1973)**, when the Geneva Conference broke down, a series of agreements laid down the path to Camp David: the agreement referred to as Kilometre 101 in November 1973, the arrangements for disengagement from the **Suez Canal** in January 1974, the first comprehensive agreement in September 1975, after which the state of war between the two was formally ended and UN troops were stationed in the demilitarized zone. The next stage in the bilateral process involved Sadat's unprecedented visit to **Jerusalem** in November 1977, to address the Israeli government and the **Knesset**— the first visit ever by the head of state of an Arab nation to Israel. Begin had become Prime Minister in May 1977, as leader of the right-wing **Likud** party, having defeated the **Israel Labour Party** for the first time since 1948, and was committed to a long-term programme to build **Eretz Israel** (Greater Israel). Sadat was committed, however, to his 'peace mission' and the two leaders met at Camp David, under the auspices of the US government to advance the process. The negotiations lasted 12 days, and concluded with two agreements. One established a framework for a peace treaty between Egypt and Israel. Israeli forces were to institute a phased withdrawal from the Sinai, and return it to Egypt within three years of signing the treaty. (Israeli ships were guaranteed right of passage through the Suez Canal.) The second agreement was more general. It called for Israel to gradually grant self-government to the **Palestinians** in the Israeli-occupied **West Bank** and **Gaza Strip** and to partially withdraw its forces from those areas in preparation for negotiations on their final status after a period of three years. The first treaty was signed in March 1979, but it was not until April 1982, after the last Israeli **settlement** in the Sinai had been dismantled, that Egypt eventually re-established sovereignty over the territory (with the exception of the disputed zone of Taba).

Cannabis

A major crop in certain parts of the region. In Morocco, for example, the crop is said to be worth US $10,000m.–$12,000m. annually. In the Rif mountains of northern Morocco as many as 800,000 people depend on its cultivation and sale, 134,000 ha are given over to the crop (known as *kif*) and as much as 47,400 metric tons is harvested. Its growth is expanding, both geographically and in terms of the area under cultivation. In all, some 1.5% of Morocco's arable land is under *kif* cultivation. In the **Beka'a Valley**, Lebanon, cannabis is also a major crop.

CARE International

International development NGO based in the USA, with programmes in more than 72 countries. One of the few organizations that had worked in Iraq for several years prior to the war in 2003, CARE initially began work in 1991 and is the only international non-governmental organization to maintain a continuous presence in southern and central Iraq.

Carter, Jimmy

Born in 1924. The 39th US President (1977–81) distinguished himself in the role of mediator, during the negotiations that led to the **Camp David Accords** of 1978, between President **Anwar es-Sadat** of Egypt and Prime Minister **Menachem Begin** of Israel, helping to mitigate and ultimately put an end to hostilities between Egypt and Israel. Carter continued his efforts to bring peace to different regions of the world out of office, setting up the Carter Center, based on the principle that everyone on earth should be able to live in peace. Jimmy Carter was awarded the Nobel Prize for Peace in 2002.

Casablanca

Largest city in Morocco, with a population of 2,940,623 (1994 census). A port and centre of industrial and commercial importance.

Caspian Sea

The largest inland lake in the world, with an area of 371,000 sq km, bordering Iran to the south.

Catholics, Armenian

Members of the Armenian Catholic Church, a semi-independent Christian church affiliated with the Roman Catholic Church. There are over 70,000 Armenian Catholics in the **Middle East**.

Catholics, Assyrian

A minority Christian group, mainly in Syria, Iraq and Lebanon.

Catholics, Greek

A minority Christian group, mainly in Syria and Lebanon.

Catholics, Maronite

Catholics belonging to the **Maronite** Church, a Christian Community centred in Lebanon, and affiliated with the Roman Catholic Church, which dates back to AD 700. There are around 1.5m. Maronites in the **Middle East**, of which 800,000 live in Lebanon, where they represent one-quarter of the population.

Catholics, Orthodox

A minority Christian group, mainly in Syria and Lebanon.

Catholics, Roman

A minority Christian group, mainly in Syria and Lebanon.

Catholics, Syrian

Catholics belonging to the Syrian Catholic Church, which is affiliated with the Roman Catholic Church. Despite its name, the Syrian Catholic Church is today strongest in Iraq and Lebanon. There are more than 100,000 Syrian Catholics in the **Middle East**.

CENTO

Central Treaty Organization, formed in 1959 after the withdrawal of Iraq following its revolution in 1958. Member states were Great Britain, Pakistan, Iran and Turkey. In 1979, following the withdrawal of Iran, Pakistan and Turkey, the alliance was dissolved.

Central Asia

An ill-defined region to the north of the **Middle East** (or West Asia) and South Asia. The southern part consists of the following countries: Turkmenistan, Afghanistan, Uzbekistan, Kazakhstan, Kyrgyzstan, Tajikistan.

Central Intelligence Agency

The main US secret service organization operating in the **Middle East**. Created in 1947 with the signing of the National Security Act by US President Truman.

Centre Party

Israeli centrist political party, founded in 1999. Formed as an alternative to **Likud** and the **Israel Labour Party**. Concerned primarily with the **peace process** and relations between religious and secular Jews. Led by Dan Meridor.

CGEM—Confédération Générale des Entreprises du Maroc

Major Moroccan business association or Chamber of Commerce.

Chadli, Benjedid

President of Algeria (1979–92). Benjedid Chadli was born in Sebaa, Algeria, in 1929. He joined the **Front de libération nationale** (National Liberation Front) shortly after the Algerian revolution began in 1954 and rose through the ranks of the guerrilla forces; by the early 1960s he was on the staff of Col (later President) **Houari Boumedienne**, and he played a decisive role in the latter's overthrow of President **Ahmed Ben Bella** in 1965. Subsequently serving in the Revolutionary Council and as acting Minister of Defence (1978), he was elected as President in February 1979 following the death of Boumedienne and re-elected in 1984 and 1988. When his democratization programme and the new multi-party system threatened to bring Islamic fundamentalists to power, he was forced to resign in January 1992 by a **military**-dominated junta, which took power as the High Council of State headed by **Mohammed Boudiaf** until January 1994.

Chador

A long garment and item of **women**'s clothing in Iran. Usually associated with an Islamist dress code and worn by women in observance of 'Islamic proprieties'. See also **veil** and **headscarf**.

Chalabi, Ahmad

Born in **Baghdad** in 1945, left in 1956. Lived at various times in Jordan, the USA and Great Britain. Member of a wealthy family with business interests in

Switzerland, London, Jordan and Lebanon. Co-founder of the failed Petra Bank in Jordan, which by the time of its crash was the third largest bank in Jordan. Chalabi was involved in a banking scandal associated with the Petra Bank but left Jordan before he could be arrested. In 1992 was tried *in absentia* and sentenced by a Jordanian court to 22 years' imprisonment on 31 counts of embezzlement, theft, misuse of depositor funds and currency speculation. In the same year he founded the **Iraqi National Congress** (INC) and became a major figure in the Iraqi opposition-in-exile during the **Saddam Hussain** years. In 1995 he travelled to northern Iraq to promote an insurrection, but the Iraqi army failed to change sides and the plan turned out disastrously. In 1998 the US Congress passed the **Iraq Liberation Act**, which allocated US $97m. to the INC, which provided the US and UK intelligence services with information from sources inside Iraq. Some of the information found its way into the report on Iraq's weapons capability that was presented by US Secretary of State Colin Powell to the UN shortly before the war of 2003. It turned out to be unreliable. In addition, the INC received funds from the US Department of State and from the Defence Intelligence Agency. Chalabi also cultivated relations with Israel and Iran. The INC maintained an office in **Tehran** and Chalabi met most of the senior government figures in Iran. He returned to Iraq in 2003 and was appointed a member of the US-appointed **Iraqi Provisional Governing Council**, holding the rotating presidency for a while. He was for a time an influential figure in post-intervention Iraq, with close links to Washington. In May 2004, however, his house was raided and US funding for his intelligence was stopped. It was believed that senior members of the INC, if not Chalabi himself, were involved in financial misdeeds, linked to the currency changeover when millions of dollars went missing during the replacement process. Increasingly, according to reports, US administrator **Paul Bremer** and other senior officials in the **Coalition Provisional Authority** regarded Chalabi as a 'loose cannon'.

Chaldean Catholic Church

Semi-autonomous Christian church, affiliated with the Roman Catholic Church. It has about a quarter of a million adherents in the **Middle East**, and is largely confined to Iraq, Syria, Lebanon and Iran.

Chamoun, Camille Nimr

Born in 1900. President of Lebanon from 1952 until 1958, after his predecessor, **Bishara al-Khuri** resigned after **corruption** charges and a general strike. Upon attaining the presidency, he broke his ties with Kamal Jumblatt of the **Progressive Socialist Party**. In 1956 Muslim leaders demanded that Lebanon sever relations with Britain and France, after the start of the Suez–Sinai War—Chamoun refused their demands. Two years later an armed rebellion broke out in Tripoli, mainly involving Muslims. The uprising soon spread to other main cities along the coast. The army refused to comply with Chamoun's order to quell the rebellion. Jumblatt supported the rebels and started to take control over large parts of the country. Soon US troops moved into Lebanon, gaining control of the country. Chamoun agreed to resign in favour of **Fuad Chehab**. He died in 1987.

Chechnya

Former republic of the Soviet Union and subsequently within the Russian Federation. Has been subject to extreme religious colonization during the 1990s. Although Chechnya had a strong secular tradition, the majority of the population were Muslims, and gradually, as the separatist movement developed, it became increasingly imbued with a fundamentalist Islamist political ideology. The first Chechen War (1994–96) destroyed the secular institutions of the state. In the political vacuum that followed, a cluster of 'state-shells' emerged, run by an Islamist militia and backed by Saudi money. In some places Islamic courts were introduced and by the end of the war, Sheikh Abu Umar—a hardline Islamist who had arrived in Chechnya in 1995, joined the *mujahidin* of Ibn ul-Khattab and introduced the principles of **Wahhabism**—had been nominated chief Islamic judge and Mufti. Some of the *mujahidin* who had fought in Afghanistan went on to Chechnya to fight there during the early 1990s.

Checkpoint

A company, established by former computer engineers from the Israeli army, that now commands 40% of the global market for network firewall systems, which protect corporations from hackers. In 1997 Checkpoint exported US $86m.-worth of such products. Israel has a relatively large number of such companies and registers more than 3,000 high-tech start-ups annually, more than any other country except the USA.

Chehab, Fuad

Born in 1902. President of Lebanon from 1958 until 1964. His presidency, following the **Lebanese civil war**, is credited for bringing stability to the country. Chehab balanced the interests of different religious and secular groups. He also instigated reforms to create a modern administration, hoping to transcend differences between members of different religions and clans. He died in 1973.

Chekad-e Azadandishan

Freethinkers Front

An Iranian political organization established in the late 1990s following the election of President **Khatami**. Had some success in the elections to the sixth **Majlis** in 2000.

Christian calendar

The calendar most widely used across the world is based on the revised Christian calendar which marks dates in terms of the supposed death of Christ (Anno Domini— the year of our Lord). This calendar also marks the Christian holy festivals of Christmas, Easter and other important events.

Christian fundamentalism

A term used to refer to those beliefs and practices which claim to emphasize the importance of the 'basic tenets' of the Christian faith by relying on the Biblical sources and interpreting them in a narrow, often literalist sense, usually in a conservative fashion. Often associated with conservative or 'right-wing' political beliefs, particularly in the USA.

Christian militia 'state-shell'

In her recent book, *Modern Jihad*, Loretta Napoleoni uses the term 'state-shells' to refer to state-like structures organized by political or paramilitary organizations within Middle Eastern states. In the late 1970s, for example, a cluster of 'state-shells' run by armed groups proliferated inside Lebanon. The Christian militia, led by the **Phalange** party of President **Amin Gemayel**, ran the Christian enclave north and east of **Beirut**. The militia levied its own customs fees at several ports of entry, costing the Lebanese government—already crippled by war—US $300m. annually in lost revenues. Under the protection of the Phalange, Christian entrepreneurs ran large and profitable smuggling businesses, from which the militia received a percentage. Inside the enclave, the Phalangists imposed their own taxation system, comprising both direct and indirect taxes. The money raised was used to support the militia in its fight against the **Palestine Liberation Organization**. An estimated 10,000–15,000 soldiers were on active duty at any given time. Revenues were also used to improve the living conditions of the residents of the enclave. The Phalange provided all the public services, including street cleaning, transportation, planting of trees, retail price control, street patrols, etc. They built car parks and ran radio campaigns to keep the city clean and even enforced noise regulations. In effect, they replaced the state.

Christians/Christianity

Christianity was adopted as the official religion of the Roman empire in AD 313 and the Christian Church came to be based on four leading cities: Rome, **Constantinople**, **Alexandria** and Antioch. From the divergent development of the four ecclesiastical provinces there soon emerged four distinct Churches: the Roman Catholic, the Greek Orthodox, the **Coptic** and the Syrian or Jacobite. Later divisions resulted in the emergence of the Armenian (Gregorian) Church in the 4th century and the Nestorian Church in the 5th century. From the 7th century onwards, followers of St Maron began to establish the foundations of the **Maronite** Church. Today, Christianity is the second largest religion in the **Middle East** and North Africa, with as many as 15m. adherents. Christianity is based upon the belief that the **Bible** contains a divine message and that Jesus represents a change in the relationship between man and God. There are differences among the various Middle Eastern churches as to how they interpret and transmit this message. The organization of the churches in the Middle East is generally hierarchical, with little congregational **democracy**. The holy places for Christianity in the Middle East include **Bethlehem**, **Nazareth**, several places in Syria and Egypt, and, most importantly, **Jerusalem**. Among the 'churches' represented in the region are various Catholic and Orthodox denominations (Armenian, **Assyrian**, Greek, Maronite, Orthodox, Roman and Syrian), as well as small numbers of Protestants. The Coptic Church is particularly important in Egypt.

Churchill Memorandum

A memorandum was produced on 3 June 1922 by Winston Churchill in his capacity as British Secretary of State for the Colonies which set out his understanding of the meaning of the **Balfour Declaration**. 'When it is asked what is meant by 'the development of the Jewish National Home in Palestine', it may be answered that it is not the imposition of a Jewish nationality upon the inhabitants of Palestine as a whole, but the further development of the existing Jewish community, with the assistance of Jews in other parts of the world, in order that it may become a centre in which the Jewish people as a whole may take, on grounds of religion and race, an interest and a pride.' He considered that this interpretation 'does not contain or imply anything which need cause either alarm to the Arab population of Palestine or disappointment to the Jews'.

Circassians

Inhabitants of an area located in the western part of the North Caucasus. Circassians are divided among three small republics of the Russian Federation: Kabardino-Balkaria (population 390,000), Karachai-Cherkessia (population 60,000), and Adygei (population 125,000). More than 2m. Circassians live in Turkey, and tens of thousands live in Jordan, Syria, and Israel.

Citi Islamic Investment Bank

A major foreign participant in Middle Eastern banking.

Citizens' Rights Movement (CRM)

Israeli movement and political party, established in 1973 by **Shulamit Aloni**, a former **Israel Labour Party Knesset** member. CRM favours strengthening civil rights in Israel and compromise in the Israeli–Palestinian conflict. Its main constituents are the Ashkenazi urban middle class and the intelligentsia. CRM won three seats in the 1973 elections and briefly joined the coalition. It was part of the **Labour Alignment** in the 1977 and 1981 elections, but broke off again in 1984. In 1984 it won three Knesset seats and another five mandates in the 1988 elections. CRM joined **Mapam** and **Shinui** to form **Meretz**/Democratic Israel in the 1992 elections.

Civil war (Lebanon)

Confrontation involving different Lebanese and foreign groups, lasting (with interruptions) from April 1975 until October 1990. The confrontation included both political and religious divides, with the **Maronite** Christians, **Shiʻa** Muslims, the **Druze**, **Palestine Liberation Organization** (PLO), and the Israeli and Syrian armies representing warring factions. The three main sides in the war were the **Lebanese National Movement** led by Kamal Jumblatt, a prominent Druze, the Lebanese Front led by **Camille Chamoun** and dominated by Maronite Christians and aided by Syria and the **Lebanese Force**, led by **Bashir Gemayel**, a Maronite Christian, allied with the PLO. The war claimed around 150,000 lives and caused grave economic and other devastation in Lebanon.

Civilizations, clash of

Neo-realist theory on the post-Cold War order by **Samuel P. Huntington**. Influential article by Samuel Huntington published in *Foreign Affairs* in the summer of 2003; later developed into a book with the same title.

Clinton, Bill

President of the USA from 1993 until 2000. He ordered the bombing of suspected **al-Qaʼida** terrorist facilities in Sudan and Afghanistan during his period of office. He also approved the bombing of Iraq at the end of 1998, under **Operation Desert Fox**, as a response to Iraq's failure to comply fully with the UN weapons inspectors and to concerns that Iraq's capacity to launch **weapons of mass destruction** remained a threat. In 1998 He reluctantly approved the **Iraq Liberation Act**, which provided support to Iraqi opposition groups.

Coalition (in Iraq)

The US-led coalition which intervened in Iraq in 2003 and established itself as the 'peace-keeping' arm of the **Coalition Provisional Authority** in 2003–04. The US forces (in early 2004, some 135,000 strong) were supported during this period by British troops (8,700) and other, smaller forces from Poland (2,500), Italy (2,500), Ukraine (1,650), Spain (1,300), the Netherlands (1,000), Thailand (900), Australia (850), the Republic of Korea (600), Japan (500), Bulgaria (480), Denmark (380), Slovenia (360), Honduras (360), Dominican Republic (300), Nicaragua (230),

Singapore (200), Mongolia (180), Czech Republic (150), Latvia (121), Slovakia (105), Portugal (100), Norway (100), New Zealand (60), Lithuania (50) and Kazakhstan (27).

Coalition Provisional Authority (CPA, Iraq)

The US-led body responsible (i.e. with executive powers and control of the budget) for immediate post-war administration and security in Iraq. The administration established by the US-led **Coalition** in the aftermath of the occupation of Iraq. Originally headed by **Gen. Jay Garner**, the CPA was intended to restore Iraq to 'normality' before handing over power to an Iraqi administration. Civilian **Paul Bremer**, an American official, soon replaced Garner and was charged with the task of directing the CPA and, in effect, running Iraq. With a staff of 6,000 (of which at one stage fewer than 20 were **Arabic** speakers, and many were on three-month contracts), the CPA had a budget considered by many to be insufficient for the task of **Iraq Post-War Reconstruction**. In December 2003 British foreign secretary Jack Straw predicted that 'an elected Iraqi transitional government should be in place by July 2004. By the end of 2005, Iraq should have a new constitution . . . and national elections'. This optimistic prediction was contested at the time it was made, but the CPA has continued to work, against the odds, to hand over responsibility to Iraqi authorities during 2004.

Collapsed states

While the governments of failed states maintain a degree of national legitimacy, despite failing to exercise exclusive control over their borders and what happens within them, collapsed states have wholly disintegrated into warring factions, armies and components. A collapsed state retains little legitimacy—it lacks government and foreign policy; war-lords and local fiefdoms with little claim to more general recognition at a national level struggle to increase their power and wealth. Collapsed states are easy prey to foreign intervention, whether economic, political or military. Lebanon, Somalia, Sierra Leone and the Democratic Republic of the Congo at various periods have had the appearance of collapsed states. In this region Afghanistan hovers between a failed state and a collapsed state. The future of Iraq remains unclear.

Colonialism

In broad terms, colonialism refers to the process and later the system whereby the major European powers intervened in, occupied, settled and defined as 'colonies' (or dependent territories of various kinds) most parts of what is now referred to as the developing world. For some, colonialism is a particular form of **imperialism**. In the **Middle East**, the process may be said to have started in the early 19th century with the French invasion of what came to be Algeria. However, colonial intervention throughout the region was uneven, and affected different parts of the region differently at different times. The period from the late 19th century until the first half of the 20th century up to the late 1950s is the major period of colonialism in the Middle East. Several territories gained nominal independence in the aftermath of the First World War, but others were brought more closely under French and British control. It was not really until the mid-to-late 1950s that political independence and political autonomy coincided, with a general rise in the tide of nationalism taking place in the aftermath of the Second World War. Some territories were retained, for specific reasons, until the 1960s or even the 1970s and the status of several territories whose local populations have struggled for self-determination, remains unresolved, even now at the beginning of the 21st century. Palestine is the most obvious example, where the independent state that was created to replace the British **Mandate for Palestine**, was that of Israel—a Jewish homeland and state—leaving the indigenous Arab population (the **Palestinians**) without a state of their own even today. The creation of the **Palestinian National Authority**, regarded by some, optimistically, as the first stage in the establishment of an independent Palestinian State, now looks more like a move to ensure Israeli domination over the **Occupied Territories**. Another case is that of the **Western Sahara**, where the **Sahrawis** have still not managed to hold the UN to its stated plan for the 'peace process' (announced in 1991) and where Morocco has copied the Israeli strategy of occupation and effective annexation of much of the disputed territory, offering only a limited autonomy to the local inhabitants, while continuing to erode any possibility of genuine independence by encouraging settlement, construction and development by Moroccans. Apart from these two territories, it could be said that colonialism and the colonial period have come to an end. Some, however, argue that former economic and political ties remain between the former colonial powers and their erstwhile colonial territories, which could be said to ensure a form of **neo-colonialism**.

Colons

French (and Spanish) settlers or colonists, mainly in North Africa and particularly in Algeria. Former *colons*, who left Algeria to settle in France, usually in the southern provinces and particularly in the vicinity of or actually in Marseilles, are still referred to as *pieds noirs* and as *colons*.

Committee on Palestine Rights

At the 30th meeting of the UN General Assembly in November 1975, **UN General Assembly Resolution 3236** was reaffirmed and a 20-nation committee—the Committee on Palestine Rights—was set up to report on the 'Exercise of the Inalienable Right of the Palestine People' by 1 June 1976. The Committee presented its report in June 1976 and recommended that Israel should withdraw from all **Occupied Territories** by June 1977. A resolution in the UN Security Council, stemming from the report, affirmed 'the inalienable rights of the Palestinians' and called for the creation of a 'Palestine entity' in the **West Bank** and **Gaza**. This resolution was vetoed by the USA on 29 June 1976. The Committee on Palestine Rights then submitted its report to the UN General Assembly in November 1976 in the form of a resolution. The resolution (No. 20 of 24 November 1976) was adopted by a vote of 90 to 16. The USA and 10 other Western countries, including the United Kingdom, opposed the resolution.

Commonwealth of Independent States (CIS)

Association of post-Soviet republics, excluding the Baltic States (Estonia, Latvia, Lithuania). The CIS was established on 8 December 1991 (effective 21 December 1991). Its aim is to co-ordinate inter-commonwealth relations and to provide a mechanism for the orderly dissolution of the former Soviet Union (USSR). The CIS has 12 members: Armenia, Azerbaijan, Belarus, Georgia, Kazakhstan, Kyrgyzstan, Moldova, Russia, Tajikistan, Turkmenistan, Ukraine and Uzbekistan.

Communist Party (Algeria)

The Socialist Vanguard Party (Parti de l'avant-garde socialiste) rallied to the **Front de libération nationale** (FLN, National Liberation Front) Government of Algeria in 1971 in support of its 'anti-imperialist' policies during its 'left turn' in the so-called socialist revolution of the early 1970s under **Boumedienne**. It maintained itself as a small, unofficial party throughout the period of FLN one-party rule.

Communist Party/Movement (Egypt)

A small, unofficial party with limited support.

Communist Party of Iran

Hezb-e Kommunist Iran

Founded in 1979 by dissident members of the **Tudeh Party**. Its secretary-general is 'Azaryun'.

Communist Party of Iraq

Established in 1934, the Communist Party is a national secular opposition group seeking to organize a popular proletarian revolution in Iraq, drawing support from **Shi'a** communities and the **Kurds**. It gained prominence in the unrest of 1948, when it organized a strike for higher wages at Haditha Petroleum pumping station that culminated in a march on **Baghdad**. In response, the regime executed the leaders of the party. It was legally recognized in July 1973 on the formation of the **National Progressive Front** (NPF). It left the NPF in March 1979. The Party provided support to Iran in the 1980–88 war. Its first secretary is Aziz Muhammad.

Communist Party of Jordan

An illegal Jordanian party.

Communist Party of Lebanon

Founded in 1924, the Party is one of the oldest multi-sectarian parties in Lebanon. For the first two decades of its existence, it controlled communist political activity in both Lebanon and Syria, until separate political parties were established in each country in 1944. The Party was outlawed in 1948 and officially dissolved, until 1970, when it experienced a resurgence, with party members contesting elections. In the 1980s the Party declined in influence. The Party's president is Maurice Nohra, its secretary-general Faruq Dahruj.

Communist Party (Morocco) – *see* Parti du progrès et du socialisme

Communist Party (Palestine)

The Palestine People's Party, or Hezb ash-Sha'ab, formerly the Palestine Communist Party, was admitted to the **Palestine National Council** at its 18th session in 1987. The Alliance of Palestinian Forces was founded in 1994 as a grouping representing the **Popular Front for the Liberaton of Palestine** (PFLP), the **Democratic Front for the Liberation of Palestine**, the **Palestine Liberation Front**, the **Palestinian Popular Struggle Front**, the Palestine Revolutionary Communist Party and the **PFLP-General Command**. It opposes the **Declaration of Principles on Palestinian Self-Rule** signed by Israel and the **Palestine Liberation Organization** in September 1993, and subsequent agreements concluded within its framework (the '**Oslo Agreements**').

Communist Party (Syria)

A bitter adversary of the **Ba'ath Party** in the late 1950s, the Syrian Communist Party was the second largest legal political party in Syria in 1987. In the early 1980s the Party was temporarily banned by President **al-Assad**. In 1986, however, it was restored to favour, partially as a concession to the Soviet Union. Nine party members were elected to the People's Council in the 1986 elections. By then the Party stressed its political and ideological independence from the Syrian regime and operated to a limited extent as a genuine opposition party. It criticized Ba'ath Party economic policies, mediated the regime's relations with the Soviet Union and, through its Committee for Solidarity with African and Asian Nations, developed relations with some Third World nations.

Confessionalism

Political system which recognizes different religious groups as potential political groupings and attempts to take this into account. Alternatively, a system in which political differences are couched in religious community differences. Lebanon provides the classic example.

Congrès national algérien

Algerian political grouping. Established in 1999. Its leader is Abdelkader Belhaye.

Congrès national ittihadi (CNI)

Moroccan political grouping. Founded in 2001. Its secretary-general is Abdelmajid Bouzoubaa.

Constantinople

Old, pre-First World War, name for **Istanbul**. Largest city in Turkey. Former capital of the **Ottoman Empire** and, before that, as **Byzantium**, of the Eastern Roman Empire.

Constantinople Agreement

Secret agreement between Russia, Great Britain and France in 1915, enabling Russia to annexe **Constantinople** to control the Straits and to be given southern Thrace, the islands of Imbros and Tenedos, and a large section of Turkey's Black Sea coast. In return, Russia was to establish the city as a free port with freedom of navigation in the Straits. Arabia and the 'holy places' were to be placed under an independent Muslim protectorate, Persia was to be divided into spheres of influence—Russian in the north and British in the south—and Russia was to be granted full freedom of action in its zone. France was to annexe Syria and Cilicia.

Constitutional Group

A quasi-political grouping representing merchants in the Kuwaiti **Majlis**.

Constitutional Monarchy Movement

An Iraqi political group, based in the United Kingdom, which supports the claim to the throne of Sharif Ali bin al-Hussein, cousin to the late King **Faisal II**.

Constitutional Revolution (Iran)

Starting in 1901, there were growing protests against the Shah's regime and against the influence of Russia in Persia/Iran's internal affairs, linked to massive debts. Eventually, in August 1906, a constitution was granted and a National Assembly established. A long struggle between the constitutionalists and the Shah ensued, and in 1908 Muhammad Ali Shah used the Cossack Brigade to suppress the National Assembly. Civil war broke out and Muhammad Ali Shah was forced to abdicate in 1909.

Containment

Policy to control Iraq after the end of the **Gulf War (1991)**. It involved three elements. The first was a disarmament process consisting of an arms embargo and international inspections to rid Iraq of what later came to be referred to as **weapons of mass destruction**. The second was the so-called **Oil for Food** programme, administered by the UN, under which Iraq was permitted to sell limited amounts of **oil** on the international market in return for which it could import specified medical and food supplies. The third element was a military enforcement regime, initially under UN sanctions over parts of northern Iraq—the so-called 'safe havens' for Kurdish refugees—but extended in 1992 by the USA, Britain and France to include what were called 'no-fly zones' in both the north and south of Iraq. Periodically, Iraq attempted to break the containment policy, and incurred retaliatory measures. One such incident occurred in June 1993, when US President **Bill Clinton** ordered a missile attack on an Iraqi intelligence centre in retaliation for an unsuccessful Iraqi assassination attempt on former US President **George Bush** during a visit to Kuwait in April. There was a further incident in September 1996, when **Saddam Hussain** moved troops into the Kurdish safe havens; on that occasion US forces fired missiles at targets in southern Iraq. The policy of containment came under continuing pressure, from the Iraqi regime, with further incidents in October 1997, February 1998 and, finally, in December 1998. The last of these led to four days of missile attacks on **Baghdad** in **Operation Desert Fox**.

Control Risks

A British security company operating in Iraq. It provides armed escorts and has 500 men guarding British civil servants.

Convention on the Elimination of All Discrimination Against Women (CEDAW)

Adopted in 1979 by the UN General Assembly, and often described as an international bill of rights for **women**. Consisting of a preamble and 30 articles, it defines what constitutes discrimination against women and sets up an agenda for national action to end such discrimination. All countries in the **Middle East** have signed the convention, with the exception of Iran, Oman, Qatar and the United Arab Emirates.

Co-operation Council for the Arab States of the Gulf – *see* Gulf Co-operation Council (GCC)

Coptic Church and Copts

The Coptic Orthodox Church and the Coptic Rite of the Roman Catholic Church both developed after **Christianity** was adopted as the official religion of the Roman Empire in AD 313. In Egypt today the Coptic Rite of the Roman Catholic Church falls under the Patriarch of **Alexandria** and at the end of December 2000 there were an estimated 217,444 adherents in the country. As for the Coptic Orthodox Church, founded in AD 61, there are an estimated 13m. adherents, in Egypt, Sudan and other African countries for the most part. They come under the Patriarch Pope Shenouda III.

Corruption

The corruption index (2002) is based on how much corruption is perceived to exist among politicians and public officials. A high ranking indicates less corruption. Israel ranks highest in the region (joint 18th with Germany), with Tunisia the next highest (36th), followed by Jordan (40th), Morocco (52nd), Egypt (62nd), Turkey (64th), Uzbekistan (68th) and Kazakhstan (88th). Other countries in the region are not ranked.

Cost of Living

Within the region, Israel and Bahrain have the highest cost of living as far as international lifestyle is concerned. The lowest cost of living is reported from **Tehran** in Iran, followed by Libya, Algeria, Tunisia, Uzbekistan, Syria and Turkey.

Council for Peace and Security

Founded in 1988 by four retired Israeli generals. Aims at an Israeli withdrawal from the **Occupied Territories** in return for peace with surrounding Arab states.

Council of Arab Co-operation – *see* Arab Co-operation Council

Council of Arab Economic Unity

Established on 3 June 1957 by a resolution of the Arab Economic Council of the **Arab League**; held its first meeting in May 1964. Its member states are Egypt, Iraq, Jordan, Libya, Mauritania, Palestine, Somalia, Sudan, Syria and Yemen. The Council's focus is regional, devoted to achieving economic integration between the member states through the framework of economic and social development. Based on a resolution passed by the Council in August 1964, the development of an **Arab Common Market** is envisaged, but there has been little progress towards this in practice. A meeting of Council ministers was convened in **Baghdad** in June 2001, which issued 'the Baghdad Declaration' on establishing, initially, a four-state free-trade area comprising Egypt, Iraq, Syria and Libya. The initiative was envisaged as the cornerstone of the **(Greater) Arab Free Trade Area (G)AFTA)** being implemented by the Arab League. It was reported in late 2001 that Palestine had also applied to join this free-trade area, which would delay its entry into force. In 2002 the Council was considering a draft general framework for Arab economic action in the areas of investment, technology, **trade** and joint ventures covering the next 20 years. The Council has seven standing committees: preparatory, follow-up and Arab Common Market development; permanent delegates; budget; economic planning; fiscal and monetary matters; customs and trade planning and co-ordination; statistics.

Council of Experts (Iran)

The first Council of Experts in Iran was a 75-member group (60 of whom were clerics) elected in August 1979 to draft the new Constitution. These elections were boycotted by opposition groups. When the Constitution was completed, the first Council was disbanded. A second 83-member Council of Experts was selected in late 1982 to choose Ayatollah **Khomeini**'s successor, seeking to avoid a political vacuum after his death. In November 1985 it chose Ayatollah Hossein-Ali Montazeri.

Council of Guardians (Iran)

Also known as the Guardian Council. The Council of Guardians was established tosafeguard Islamic rules and the Constitution of Iran. The Council has a dozen members; six clerics who have attained the Islamic rank of **Ayatollah** appointed by the *faqih* or Leadership Council and six jurists, nominated by the High Judicial Council and voted on by the **Majlis** (or National Assembly). Members are appointed for six-year terms, but, in order to stagger the terms, three of the original members were dropped in 1983. The body is in charge of screening the acts ratified by the Majlis so that they are not in conflict with either Islamic laws or the Constitution. Should the Council find any legislation made by the parliament in conflict with **Islam** and the Constitution, it will reject them. The group has refused at times to accept measures passed in the Majlis, notably those on land reform.

Courage to Refuse

A movement of **military** personnel in the **Israeli Defence Force** and conscripts who refuse to serve in the **Occupied Territories**. Known as 'refuseniks', they may be sent to prison for their beliefs. Increasing in numbers during the last few years, they are becoming more organized and more vocal.

Croatian Pipeline

In 1991 US, Turkish and Iranian intelligence set up the Croatian Pipeline using the blueprint of the Afghan Pipeline. Iranian and Turkish arms were flown into Croatia by Iran Air and, later, by a fleet of C-130 *Hercules* transports. Saudi Arabia paid for the weapons and equipment. Other Muslim states—Brunei, Malaysia, Pakistan, Sudan and Turkey—provided funds, arms and equipment. To supply the pipeline, the USA broke the UN embargo against Bosnia. With the arms entering Bosnia came Iranian **Revolutionary Guards**, spies of **VEVAK**, and *mujahidin.* In April 1994, at the suggestion of future US **Central Intelligence Agency** chief, Anthony Lake, and the US Ambassador to Croatia, Peter Galbraith, US President **Bill Clinton** personally approved this policy of co-operation with Iran in Bosnia. The **Third World Relief Agency**, a Sudan-based supposedly humanitarian organization, was used as an intermediary for the suppliers and fighters in Bosnia.

Curiel, Henri

Born in **Cairo** on 13 September 1914, Curiel helped to found the Egyptian communist movement. Exiled to France in 1950 by King **Farouk**. *Le Point* published an article by Georges Suffert in its issue of 21 June 1976 that accused Curiel of being 'the head of the terrorist support networks'. He was assassinated on 14 May 1978.

Cyprus, Turkish Republic of Northern

The head of state is **Rauf Denktash**, who has been President of the Turkish-Cypriot area since 13 February 1975 (the President is elected by popular vote for a five-year term); the most recent elections were held on 15 April 2000 (the next elections are scheduled to be held in April 2005); Dervis Eroglu has been Prime Minister of the Turkish-Cypriot area since 16 August 1996; there is a Council of Ministers (Cabinet) in the Turkish-Cypriot area. The legislative branch is unicameral.

The Assembly of the Republic, Cumhuriyet Meclisi, is a 50-member body to which members are elected by popular vote to serve five-year terms. The most recent elections were held on 6 December 1998. With regard to the judiciary, Supreme Court judges are appointed jointly by the President and the Vice-President; there is also a Supreme Court in the Turkish-Cypriot area. The legal system is based on common law, with civil law modifications.

Political Parties and Groups

Turkish-Cypriot area:

Communal Liberation Party; Leader Huseyin Angolemli
Democratic Party; Leader Salih Cosar
National Birth Party; Leader Enver Emin
National Unity Party; Leader Dervis Eroglu
Our Party; Leader Okyay Sadikoglu
Patriotic Unity Movement; Leader Izzet Izcan
Republican Turkish Party; Leader Mehmet Alitalat

Confederation of Cypriot Workers; pro-West
Confederation of Revolutionary Labour Unions
Federation of Turkish Cypriot Labour Unions
Pan-Cyprian Labour Federation; communist

Media

The Cypriot media mirror the island's political division, with the Turkish-controlled zone in the north operating its own press and broadcasters. State-run services operate side by side with a large number of independent/private television and radio stations.

Newspapers on both sides of the divide are highly politicized and frequently critical of the authorities. There are six television stations, one of which is state-controlled. There are five radio stations, one of which is state-controlled. In 2000 there were six internet service providers. In 2002 there were 150,000 internet users.

History

The struggle for independence continued throughout the 1950s. By 1956 Britain had removed its military base from the **Suez Canal** zone to Cyprus. The nationalist struggle involved demands for union with Greece (enosis) by the Greek Cypriots and gave rise to bitter communal conflict between Cypriots of Greek and Turkish origin and affiliation. Independence was achieved in 1960 with constitutional guarantees by the Greek-Cypriot majority to the Turkish-Cypriot minority, and Archbishop Makarios became the island's first President. Cyprus remained in the Commonwealth. In 1974 a Greek-sponsored attempt to seize the government was met by military intervention from Turkey, which soon controlled almost 40% of the island. This led to the effective partition of the island. In 1983 the Turkish-held area declared itself the 'Turkish Republic of Northern Cyprus' (TRNC), but this is recognized only by Turkey. In 2001 President Clerides visited the TRNC and in January 2002 UN-led direct reunification talks—the first since the hostilities of 1974 divided the island into two *de facto* autonomous areas, a Greek-Cypriot area controlled by the internationally recognized Cypriot Government (59% of the island's land area) and a Turkish-Cypriot area (37% of the island), that are separated by a UN buffer zone (4% of the island)—were initiated. In mid-December 2003 Turkish-Cypriot opposition parties failed to secure a majority in elections widely regarded as a referendum on UN proposals to reunite the island, despite winning 48% of the vote, 2% more than the government party supporting Rauf Denktash, the 'hardliner'. The pro-government and pro-reunification parties divided the 50 parliamentary seats equally, in a dead heat. Denktash, who has the army's backing, pledged to call another election within 60 days and indicated that he might step aside for a new government representative if and when UN negotiations on the future of Cyprus are resumed.

Cyprus, economy

Economic affairs are affected by the division of the country. The Greek-Cypriot economy is prosperous but highly susceptible to external shocks. Erratic growth rates in the 1990s reflect the economy's vulnerability to fluctuations in the number of tourist arrivals, caused by political instability in the region, and fluctuations in economic conditions in Western Europe. Economic policy is focused on meeting the criteria for admission to the **European Union**. As in the Turkish sector, **water** shortages are a perennial problem; a few desalination plants are now online. The Turkish-Cypriot economy has less than one-half the per caput gross domestic product (GDP) of the south. Because it is recognized only by Turkey, it has had much difficulty arranging foreign financing, and foreign firms have hesitated to invest there. It remains heavily dependent on **agriculture** and government services, which together employ about one-half of the workforce. To compensate for the economy's weakness, Turkey provides substantial direct and indirect **aid** to **tourism**, **education**, **industry**, etc.

Strengths

Strong tourism sector (provides about 20% of GDP). Manufacturing sector and provisioning of services to Middle Eastern countries.

Weaknesses

Pressure for tighter supervision of offshore finance and for a crackdown on tax evasion. The TRNC is starved of foreign investment.

D

Ad-Da'awa al-Islamiyya – *see* Islamic Da'awa Party

Ould Daddah, Mokhtar

Born in the south-east of Mauritania into a religious family. After a traditional Muslim and French primary education, Mokhtar moved to France, where he completed his secondary education, took a degree in law and met his future wife, whom he married in 1959. He returned to Mauritania, ran as a political candidate on a list of the Progressive Mauritanian Union (Union progressiste mauritanienne) and was elected territorial councillor of Adrar in March 1957. In May he was nominated as vice-president of the Council of the Government. In 1958 he campaigned for a 'yes' vote in the referendum held by de Gaulle to keep the former French African colonies in the French-African Community. In 1961 he was elected as the first President of the independent Islamic Republic of Mauritania. He remained President of what was effectively a one-party state in Mauritania from 1961 until 1978 when he was overthrown by a **military** coup, after some years of economic crisis, exacerbated by drought and Mauritania's alliance with Morocco to take control of the former **Spanish Sahara** which led them to a costly war with the **POLISARIO Front**, the political movement fighting for **Sahrawi** self-determination. In 1969 he secured the assistance of Algeria in the Organization of African Unity to secure recognition of Mauritania's sovereignty, which was previously disputed by Morocco, but from 1976 embroiled Mauritania in a war in the **Western Sahara** led by Morocco against the POLISARIO Front. After his overthrow in 1978 he was detained for more than a year without trial in a remote fort by the leaders of the Military Committee for National Recovery (later the National Salvation Committee) who replaced him. However, he was allowed to travel to France for medical treatment after the intervention of French President Giscard d'Estaing, the Kings of Morocco, Saudi Arabia and Jordan, and some African leaders, and to remain there in exile. In his absence he was sentenced to hard labour for life, for treason, violation of the Constitution and undermining national economic interests. He spent the next 15 years in exile before the establishment of a multi-party regime in Mauritania encouraged him to consider a political comeback. There was still support for him within the country and for a while it seemed that he might be prepared to try. However, despite calls from some opposition groups for his return to Mauritanian politics, he eventually abandoned hope of this. He returned finally to Mauritania, after 22 years in France, in July 2001, and died there in October 2003.

Dallah al-Baraka Bank (DAB)

A major Saudi bank, founded in 1981 thanks to the initiative of Saleh Abdullah Kamel, Saudi magnate and the King's brother-in-law. According to *Forbes Magazine*, Saleh is the 137th richest man in the world, with a fortune worth US $4,000m. The DAB has 23 branches and several investment companies in 15 countries.

Damascus

Capital of Syria, with 1.7m. inhabitants. Ancient town, modern industrial and commercial centre. Damascus is one of the world's oldest continuously inhabited cities, dating back more than 3,500 years. The city is divided into several areas—the market area, the Muslim area, the Christian area, and the Jewish area. There are more than 200 mosques, a university, an international airport, and many cultural and historical attractions. The city was declared capital of the new state of Syria in 1919, but became the real capital in 1946 after the end of the League of Nations Mandate and the withdrawal of French troops.

Dar al-Islam

Literally 'the house of Islam'. The part of the world where **Islam** reigns.

Dar al-Mal al-Islami (DMI)

Saudi bank founded in 1981 by Mohammed al-Faisal, brother of Prince Turki. Today it is chaired by Prince Mohammed al-Faisal as-Saud, a cousin of King **Fahd**. This giant banking conglomerate is the primary vehicle used by the Saudis to finance the dissemination of **Islamic fundamentalism**. One of its subsidiaries is the ash-Shamil Islamic Bank in Sudan. The US Department of State claimed that **Osama bin Laden** controlled this bank after paying US $50m. towards its ownership, although it is more likely that he was just a large shareholder. Nevertheless, Jamal Ahmed Mohammed al-Fadli, a former business associate of bin Laden who testified at the trial of **al-Qa'ida** operatives responsible for the 1998 bombing of the two US embassies in east Africa, revealed that bin Laden used the ash-Shamil Islamic Bank, along with two other banks, the Tadamon Islamic Bank and the **Faisal Islamic Bank**, to move funds around the world.

Ad-Dawr

Small village just south of **Tikrit** in Iraq where **Saddam Hussain** was finally captured in mid-December 2003.

Dayan, Moshe

Israeli military and political leader. Born in 1915, Dayan was chief of general staff in 1953–58 and conducted the Sinai campaign. He was agriculture minister from 1959 until 1964, and was Minister of Defence during the **Six-Day War** of 1967 and the **Yom Kippur War** of 1973. From 1977 until 1979 he was foreign minister, playing a key role in the negotiation of the **Camp David Accords** and the Israel-Egypt Peace Treaty.

Debt

A major problem for many countries in the region. The debt problem arose during the 1970s, when many economies which had borrowed significantly from public and private lending agencies and banks, as well as from the **international financial institutions**, began to experience difficulties in repaying the interest, let alone the capital borrowed. Countries with substantial foreign debts include some of the most important participants in the political economy of the **Middle East**. Israel has one of the highest per caput debts, with a very large proportion owing to institutions in the USA, which regards Israel as a major client state to be supported economically and financially as well as diplomatically, politically and militarily. Other states with substantial debts to the USA include Turkey, Egypt and Morocco. Iraq, which received very considerable support (military, technical and financial as well as diplomatic and political) from the West and from the Soviet Union during its war against Iran, began to experience financial difficulties towards the late 1980s and was seriously affected by the regime of sanctions applied against it in the 1990s following the **Gulf War (1991)**. Its debt of US $125,000m. (£72,000m.) in the aftermath of the **Gulf War (2003)** was one of the largest in the region. During the final months of 2003 the USA was trying to create support for writing off the Iraqi debt; other states were less enthusiastic.

Debt relief (Egypt)

Major concessions regarding its foreign **debt** were accorded to Egypt by the USA after Egypt's role in supporting the US-led alliance in the **Gulf War (1991)**. Concerns were expressed then, as in the case of Iraq, that much-needed debt relief for poor developing countries in Africa and Asia was being sidelined for political reasons rather than humanitarian or development considerations.

Debt relief (Iraq)

In December 2003 France, Germany, Britain and the USA agreed to offer substantial **debt** relief to Iraq. Iraq owes US $8,000m. to Russia (which is ready to write off 65%); Japan is owed $4,100m., with another $3,000m. in interest and penalties (and promises to forgive 'the vast majority' if others do the same); Germany is owed $5,400m. (and is open to forgiving part of the amount); France is owed about $3,000m. (and agrees to an unspecified amount being written off); Britain is owed $2,000m. (and agrees on the need to reduce Iraq's debt); Italy is owed $1,700m., excluding interest (and backs a plan to relieve Iraq of its debt); and China is owed $1,100m. (and is considering forgiving part of it).

Declaration of Independence (Palestine)

The Declaration of the independent State of Palestine, with the holy city of **Jerusalem** as its capital, was made at the 19th session of the **Palestine National Council** in November 1988. It was followed by a political communiqué calling for an international conference on the question of Palestine to be held under the auspices of the United Nations, and with the participation of the permanent members of the UN Security Council and all parties to the conflict in the region, including the **Palestine Liberation Organization** (PLO), as the sole legitimate representative of the Palestinian people, on an equal footing. This was followed by a number of other requests, demands and suggestions, to friendly and sympathetic countries, to the peace forces in Israel and to the USA. The opportunity for the PLO to assert sovereignty over a specific area arose through the decision of King **Hussein** of Jordan, in July 1988, to sever Jordan's 'administrative and legal links' with the **West Bank**. The Declaration of Independence cited **UN General Assembly Resolution 181** of 1947, which partitioned Palestine into two states, one Arab and one Jewish, as providing the legal basis of the right of the Palestinian Arabs to national sovereignty and independence.

Declaration of Principles on Palestinian Self-Rule

The government of the State of Israel and the Palestinian team in the Jordanian-Palestinian delegation to the **Middle East Peace Conference** agreed on 13 September 1993 a Declaration of Principles (DoP) relating to Palestinian self-rule. They agreed to establish a Palestinian Interim Self-Government Authority, an elected Council for the Palestinian people in the **West Bank** and **Gaza Strip**, for a transitional period, not exceeding five years, leading to a permanent settlement based on **UN Security Council Resolution 242** and **UN Security Council Resolution 338**. The Israeli government committed itself, after the entry into force of the DoP and not later than the holding of elections for the Council, to a redeployment of Israeli military forces in the West Bank and Gaza Strip, in addition to the withdrawal of forces from the Gaza Strip and **Jericho** area. It foresaw further redeployments to specified locations to be gradually implemented commensurate with the assumption of responsibilities for public order and internal security by the Palestinian police force. The DoP was followed by two protocols—one on Israeli-Palestinian co-operation in local economic and development programmes and the other on Israeli-Palestinian co-operation concerning regional development programmes.

Declaration on the Middle East

The European Council published a Declaration on the **Middle East** in June 1989, which recalled that 'the policy of the Twelve on the Middle East conflict is defined in the **Venice Declaration** of June 1980 and other subsequent declarations. It consists in upholding the right to security of all states in the region, including Israel ... and in upholding justice for all the peoples of the region, which includes recognition of the legitimate rights of the Palestinian people, including their right to self-determination with all that this implies'. The European Council welcomed the support given by the Extraordinary Summit Meeting of the **Arab League**, held in **Casablanca**, to the decisions of the **Palestine National Council** in **Algiers**, involving acceptance of **UN Security Council Resolutions 242** and **338**, which resulted in the recognition of Israel's right to exist, as well as the renunciation of **terrorism**. It also called on the Israeli authorities to put an end to repressive measures, to respect the provisions of the Geneva Convention on the protection of civilian populations in times of war, to implement **UN Security Council Resolutions 605**, **607** and **608**, and to recognize the right of the Palestinian people to exercise self-determination. It called upon the Arab countries to establish normal relations of peace and co-operation with Israel.

Defence spending

States in the region tend to have high defence expenditure as a proportion of gross domestic product (GDP). Highest in the region (and third highest in the world) is Oman with defence accounting for 14.4% of GDP. Saudi Arabia is next, followed by Afghanistan (12.2%) and Kuwait (12.1%). Syria spends 10.9% of its GDP on defence, Israel 9.5% and Iraq (under **Saddam Hussein**) 9.3%. Jordan spends 8.5% and Yemen 8.1%. Qatar spends 7.1%, Algeria 6.3% and Iran 5.8%. Turkey spends 5%, Bahrain 4.8%, Egypt 4.7%, the United Arab Emirates 4.6% and Libya 4.1%. The spending is largely, but not entirely, on the **armed forces** and defence equipment

Deforestation

Deforestation is far advanced in most countries in the region. Oman, Egypt, Qatar, Libya, Kuwait, Mauritania, Saudi Arabia, Algeria and Yemen all have less than 1% of their land area under forest. Jordan and Iraq have 1% and 1.8% respectively and

Afghanistan has just over 2% under forest. Most have some commitment to reforestation, and some of the most severely denuded are making most effort: the annual rate of reforestation (in 1990–2000) in Oman, for example, was 9.6%; in Israel it was 4.9%, in Kuwait 3.5 %, in Egypt 3.3%, in the United Arab Emirates 2.8%, in Kyrgyzstan 2.6% and in Kazakhstan 2.2%. A few countries have placed land under protected status—Saudi Arabia, for example, has placed 34 % of its land area under protection—but most of the countries in the region have failed to protect much of their land. Kuwait, for example, has just over 1% of its land under protection, Turkey 1.2%, Uzbekistan 1.8%, Algeria 2.4%, Kazakhstan 2.7% and Jordan 3.1%. Mauritania is one of the few severely deforested countries in the region that is continuing to deteriorate, at the annual rate of 2.7%.

Degel Ha Torah

A political grouping in Israel formed in 1988 as a breakaway group by the anti-Hassidic **Ashkenazim** of the **Agudat Israel**. Mainly orthodox Western Jews. Gained two seats in the **Knesset** in 1988.

Demirel, Süleyman

Leader of the **Turkish Justice Party** in the 1970s and of the **True Path Party** in the late 1980s after the ban on pre-1980 politicians was lifted. From provincial origins, after local schooling he was educated as an engineer in **Istanbul**. Learned English late in life. Did not belong to the Westernized élite and retained strong links to his provincial roots. Became President of Turkey in April 1993.

Democracy

Although most Middle Eastern regimes hold periodic presidential, national and local elections, relatively few of the states of the region have well-developed functioning democratic political systems. Israel has the best claim to be a fully functioning political democracy, with a wide range of political parties and movements; but its continuing illegal occupation of the **West Bank** and **Gaza Strip** casts doubts on its overall political complexion. Turkey has for many decades operated a multi-party political system, but periodic **military** coups and the continuing significance of the military marks a strong centralist tendency.

Democratic Arab Party (DAP)

Founded in 1988. Aims to unify Arab political forces so as to influence Israeli and Palestinian policy. Argues for international recognition of the Palestinian people's right to self-determination, the withdrawal of Israel from all territories occupied in 1967, including **East Jerusalem**. Also aims for full equality between Arabs and Jewish citizens of Israel, to eliminate discrimination and improve the social, economic and political conditions of the Arab **minority** in Israel. Contested the

1999 **Knesset** elections as part of the coalition of the **United Arab List**, which gained five seats with 3.5% of the vote. Its director is Muhammad Darawshe.

Democratic Party (DP)

Major opposition party to the **Republican People's Party** (RPP) in Turkey in the post-war period. Led by Adnan Menderes, the DP won a landslide victory in the general elections of 1950, having made a strong showing in the general elections of 1946. Opposed to the strongly statist and 'socialist' orientation of the Kemalist RPP, the DP maintained a liberal regime and presided over a strong economy during the first half of the 1950s. In 1957, when the 'economic miracle' had begun to fade, Prime Minister Menderes began to woo the Muslim vote, looking to gain the support of the religious leader Said I-Nursi. Menderes won the election, but with a greatly reduced majority. In May 1960 the DP was overthrown by a **military** coup. The new junta, which established a **National Unity Committee**, although strongly committed to the Kemalist tradition, recognized the importance of **Islam** in Turkey and made no attempt to undo the liberalization of the 1940s and 1950s.

Democratic Front (Algeria)

Algerian political party, established in 1999. Led by Sid-Ahmed Ghozali.

Democratic Front (Kuwait)

Kuwaiti quasi-political grouping.

Democratic Front for the Liberation of Palestine (DFLP)

Marxist-Leninist organization founded in 1969, when it split from the **Popular Front for the Liberation of Palestine (PFLP)**, with approximately 500 members. Believes Palestinian national goals can be achieved only through revolution of the masses and continues to oppose the Israel-**Palestine Liberation Organization** peace agreement. In the 1970s it carried out numerous small bomb attacks and minor assaults and some more spectacular operations in Israel and the **Occupied Territories**, concentrating on Israeli targets. In the early 1980s it occupied a political position midway between **Yasser Arafat** and the so-called rejectionists. Split into two factions in 1991. Involved only in border raids since 1988 and conducts occasional guerrilla operations in southern Lebanon. Joined with other rejectionist groups to form the Alliance of Palestinian Forces (APF) to oppose the **Declaration of Principles on Palestinian Self-Rule** signed in 1993. Broke from the APF—together with the PFLP–owing to ideological differences. Has made limited moves toward merging with the PFLP since the mid-1990s. Operates from Syria, Lebanon, and the Israeli-occupied territories, with the terrorist attacks for which it has been responsible taking place entirely in Israel and the Occupied Territories. Receives limited financial and military aid from Syria. **Nayef**

Hawatmah leads the majority and more hardline faction, which continues to dominate the group.

Democratic Front for Peace and Equality

Israeli political grouping with support from **Arab Israelis**. Otherwise known as **Hadash**. Led by Muhammad Baraka.

Democratic Gathering

Iraqi political group, led by Saleh Doublah.

Democratic Movement

Israeli political grouping, led by Roman Bronfman.

Democratic National Rally (RND)

Algerian political grouping, led by Ahmed Ouyahia (chairman).

Democratic Party of Iranian Kurdistan

Iranian opposition party, founded in 1945. Seeks autonomy for the Kurdish area of Iran. Member of the **National Council of Resistance**, based in Paris, France. Has some 55,000 members.

Democratic Party of the Iranian People

Political grouping formed by dissidents of the **Tudeh Party** in Paris, France, in February 1988.

Democratic Party of Kurdistan

A political party of the **Kurds** in Turkey, sister party to the **DPK** in Iraq. Supported the struggle for the autonomy of Turkish **Kurdistan**. Banned in 1971.

Democratic People's Party

Egyptian political party, established in 1992. The Party's chairman is Anwar Afifi.

Democratic Progressive Forum (DPF)

Political grouping in Bahrain with leftist antecedents within the Communist Party,

Democratic Unionist Party

Egyptian political party, founded in 1990. The Party's president is Ibrahim Abd al-Moneim Turk.

Demographic structure

In terms of gender structure, most countries in the region have a ratio of males to females that is more than one-to-one (100), in part because of heavy reliance on male immigrant workers (in the case of the **Gulf States**), and in part because of significant discrimination against **women**. They are: United Arab Emirates (186), Qatar (173), Kuwait (151), Bahrain and Oman (135), Saudi Arabia (116), Jordan (109), Afghanistan (109), Libya (107), Iran, Iraq, Yemen and the **West Bank** and **Gaza Strip** (103). Some have very high fertility rates: Yemen (7.01 children per woman), Afghanistan (6.80), the West Bank and Gaza Strip (5.57), Oman (4.96) and Iraq (4.77). Regarding crude birth rates, Yemen has one of the world's top 10 highest average live birth rates per 1,000 population, with 48.8, behind eight countries in sub-Saharan Africa. Within the region, annual population growth is most rapid in Afghanistan (3.88%), the West Bank and Gaza Strip (3.57%), Yemen (3.52%) and Kuwait (3.46%).

Denktash, Rauf

Turkish Cypriot leader and President of the Turkish Republic of Northern Cyprus (recognized only by Turkey). Born in Baf, Cyprus, in 1924. Formed the National Unity Party and went on to win the presidency.

Desert Shield – *see* Operation Desert Shield, Gulf War (1991)

Desert Storm – *see* Operation Desert Storm, Gulf War (1991)

Destour Party

The first party to challenge French colonial rule in Tunisia. The Destour was essentially a party of Tunisia's traditional leadership, based in the capital, **Tunis**: administrators, religious leaders, merchants, leaders of the most respected crafts and notables of the Ottoman **beys**. It was formed just after the end of the First World War. Active during the 1920s, it failed to mobilize popular support and was supplanted in the 1930s by the **Neo-Destour**, led largely by a new intelligentsia of modest social origins, with a significant power base in the provinces.

Devrimci Sol

Formed in 1978, Devrimci Sol (popularly known as Dev Sol) changed its name to the Turkish Revolutionary People's Liberation Front in 1994 after factional infighting. It originally broke off as a splinter group from the Turkish People's Liberation Party or Front.

DFLP – *see* Democratic Front for the Liberation of Palestine

Direct Path (also known as Righteous Path)
Assirat al-Moustaquim

On 16 May 2003 13 suicide bombers killed themselves and 28 other people in a co-ordinated attack on five tourist and Jewish targets in **Casablanca**, Morocco. The worst carnage was in the Casa de España, a popular private club; other targets were the Israeli Alliance Club, a major business hotel, the Belgian consulate and a Jewish cemetery. A fourteenth suicide bomber, who fled from the attack on the hotel, identified eight colleagues, some of them Moroccans living abroad. According to Morocco's justice minister, 'he gave information on his criminal accomplices and helped identify those involved'. Some indications suggest they were linked to a group calling itself Assirat al-Moustaquim (Direct Path). This group—several of whose members have recently been jailed—is believed to be a splinter group of another radical Islamist organization, **Salafist Jihad**. One of Salafist Jihad's main spiritual leaders, 28-year-old Ould Mohamed Abdelwahab Raqiqi, alias 'Abu Hafs', was jailed earlier in the year for inciting violence against westerners.

Doha

Capital of Qatar, Doha lies on the eastern side of the peninsula of Qatar, and is by far the largest city in the country, with its population of 400,000 totalling more than the populations of other parts of the country combined. The economic base of Doha resides in **petroleum** exports, shrimp processing, finance and administration. Doha's Qatar University was founded in 1973.

Dome of the Rock

The great Dome of the Rock (**Arabic**: Qubbat as-Sakhrah) is a famous Islamic mosque in **Jerusalem**. This is the oldest Muslim building, which has survived basically intact in its original form. It was built by the Caliph Abd al-Malik and completed in AD 691. The building encloses a huge rock located at its centre, from which, according to tradition, the **Prophet Muhammad** ascended to heaven at the end of his Night Journey. In the Jewish tradition this is the Foundation Stone, the symbolic foundation upon which the world was created, and the place of the Binding of Isaac. (See also **al-Aqsa Mosque**.)

Dostum, Abdul Rashid

Ethnic **Uzbek** warlord, who once worked with Soviet forces against **Masoud** but joined him in the alliance after the fall of **Kabul** to the **Taliban**. Maintained control over much of northern Afghanistan since aiding the US forces to oust the Taliban in 2001. During April 2004 he advanced further into Faryab province in northern

Afghanistan after having captured the provincial capital Maimana. Government troops repossessed the city but Dostum remained in control of much of the province. Gen. Dostum, who is nominally an adviser to the Government of President **Hamid Karzai**, has changed sides repeatedly throughout two decades of conflict in Afghanistan, but remains a regional warlord of the north. He has insisted that Karzai dismiss some officials, including his defence minister, Mohammad Qasim Fahim. 'If he does not, his government will fail', Dostum told Reuters.

DPK

Democratic Party of **Kurdistan** in Iraq.

Drugs

There are several regions within the **Middle East** where crops such as **cannabis** and **opium** are grown for the market and are associated with major drugs trade and smuggling, notably Afghanistan and the **Beka'a Valley** in Lebanon.

Druze

The Druze are a small religious community, with members in Syria, Lebanon and Israel. They speak **Arabic** but consider themselves neither Arabs nor Muslims. They do not intermarry with Muslims or Jews. Some 300,000 Druze live in the **Middle East** today. The origins of the sect/religion are still unclear, but it seems to have developed from that of the 'Fatimid **Ismailis**', a distinctive branch of the Ismailis that emerged in the Fatimid **Caliphate** during the 11th century. The Druze religion is a mystery religion that does not allow its teachings to be revealed to outsiders. The three principles of the Druze faith are: guarding one's tongue, protecting one's brother and belief in one God (monotheism), like **Judaism**, **Christianity** and **Islam**. The Druze appear to believe that God may be able to become incarnate in human form—his last incarnation was in the person of the Fatimid Caliph al-Hakim (who disappeared in 1020); they also believe in reincarnation for all deserving members of the community. They have very few religious ceremonies or prayer books. Druze believe in seven prophets: Adam, Noah, Abraham, Moses, Jesus, **Muhammad**, and Muhammad ibn Ismail ad-Darazi. They also have a special affinity with Shueib, or Jethro, the father-in-law of Moses. Individual prayer, as in Islam, does not exist. Smoking, alcohol, and the eating of pork are banned. The only way to become a Druze is to be born one—they do not accept converts. The Druze in Lebanon have fought ardently in recent decades against Israeli forces and their Christian allies.

Dubai

City and emirate in the United Arab Emirates (UAE), with more than 700,000 inhabitants. Dubai is situated on the **Persian (Arabian) Gulf** and is divided into two parts by the Dubai Creek. Dubai proper lies on the western side. It is the second largest emirate in the UAE after Abu Dhabi.

Dubai International Financial Centre (DIFC)

Dubai—the **Persian (Arabian) Gulf**'s commercial and **tourism** hub—aims to become a force in global banking. The multi-billion dollar DIFC project will provide asset management, back-office administration, reinsurance, Islamic finance and niche banking services to a wider region extending from the Gulf and East Africa to **Central Asia** and the Indian subcontinent. DIFC is expected to be operational by the end of 2004, thus enabling Arab investors to trade in global stocks/bonds without having to use New York or London exchanges. There are plans to create a regional electronic stock market—fully open to foreign portfolio investors—and an energy derivatives exchange as part of the DIFC hub. DIFC will be supervised by a 'two-tier' independent regulator comprising a regulatory council (headed by Ian Davidson, former chief executive of Lloyds of London) and a regulatory commission (chaired by Philip Thorne, former managing director of the United Kingdom's Financial Services Authority). Reputable institutions represented on DIFC's advisory board are HSBC, Citigroup, Goldman Sachs and Deutsche Bank. So far, more than 20 companies have expressed interest in obtaining DIFC licences. Dubai argues that Bahrain's position as an offshore banking sector will not be undermined by DIFC, but it has nevertheless given rise to concern in Bahrain.

Durrani

Major Afghan tribal division.

E

East Bank (of the Jordan river)

The terms East Bank and **West Bank** apply to the **Jordan river**. The territory on the East Bank belongs to Jordan; the West Bank, which belonged to Jordan prior to the **Arab–Israeli War (1967)**, is now occupied by Israeli defence forces.

East Jerusalem

The capital of Palestine, defined as the territory under the jurisdiction of the **Palestinian National Authority**, is **East Jerusalem**. The population of East Jerusalem is about 177,000, with 29 Israeli **settlements** (February 2002 estimate). The eastern part of Jerusalem remained part of the **Occupied Territories** after 1967, when Jerusalem was divided. **West Jerusalem** is within Israel itself, as defined by the 1967 borders. The future of Jerusalem, East Jerusalem included, proved to be the principal obstacle to the achievement of a peace agreement in the talks at **Camp David** in July 2000. In late September 2000 the holy sites of East Jerusalem were the initial focal point of a renewed uprising by **Palestinians**, which became known as the **al-Aqsa** *intifada*.

Eastern Turkestan

Term used to refer to the areas in north-western China inhabited predominantly by the Muslim Uigurs, who regard themselves, increasingly, as being linked to other Turkic-speaking peoples and have seen several groups and institutions emerge which support the idea of Uigur autonomy within Eastern Turkestan. Following the death of the exiled East Turkestan leader, Isa Yusuf Alptekin, who advocated non-violence and was called the Turkic Dalai Lama, no one has had the authority to prevent militant resistance against Chinese rule in **Xinjiang.**

Eastern Turkestan National Freedom Centre

Anwar Yusuf, president of the Eastern Turkestan National Freedom Centre, was one of several independence movement leaders who gathered in the Republic of China (Taiwan) in February 1998 for public and private meetings and numerous press interviews. Invited by the World Federation of Taiwanese Associations in the U.S., Yusuf was joined by prominent political activists from around the world.

Eban, Abba

Born 1915, Israeli politician and prominent foreign minister in 1966–74. Eban was central in Israeli politics during both the **Arab–Israeli War (1967)** and the **Arab–Israeli War (1973)**. He has published several books.

Ecevit, Bülent

Turkish Prime Minister on several occasions and leader of the **Republican People's Party** for many years. Major political rival of **Süleyman Demirel**, who led the **Justice Party** during the 1960s and 1970s. A member of the Westernized urban élite; born into an **Istanbul** family of the Kemalist élite, he learned English as a boy at the exclusive Robert College.

Economic Commission for Africa

The Economic Commission for Africa was founded in 1958 by a resolution of the UN Economic and Social Council to initiate and take part in measures for facilitating Africa's economic development. The Commission is based in Addis Ababa, Ethiopia, but a subregional development centre for northern Africa is based in Tangier, Morocco. The Information Technology Centre for Africa, located in Addis Ababa, is an associated body.

Economic Co-operation Organization (ECO)

Established 27–29 January 1985 as the successor to the Regional Co-operation for Development, founded in 1964. Its aim is to promote regional co-operation in trade, transportation, communications, **tourism**, cultural affairs and economic development. Member states are Afghanistan, Azerbaijan, Iran, Kazakhstan, Kyrgyzstan, Pakistan, Tajikistan, Turkey, Turkmenistan and Uzbekistan. In addition, the Turkish Republic of Northern Cyprus has the status of associate member. The first summit meeting was held in February 1992; the seventh summit meeting in October 2002. Convening in conference for the first time in early March 2000, ECO ministers of trade signed a Framework Agreement on ECO Trade Co-operation , which envisaged the eventual adoption of an ECO Trade Agreement providing for the gradual elimination of barriers between member states. The first meeting of ECO ministers of energy and petroleum was held in November 2000 and adopted a plan of action for regional co-operation on **energy** and **petroleum** matters in 2001–05. The first meeting of ministers of **agriculture** in July 2002 adopted a declaration on future co-operation in the agricultural sector, and agreed to contribute to agricultural rehabilitation in Afghanistan. In November 2001 the UN Secretary-General had requested ECO to take an active role in efforts to restore stability in Afghanistan;

and in June 2002 the ECO secretary-general participated in a tripartite conference on co-operation for development in Afghanistan, with representatives from Afghanistan, Iran and Pakistan.

Economic and Social Commission for Western Asia (ESCWA)

The UN Economic Commission for Western Asia was established in 1974, aimed at promoting economic and social development through regional and subregional co-operation and integration, to provide facilities of a wider scope for those countries previously served by the UN Economic and Social Office in **Beirut**. The current name was adopted in 1985, but the office remains in Beirut. According to the UN itself, ESCWA formulates and promotes development assistance activities and projects commensurate with the needs and priorities of the region. It also undertakes or sponsors studies of economic and social development issues. It works within the framework of medium-term plans, divided into two-year programmes of action and priorities.

Education

Levels of education vary enormously by country across the region. Gender differences in access to education are also particularly marked in the region, with girls' enrolment at school generally significantly lower than that of boys. The highest spending on education as a proportion of gross domestic product (GDP) in the region is in Yemen (10%) and Saudi Arabia (9.5%). This makes those countries respectively the third and fourth highest spenders on education in the world. Both, however, are among the 25 countries with the lowest primary school enrolment (Saudi Arabia 14th and Yemen 22nd). Also with low enrolment at primary level are Oman and Uzbekistan. The countries with the lowest spending include the United Arab Emirates (2% of GDP), Tajikistan (2.1%) and Egypt (2.3%). The least literate countries are Mauritania (only 40% of adults literate), Yemen (46%), Morocco (49%) and Egypt (55%). Countries with the highest primary school enrolment include Tunisia, Libya, Algeria and Israel.

Egypt, Arab Republic of

Jumhuriyat Misr al-Arabiyah

Located in north-east Africa, bordering the **Mediterranean** Sea, between Libya and the **Gaza Strip**. It borders Israel to the east, across the Sinai Peninsula, and Sudan to the south. Egypt controls the Sinai—the only land bridge between Africa and Asia—and the **Suez Canal**, which provides the shortest sea link between the Mediterranean and the Indian Ocean. It has an area of 1,001,450 sq km (of which 6,000 sq km is **water**). The capital is **Cairo**. For administrative purposes Egypt is divided into 26 governorates (*muhafazah*, plural *muhafazat*): Ad-Daqahliyah, Al-Bahr al-Ahmar, Al-Buhayrah, Al-Fayyum, Al-Gharbiyah, Al-Iskandariyah, Al-Isma'iliyah, Al-Jizah, Al-Minufiyah, Al-Minya, Al-Qahirah, Al-Qalyubiyah,

Al-Wadi al-Jadid, Ash-Sharqiyah, As-Suways, Aswan, Asyut, Bani Suwayf, Bur Sa'id, Dumyat, Janub Sina', Kafr ash-Shaykh, Matruh, Qina, Shamal Sina' and Suhaj. In July 2002 the population was estimated at 70,712,345, of which Egyptians, **Bedouins** and **Berbers** constituted 90%, while Greeks, Nubians, **Armenians** and other Europeans (primarily Italian and French) accounted for 10%. The majority (94%) are Muslims (mostly **Sunni**), with **Coptic** Christians and 'others' accounting for the remaining 6%. **Arabic** is the official language. English and French are widely understood by educated classes.

Political profile

Egypt is a republic. The head of state is President **Hosni Muhammad Said Mubarak** (since 14 October 1981), the head of government is Prime Minister Atef Mohammed Abeid (since 5 October 1999). The Prime Minister is appointed by the President, as is the Cabinet. Presidents are nominated by the People's Assembly for a six-year term. The nomination must then be validated by a national, popular referendum. A national referendum was last held on 26 September 1999 and the next is due to be held in October 2005. The legislative bicameral system consists of the People's Assembly or **Majlis** ash-Sha'b (454 seats; 444 elected by popular vote, 10 appointed by the President; members serve five-year terms) and the Advisory Council or Majlis ash-Shura—which functions only in a consultative role—(264 seats; 176 elected by popular vote, 88 appointed by the President). The People's Assembly is elected through a system of three-phase voting—elections were last held on 19 October, 29 October and 8 November 2000 (the next elections are scheduled to be held in November 2005). Elections to the Advisory Council were last held on 7 June 1995. The legal system is based on English common law, **Islamic Law** and Napoleonic codes. Judicial review is by the Supreme Constitutional Court and the Council of State (which oversees the validity of administrative decisions). Egypt accepts compulsory International Court of Justice jurisdiction with reservations. The formation of political parties and NGOs must be approved by the government. There is a constitutional ban on religious-based parties, but the proscribed **Muslim Brotherhood** nevertheless constitutes the most significant political opposition to the government. Civil society groups are officially sanctioned, but constrained in practice; trade unions and professional associations are officially sanctioned.

Recognized political parties include:

- Nasserist Arab Democratic Party; Leader Dia' ad-din Dawud
- **National Democratic Party**; Leader Pres. Muhammad Hosni Said Mubarak; the governing party, formerly the **Arab Socialist Union**
- **National Progressive Unionist Group** (Tagammu); Leader Khalid Muhi ad-Din
- **New Wafd Party**; Leader No'man Goma; nationalist party
- **Socialist Liberal Party**

Religious parties and groups:

- Muslim Brotherhood
- **Al-Jihad**
- **Takfir wal-Hijra**

Egypt has numerous NGOs and informal groups. Some of the most vocal and prominent have been the informal **Popular Committees** supporting the Palestinian people and the Iraqi people and fighting against US aggression.

Media

There are 17 daily newspapers, *al-Ahram* (government organ) and *al-Akhbar* being the most widely read. There are also several weeklies, (e.g. the *Cairo Times*). In 2000 there were 50 internet service providers, and in 2002 there were 600,000 internet users.

History

A unified kingdom first arose along the **Nile** in 3000-4000 BC and a series of dynasties ruled in Egypt for the next three millennia. The last native dynasty fell to the Persians in 341 BC, who in turn were replaced, in succession, by the Greeks, Romans, and Byzantines. It was the Arabs who introduced **Islam** and the Arabic language in the 7th century and who ruled for the next six centuries. A local military caste, the Mamluks, took control in about 1250 and continued to govern after the conquest of Egypt by the Ottoman Turks in 1517. Following the completion of the Suez Canal in 1869, Egypt became an important world transportation hub, but also fell heavily into debt. Ostensibly to protect its investments, Britain seized control of Egypt's government in 1882, but nominal allegiance to the **Ottoman Empire** continued until 1914. Partially independent from the United Kingdom in 1922, Egypt acquired full sovereignty following the Second World War. In 1951 the Egyptian Government abrogated the 1936 treaty with Britain and British troops occupied the Canal Zone. In 1952 Gen. **Muhammed Neguib** and Col **Gamal Abdel Nasser** seized power, ousting King **Farouk** in a **military** coup. In 1954 Nasser took full control. An Anglo-Egyptian agreement on the Canal Zone stipulated that the British base was to be evacuated within 20 months. In January 1956 Britain granted independence to Sudan in part as a move to pre-empt any union between Egypt and Sudan. The **World Bank**, the USA and Britain withdrew their offer of aid for the construction of the **Aswan High Dam**; instead the Soviet Union offered to build it. The completion of the Aswan High Dam in 1971 and resultant Lake Nasser only increased the significance of the Nile in the **agriculture** and ecology of Egypt. A rapidly growing population, limited arable land, and dependence on the Nile all continue to create constraints and pressures. The government has struggled to prepare the economy for the new millennium through economic reform and massive investment in communications and physical infra-structure.

Egypt, economy

Egypt has the fifth largest economy in the **Middle East** (after Saudi Arabia, Turkey, Iran and Israel), with a gross national product of US \$98,500m. Egypt improved its macroeconomic performance throughout most of the last decade by following the advice of the **International Monetary Fund** on fiscal, monetary and structural reform policies. As a result, it managed to bring inflation under control, reduce budget deficits and attract increased foreign investment. In the past three years, however, the pace of reform has slackened, and excessive spending on national infrastructure projects has widened budget deficits again. Lower foreign-exchange earnings since 1998 have resulted in pressure on the Egyptian pound and periodic dollar shortages. Islamist terrorist acts have had a negative impact on tourism. The country is dependent on imported technology. Monetary pressures have increased since 11 September 2001 because of declines in **tourism**, **Suez Canal** tolls, and exports, and Egypt has devalued the pound several times in the past year. The development of a **gas** export market is a major positive element of future prospects for growth. Other strengths include **oil** and gas, a well-developed tourist industry, **remittances** from Egyptians working in the **Gulf**, Suez Canal tolls, cotton, light **industry** and manufacturing.

International relations

Egypt and Sudan each claim to administer triangular areas which extend north and south of the 1899 Treaty boundary along the 22nd Parallel (in the north, the 'Hala'ib Triangle' is the largest, comprising 20,580 sq km); in 2001 the two states agreed to discuss an 'area of integration' and to withdraw military forces in the overlapping areas.

Egyptian Arab Socialist Party

Centrist party established by the **Sadat** regime in 1976, after a decision to 'open up' Egyptian politics. Its leader was Abu Wafa, who was related by marriage to Sadat. In 1978 it was renamed the **National Democratic Party**. **Hosni Mubarak** became its secretary-general, a post he retained on succeeding Sadat as President.

Egyptian-Israeli Peace Treaty

Treaty between Egypt and Israel, signed in March 1979, following the **Camp David Agreements**. The Treaty established a linkage between peace with Egypt and Palestinian autonomy. Though it was not fully implemented, the principle of recognition of the rights of **Palestinians** as well as that of the return of all territories implicit in the Treaty greatly influenced subsequent negotiations with the Palestinians and with Syria. On the other hand, Egypt was expelled from the **Arab League** and financial and economic assistance to Egypt from other Arab states was cancelled. Diplomatic relations were severed, with only Sudan, Somalia and Oman (all having a continuing dependence on Egypt) refusing to join in Egypt's effective exclusion. **Sadat**'s political and economic strategy, designed to bring Egypt more fully within the orbit of the USA and introduce economic reforms, also exposed him to opposition from within the country. It has been suggested that Sadat's assassination in 1981 was the most significant consequence of the Egyptian-Israeli Treaty.

Ein Saheb

A civilian refugee camp to the north-west of **Damascus**, Syria. It was attacked by the Israeli air force in October 2003—the first attack in nearly three decades against targets on Syrian territory. Israel claimed that Ein Saheb was a training camp for the **Palestinian Islamic Jihad** (PIJ), and regarded the attack as an act of self-defence in response to a PIJ suicide bombing in **Haifa** in which 19 people were killed and 60 wounded. In fact, the air strike seems to have been made against a military installation of the **Popular Front for the Liberaton of Palestine-General Command** (PFLP-GC) that had been defunct since late 2000. The camp at Ein Saheb is a known stronghold of the **PFLP** and the PFLP-GC, but there is no known organized activity there by either the PIJ or **Hamas**.

Einstein, Albert

World-famous physicist and Nobel Prize winner. Jewish by descent, Einstein was also a committed Zionist. In the face of the Nazi threat and the Holocaust, he was actively involved in the debates over the development of the nuclear bomb by the USA. He renounced pacifism and argued that the USA should develop the atomic bomb, but he also warned of the dangers of nuclear war and proposed international control of nuclear weaponry. His vocal support of the Zionist cause was duly recognized in 1952, when he was offered the presidency of the new State of Israel. He declined, on the grounds of political naivety.

Eisenhower Doctrine

US foreign policy doctrine, named after and instituted by former US President Dwight Eisenhower, who refused to support Anglo-French action against **Nasser** in Egypt. Eisenhower's Secretary of State, John Foster Dulles, was also concerned about the growing influence of the Soviet Union in the **Middle East**. In January 1957 Eisenhower made a speech calling for the use of US forces to protect Middle Eastern states against overt aggression from nations 'controlled by international communism'. He also urged the provision of economic aid to those countries with anti-communist governments. The new foreign policy became known as the Eisenhower Doctrine. In April 1957 help was given to King **Hussein** of Jordan who was under threat from left-wing groups. In the following year 10,000 marines were deployed in Lebanon to protect President **Camille Chamoun** from Muslim extremists. These two interventions created a great deal of anti-American feeling in the Middle East. By the end of the decade the Doctrine had been phased out. See also **US policy in the Middle East**.

El Al

Israeli national airline. See **El Al hijacking**.

El Al hijacking

On 23 July 1968 an El Al passenger aircraft *en route* to **Tel-Aviv** from Rome, Italy, was hijacked by members of the **Popular Front for the Liberation of Palestine** (PFLP) and diverted to **Algiers**. All of the passengers were released except for 12 Israeli men who were held hostage for 39 days until the demand of the hijackers for the release of 15 jailed **Palestinians** was met. The **hijacking** was planned by **Wadi Haddad**, founder of the **Movement of Arab Nationalists** and (later) of the PFLP.

Emir (or Amir)

Traditional title meaning 'leader'. May refer to a head of state of one of the United Arab Emirates. In Morocco, the sultans and subsequently the kings (**Hassan II** and **Mohammed VI**) have also been referred to, in their capacity as religious leaders, as Emir of the Faithful (Amir al-Muminin). In Algeria, the leaders of the various Islamist groups within the **GIA—Groupe islamique armé** (Armed Islamic Group) and the **GSPC—Groupe salafiste pour la prédication et le combat** (Salafist Group for Call and Combat) are referred to as 'emirs'.

Energy

Saudi Arabia is the largest producer of energy in the region (488m. metric tons **oil** equivalent in 2000), ranking fourth in the world. Iran ranks eighth in the world, producing 242m. tons oil equivalent and Algeria 15th with 150m. tons. The United Arab Emirates (UAE) ranks 17th, producing 144m. tons oil equivalent, Iraq 20th with 134m., Kuwait 22nd with 111.5m., Kazakhstan 27th with 78m. and Libya 30th with 74m. Saudi Arabia is also the largest consumer of energy in the region, accounting for 108m. tons oil equivalent, with Turkey and Uzbekistan consuming 77m. and 50m. respectively. The highest net energy importers are Israel, Lebanon, Jordan and Morocco. Morocco is one of the most efficient users of energy (sixth in the world), Uzbekistan one of the least efficient (second equal with Nigeria and Zambia), followed by Turkmenistan, Bahrain and Kuwait. The more profligate users of energy are, not surprisingly, the energy-rich states—led by Qatar, with the world's highest rate of consumption at almost 27,000 kg of oil equivalent per head. Others include, in order, Kuwait, the UAE, Bahrain, Saudi Arabia and Oman. Among the lowest net energy importers are Yemen, Oman, Kuwait, Algeria, the UAE, Iraq, Saudi Arabia, Libya, Qatar, Turkmenistan, Iran, Kazakhstan and

Syria—most because they are themselves energy-rich, but some (e.g. Yemen and Syria) because of relatively low levels of energy use.

Erbakan, Necmettin

Member of the Turkish Islamist **National Salvation Party** during the 1970s and subsequently of the **Welfare Party** (Refah). The referendum of September 1987 lifted the ban on pre-1980 politicians, allowing Erbakan to lead his party in the election campaign, though to little effect.

Erbil – *see* Irbil

Erdoğan, Recip Tayyip

Prime Minister of Turkey, and leader of the **Justice and Development Party** (AKP), an organization that developed out of the pro-Islamist regime that the army deposed in the 'soft coup' of 1997.

Erekat, Saeb

Palestinian minister in charge of official negotiations regarding the so-called **Road Map to peace** with Israel.

Eretz Israel

'Greater Israel'—a dream of some Zionists: an Israel incorporating not only the present State of Israel and the **Occupied Territories** of the **West Bank** and **Gaza**, but also parts of Lebanon, Jordan and even beyond.

ESCWA

UN Economic and Social Commission for Western Asia.

Esfahan – *see* Isfahan

Eshkol, Levi

Prime Minister of Israel in 1963–69.

Ethnic groups and ethnicity

Many of the states in the region are characterized by societies of considerable ethnic diversity. That is to say that within the boundaries of the nation state and within the broader structure of 'national' identity, many people regard themselves as members of more specific groups—defined essentially by linguistic, cultural and/or tribal affiliations—which could be referred to as 'ethnic groups'. This form of affiliation is called 'ethnicity'. These groups are sometimes referred to as 'primordial groups' in the sense that loyalties to these groups often come first and run deeper than those to the nation state and its values and priorities. Examples in the region would include large groups (which some might describe as 'peoples' or even 'nations'), such as the **Berbers** and the **Kurds**, and essentially 'tribal' confederations, such as **Baluchis**, **Pashtuns**, etc., whose 'homeland' crosses state boundaries. It could even be argued that Turks and Arabs constitute ethnic groups.

Euphrates

A major river whose headwaters are in Turkey and which traverses Syria and Iraq to the sea where it disgorges into the **Shatt al-Arab**. The Euphrates is 2,735 km in length and covers a surface of 450,000 sq km.

Euro-Arab Dialogue

The 'Euro-Arab Dialogue' was initiated in 1973, initially to provide a forum for the discussion of economic issues. After the Egypt-Israel peace agreement in 1979 all activity was suspended at the request of the **Arab League**. In December 1989 a meeting of ministers of foreign affairs of European Community (EC) and Arab countries agreed to reactivate the Dialogue. Meetings were suspended as a result of Iraq's invasion of Kuwait in August 1990. In April 1992 senior officials from the EC and Arab countries agreed to resume the Dialogue once more. In 1992 the EC was involved in the **Middle East** peace negotiations. In September 1993, following the signing of a peace agreement between the Israeli Government and the **Palestine Liberation Organization**, the EC committed ECU 33m. in immediate humanitarian assistance and proposed a five-year programme of development **aid**, to comprise ECU 500m. in grants and loans for the **Occupied Territories**, from 1994 to 1998. Further assistance, totalling ECU 100m., was disbursed during these years. In November 1998 an assistance programme totalling ECU 250m. was approved for the period 1999–2003. The **European Union** (EU) was—and remains—the largest donor to the **Palestinian National Authority** (PNA). An interim Euro-**Mediterranean** agreement on **trade** and co-operation was signed with the Palestinian authorities in January 1997 and entered into force on 1 July. The EC-Palestinian joint committee, established under the interim agreement, met for the first time in May 2000. Implementation of the agreement has been slow, partly owing to Israeli obstruction of Palestinian trade. Following the outbreak of the (renewed) *intifada* in late 2000, and the economic difficulties that ensued, the EU granted emergency loans to cover the PNA's running costs. The European Parliament decided in June 2002 to continue this support.

Euro-Mediterranean Economic Area (EMEA)

In June 1995 the European Council endorsed a programme to reform and strengthen the **Mediterranean** policy of the **European Union** (EU). It envisaged the establishment of a Euro-Mediterranean Economic Area, preceded by a gradual liberalization of **trade** within the region through bilateral and regional free-trade arrangements and through structural reforms in the countries of the Mediterranean involved. In November 1995 a conference of ministers of foreign affairs of the EU member states, eleven Mediterranean non-member countries (excluding Libya) and the Palestine authorities was convened in Barcelona, Spain. The conference endorsed the agreement on the EMEA and resolved to establish a permanent Euro-Mediterranean ministerial dialogue. The Barcelona Declaration set the objective of a Euro-Mediterranean Free Trade Area by 2010. This was the so-called **Euro-Mediterranean Partnership**.

Euro-Mediterranean Partnership (EMP)

The 15 foreign ministers of the **European Union** (EU) met with their counterparts—from Algeria, Cyprus, Egypt, Israel, Jordan, Lebanon, Malta, Morocco, Syria, Tunisia, Turkey and the **West Bank** and **Gaza Strip**—in Barcelona, Spain, in November 1995 to launch a Euro-**Mediterranean** Partnership initiative, which called for a full liberalization of non-agricultural trade among the partner countries by 2010. Libya, until 1999 restricted by UN sanctions for its supposed part in the **Lockerbie** disaster, would have observer status. The EU supported the Barcelona Declaration with a budgetary commitment over four years (1996–99) of ECU 4,700m. (US \$5,000m.) in grants to finance projects preparing for free trade as well as for other social and developmental objectives. The funds, however, are limited (the actual allocation for the four years in question was ECU 3,800m. (\$3,200m.)—a sum probably less than that remitted annually by migrant workers from the **Maghreb** countries—and states in the region are in effect surrendering their preferential access to European agricultural markets while progressively allowing the EU free access to their own markets for industrial products. From the perspective of the Mediterranean 'partners', the EMP appears somewhat unequal. Participation agreements have been signed with Tunisia (July 1995), Morocco (February 1996) and Israel (1999–2000); agreements have also been signed with Jordan and the **Palestinian National Authority**. Negotiations with Egypt have been completed and some of the programmed bilateral funds have reached Algeria, Lebanon and Syria, without formal agreements. The primary financial instrument for the implementation of the EMP is the MEDA programme. Under MEDA II (the revised version of MEDA I), a long-term strategy for 2000–2006 was drawn up and a budget of €5,350m. was allocated. Libya was gradually readmitted in 1999–2002 as its wider 'post-Lockerbie' rehabilitation took place.

EU – *see* **European Union**

European Union (EU)

Since its creation the EU has sought to establish a special relationship with a significant number of countries in the region, through a variety of mechanisms and institutional frameworks and agreements, including the **Euro-Mediterranean Partnership** initiative. Individual partnership agreements signed with Tunisia (July 1995), Morocco (February 1996) and Israel have been ratified, as have agreements with Jordan and the **Palestinian National Authority**. Negotiations with Egypt have been completed and some of the programmed bilateral funds have reached Algeria, Lebanon and Syria without formal agreements. Rapid reformers are supposed to receive greater shares of the allocated funds than the more reluctant states. Funds are in any case limited and states in the region are surrendering their preferential access to European agricultural markets while progressively allowing the EU free access to their markets for industrial products.

EU-Mauritania

Relations between the **European Union** and Mauritania fall outside the **Euro-Mediterranean Partnership** (EMP) framework, despite the fact that Mauritania belongs to the **Arab Maghreb Union**, all other members of which, apart from Libya, are fully involved in various arrangements under the EMP. Mauritania is classified by the EU as one of the African, Caribbean and Pacific countries with which successive treaties and agreements have been negotiated under the heading of the Lomé Convention and the Cotonou Agreement. It is the only Arab country within this grouping. In August 2001 the EU signed its biggest fishing agreement with Mauritania, with potentially disastrous ecological consequences and considerable implications for EU-Mauritania relations.

EU-Yemen

A co-operation agreement between the European Community (EC) and the Yemen Arab Republic covering commercial, economic and development co-operation was signed in October 1984, entering into force in January 1985, initially for a five-year period. In June 1992 the European Council agreed to extend the original co-operation agreement to include the whole of the new Republic of Yemen (unified in 1990). During 1994 EC projects in Yemen were suspended owing to civil conflict, although humanitarian **aid** was provided. In March 1995 the **European Union**-Yemen Joint Co-operation Council convened for the first time since early 1993. A new co-operation agreement, incorporating a commitment to democratic principles and respect for human rights, was approved in April 1997 and entered into force in July 1998. Yemen received assistance under the ECHO programme for **refugees** and other vulnerable groups in 2000.

Evren, Col Kenan

Led a **military** coup in September 1980 against the civilian Turkish Government, and was head of state of Turkey first in his capacity as leader of the military junta (from September 1980 until 1982) and then as President until October 1989.

Exxon-Mobil

Exxon-Mobil is the largest **oil** company in the world and the second largest corporation in the world after Wal-Mart Stores, with annual sales figures of some US $192,000m. One of the major oil corporations, the so-called 'seven sisters', operating in the region.

F

Fadhlallah, Ayatollah Sayyid Muhammad Husayn

Born in 1935, **Shi'ite** cleric and spiritual leader of **Hezbollah**, the 'Party of God', in Lebanon. Born in Iraq of Lebanese parents, he moved to Lebanon in 1966 and quickly established a reputation as a leading religious authority. Hezbollah, founded after the 1982 Israeli invasion of Lebanon, became public in 1985. Fadhlallah's eloquence led many to believe that he was Hezbollah's leader, but both he and the Party of God deny this, while acknowledging his strong spiritual influence. While agreeing with many of Hezbollah's positions, he has opposed others. In 1985 it was widely reported that he was the target of an aborted US-Saudi car-bomb assassination attempt, a charge denied by US and Saudi authorities.

Al-Fadl, Ahmed

Involved in a plot to kill US soldiers in Somalia in 1992. When interrogated, he described the **al-Qa'ida network** organized by **Osama bin Laden**, bin Laden's aim of attacking the USA and his efforts to obtain uranium. Al-Fadl's revelations were passed on to every anti-terrorist agency in the USA, but the US Department of State failed to add **al-Qa'ida** to its list of terrorist organizations.

Fahd ibn Abdul Aziz

Fifth king of Saudi Arabia (1982–). Son of the founder of the Saudi kingdom, King **(ibn Saud) Abdul Aziz as-Saud**. Born in 1923, 30 years later he became Saudi Arabia's first Minister of Education; in 1962 he was appointed Minister of the Interior; in 1975 he became Crown Prince and Deputy Prime Minister under King **Khalid ibn Abdul Aziz**. In 1981 Fahd developed an eight-point Peace Plan to resolve the **Arab–Israeli Conflict**. It required the withdrawal of Israel from the **Occupied Territories** and the abandonment of all Jewish **settlements** in the area. In 1982 Fahd became King of Saudi Arabia after the death of Khalid and the **Fahd Plan** was adopted by the **Arab League**. Among King Fahd's international achievements is the historic **Ta'if Agreement**. In 1989 Lebanese parliamentarians met in Ta'if, Saudi Arabia, and established a national reconciliation government to end 15 years of civil war in Lebanon. King Fahd has also been an active supporter of

Lebanon's reconstruction efforts, providing financial **aid** and other forms of assistance. In the weeks before the Iraqi invasion of Kuwait on 2 August 1990 King Fahd sought to mediate in the dispute between Kuwait and Iraq. In co-operation with US President **George Bush**, he helped put together a coalition of Arab, Islamic and other countries to implement UN Security Council resolutions to liberate Kuwait following the Iraqi invasion. An advocate of peace, he has supported the **Middle East** peace process, including the **Declaration of Principles on Palestinian Self-Rule** concluded by the **Palestine Liberation Organization** and Israel in Washington, DC, on 13 September 1993, as a first step towards achieving a just and comprehensive settlement of the Arab–Israeli Conflict. Domestically, King Fahd has introduced a number of reforms aimed at facilitating the continued development of Saudi Arabia, particularly in the area of higher **education**. More conservative in political matters, in 1993 he established a Council of Ministers (**Majlis ash-Shura**) composed of 60 members with a wide diversity of experience to give advice on the formulation of future policy. He suffered a series of strokes in 1995 and his half-brother, Crown Prince Abdullah, effectively took over as ruler. The king rules by decree and serves as Prime Minister as well as supreme religious leader. A recent decision to limit ministerial tenure to four years ensures a periodic renewal of the government and probably strengthens the hand of the monarch over his ministers.

Fahd Plan

The Fahd Plan, launched in August 1981 by Crown Prince Fahd of Saudi Arabia, called for:

1. Israeli withdrawal from all Arab territories taken in the Six-Day War, including Arab (East) Jerusalem.
2. The dismantling of Israeli settlements in the territories captured in 1967.
3. The assurance of the freedom of worship for all religions in the holy sites.
4. The emphasis of the rights of the Palestinian nation, including compensation for those who do not wish to return.
5. A brief transition period for Gaza and the West Bank under the auspices of the United Nations.
6. The establishment of an independent Palestinian state with Jerusalem as its capital.
7. The right for all nations in the area to live in peace.
8. The UN or some of its members to guarantee the implementation of the above-mentioned principles.

Some Arab states showed their support, but failure to agree on the Fahd Plan caused the collapse of the Fez Arab summit in November 1981 only a few hours after it had opened.

Fahim, Mohammed

Afghan defence minister and member of the **Northern Alliance**.

Failed states

A term used to refer to states whose 'national' governments are no longer able to maintain exclusive control over their territory and population. Madeleine Albright, former US Secretary of State, defined them as 'countries with a weak or non-existent central authority'. Often, in a failed state, several competing authorities exercise varying degrees of power in different regions. It is generally argued that failed states arise from the political and economic disintegration of pre-existing states, under exceptional internal or external conditions. Arguably they may be the result of failed attempts to construct new regimes under inappropriate conditions. Loretta Napoleoni has used the term 'state-shells' to refer to emerging state-like forms within failed or disintegrating states which may develop their own economic and political and **military** regimes. Armed groups fill what is left of 'a mere geographical expression, a black hole into which a failed polity has landed'; they gain control of regions, create their own infrastructure, regulate markets and **trade** flows, and even attempt to establish foreign relations with neighbouring states. Failed states, however, retain some of the outward elements of sovereignty; even if they cannot retain control of their borders, or of all that occurs within them, they maintain the 'footprint' of territoriality. Failed states maintain diplomacy and a degree of legitimacy. Some would argue that this distinguishes them from **collapsed states**.

Faisal, ibn Abdul Aziz as-Saud

Became king of Saudi Arabia in 1954 after the death of **Ibn Saud**; assassinated in 1975 and succeeded by Crown Prince Khalid ibn Abdul Aziz as-Saud, who was king until his death in 1982.

Faisal I, King (ibn Hussein al-Hashem) (1885–1933)

In 1916 Faisal led an **Arab Revolt** in **Hejaz** against the Ottomans that resulted in independence for Hejaz when his father became king. In 1919, at the Paris Peace Conference, Faisal unsuccessfully claimed the right to establish an Arab kingdom or a federation of Arab emirates. In March 1920 Faisal was elected king of greater Syria (present-day Syria, Lebanon, Jordan, Israel and Palestine) by the Syrian National Council, but in the following month the French authorities were given the Mandate to administer Syria and Lebanon by the League of Nations. In July he was forcibly expelled by the troops of French Gen. Gouraud who occupied **Damascus** in July. Faisal was exiled to Britain and the country divided into six. However, by 1921 Britain was experiencing opposition to its presence in Iraq. An agreement to make him king of Iraq was forged with Faisal in 1921 and in 1923 the title of constitutional monarch was conferred on him by the Iraqi National Assembly. In 1930 Faisal signed an agreement with Britain that was intended to lead to the independence of Iraq. The agreement secured the basing of British troops in Iraq and ensured that Iraqi foreign policy followed the British political line. In 1932 Iraq became independent and joined the League of Nations. On his death in 1933, Faisal was succeeded by his son, Ghazi ibn Faisal, who was king for only three years, until 1939, when he was succeeded by his son, Faisal ibn Ghazi (as **Faisal II**).

Faisal II, King (ibn Ghazi ibn Faisal al-Hashem) (1935–58)

King of Iraq in 1939–58. Succeeded his father Ghazi ibn Faisal al- Hashem, initially under the regency of his uncles until he came of age. He was assassinated in July 1958 during a coup mounted by republican officers.

Faisal Islamic Bank

Osama bin Laden made use of the Faisal Islamic Bank to channel funds across the world. The chairman of the bank is Prince Mohammed al-Faisal as-Saud. Among the founders of the bank is Saleh Abdullah Kamel, Saudi magnate and the King's brother-in-law. It was thanks to him that in 1981 the Dallah al-Baraka holding group, one of the twin pillars (together with the **Dar al-Mal al-Islami**) of the Saudi banking establishment, was founded.

Faithful Resistance

Al-Muqawma al-Mu'mina

An **Amal** splinter group, seemingly independent. It carried out a *Katyusha* rocket attack on northern Israel in January 1986, at a time when **Shi'a** Islamists accused Amal of having entered into a secret agreement with Israel. Believed to have almost 200 members.

Falluja

Predominantly **Sunni** town to the west of **Baghdad**, Iraq. Emerged during the latter part of 2003 and early 2004 as a centre of resistance to the **coalition** occupation of Iraq. During April 2004 US marines were involved in heavy fighting to regain control of Falluja from guerrilla forces and there were serious civilian casualties.

Fanon, Frantz

Born in Martinique in 1925. French West Indian psychiatrist, author, revolutionary, and leader of the Algerian National Front. Educated in France, he subsequently travelled to Algeria (1953) to practise psychiatry. Sympathetic to the Algerian revolution from its inception (1954), Fanon resigned his medical post (1956) to become editor of the Algerian National Front's newspaper. Author of several books on the colonial experience. Died in 1961.

FAO

UN Food and **Agriculture** Organization. It has numerous activities in the region, and a number of regional commissions, including the Commission for Controlling the Desert Locust in the **Near East**, the Commission for Controlling the Desert Locust in North West Africa, the General **Fisheries** Council for the **Mediterranean**, the Near East Forestry Commission, the Near East Regional Commission on Agriculture, the Near East Regional Economic and Social Policy Commission, and the Regional Commission on Land and **Water** Use in the Near East. The FAO is also responsible for the **WFP**, the UN World Food Programme, and its operations in the region.

Farouk

Born in 1920, died in 1965. King of Egypt in 1936–52. Son and successor of **King Fuad** I. After a short regency period he acceded to the throne in 1937. A constitutional monarch, Farouk was frequently at odds with the **Wafd Party**, the largest Egyptian party. Because of his pro-Axis sympathies during the Second World War, Britain imposed upon him a pro-British premier in 1942. Egypt's defeat in the **Arab–Israeli War (1948–49)** and Farouk's own decadent lifestyle eventually led to the **military** coup of 1952, headed by Abdul al-Hakim and **Gamal Abdel Nasser**. Farouk was forced to abdicate; he fled the country and found refuge abroad.

Fars (Province of Iran)

Located in southern Iran and covering an area of 133,000 sq km, Fars is bounded on the north by Yazd and **Isfahan**, on the west by Kohgilouyeh va Boyr Ahmad, on the south by Hormozgan and Bushehr, and on the east by Kerman.

Dating back to antiquity, Fars province has been a significant centre of the Persian culture and civilization. During some important Iranian dynasties, including the Achaemenids, Fars was the capital of the country. Some of the greatest Iranian poets and philosophers are from this province. The religious minorities are **Zoroastrians**, Jews and Christians. One of the largest Iranian tribes, the Qashqai, live in Fars.

Farsi

The most widely spoken member of the Iranian branch of the Indo-Iranian languages, a subfamily of the Indo-European languages. It is the language of Iran (formerly Persia) and is also widely spoken in Afghanistan and, in an archaic form, in Tajikistan and the Pamir Mountain region. There are significant populations of speakers in other **Persian (Arabian) Gulf** countries (Bahrain, Iraq, Oman, Yemen, and the United Arab Emirates), as well as large communities in the USA. About 50% of Iran's population, some 30m. people, are Farsi speakers. There are more than 7m. Dari Persian speakers in Afghanistan (some 25% of the population), and about 2m. Dari Persian speakers in Pakistan.

Al-Fassi, Allal

Allal al-Fassi was one of the leading bourgeois nationalist leaders of Morocco. He was a member of the initial nationalist group, which was established in Fez, in the early 1930s, as if it were a religious brotherhood: the nucleus was known as the *zawiya* (religious lodge or fraternity) and the wider organization (responsible for seeking and screening recruits) as the *taifa*. He was a member of the Moroccan Action Committee formed in 1934 and of the National Party (**Istiqlal**), established in 1936. The nationalists maintained close relations with the palace during the war.

Al-Fatah (also known as Al-'Asifa—Palestinian National Liberation Movement)

Founded in 1958 by **Yasser Arafat**, al-Fatah was committed to achieving self-determination and political independence for **Palestinians**. Its original aim was to establish a democratic secular state in the area of the British Mandate of Palestine with equal rights for Jews, Muslims and Christians. It was initially supported and strongly directed by the secret services of Egypt and Syria, which supplied funds, arms and training. From the outset, Arafat was concerned to break away from state sponsorship and gain independence for the Palestinian movement. Al-Fatah became increasingly important in the **Palestine Liberation Organization** (PLO) during the 1960s, and gained effective control over the PLO in 1969, when Arafat was elected as chairman of the PLO's Executive Committee. Its leaders were expelled from Jordan, where they had established themselves after 1967, following violent confrontations with Jordanian forces in 1970–71, beginning with **Black September** in 1970. During the 1970s al-Fatah and the PLO gained a high degree of independence from their Arab sponsors and established an economic and financial base, as well as a military base, in Lebanon. It maintains several military and intelligence wings that have carried out terrorist attacks, including **Force 17** and the Western Sector. Two of its leaders, **'Abu Jihad'** and **'Abu Iyad'**, have been assassinated in recent years. The Israeli invasion of Lebanon in 1982 led to the group's dispersal to several Middle Eastern countries, including Tunisia, Yemen, Algeria and Iraq. Al-Fatah has had close political and financial ties to Saudi Arabia, Kuwait, and other moderate **Gulf states**. These relations were disrupted by the Gulf crisis of 1990–91. It has also had links to Jordan. Al-Fatah received weapons, explosives and training from the former USSR and the former Communist regimes of East European states. The People's Republic of China and North Korea have reportedly provided it with some weapons.

In the 1960s and 1970s Fatah offered training to a wide range of European, Middle Eastern, Asian, and African terrorist and insurgent groups. It carried out numerous acts of international **terrorism** in western Europe and the Middle East in the early-to-mid-1970s.

Arafat signed the **Declaration of Principles on Palestinian Self-Rule** with Israel in 1993 and renounced terrorism and violence. There has been no authorized terrorist operation since that time. However, in 1990 al-Fatah's leaders supported Iraqi President **Saddam Hussain** when, Iraq having occupied Kuwait in August, he tried to link Israel's withdrawal from the **West Bank** and **Gaza** with Iraq's withdrawal from Kuwait.

Fatah's constitution requires leadership elections every five years, but none have been held for 15 years. Many are critical of the central committee and of Yasser Arafat.

Al-Fatah Revolutionary Council (FRC) – *see* ANO—Abu Nidal Organization

Fatwa

A legal pronouncement in **Islam**, issued by a religious legal authority, on a specific issue. Usually a *fatwa* is issued at the request of an individual or a judge to settle a question where *fiqh*, (**Islamic jurisprudence**) is unclear. Because there is no central Islamic priesthood, there is no generally accepted method to determine who can issue a *fatwa* and who cannot. Thus, in both theory and practice, different Islamic clerics can issue contradictory, or competing, *fatwas*. What happens subsequently depends on whether one lives in a nation where **Islamic Law** is the basis of civil law or whether one lives where Islamic Law has no legal status. In nations based on Islamic Law, *fatwas* by the national religious leadership are debated before being issued and are decided upon by consensus. In such cases they are rarely contradictory, and they carry the status of enforceable law. If two *fatwas* are contradictory, the ruling bodies (which combine civil and religious law) effect a compromise interpretation which is followed as law. In nations that do not recognize Islamic Law, religious Muslims are often confronted with two competing *fatwas*. In such a case, they would follow the *fatwa* of the leader in the same religious tradition as themselves. Thus, for example, **Sunni** Muslims would not adhere to the *fatwa* of a **Shi'ite** or Sufi.

Fedaiyan-e-Islam

Devotees of Islam

Founded in 1945. A semi-secret Iranian religious political group; in 1948 it claimed responsibility for the murder of pro-British and **Baha'i** minister Abdul Hussein

Hazir and of the secular historian Ahmad Kasravi. In 1955 the group's attempted assassination of the Shah's Prime Minister, Hussein Ala, led to the execution of its main leaders, including Nyab Safavir. The assassination of Mustafa Shafiq, nephew of the Shah, in Paris in 1979 was attributed to Fedaiyan-e-Islam.

Fedayan—Organization of the Guerrilla Devotees of the Iranian People

Sazman-e Cherik-ha-ye Fada'i-ye Khalq-e Iran

Popularly known as the Fedayan, this Marxist coalition was formed in 1971 from three different groups, which originated in the mid-1960s. Bijan Jazani, previously a member of the **Tudeh Party**, formed his own group in 1964, which later merged with two others, one led by Mas'ud Ahmadzadeh and the other by Behruz and Ashraf Dehqani (brother and sister). The Fedayan began as a leftist guerrilla movement inspired by Che Guevara and others; many cadres were trained by the **Palestine Liberation Organization**, and some by the People's Republic of China, Cuba and **South Yemen**. Their first assault on the Shah's regime was an attack on a village in the Caspian region in February 1971. From then onwards their area of operations tended to be concentrated in the north of the country, although they focused more on the urban areas. In June 1980 the Fedayan split, with the majority (Aksariyyat) accepting the rule of the **Islamic Republic(an) Party** and the minority (Aqaliyyat) continuing the armed struggle against the **Khomeini** regime. Despite their decision, the Aksariyyat were heavily repressed by the government from 1983 onwards.

Fedayeen

In **Arabic**: 'one who sacrifices himself'; 'martyr'. Guerrilla, paramilitary group. In the mid-20th century the term was applied to Palestinian guerrillas operating from Jordan and southern Lebanon. It was associated during the **Gulf War (2003)** with **Uday Hussain**'s militia, the *Fedayeen* **Saddam** (sacrificers of Saddam). *Fedayeen* was a link of support between the Palestinian communities who had been forced to flee their country during the **Arab–Israeli War (1948–49)**. The *Fedayeen* were based in Egypt, Lebanon and Jordan. The Israeli view is that the *Fedayeen* were recruited, armed and trained mainly by Egypt's security forces under the control of Egyptian President **Gamal Abdel Nasser** to kill as many Israeli civilians as they could ambush on roads and in isolated communities. The *Fedayeen* name was later selected by **Saddam Hussein** to designate his *Fedayeen* Saddam, in part to imply a connection to the Palestinian resistance.

Fedayeen Saddam – *see also* *Fedayeen*

In **Arabic**: 'sacrificers of Saddam'. The *Fedayeen* Saddam were **Saddam Hussein**'s most trusted paramilitary unit, comprising a 30,000–40,000-strong militia in Iraq headed by Hussain's eldest son, Uday. The name was selected to imply a conceptual relationship to the *Fedayeen* of the Palestinian resistance. **Uday Hussain** formed the group in 1995, but lost control of it in 1996, apparently after supplying the group with sophisticated weapons from the Republican Guard without Saddam Hussain's permission. Subsequently Saddam's younger son, Qusai, is believed to have taken control of the group for some time. In the years that followed the force was once again placed back in Uday's control. The group is suspected to be directly responsible for many of Saddam Hussain's regime's most brutal acts, including beheadings and other executions. It is believed that the *Fedayeen* Saddam is one of the most active and sophisticated (pro-Saddam) guerrilla groups fighting against the US and UK occupation of Iraq.

Fedayin-e Khalq
Warriors of the People

Iranian political party, formed in 1970. Received training from the **Popular Front for the Liberation of Palestine**. After the **Iranian Revolution** of 1979, Ayatollah **Khomeini** rejected the party's demand for a share of power and many of its activists joined the Kurdish guerrilla movement. Subsequently underwent many divisions and was formally dissolved in 1987.

Federation of Egyptian Industries (FEI)

Established in 1922, the FEI represents the industrial community in Egypt. Its main offices are in **Cairo** and **Alexandria**.

Federation of South Arabia

The Federation of South Arabia came into being in February 1959 when the 17 leaders of the various states and tribes of the Western **Aden** Protectorates who had requested British assistance in forming a federation agreed a treaty whereby the British extended to the new entity as a whole the protectorate treaties previously concluded with its individual members. The Federation was never recognized by the governments of any existing Arab state, but appeared to be an instrument of British foreign policy while having the ultimate stated aim of independence. The former state and tribal leaders, sitting as the Supreme Council, constituted its only political and legislative organ, the chairmanship of which rotated on a monthly basis. The important states of the Eastern Aden protectorates refused to join, but by 1961 the Federation had made some economic progress and had developed its own **armed forces**. A constitutional conference took place in 1964 at which it was announced that independence would come in 1968, and that in the mean time there would be various reforms to increase political representation. These were never implemented and, as the struggle for the liberation of South Arabia by the **National Liberation Front** (NLF) and the **Front for the Liberation of Occupied South Yemen**—which had started in 1963—became more intense, the federal government and army began to join forces with the rebels. In September 1965 the British Governor, Sir Richard Turnbull, suspended the Constitution and imposed direct colonial rule. In December 1966 the NLF declared itself the sole representative of the people of South Arabia, and in September 1967 the British High Commissioner declared that the federal government had ceased to exist. **South Yemen** now came into existence.

Fergana Valley

The Fergana Valley is 200 miles long and 70 miles wide. It is the economic heart of south **Central Asia**. It houses the densest concentration of population in the region—about 10m. inhabitants (20% of the total population of Central Asia). The Fergana Valley has been a traditional hub of **Islam**. It is also the birthplace of the **Islamic Movement of Uzbekistan** (IMU). The disintegration of the Soviet Union has hit the region hard: the birth of the republics and their detachment from Moscow set in motion a process of decentralization and fragmentation, which has destroyed much of the industrial and agricultural infrastructure. **Trade** between the Fergana Valley and Tashkent, the largest and most important Central Asian market, was disrupted as this market was no longer freely available. The local **tribes** were ready to support the IMU in its fight against the newly formed governments of the republics of Central Asia and particularly against the government of **Uzbek** President **Karimov**, which is widely viewed as having failed to promote the development of the Fergana Valley and its people. In the Fergana Valley unemployment has reached 80% in recent years and inflation is rampant; given that 60% of the population is below 25 years of age, it is a fertile ground for recruitment to armed Islamist groups. Namangiania of the IMU pays between US $100 and $500 a month to its recruits.

Fertility rates

Fertility rates tend to be high throughout the region in comparison with most other regions in the developing world. Changes are, however, taking place in some countries, particularly where gender inequality is improving. In Iran, for example, where **women** tended to have, on average, 5.3 children in 1981, by 2001 the average number was 2.6. In Tunisia the decline over two decades was from five to 2.3. (See also **Democratic structure and change**.)

Fez Plan

An Arab summit meeting was held in Fez, Morocco, in September 1982. It produced a set of proposals for resolving the **Arab–Israeli Conflict** in the **Middle East**, which came to be known as the Fez Plan. The summit demanded: the withdrawal of Israel from all **Arab** territories occupied in 1967, including **East Jerusalem**; the dismantling of **settlements** established by Israel on the Arab territories after 1967; the guarantee of freedom of worship and practice of religious rites for all religions in the holy shrine; the reaffirmation of the Palestinian people's right to self-determination and the exercise of its imprescriptible and inalienable national rights under the leadership of the **Palestine Liberation Organization**, its sole and legitimate representative, and the indemnification of all those who do not desire to return; the placing of the **West Bank** and **Gaza Strip** under the control of the United Nations for a transitional period not exceeding a few months; the establishment of an independent Palestinian state with **Jerusalem** as its capital; that the UN Security Council should guarantee peace among all states of the region, including the independent Palestinian state; and that the Security Council should guarantee the respect of these principles.

Fighting Islamic Group (FIG)

Al-Jama'a al-Islamiyyah al-Muqatilah bi-Libya

Emerged in 1995 among Libyans who had fought against Soviet forces in Afghanistan. Declared the Government of Libyan leader **Muammar al-Qaddafi** unIslamic and pledged to overthrow it in order to establish an Islamic regime. Some members maintain a strictly anti-Qaddafi focus and organize against Libyan Government interests, but others are aligned with **Osama bin Laden**'s **al-Qa'ida** organization or are active in the international *mujahidin* network. Claimed responsibility for a failed assassination attempt against Qaddafi in 1996 and engaged Libyan security forces in armed clashes during the mid-to-late 1990s. Continues to target Libyan interests and may engage in sporadic clashes with Libyan security forces. Probably maintains a clandestine presence in Libya, but since the late 1990s many members have fled to various Middle Eastern and European countries.

Fiqh – *see* Islamic jurisprudence

First Islamic Bank

Bahrain-based First Islamic Bank and London-based Englefield Capital combined in January 2004 to take a one-third stake each in National Wind Power, Britain's leading operator of wind farms. Innogy, the British electricity arm of German multi-utility RWE, will retain one-third of the company. First Islamic, working through Crescent Capital, its private equity arm based in Atlanta and London, is supported by 100 prominent Middle Eastern institutions and families controlling funds worth more than US $100,000m. The Bank is contributing equity rather than debt because **Shari'a** law forbids it from receiving payments of interest.

FIS—Front islamique du salut
Islamic Salvation Front—al-Jibhat al-Inqath

An Algerian Islamist political party, founded in **Algiers** in 1989, after the riots of October 1988, and legalized in September 1989, the FIS quickly emerged as a force capable of mobilizing large numbers of supporters and sympathizers, possessing a nation-wide organization and appeal, extending its influence to other cities, such as Oran, Mostagenem and Blida, over the period from 1989 until 1992 In June 1990 it took control of the popular assemblies in 32 out of Algeria's 48 provinces (*wilayat*) and in 853 out of the 1,539 communes, winning a landslide majority in virtually all of the major cities in particular. It received at least 54% of the vote in an electoral turn-out of 65%; the support, therefore, of about one-third of the total electorate. It won nearly twice as many votes as the official **Front de libération nationale** (FLN, National Liberation Front), which came second, with six provinces and 487 communes. Intoxicated by their triumph, the FIS demanded that the general parliamentary elections be brought forward and that the election laws be amended. Taking to the streets, their slogans were often openly anti-democratic and they were involved in clashes with the state security forces. While generally supporting the Algerian government's economic policy, the FIS—like **Hamas**, the **Mouvement de la renaissance islamique** (MRI) and Rabita—has been primarily concerned with the reconstruction of the state on the basis of the **Shari'a** (**Islamic Law**) and with introducing the Islamic notion of *shura* in place of Western conceptions of pluralism and representative **democracy**. It differed from the other three movements in three main respects. It placed more emphasis on the capture of political power as the prerequisite for the reform of society on Islamic lines. It may be considered, therefore, to have been more 'revolutionary' than its main rivals, although it was prepared to operate within the framework of the 1989 Constitution, while reserving its right to state its principled objections to this Constitution as unIslamic. It was by far the most populist of the Islamist movements and parties in its political style and strategy. Its **populism** and its doctrinal eclecticism, while endowing it with a greater capacity than the other movements to gain and mobilize wide support, obliged it to accommodate a relatively high degree of social and political heterogeneity within its ranks. At the top of the FIS was a consultative council (*majlis ash-shura*) whose membership was highly guarded. It probably included Hachemi Sahnouni, an imam in Algiers and Ben Azzouz Zebda, editor of the FIS newspaper *al-Munqidh* (*The Saviour*). More was known of the group's two main leaders, Professor **Madani Abbasi** (born 1931) and Sheikh **Ali Belhadj** (born 1954). Madani Abbasi (as he was known) represented the 'old guard', while Sheikh Ali Belhadj, the imam of the al-Sunna mosque in the popular quarter of Bab el-Oued in Algiers, personified the younger generation of the FIS, with a powerful appeal to the deprived and frustrated urban youth.

The FIS had ties with Saudi Arabia and other **Gulf** regimes, and is known to have received substantial financial support from them. After Iraq's invasion of Kuwait, the FIS initially adopted a balanced, if not ambiguous, stand, with Madani condemning the invasion early on, but also stating at a meeting on 17 August 1990 that there was no reason for frontiers to exist between Muslim countries, and Belhadj referring to **Saddam Hussain** in a derogatory fashion before denouncing the Kuwaiti regime for having amassed colossal fortunes 'against God's will'. He also suggested that the Holy Places belonged to all Muslims and that their management should be entrusted to the *ulema*—a not so veiled attack on the Saudi royal family. The FIS maintained this attitude for several weeks. At a press conference in Algiers on 13 September 1990, Madani announced that the FIS was engaged in an effort at mediation and declared himself in favour of an Arab solution. He and Ali Belhadj travelled to the Gulf, visiting **Jiddah** three times and **Baghdad** twice in the hope of using the close link of the FIS with the Saudis to good effect. Their efforts were unsuccessful but the FIS persisted in its ambivalent posture, articulating the general view of its popular constituency without breaking the Saudi connection. As popular feelings moved towards support for Iraq, the FIS was also obliged to move steadily towards a pro-Iraqi position. It did this by making the Western military presence the major issue, stopping short of backing Baghdad. Once the war started, however, the FIS emerged as the most vociferous and militant supporter of Iraq, notably at the huge demonstration held in Algiers on 18 January, which reportedly mobilized some 400,000 people and in which virtually all Algerian political parties took part. The FIS marched in this demonstration to slogans and under banners which were explicitly pro-Iraqi and which called on the government to set up training camps for volunteers wishing to go to Iraq to fight. It continued to show its strength, with another demonstration on 31 January, which mobilized some 60,000 supporters (some sources claim 100,000), with other parties staying away. In addition to calling for 'victory to **Islam** and the Muslims' in the war, the demonstrators also made clear the internal political issues at stake, by calling for a date to be fixed for the elections to the national assembly. Despite the outcome of the war in Iraq, the FIS was able to maintain its political momentum within Algeria. The government decided that the elections to the national assembly were to be held in two rounds, but measures were introduced which were designed to hamper, if not provoke, the FIS. Only the two parties winning the most votes in the first round would be allowed to contest the second in each constituency. This provision would have favoured the FLN across the country, and the FIS only where its support was safe from inroads from the other Islamist movements or the **Mouvement pour la démocratie en Algérie**. Moreover, in raising the number of constituencies from 295 to 542, the new law would have given much greater weight than before to the rural districts, where it was felt the FLN was relatively strong. Despite this, the FIS was able to maintain its high level of support, by prioritizing its popular base at home rather than its links with the **Gulf states** abroad. The FIS now made it very clear that, whatever the outcome of the war in Iraq, their objective was (as their president Abbsi Madani declared) 'the building of an **Islamic state** in Algeria in 1991'. This may have cost it its formerly close links with Saudi Arabia in particular (although this is not certain), but it enabled it to mobilize considerable support in the first round of the elections for the national assembly. On 30 June 1991 Abbasi Madani and Ali Belhadj were both arrested and charged with conspiring to overthrow the government; they were subsequently released. Parliamentary elections, however, were to go ahead in December 1991. The turn-out was low, but the success of the FIS was startling. They won 188 out of 231 seats, with 28 seats only left for a second round of voting that was to have been held on 1 January 1992. This did not take place. A military-backed 'palace coup' took place and the elections were stopped. A state of emergency was declared in February, and in March the FIS, together with other Islamist movements, was banned. Only the **MRI** and **Hamas** (since April 1997 the **Mouvement de la société pour la paix**) remained able to operate legally. During the widespread unrest which followed, most of the leadership of the FIS—including Abbasi Madani and Ali Belhadj, were arrested. The FIS claimed that as many as 30,000 were arrested and detained, and that 150 people were killed. The government dissolved the 411 FIS-controlled local and regional authorities. Abbasi Madani and Ali Belhadj were arrested in June 1991, and in July 1992 were sentenced to 12-year terms of imprisonment. Abdelkader Hachani, in exile in Germany, directed the executive branch of the FIS. In February 1993 the state of emergency was renewed for an indefinite period. The FIS leadership was placed under house arrest in September 1994, but Belhadj was later returned to prison, where he remains. In the following years, the Islamist opposition in Algeria became fragmented and increasingly radicalized. Several groups emerged with more or less direct links with the FIS. In the minds of many Algerians, however, the FIS continued to be the dominant Islamist force within the country and these other groups were often thought to be no more than splinter groups of the FIS. The **AIS**— **Armée islamique du salut** (Islamic Salvation Army) was the armed wing of the banned FIS. Other paramilitary Islamist groups that emerged in the first few years included the Armed Islamic Group (or Groups) (Groupe(s) islamique(s) armé(s)— **GIA**), from which, later, in 1998, the **GSPC—Groupe salafiste pour la prédication et le combat** (Salafist Group for Call and Combat) was to split off. In 1996 Algeria introduced a new constitution which banned parties that defined themselves in exclusively religious or ethical terms. In 1997 the AIS took advantage of a government amnesty, accepted a cease-fire, and, in 1999, dissolved itself. At the end of January 1997 the executive branch of the FIS in exile condemned the wave of violent attacks perpetrated mainly by the GIA but also by some paramilitary sections of the FIS, and called for the formation of a national government. In mid-March 1997 the FIS excluded from membership some 40 of its leaders, who had refused 'to make peace at any price'. Its spokesman abroad, Abdelkrim Ould Adda, declared that the FIS did not want a religious state or a theocracy in Algeria. However, according to a statement at the beginning of April 1997 by the same spokesman, the FIS would boycott the parliamentary elections. In November 1999, Abdelkader Hachani, who had returned from exile abroad, was killed in Algiers. The spokesperson for the FIS in exile became Annouar Haddam. FIS leader Abbasi

Madani remained under house arrest, allowed to receive visits but not to travel abroad, while Belhadj remained in prison. In 2000 the government refused to approve the new **Wafa** party, on the grounds that it contained large numbers of FIS members. In August 2002 Rabeh Kabir, a former member of the FIS leadership, was ousted from party management at a Congress held in Belgium. At a further meeting in October, in Switzerland, Mourad Dhina was named as interim head of the party's executive.

Fisheries

Most of the countries of the region that have significant coastlines are involved in fishing and many of these rely to an important degree on the fisheries sector for exports as well as domestic consumption. The major concerns are increasing **pollution** and over-fishing. For countries for which fisheries constitute a major sector, particularly those with an Atlantic seabord (Morocco, **Western Sahara** and Mauritania), over-fishing by foreign fleets is the main menace. In November 2002 the **European Union** (EU) signed a major agreement with Mauritania. This permits some 250 boats from the EU fleet to fish in Mauritanian waters for around £54m. annually for five years. Hailed as being 'of mutual benefit' to both sides, the fact of the matter is that the Mauritanian government is desperate to secure foreign exchange with which to pay its crippling foreign debts, while Europe wants more fish as catches in the North Sea and the North Atlantic become more difficult and fish stocks there are depleted. International scientists have long voiced concern that the fish stocks off west Africa are threatened by foreign fleets and industrial fishing—one expert has stated that 'foreign trawlers are strip-mining African waters of their fisheries resources. It's a scandal. It's almost international piracy. Having seriously mismanaged its home fisheries, the EU is now exporting the problem elsewhere and robbing people of their future'. The Worldwide Fund for Nature has called the level of fishing off Mauritania 'unsustainable'. The Mauritanian National Fisheries Federation, which represents Mauritania's 20,000 fishermen, believes the deal to be the basis for an ecological and human disaster.

Fitna

Literally 'disorder'—the very last thing that a Muslim feels obliged to endure as a result of the failure of government to maintain order in a legitimate fashion.

Five Pillars of Islam

Muslims submit to Allah through *arkan ad-din*, the five basic requirements or 'pillars' of **Islam**; *shahaddah* (statement of faith), *salah* (prayer), *zakat* (charity/alms-giving), *saum* (fasting) and *hajj* (pilgrimage).

Fiver Shi'ites – *see* Zaidis

Front de libération nationale (FLN)

National Liberation Front

The Algerian FLN was established in 1954 and became the driving force of the national liberation struggle against French colonial rule in Algeria. Its military branch was the Armée de libération nationale (ALN). In 1958 the FLN leaders formed the Provisional Government of the Algerian Republic (GPRA) and 'moderate' **Ferhat Abbas** was appointed as its first premier, the government-in-exile being based in **Tunis**. Eventually successful in July 1962 in gaining political independence for Algeria, the FLN was recognized as the sole legal representative of the Algerian people. Ben Youssef Ben Khedda, former secretary-general of the Movement for the Triumph of Democratic Freedoms, led by Ahmed Messali Hadj, had become president of the GPRA in 1960 and he and his Cabinet moved the provisional government to **Algiers**. However, they faced opposition from more radical FLN leaders, including **Ahmed Ben Bella** and **Houari Boumedienne**, who set up a politburo in Tlemcen to compete with the GPRA. When independence came, Ben Bella and his ALN fighters advanced on Algiers in September 1962 and effectively took power. Ben Khedda and the 'centralists' were purged from a single list of candidates to the new Constituent Assembly, as were members of the Communist Party, 'Messalists' (supporters of Ahmed Messali Hadj) and left-wing socialists who followed **Mohammed Boudiaf**. A new Constitution, shaped by Ben Bella, declared the FLN to be the single party of the new state. It has remained, in effect, the ruling party ever since, although for a period in the late 1980s and early 1990s it recognized other political parties.

Force 17

Formed in the early 1970s, the group was originally a personal security force for **Yasser Arafat** and other leaders of the **Palestine Liberation Organization** (PLO). In 1985 its operations were expanded to include terrorist attacks against Israeli targets. Based in **Beirut** before 1982 and since dispersed in several Arab countries, it now operates in Lebanon, other Middle Eastern countries and Europe. The PLO is its main source of support. It has not been responsible for any confirmed terrorist activity outside of Israel and the **Occupied Territories** since September 1985, when it claimed responsibility for killing three **Israelis** in Cyprus, an incident that was followed by Israeli air raids on PLO bases in Tunisia.

Forward (Morocco)

Moroccan radical left-wing political grouping (**Arabic**: Ilal Amam). Founded in 1970 in a split from the Party of Liberation and Socialism (PLS), a Moroccan communist party, over the issue of the **Western Sahara**. Forward supports **Sahrawi** self-determination and the **POLISARIO Front**. Banned from the start, and heavily repressed throughout its existence, the group operated underground. Many members, including its principal leader, Abraham Serfaty, were jailed.

FLAM (African Liberation Forces of Mauritania)

Organized in 1983 in opposition to what were perceived as repressive policies towards Blacks, FLAM was believed to be responsible for an 'Oppressed Black' manifesto which in 1986 was widely distributed within Mauritania and at the **Non-Aligned Movement**'s summit meeting in Zimbabwe. Based partly in Dakar, Senegal, the group also condemned reprisals against Blacks by the **Ould Taya** regime following an alleged coup attempt in 1987. Many FLAM supporters were reported to be among those who fled or were expelled to Senegal in 1989. Subsequently engaged in guerrilla activity, FLAM leaders announced in July 1991 that they were suspending 'armed struggle' in response to the government's general amnesty and the promulgation of a new Mauritanian constitution. FLAM endorsed Ahmed Ould Daddah in the January 1992 presidential election, after which it renewed its anti-governmental military campaign near the Senegalese borders. Leaders of the group stated in early 1995 that they were neither secessionists nor terrorists, reiterating their support for the establishment of a federal system that would ensure an appropriate level of Black representation in government while protecting the rights of Blacks throughout Mauritanian society.

For a Free Eastern Turkestan – *see* Islamic Movement of Uzbekistan

Fraksion-e Hezbollah

Iranian political grouping, formed in 1996 by deputies in the **Majlis** who had contested the 1996 legislative elections as a loose coalition known as the Society of the Combatant Clerics. Its leader is Ali Akbar Hosseini.

Franco-Syrian Treaty of 1936

Also known as the Franco-Syrian Treaty of Friendship and Alliance. An agreement that the French Mandate over Syria would end within three years, signed in Paris by Syrian and French representatives. All Syrian administrative units, with the exception of Alexandretta, were consolidated and made into a single Syrian state. France was granted supervision of Syrian foreign affairs and defence and received the right to use Syrian bases upon the outbreak of war, thus maintaining its influence. Syria was also promised admission to the League of Nations within three years. Owing to divisions among the Syrian leadership and opposition to the Treaty within France, the pact remained unratified.

Franjieh clan.

One of Lebanon's strongest **Maronite** clans, based in the Zghorta region.

Franjieh (Franjiyya), Suleiman

Born in 1910. President of Lebanon in 1970–76. The Franjieh family was one of Lebanon's strongest clans. A **Maronite** Christian, he supported parliamentary reform in 1976 that would have given Muslims more influence; however, this was not implemented until 1989, as part of the agreement that led to the end of the **Lebanese civil war**. He died in 1992.

Free Centre Party

Founded in 1967 by Shmuel Tamir (born 1923) when he and two other **Knesset** members split from the **Herut** party. The Free Centre rejoined Herut in 1973. Subsequently, the larger portion of the former Free Centre, excluding Tamir, joined the La'am faction (organized in 1977) within **Likud**. At the same time, Tamir joined the **Democratic Movement.**

Free Iraq forces

The Free Iraq forces are the troops loyal to **Ahmad Chalabi**, a member of the **Iraqi Provisional Governing Council** after the fall of **Saddam Hussain**, and a politician close to the US administration. During April 2004 the Free Iraq forces and Kurdish *peshmergas* were the only Iraqis to fight alongside US forces.

Free Man—El Hor (Mauritania)

This political grouping in Mauritania is an organization of *harratin*—freedmen or ex-slaves of the Moorish ruling élite. Established in the late 1970s, El Hor was opposed to the continuing existence of slavery in Mauritania despite legislation to ban the practice. Its activities led to the formal abolition of slavery (not for the first time) in July 1980. The group continued to campaign against the effective continuation of slavery and of discrimination against freedmen and ex-slaves.

Free Officers' Movement (Egypt)

Following the 1948 Palestine war, the Free Officers' Movement was formed in 1949 from a revolutionary cell within the army, composed of élite young officers hostile to and suspicious of the reigning political order, which called for political reforms as well as deep-seated change in the structure of Egyptian society. **Gamal Abdel Nasser** became chairman of the organization in January 1950, and Gen. **Muhammed Neguib** was elected president in December 1951. On 23 July 1952 the Movement, led by Nasser, seized power in a bloodless revolution. King **Farouk** was forced to abdicate in favour of his son and left the country for exile in Italy. The nine men who had constituted themselves as the committee of the Movement and led the 1952 revolution were Nasser, Maj. Abd al-Hakim Amir, Lt-Col **Anwar es-Sadat**, Maj. Salah Salim, Maj. Kamal ad-Din Husayn, Wing-Commander Gamal Salim, Squadron Leader Hasan Ibrahim, Maj. Khalid Muhi ad-Din and Wing-Commander Abd al-Latif al-Baghdadi. Maj. Husayn ash-Shafii and Lt-Col Zakariyya Muhi ad-Din also joined the committee later.

Free Officers' Movement (Iraq)

Led by Brig.-Gen. Najib as-Salihi. The Movement was established in 1996. As-Salihi was a commander of an armoured division of the **Republican Guard**. He defected in 1995. In June 2002 the Movement signed a confederation agreement with the Assyrian National Congress. As-Salihi has avoided giving the impression of being hungry for power, and at conferences with the USA he has argued that the **military** should not be directly engaged in politics. He emerged as front-runner in an internet poll conducted by Iraq.net to discover who the Iraqi people would prefer to lead a transitional government. The poll was abandoned after a few days, allegedly because of suspicious voting activity, but possibly because it revealed little popular support for other prominent figures. The Movement has the support of the **Shi'a** Muslims in southern Iraq. Its name is deliberately reminiscent of that led by **Nasser** which brought about the revolution in Egypt.

Freethinkers' Front

Political grouping in Iran.

French policy in the Middle East

France has had an interest in the **Middle East** since the time of the Crusades, but modern French policy in the region could be said to have been initiated by Napoleon Bonaparte. The last major direct French intervention in support of European colonial policy in the Middle East was at the time of the 'Suez crisis', when France joined the United Kingdom and Israel in attempting to reverse by force the Egyptian nationalization of the **Suez Canal**.

French Protectorate of Morocco

Established in 1912, the French Protectorate in Morocco was the formal outcome of a gradual process of intervention and infiltration which had begun during the latter part of the 19th century. It involved most of Morocco, with the exception of the north, which came under Spanish rule (as 'the Spanish Protectorate). Use of the term 'protectorate' enabled France to maintain that its interest was essentially to 'protect' the Moroccan sultanate, although it became in effect a settler colonial state, with a substantial European (mainly French) expatriate community. The Protectorate came to an end in 1956 after many decades of growing pressure from the Moroccan nationalist movement.

Frente Popular para la Liberación de Saguia el-Hamra y Río de Oro – *see* POLISARIO Front

Front des forces démocratiques

Moroccan political grouping. Formed in 1997 after a split from the **Parti du progrès et du socialisme**. Its secretary-general is Thami el-Khiari.

Front des forces socialistes

Algerian political party, established in 1963 and revived in 1990. It is led by **Hocine Aït Ahmed**.

Front for the Defence of Constitutional Institutions (FDIC)

Moroccan political grouping, also (somewhat misleadingly) known as the Royalist Front. The FDIC was established in 1963, but its antecedents have a much longer lineage. A loose coalition whose aim was to counterbalance both the **Istiqlal** and the **monarchy**, to ensure an effective multi-party democracy, the leadership of the FDIC regarded themselves as liberal democratic constitutionalists. Their *zaim*, or mentor, was Rachid Mouline and their predecessor was the party of the Liberal Independents, established in 1955 by 'the friends of Rachid Mouline', an informal grouping around Mouline which had refused to pick sides when the nationalist movement split in 1937 between the followers of Hassan al-Wazzani and **Allal al-Fassi.**

Front for the Liberation of Occupied South Yemen (FLOSY)

The FLOSY was an amalgamation in 1965 of the **National Liberation Front** (NLF, established in 1963) and the leadership of the old **Federation of South Arabia** (notably former chief minister of **Aden** under the British, Abd al-Qawi Makkawi). It was provided with support and financial assistance by the Egyptian government. FLOSY organized the opposition to continuing British rule during 1965 and 1966, but the divisions between the more militant NLF and the FLOSY leadership became more acute, and eventually, in December 1966, the NLF declared itself the sole representative of the people of South Arabia. FLOSY continued to exist, but as the NLF began to gain control in the hinterland and Egypt withdrew its support as a result of the Egyptian withdrawal from Yemen, FLOSY lost ground. Although the NLF was known to have extreme left-wing views, the British preferred it to the pro-**Nasser** FLOSY and assisted its assumption of power. FLOSY was defeated with heavy losses after the army of the Federation of South Arabia declared support for the NLF. In 1967 the NLF took formal control of South Arabia and declared **South Yemen** a unitary state. The FLOSY supporters were repressed brutally and their leaders marginalized.

Fuad, King

King of Egypt from 1917 until 1936.

Fundamentalism

The *Concise Oxford Dictionary of Current English* defines fundamentalism as the 'strict maintenance of ancient or fundamental doctrines of any religion, especially **Islam**'. The term originated as a description of strict adherence to Christian doctrines based on a literal interpretation of the **Bible**. This usage derives from a late 19th–early 20th century transdenominational Protestant movement that opposed the accommodation of Christian doctrine to modern scientific theory and philosophy. However, the term fundamentalist has been misused by the media to refer to terrorists who happen to be Muslims, or to anti-American Muslims. Fundamentalist Islam is simply the conservative wing of Islam, just as Fundamentalist **Christianity** is the conservative wing of Christianity

Fursan Salah ad-Din

An Iraqi Kurdish military force created and supported by the Iraqi **Ba'ath** regime in the early 1960s to fight the *peshmerga* forces of **Mustafa Barzani**, the leader of the Kurdish movement and of the **Kurdish Democratic Party** (KDP) in Iraq from the mid-1950s until the collapse of the movement in March 1975, following the **Algiers Accord** between the Shah of Iran and **Saddam Hussain**, then Iraqi Prime Minister.

The Fursan was made up mainly of Barzani's tribal enemies, led by the Ahmad Talabani faction. Ahmad Talabani belonged to the same **tribe** as **Jalal Talabani**, the present leader of the **Patriotic Union of Kurdistan** (PUK), which fought a long civil war against the KDP. One of the main demands of the Kurdish movement under Barzani, during the negotiations that took place in the late 1960s between Barzani and the Iraqi regime, was the dissolution of the Fursan and an end to the regime's support for them. The regime continued, however, to support the Fursan, although to a considerably lesser extent after 1975. Fursan, and other 'fifth column' groups operating against the **Kurds**, are commonly referred to as *jash*, meaning 'little donkey'—indicating the contempt that most Kurds feel towards these 'traitors'. *Jash* forces continued to operate and to receive support from the Iraqi regime until 1990. After the **Gulf War (1991)** and the Kurdish uprising that followed it, many of the *jash* leaders, along with their men, joined either the PUK or the KDP, depending on their tribal affiliations and other factors.

G

Gaddafy – *see* al-Qaddafi, Col Muammar Abu Minyar

GAFTA – *see* (Greater) Arab Free Trade Area

Gahal

The **Herut-Liberal** bloc in Israeli right-wing politics, created in 1965.

Galilee

Galilee is the northern region of Palestine, assigned by the partition plan of 1947 to the future Arab state and annexed by Israel at the end of the war of 1948–49. It is where the majority of **Israeli Arabs** have tended to live, though the inexorable process of settlement has affected the demography of the region over time. The Galilee is rich in religious history. It was the centre of **Judaism** and of Jesus' preaching. The town of **Nazareth** is in the Galilee, as is Lake Galilee, which is associated with many incidents in the life of Jesus. As a border region adjoining Lebanon, it has frequently been the target of attacks by the **Palestine Liberation Organization**. It was in the name of 'Peace for Galilee' that **Menachem Begin** launched the Israeli invasion of Lebanon in 1982.

Al-Gama'a al-Islamiyya
Egyptian Islamic Group

Egypt's largest militant group, active since the late 1970s; it appears to be loosely organized. It has an external wing with a world-wide presence. The group announced a cease-fire in March 1999, but its spiritual leader, Sheikh **Omar Abdul ar-Rahman**, incarcerated in the USA, withdrew his support for the cease-fire in June 2000. The Gama'a has not conducted an attack inside Egypt since August 1998. Rifa'i Taha Musa—a hardline former senior member of the group—signed **Osama bin Laden**'s *fatwa* in February 1998 that called for attacks against US civilians. The Gama'a has since publicly denied that it supports bin Laden and frequently differs with public statements made by Taha Musa. Taha Musa has, in the last year, sought to push the group towards a return to armed operations, but the Gama'a, which is still led by Mustafa Hamza, has yet to break the unilaterally declared cease-fire. In late 2000 Taha Musa appeared in an undated video with bin Laden and **Ayman az-Zawahiri**, threatening retaliation against the USA for Abdul Rahman's continued incarceration. The Gama'a's primary goal is to overthrow the Egyptian government and replace it with an **Islamic state**, but Taha Musa also may be interested in attacking US and Israeli interests. The Egyptian Government believes that Iran, bin Laden and Afghan militant groups support the organization. It may also obtain some funding from various Islamic non-governmental organizations.

GAP – *see* **Guneydocu Anadolu Projesi**

Garner, Gen. Jay

US Chief of Staff responsible for the Office of Reconstruction and Humanitarian Assistance (ORHA) and the reconstruction of Iraq in January–May 2003. He was replaced shortly after the end of the war by US civilian administrator, **Paul Bremer**. In retrospect, many local Iraqi observers believe that his initial policy, which was more inclusive than that of his successor and envisaged a role for a reconstituted Iraqi army and the **Ba'ath Party**, would have proved more successful than that which was followed subsequently. Garner claims that insufficient resources were allocated to ORHA by the military in the early days.

Gas – *see* **Natural gas**

Gaza – *see* **Gaza Strip**

Gaza Strip

Qita Ghazzah

Gaza is a narrow strip of land (360 sq km in area) with 20 km of coastline bordering the **Mediterranean** Sea, between Egypt and Israel. Before 1967 and its occupation by Israeli forces, it came under the administration of **Cairo**, but was not annexed to Egypt; and before 1948–49 it was a part of the British Mandate of Palestine. Highly urbanized and with several major refugee camps, the population was estimated at 1,225,911 in July 2002. The overwhelming majority are Palestinian Arabs, of whom approximately one-third live in refugee camps, with a minority Jewish settler population comprising 0.6%. There are some 25 major Israeli settlements and civilian land-use sites in the Israeli-occupied Gaza Strip, with a total of about 5,000 Israeli settlers. The vast majority (98.7%) of the people of Gaza are Muslims (predominantly **Sunni**), with small minorities of Christians (0.7%) and Jews (0.6%). Languages spoken are **Arabic**, **Hebrew** (spoken by Israeli settlers and many **Palestinians**) and English (widely understood). Occupied during the **Arab–Israeli War (1967)**, the Gaza Strip has been consistently linked since that time with the idea of a future Palestinian state. The Israel-**Palestine Liberation Organization** (PLO) **Declaration of Principles on Palestinian Self-Rule** (DoP), signed in Washington, DC, on 13 September 1993, provided for a transitional period (not exceeding five years) of Palestinian interim self-government in the Gaza Strip and the **West Bank**. Under the DoP, Israel agreed to transfer certain powers and responsibilities to the **Palestinian (National) Authority** (P(N)A), which included the Palestinian Legislative Council elected in January 1996, as part of the interim self-governing arrangements. A transfer of powers and responsibilities for the Gaza Strip and **Jericho** took place pursuant to the Israel-PLO 4 May 1994 **Cairo Agreement on the Gaza Strip and Jericho** and in additional areas of the West Bank pursuant to the Israel-PLO 28 September 1995 Interim Agreement, the Israel-PLO 15 January 1997 Protocol Concerning Redeployment in **Hebron**, the **Israel-PLO 23 October 1998 Wye River Memorandum**, and the 4 September 1999 **Sharm esh-Sheikh Agreement (Memorandum)**. The DoP provides that Israel will retain responsibility during the transitional period for external security and for internal security and public order of settlements and Israeli citizens. Direct negotiations to determine the permanent status of Gaza and the West Bank had begun in September 1999 after a three-year hiatus, but were interrupted by a second *intifada* (the **al-Aqsa** *intifada*) that broke out in September 2000. The resulting widespread violence in the West Bank and Gaza Strip, Israel's military response, and instability within the P(N)A continue to undermine progress toward a permanent agreement. During 2003–04 the Israeli government initiated a process aimed at eventually dismantling many of the settlements in the Gaza Strip.

Gaza Strip, economy

Economic output in the Gaza Strip—under the responsibility of the **Palestinian National Authority** (PNA) since the **Cairo Agreement on the Gaza Strip and Jericho** of May 1994—declined by about one-third in 1992–96. The downturn was largely the result of Israeli closure policies—the imposition of generalized border closures in response to security incidents in Israel—which disrupted previously established labour and commodity market relationships between Israel and the **West Bank** and Gaza Strip. The most serious negative social effect of this downturn was the emergence of high unemployment: unemployment in the West Bank and Gaza Strip during the 1980s was generally under 5%; by 1995 it had risen to more than 20%. Israel's use of comprehensive closures decreased during the next few years and, in 1998, Israel implemented new policies to reduce the impact of closures and other security procedures on the movement of Palestinian goods and labour. These changes fuelled economic recovery lasting almost three years in the West Bank and

Gaza Strip; real gross domestic product (GDP) grew by 5% in 1998 and by 6% in 1999. Recovery ended in the final quarter of 2000, however, with the outbreak of Palestinian violence, triggering stringent Israeli closures of Palestinian self-rule areas and a severe disruption of **trade** and labour movements. In 2001, and even more severely in early 2002, internal turmoil and Israeli military measures in PNA areas resulted in the destruction of capital plant and administrative structure, widespread business closures, and a sharp drop in GDP. Another major loss has been the decline in income earned by Palestinian workers in Israel. West Bank and Gaza Strip are Israeli-occupied with current status subject to the **Israeli-Palestinian Interim Agreement**—permanent status to be determined through further negotiation.

GCC – *see* **Gulf Co-operation Council**

Gemayel, Amin

President of Lebanon from 1982 until 1988. Following the assassination of his brother Bashir in 1982, Amin was elected as President. A central dilemma to his politics was the need to meet the demands of Muslims, without alienating support from his own Christian community. Balancing the interests towards Syria was another challenge, and although he was helped to power by Syria, he lost its support after two years. A large part of Lebanon was outside his jurisdiction; in the north, pro- and anti-Syrian groups fought and in the southern Israeli-dominated area, Phalangists and **Druze** were in conflict. Even in the government-controlled areas in central Lebanon, many militia groups were fighting each other. In 1984 Gemayel deployed the army against the **Shi'a** strongholds of west **Beirut**, but it failed to bring them under government control. Instead, the Lebanese army started to split according to its religious divisions. At the end of his term of office in 1988 Gemayel moved to the USA and Europe, but he returned to Lebanon in 2000 to become, once again, politically active.

Gemayel, Bashir

Born in 1947. Son of **Pierre Gemayel**. Lebanese politician and President-elect in 1982. Architect of the secret pact with Israel to remove **Palestinian Liberation Organization** (PLO) guerrillas from Lebanon. With the outbreak of the **Lebanese civil war** in 1975, he joined the Phalangist militia fighting the PLO forces and was subsequently appointed head of the unified command of the Lebanese forces, a coalition of Christian militias of the Phalange Party, the national **Liberal Party**, the Tanzim and the Guardians of the Cedars. In January 1976, in an extraordinary alliance with **Ali Hassan Salameh** (head of **al-Fatah** security), he organized a 48-hour truce with al-Fatah (with which the Israeli-backed Christian militia had been fighting savagely for years) in order to rob the British Bank of the Middle East in

Beirut. In 1978 he was allegedly involved in the assassination of Tony Franjieh, the son of the then Lebanese President, and in 1981 he became the chief of the Phalange Security Council and a member of the party's politburo. In the following year he was elected as President of Lebanon with 57 out of 65 votes and prepared to establish diplomatic relations with **Menachem Begin** of Israel. In September of 1982, however, he was killed in a bomb attack on the Phalangist headquarters in Ashrafiyya, Beirut, together with 26 others. This was only eight days before he was due to be installed in office. It was later discovered that the bomb had been placed at the headquarters by *Syrian* agents.

Gemayel, Pierre

Born in 1905. Lebanese politican and founder of the Phalange Party in 1936. Father of **Bashir Gemayel** and **Amin Gemayel**. Died in 1984, two years after his son Bashir was assassinated.

General People's Congress (Yemen)

Ruling party in Yemen. Won an emphatic victory in the most recent election.

General Security Service (GSS)

Israeli security and intelligence service, known as Shabak. It has been particularly effective since September 2000, during the recent **al-Aqsa** *intifada*. GSS, which used to rely largely on human intelligence, has now developed extensive technical capacity for 'signals intelligence', which has assisted it considerably in recent operations.

Geneva Accord

A 50-page plan covering a set of points of agreement reached between Palestinian and Israeli representatives, led by **Yossi Beilin**, a former Israeli Cabinet minister, and Yasser Abed Rabbo, a former Palestinian Cabinet minister, after unofficial discussions held in Geneva, Switzerland, during November 2003. The plan was launched at the beginning of December with a ceremony involving former US President **Jimmy Carter**. Former Soviet leader **Mikhail Gorbachev** and 56 other presidents, prime ministers, foreign secretaries and other leaders offered their support in a jointly published letter. The accord received only qualified public support from **Yasser Arafat**; two leading members of the Palestinian team that negotiated the Accord withdrew from the ceremony after Arafat refused to give written confirmation of his backing for the so-called Geneva process. The **al-Aqsa Martyrs' Brigade** denounced the delegation as 'collaborators with Israel'. **Ariel Sharon**'s official spokesman dismissed the Accord as 'a Swiss golden calf', or false idol. The Accord proposes the creation of a wholly independent Palestinian state. **Palestinians** would recognize Israel as a Jewish state and end violence against it.

There would be compensation for the 3.5m. Palestinians whose land has been appropriated by Israel. In return, the Palestinians would, for the most part, give up their claim to a right of return. Israel would incorporate about 25% of the illegal Jewish **settlements** on the **West Bank** and leave the remaining 75% inside the Palestinian state. **Jerusalem** would be divided, with **East Jerusalem** incorporated into the Palestinian state. Israel would cede sovereignty over the site in Jerusalem's old city known to Jews as Temple Mount and to Muslims as al-Haram ash-Sharif.

Gesher

Israeli political grouping founded in 1996. It is led by David Levi

Ghaith, Sulaiman Abu

Kuwaiti-born Abu Ghaith was an imam and member of the **Muslim Brotherhood** before travelling to Bosnia to fight alongside Muslim forces there. Pictured seated alongside **Osama bin Laden** during his interview on **al-Jazeera** television after the attacks on US targets on 11 September 2001, Abu Ghaith is considered a trusted insider and chief spokesman for **al-Qa'ida**. It is believed that he is among those al-Qa'ida members held by the Iranian authorities, along with other leaders, including possibly Saif al-Adel (also known as **Mohamed Makkawi**), the latest chief of al-Qa'ida military operations.

Ghanim, Shukri Muhammad

Libyan Prime Minister since June 2003, when he replaced Mubarak Abdallah ash-Shamikh. An economist and former Minister of Economy and Trade, Ghanim is in favour of a more liberal economic regime in Libya. Col **Qaddafi** has recently spoken of his desire to open up the Libyan economy to foreign investment and even talked about privatizing upstream **oil** and **gas** assets. The appointment of Ghanim undoubtedly reflects this new thinking.

Ghashmi, Ahmad Hussein

President of **North Yemen** from 1977 until 1978, when he was overthrown in a coup and replaced by **Ali Abdullah Salih**.

Abu Ghraib

Notorious Iraqi prison complex where the Iraqi regime of **Saddam Hussain** incarcerated political prisoners, mistreating and torturing them. It also became a focus of attention when pictures and accounts were released and published world-wide during May 2004 that revealed gross abuse of Iraqi prisoners by US troops. US President **George W. Bush** apologized, in a speech made shortly after the reports of US torture of Iraqi prisoners had been made public, and promised that he would finance the destruction of the old prison and the construction of a new one, if so requested by the Iraqi authorities.

Gibraltar Straits

The narrow waterway between Tangier in Morocco and Gibraltar (and Spain) in the Iberian Peninsula, western Europe. Links the **Mediterranean** Sea with the Atlantic Ocean.

GIA—Groupe islamique armé

Armed Islamic Group, Algeria

An Algerian Islamic extremist group, aiming at the overthrow of the secular regime in Algeria and its replacement with an **Islamic state**. The GIA began its violent activity in 1992–93 after the government had nullified the success of the **FIS—Front islamique du salut** (Islamic Salvation Front), the largest Islamic opposition party—in the first round of legislative elections in December 1991. It claimed to be involved in a *jihad* or holy war. It was led initially by Abdelhak Layada. Many members of the banned FIS joined its ranks. Some of its members are thought to have been trained and to have fought in Afghanistan. It has also been suggested that some have had experience in Pakistan, Yemen, Syria, Sudan, Bosnia and **Chechnya**. The Algerian Islamist Khamareddine Kherbane, an Afghan veteran, was close both to the GIA and to the leadership of **al-Qa'ida**. At the outset the GIA focused its attention on the assassination of specific individual targets, particularly diplomats, clergy, industrialists, intellectuals, feminists, journalists, priests and foreigners. The intelligentsia, especially those thought to have been influenced by Western values (which often included **Berbers**), were branded 'false Muslims' or 'anti-Islamic civilians' and selectively targeted. After announcing a campaign of terror against foreigners living in Algeria in 1993, the GIA killed more than 100 expatriate men and women—mostly Europeans. It developed cells and networks among expatriate Algerians in Europe, mainly in France. In 1994 it hijacked an Air France flight to **Algiers**. In July 1995 one of its leaders, Zitouni, who had been in charge since October 1994, was assassinated. In 1996 there were splits within the GIA that led to a number of groups being formed. Antar Zouabri emerged as the leader of the main faction. From 1996 onwards the GIA campaign broadened in scale and scope. The group uses assassinations and bombings, including car bombs; many thousands of Algerian civilians have been killed, individually and in groups. There were massacres of whole communities. The level of violence associated with the GIA prompted four other north African Islamist groups—including the **Libyan Islamic Fighting Group** and Egyptian **Islamic Jihad**—to issue communiqués denouncing the cult of violence and by mid-1996 to withdraw their support from the GIA. On 8 September 1997 the GIA issued a declaration justifying the massacres, stating that the Algerian people were 'kaffirs [unbelievers], apostates and hypocrites' because they did not support the GIA against the government. It was claimed that all of its extreme actions were 'for the cause of Allah'. Al Qa'ida severed its links with the GIA leadership, denounced Antar Zouabri and encouraged Hassan Hattab, the head of the GIA's European network (who also disagreed with Muslims killing each other), to break way and join the **GSPC—Groupe salafiste pour la prédication et le combat** (Salafist Group for Call and Combat), a group formed in May 1998 with several hundred former GIA members. Thereafter, al-Qa'ida support was concentrated on the GSPC, which it penetrated during the two years between 1998 and 2000. The GIA was led by nine 'emir' generals during its first eight years, all of whom were either killed or imprisoned. Antar Zouabri, the main 'emir' at the time, was killed along with two of his henchmen by security forces in February 2002 in his home town of Boufarik, near Algiers. According to unconfirmed reports, his successor, Rachid Abou Tourab, was killed by security forces in June 2002. The total number of GIA members is unknown. Estimates vary between 200 and several thousand. An estimated 1,000 GIA members surrendered to the Algerian authorities within the framework of the Law of Civil Harmony (Accord) in 1999–2000, but there remained an active hard core which continued to operate throughout the first half of the new decade. It is generally thought that the GIA recruits heavily from among the unemployed youth of the urban poor, but in fact relatively little is known in detail of its membership. Although in recent years, its activities have been reduced, there remain active cells in many parts of the country, including several of the larger towns, particularly Algiers—usually in the popular quarters (e.g. Bab el Oued, etc.).

Giza

Al-Jiza, the third largest city in Egypt, with some 3m. inhabitants.

Global Risk Strategies (GRS)

A London-based security company operating in Iraq. Until the invasion of Afghanistan, GRS was a two-man team. In 2003–04 it employed more than 1,000 guards in Iraq—a greater force than those of many of the countries taking part in the occupation and security maintenance operations—manning the barricades of the **Coalition Provisional Authority**. In 2003 it won a contract to distribute the new Iraqi currency.

Globalization

A term increasingly used during the 1990s and early years of the 21st century to refer to the process of global economic (and social) integration as a consequence of international liberalization and domestic economic reforms and privatization.

Glubb, (Pasha) Sir John Bagot

Born in 1897, died in 1986. He served in France during the First World War and in 1920 was posted to Iraq, where he lived among Arab **Bedouins** and studied their language and culture. After serving as administrative inspector for the Iraqi government from 1926 until 1930, Glubb was transferred to Jordan and attached to the Arab Legion, of which he assumed command in 1939. He was replaced by a Jordanian general in the 1950s.

Golan Heights

The Golan Heights is a plateau on the border of Israel, Lebanon, Jordan and Syria. It is one of the territories captured by Israel during the **Arab–Israeli War (1967)**. The Golan Heights are currently under Israeli control, though claimed by Syria. The Syrian and Israeli governments are still contesting the ownership of the Heights, but have not used overt military force since 1974. The great strategic value of the Heights both militarily and as a source of **water** means that an agreement is uncertain. The Heights were controlled by the Israeli army from 1967 until 1981, when the **Knesset** annexed the land by the Golan Heights Law. This annexation has not been internationally recognized, and the Golan is generally considered occupied territory. The final status of the Golan Heights is to be determined as part of a peace agreement between Israel and Syria. The 1981 law awarded Israeli citizenship to the Syrian citizens who remained in the area after the 1967 war. The Israeli position has been a source of criticism from the international community, which demands withdrawal. In addition, the international community demands that the original inhabitants made **refugees** by the invading Israeli army should be allowed to return. By 1991 there was a Jewish settler population of about 12,000 in 21 **settlements** and a predominantly **Druze** population of about 16,000 living in the six remaining villages. Talks on the future of the Golan collapsed in 1999 after the start of the **al-Aqsa** *intifada*. Renewed interest on the part of Syria in reviving talks on the Golan Heights, as part of President **Bashar al-Assad**'s call, towards the end of 2003, for the renewal of peace negotiations, was met with Israeli plans to double the number of settlers on the Golan Heights. The Israeli Cabinet committee on settlements approved a plan by the Israeli agriculture minister, Yisrael Katz, to spend £40m. on housing for more than 10,000 new settlers, who will be encouraged by land grants and tax incentives.

Gold

Gold is one of the most secure means of exchange and mediums in which to hold assets. It is widely used in the region by government central banks to back currencies and by private banks to support their activities. The value of currencies associated with paper money depend on the faith in the governments or authorities which issue them; often these are dependent on guarantees of gold reserves and holdings. An example is that of the **Taliban** Government in Afghanistan, which demanded that taxes on **opium** production and other **income** be paid in gold, not in cash. Indian and Pakistani trucking companies operating in Afghanistan had to pay road access taxes in gold. Often donations to **Osama bin Laden** and his followers in Afghanistan would arrive in the form of gold—boxes of gold bullion were flown from Dubai to **Kandahar** on Ariana, the Afghan airline, aboard regular scheduled flights. When the Taliban regime collapsed, **al-Qa'ida** shipped several containers of gold to Sudan. The Taliban took an estimated US $10m.-worth of gold out of the country—one of the couriers was the Taliban consul-general in Karachi, Kaka Zada, who carried at least one shipment worth $600,000 to Dubai, where the bulk of the Taliban's gold and foreign exchange had been transferred before the 2001 war in Afghanistan. Dubai is a major centre of gold trading and gold smuggling as well as a major financial centre for the region as a whole.

Governing Council (Iraq) – *see* Iraqi Provisional Governing Council

Gnosticism

Gnosticism is a philosophical and religious movement which developed in pre-Christian times. The term is derived from the Greek word gnosis which means 'knowledge'. Gnostics claimed to have secret knowledge about God, humanity and the rest of the universe of which the general population was unaware. It became one of the three main belief systems within 1st century Christianity, and was noted for three factors which differed from other branches of Christianity:

- Novel beliefs about Gods, the **Bible** and the world which differed from those of other Christian groups.
- Tolerance of different religious beliefs within and outside of Gnosticism.
- Non-discrimination against **women**.
- A belief that salvation is achieved through knowledge.

The movement and its literature were essentially wiped out by the end of the 5th century CE by heresy hunters from mainline Christianity. However, its beliefs are still alive in the contemporary world.

Gorbachev, Mikhail

Born in 1931, Gorbachev was the last leader of the Soviet Union. From 1985 until 1991 he was the general secretary of the Communist Party. He also served as deputy chairman of the Supreme Soviet in 1970–90 and acted as chairman for the Foreign Affairs Committee of the Soviet of the Union in 1984–85. From 1985 until 1990 he was a member in the Presidium of the Supreme Soviet of the USSR, serving as its president in 1989–90. He was President of the USSR in 1990–91. He inherited the

Soviet intervention in Afghanistan, and for several years pursued the war. He initiated the policies of *perestroika* and *glasnost*, which led to an upsurge of ethnic nationalism in the southern Muslim republics of **Central Asia**, as well as a rebirth of **political Islam**. In 1989 he ordered the withdrawal of Soviet forces from Afghanistan.

Great Eastern Islamic Raiders' Front

A small fundamentalist group in Turkey which claimed responsibility for the bombing of the Neve Shalom and the Beth Israel synagogues in **Istanbul** in November 2003.

Great Game

Refers to the colonial enterprise in **Central Asia**, and, in particular, to the struggle between Russia and Britain for supremacy in Asia. The term was coined by one of the Great Game's Russian participants.

Greater Syria

Term used to designate the region that included, approximately, the present-day states of Jordan, Israel, Lebanon, and Syria before those states were formed. In present-day Syria there are still political elements that favour the formation of a Greater Syria, or at least of a Syria that includes Lebanon.

Greek Cypriotic Republic of Cyprus – *see* Cyprus

Green Book

Libyan leader Col **Qaddafi**'s two-volume series outlining his views, influenced by **Islam**, **socialism** and **Arab nationalism**. (See also **Third International Theory**.)

Green Leaf Party

Israeli political grouping.

Green march

In late 1975 King **Hassan II** of Morocco urged Moroccans to march *en masse* across the border into the former **Spanish Sahara** (**Western Sahara**) to lay claim to the territory, whose inhabitants, the **Sahrawis**, were calling for self-determination and had been fighting since 1973 for their independence.

Green Party

Egyptian political party, founded in 1990. The Party's chairman is Dr Abd al-Moneim el-Aasar.

Green Party

Israeli environmentalist party.

Groupe islamique armé – *see* GIA

Groupe islamique des combatants marocains (GICM)

A Moroccan Islamist group believed to be behind bomb attacks in **Casablanca** in May 2003, which killed 33 people and led to the deaths of 12 suicide bombers. The GICM is also thought to have been associated with the bombings in Madrid, Spain, in March 2004. Some six Islamists suspected of carrying out the Madrid train bombings blew themselves up after being cornered by the police in a flat in the Madrid suburb of Leganes on 3 April. Shortly prior to that, explosives had been found on the Madrid–Seville high-speed railtrack. A total of 16 suspects were taken into custody; 15 were charged, 11 of them Moroccans.

GSPC—Groupe salafiste pour la prédication et le combat

Salafist Group for Call and Combat, Algeria

The GSPC was formerly a faction of the **Groupe islamique armé** (Armed Islamic Group), from which it split in mid-1998. Its leader was Hassan Hattab. It has a fearsome reputation, but has pledged to avoid attacks on civilians as far as possible. It is linked to the radical wing of the **FIS—Front islamique du salut** (Islamic Salvation Front) and is thought to have links to **al-Qa'ida**. It responds to preaching by **Ali Belhadj**, one of the most prominent leaders of the banned FIS. It began operations in the region east of **Algiers** and Kabylia—in the region between Boumerda province and Kabylia. Some of its 'emirs' are of **Berber** (Kabyle) origin. It is now reported to have groups in eastern Algeria, notably Jijel, Tizi Ouzou, Sétif and the area around Constantine. A GSPC group also operates in the Lakhdaria-Kadiria region, 70 km south of Algiers. The local 'emir' of this el-Farouk group is reportedly Ahmed Djebri. The GSPC operates in some cities, such as Boghni. Its numerical strength is unknown. Estimates range from several hundreds to several thousands inside Algeria. The GSPC has networks outside Algeria, notably in Europe. About 90 members reportedly surrendered under an amnesty in 1999–2000.

Gulf (Persian/Arabian)

The waterway which serves as a major passage for **oil** and other exports from southern Iraq, Kuwait, southern Iran and the United Arab Emirates.

Gulf Co-operation Council (GCC)

Also known as the Co-operation Council for the Arab States of the **Gulf**. It was established on 25 May 1981, with the aim of promoting regional co-operation in economic, social, political and military affairs. Its member states are Bahrain, Kuwait, Oman, Qatar, Saudi Arabia and the United Arab Emirates. A **Gulf Investment Corporation** was set up at the same time. A common minimum customs levy on foreign imports was imposed from 1986. In May 1992 the GCC **trade** ministers announced the objective of establishing a GCC common market, but progress was slow. The technical committee charged with considering the practicalities of establishing a customs union met first in June 1998. In November 1999 the Supreme Council of the GCC concluded an agreement to establish such a union by 1 March 2005. In December it was agreed to bring the date forward to 1 January 2003. The agreement also provided for the introduction, by 1 January 2010, of a GCC single currency, linked to the US dollar.

Gulf crisis

The term refers to the events leading to the Iraqi invasion of Kuwait (see also **Gulf Wars**). Although Iraq had claimed Kuwait as a lost territory on numerous occasions, it had no legitimate historical claim to the country. Iraq wanted access to the **Gulf**. After failing to obtain that access in its war with Iran, Iraqi attention returned to Kuwait. Iraq had amassed a substantial war **debt**, and Kuwait was one of its creditors. The Iraqi economy was in crisis, and Iraq lacked the funds to rebuild its infrastructure, or even to import the food it needed. Also, Iraq perceived itself as having defended and sacrificed its own people to protect the other, wealthier Arab nations from Iranian **fundamentalism**.

As soon as the **Iraq–Iran War** ended, Kuwait started over-producing **oil**. This drove the price of oil down just when Iraq most needed **income** from oil sales. Moreover, Kuwait was in all likelihood pumping oil from the Iraqi side of a shared oilfield. Unlike Saudi Arabia, Kuwait refused to forgive Iraqi war debts. Kuwait had supported Iraq during the war with Iran. After the war ended, Kuwait began to strengthen its ties with Iran, while opposing Iraqi membership of the **Gulf Co-operation Council**. Kuwait viewed compromise with Iraqi demands as capitulation to threats and intimidation, and so took a hardline stance against Iraq's demands. **Saddam Hussain** gave a number of warning signals between February 1990 and the time of the Iraqi invasion on 2 August 1990. In a speech made on 17 July he threatened, 'if words fail to protect Iraqis, something effective must be done'. However, only the USA and the other Arab nations made any attempts at preventative diplomacy. The USA sent mixed and confusing signals to Iraq. The USA believed that Iraq was simply bluffing and threatening. If there were an invasion, it would be a limited one. On the same day that the Department of State stressed the USA's strong commitment to 'supporting the individual and collective self-defence of our friends in the Gulf', another Department of State spokesperson stated that 'we do not have any defence treaties with Kuwait, and there are no special defence or security commitments to Kuwait'. Saudi Arabia, backed by other Arab nations, exerted pressure on Kuwait to negotiate and settle the dispute with Iraq. The leaders of Saudi Arabia, Jordan and Egypt engaged in active, if ineffective, diplomacy, travelling extensively between **Baghdad** and the other Arab capitals. Misperceptions and ambiguous signals led the Arab nations to underestimate the likelihood of an Iraqi military invasion. Saudi Arabia arranged a meeting between Kuwaiti and Iraqi representatives on 31 July 1990. Kuwait offered some concessions, but the meeting ended inconclusively. Saddam Hussain appears to have viewed that meeting as Kuwait's last chance to address Iraq's demands.

Gulf International Bank

Established in 1976 by the six member states of the **Gulf Co-operation Council** and Iraq. In 1991 it became a wholly-owned subsidiary of the **Gulf Investment Corporation** (without Iraqi shareholdings). In 1999 it merged with the Saudi Investment Bank.

Gulf Investment Corporation

Established in 1983 by the six member states of the **Gulf Co-operation Council** for investment, chiefly in the **Gulf**, and for industrial, trading and banking operations and activities. Its resources come from contributions by member states.

Gulf Rapid Deployment Force

Initially deployed in the **Gulf** area to safeguard the supply of **oil**. Now there is an expanded Rapid Deployment Force, the US Central Command that will serve approximately the same purpose, though its theatre of operations has been expanded to include south-west Asia.

Gulf states

Though there are eight countries with coasts to the **Gulf**, it is the six **monarchies**, emirates and sheikhdoms of Bahrain, Oman, Kuwait, Qatar, Saudi Arabia and the United Arab Emirates that are normally designated by this term. The two countries excluded are Iran and Iraq.

Gulf War (1991)

The Gulf War (1991) followed Iraq's invasion of Kuwait in August 1990 and the assembly of a coalition force led by the USA in the aftermath of that invasion between September 1990 and January 1991. US President **George Bush** eventually stipulated that **Saddam Hussain** must withdraw Iraqi troops from Kuwait by 16 January 1991. Hussain's failure to comply with that demnd led the US Administration to initiate the war with heavy aerial bombing of **Baghdad** and other strategic targets, followed, after 39 days and 91,000 air missions, by a ground offensive against the Iraqi forces. The ground war lasted five days and the Iraqi forces were overwhelmed. President George Bush announced the end of the war on 27 February 1991 and Iraq agreed to a cease-fire on the following day. See also **Iraq War (1991)**.

Gulf War (2003)

Throughout the years between 1998 and 2003, the US administration was increasingly persuaded that military intervention against Iraq was needed. A letter from a group of 'neo-conservatives' to President **Bill Clinton** in January 1998 remarked that the policy of **containment** had been eroding, that the **Gulf War (1991)** coalition had fallen apart and that the weapons inspection regime in Iraq was becoming increasingly ineffectual. US policy, they stated, should no longer be crippled by a misguided insistence on unanimity in the UN Security Council. The only acceptable strategy, they argued, was one that eliminated the possibility that Iraq would be able to use or threaten to use **weapons of mass destruction**. In the near term this meant undertaking military action, and in the long term removing **Saddam Hussain** from power. This lobby successfully pursued the enactment of the **Iraq Liberation Act** (signed into law reluctantly by Clinton) in October 1998 and set the scene for the subsequent military intervention. The presidential campaign intervened, but during 2001 US policy was increasingly driven by the thinking that lay behind the Iraq Liberation Act and, after the attacks on Washington, DC, and New York in September 2001, the US Administration effectively decided to go to war against Iraq. The war plan against Afghanistan reached the President's desk on 17 September 2001; he signed it at once, but at the end of the document was a direction to the Pentagon to draw up military options for an invasion of Iraq. In a speech at West Point on 1 June 2002, President **Bush** unveiled what was to become 'the Bush doctrine' of pre-emptive military action. By August the die was cast. The issue was now not whether to attack Iraq but when and how. In early September 2002 President Bush and UK Prime Minister Tony Blair met at **Camp David** in Maryland. The British Prime Minister in particular was all too aware that, internationally, there was considerable anxiety regarding the legitimacy of any military intervention in Iraq beyond the kind of operations that had been continuing throughout the 1990s. The British government, although supporting the US administration, was concerned to secure an additional UN resolution, to provide evidence of commitment on the part of the international community as a whole. Bush seemed to agree. However, the additional UN resolution was not forthcoming and a number of states (including Germany, France and Russia) actively opposed military intervention, as did many ordinary people in most Western countries, including Britain. Despite this, the US administration was now visibly moving towards military intervention in Iraq, with a view to overthrowing Saddam Hussein and his regime. At the end of September 2002 Blair argued before the British Parliament that Saddam Hussein represented a clear and present danger and promised to publish a dossier proving that he had weapons of mass destruction and was preparing to use them. In the mean time efforts to secure a UN resolution to cover further action against Iraq continued. On 8 November 2002 the UN finally agreed the ambiguous Resolution 1441, which was generally regarded as not in itself sufficient to authorize a military intervention in Iraq.

Gulf Wars

Refers to the three Gulf Wars; Iraq has been involved in all of them. The first was the **Iran–Iraq War** (1980–88). The second was the **Gulf War (1991)**, the UN-sanctioned war against Iraq in 1991 after its occupation of Kuwait in 1990. The third **Gulf War (2003)** refers to the US/UK war on Iraq that ousted the regime of **Saddam Hussein** in 2003.

Guneydocu Anadolu Projesi (GAP)

A major investment and development project in south-eastern Turkey, in the Kurdish area. It involves the construction of a major dam complex (which will affect the flow of the **Tigris** and **Euphrates** rivers and, hence, relations with Syria and Iraq), irrigation facilities, hydro-electric power facilities and other infrastructure.

Gürsel, Gen. Cemal

Involved in the **military** coup which overthrew Turkish President Bayar in 1960. Held power from May 1960 until October 1961 and, subsequently, as President, until 1966.

Gush Emunim

A **Hebrew** term translated as 'Bloc of the Faithful'. A right-wing Israeli political-religious movement, calling for the right of Jews to settle everywhere in **Eretz Israel**. Founded in 1974, it was spawned from the **National Religious Party**, which in 1970 captured attention by establishing an unauthorized **settlement** at Kiryat Arba near **Hebron**. In the 1970s it was actively involved in raids and illegal occupations in heavily populated Palestinian Arab areas. On the eve of **Menachem**

Begin's electoral victory in 1977 five settlements had been formed in this way. It has had close links with various right-wing Israeli governments and has been involved in acts of **terrorism** against **Palestinians**. Its influence began to wane after the Palestinian *intifada*. It opposed the Oslo process and applauded the massacre by Baruch Goldstein (a resident of Kiryat Arba settlement) of 29 Palestinians at prayer in Hebron. It shared with **Kach** a twofold demand: the annexation of the **Occupied Territories** and the expulsion of their Palestinian inhabitants. Gush Emunim is led by Rabbi Moshe Levinger.

H

Ha'aretz

Leading Israeli daily newspaper, often critical of the Israeli government.

Habash, George

Born *c.* 1925–26 in Lydda, Palestine (now Lod, Israel). Militant Palestinian and leader of the **Popular Front for the Liberation of Palestine**.

Habibi, Hassan

Member of the **Council of Guardians** (Iran).

Hadash

Left-wing Israeli political grouping. Also known as the **Democratic Front for Peace and Equality**—or the Communist Party of Israel. Descended from the Socialist Workers Party of Palestine founded in 1919, the **Israel Communist Party** (**Maki**), founded in 1948, and a pro-Soviet anti-Zionist group which formed the New Communist Party of Israel (**Rakah**) in 1965. Hadash has Jewish and Arab members and aims for a socialist system in Israel, a lasting peace between Israel and the Arab states and the Palestinian Arab people. It favours the full implementation of **UN Security Council Resolution 242** and **338**; Israeli withdrawal from all Arab territories occupied since 1967; the formation of a Palestinian Arab state in the **West Bank** and **Gaza Strip** (with **East Jerusalem** as its capital); the recognition of the national rights of the State of Israel and of the Palestinian people; and democratic rights and the defence of working-class interests. Hadash also demands an end to discrimination against the Arab **minority** in Israel and against oriental Jewish communities. It is led by Muhammad Baraka. The Communist Party is led by Muhammad Nafah and Hadash by Odde Bsharat.

Haddad, Wadi

Palestinian graduate in medicine from the American University of **Beirut**. Together with some of his student colleagues—including **George Habash** and Ahmad al-Khatib—he founded the **Movement of Arab Nationalists** (MAN). In 1968 Haddad and Habash transformed the MAN into the **Popular Front for the Liberation of Palestine**.

Hadith

The body of traditions about the sayings and acts of the **Prophet Muhammad** that delineate proper Muslim behaviour and, together with the **Koran**, constitutes the basis for **Shari'a**.

Al-Hafiz, Amin

Head of state of Syria in 1963–66.

Haganah

Haganah was the forerunner of the **Israeli Defence Force** and the heir of **Hashomer**. It was an underground intelligence organization serving the interests of the Jews in Palestine. There were various factions and splits within Haganah and eventually one splinter group, Haganah B, united with the youth group of **Vladimir Jabotinsky** to form the so-called counter-terrorist organization **Irgun Zvai Leumi**, which was in effect a paramilitary organization with its own intelligence network, under David Raziel. However, the mainstream Haganah was intent upon the pursuit of peaceful policies and opposed Jewish vigilantism as a response to Arab attacks.

Haichud Haleumi

National Unity

Israeli right-wing coalition, formed in 1999, comprising the **Herut**, **Moledet** and Tekuma parties. In February 2000 Herut withdrew from this coalition, which subsequently merged with **Israel B'Aitainu**.

Ould Haidalla, Lt-Col Khouna

Head of state of Mauritania from January 1980 until December 1984, when he was overthrown by Col **Maaouiya Ould Sidi Ahmed Taya**.

Haifa

Centre of the **Baha'i** faith. Pilgrims visit the Baha'i holy places in Haifa and in and around **Acre** throughout the year (except for the months of August and September).

Al-Hairiu, Kazim al-Husseini

Iraqi **Shi'ite** religious leader who supports the reinstatement of an Islamic government in Iraq.

Hajj/Hagg

In **Arabic** the word means 'pilgrimage'. The annual pilgrimage to **Mecca**, a religious rite to be performed by every Muslim at least once if economically posssible. The *Hajj* is one of the **Five Pillars of Islam**.

Al-Hakim, Abd al-Aziz

A **Shi'ite** Muslim member of the **Supreme Council for the Islamic Revolution in Iraq** (SCIRI). Abd al-Aziz is the brother of SCIRI leader **Ayatollah Muhammad Baqir al-Hakim**. SCIRI opposes the US-led administration in Iraq, but Abd al-Aziz is also a member of the Iraqi **Governing Council** which was inaugurated in **Baghdad** on 13 July 2003, marking the first step towards the formation of a democratic government in Iraq.

Al-Hakim, Ayatollah Muhammad Baqir

Shi'ite cleric and political leader (Iraq). Born in **Najaf**, where his father was a senior cleric, al-Hakim received a traditional Shi'ite cleric's training. He was arrested and tortured for his beliefs by the forces of **Saddam Hussain** in 1972. Five of his brothers and another dozen or so of his relatives were killed by the Ba'athist regime. He belonged to the Shi'ite **ad-Da'awa** (Call) group, which periodically launched attacks on the regime. In 1980 he fled to Iran, just as the **Iran–Iraq War** began. In **Tehran** he created the **Supreme Council for the Islamic Revolution in Iraq** (SCIRI), an umbrella group encompassing ad-Da'awa and other organizations. He was angry with what he referred to as US President **George Bush**'s 'betrayal' of the Shi'ites in Iraq when in 1991 he encouraged them to rise up against the regime of Saddam Hussain, but failed to provide support, leaving the rebels at the mercy of the Iraqi Republican Guard. Tens of thousands of southern Iraqi Shi'ites may have been killed as a consequence. Al-Hakim had spent 23 years in exile in Tehran before returning to Iraq on behalf of SCIRI after the 2003 conflict, and has sometimes been accused of having fallen under the influence of Iranian clerics, such as Ayatollah **Ali Khameini**. However, he has taken pains to emphasize the pluralism of the Shi'ite movement. After 2001 he also suggested that he no longer proposed an Iranian-style *velayat-i faqih* (rule by clerics) for Iraq. Al-Hakim returned to Iraq, and to Najaf, in May 2003 to considerable acclaim and adulation. In July he agreed to nominate a representative to the new US-appointed **Governing Council**. He encouraged his brother, Abdul Aziz, to sit on the provisional Governing Council, despite the fact that the latter also heads SCIRI's Iranian-based **Badr Brigade**, which US defence secretary Donald Rumsfeld warned not to intervene during the allied invasion of Iraq. He admonished his supporters not to use violence against the foreign invaders and occupying forces. However, there were Shi'ite elements who opposed him. Al-Hakim was killed together with 124 other people by a car bomb in Najaf in August 2003. His brother is now a member of Iraq's Governing Council.

Al-Hakim, Ayatollah Mohammed Saeed

Shi'a cleric and uncle of **Muhammad Baqir al-Hakim**, leader the **Supreme Council for the Islamic Revolution in Iraq**.

Al-Hakim, Muhsin

Born in **Najaf**, Iraq, in 1889. The leader of **Shi'a** Muslims around the world from 1955 until 1970. When he declined to side with the Ba'athist Government of Iraq in 1969, his son was sentenced to death and funds belonging to his *hawzah* (theological centre) were confiscated. He died in 1970.

Halabja

Town in northern Iraq in Kurdish territory. Notorious as the location for the use by the regime of **Saddam Hussain** of chemical weapons against Iraqi civilians in September 1988. Later, the centre of the activities of the **Ansar al-Islam**.

Halliburton

Major US energy corporation (once headed by US Vice-President Dick Cheney), whose subsidiary, KBR, was awarded a contract in 2003 without competition to manage the **oil** industry in post-war Iraq. Revealed by a defence department audit towards the end of 2003 to have been substantially overcharging for oil (US $2.64 per gallon for fuel transported from Kuwait instead of $1.18 per gallon—the price for fuel from Turkey—or less) during the **Gulf War (2003)**. US President **George W. Bush** stated that it should repay the government if its subcontractor is found to have overcharged, as alleged, by $61m. Replaced by the US forces fuel agency, the Defence Energy Support Centre at the Pentagon, in 2004.

Hamah

Ancient city in west central Syria, on the banks of the Orontes river. Frequently referred to in the **Bible** as Hamath, Hamah was once an important centre of the Hittites. The city was the leading centre of the **Sunni** religious establishment, and major skirmishes have taken place there between Islamists and security forces of the **Ba'ath Party**, especially in 1964 and in 1980. In 1984 the so-called **Hamah revolts** took place there.

Hamah revolts

In February 1982 an Islamist-inspired revolt took place in the Syrian city of **Hamah**. The security forces of the Syrian **Ba'ath Party** crushed the revolt in an operation that cost the lives of some 5,000–10,000 people, including 1,000 soldiers. The city was shelled with heavy artillery and a substantial part of the old quarter was destroyed.

Hamas (Algeria) – *see also* Mouvement de la société pour la paix

Movement for an Islamic Society

Al-Haraka li-Mujtama' Islami evolved from a previously non-political Islamic association, **al-Irshad wa'l-Islah** (Guidance and Reform), founded by Sheikh Mahfoud Nahnah. The new Hamas was established in December 1990, two months after a meeting (on 20 September) organized by Sheikh Nahnah, and attended, at his invitation, by more than 300 local Islamic associations and several minor parties which sought to unify the Islamist movement. Hamas was expected eventually to function like a political party. Its name was a direct allusion to the principal Islamist movement involved in the uprising (*intifada*) in the **Occupied Territories** of the **West Bank** and the **Gaza Strip**. In outlook Hamas could be situated in the tradition of the **Muslim Brotherhood** in the **Middle East**, but on the left wing of that tradition. It was anticipated that it would be likely to adhere to the evolutionary perspective of its predecessor, al-Irshad wa'l-Islah, which tended to emphasize the need to reform society through Islamic missionary activity before it would be possible to reform the state in accordance with Islamic principles. This was in marked contrast to the 'revolutionary' perspective of the **FIS—Front islamique du salut** (Islamic Salvation Front. Sheikh Nahnah expressed a more principled acceptance of the rules of the pluralist political process, in contrast to the purely tactical acceptance of it by the FIS. These differences, however, did not prevent Sheikh Nahnah from urging his followers to vote for Islamists in the June 1990 elections held in Algeria, and so, by implication, for the FIS, but they probably explain the decision to establish a distinct, rival party after the September 1990 meeting. The move was denounced as divisive by the FIS, which did not attend the meeting. Hamas had a strong following in Blida, a large town some 30 miles south of **Algiers**, where Sheikh Nahnah himself was based. It held well-attended meetings in southern Algeria and is reported to have expanded its membership throughout much of central Algeria. It was also reported in the early 2000s to have a nation-wide network of offices. Little information was available, however, concerning Hamas' leadership, other than that Sheikh Nahnah's deputy was Muhammad Bouslimani.

Hamas—Harakat al-Muqawama al-Islamiyya

Islamic Resistance Movement, Lebanon

Hamas has approximately 500 members in Lebanon. In 1973 Sheikh **Ahmed Yassin** founded the Islamic Assembly (al-Mujamma' al-Islami), an activist offshoot of the **Muslim Brotherhood**, in **Gaza**. Soon after the onset of the *intifada* in December 1987, he established Hamas, the leading Palestinian Islamist movement. Hamas also has a presence in the Palestinian camps of south Lebanon, under the leadership of 'Imad al-'Ali.

Hamas—Harakat al-Muqawama al-Islamiyya

Islamic Resistance Movement, Palestine

HAMAS (an acronym, in **Arabic**, that stands for 'Harakat al-Muqawama al-Islamia', and a word meaning courage and bravery, zeal or enthusiasm) is a radical Islamic fundamentalist organization which became active in the early stages of the Palestinian *intifada*, operating primarily in the **Gaza** district, but also in **Judea and Samaria**. It was formed in late 1987 during the early stages of the *intifada* as an outgrowth of the Palestinian branch of the **Muslim Brotherhood**. Its inspiration has been the Muslim Brotherhood and the **Islamic Jihad** of Egypt and Jordan, and it has links with these and other Islamist groups, such as the Lebanese **Hezbollah**. It does not recognize the right of the **Palestine Liberation Organization** (PLO) to create a secular state and therefore does not accept the PLO's role in peace negotiations with Israel. Hamas calls for the destruction of the State of Israel and its replacement by a pan-Islamic Palestinian state stretching from the **Mediterranean** to the River Jordan. Various Hamas elements have used both political and violent means, including **terrorism**, in pursuit of its goals. Hamas is loosely structured, with some elements working clandestinely and others working openly through mosques and social-service institutions to recruit members, raise money, organize activities and distribute propaganda. Hamas' strength is concentrated in the Gaza Strip and a few areas of the **West Bank**. It has also engaged in political activity, such as presenting candidates in West Bank Chamber of Commerce elections. Hamas activists, especially those in the **Izz ad-Din al-Qassam Brigades**, have conducted many attacks—including large-scale suicide bombings—against Israeli military and civilian targets. In the early 1990s they also targeted suspected Palestinian collaborators and **al-Fatah** rivals.

When, at the onset of the **Gulf War (1991)**, **Yasser Arafat** supported **Saddam Hussain**, Saudi Arabia retaliated by terminating its financial assistance to the PLO; money sent to the **Occupied Territories** went to fund Hamas instead. Because of its opposition to the PLO, Hamas initially also received funding from Israel. Arafat declared that 'Hamas is a creature of Israel, which at the time of Prime Minister Shamir gave it money and [funded] more than 700 institutions, among them schools, universities and mosques'. Hamas' leadership used the unexpected income to strengthen its self-financing capability and to challenge Arafat's leadership in the Occupied Territories. As money flowed in, Hamas provided its supporters with an alternative 'state-shell'. It increased its operational activity in 2001–02 claiming responsibility for numerous attacks against Israeli interests. The group has not targeted US interests—although some US citizens have been killed in Hamas operations—and it continues to confine its attacks to Israeli military and civilian targets inside Israel and in the West Bank and Gaza Strip. The group's leadership is dispersed throughout the Gaza Strip and West Bank, with a few senior leaders residing in Syria, Lebanon and the **Gulf states**. Hamas delivered a blow to the so-called **Road Map to peace** in June 2003 when it broke off talks aimed at establishing a cease-fire. The group issued an uncompromising statement condemning the summit meeting held at the beginning of that month between US President **George W. Bush**, Israeli Prime Minister **Ariel Sharon** and his Palestinan counterpart, **Mahmoud Abbas** ('Abu Mazen') as a US attempt to dictate peace terms. Hamas urged the Palestinian people and the **Arab World** to unite against the Road Map embraced by Abbas and the Palestinian leadership. Hamas backed its stand with a series of rallies in Gaza. During 2003 and 2004 it was responsible for a number of bomb attacks on Israeli targets. In March 2004 its spiritual leader, Sheikh **Ahmed Yassin**, was assassinated by a missile launched from an Israeli army helicopter.

Hamdi, Ibrahim

President of **North Yemen** from 1974 until 1977.

Hamrouche, Mouloud (1943–)

Prime Minister of Algeria in 1989–91. Led a government committed to democratic political reforms and economic liberalization under the presidency of **Benjedid Chadli**.

Hanafi Code

The Code of one of the four main legal schools (*madhabs*) of **Sunni Islam**. The differences between the schools are mainly confined to questions concerning prayer, marriage and **women**'s rights, with the Hanafis taking a relatively liberal position. Jurists from three of the main schools continued to exercise *ijtihad* (reason) for many centuries—the Hanbalis were the exception. It was long argued, however, that the 'gates of reason' had been closed after the third Muslim century. More recent scholarship (from the latter part of the 19th century onwards) suggests that these 'gates' were never completely closed and that *ijtihad* was at least acceptable. See also **Hanbali Code**, **Maliki Code** and **Shafi'i Code**.

Hanbali Code

The Code of one of the four main legal schools of **Sunni Islam**. Generally more conservative than the other schools (see **Shafi'i Code**, **Hanafi Code** and **Maliki Code**), the Hanbali Code is particularly conservative and restrictive with regard to marriage, inheritance and **women**'s rights. It also considered that 'the gates of *ijtihad*' (reason) had closed irrevocably after the third Muslim century.

Haolam Hazeh – *see* Israel Communist Party

Har Homa

At the end of February 1997 Israel's Ministerial Committee on **Jerusalem** announced the construction of the 6,500-unit **settlement** of Har Homa, south-east of **Jerusalem** at Jabal Abu Ghunaim. The decision provoked international condemnation. US President **Bill Clinton** agreed with a statement issued by the **European Union** to the effect that the construction of Har Homa was an obstacle to peace. **Palestinian National Authority** officials warned that the proposed settlement could signify 'the end of the peace process' and Crown Prince Hassan of Jordan cancelled an official visit to **Tel-Aviv** in protest.

Harakat Amal – *see also* **Amal** and **Lebanon**

Founded in 1975, this group has subsequently changed character considerably to evolve into a **Shi'a** political movement, headed by **Nabih Berri** (who holds a leading political position in the Lebanese parliament). Harakat Amal was originally one of the many militant Islamic groups in Lebanon in the 1970s. Its founder, Imam **Musa as-Sadr**, disappeared in 1978, and subsequent leaderships eventually adapted its radical outlook into a more mainstream approach. Amal provided a counterweight to **Hezbollah**. Although both groups are **Shi'ite**, their agendas are perceived differently by Lebanese Shi'a communities. Some consider Amal and Berri to represent a nationalist Shi'a interest in the defence of Lebanon.

Harakat e Enqelab e Islami

Islamic Movement of Afghanistan

A **Shi'a** party led by **Ayatollah** Muhammad Asif Muhsini, whose support was strongest in south-west and eastern Afghanistan.

Al-Haraka li-Mujtama' Islami – *see* **Hamas (Algeria)**

Harakat al-Muqawama al-Islamiyya – *see* **Hamas**

Harakat at-Tawhid (Lebanon)

Sunni group which split from the **Jama'a al-Islamiyya** in 1982 and is led by Sheikh Said Sha'ban.

Haramain sharifain

The holy shrines of **Mecca** and **Medina**. From **Arabic** *haram*, meaning 'forbidden' or 'sacred'.

Al-Hariri, Rafiq

Lebanon's billionaire Prime Minister, who came to power in 1992 under President **Elias Hrawi**. Al-Hariri eventually resigned from office in 1998 (to be replaced by Salim al-Hoss) after his private empire had acquired effective control of much of the banking system and the real economy of Lebanon. He had earlier made his fortune in Saudi Arabia and came to office offering his countrymen a vision of a modern, dynamic Lebanon, with substantial foreign direct investment and loans on favourable terms to reconstruct the economy and the country. During his period of office, however, the interface between the private and public sectors was dangerously eroded. His former stockbroker at Merrill Lynch became the head of the central bank, while the Ministry of Finance was allocated to the chief financial officer of al-Hariri's own business conglomerate. Solidère, a private company founded and controlled by al-Hariri, was given ownership of central **Beirut**, and the Council for the Development and Reconstruction of Lebanon, nominally a government agency but in fact under the direct control of al-Hariri's team, was awarded a virtual monopoly over governmental construction. From this public/private-sector base, al-Hariri constructed a business empire alongside the Lebanese state. Over the years his private empire came to control a larger share of the public purse than did the official state. Increasingly, al-Hariri was obliged to 'buy' a sufficient bloc of deputies in the Lebanese parliament to enable him to continue. His take-over of the state was increasingly criticized and eventually al-Hariri was shown to be unable to maintain the momentum of economic development promised to the Lebanese people. He was successful again in the September 2000 elections and it remains to be seen how Lebanon's development and the position of al-Hariri fare in coming years.

Hashemites/al-Hashem/Banu Hashem

Jordan's ruling dynasty. Named after Hashem ibn Abdul Manaf, the great grand-father of the **Prophet Muhammad**. The Banu Hashem clan was part of the Quraish tribe of Arabia. In the 10th century the Hashemites became the ruling family of **Mecca** and the surrounding province of **Hejaz**. The Hashemite royal family established the modern state of Jordan in 1921.

Hashomer

In 1909 Hashomer ('the Watchman'), a defence society, was established by Jews in Palestine and thereafter acted as an intelligence nucleus. It was dominated by Marxist-oriented Russian Jews and had both revolutionary and fervent militant socialist characteristics. It sought to protect Jewish villages from Arab attacks and to propound its own brand of socialist **Zionism**. It was disbanded in 1925, but its influence lived on, through **Haganah**, in the 1930s.

Hassan, Crown Prince (of Jordan)

Born in 1947. Crown Prince of Jordan in 1965–99. Brother of former King **Hussein** and uncle of the current King **Abdullah II**. In 1965 Hassan was named Crown Prince of Jordan, deposing his nephew, the three-year old Abdullah. The background to this change was that Hussein had been the target of a number of assassination attempts and did not want to take the risk of leaving Jordan in the hands of an infant. In 1999, however, Abdullah was appointed Crown Prince, replacing Hassan. On the death of King Hussein in 1999 Abdullah became king.

Hassan II (Moulay Hassan Muhammadi ibn Yussuf)

Born in 1929, died in 1999. King of Morocco in 1961– 99. Formerly crown prince until he succeeded his father as king. In 1960 Hassan was appointed as Minister of Defence and deputy Premier and successfully led the negotiations with France, Spain and the USA which ensured the withdrawal of foreign troops from Morocco. Coming to the throne in 1961, he was an authoritarian ruler, who made maximum use of his status as Commander of the Faithful as well as head of state to ensure his religious and political dominance in Morocco. The main religious authorities (e.g. the *ulema*) and the political parties were orchestrated by him to establish what appeared to be a relatively open society but was in reality a highly controlled system of patronage and coercion. The survivor of three attempted assassinations, Hassan II was regarded with mixed feelings by his subjects. An effective secret police and heavy reaction to political opposition ensured political stability, or, rather, the absence of political activity and Hassan II was at times fiercely criticized by organizations in other countries for what were regarded as violations of human rights, political oppression and the cruel punishment of prisoners. However, he is also recognized as having been one of the more important participants in the peace process in the **Middle East** that was contemporaneous with more than 10 of the final years of his rule. Under Hassan II Morocco's relations with neighbouring countries (Algeria and Mauritania) were at times tense, and inside Morocco every effort was made to uphold the King's position and maintain the stability of the country. In 1962 he introduced a new constitution, which permitted a popularly elected legislature. In 1975 he initiated the **Green March**, whereby 350,000 civilians marched into the former Spanish colony, later named **Western Sahara**, claiming the territory as Moroccan and taking control over the northern two-thirds of it. By 1976 the part of Western Sahara occupied by Morocco in the preceding year had been officially annexed. The annexation is not recognized by any foreign state, however. In 1979, following the Mauritanian withdrawal from the southern part of Western Sahara, Morocco annexed the remainder of the territory, without taking control of the border town of La Gouera. The politics of Hassan II were among the most Western-friendly in North Africa, and in many cases Hassan played an important role in international affairs. In 1991 Morocco was the only **Maghreb** country to contribute troops to the UN actions against Iraq in Kuwait. Much of

Hassan's domestic success, in particular his confrontation of Islamist elements, rested on his family's claim to be sharifs, descendants of the **Prophet Muhammad**, a claim that was widely accepted in Morocco as well as abroad. Moreover, Hassan took pains to preserve Moroccan heritage and religion. The world's highest mosque, completed in 1993, was built on his initiative and is named after him. Morocco, at the time of Hassan's death, suffered from high unemployment, an inappropriate educational system, an unresolved situation in Western Sahara and strong tensions within the population. On the other hand, Morocco had during the last decades of his rule developed an excellent infrastructure, and in some sectors, such as **information technology** and **tourism**, the Moroccan economy had achieved very positive growth.

Hassidism

The beliefs and practices of several ultra-orthodox Jewish sects whose leadership tends to be hereditary.

Hawala

Traditional system of informal money transfers, widely used in the **Middle East** and in South Asia (where it is referred to as the *hundi* system) for channelling money from one country to another. Originally invented, it appears, by the ancient Chinese—who called it *fei qian* ('flying money')—the system was adopted by Arab traders to avoid robbery on the Silk Route. With the growth of international migration from developing countries (particularly from the Middle East and South Asia) to Europe and, latterly, to the **Gulf**, the *hawala* system has been increasingly used for repatriating the **remittances** of migrant workers and overseas businessmen. Confidentiality, trust and the speed of transactions commend the system to those who wish to transfer money internationally; the fact that it is informal and often secret means that it avoids regulation, taxation and the other concomitants of formal money transfer systems. These are also qualities that ensure its popularity with international terrorist organizations. There are numerous reports suggesting that Islamist extremists make widespread use of the *hawala* system for international money transfers. *Hawala* networks in the Middle East and South Asia—and even outside these regions—tend to be dominated by Pakistani and Indian *hawaladars* (*hawala* dealers). According to the United Nations, the annual turnover of the *hawala* industry is US $200,000m. Official figures suggest that in Pakistan alone $5,000m. move annually through the *hawala* network. At the end of the 1990s there were 1,100 known *hawaladars* in Pakistan, some handling single transactions as large as $10m. The system is widely used in countries such as Somalia and Afghanistan, where the formal banking system is poorly developed. Until the end of 2001, in addition to the **Taliban** currency, there were four different Afghan banknotes in circulation. **Gold** was the most reliable means of exchange. *Hawaladars* commonly used gold to balance their books. Since 11 September

2001 there has been growing concern regarding the use of these informal money transfer systems by international terrorist organizations, and efforts are being made, particularly by the USA, to initiate a global clampdown on such systems. That this is possible is shown by the success of Indira Gandhi in crippling the system in India, where today *hawala* transactions are reportedly relatively limited.

Al-Hawali, Safar

Sheikh Safar al-Hawali was, with Salman al-'Auda, one of the two best-known imprisoned *ulama* in Saudi Arabia. Born in 1950 south of at-Ta'if, he studied at the Islamic University in **Medina** and at Umm al-Qurra' University in **Mecca**, eventually rising to be head of a department at that university. His academic work has focused primarily on a critique of secularism and Westernism; Mamoun Fandy has identified affinities in his work with **Samuel P. Huntington**'s notion of the 'clash of civilizations', presenting the Muslim point of view. His books have focused less on criticism of the Saudi government as such (the focus of much of 'Auda's preaching), but rather on portraying the West as the enemy of **Islam**. The author of a number of books, Hawali's work has tended to be more intellectual while 'Auda has been primarily a preacher. He and al-'Auda were reportedly arrested in 1994, at the time of the Bureida demonstrations.

Hawatmah, Nayef

Palestinian politician and leader of the **Democratic Front for the Liberation of Palestine** (DFLP), Hawatmah was born to a Greek Catholic peasant family on 17 November 1935 in Salt, on the eastern bank of the Jordan river. In 1954 he began his higher education studies in **Cairo** and joined the **Arab Nationalist Movement** (ANM) of **George Habash** in the same year. Following his return to Jordan in 1956 he became involved in revolutionary activity which led to his being sentenced to death *in absentia*. In 1958 he fought in the civil war in Lebanon. Afterwards he took refuge in Iraq where he directed the local section of the ANM for five years. From 1963 until 1967 he participated in the freedom struggle against the British in **South Yemen**. After the **Six-Day War** he was pardoned and returned to Jordan where he joined the **Popular Front for the Liberation of Palestine**. He took over the leadership of the left wing of the organization. In February 1969 the movement split and Hawatmah created the Popular Democratic Front for the Liberation of Palestine, which was renamed the DFLP in August 1974. Long before **Yasser Arafat** Hawatmah was the first Palestinian leader to advocate the coexistence of a Palestinian state and Israel. He recently expressed a wish to return and settle in the Palestinian Territories, but Israel's **Netanyahu** Government totally opposed the idea. Through his capacity for analysis and independence *vis-à-vis* Arab regimes, Nayef Hawatmah has made the DFLP stand out from other Palestinian movements. He is currently residing in **Damascus**.

Hazaras

Ethnic group in Afghanistan. The literal meaning of the word *hazara* is 'thousand' as their ancestors were a garrison of 1,000 Mongolian troops (Djengis Kahn). They are **Shi'a** and the **Hizb-i Wahdat** is made up of Hazaras. This group received support from Iran during the **Afghan civil war**. The Hazaras were persecuted by the largely Pashtu **Taliban**, who ethnically cleansed some Hazara villages.

Headscarf

Widely worn by Muslim women (and, indeed, by Roman Catholic women) in public. The subject of considerable social, cultural and political debate, particularly as a symbol of Islamic faith. In late 2003 President Chirac of France announced that Muslim headscarves and other religious symbols were to be banned from French schools and public buildings. In France secularism is a constitutional guarantee. In many countries in the **Middle East** and North Africa **women** are virtually obliged to wear specific 'Islamic dress', that usually covers most parts of the body, including the face. Those ethnic and cultural **minorities** which have historically tended not to adopt 'Islamic dress' are increasingly condemned by Islamists as unIslamic and may be subject to hostile and aggressive treatment. In Algeria women not wearing the *hejab* or *hijab* (headscarf) run the risk of verbal abuse, harassment, physical violence and even assassination as a consequence.

Health

Health expenditure as a proportion of gross domestic product (GDP) is high in a number of countries in the region. It is highest in Lebanon, where it represents 12.2% of GDP (the third highest percentage in the world, after the USA and Nicaragua. The proportion of GDP devoted to health expenditure in Saudi Arabia (11%) is the fourth highest in the world. The United Arab Emirates (UAE) and Israel spend 9.5% and 9.4% respectively on health; Jordan spends 8%, the same proportion as New Zealand. At 2.5% of GDP, spending on health is lowest in Syria. If the number of people per doctor is regarded as a useful indicator for health-care provision, then the former Soviet republics of **Central Asia** emerge as those with the best health services. Israel is also high on the list of countries with low numbers per doctor. Saudi Arabia, the UAE and Kuwait, however, all have large numbers per doctor, yet have the reputation of providing excellent health-care.

Hebrew

Semitic language with strong links to **Arabic**. The language is widely spoken in Israel by both Jews and Arabs. Hebrew is the official language of Israel.

Hebron

Important town in the **West Bank**. Hebron's population largely comprises Palestinian Arabs, but there is also a small core of Israeli settlers. The Mosque of Abraham (al-Khalil—the 'Friend of God') is built over the tomb of Abraham, the Cave of Machpelah; it also contains the tombs of Sarah, Isaac, Rebecca, Jacob and Leah. The shrine is revered by Muslims and Jews and is also important to Christians.

Hejab – *see* headscarf, veil

Hejaz

Hejaz is a region and province in the north-west of present-day **Saudi Arabia**. The most prominent city in the region is **Mecca**. Its area totals 388,500 sq km. The Hejaz is the birthplace and spiritual centre of **Islam**. It is also the location of **Medina**, the first Muslim city and burial place of the **Prophet Muhammad**, as well as **Jiddah** and at-Ta'if. It was the centre of the early Islamic empires. For most of its history it was under the control of regional powers (e.g. Egypt and the **Ottoman Empire**). The Hejaz enjoyed a brief period of political independence in the early 20th century. In **1916** its independence was proclaimed by Husain ibn Ali, the sherif of Mecca. In **1924**, however, ibn Ali's own authority was usurped by ibn Saud of the neighbouring nation of **Najd**. This annexation was instrumental in the creation of the Saudi Arabian state.

Hekmatyar, Gulbuddin

Born in Baglan, Kunduz, in Afghanistan, probably in 1947. A **Pashtun**, Hekmatyar was a leader of the **Muslim Brotherhood** movement in **Kabul** in the early 1970s. He later moved to Pakistan to organize an Islamic opposition movement against the Daud regime. In 1975 he led a major insurrection in the **Panjshir Valley**, near Kabul, which was sponsored by the Pakistani government in response to Daud's support of the Pashtunistan movement inside Pakistan. Leader of **Hizb-i Islami**.

Herat

Major town in western Afghanistan, under the control of a governor. Now receiving considerable **aid** from Iran for rebuilding its infrastructure. In August 2003 Iran began supplying electricity to the streets, government buildings and the hospital, extending the Iranian system at the cost of some US $15m. and selling at a loss.

Hergirtin Party
Hevgertina Gel a Kurd li Suriya

Political party founded in 1975 as the Partya Demokrati Kurd a Cep li Suriya. It has been known as Hevgertina Gel since 1980. In Syria Kurdish parties are perceived as separatist and involvement with such parties is regarded as a serious crime.

Heroin

Afghanistan has always been a source of **opium**, sold largely to local regional markets. During the war against the Soviet Union and subsequently, it became a major centre of production of opium for conversion into heroin for the international trade in narcotics. The Pakistani **Inter-Services Intelligence** (ISI), with support from the US **Central Intelligence Agency** (CIA), provided support for the *mujahidin* and merchants to encourage farmers to increase their output of opium and expertise at refining it into heroin. In less than two years there was a massive expansion in opium production. Soon the narcotics-based economy took over from traditional crop production and sale and, with the help of the ISI, the *mujahidin* opened hundreds of heroin laboratories. Within two years the Pakistan-Afghan borderland had become the biggest centre for the production of heroin in the world and the single greatest supplier of heroin on the streets of Europe and the USA, meeting 60% of US demand for narcotics. By 1991 annual production from the tribal areas under the control of the *mujahidin* had risen to an astonishing 70 metric tons of premium quality heroin, an increase of 35% compared with the previous year. Annual profits were estimated at between US \$100,000m.–\$200,000m. In 1995 the former CIA director of the Afghan operation, Charles Cogan, admitted that the CIA had sacrificed the **drugs** war to fight the Cold War. In fact it had directly promoted the drugs trade. The preferred smuggling route traversed Pakistan. The ISI used the army to transport drugs across the country, while the **Bank of Credit and Commerce International** provided financial and logistical support for the whole operation.

Herut

Menachem Begin founded Herut in June 1948 in order to advocate the revisionist programme in Israel. Herut's organization is highly complicated, varying from place to place, institution to institution, and election to election. A small leadership determines party policy, which advocates a free enterprise economy and the inalienable right of Jews to settle anywhere in Israel (in its broader sense), including **Judea and Samaria** (the **West Bank**). Begin was a leading figure in Herut. When he retired **Itzhak Shamir** (born 1915) became party leader and Prime Minister, although he was challenged within Herut by **Ariel Sharon** (born 1928), the current Prime Minister, and David Levy (born 1938). Sharon brought the **Free Centre Party**, the **State List**, and the Land of Israel Movement into the Herut-Liberal alliance in 1973 to form **Likud**. Herut was reconstituted in 1998. A right-wing nationalist party, it is opposed to further Israeli withdrawal from the **Occupied Territories**.

Herzl, Theodor

Journalist who became the founder of modern political **Zionism**. Born in Budapest, Hungary, in 1860, he subsequently settled in Vienna, Austria, and was educated there in law. However, he devoted himself almost exclusively to journalism and literature. His early work was in no way related to Jewish life. From April 1896, when the English translation of his *Judenstaat* (*The Jewish State*) appeared, his career and reputation changed. Herzl was moved by the Dreyfus affair, a notorious anti-Semitic incident in France. In 1897 he planned the first Zionist Congress in Basel, Switzerland. He was elected president, and was re-elected unanimously at every congress until his death in 1904.

Hevgertina Gel – *see* Hergirtin Party

Hey'at Peygiri-ye Qanun Asasi va Nezarat Bar An

Committee for Ensuring and Supervising the Implementation of the Constitution, Iran

Institution established by President **Khatami** of Iran in November 1997. The five members are appointed for a four-year term.

Hezb-e E'tedal va Towse'eh

Moderation and Development Party, Iran

Political organization established in the late 1990s after President **Khatami** was elected. It had some success in the elections to the sixth **Majlis** in 2000.

Hezb-e Hambastegi-ye Iran-e Islami

Islamic Iran Solidarity Party

Iranian political organization, established in the late 1990s after the election of President **Khatami**. It had some success in the elections to the sixth **Majlis** in 2000.

Hezb-e Islami

The Hezb-e Islami is a faction of warlord **Gulbuddin Hekmatyar** and allied with remnant members of the **Taliban** in Afghanistan, especially around **Kandahar**.

Hezb-e Jomhuri ye Eslam (Iran) – *see* Islamic Republic(an) Party

Hezb-e Kargozaran-e Sazandegi

Servants of Construction Party, Iran

Political grouping established in the late 1990s after the election of President **Khatami**. It had some success in the elections to the sixth **Majlis** in 2000.

Hezb ash-Sha'ab

Palestinian People's Party

Formerly the **Palestine Communist Party**, admitted to the **Palestine National Council** at its 18th session in 1987. Its secretary-general is Sulayman an-Najjab.

Hezbollah (Iran)

The 'Party of God' in Iran is not a political party in the usual sense, but consists of organized street gangs, allied to the clerics, that, in the early years of the Islamic Republic, used to patrol large cities and maintain order 'in the name of the Imam'. Referred to by Bani Sadr as 'the club-wielding thugs of the clerics', they were particularly active in the summer and autumn of 1981 in battles with leftists.

Hezbollah (Lebanon)

In **Arabic**: 'Party of God'. An umbrella organization of radical groups, including **Islamic Jihad**, **Revolutionary Justice Organization**, Organization of the Oppressed on Earth and Islamic Jihad for the Liberation of Palestine. Formed in 1982 in response to the Israeli invasion of Lebanon, this Lebanon-based radical **Shi'a** group takes its ideological inspiration from the **Iranian Revolution** of 1979 and the teachings of the late Ayatollah **Khomeini**. The Majlis ash-Shura, or Consultative Council, is the group's highest governing body and is led by secretary-general **Hassan Nasrallah**. Hezbollah is dedicated to liberating **Jerusalem**, ultimately eliminating Israel, and has formally advocated the ultimate establishment of Islamic rule in Lebanon. None the less, Hezbollah has actively participated in Lebanon's political system since 1992. It operates mainly out of the southern suburbs of **Beirut**, the **Beka'a Valley** and southern Lebanon, but has also established cells in Europe, Africa, South America, North America and Asia. Hezbollah is closely allied with, and often directed by, Iran, but may have conducted operations that were not approved by the Iranian authorities. While Hezbollah does not share the Syrian regime's secular orientation, the group has also been a strong tactical ally in helping Syria advance its political objectives in the region. Hezbollah is known or suspected to have been involved in numerous anti-US and anti-Israeli terrorist attacks, including the suicide truck bombings of the US embassy and US marine barracks in Beirut in October 1983 and of the US embassy annex in Beirut in September 1984. Three members of Hezbollah, 'Imad Mughniyah, Hasan Izz-ad-Din, and Ali Atwa, are on the US Federal Bureau of Investigation's list of 22 Most Wanted Terrorists for the **hijacking** in 1985 of TWA Flight 847 during which a US navy diver was murdered. Elements of the group were responsible for the kidnapping and detention of US citizens and other Westerners in Lebanon in the 1980s. Hezbollah also attacked the Israeli embassy in Argentina in 1992 and the Israeli cultural centre in Buenos Aires in 1994. In 2000 it captured three Israeli soldiers in the Shab'a Farms and kidnapped an Israeli non-combatant whom it may have lured to Lebanon under false pretences. Suicide operations were pioneered in the 1980s by Hezbollah.

Hezbollah has almost 15,000 members. The Israeli invasion of Lebanon in June 1982 provided the crisis that won Shi'i radicalism a mass constituency. It subscribes to Khomeini's theory that a religious jurist (*velayat-i faqih*) should hold ultimate political power. The authority of this jurist, both spiritual and political, may not be challenged; he must be obeyed. Hezbollah considers itself to be fulfilling the messianic role of turning Lebanon into a province of **Islam**. In an open letter in February 1985 Hezbollah declared that Muslims must 'abide by the orders of the sole wise and just command represented by the supreme jurisconsult, who is presently incarnate in the imam Ayatollah Khomeini'. It also called for a battle with vice, a reference to the USA, and for the destruction of Israel to make way for Palestine.

Hezbollah built a powerful presence in Lebanon, so that it now has 5,000 active fighters in its combat organization, the Islamic Resistance (*al-Muqawama al-Islamiyya*). It administers three hospitals, 17 medical centres and a commercial network that includes supermarkets, gas stations, department stores, and construction companies. Hezbollah's social-welfare activities won it additional members, especially after 1984, when Iran financed 90% of Hezbollah's social programme. None of Lebanon's Shi'i religious leaders has established a Khomeini-like pre-eminence, but **Muhammad Husayn Fadlallah** is recognized as Hezbollah's spiritual guide (*al-murshid ar-ruhi*), though he keeps himself apart from Hezbollah's activities and regards his mission as transcending specific Shi'i groupings to embrace the whole Muslim community if possible. Despite Hezbollah's appeals for Islamic unity and efforts to recruit non-Shi'i Muslims, its membership remains limited to Shi'a. Not only Christians and **Druze** rejected its declared aim to establish an Islamic order along Iranian lines, so too did most **Sunnis**. **Amal** resisted its goal of establishing an **Islamic state** and its moves to dominate the south. Hezbollah's militant anti-Israeli stance led to bloody conflicts with Amal in 1985–89, as the latter feared that Hezbollah would resort to *jihad* (holy war) against Israel as a pretext to undermine its strength. Symbolic of Hezbollah's limited appeal, its representation in the Lebanese parliament amounted to just eight seats in the 1992 parliamentary elections and seven in the elections of 1996.

Hezbollah (Turkey)

The **Islamic Great Eastern Raiders' Front** was the first group to claim responsibility for the November 2003 bombings in **Istanbul**. Responsibility was also claimed by the **Abu Hafs al-Masri Brigade**. Most of those charged so far, however, appear at some time to have been connected to Turkey's indigenous Hezbollah movement—which is not linked to the Lebanese group of the same name. This group was largely Kurdish and at its most violently active during the late 1980s and 1990s, engaged chiefly in a bitter struggle against the more secular and Marxist-oriented **Kurdish Workers' Party** (PKK). Although its aspiration was to establish an Islamic regime in south-eastern Turkey, it is widely believed to have been armed and funded by elements of Turkey's security forces, which used it as a weapon in their own struggle against the PKK. Turkish Hezbollah was widely believed to have been broken when it was targeted by the security forces in the wake of the capture, in 1999, of the PKK's leader **Abdullah Öcalan**. This culminated in a bloody gunfight in Istanbul in 2000, during which its presumed leader was killed. Many of its activists, however, were never apprehended, and Turkey is now discovering what happened to them. Some joined splinter groups, such as **Islamic Action** or a still more obscure group called **Beyyat al-Islam**. These groups have overlapping memberships and are also thought to have links with Iran. It is perhaps significant that Turkish foreign minister Abdullah Gul praised both Syria and Iran for their co-operation in the hunt for the suspects. The Turkish authorities now believe that more than 1,000 Turkish nationals have in some way or another engaged in international activities of the kind now commonly associated with **al-Qa'ida**. In connection with the Istanbul bombings, among those charged, detained or still at large are veterans of armed conflict in Bosnia, **Chechnya** and Afghanistan, and of Pakistani training camps.

Higher Economic Council (HEC—Saudi Arabia)

Established in 1999 by and under the chairmanship of Crown Prince Abdullah of Saudi Arabia, the HEC is the key strategic economic decision-making body in the kingdom. It includes a consultative committee of 10 private-sector representatives as well as the economic ministers and the governor of the central bank.

Hijacking

An instrument of various terrorist groups involving the seizure of an aircraft (or, more rarely, a ship), its diversion from its normal route and the taking of hostages from those aboard as leverage for negotiations. One of the earliest instances in the region was the **El Al hijacking** in July 1968, which involved the seizure by members of the **Popular Front for the Liberation of Palestine** (PFLP) of an aircraft belonging to the Israeli national airline, El Al, *en route* from Rome, Italy, to **Tel-Aviv**, Israel. Another was the hijacking of the *Achille Lauro* (a passenger liner), which resulted in the death of a disabled American passenger. A German Lufthansa aircraft was hijacked by the PFLP in **Aden** in 1972.

Hijaz – *see* **Hejaz**

Hijra

The Hijra, or withdrawal, refers to the emigration of the **Prophet Muhammad** and his followers to the city of **Medina** in AD 622. Muhammad, preaching the doctrines of one God (Allah) and the threat of the Day of Judgment, did not have much success in the city of **Mecca**. The Quraysh (Muhammad's tribe) was in charge of the Kaaba (a shrine to pagan gods) and persecuted and harassed him continuously. Muhammad and his followers emigrated to the city of Yathrib, later called Medina, on 16 July 622. This event marks the beginning of the Islamic calendar (AH 1, *anno Hegirae*, or 'in the year of the *hijra*').

Hilu, Charles

President of Lebanon from 1964 until 1970.

Hisb-i Wahdat – *see* **Hizb-i Wahdat**

Histadrut

The Israeli Labour Federation. A major organization within the Israeli economy. Many Jewish businesses were established and heavily subsidized during the colonial period in Palestine by the Histadrut, the Zionist labour federation. In the 1980s Histadrut-controlled companies accounted for about one-fifth of all employment in Israel and for an equal share of the country's gross national product (GNP), bringing the public sector's total share of ownership of large companies to more than one-half, its share of total employment to more than one-third and its contribution to GNP to just less than one-half of the national total. The Histadrut owned the **Bank Ha'Poalim** until 1983, when it came under direct government control.

HIV/AIDS

HIV/AIDS is a growing **health** problem in the region, but the level of infections per head is significantly lower than in most parts of the world.

Hizb ad-Da'awa al-Islamiyya (Da'awa Party) – *see* **Islamic Da'awa Party**

Hizb al-Haq

Legal opposition party in Yemen.

Hizb-i Islami

Islamic Party, Afghanistan

Afghan political grouping. One faction (Hizb-i Islami Gulbuddin), led by **Gulbuddin Hekmatyar**, was originally associated with the **Muslim Brotherhood**. It has support in Wardak, Ghazni, Kabul and Kundiz provinces. Another faction is led by Mohammed Yunus Khalis and has support in the **Pashtun** provinces, especially Paktia, Nangrahar and Jalalabad. The Hizb-i Islami was initially one of the most disciplined of the guerrilla groups that fought against Soviet occupation. Even though Hizb-i Islami received millions of dollars-worth of military and financial **aid** from the USA, it still failed to liberate Afghanistan from the Communists. The major Afghan political factions are largely based on the former resistance organizations. **Hizb-i Islami Gulbuddin** and President **Burhanuddin Rabbani**'s **Jamiat-i Islami** (Islamic Society) have been bitter rivals for political influence in Afghanistan. Following the Soviet withdrawal, the Pakistani **Inter-Services Intelligence** (ISI) initially supported the Hizb-i Islami under Prime Minister Gulbuddin Hekmatyar to dislodge the Rabbani Government. Pakistan feared that the exclusively non-Pashtun character of that Government would lead Afghanistan's Pashtuns to revive the demand for Pashtunistan. On 1 January 1994 troops in **Kabul** commanded by the leader of the National Islamic Movement, Gen. **Abdul Rashid Dostum**, hitherto aligned with President Rabbani, transferred their allegiance to Gulbuddin Hekmatyar. Aided by forces loyal to Hekmatyar, they attempted to stage a *coup* d'état against President Rabbani. The President's forces quickly countered and the coup attempt was foiled. However, protracted fighting caused heavy civilian casualties and the destruction of much of Kabul, and subsequently engulfed much of the north of the country. In February 1994 Hekmatyar imposed a food blockade on northern Kabul, the area controlled by President Rabbani's troops. In July 1994 Commander Naser of Laghman province, who was affiliated with Hekmatyar's party, and 10 of his bodyguards were reportedly murdered as Naser traveled to meet with a rival. In September 1994 Commander Sadiq, also a follower of Hekmatyar, and his bodyguard were murdered in Nangarhar province while returning from a visit to Pakistan. Sadiq was rumored to have been involved in **drugs**-trafficking, a Pashtun intra-tribal dispute, and the factional fighting in Kabul—any of which may have provided the motive for his murder. On 12 August 1994 President Rabbani's forces apparently targeted Hekmatyar himself in an air raid that demolished his living quarters. Subsequent air attacks were made on a hospital facility where Hekmatyar was thought to be receiving treatment for injuries sustained in the 12 August air raid; in fact he had escaped serious injury. Eventually, the remarkable success of the **Taliban**, and economic considerations, led Pakistan in 1994–95 to transfer its support to the Taliban. In February 1995 the Taliban drove former Prime Minister Hekmatyar's forces out of southern Kabul and disarmed Hizb-i Islami **Shi'a** forces allied with him.

Hizb-i Islami Gulbuddin

Gulbuddin Hekmatyar founded Hizb-i Islami Gulbuddin (HIG) as a faction of the **Hizb-i Islami** party in 1977, and it was one of the major *mujahidin* groups in the war against the Soviet occupation. HIG has long-established ties with **Osama bin Laden**. In the early 1990s Hekmatyar administered several terrorist training camps in Afghanistan and was a pioneer in sending mercenary fighters to other Islamic conflicts. Hekmatyar offered to shelter bin Laden after the latter fled from Sudan in 1996. HIG has staged small attacks in its attempt to force US troops to withdraw from Afghanistan, overthrow the Afghan Transitional Administration and establish a fundamentalist state. Its areas of operation are eastern Afghanistan, particularly Konar and Nurestan provinces, and adjacent areas of Pakistan's tribal areas.

Hizb-i-Wahdat

Unity Party, Afghanistan

An anti-communist party, comprising mainly **Hazaras** and based in **Mazar-i Sharif**. The **Shi'a** minority in Afghanistan (*c.* 20% of the population) is concentrated in central and western Afghanistan, and is among the most economically disadvantaged groups in the country. The Shi'a **minority** wishes a national government to grant them equal rights as citizens. In 1988 Iran united eight Shi'a parties (all but Harakat-i Islami) into Hizb-i Wahdat, primarily consisting of the political representatives of ethnic Hazara chiefs. In January 1996 Iran announced it had reconciled them under President **Rabbani**. Hizb-i Wahdat effectively controls central Afghanistan. In February 1995 Commander **Masoud** defeated the Hizb-i Wahdat forces in **Kabul** after its ally, **Hizb-i Islami**, had been defeated by the **Taliban**. Hazarajat remains under the control of Hizb-i Wahdat, though initially the Jamiat government and later the Taliban contested its power in the town of Bamiyan. By November 1997 the Taliban-imposed blockade on the Hazarajat region ruled by Hizb-i Wahdat had brought the population (of about 1m.) to the verge of starvation. Iran considered itself the protector of the Shi'a Hazaras from the Taliban, which was **Sunni** and militantly anti-Shi'a. Hizb-i Wahdat is the instrument of the interests of the Iranian regime in Afghanistan. These interests run counter to those of Pakistan, which are currently expressed through the Taliban. Hizb-i Wahdat is alleged to provide espionage and *agent provocateur* services to the Iranian regime. The government of Iran has recognized Rabbani as the President of Afghanistan and diplomatic relations have been maintained through the Iranian consulate in Taloquan, in the Tajik-controlled north-east of Afghanistan, and not through Kabul, which was captured by the Taliban militia. Iran is providing Rabbani-**Dostum**-Masoud forces with thousands of antipersonnel mines that are being deployed in Badghis province and the Bala Murghab area.

Hizb al-Watan

Homeland Party, Iraq

Iraqi political group.

Hizb al-Wifaq al-Qawmi

National Accord Party, established in 2000.

Hizb ut-Tahrir (HT)

The HT (Islamic Liberation Party), which did not even have a foothold in the region in 1991, when the disintegration of the Soviet Union began, appears to have expanded its underground network into all five Central Asian Republics. It is a non-violent movement, preaching a peaceful *jihad*, which will persuade the Muslim peoples of **Central Asia** to rise up in the name of **Islam**. It seeks to reunite the Central Asian states and eventually the whole Muslim world by non-violent means, with the ultimate aim of establishing a **Caliphate** similar to that established after the death of the **Prophet Muhammad** in **Arabia** in the 7th century AD. It is particularly popular among college and university students. It produces an abundance of literature on its aims and methods. It is critical of the current regimes of the region and, particularly, of US influence and presence. It has mobilized resources to issue leaflets in Uzbekistan and Kyrgyzstan criticizing the US military presence, and appears to be developing a strategy to mobilize even greater support for its campaign to overthrow the existing regimes, by emphasizing their complicity with the USA in viewing all Islamic movements as part of an international terrorist network. Although the USA has so far (2002) not classified the HT as a terrorist group, it has tended to regard it as linked to the **Taliban** and to **al-Qa'ida** and has made few efforts to stop the increased arrest and detention of HT members across the region. The suppression of secular democratic parties and, particularly, of the HT and its supporters—Central Asian prisons contain more members of the HT than of any other movement—is having the effect of increasing support for more militant Islamist groups, such as the **Islamic Movement of Uzbekistan**.

HNWIs

High net worth individuals. *World Wealth Report 2002* revealed that there were about 300,000 HNWIs in the **Middle East**, holding investable assets of US \$1,100,000m. This figure represents 309% of the **Gulf Co-operation**

Council region's annual output, or 11% of US gross domestic product. See also **Income**.

Holy Land

Term given to the region described in the **Bible**. For many Jews it means **Judea and Samaria**. For most non-Arab Christians as well as for Arab Christians, it means the land in which Jesus was born, grew up, preached and died, marked by places referred to in the Bible and fought for during the Crusades. For Palestinian Muslims it is a territory in which there are many holy places associated with their 'national' as well as their religious identity. For all **Palestinians**, Palestine is a special land, their homeland.

The Holy Land Foundation for Relief and Development (HLF)

Founded in 1992 with a large cash donation from **Hamas**, the Foundation collected US $42m. between 1994 and 2000, according to its tax returns. In 2000 it raised an estimated $13m. in the USA alone (having raised $5.8m. in 1998 and $6.3m. in 1999). The HLF also received money from other charitable organizations across North America. In the early 1990s, for example, the Woodridge Foundation, a custom-built subdivision of houses worth $300,000–$500,000 in DuPage County, was used by the **Qur'anic Literacy Institute** to launder money from wealthy Saudi supporters of Hamas. In 1994 a meeting of the **Muslim Arab Youth Association** in Los Angeles raised over $200,000 for the families of Hamas fighters. During Thanksgiving 2000 the **Islamic Association for Palestine**, the voice of Hamas in the USA, organised a conference to raise $200,000 for Palestinian martyrs. In December 2001 South African intelligence revealed that a contribution to the HLF had been made by the Jerusalem Fund, a Canadian **aid** organization. The HLF has supported medical clinics, orphanages, schools, refugee camps and community centres in the **West Bank** and **Gaza Strip**. It also supports Hamas itself, enabling it to operate throughout Israel and in the **Occupied Territories.**

Home of East Turkestan Youth

Branded as '**Xinjiang**'s Hamas', the Home of East Turkestan Youth is a radical group committed to achieving the goal of independence through the use of armed force. It has some 2,000 members, some of whom have undergone training in using explosive devices in Afghanistan and other Islamic countries.

Homeland Security Advisory System

Established by US President **George W. Bush** in September 2001 in the immediate aftermath of the bombing of the **World Trade Center** and the Pentagon. It was to be 'the foundation for building a comprehensive and effective communication structure for the dissemination of information regarding the risk of terrorist attacks to all levels of government and American people'.

House of Saud

Royal family of **Ibn Saud** and his descendants.

Hrawi, Elias (1930–)

Lebanese politician, and President in 1989–98. As Hrawi's Zahle region was under Syrian control through most of the civil war, he developed good relations with Syria. This came to be central both to his rise to success, which was aided by Syria, and the direction of his politics through the nine years of his presidency. However, his pro-Syrian politics provoked many Lebanese nationalists. Born into a land-owning **Maronite** Christian family in the Zahle region, Hrawi was elected as President in 1989 with 90% of the votes from the parliament. His first challenge was **Michel Aoun**, the 'temporary' Prime Minister, who did not acknowledge his presidency. This led to a bitter struggle, but in 1990 Hrawi was central in securing support for the forthcoming negotiations for the National Reconciliation Charter to be held in Ta'if, Saudi Arabia, and, together with his Syrian allies, Hrawi inflicted a heavy defeat on Aoun. This victory marked the end of the **Lebanese civil war** and allowed Hrawi to create Greater **Beirut**, which came totally under his Government's control. At the next elections in 1992 Hrawi's supporters gained more seats, increasing his power. In 1995 he had his presidency prolonged for three years, followinga change in the Constitution, but in 1998 he stepped down and was succeeded by **Emile Lahoud**.

HSBC Amanah Finance Company

A major foreign participant in Middle Eastern banking.

Human Development Index (HDI)

Before the development of the Human Development Index by the United Nations (first used in 1990), international organizations commonly focused on a nation's economy as the sole indicator of its development status. Gross national product was the only measurement used to compare international development between countries. Critics claimed that a country's basic standard of living should be analysed with more than economic growth in mind.

The HDI attempts to broaden the definition of development by including both economic and social indicators. The index combines three factors: opportunity for long and healthy live (life expectancy), educational attainment (adult **literacy** rate and school enrolment), and standard of living (gross domestic product). The index is calculated by averaging the values of the three components to produce a final ranking. The HDI is helpful in assessing a country's development status through measurements of the quality of life as well as economic strength..

The HDI ranks countries from 1-174, the first being the most developed and the 174th the least. In the *Human Development Report 2003* Norway ranked first and Sierra Leone 174th.

Human Development Report

The *Human Development Report*'s primary purpose is to assess the state of human development world-wide and to provide a critical analysis of a specific theme each year. It combines thematic policy analysis with detailed country data that focus on human well-being, not just economic trends. The indicators in the Report reflect the rich body of information available internationally. To allow comparisons across countries and over time, where possible the indicator tables in the Report are based on internationally standardized data, collected and processed by sister agencies in the international system or, in a few cases, by other bodies. These organizations, whether collecting data from national sources or through their own surveys, harmonize definitions and collection methods to make their data as internationally comparable as possible. In a few cases where data are not available from international organizations—particularly for the human development indices—other sources are used. Data on all of the countries of the **Middle East** are available. (See also **Arab Human Development Report**.)

Human Poverty Index

HPI-1 is used for measuring the level of poverty in developing countries. It reflects three aspects of impoverishment: life expectancy; the knowledge level, measured by the adult population illiteracy ratio indicator; and the general level of economic well-being, measured by the percentage of the population that does not have access to a modern **water** supply and the percentage of children under five years of age who are underweight. As the level of impoverishment of individuals depends on their relationship to the wider society of which they are a part, a separate indicator was developed—HPI-2—to estimate the poverty level of the population in countries of the OECD. HPI-2 is calculated on the basis of the three components used in calculating HPI-1 plus one additional component, the social isolation factor, which is based on expectancy at birth of death before 60; the coefficient of functional illiteracy of the adults; the percentage of the population living below the poverty line, and the coefficient of long-term unemployment (12 months and more).

Huntington, Samuel P.

Right-wing/conservative academic who coined the term and theory of the Clash of Civilizations first in the journal *Foreign Affairs*, and subsequently expanded it in his publication, *The Clash of Civilisations and the Remaking of World Order*.

Husayn Suicide Squads

The Husayn Suicide Squads (Majmu'at Husayn al-Intihariya) comprised about 100 members. The organization was obscure except for the name of its leader, Abu Haydar al-Musawi. It emerged in 1982 when it claimed responsibility for attacks against the South Lebanese Army in protest against its collaboration with Israel.

Hussain, Saddam

President and Prime Minister of Iraq, 1979–2003. Born in **Tikrit**, north-west of **Baghdad**, son of a landless peasant, Saddam Hussain first joined the Iraqi branch of the **(Arab) Ba'ath(ist) Socialist Party** in 1956 at the age of 19. Two years later he was sentenced to prison, subsequently serving a six-month sentence, for political activities against the regime. In 1959 he participated in the coup and assassination attempt against Prime Minister **Abdul Karim Kassem.** The plot was discovered and Saddam fled first to Syria and then to Egypt and was sentenced to death *in absentia* in 1960. On 8 February 1963, following the **Ramadan** revolution, he returned to Iraq and joined the leadership of the Ba'ath Party, but was arrested in a campaign against Ba'ath Party members. Whilst still in prison, Saddam was elected as deputy secretary-general of the Ba'ath Party. He escaped from prison in 1967, was involved in the 1968 Ba'athist *coup d'état* and was subsequently made responsible for Iraqi internal security. In November 1969 he was elected as vice-chairman of the **Revolutionary Command Council** (RCC), and formed an alliance with his second cousin, **Ahmad Hassan al-Bakr**, the Council's chairman and Iraq's President.

In June 1972 Saddam led the process of nationalizing the **oil** resources of Iraq, which had been under the control of Western companies. In 1975 he signed the **Algiers Accord** with Iran (which, among other matters, regulated the border questions), an act that indicated that he had gained a stronger position than al-Bakr and was effectively the major power in the government. In June 1979 he took over as President, after he had discovered that al-Bakr had initiated negotiations on unity between Syria and Iraq. Al-Bakr was stripped of all positions, and placed under house arrest. In 1980 Saddam initiated a process to restore some semblance of parliamentary **democracy** in Iraq; elections to the Iraqi national assembly took place in June and the assembly held its first session at the end of the month. Despite growing opposition, Saddam was re-elected as chairman of the RCC and during the next few years consolidated his position—despite opposition within the Ba'ath Party, the army and the administration—in ruthless fashion. No formal political opposition was permitted; little informal opposition was allowed either. In September 1980 he effectively terminated the Algiers Accord, on the grounds of continuing disagreements over territories occupied by Iran in 1973, thereby provoking a war that was to last eight years and prove enormously costly.

At the same time, he was involved throughout the first half of the 1980s in a protracted struggle to resolve 'the Kurdish question' through a combination of negotiations and military force. Throughout the **Iran–Iraq War (1980–88)** Saddam continued to deal aggressively with the Kurdish separatist movement in the north. Throughout the war, the West (and the Soviet bloc) provided substantial financial and material support to Iraq, viewing Iran as a major threat to the stability of the **Middle East**. Saddam Hussain made use of this almost universal external support to build a massive military capacity (including chemical weapons, which were used not only against Iran but also against the **Kurds** at **Halabja** in 1988). Despite the support received, Iraq was unable to achieve a lasting success in the war; but eventually, in July 1988, Iran accepted the terms for a cease-fire of UN Security Council Resolution 598 and two years later, in September 1990, peace was declared as Iraq and Iran agreed to resume diplomatic relations.

As the war with Iran came to an end, Saddam Hussain moved to consolidate his position at home. While continuing to maintain an extremely repressive regime involving a pervasive secret service and significant violations of human rights, in November 1988 he also announced a programme of political reforms, including the introduction of a multi-party system. In January 1989 he established a committee to draft a new constitution. Elections to the national assembly were held in April 1989 for the third time since its creation in 1980. The 250 seats were reportedly contested by more than 900 candidates, including independents and members of the **National Progressive Front** as well as members of the Ba'ath Party. It was estimated that 75% of Iraq's electorate took part in the elections and that one-half of the deputies elected were members of the Ba'ath Party. A new draft constitution was approved by the national assembly in July 1990 and its provisions were published. Before these proposed reforms could be implemented (or the commitment of the President to the reforms tested), however, Iraq invaded Kuwait at the beginning of August 1990. The invasion was widely condemned. The UN Security Council adopted Resolution 660, which condemned the invasion, demanded Iraq's immediate withdrawal and appealed for a negotiated settlement; and Resolution 661, which imposed mandatory economic sanctions on Iraq. The US Administration led moves to deploy military forces in the **Gulf** under **Operation Desert Shield**, in accordance with Article 51 of the UN Charter. Saddam Hussain proposed an initiative for the resolution of the conflict in the Gulf, linking Iraq's occupation of Kuwait with Israel's occupation of the **West Bank** and **Gaza Strip** and the Palestinian question. This was repeatedly rejected by the US Administration. Successive diplomatic efforts made between August 1990 and January 1991 foundered, virtually without exception, on Saddam Hussain's refusal to withdraw from Kuwait. **Operation Desert Storm**—in effect, war with Iraq to achieve the liberation of Kuwait—was initiated on the night of 16–17 January 1991 on the basis of UN Security Council Resolution 678, which authorized 'all member states . . . to use all necessary means to uphold and implement UN Security Council Resolution 660 and all subsequent relevant resolutions and to restore peace and security in the area'. Although Saddam Hussain himself predicted fierce resistance by Iraqi forces and 'the mother of all battles', the US-led military intervention—air raids first on Baghdad and then on the

Iraqi forces, followed by a ground assault—resulted in defeat for Iraq within a few weeks, and by the end of February 1991 US President **George Bush** announced that the war to liberate Kuwait had been won.

Encouraged by the defeat of the regime and in anticipation of further external support, rebellion broke out almost immediately both in the north, among the Kurds, and in the south, among the Iraqi **Shi'ite** population. By mid-March the uprising in the south had been brutally crushed, but there was international support to establish 'safe havens' for the more clearly distinctive Kurds and Saddam Hussain's regime proved unable to control political developments in the north—which included not only a degree of effective autonomy for the Kurds as a whole and the intervention of foreign agencies (including relief and humanitarian **aid** organizations) on a significant scale, but also considerable conflict between the major Kurdish factions, the **Patriotic Union of Kurdistan** (PUK) and the **Kurdish Democratic Party** (KDP) and the involvement of Turkish forces—throughout the remainder of the decade.

Within the country at large, Saddam Hussain appeared more secure politically even than before the 'war'. Despite several alleged attempts at military coups, the government's control of the army looked as firm as ever while a reshuffle of the Council of Ministers in March 1991, and additional government adjustments later in the year and in February and August 1992, brought his closest supporters and family members into the most important positions. In September 1991 the government introduced legislation providing for the establishment of a multi-party political system, in accordance with the draft of the new permanent Constitution, resuming a process that had begun before the invasion of Kuwait. In the same month the Ba'ath Party held its 10th Congress—the first since 1982—and Saddam Hussain was re-elected as secretary-general of the Party's powerful regional command. Assured of his position at home, Saddam Hussain continued in effect to defy the international community, flouting, ignoring and 'playing fast and loose' with UN requirements and resolutions, and lobbying for the lifting of economic sanctions. The USA and Britain remained adamant, although other states were showing increasing willingness to compromise by the mid-1990s. By this time, however, the regime was under pressure at home as well as abroad. In May 1994 Saddam Hussain had assumed the post of Prime Minister in a reshuffle of the Council of Ministers and austerity measures were in force. Dissatisfaction within the army surfaced in early 1995. An unsuccessful coup in January resulted in a comprehensive reorganization of military ranks and the appointment of a new chief of the general staff. In March another coup attempt was thwarted. Civil disturbances led to the dismissal of the Minister of the Interior. Major opposition from within the army and clans traditionally supportive of Saddam Hussain began to develop and there were defections (to Jordan) by two of his sons-in-law. In September 1995 the RCC approved an amendment to the Constitution whereby the elected chairman of the RCC would automatically assume the presidency of the republic, subject to the approval of the national assembly and endorsement by a national plebiscite. Saddam Hussain's candidature was endorsed by the national assembly and a referendum took place in

October in which 99.5% of the electorate reportedly participated, of whom 99.9% reportedly endorsed the President's continuance in office for a seven-year renewable term. At the end of the month further elections and 'more democratization' were promised. There were further changes in the Council of Ministers at the end of the year. In February 1996 the two sons-in-law who had defected to Jordan returned to Baghdad and were immediately assassinated. There was conflict within the ruling élite, and in March the chief of staff of the Iraqi army during the **Gulf War (1991)** fled to **Amman**, Jordan, and joined the **Iraqi National Accord** (an expatriate opposition group). In June there were reports of another coup attempt and large numbers of army officers were arrested and executed. Elections to the national assembly were held in March 1996, and elections to municipal councils in May, but these were widely condemned as a farce. There was continuing repression of the Shi'ites in the south, particularly affecting the **Marsh Arabs**. Saddam's absence from celebrations for his 60th birthday in April 1997 prompted speculation that security concerns had intensified since the assassination attempt on his son, **Uday Hussain**, in December 1996. In mid-1997 a number of changes were made to senior military posts and in the second half of the year a number of senior military officers and Ba'ath Party members were executed, as were an estimated 800 political prisoners. Many mid-level and senior Ba'ath Party officials were replaced in a political purge.

During 1998 and 1999 the US Administration substantially increased its support for Iraqi opposition groups in exile after President **Clinton** reluctantly approved the **Iraq Liberation Act**. The Iran-based Shi'ite opposition group, **the Supreme Council for the Islamic Revolution in Iraq**, refused involvement in any US-sponsored plan to overthrow Saddam Hussain, but continued to mount its own attacks inside Iraqi territory. The response of the regime was continued repression in the predominantly Shi'ite south. In the Kurdish enclave the rival factions of the PUK and KDP had managed to achieve a fragile cease-fire, and in September 1998 the USA brokered a peace agreement between them. By late 1999, however, little progress had been made in implementing the 'Washington Accord' and in February 2000 a group of State Department officials visited the area. Saddam Hussain had maintained relations with the two Kurdish factions and had shown himself prepared to envisage a regional Kurdish government, but unwilling to allow Kurdish control over oil-rich **Kirkuk**. In December 2000 the Iraqi army advanced briefly into the Kurdish enclave while the administration continued a policy of '**Arabization**' of those parts of northern Iraq controlled by Baghdad.

UN sanctions imposed from August 1990 onwards against the Iraqi regime, under the terms of **UN Security Council Resolution 687**, had continued throughout the first half of the 1990s, although from late 1992 onwards there had been increasing disagreement both within the UN and among the members of the international community regarding this strategy, with Russia, France, China and Spain more open to change and the USA and Britain taking a harder line. Already by the mid-1990s there was evidence that, while the sanctions seriously affected the

Iraqi economy, leading to food shortages, declining public **health** services and great hardship for the Iraqi people, they did little to weaken Saddam's political power and could even have had the effect of increasing his reputation both at home and abroad, and his effective grip on domestic politics. In November 1994 the Iraqi national assembly voted to recognize Kuwait within the borders defined by the UN, but sanctions were renewed in the same month, and again in January 1995, despite the report by the head of **UNSCOM** in December that he was confident Iraq no longer had any nuclear, chemical or ballistic weapons. In October 1995, however, UNSCOM reported that Iraq had concealed evidence of biological weapons development, chemical missile flight tests and work on missiles with nuclear capability and that, consequently, its work was far from over. In December 1996 the UN agreed to implement Resolution 986 making possible an 'oil-for-food agreement', but difficulties remained regarding the relationship between UNSCOM and the Iraqi regime. Throughout 1998 the debate continued, both with regard to sanctions and with regard to Iraq's 'non-compliance' with the requests of UNSCOM for full disclosure of weapons and weapons programmes. In September 1998 the Iraqi government formally halted its co-operation with UNSCOM until the sanctions regime was reviewed. In December 1998, as the UN Security Council considered yet another critical report by UNSCOM, the USA and Britain launched an intensive bombing campaign against Iraq with the stated aim of diminishing and degrading Saddam Hussain's ability to deploy and use **weapons of mass destruction**. The bombings of **Operation Desert Fox** revealed the divisions within the UN Security Council regarding policy towards Iraq. Over the next two years, the sanctions regime was progressively eroded as opposition to its continuance increased, UNSCOM was replaced by **UNMOVIC**, and the position of the USA and Britain hardened against what they considered to be an appeasement policy towards Saddam Hussain's regime.

The election of a Republican US President, **George W. Bush**, son of the President who had gone to war against Iraq 10 years earlier, also served to stiffen US resolve. After his nomination as Secretary of State in the new Bush Administration, Colin Powell, who had been chairman of the joint chiefs of staff at the time of the Gulf War (1991), asserted that Saddam Hussain's regime was a menace to Iraq's neighbours and to its own people. In February 2001 US and British aircraft attacked targets inside Iraq, in the first major assault since Operation Desert Fox in 1998. Further air strikes took place during the year. At the same time, the US Administration proposed a tighter, 'smart' sanctions regime against Iraq.

In October 2002 Saddam Hussain stood as the sole candidate in presidential elections, in which, in a reported 100% turn-out, 100% of the votes cast were for him. The result was ridiculed by most external observers. In March 2003 US President George W. Bush demanded that Saddam leave Iraq together with his sons. Saddam failed to respond, and the USA, together with Britain, attacked Iraq, first with massive aerial bombardments and then with land forces under the control of the USA. In April Saddam Hussain and his immediate supporters went into hiding, and the Ba'ath Party lost effective control of the country, the administration of which was assumed by the '**coalition**' forces. On 13 December 2003 Saddam Hussain was captured by US military forces. He is now due to be tried before a Iraqi court, whose proceedings it is anticipated that he will attempt to politicize by, in a way similar to that pursued by the former Yugoslav President Slobodan Milošević, attempting to call to account former Western government leaders for the support they offered him prior to the Gulf War (1991). The US Secretary of Defense, Donald Rumsfeld, who visited Saddam in 1983 and 1984, is among those who could face unwelcome questioning.

Hussain, Qusay Saddam

Saddam Hussain's second eldest son who may have been designated as his successor. He was deputy commander-in-chief of Iraq's armed forces and head of security, supervising the **Republican Guard**. He was killed by **coalition** forces, together with his brother, Uday, in July 2003.

Hussain, Uday Saddam

Saddam Hussain's eldest son, who was in charge of the *Fedayeen*, an armed militia. He was shot and temporarily paralysed in 1996. He was regarded as unstable and unlikely to succeed Saddam Hussain. He was killed by **coalition** forces, together with his brother, Qusay, in July 2003.

Hussein I (Hussaynu ibn Talali Hashim)

Former King of Jordan. Educated in Egypt and at the British Royal Military Academy at Sandhurst, the 18-year-old Hussein ascended the throne as King of Jordan in 1953 following the death of his father, **Talal**. Talal had succeeded to the throne himself only two years before on the death by assassination of his father King **Abdullah** (in July 1951), only five years after his own accession to the throne, in May 1946. The new Constitution of 1952 defined the king of Jordan as a constitutional monarch, but one with considerable powers. Hussein was concerned to establish good relations with other **Arab** states, of whatever political orientation, and not to make too heavy a commitment to any particular alliance or pact. He was unwilling to adhere either to the Egyptian-Syrian-Saudi Arabian grouping or to the **Baghdad Pact** that Britain was trying to establish. His relationship with Britain in particular was a delicate balancing act. In December 1954 a financial **aid** agreement was signed; but agreement over the revision of the **Anglo-Jordanian Treaty of 1948**, which gave Britain certain peace-time military privileges, was precluded by British insistence that any new pact should fit into a general Middle Eastern defence system. During 1955 military co-operation was agreed with Syria, Lebanon and Egypt and **Glubb** Pasha, the British commander-in-chief of the Jordanian army, was dismissed in favour of a Jordanian. Tension between Jordan and Israel was not helped by the Suez crisis in 1956, but British policy in the **Middle East** was dramatically affected and by mid-July 1957 the last of the British troops deployed in Jordan had left.

At home Hussein's plans for limited political representation included elections, which were held in October 1956. These resulted in the inclusion of Arab nationalists and communists in the Cabinet. Political divisions developed and a rift between King Hussein and Prime Minister Nabulsi over the latter's inclination towards the USSR led to his resignation. In 1957, after an attempted military coup led by his chief of staff, Hussein dissolved parliament, banned political parties and introduced martial law introduced. From now on King Hussein was to keep firm control of the political process, although he was prepared to experiment with limited forms of political representation. In 1965 he appointed his brother, Hassan, as crown prince, thereby excluding his own children from the succession to the throne.

In 1967 he took Jordan into war with Israel (the **Six-Day War**), which resulted in the loss of the **West Bank** to Israel. This was a blow to Hussein's hope for formal recognition of the West Bank as part of Jordan and a further source of tension between Jordan and the other Arab states (and the **Palestine Liberation Organization**—PLO) regarding the status of **Palestinians** in Jordan. In 1970 fighting between Palestinian guerrillas operating from Jordan and Jordanian gov-ernment forces led to a major conflict (**Black September**) and the eventual expulsion, in 1971, of the PLO guerrillas from Jordan. Jordan's relations with the PLO and other Arab states deteriorated and Jordan participated only marginally (sending troops to support Syria on the **Golan Heights**) in the **Arab-Israeli War (1973)**. Relations with the PLO and other Arab states improved after the **Rabat** Summit of 1974 when representatives of 20 Arab heads of state (including King Hussein) unanimously recognized the PLO as the sole representative of the Palestinians and its right to establish a national authority over any liberated Palestinian territory (including the West Bank).

Hussein had experimented with various forms of political representation during the early 1970s—in 1971 he announced the creation of a tribal council and the establishment of the Jordanian National Union, which (renamed the Arab National Union in 1972) was to become Jordan's only legal political organization (Hussein was its president and appointed its Supreme Executive Council). However, after internal security was threatened by an attempted military coup in 1972, he began to take more powers into his own hands and limited political representation still further. In 1974 the national assembly was dissolved; in 1975 elections were postponed; and in 1976 a constitutional amendment was enacted to suspend elections indefinitely. In June 1978, at the age of 43, Hussein married Lisa Najeeb Halaby, who took the name Queen Noor.

Hussein refused to allow Jordan to be drawn into the '**peace process**' involving the USA, Israel and Egypt. After Israel's invasion of Lebanon in 1982, however, he found himself a key part of US President Reagan's peace plan that involved the creation of an autonomous Palestinian authority on the West Bank in association with Jordan. In 1985 Hussein apparently reached an agreement with the PLO on a future confederation of a Palestinian state and Jordan. In July 1988, however, he ceded all Jordanian claims to Israeli-occupied West Bank to the PLO.

In 1989, in the aftermath of extensive popular protest against rising prices and the government's economic policies, Hussein announced that a general election would be held for the first time since 1967. An election to the national assembly (suspended in 1974, but reconvened in 1984) or house of representatives duly took place in November 1989. The ban on political parties (in force since 1963) remained in force and most candidates stood as independents. Islamists won 34 of the 80 seats. Under increasing pressure to allow greater political freedom, Hussein appointed a Royal Commission in April 1990 to draft a **National Charter** and in 1991 the Charter was approved. Among other things, it revoked the ban on political parties in return for their allegiance to the **monarchy**. In 1991 Hussein repealed the provision for martial law that had been in force since 1967. Elections were held in 1993.

During the Iraq crisis, Hussein made every effort to maintain neutrality, but persistently argued for an Arab solution and opposed the deployment of a multi-national armed force in the **Gulf** region. He also made major efforts to contribute to the peace process in the Middle East, meeting secretly with **Shimon Peres** in November 1993 and with **Itzhak Rabin** in May 1994, and eventually signing the Washington Declaration at the White House ending the state of war between Jordan and Israel which had existed since 1948. At home, the promise of greater **democracy** had not substantially materialized; there was growing disillusionment with the role of the national assembly which was perceived to have little or no influence over important issues, and many parties decided to boycott elections held in 1997 in which there was a low turn-out. In 1988 Hussein began to undergo treatment in the USA for lymphatic cancer and transferred responsibility for certain executive duties to his brother, the crown prince. In January 1999, however, he dismissed his brother and issued a royal decree naming his eldest son, **Abdullah**, as Crown Prince of Jordan. In February Hussein died and his son Abdullah was sworn in as the new King of Jordan.

I

IAEA – *see* **International Atomic Energy Agency**

Ibadis

Followers of the Islamic sect of **Ibadism**. Ibadis refer to themselves as 'the Muslims' or 'the people of straightness' (*ahl al-istiqama*).

Ibadism

Ibadism is a distinct sect of **Islam** that is neither **Sunni** nor **Shi'i**. It exists mainly in Oman (where it is the majority religion), in Zanzibar, East Africa, and in the **Maghreb**—in the Nafus mountains of Libya, the island of Jerba in Tunisia and the Mzab valley of Algeria. The sect developed out of the 7th-century Islamic sect known as the Khawarij, and shares with that group the desire to found a righteous Muslim society and the belief that true Muslims are only to be found in their own sect. The **Ibadis** broke off early from the mainstream of Islam and are usually regarded as heretics.

IBDCA-C – *see* **Islamic Great Eastern Raiders' Front**

Ibn Saud

Born *c*. 1879, Abdul Aziz Abdul Rahman as-Saud was the founder of the modern state of Saudi Arabia. A decade after the expulsion of his family from **Najd** by the Rashidis in 1891, when he was in his early twenties, Ibn Saud (as he came to be widely known) sought to regain the family territories. At the head of a small force of tribesmen, he began to raid areas under Rashidi control north of **Riyadh**, and in 1902 seized Riyadh in a surprise attack. He was subsequently defeated by Ottoman troops, but when the Ottomans departed in 1912 he was able to build up his support. His followers included the zealous religious-military **Ikhwan** (Brothers) who provided the shock-troops of his forces. He gradually gained control of the Hasa region (modern Kuwait and Qatar). After the First World War, in 1921 he was able to defeat the Rashidis at Hail. He gained control of the Asir region between **Hejaz**

219

and Yemen, with the assistance of his ablest son Faisal, and the northern region of what is now Saudi Arabia. He defeated Hussein, Sherif of **Mecca.** By 1926 he was able to assume the title of King of the Najd and the Hejaz. By 1932, he had achieved effective control over the different parts of **Arabia** for the first time, and took the title of King of 'Saudi' Arabia, stamping his family's name on the new state he had established. In 1933 he granted the Standard Oil Co a concession to search for **oil** in 'Saudi Arabia'. The discovery of the world's largest oilfields transformed thestatus of the regime, the country and the region. The US companies operating in the new Saudi Arabia were combined to constitute the Arabian Oil Company (**ARAMCO**), which maintained an effective monopoly over Saudi Arabia's oil **industry**; it was not until 1980 that Saudi Arabia was to take over control of ARAMCO. Ibn Saud played a key role in establishing the **Arab League** in **Cairo** in 1945, while his meeting in the same year with US President Roosevelt consolidated the close relationship between Saudi Arabia and the USA which was to prove enduring. After his death in 1953, the kingdom passed through a decade of instability, which ended with the coronation of **Faisal** in November 1964.

Ibrahim, Izzat

Deputy chairman of the Iraqi **Revolutionary Command Council** and leader of the powerful ad-Douri clan. A close associate of **Saddam Hussain** since the early days of the **Ba'ath Party**.

IDF – *see* Israeli Defence Force

Idris I, Said Mohammad

Born in 1890, Said Mohammad Idris as-Sanussi was the first King of Libya, who reigned in 1951–69. A grandson of the founder of the Sanussi Muslim order, he became its leader in 1917. In 1920 he was acknowledged by Italy as Emir of Cyrenaica and, in 1921, after joining forces with the Tripolitanians, as Emir of Libya. He was forced to flee to Egypt in 1922 after quarrelling with the Italian Fascists. He was restored to power by Great Britain in 1943 and became Libya's first king when independence was granted in 1951. He was deposed in September 1969 by the Libyan army under the leadership of Col **Mu'ammar al-Qaddafi** in a bloodless coup. He went into exile in Egypt, where he remained until his death in 1983.

IFAD – *see* International Fund for Agricultural Development

IFIs – *see* **International financial institutions**

IG – *see* **Islamic Group**

IGC – *see* **Iraqi Provisional Governing Council**

Ijma

In **Arabic**: means 'consensus'. Consensus of the opinions of the recognized religious authorities at any given time concerning the interpretation (***ijtihad***) and application of the teachings of the **Koran** and the **Hadith** in any particular situation. One of the four components of the **Shari'a**—the others being the Koran, Hadith and Ijtihad.

Ijtihad

Individual reasoning, or interpretation of the Holy Scriptures (the **Koran** and **Hadith** and other texts). Considered by many as a crucial component of a 'rational' approach to Islamic beliefs and practices.

Ikhwan

Generally (in **Arabic**) means brotherhood or brethren.

Ikhwan

The Brotherhood

An Islamic military movement in **Arabia**. **Ibn Saud** (Abdul Aziz ibn Abdul Rahman as-Saud), the ruler of **Najd**, had the idea of teaching the tenets of **Islam** to the nomadic **tribes** of Arabia. He wanted to replace their customary law with **Islamic Law**, or **Shari'a**, and their traditional tribal bonds with religious ones. He would do this first and foremost by settling the tribes. The settlers were known as al-Ikhwan. Their settlements became the primary source of soldiers to as-Saud, and the Ikhwan helped him conquer almost four-fifths of the **Arabian Peninsula**. Helped by his army, Great Britain recognized him as King of the **Hejaz** and Sultan of Najd in exchange for his respect for Britain's status as protector of Oman and the **Gulf** principalities, as well as the territorial integrity of Iraq and **Transjordan**.

Al-Ikhwan al-Muslimin – *see* Muslim Brotherhood

Ilal Amam – *see* Forward (Morocco)

Imam

Has the contemporary meaning of prayer leader at a mosque. Historically, the term refers to one of the legitimate descendants of the **Prophet Muhammad**.

Imperialism

A term that is generally used to refer to a system of political and economic domination. Usually prefaced by reference to a particular dominant or imperialist state—e.g. US imperialism, British imperialism, Soviet imperialism. In the Marxist tradition the term is used more precisely to refer to 'the highest stage of capitalism' (following Lenin) and is usually associated with the period from 1870 until the First World War. In this context, **colonialism** refers to a particular form of imperialism associated with the annexation of territory, the creation of 'colonies' or 'colonial territories' and, in some cases, the establishment of settler colonial states.

IMU – *see* Islamic Movement of Uzbekistan

INA – *see* Iraqi National Accord

INC – *see* Iraqi National Congress

Income

Average annual income per caput in the **Middle East** is currently some US $1,375. However, this figure obscures enormous income differentials between and within individual countries in the region. In the wealthiest sub-set of countries, the members of the **Gulf Co-operation Council** (GCC), income from exports of **petroleum** drives annual income per caput up to $11,605. In 2002 the *World Wealth Report* estimated that there were some 300,000 so-called **high net worth individuals** in the region, holding investable assets of $1,100,000m., equivalent to 309% of the GCC countries' output, or to 11% of US gross domestic product. Even average annual per caput income in the **Gulf states**, however, is still well below average annual per caput income in Europe ($19,740) and the USA ($34,800). Income distribution is unequal in most countries within the region.

Independent Liberal Party (ILP)

Israeli political party established in 1965 when seven of the members of the **Liberal Party** in the **Knesset** refused to join **Gahal**, the result of a merger between the Liberal Party and **Herut**. From 1965 until 1977 the ILP received, on average, about

3.5% of the vote and retained four–five Knesset seats. In 1971 it won only one seat and in 1981, with only 0.6% of the vote, it forfeited its representation in the Knesset.

Independent Nasserite Movement

Lebanese political grouping, also known as **Murabitun** or the **Sunni Muslim** militia. Its leader is Ibrahim Qulayat.

Industry and industrial output

Saudi Arabia is the largest industrial economy in the region, ranking 17th in the world in terms of industrial output, one place ahead of the Republic of China. In regional terms, Israel follows Saudi Arabia (ranking 30th in the world), and is followed in turn by Iran and the United Arab Emirates (joint 32nd in the world), Turkey (36th), Egypt (38th) and Algeria (40th). Israel is the country with the largest manufacturing output in the region (26th in world terms), followed by Saudi Arabia and Turkey (joint 34th in the world), Iran (37th) and Egypt (39th). Syria experienced the highest rate of industrial growth of the economies of the region in 1991–2001, with an average annual rate of 8.5%.

Infitah

The term literally means 'open door'. In economic terms it refers to liberalization. It is normally used in connection with **Anwar Sadat's** policies after the **Arab–Israeli War (1973)** when he began relaxing government controls on the Egyptian economy. In this way he hoped to encourage the private sector and stimulate foreign investment in Egypt.

Informal money transfer systems (IMTS)

There are many IMTS in operation in the region. The best known is the *hawala* system. Others include the movement of funds through multiple points in a chain of banking services so as to obscure the origin and final destination of the funds being transferred—this is often referred to as '**money-laundering**'; and smuggling cash, bullion or goods in kind across borders.

Information technology

Access to and use of information and computing technology (ICT) is very limited in the region as a whole. Only 0.6% of the population of the **Arab World** uses the internet and the personal computer penetration rate is only 1.2%, according to the *Arab Human Development Report*. Israel has the highest commitment to, and use of, information technology in the region, ranking 15th in the global information and communications technology index (a measure of ICT usage that includes per caput measures of telephone lines, internet usage, personal computers and mobile phone users). No other country in the region features in the top 40 places of the index. Companies such as **Checkpoint** account for a very large proportion of the 109 Israeli firms listed on US stock markets, which have a total value of US $29,000m. Israel has more than 3,000 high-technology start-ups annually, more than any other country, except the USA.

Inonu, Ismet

President of Turkey from 1938 until 1950.

Intégrisme

The term properly refers to a dissident tendency within the Roman Church, but it is widely used as the French equivalent to Islamic **fundamentalism** or radical Islam.

Inter-Arab Investment Guarantee Corpn

Established in 1975, and based in Kuwait, the Corporation insures **Arab** investors for non-commercial risks and export credits for commercial and non-commercial risks. It also undertakes research and other activities to promote inter-Arab trade and investment.

Inter-Services Intelligence (ISI)

Pakistan's intelligence services, operating both within Pakistan and outside the country.

International Atomic Energy Agency (IAEA)

An agency of the United Nations responsible for monitoring nuclear programmes world-wide. It undertakes the supervision of national nuclear programmes and ensures that, where these are being designed to develop nuclear weapons and not just nuclear power for peaceful purposes, the governments of the states in question are reported to the UN and that teams are dispatched to inspect the relevant plants and sites in order to determine how far the weapons programme has advanced. Syria is the only Arab member state. Representatives of the IAEA were among the UN weapons inspectors sent to Iraq in the 1990s to investigate that country's programme for the development of **weapons of mass destruction**. In November 2003 the head of the IAEA, Mohammed El Baradei, informed the board of the Agency that Iran was guilty 'of many breaches and failures to comply with its obligations' and accused that country of conducting 'a deliberate counter-effort that spanned many years to conceal materials, facilities and activities that were required to have been declared'. The IAEA is currently inspecting Libyan and Iranian facilities. In December 2003 it put forward a proposal to focus attention on Israel, which is widely believed to have between 100 and 200 nuclear warheads as part of its arsenal of weapons of mass destruction.

International Centre for Agricultural Research in the Dry Areas (ICARDA)

Established in 1977 and based in **Aleppo**, Syria, ICARDA aims to improve the production of lentils, barley and fava beans throughout the developing world. It supports the improvement and development of dryland farming and on-farm **water** efficiency use, rangeland and small ruminant production in all dry area developing countries. Within the West Asia and North Africa regions it promotes the improvement of bread and durum wheat and chickpea production and of dryland farming systems generally. It undertakes research, training and dissemination of information, in co-operation with national, regional and international research institutes, universities and ministries of **agriculture**, in order to enhance production, alleviate poverty and promote sustainable natural resources management practices. It is a member of the network of 16 agricultural research centres supported by the Consultative Group on International Agricultural Research.

International Conference on Population and Development (ICPD)

UN conference, held in **Cairo**, Egypt, on 5–13 September 1994, which led to a declaration, by 179 countries, that population and development are inextricably linked, and that empowering **women** and meeting people's needs for **education** and **health**, including reproductive health, are necessary for both individual advancement and balanced development. The conference adopted a 20-year Programme of Action, which focused on individuals' needs and rights, rather than on achieving demographic targets. Advancing gender equality, eliminating violence against women and ensuring women's ability to control their own fertility were acknowledged as cornerstones of population and development policies. Concrete goals of the ICPD centred on providing universal education; reducing infant, child and maternal mortality; ensuring universal access by 2015 to reproductive health care, including family planning and assisted childbirth; and the prevention of sexually transmitted infections, including **HIV/AIDS.**

International financial institutions

International lending agencies, such as the **International Monetary Fund** and the International Bank for Reconstruction and Development, better known as the **World Bank**, established at Bretton Woods in 1944, and now lenders of last resort and major influences on macroeconomic policy throughout the developing world, including the **Middle East**. The term is sometimes also used with reference to UN institutions such as the **International Fund for Agricultural Development**. It is also used for regional banks such as the Asian Development Bank, the African Development Bank and European Development Bank.

International Food Policy Research Institute (IFPRI)

The mission of IFPRI is to identify and analyse policies to meet the food needs of the developing world. IFPRI is one of 16 food and environmental research organizations known as the Future Harvest centres. These centres, located around the world, conduct research in partnership with farmers, scientists, and policy-makers to help alleviate poverty and increase food security while protecting the natural resource base. They are principally funded through the 58 countries, private foundations, and regional and international organizations that make up the Consultative Group on International Agricultural Research.

International Fund for Agricultural Development (IFAD)

An organization of the UN established in 1977, following a decision by the 1974 UN World Food Conference, with a mandate to combat hunger and eradicate poverty on a sustainable basis in low-**income**, food deficit regions of the world. Funding operations began in January 1978. The bulk of its funding and support for its activities came from countries that were members of the **Organization of Petroleum Exporting Countries** and from the members of the **European Union**. The governance structure of the Fund, however, was amended in February 1997, on the occasion of the fourth replenishment of its resources, in order to give more weight to the industrialized countries so that their financial contribution was better reflected. The Fund makes available additional resources on concessionary terms for agricultural development in poor member states. In allocating resources, IFAD is guided by the need to increase sustainable food production in food deficit countries and regions, and to provide support for developing sustainable livelihoods among the poor and vulnerable in developing countries. It may commit funds in the form of grants as well as loans. It is a leading agency in both research and practical work in the field of rural poverty and hunger alleviation.

International Islamic Front

The International Islamic Front for Jihad against Jews and Crusaders was launched in February 1998 by **Osama bin Laden**. Notice of its creation was given in the London-based **Arabic** newspaper *Al-Quds al-Arabi*. (The United Kingdom's press laws protected a statement banned in many parts of the **Arab World**.)

International Labour Organization (ILO)

A specialized agency of the UN whose aim is to facilitate the improvement of conditions of labour and living standards throughout the world. The ILO was created in 1919, after the First World War, by the Treaty of Versailles as an affiliated agency of the League of Nations. After the establishment of the UN during the Second World War, the ILO became the first specialized agency to be affiliated with it, in 1946. The functions of the ILO include the development and promotion of standards for national legislation to protect and improve conditions of work and standards of living. It provides technical assistance in social policy and adminis-tration and in workforce training, and fosters co-operative organizations and rural industries. It compiles labour statistics and conducts research on the social problems of international competition, unemployment and under-employment, labour and industrial relations, and technological change (including automation). It is con-cerned with the protection of international migrants and the safeguarding of trade-union rights. The ILO was awarded the Nobel Prize for Peace in 1969 in recognition of its activities.

International Monetary Fund (IMF)

Established in July 1944 at the Bretton Woods Conference, the IMF is a multilateral institution based in Washington, DC, USA, that lends money to governments to stabilize currencies and maintain order in international financial markets. For many decades the Fund has imposed stringent loan conditions designed to improve financial stability and macroeconomic indicators. It is criticized by its opponents for advocating measures that tend to lead to austerity, worsening **income** inequality and conditions for the majority of the population in the affected countries. Even more than its partner, the **World Bank**, the Fund is known for its rigid orthodoxy and often high-handed approach to indebted countries. Its performance in the **Middle East**, as well as in the Asian crisis and in Latin America, has led to charges that 'its medicine was worse than the disease it was supposed to treat'.

International Security Assistance Force (ISAF)

Eighteen countries are contributing to ISAF, the peace-keeping mission in Afghanistan sanctioned by UN Security Council Resolution 1386 of 20 December 2001. The ISAF works closely with the United Nations and the **Afghan Interim Authority** (AIA) in the performance of three principal tasks: aiding the interim government in developing national security structures; assisting the country's reconstruction; and assisting in developing and training future Afghan security forces. In agreement with AIA, ISAF has 'complete and unimpeded freedom of movement throughout the territory and airspace of Afghanistan'. The mission of the ISAF is currently limited to **Kabul** and its environs. Although Afghan Prime Minister **Hamid Karzai** favours the deployment of international peace-keepers throughout Afghanistan, US military officials remain wary of dis-patching peace-keepers to other cities while the military campaign is ongoing. An amendment to the UN resolution would be needed to expand the ISAF's operations beyond the Afghan capital.

International Solidarity Movement (ISM)

The ISM is a Palestinian-led movement of Palestinian and international activists working in the **Occupied Territories** to raise awareness of the struggle for Palestinian freedom and for an end to Israeli occupation. ISM utilizes non-violent, direct-action methods of resistance to confront and challenge illegal Israeli occupation forces and policies. The ISM supports the Palestinian right to resist the occupation, as provided for by international law, and urges an immediate end to the occupation and immediate compliance and implementation of all relevant UN resolutions. In addition, it urges immediate international intervention to protect the Palestinian people and ensure Israel's compliance with international law.

International terrorism

Attempts to forge strategic alliances between the various armed terrorist organizations of Europe and the **Middle East** began in the 1970s. In Lebanon in 1972 **George Habash** hosted one of the first international summits to form a common front against **Zionism** and Western **imperialism**. Representatives of the Japanese Red Army, the **Iranian Liberation Front**, the Irish Republican Army, the Bader-Meinhof Gang and the Turkish **Revolutionary People's Liberation Front** attended the conference. The participants agreed to establish an international network, which included economic and financial co-operation, the exchange of intelligence, sharing safe houses, joint training programmes and arms purchases. During the 1970s and 1980s the radical factions of the Palestinian nationalist movement were heavily involved in terrorist activities. During the 1980s a number of Middle Eastern states, including Iran, Israel, Libya, Saudi Arabia and Syria, were alleged to be involved in sponsoring and supporting freedom fighters/terrorist groups operating in the Middle East and Europe. An international network of such groups continued to exist, albeit in a less than systematic fashion, throughout the 1980s and into the 1990s. The emergence of **al-Qa'ida** from the mid-1980s onwards, and particularly since its dispersal after the withdrawal of Soviet troops troops from Afghanistan in 1989, has provided new impetus for the development of an international terrorist network, this time exclusively Islamist. The activities of al-Qa'ida during the 1990s, which included the bombing of US embassies in Kenya and Tanzania, led US President **Bill Clinton** to order attacks on Sudan, which was thought to be hosting **Osama bin Laden**, and on Afghanistan, which continued to provide support and a safe haven to al-Qa'ida. The attacks on the twin towers of the **World Trade Center** building in New York and on the Pentagon in September 2001, by terrorists linked to al-Qa'ida, provided the impetus for US President **George W. Bush**'s 'war on terror', which led to the mass bombing of Afghanistan, the overthrow of the **Taliban** regime and, eventually, in 2003, to intervention in Iraq.

Intifada

In **Arabic**: means 'shaking off' or 'shivering' because of fear or illness. It also has the meanings of 'sudden waking from sleep' and 'uprising'. There have been two uprisings in the Palestinian occupied territories of the **West Bank** and **Gaza Strip** in the last 20 years: the first from 1987 until 1993 and the second, known as the **al-Aqsa** *intifada*, from 2000 (see below). The first *intifada* began as demonstrations, strikes, riots and violence in the refugee camps, but it spread rapidly across the whole of Palestinian society in the West Bank and Gaza Strip. On 6 December 1987 an Israeli was stabbed to death while shopping in Gaza. On the following day four residents of the Jabalya refugee camp in Gaza were killed in a traffic accident. Rumours that the four had been killed by **Israelis** as a deliberate act of revenge began to spread among **Palestinians**. Mass rioting broke out in Jabalya on the morning of 9 December, in which a 17-year-old youth was killed by an Israeli soldier after throwing a Molotov cocktail at an army patrol. This sparked a wave of unrest that engulfed the West Bank, Gaza and **Jerusalem**. Over the following week rock-throwing, blocked roads and tyre burnings were reported throughout the territories. By 12 December six Palestinians had been killed and 30 injured in the violence. On the following day rioters threw a gasoline bomb at the US consulate in **East Jerusalem**. No one was hurt in the bombing. Israel attempted to suppress the *intifada*, with more police and army forces, the closure of universities, deportations and restrictions on economic activities. There were three principal groups behind the *intifada*—the **Palestine Liberation Organization** (PLO), **Hamas** (founded in 1988) and **Islamic Jihad** (Jihad al-Islamiyya). Hamas and Islamic Jihad called for an **Islamic state** in the entire region of (former) Palestine. Throughout the *intifada*, the PLO-dominated Unified Leadership of the *Intifada* (UNLI) co-ordinated and orchestrated the uprising, but what distinguished it from earlier protest movements was the widespread support for it, its duration and the active involvement of Islamist groups. The *intifada*, and the associated change of public opinion, was one of the reasons for the **Oslo Agreement** of 1993. The *intifada* gradually became weaker, with less widespread popular support from 1991, and broke up into a more divided and factional struggle after the Oslo Agreement. In 1989–92 many Palestinians died at the hands of other Palestinians. During this period only 16 Israeli civilians and 11 soldiers were killed by Palestinians in the territories, but more than 1,400 Israeli civilians and 1,700 Israeli soldiers were injured. As the *intifada* waned, the number of Palestinians killed for political and other reasons by death squads came to exceed the number killed in clashes with Israeli troops. The PLO began to call for an end to the violence, but murders by its members and rivals continued.

Intifada, **al-Aqsa**

The second *intifada* is known as the al-Aqsa *intifada*, which started in September 2000 after Israeli politician **Ariel Sharon** very publicly visited—and, as far as **Palestinians** were concerned, violated—the holy places in **Jerusalem**. There was increasing violence and protest in the years that followed. After 1,000 days of violence, the deaths of more than 3,000 people (2,400 Palestinians and 700 **Israelis**) and a toll of nearly 30,000 injured (23,000 Palestinians and 4,800 Israelis), the bitter and longstanding conflict between the Palestinians and Israel degenerated into a state of bitter mutual enmity that had never been so pervasive. Massive destruction of property and assaults on the lives and livelihoods of the Palestinians in the **Occupied Territories** by the **Israeli Defence Force** resulted in a wave of suicide bombings inside Israel. The Israeli government refused to talk with the Palestinian leadership and initiated a strategy of assassination with respect to the militant Islamist groups. The construction, begun in the summer of 2003, of a fence (known as '**the wall**'), ostensibly to protect Israel from attacks by Palestinian suicide bombers, but also enclosing an additional area of the **West Bank**, marked a further stage in the division of Israel from the Occupied Territories.

Invasion of Kuwait

In August 1990 Iraqi forces invaded Kuwait. This produced an immediate diplomatic and political response from the **Arab World** and the international community. The UN called on Iraq to withdraw. Iraq began to establish itself in Kuwait. While diplomatic efforts to resolve the crisis were taking place, the US Administration under President **George Bush** commenced a military deployment—**Operation Desert Shield**—to protect Saudi Arabia and build up its forces in the region. The US Administration warned Iraq that it would proceed to military action if Iraq did not withdraw from Kuwait, announcing a deadline of January 1991 by which it must do so. In the mean time it continued to build up its forces in the **Gulf** and to construct a coalition of Arab and other states to apply pressure on the regime of **Saddam Hussein**. Iraq failed to withdraw within the stipulated deadline and, in spite of intense continuing diplomacy, a US-led coalition of forces, under UN auspices, launched an assault on Iraqi forces—**Operation Desert Storm**—designed to secure their withdrawal from Kuwait.

Iran, Islamic Republic of

Jomhuri-ye Eslami-ye Iran

Lying between Iraq and Turkey to the west and Pakistan and Afghanistan to the east and north-east respectively, Iran is also bordered to the south by the Gulf of Oman, the Straits of Hormuz and the **Persian (Arabian) Gulf**, and to the north by the Caspian Sea. The Persian (Arabian) Gulf is a vital maritime route for the **transport** and export of crude **oil** from Iraq and Iran as well as from the **Gulf states**. Iran has an area of 1.648m. sq km, of which 12,000 sq km is **water**. The capital is **Tehran**, and the main administrative regions are the 28 provinces (*ostan, plural ostanha*) into which the country is divided: Ardabil, Azarbayjan-e Gharbi, Azarbayjan-e Sharqi, Bushehr, Chahar Mahall va Bakhtiari, Esfahan, Fars, Gilan,

Golestan, Hamadan, Hormozgan, Ilam, Kerman, Kermanshah, Khorasan, Khuzestan, Kohkiluyeh va Buyer Ahmad, Kordestan, Lorestan, Markazi, Mazandaran, Qazvin, Qom, Semnan, Sistan va Baluchestan, Tehran, Yazd, and Zanjan. The total population was estimated at 66,622,704 in July 2002, of which some 51% are Persian, 24% Azeri, 8% Gilaki, 8% Mazandarani, 7% **Kurd**, 3% Arab, 2% Lur, 2% Baluch, 2% Turkmen, and 1% 'other'. The population is divided among Iran's various religious groups in the following proportions: **Shi'a** Muslim 89%, **Sunni** Muslim 10%, and **Zoroastrian**, Jewish, Christian and **Baha'i** 1%. The main languages are Persian and Persian dialects (58%), Turkic and Turkic dialects (26%), Kurdish (9%), Luri (2%), Baluchi (1%), **Arabic** (1%), Turkish (1%), and 'other' (2%).

Political profile

Iran is a republic, governed by clerics. The head of state and leader of the **Islamic Revolution** is **Ayatollah Sayed Ali Khamenei** (since 4 June 1989). The leader of the government and President is Dr **Sayed Muhammad Khatami** (since 3 August 1997). The First Vice-President is Muhammad Reza Aref (since 26 August 2001). The Council of Ministers is selected by the President with legislative approval. The leader of the Islamic Revolution is appointed for life by the **Assembly of Experts**. The President, on the other hand, is elected by popular vote for a four-year term. Presidential elections were last held in June 2001. The legislature is the unicameral **Majlis-e-Shora-ye-Islami** (Islamic Consultative Assembly). It is a 290-member body (increased by 20 members for the 18 February 2000 election) whose members are elected by popular vote to serve four-year terms. Elections to the Majlis were held in February–April 2000 and again in February 2004. There was a low turn-out in 2004, largely because most of the reformist candidates were barred from contesting the election. The main reformist parties, including one led by the President's brother, boycotted the poll. The legal system is based on Islamic principles of government as laid out in the Constitution. Its apex is the Supreme Court. Political parties and groups include: the **Assembly of the Followers of the Imam's Line**, the **Freethinkers' Front**, the **Islamic Iran Participation Front**, the **Moderation and Development Party**, the **Servants of Construction Party**, and the **Society of Self-sacrificing Devotees**. Active student groups include the pro-reform Organization for Strengthening Unity and the Union of Islamic Student Societies. Groups that generally support the Islamic Republic include **Ansar-e Hezbollah**, Mujahidin of the Islamic Revolution, Muslim Students Following the Line of the Imam, and the Islamic Coalition Association. Opposition groups include the **Liberation Movement of Iran** and the Nation of Iran party. Armed political groups that have been almost completely repressed by the government include the **Mujahidin-e Khalq Organization**, the People's Fedayeen, the **Democratic Party of Iranian Kurdistan** and the Society for the Defence of Freedom.

Media

Radio and television are state-controlled and satellite dishes are banned. The regime has closed several reformist newspapers and initiated legal proceedings against their editors. There is one state-controlled radio service and one state-controlled television service. In 2002 there were eight internet service providers and 420,000 internet users.

History

Known as Persia until 1935, Iran became an Islamic republic in 1979 after the Shah was overthrown by a popular revolution and forced into exile. Clerical forces managed to gain direction of the revolution and to establish dominance over both left-wing forces and forces in favour of 'Western-style' development. Militant Iranian students seized the US embassy in Tehran on 4 November 1979 and held it until 20 January 1981. During 1980–88 Iran fought a bloody, indecisive war with Iraq over disputed territory. Since the end of the 1980s there has been a continuing struggle between the clerical conformists ('conservatives') and those wishing to undertake social, political and economic reforms. After more than two decades the key issues affecting the Islamic Republic still include the pace of economic and social reform and the reconciliation of clerical control of the regime with popular participation in government and wider political reform. The debate continues, erupting periodically in the form of overt protest. Another crucial issue is that of Iran's international relations, including those with 'the West'—in particular with the USA. In the aftermath of the **Gulf War (2003)**, the USA turned its attention to Iran and Syria, alleging that the former was developing **weapons of mass destruction** and harbouring **al-Qa'ida** operatives. After intense diplomatic pressure Iranian officials signalled that they would submit the country's nuclear programme to UN inspection, and that they would consider signing an additional protocol to the nuclear non-proliferation treaty.

International relations

To its west and south, despite the restoration of diplomatic relations in 1990, Iran lacks an agreed maritime boundary with Iraq, with which it remains in dispute over land boundaries, navigation channels and other issues arising from the **Iran–Iraq War**. In the south, the United Arab Emirates (UAE) seeks **Arab League** and other international support against Iran's occupation of Greater **Tunb Island** (known as Tunb al-Kubra in Arabic and Jazireh-ye Tonb-e Bozorg in Persian) and Lesser Tunb Island (Tunb as-Sughra in Arabic and Jazireh-ye Tonb-e Kuchek in Persian) and its attempts to occupy completely a jointly administered island in the Persian (Arabian) Gulf (called **Abu Musa** in Arabic and Jazireh-ye Abu Musa in Persian). To the north, Iran insists on the division of the Caspian Sea into five equal sectors while Azerbaijan, Kazakhstan, Russia and Turkmenistan have generally agreed upon equidistant seabed boundaries. Iran threatens to conduct **oil** exploration in waters claimed by Azerbaijan, while interdicting Azerbaijani activities. Despite substantial external pressure, Iran remains a key entrepôt for **heroin** smuggled from **Central Asia** to Europe; domestic narcotics consumption remains a persistent problem and Iranian press reports estimate that there are at least 1.8m. drug users in the country.

Iran, economy

Iran is one of the largest economies in the **Middle East** (third after Saudi Arabia and Turkey), with a gross national product of US $114,100m. Iran's economy is a mixture of central planning, state ownership of **oil** and other large enterprises, village **agriculture**, and small-scale private trading and service ventures. President **Khatami** has continued to follow the market reform plans of former President **Rafsanjani** and has indicated that he will pursue the diversification of Iran's oil-reliant economy, although he has made little progress towards that goal. The strong oil market in 1996 helped ease financial pressures on Iran and allowed it to make timely **debt**-service payments. Iran's financial situation deteriorated in 1997, however, and worsened again in 1998 owing to lower oil prices. Subsequent rises in oil prices have relieved the fiscal pressure on Iran, but do not solve the country's structural economic problems, including a lack of foreign investment and high inflation. Iran is the **Organization of Petroleum Exporting Countries**' second largest oil producer. The country has considerable potential for oil-related industries and increased production of traditional exports (such as carpets, pistachio nuts and caviar). Weaknesses include high unemployment and inflation, and a sizeable foreign debt.

Iran-*Contra* affair

Also known as Irangate. A scandal involving the secret sales of US arms to Iran in 1985–87, in which many high-ranking US officials, including President Reagan himself, were implicated. In 1986 it was discovered that the Reagan Administration had sanctioned a scheme to sell arms to Iran, despite an embargo on such sales, and then used the profits to finance paramilitary operations by the right-wing '*contras*' in Nicaragua and El Salvador. This was a direct violation of Congress' ruling, in the 1984 Boland Amendment, that no US funds should be used on further military activities, whether overt or covert, in Nicaragua. Israel, which had for some time been supplying arms to both the '*contras*' and Iran, was also involved. In exchange for US-made missiles delivered to Iran by Israel, the USA would obtain the liberation of the hostages held in Lebanon by Iranian-backed militias, increase the chances of a moderate regime in Iran and recoup substantial profits for their '*contra*' protégés. Money even flowed to the '*contras*' from the Pentagon's own secret fund (part of the Black Budget originally set up during the Second World War by President Roosevelt to finance 'Project Manhattan', which led to the development of the atomic bomb and, eventually, the bombing of Hiroshima and Nagasaki).

The Tower Commission was charged with investigating Irangate, but little resulted from its months of hearings and final report.

Iran hostage crisis

Shortly after the **Iranian Revolution**, US embassy personnel were taken hostage by **Revolutionary Guards** in **Tehran**. An attempt to free the hostages, involving a military operation undertaken by the US Administration under President **Jimmy Carter**, proved abortive. The hostages were only finally freed after all of the funds frozen in the USA at the outbreak of the Revolution and most of the US $3,500m. in property held by the former Shah in the USA had been secretly released and made available.

Iran-e Novin

Pro-government party established by the Shah of Iran in 1963 to replace **Mellioun**, as part of an attempt to create the impression that multi-party political debate existed in Iran. It was set against a loyal opposition party, called **Mardom**. Both parties were led by friends of the Shah.

Iran–Iraq War

Fighting began between Iraq and Iran after Iran ignored Iraq's demand that it withdraw its forces from Zain ul-Qos, in Diali province on their joint border, which Iraq maintained should have been returned to it under the 1975 **Shatt al-Arab** Agreement. Iraq therefore abrogated the agreement and invaded Iran in September 1980. Despite Iraq's superiority in equipment and *matériel*, Iran put up an effective resistance and a stalemate was soon reached along a 480-km front. In the spring of 1982 Iran launched two offensives, which had considerable success. Iran recaptured Khorramshahr and took the war into Iraqi territory. In February 1983 Iran launched another offensive, and then yet another in April and another in July. Iran was able to prevent Iraq from exporting **oil** through the **Gulf** and a pipeline through Syria was cut off. During the second half of 1983 Iraq intensified its missile and aircraft raids on Iranian towns and petroleum installations with new weapons purchased from abroad (*Exocet* missiles and French *Super Etendard* fighter aircraft). Iraq was receiving substantial financial assistance from various quarters during the war years, but so too was Iran, albeit more covertly. During the spring of 1984 Iran mounted another offensive into the marshlands, at great human cost. Iraq used mustard gas to counter the offensive. Iraq now attacked tankers using the Kharg Island oil terminal at the north-east end of the Gulf. Iran retaliated with assaults on Saudi Arabian and Kuwaiti tankers in the Gulf. Iranian oil exports were effectively reduced during 1984, causing the government to suspend imports temporarily. In March 1985 Iran launched a thrust towards the Iraqi marshlands, but this failed to have the intended decisive effect, although Iranian forces crossed the **Tigris** and closed the **Basra–Baghdad** road. Iraq continued, meanwhile, to bombard Iranian cities, including **Tehran**, and launched a counter-offensive, which pushed back the Iranians, causing heavy casualties on both sides. Iraq was again accused of using chemical weapons during this encounter. Iran shelled Basra and other Iraqi towns, and struck Baghdad with ground-launched missiles. Attempts by the UN to secure a cease-fire proved unsuccessful. In August 1985 Iraq made the first of a series of attacks on Kharg Island, severely affecting Iranian oil exports. In February 1986 Iran launched the Wal-Fajr (Dawn) 8 offensive and Iranian forces crossed the Shatt al-Arab, occupied the Iraqi port of Faw and 800 sq km of the Faw peninsula. When Iraq launched a counter-offensive, Iran opened up a second front in Iraqi **Kurdistan**. In Resolution 582, the UN Security Council, while urging a cease-fire, for the first time cited Iraq as the aggressor. In May 1986, ignoring the Security Council resolution, Iraq made its first incursions into Iran since 1982 and launched the first air-raid on Tehran since June 1985. In December 1986 Iran launched an offensive (Karbala-4) in the region of Basra, but failed to penetrate Iraqi defences. In January 1987, a second, two-pronged attack (Karbala-5) was launched towards Basra. The threat to tankers operating in the Gulf increased, the USA and USSR intervened to protect foreign shipping, and Iran stated that it regarded the US naval presence in the Gulf to be provocative. The UN Security Council adopted a 10-point resolution (No. 598) urging an immediate cease-fire, the withdrawal of all forces to internationally recognized borders and the co-operation of Iran and Iraq in efforts to achieve a peaceful settlement. As Iran temporized, Iraq lost patience and attacked Iranian oil installations and industrial targets. Iran agreed to a formal cease-fire, but only if Iraq's responsibility for starting the war were acknowledged first; it also agreed to a *de facto* cease-fire while a UN-appointed commission of enquiry determined responsibility. Iraq rejected these terms. The so-called 'tanker war' continued and losses mounted, despite the growing involvement of the US navy in the Gulf. At the end of February 1988 the so-called 'war of cities' was resumed in which civil and economic targets were attacked on both sides. During the first half of 1988 Iran began to lose ground seriously on all fronts and suffered a number of military reverses, offsetting the gains it had made in previous years. In July 1988 Iran announced its acceptance of the terms of Resolution 598, and a cease-fire came into effect in August. It was monitored on the ground by a specially-created UN observer force, the UN Iran-Iraq Observer Group (**UNIIMOG**). Progress in the peace negotiations was slow and difficult. By the end of the year, while the cease-fire held, that was the only element of the resolution to have been successfully implemented. In August 1990, on the eve of Iraq's invasion of Kuwait, **Saddam Hussein** abruptly sought an immediate, formal peace with Iran by accepting all of the claims Iran had pursued since the declaration of the cease-fire, and in September 1990 Iran and Iraq re-established diplomatic relations.

Iran-Libya Sanctions Act (ILSA)

This US Act was introduced to ban large-scale investment in the two countries named, in response to their alleged support for **terrorism**. It has recently been renewed and tightened, despite opposition from US oil companies and efforts on various fronts by the regimes of both countries to show themselves not to be 'rogue states'. Pressure for a change in policy is likely to come from the Oasis consortium of US companies, which held major assets in Libya at the time sanctions were first imposed. These have been 'frozen' by the Libyan Government and held in trust, despite repeated threats to reallocate operating licences to other foreign companies. At present, firms such as ConocoPhillips and Marathon Oil have until 2005 to resume work or risk losing their assets. The promised payout to the **Lockerbie** victims could also moderate the US administration's position on sanctions, at least as far as Libya is concerned.

Iran Nationalist Party

Member of the **National Front** or Union of National Front Forces, based in Paris, France, since 1978.

Iranian Central Bank

In the 1990s the Iranian Central Bank led the movement to invest in Albania, regardless of poor profits or high risks. Iranian banking institutions soon became a primary source of hard currency in Albania. They promoted links between local importers, exporters and Islamic trading companies; and they encouraged and facilitated **trade** with Iranian businessmen. Local banks and financial institutions were restructured to manage relations with Islamic banks. Within a few years the Iranian presence in the Albanian domestic banking and finance sector was not merely widespread, but had became part of the establishment.

Iranian Liberation Front – *see* Nehzat-e Azadi-ye Iran

Iranian Revolution

In 1979 the Shah of Iran's regime was overthrown by a mass uprising. A combination of social forces was involved but the clerics gained the upper hand over the direction of the popular movement and an Islamic republic was declared.

Iraq, Republic of

Al-Jumhuriyah al-Iraqiyah

Located between Iran (to the east), Turkey (to the north), Syria and Jordan (to the north-west and west, respectively), and Saudi Arabia and Kuwait (to the south), Iraq has an area of 437,072 sq km (of which 4,910 sq km is **water** and marshland) and a southern outlet into the **Shatt al-Arab** waterway and the **Persian (Arabian) Gulf**. Formerly a part of the **Ottoman Empire**, it was part of **Transjordan**, under British control after the First World War, before being separated from Jordan to become a distinct colonial territory. Independence was eventually achieved in 1932. The capital is **Baghdad** and the administration comprises 18 governorates (*muhafazah*, plural *muhafazat*): Al-Anbar, Al-Basrah, Al-Muthanna, Al-Qadisiyah, An-Najaf, Arbil, As-Sulaymaniyah, At-Ta'mim, Babil, Baghdad, Dahuk, Dhi Qar, Diyala, Karbala', Maysan, Ninawa, Salah ad-Din and Wasit. In 2003 the population was estimated at 24,683,313, of which 75%–80% are Arabs, 15%–20% **Kurds**, and 5% Turkomans, **Assyrians** or 'other'. The vast majority of the population are Muslims, with the majority **Shi'a** (60%–65%) and the minority **Sunni** (32%–37%) or Christian or 'other' (3%). **Arabic** is generally the official language, although in the Kurdish areas it is Kurdish. Other languages include Assyrian and Armenian. Formerly a military dictatorship under **Saddam Hussain**, Iraq is currently under the administration of the **Coalition Provisional Authority** (CPA). Following the US-led intervention and occupation of Iraq, the government of the country came under the CPA after May 2003, when US President **Bush** announced that 'the war' was over. The CPA appointed a provisional **Governing Council** to identify an interim government and draft a new constitution that was to be submitted for approval by the electorate in 2004 or 2005. It was planned that the CPA would formally relinquish power to an Iraqi interim government at the end of 2003.

Politics and administration

After the overthrow of Saddam Hussain in 2003, the US occupation force appointed **Paul Bremer** as the chief civilian administrator in Iraq (in place of **Gen.** (retd) **Jay Garner**) and head of the CPA. It was envisaged that the CPA would administer during a transitional period while preparations were made for a representative Iraqi government. The CPA appointed a 25-member provisional Governing Council, which in turn appointed a 25-member ministerial Cabinet. The USA has committed itself to withdrawal from Iraq by the end of June 2004. It is hoped that an effective government will be in place by then. In the mean time, the US chief civilian administrator has veto power over any government, especially with regard to matters of economy and security. Local caucuses have resulted in a form of representative government at local level, but the 'national' government remains representative only in terms of its regional and sectarian balance. Even this is questioned by some, who point to the essentially undemocratic procedures which led to the selection both of the Governing Council and of the ministers. Shi'a representatives in particular have expressed a wish to see genuine elections (the Shi'ites are the largest confessional grouping within the population), while Sunnis are concerned that they have been excluded owing to their association with the former regime, and Kurds are worried about the future of the north.

Political parties and groups (leaders):

After the fall of Saddam Hussain, myriad groups and parties have become involved in politics. These include the **Iraqi National Congress** (**Ahmad Chalabi**), the Shi'ite **ad-Da'wa al-Islamiyya**, the **Supreme Council for the Islamic Revolution in Iraq** (SCIRI, **Muhammad Baqir al-Hakim**). There are also informal militias and groups, supporting various religious and political leaders, such as the so-called Mahdi's Army of **Moqtada as-Sadr**. Influential political figures in the aftermath of the **Iraq War (2003)** included: **Adnan Pachachi**, the former Iraqi foreign minister, currently adviser to the United Arab Emirates government, who recently gained the backing of the USA as a Sunni elder who could play a future role in a new Iraqi government; he is regarded as acceptable by Saudi Arabia and other **Gulf states**; Pachachi has no party affiliation or power base; **Jalal Talabani**, leader of the **Patriotic Union of Kurdistan** (PUK); the PUK controls 25,000 fighters in the eastern part of Iraqi **Kurdistan** from Sulaymaniyah; **Naguib as-Salahi**, former divisional commander of Saddam Hussain's **Republican Guard**, who defected in 1995; as-Salahi heads the Iraqi **Free Officers' Movement** and has close links with the Iraqi army and with the US **Central Intelligence Agency** (CIA) and the US Department of State; **Masoud Barzani**, leader of the **Kurdistan Democratic Party** (KDP) which controls the Western part of Iraqi Kurdistan from Arbil; the KDP has a combat strength of approximately 35,000 fighters; Muhammad Baqir al-Hakim, a senior Shi'a cleric who was imprisoned and tortured as an opposition leader during the 1970s; al-Hakim leads the SCIRI which claims to represent the majority of Shi'ites in Iraq; he also controls the **Badr Brigade**, which maintains a force of thousands of troops in Iran; Sharif Ali bin-Hussain, cousin of former King **Faisal**, who leads the **Constitutional Monarchy Movement**; **Ayad Allawi**, a former member of the **Ba'ath Party** who formed the opposition **Iraqi National Accord** in 1976; Allawi claims to have support in the Iraqi diaspora and among disillusioned party officials inside Iraq; he has worked closely with the CIA and MI6, and received funding from Saudi Arabia.

Media

The fall of Saddam Hussain encouraged an influx of media organizations. However, the occupation regime has imposed strict censorship, and has criticized some Arab broadcasters, such as **al-Jazeera** and **Abu Dhabi TV**, on the grounds that they are 'biased' and 'incite violence against American and British troops'. In 2000 there was one internet service provider, and in 2001 there were 12,500 internet users.

History

Formerly part of the Ottoman Empire, Iraq became an independent kingdom in 1932. A republic was proclaimed in 1958, and thereafter the country was ruled by successive military 'strongmen', the most recent having been Saddam Hussain. Territorial disputes with Iran led to an inconclusive and costly eight-year war

(1980–88). In August 1990 Iraq seized Kuwait, but was expelled by a US-led UN coalition force in the **Gulf War (1991)**. Following Kuwait's liberation, the UN Security Council required Iraq to destroy all of its **weapons of mass destruction** and long-range missiles and to allow UN verification inspections. In addition, Iraq was subjected to UN sanctions for 12 years, and these have impoverished its population. In March–May 2003 a US-led intervention in Iraq ousted the regime of Saddam Hussein. Coalition forces subsequently occupied Iraq and established the CPA.

International relations

Despite the restoration of diplomatic relations in 1990, disputes with Iran over maritime and land boundaries, navigation channels and other issues from the eight-year war persist. The demarcation of land and **Shatt al-Arab** boundary questions eventually ended Iraq's claims to Kuwait and to the Bubiyan and Warbah Islands, but no maritime boundary exists with Kuwait in the Persian (Arabian) Gulf. Iraq has also expressed concern regarding Turkey's hydrological projects to regulate the **Tigris** and **Euphrates** rivers upstream for the major **GAP** programme in south-eastern Turkey.

Iraq, economy

Iraq's economy is dominated by the **oil** sector, which has traditionally provided about 95% of foreign exchange earnings. In the 1980s financial problems caused by massive expenditures in the eight-year war with Iran and damage to oil export facilities by Iran led the government to implement austerity measures, borrow heavily and, later, reschedule foreign **debt** payments. Iraq suffered economic losses from the war of at least US $100,000m. After hostilities ended in 1988 oil exports gradually increased with the construction of new pipelines and the restoration of damaged facilities. Iraq's seizure of Kuwait in August 1990, subsequent international economic sanctions, and damage from military action by an international coalition beginning in January 1991 drastically reduced economic activity. Although government policies supporting large military and internal security forces and allocating resources to key supporters of the regime have hurt the economy, the implementation of the UN's so-called **Oil for Food** programme from December 1996 helped improve conditions for the average Iraqi citizen. Iraq was allowed to export limited amounts of oil in exchange for food, medicine, and some infrastructure spare parts. In December 1999 the UN Security Council authorized Iraq to export under the programme as much oil as required to meet humanitarian needs. Oil exports have recently risen to more than three-quarters of the pre-war level. However, 28% of Iraq's export revenues under the programme have been deducted in order to meet UN Compensation Fund and administrative expenses. The decline in gross domestic product in 2001–02 was largely the result of the global economic slowdown and lower oil prices. Per caput food imports increased significantly, while medical supplies and **health**-care services steadily improved. Per caput output and living standards were still well below the pre-war level, but any estimates have a wide range of error. The military victory of the US-led coalition in March–April 2003 resulted in the closure of much of the central economic administrative structure and the loss of a comparatively small amount of capital plant. Iraq has the second largest crude oil and **natural gas** reserves within the **Organization of Petroleum Exporting Countries** and a large labour force. However, the economy and infrastructure has been devastated by the three major Gulf wars: the **Iran–Iraq War (1980–88)**, **the Iraq War (1991)** and the **Iraq War (2003)**, as well as by 12 years of sanctions imposed by the UN between the Gulf Wars. The formal economy is in ruins and a huge proportion of the population are unemployed. Massive, forced privatization of Iraqi state assets may lead to capital flight, and the huge scale of reconstruction might cause the country to accumulate an enormous foreign debt.

Iraq Cabinet of Ministers

In September 2003 Iraq's provisional **Governing Council** appointed a Cabinet comprising 25 ministers. The ministers were to serve until elections were held. Of the 25, 13 were **Shi'ites**, five **Sunnis**, five **Kurds**, one an ethnic Turk and one an **Assyrian** Christian. Only one, Nisrin Barwari, a Kurd—the Minister for Public Works—was a woman.

Iraq – the 'democratic transition'

The official programme for the 'transition to **democracy**', devised by the **Coalition Provisional Authority** (CPA) in control of Iraq after the overthrow of the regime of **Saddam Hussain**, involved the establishment of a Basic Law prepared by the **Iraqi Provisional Governing Council** (IGC) to function as a temporary constitution, to be followed by the formation of a transitional national assembly. The plan envisaged a three-stage selection process, based on governorate boundaries, with the IGC and CPA choosing individuals for the first stage. The transitional assembly was to be elected by the end of May 2004, and to assume full sovereign powers for governing Iraq by 30 June, at which point the CPA would formally cede power to the new Iraqi government. Despite the claim that Iraqi democracy would soon be restored, it seemed likely that the members of the CPA-appointed IGC and its selected ministers would be at the core of the next government, which would almost certainly continue to be run by US officials behind the scenes for at least some time.

Iraq – interim government

At the beginning of September 2003, the **Iraqi Provisional Governing Council** (IGC) nominated a 25-member Cabinet (interim government) to take official charge of a range of ministerial domains. US officials continued in practice to administer all of the ministries. The interim government of Iraq was extended to planning, communications, public works, construction and housing, **trade**, **education**, higher education, culture, foreign affairs, the interior, justice, human rights, **agriculture**, **industry** and **minerals**, **oil**, **water** resources, the environment, **transport**, science and technology, electricity, finance, work and social affairs, sport and youth, **health**, immigration and **refugees**. In terms of ethnic-religious affiliation, roughly one-half (13 of 25) of the positions went to **Shi'ites**, five to **Kurds**, five to **Sunnis**, one to an ethnic Turk and one to an **Assyrian** Christian; only one (public works) was assigned to a woman.

Iraq Islamic Party

Led by Mohsen Abdel Hamid and other **Sunni** Islamists (including some clerics) who opposed **Saddam Hussain**'s regime but remained in the country, unlike many senior members of the **Iraqi Provisional Governing Council**. A potentially influential force in post-intervention Iraq.

Iraq Liberation Act

Came into effect in October 1998 when signed, reluctantly, by US President **Bill Clinton**. It baldly stated that US policy was to support efforts to remove the regime headed by **Saddam Hussain** from power. It suggested an important role for Iraqi opposition groups, which the USA would train and arm, and provided a mechanism to enable the US administration to channel money and military aid towards those groups. Its proponents seemed to believe at the time that the liberation of Iraq would be best achieved by creating large liberated areas within central and southern Iraq, protected by US air power, from which attacks would be launched by Iraqi opposition forces into the parts of the country remaining under Saddam Hussain's control. In February 2001, less than one month after he had assumed office, US President **George W. Bush** ordered the bombing of Iraqi command and control centres near **Baghdad**. US policy 'continues to be driven by the Iraq Liberation Act', Donald Rumsfeld told a congressional committee, and the Iraqi opposition began to receive weapons training from US special forces based at College Station in Texas.

Iraq-Najd Neutral Zone

The **Najd** (Saudi Arabia) frontier with Iraq was defined in the Treaty of Mohammara in May 1922. A neutral zone of some 7,000 sq km was established adjacent to the western tip of the Kuwait frontier. No military or permanent buildings were to be erected in the zone and the nomads of both countries were to have unimpeded access to its pastures and wells. A further agreement concerning the administration of this zone was signed in May 1938.

Iraq post-war peace-keeping

The US-led **coalition** in Iraq—essentially US and British forces—became involved in 'peace-keeping' and security operations in Iraq as soon as the war officially ended in May 2003. As the difficulty of this task became more evident during the summer, there was increasing pressure to involve other countries of the coalition. Eventually 30 countries promised to send troops, although some contributions were less than 100 in strength and were thus symbolic rather than significant in practical terms. Control of the **Shi'a**-dominated south central region was transferred to Polish forces in September 2003. The multinational force (about 10,000 strong) includes soldiers from Poland, Spain, Ukraine, Thailand, Albania, Mongolia and Honduras. Further south, in the vicinity of **Basra**, a UK-controlled force consists of British (some 11,000) as well as Italian (some 3,000), Dutch, Czech, Romanian, Portuguese, Norwegian, Lithuanian and New Zealand troops. Attempts to persuade Turkey to deploy troops have not been successful and there is some controversy about where they would serve.

Iraq post-war reconstruction

In October 2003 US President **Bush** requested Congress to grant funds of US $87,000m. in addition to the $79,000m. already approved for Iraq. Some $18,600m. was for post-war reconstruction. The **European Union** pledged $235m. for 2003–04. In the same month the **World Bank** and the UN indicated that an additional $55,000m. would be needed for basic reconstruction over the next five years. US administrator **Paul Bremer** himself had estimated in September that he would need 'tens of billions of dollars more' for post-war reconstruction. The **Coalition Provisional Authority** (CPA) has already allocated $680m. for reconstruction, of which $229m. is to be used for electric power rehabilitation. Some estimate that the rehabilitation of electricity services will require $17,000m., and that of **water** and sewage services $27,000m. Even CPA experts considered that it would require $10,000m. to meet the full demand for electricity over three years. The water systems were largely operational by the end of 2003, but it was estimated that it would take one year at least to restore the sewage system. **Transport** infrastructure was relatively undamaged during the war, and road and bridge reconstruction should be completed by March 2004, at a cost of $12m.. As far as the rehabilitation of the human resource component of the public services is concerned, the CPA was criticized for its initially anti-Ba'athist stance and its rapid disbanding of the army and internal security services (such as the police). Bremer set a target of 18 months to raise the strength of the police force to 65,000, but the process was slower than anticipated and total estimated costs rose well beyond the budget of the CPA. Intimidation of potential recruits was achieved by the bombing of police stations and police recruitment centres during 2003 and 2004. In a change of policy, the CPA began in August 2003 to recruit members of the **Mukhabarat**, the former regime's feared secret service. In September, after the **Iraqi Provisional**

Governing Council had set aside $200m. for this purpose, the newly appointed Iraqi interior minister began to set up an anti-terrorist paramilitary force (a civil defence battalion) with a strength of 7,000–10,000, to be recruited and trained by the end of 2003. The strength of the army was planned at 40,000, of which 30,000 were due to be in place by September 2004. Members of the former Iraqi army were to be encouraged to join. By April 2004 it was reported that the USA had trained 200,000 police, border guards, members of the new civil defence corps and soldiers. Most hospitals were reported to be back to or above pre-war levels of service by the end of August 2003, but it was estimated that it would take five years for **health-care** in Iraq to reach the level it had achieved by the end of the 1980s. The Red Cross withdrew from emergency health work for security reasons, and most of the work was then undertaken through the Iraqi Ministry of Health, with the salaries of doctors and nurses being paid by the ministry from the end of the summer of 2003. Food distribution was reported to have risen to 95% of the capacity achieved under the UN's **Oil for Food** programme, with stocks arriving at the port of **Umm Qasr** and being transported onwards by road. In January 2004 the Pentagon invited bids for 17 construction contracts worth $5,000m., the first in a series of deals funded by the $18,600m. allocated for reconstruction.

Iraq Survey Group

US organization established to replace **UNMOVIC**, which had in turn replaced **UNSCOM** in 1999, to search for **weapons of mass destruction** and other Iraqi military *matériel*. It was significantly downgraded in December 2003–January 2004.

Iraq War (1980–88) – *see* Iraq–Iran War

Iraq War (1991)

The Iraq War (1991) was the direct outcome of Iraq's invasion, in August 1990, and subsequent occupation, from August 1990 to January 1991, of Kuwait. During the summer of 1990 there had been disagreement within the **Organization of Petroleum Exporting Countries** regarding production levels and **oil** prices, and Kuwait decided to increase production above its quota level, thereby effectively undermining the agreed price. **Saddam Hussain** stated that he regarded this as a hostile act, and it would appear to have been one of several factors which led him to decide to invade Kuwait. The invasion resulted in intense diplomatic pressure on Iraq to withdraw: the UN (in Resolution 660) and most countries condemned the invasion and demanded that Iraq withdraw from Kuwait. The USA immediately began to construct a coalition of forces to compel Iraq to withdraw, including allies in the **Arab World** (notably Egypt and Syria), and to build up its forces in the region under **Operation Desert Shield** (designed, among other things, to protect

Saudi Arabia). As the months progressed, the US Administration became increasingly adamant regarding the need to back up diplomacy with force, if necessary, and warned that if Iraq had not withdrawn by, at the latest, January 1991, it would deploy the coalition to launch an attack on the Iraqi forces occupying Kuwait. Iraq failed to withdraw by the stipulated deadline and in January 1991 the coalition embarked on a major assault—**Operation Desert Storm**—on the Iraqi forces in Kuwait and on installations and equipment in Iraq, first with a massive aerial bombardment and then with a ground attack. The coalition force (primarily the US and UK contingents) proved overwhelmingly superior and the assault destroyed large sections of the Iraqi air and ground forces. At the end of February 1991 US President **Bush** declared that the war to liberate Kuwait had been won and declared a cease-fire. Iraq agreed to renounce its claim to Kuwait and to release all prisoners of war. It also indicated that it would comply with the remaining relevant UN Security Council resolutions. On 3 March 1991 Iraq accepted the cease-fire terms dictated by the commander of the multinational force, **Gen. Norman Schwarzkopf** of the US army.

Iraq War (2003)

A US-led **coalition** was, with difficulty, assembled during the latter part of 2002 and early part of 2003 to launch a war against the regime of **Saddam Hussain**, on the grounds that it had failed to disarm and possessed **weapons of mass destruction** which posed a major threat to international security. On 17 March 2003 US President **George W. Bush** issued an ultimatum to Saddam Hussain to leave Iraq with his sons or face war. The ultimatum was opposed by France, Germany, Russia, Canada and the Vatican. The British Parliament backed UK Prime Minister Tony Blair, who supported Bush. On 19 March Hans Blix delivered the final weapons inspection report to the UN Security Council. US and British forces moved into the demilitarized zone on the Kuwaiti border with Iraq. The war began on 20 March when US and UK forces moved into southern Iraq, launching air, sea and land assaults. On 22 March 200,000 people marched in London in the biggest ever peace-time protest. Major demonstrations took place in other countries around the world. Capturing the strategic port of **Umm Qasr** and the Faw Peninsula in the first week of the war made the task of the combined US-UK forces easier—British forces declared Umm Qasr 'safe and open' on 25 March. Meanwhile coalition forces moved north as heavy bombing of **Baghdad** took place. British forces attempted to secure **Basra** while US troops headed north to **Najaf** and Nassiriya, where they encountered significant resistance. By 1 April British forces had largely secured southern Iraq and were patrolling with 'helmets off, berets on'. US forces continued to encounter resistance on the ground, but also to bombard targets from the air in central and northern Iraq. On 4 April the US 3rd Infantry captured Saddam International Airport and on the next day entered Baghdad itself. On 6 April British forces moved into central Basra, while US forces captured **Karbala**. On 7

April some 700 Iraqi opposition fighters, led by **Ahmad Chalabi**, arrived in Nassiriya. On 9 April viewers around the world saw television footage of crowds pulling down statues of Saddam Hussain in central Baghdad. On 10 April Kurdish fighters captured the northern **oil** centre of **Kirkuk**; on the following day combined Kurdish and US forces captured **Mosul** without a fight. On 13 April US forces engaged with remnants of the Iraqi army in **Tikrit**, the home town of Saddam Hussain. On 14 April Tony Blair told the British Parliament that '. . .we are near the end of the conflict. But the challenge of the peace is now beginning'. President Bush declared the end of major combat on 1 May 2003.

Iraqi Communist Party (ICP)

The ICP joined the **National Progressive Front** in July 1973. It experienced severe repression in mid-1979 and went underground, where it subsequently mainatained a consistent, illegal opposition to the regime of **Saddam Hussain.**

Iraqi Democratic Conference

Iraqi political coalition formed after the **Iraq War (2003)**, comprising some 21 political parties. Participants from a workshop at Hilla subsequently organized a larger conference of 192 political parties and movements, civil society organizations and unions in **Baghdad.**

Iraqi Fund for Development

After the occupation of Iraq, **oil** revenues were to be diverted to a new Iraqi Development Fund for rebuilding the country, controlled by the coalition of the USA and the United Kingdom, headed by Peter McPherson, formerly deputy US Treasury Secretary and Bank of America executive, and overseen by an international board. **UN Security Council Resolution 1483** required all UN member states to identify, 'freeze' and immediately transfer to the Development Fund all funds, financial assets or economic resources in their jurisdictions that were established or held by the previous Government of Iraq. The **Oil for Food** programme was to be phased out over six months. Once again, the disbursement of the money in this Fund, estimated at some US $10,000m., was to be administered by the **Coalition Provisional Authority**. The following are the main terms of the new US draft resolution. The USA and United Kingdom submitted letters to the Security Council recognizing their obligations as occupying powers. The draft refers to them as the 'authority'.

- The resolution would establish a 'Development Fund for Iraq' for reconstruction and humanitarian purposes to be held by the central bank of Iraq and to be audited by independent accountants approved by an international advisory board.

- The board includes envoys from the UN, the International Monetary Fund, the **Arab Fund for Economic and Social Development** and the **World Bank**.
- All proceeds from oil sales would be paid into the proposed Development Fund until an 'internationally recognized' Iraqi government is established. The money would be 'disbursed at the direction' of the authority, in consultation with the Iraqi interim authority.
- Five per cent of the oil revenues are to be deposited into a compensation fund (compared to the current 25%) for claims resulting from Iraq's 1990 invasion of Kuwait.
- The resolution phases out the UN Oil for Food programme over a period of six months. Some $13,000m. from Iraq's past oil revenues are now in the programme, administered by the UN. Whatever is not spent would be deposited into the new Development Fund.
- All monies from Iraq's oil sales or those in the Development Fund are immune from claims and lawsuits until an internationally recognized Iraqi government is established.

Iraqi Islamic Party

A proxy in the early 2000s for one of the oldest **Sunni** movements in Iraq, the **Muslim Brotherhood**.

Iraqi Istiqlal (Independence) Party

Iraqi political party active during the colonial period. It operated from Iraq and advocated the unification of Iraq, **Transjordan**, Syria and Palestine.

Iraqi Kurdistan Front – *see* Kurdistan Iraqi Front (KIF)

Iraqi National Accord (INA)

Iraqi political party, led by **Ayad Allawi** (Salah esh-Shaykh), who was appointed iterim Prime Minister of Iraq in May 2004.

Iraqi National Congress (INC)

Established in London, United Kingdom, during the 1990s as a coalition of political forces opposed to **Saddam Hussain**, the INC agreed the principal of a collegiate leadership at a conference held in London in April 1999. In November a seven-man leadership was elected by the *c.* 300 delegates, as was a 65-member central council. These included: **Ayad Allawi** of the **Iraqi National Accord**; Sharif Ali bin al-Hussein of the **Constitutional Monarchy Movement**; Latif Rashid of the **Patriotic Union of Kurdistan**; Hoshyar az-Zibari of the **Kurdish Democratic Party**; and three independents—Sheikh Muhammad Muhammad Ali, Riyad al-Yaar and

Ahmad Chalabi. Several leading members of the INC then relocated to the USA, including Chalabi, who became the leading representative of the INC as far as the US administration was concerned. One of the most important opposition groups in exile during the period of Saddam Hussain's regime, the INC was identified by the US administration as a major potential force for change in Iraq and was liberally funded through the 1990s by them. Close relations were maintained during the 1990s between the US administration and the INC, as well as with other opposition political groups. Many received military and other forms of training. Reputedly paid US $340,000 a month to provide military and political intelligence on the regime and the situation in Iraq, both before and after the **Iraq War (2003)**, the INC has received a total of about $33m. from the US Department of State and $6m. from the Defense Intelligence Agency. The INC provided a stream of intelligence, some of which was influential in the commitment of the US administration to intervention in Iraq, but not all of which was very reliable. As a leading member of the INC and an influential figure in his own right, Ahmad Chalabi was considered by the USA as a potential leader of post-reconstruction and post-independence Iraq and was strongly supported by the US **Coalition Provisional Authority** during 2003 and 2004. He was appointed to the **Iraqi Provisional Governing Council** in July 2003 and became one of its most prominent members. In May 2004 allegations of **corruption** resulted in a dramatic raid on Chalabi's house. Senior members of the INC had been accused of involvement in fraud and corruption earlier in the year. In March 2004 Sabah Nouri, a leading member of the INC and head of the ministry's bank audit, was arrested and jailed. The raid on Chalabi's villa was reported to be part of the continuing investigation of 15 people in connection with fraud, kidnapping and associated matters, although Chalabi himself was not charged. The Pentagon announced that it was ending the monthly payments to the INC.

Iraqi National Joint Action Committee

Group formed in **Damascus**, Syria, in 1990, bringing together the **Supreme Council for the Islamic Revolution in Iraq**, the four principal Kurdish parties belonging to the **Kurdistan Iraqi Front**, **ad-Da'awa al-Islamiyya**, the Movement of the Iraqi *Mujahidin* (based in **Tehran**), the Islamic Movement in Iraq (a **Shi'ite** group based in Tehran), **Jund al-Imam**, the **Islamic Action** organization (based in Tehran), the Islamic Alliance (based in Saudi Arabia), the Independent Group, the **Iraqi Socialist Party**, the Arab Socialist Movement, the Nasserite Unionist Gathering and the National Reconciliation Group.

Iraqi Provisional Governing Council

A 25-member body appointed by the US-led **Coalition Provisional Authority** (CPA) from among non-Ba'athist and opposition Iraqi leaders in July 2003, in order to initiate a process of transfer of power from the CPA to an Iraqi government. The CPA maintained strict control over the IGC and, although it had some power, **Paul**

Bremer, the US administrator of Iraq, retained a veto on its decisions. Defence and security remained officially in the hands of the CPA, but it was expected that the Council would have an increasing role in policy-making. Chaired by Mohammed Bahr al-Uloum, a 'moderate' **Shi'a** cleric recently returned from exile in London, United Kingdom, it included 13 Shi'a Muslims, five **Sunni** Muslims, five **Kurds**, one Turkmen and one Christian, 22 men and three **women**, designed to represent Iraq's diverse ethnic, religious, gender and political composition. At least nine of the 18 Arab members of the Council and eight out of the nine members of the rotating presidency had not been based in south-central Iraq since 1991. Among the better known political figures were the leaders of the main Kurdish groups, **Masoud Barzani** and **Jalal Talabani**, prominent exiles such as **Ahmad Chalabi** and **Ayad Allawi**, and leaders of the Shi'a parties. Also included was Abu Hattem, known as 'the lord of the marshes', who waged a guerrilla campaign in the 1990s on behalf of the **Marsh Arabs** and others in order to prevent the draining of the marshlands of southern Iraq. According to the definition of the Council's authority and responsibilities, its activities were to include appointing interim ministers, working with the CPA on policy and budgets, and establishing procedures to write a new constitution. The IGC had generally only qualified support from the mass of the Iraqi population. It was reputed to be corrupt and nepotism appears to have infiltrated it at the highest level—eight ministers are close relatives of IGC members. Several members of the IGC maintained their own militias—including the troops of Ahmad Chalabi, the ex-Ba'athist **Mukhabarat** under Ayad Allawi's **Iraqi National Accord**, the **Badr Brigade** of the **Supreme Council for the Islamic Revolution in Iraq**, the so-called Mahdi's Army of **Moqtada as-Sadr** and the *peshmergas* of the two main Kurdish parties.

Iraqi Socialist Party

Iraqi political grouping, led by Gen. Hassan an-Naquib.

Iraqi Turkmen Front

Party representing the Turkmen **minority** in the area around **Kirkuk** in northern Iraq.

Turkmens and **Kurds** began competing for power in Kirkuk almost as soon as **Saddam Hussain**'s regime had fallen.

Irbil

Major town in Iraqi **Kurdistan**.

Irgun Zvai Leumi

A Jewish paramilitary group originating in a split of the **Haganah** in the early 1930s. A splinter group, Haganah B, united with the youth group of **Vladimir**

Jabotinsky to form the Irgun Zvai Leumi under the leadership of David Raziel. Raziel had been educated at the Hebrew University, where he read mathematics and philosophy, but devoted all his spare time to studying military history, tactics and strategy. He was soon writing textbooks with **Avraham Stern** on small arms, and teaching his underground movement guerrilla tactics and how to manufacture bombs. Irgun's attacks were initially directed more against the Arabs than against the British, but both Raziel and Stern (his deputy) were arrested on the eve of the Second World War. They were released from prison in 1941 but Raziel was killed in a bomb attack shortly afterwards. His deputy, Stern, had founded a more extreme group, called **Lechi** (Lohamei Herut Israel) but referred to by the British as the 'Stern Gang'. Stern himself was hunted down by the British, located in a flat in central **Tel-Aviv** and 'shot while trying to escape'. His 'gang' was responsible for the assassination of the anti-Semitic Lord Moyne, the British resident minister in **Cairo** who had been colonial secretary in the British government after Lord Lloyd.

Al-Irshad wa'l Islah

Movement for Guidance and Reform, Algeria

Algerian 'non-political' Islamic movement, founded in 1974 by Mahfoudh Nahnal. Regarded increasingly as a political movement by the Algerian authorities, especially during the 1990s, when they cracked down on al-Irshad wa'l Islah activities and its adherents.

Al-Iryani, Abdul Rahman

President of **North Yemen** from 1967 to 1974.

ISAF (Afghanistan)

The international peace-keeping force in **Kabul**, Afghanistan. Placed under the strategic command of NATO in August 2003, with Canada taking tactical control. This force, of some 5,000 peace-keepers from 30 nations, previously under, at different times, British, Dutch, German and Turkish command, operates separately from the 11,000-strong US-led coalition force still in the country under **Operation Enduring Freedom**. The extension of ISAF operations to the provinces remains politically problematic. Instead, the extension of security was to be achieved by the deployment of **Provincial Reconstruction Teams (PRTs)**, clusters of lightly armed troops meant to assist the international development agencies and other organizations in reconstruction work throughout the country. PRTs are not part of ISAF, but draw on ISAF experience; they are not part of the coalition force, but receive air support from the coalition.

Isfahan

City in southern central Iran, on the Zaindeh Rud river, famed for its mosaics and tiled mosques. It is said that 'he who has not seen Isfahan has not seen half the world'.

Islah

The Islamic reform movement that developed in the region during the latter part of the 19th century. Major influences include Jamal ad-Din al-Afghani and **Muhammad Abduh**. The Islah movement began in Algeria in 1903 with the visit of Muhammad Abduh and was developed subsequently by Sheikh **Abdelhamid Ben Badis** of Constantine. Many political parties and movements throughout the region have used this term in their names to signify a distinctive approach to progress and change.

Islah Party (Morocco)

Nationalist movement founded in the northern Spanish Protectorate of Morocco in the 1920s.

Al-Islah Party (Yemen)

Yemeni political party. Consists mainly of the northern Hashed tribe with support from the **Muslim Brotherhood**. Produces the *as-Sahwa* newspaper. Strengthened its position after the 1994 civil war with the south. Its rather narrow tribal base prevented it from securing more than 53 seats in the legislative elections of 1997, compared with 187 gained by the ruling **General People's Congress**.

Islam

In **Arabic** means 'submission'. Major religion of the **Middle East**. Established by the **Prophet Muhammad** (revered by Muslims as the Prophet of Allah). After his death in AD 632, his successors, the caliphs, spread Islam across the known world from north Africa to Spain, into eastern and central Europe, and eastwards to India and China. Islam is the fastest growing religion in the world. In the mid-1990s the annual growth of the Muslim population was 6.4%, compared with a growth rate of 1.46% for the Christian population.

Islamic Action

A Turkish Islamist splinter group. Linked by overlapping membership with **Beyyat al-Islam**.

Islamic Action Front

The Islamic Action Front is the political arm of the **Muslim Brotherhood** in Jordan. Established in 1992, the Islamic Action Front had 350 founder members, with the main initiators of the movement being Ahmed Azaida, Dr Ishaq Farhan and Dr **Abd al-Latif Arabiyat**. The present leader is Hamza Mansoor. It first achieved representation in the general election of November 1993, when it became the largest single party in the House of Representatives. The party seeks to introduce strict **Islamic Law** and to achieve an abrogation of the peace treaty with Israel that was agreed to by the Jordanian government in 1994. In elections held in 2003/04 elections the Islamic Action Front secured 18 of the 110 parliamentary seats, according to the final results provided by the interior ministry. Its representation is likely to be enhanced by the presence of six Islamic Action Front sympathizers who were former members of the party but secured their seats as independents.

Islamic Amal

A Lebanese political grouping, headed by Hussain al-Moussavi, who left the **Amal** movement in 1982 in protest at its secular orientation. Moussavi, a former school teacher, made Islamic Amal a devoted follower of Ayatollah **Khomeini**'s ideology, including his theory of the religious jurist and strong opposition to the West. Principally based in **Ba'albek**, with close ties historically to the Iranian **Revolutionary Guards**—a militia sent to Lebanon in 1982 and mostly withdrawn in late 1991. Islamic Amal has perhaps 500 supporters.

Islamic Army of Aden/Abyan (IAAA)

The Islamic Army of Aden/Abyan (IAAA) emerged publicly in mid-1998 when the group released a series of communiqués that expressed support for **Osama bin Laden**, and appealed for the overthrow of the Yemeni Government and the commencement of operations against US and other Western interests in Yemen. It operates in the southern Yemeni governorates—primarily **Aden** and Abyan—and engages in bombings and kidnappings to promote its goals. It had links with the so-called Supporters of **Shari'a** organization run by Sheikh Abu Hamza al-Masri (whose real name is Mustafa Kamel), the cleric at the Finsbury Park mosque in north London, and with eight young British Muslims who travelled to Yemen in December 1998 with plans to attack the British consulate in Aden, the Anglican church and a hotel. They were captured by the police. In revenge for the arrests, the organization kidnapped 16 British, Australian, and US tourists in late December 1998 near Mudiyah in southern Yemen. The gang was tracked down and the Yemeni security forces attacked their hide-out, capturing many of the hostage-takers, including the gang's leader, Zein al-Abidine al-Mihdar (also known as 'Abu Hassan'), but leaving four of the hostages dead. Since the capture and trial of the Mudiyah kidnappers and the execution in October 1999 of 'Abu Hassan'), individuals associated with the group have remained involved in terrorist activities. Kidnappings of foreign nationals have continued and in October 2000 Hatim Muhsin bin Farid, alleged to be the new leader of the IAAA, was convicted on kidnapping charges and sentenced to seven years' imprisonment. In 2001 the Yemeni Government convicted an IAAA member and three associates for their roles in the October 2000 bombing of the British embassy in **Sana'a**.

The Islamic Association

Al-Jama'a al-Islamiyya

An international Islamist group active mainly in Lebanon, where it has 5,000 members. Its origins can be traced to **Gamal Abdel Nasser**'s efforts to achieve Arab unity in 1964, when members of an older organization established the Islamic Association in Tripoli. Following the Arab defeat in 1967 and the decline of **Nasserism**, the Islamic Association and other Islamist groups throughout the **Arab World** gained strength. During the **Lebanese civil war** its militia (the *mujahidin)*, fought with the **Lebanese National Movement** against Christian **Maronite** forces. In 1982–83 it participated in fighting the Israeli forces. The Islamic Association follows the doctrines of militants among the **Muslim Brotherhood** in Egypt and Syria. Fathi Yakan, a follower of **Sayyid Qutb**'s radical brand of Islamist thought, is its main ideologue. Yakan joined Sa'id Hawwa of Syria's Muslim Brotherhood in the wake of the 1967 war to advocate a holy war (*jihad al-muqaddas*) against the Western and Israeli 'crusaders'. Later, the Islamic Association tacitly rejected **Hezbollah**'s model of an **Islamic state**. It believes in achieving an Islamic order based on the **Shari'a** (Islamic sacred law) through *jihad* of the heart (spiritual struggle), *jihad* by word (education and propaganda), and *jihad* by hand (economic, political and military action). The Islamic Association engages in internecine struggles with the **Ahbash** and the **Tawheed Islami**, as well as with the traditional **Sunni** religious establishment as represented by Juridical Office (*Dar al-Ifta'*) and traditional leaders (the Karamis of Tripoli, the Salams of **Beirut**, and the newly-emerged Hariris of Sidon), whom it regards as the instruments of foreign interests. Its members tend to live in Lebanon's urban centres where there are large concentrations of Sunnis—Tripoli, Beirut, and Sidon. It recruits the young via the Muslim Students Association (Rabitat at-Tullab al-Muslimin). The Islamic Association offers social welfare services, though less sophisticated ones than Hezbollah provides, but has not succeeded in attracting many Sunni votes; it won three seats in the 1992 parliamentary elections and just one seat in 1996.

The Islamic Association for Palestine

An organization effectively representing **Hamas** in the USA. During Thanksgiving 2000 it raised US $200,000 for the Palestinian 'martyrs' at a conference.

Islamic Associations (Iran)

Islamic associations (*anjoman-e eslami*) were established in revolutionary Iran by supporters of the new Islamic government in schools, workplaces and many neighbourhoods. They monitored others for ideological (Islamic) purity and tended to harass those who appeared lax in their religious beliefs and practices or reluctant to join rallies and demonstrations in favour of the regime. They played a key role in the distribution of goods and food ration coupons through local mosques, particularly in poorer neighbourhoods, and were able both to exercise a measure of social control and to provide valuable welfare services.

Islamic Bank for Development – *see* Islamic Development Bank

Islamic banking

Usury or the taking of interest for loans is forbidden in **Islam**, so Islamic banking involves various different strategies to ensure viability and profitability.

Islamic banks have grown and become more significant within the region in the years since the collapse of the Soviet Union and the demise of state socialism in eastern Europe. Unlike their Western counterparts, Islamic financial institutions were quick to come to the rescue of many former 'socialist' regimes which, deprived of support from Moscow, became highly dependent on Islamic finance; they have also become more involved in other regions where Western banks have been reluctant to invest—Africa, the Caucasus, parts of the Balkans and **Central Asia**, in particular. The fall of the Soviet system provided Islamic finance with its greatest opportunity for growth since its earlier revival in the mid-1970s. One of the most successful of the private Islamic banks, until its collapse, was the **Bank of Credit and Commerce International**. Inter-governmental banks also, such as the **Islamic Development Bank**, have proved very successful. The body that oversees modern Islamic finance is the **Shari'a** Supervisory Board of Islamic Banks and Institutions, better known as the Shari'a Committee. Today, Islamic banks operate all over the world, offering their services to the international Muslim community. More than 200 Islamic banks are active in the USA, and there are thousands in Europe, Africa, the Arab countries and Asia. In 1998 the total liabilities of Islamic financial institutions were estimated at US $148,000m.—more than the gross domestic product of Saudi Arabia in that year ($138,000m.).

Islamic calendar

The Islamic calendar records dates from the death of the **Prophet Muhammad**.

Islamic Constitutional Movement

A quasi-political grouping in the Kuwaiti **Majlis** representing **Sunni** Muslims.

Islamic Consultative Assembly (Iran) – *see* **Majlis**

Islamic Da'awa Movement

Iraqi, predominantly **Shi'a**, political group, strongly identified with the **Iranian Revolution** and formed initially by Izzedin Salim, at around the time of the revolution in Iran as a breakaway group as a result of a split with the **Islamic Da'awa Party**, the leading religious party in the Iraqi Shi'a community. Izzedin Salim was at that time in exile in Iran, where he also set up an Islamic centre for political studies. It maintained itself throughout the Saddam years and was dramatically revived during 2002 when Izzedin Salim was selected to represent the group at the London exiles conference, and was growing in influence during the American-British occupation of Iraq, until the assassination in May 2004 of Izzedin Salim, who had been appointed a member of the **Iraqi Provisional Governing Council** in July the previous year.

Islamic Da'awa Party

Hizb ad-Da'awa al-Islamiyyaa

Iraqi political party. In **Arabic** '*da'awa*' means the 'call'. The Party's official title, Hizb ad-Da'awa al-Islamiyya, may be translated as Islamic Call Party, or the Voice of Islam Party. Established in October 1957 in **Najaf**, by the **Shi'ite** religious authority, Ayatollah **Muhammad Baqir as-Sadr** (1933–80), this is one of the two most important political organizations among the fundamentalist Shi'ite opposition groups in Iraq. Orginally, it was led by a group of young religious scholars (***ulema***) under as-Sadr's guidance and with the financial help of the then chief *mujtahid*, Grand Ayatollah **Muhsin al-Hakim**. Its main activity was directed towards lay intellectuals—mainly university students, graduates and urban professionals. It experienced increasing harassment—as did Islamic institutions and Shi'a clerics generally, following the Ba'athists' seizure of power in 1968. In December 1974, after Shi'a religious processions had turned into anti-government demonstrations, five ad-Da'awa leaders were executed. Following the **Iranian Revolution** in 1979, the new leadership in **Tehran** decided to encourage an Islamic movement in Iraq and provided assistance to ad-Da'awa. Membership of ad-Da'awa was made a capital offence in Iraq. In March 1980 50 members of ad-Da'awa were executed. In the following month ad-Da'awa militants tried but failed to assassinate the Iraqi deputy premier, **Tariq Aziz**, a **Christian**. After the death of as-Sadr at the hands of the Ba'athist authorities in April 1980, and its severe repression by the Ba'ath regime, the Party was deprived systematically of most of its religious leaders— some were executed, others disassociated themselves from the Party. After the outbreak of the **Iran–Iraq War** in September 1980, ad-Da'awa intensified its sabotage and assassination campaign within Iraq, with support from Iran. After Iranian forces had entered Iraq in June 1982, however, it became easier to label members of ad-Da'awa as traitors and allies of the Iranian enemy. This made their suppression easier, and practical support for ad-Da'awa declined. Many went into exile in Iran. In November 1982 ad-Da'awa members in Iran co-operated with other Islamic organizations, including the breakaway **Islamic Da'awa Movement** under Izzedin Salim, to form the Supreme Assembly of Islamic Revolution in Iraq, in Tehran. In 1985 ad-Da'awa allied itself with the secular Iraqi opposition, especially the **Kurdish Democratic Party**, which provided it with refuge in the Kurdish region to carry out attacks on the Ba'athist regime. In April 1987 ad-Da'awa militants made an unsuccessful attempt to assassinate **Saddam Hussain** on the outskirts of Mosul. Ad-Da'awa's activities subsided with the end of the Iran–Iraq War in August 1988, but revived in March 1991 when the Shi'a population of southern Iraq rose up in response to the call from the USA, following the withdrawal of 'allied forces' from Iraqi territory at the end of **Operation Desert Storm**. With the failure of the uprising, ad-Da'awa was once again largely marginalized. In December 1993 ad-Da'awa supporters detonated five bombs in Kuwait, which had aided Iraq during the war. Ad-Da'awa is the oldest Shi'a political party in Iraq and one of the most mature. During the US-British occupation of 2003–04 it tried to maintain some degree of balance between the **coalition** and the Shi'a population, and discouraged its supporters from allying themselves with **Moqtada as-Sadr**.

Over the last two decades lay intellectuals have come to constitute the majority of the two supreme bodies of the Party—the highest body (7–12 people) and a subordinate body (a group of some 100 representatives sent by the various regional branches), which elects the highest body. Below these are the regional branches that operate according to circumstances. Inside Iraq ad-Da'awa has been, until 2003, highly clandestine—mere membership of the Party was punishable by the death penalty. The Party or Movement was organized in cells (*halaqat*) beneath which were the basic units—'families' (*usar*). Outside Iraq the Party has maintained branches in Iran, Syria, Lebanon, Afghanistan and Britain. While monitored by the authorities in the first two of these countries, party work is generally not hindered and activity is relatively free. Branches in Iran and Syria hold open general meetings and conduct open political, educational and social activities. The Party's main spokesman has been Hojjatulislam Muhammad Mahdi al-Asifi (also known as Sheikh al-Assefie), who was also a member of the highest body. The Party's senior representatives in London were Dr Muwaffaq ar-Rubayi, a physician working in a London hospital, and Hojjatulislam Hussein as-Sadr. Ad-Da'awa sources are reluctant to disclose the names of the members of leading bodies, but party press reveals some of them. In many cases they are *noms de guerre*. Thus ad-Da'awa's most senior member in **Damascus** is reported to be Prof. 'Abu Bilal'. In Iran, Prof. 'Abu Mujahid ar-Rikabi', Dr 'Abu Yasir', Dr 'Abu Nabugh', Dr Abu Ahmed al-Jafari, 'Abu Fatima' and as-Sayyid Hasan Shubbar are all lay intellectuals. Besides al-Asifi and as-Sadr, among the party leadership there are a few other members of the *ulema*—Muhammad Baqir an-Nasiri and **Ayatollah** Kazim al-Husseini al-Hairi, among others. In Europe, the movement's main activities are political and cultural, and aimed at the Party's traditional constituency—university students and professionals. The situation is different in Iran, where the vast majority of members have been Iraqi expatriates from the lower social classes and strata. There the party maintains a range of groups and associations that provide practical as well as moral and religious support. These organizations include the Association of the Islamic Women of Iraq, the Islamic Union of Iraqi Workers, the Islamic Medical Association of Iraq, the Islamic Union of Iraqi Engineers, and traditional Shi'ite social institutions adjacent to mosques. These groups provide supporters (*al-ansar*), who are meant to serve as a protective shield around the central cadre.

Islamic Development Bank (IDB)

The IDB is an international financial institution, based in Saudi Arabia, established in pursuance of the Declaration of Intent issued by the Conference of Finance Ministers of the Islamic Conference held in **Jiddah** in December 1973. The inaugural meeting of the Board of Governors took place in Rajab in July 1975, and the Bank was formally opened on 20 October 1975. The present membership of the Bank comprises 54 countries. It has regional offices in Kazakhstan, Malaysia and Morocco. The basic condition for membership is that the prospective member country should be a member of the **Organization of the Islamic Conference**, pay its contribution to the capital of the Bank and be willing to accept such terms and conditions as may be decided upon by the Board of Governors. The purpose of the Bank is to foster the economic development and social progress of member countries and Muslim communities individually as well as jointly in accordance with the principles of **Shari'a**. The functions of the Bank are to participate in equity capital and grant loans for productive projects and enterprises besides providing financial assistance to member countries in other forms for economic and social development. The Bank is also required to establish and operate special funds for specific purposes including a fund for assistance to Muslim communities in non-member countries, in addition to setting up trust funds. It is also charged with the responsibility of assisting in the promotion of foreign **trade**, especially in capital goods, among member countries; providing technical assistance to member countries; and extending training facilities for personnel engaged in development activities in Muslim countries to conform to the Shari'a. In 1993 Saudi Arabia offered money to the Egyptian Government of **Hosni Mubarak** on condition that it encouraged the Islamization of Egyptian society. Large sums of Saudi **oil** revenues have been channelled into the IDB, which in turn has used its funds to promote the proliferation of Islamic investment houses and banks. Loans are conditional on strict adherence to Islamic laws and traditions. The Bank is used not only for strictly financial and banking purposes but also as a vehicle for the propagation of the Saudi fundamentalist interpretation of **Islam**, known as **Wahhabism**. One of its associated organizations, ar-Rayan, paid female students 15 Egyptian pounds to adopt the **veil**. Similar 'incentives' to **women** have been offered in other Muslim countries. It has wider political concerns as well, particularly where Islamic regimes are concerned. In 1998, several years after the closure of the **Bank of Credit and Commerce International**, it helped meet the economic penalties imposed on Pakistan for carrying out nuclear tests.

Islamic Front

Al-Jabha al-Islamiyya

This Lebanese umbrella group, with almost 100 members, was founded in 1985 by Sheikh Mahir Hammud. It brought together sheikhs and lay leaders. Its programme is generally critical of the West, its Arab allies and their willingness to make peace with Israel.

Islamic Front of the Armed Jihad (FIDA)

Front islamique pour le jihad armé (FIJA)

It is believed that the Algerian FIDA is the armed wing of al-Djazaraa, an Islamist group, and that its members are from the educated élite. The leader of this group is Omar el-Fidai. The group has been responsible for the assassination of prominent intellectuals, celebrities and politicians. It claimed responsibility for the assassination of the leader of the General Union of Algerian Workers, Abd al-Haq bin-Hamouda, in January 1997.

Islamic fundamentalism

A term widely used to refer to interpretations of **Islam** that urge a return to basic principles and, usually, to the more orthodox, conservative interpretations of the **Koran** and the **Hadith**. It can refer to both **Sunni** and **Shi'a** Islamic traditions.

Islamic government

Generally, government in accordance with principles derived from the **Koran**. In the case of the Islamic Republic of Iran, it has sometimes meant that the state is to be guided by a learned cleric (***velayat-i faqih***) who rules in the absence (on behalf) of the Twelfth Imam. Under Ayatollah **Khomeini**, the position of *faqih* (which he held) was ambiguous—it was provided for in the Constitution, but was not formally part of the government.

Islamic Great Eastern Raiders' Front

A militant Turkish Islamist group, which claimed responsibility for two major suicide bombings in **Istanbul** on 20 November 2003 that destroyed buildings and killed at least 27 and injured some 450 people when the HSBC Bank and the British consulate were attacked. It also claimed responsibility for bomb attacks on two synagogues, also in Istanbul, on the previous weekend. The group is believed to have close links with **al-Qa'ida** and also be connected to Turkish **Hezbollah**.

Islamic Group

Al-Jama'a al-Islamiyya

An Islamist political group in Morocco.

Islamic Group (IG)

Al-Gama'a al-Islamiyya

Egypt's largest militant group, active since the late 1970s. The group conducted armed attacks against Egyptian security and other government officials, **Coptic** Christians, and Egyptian opponents of Islamic extremism before it declared a cease-fire in March 1999. From 1993 until the cease-fire, al-Gama'a launched attacks on tourists in Egypt, most notably the attack in November 1997 at Luxor in which 58 foreign tourists died. It also claimed responsibility for the attempt in June 1995 to assassinate Egyptian President **Hosni Mubarak** in Addis Ababa, Ethiopia. It appears to be loosely organized. The group issued a cease-fire in March 1999, but its spiritual leader, Sheikh **Omar Abdul ar-Rahman**, imprisoned for life in January 1996 for his involvement in the 1993 bomb attack on the **World Trade Center** and incarcerated in the USA, rescinded his support for the cease-fire in June 2000. The Gama'a has not, however, conducted an attack inside Egypt since August 1998. Senior members signed **Osama bin Laden**'s *fatwa* in February 1998 calling for attacks against the USA. Unofficially split in two factions, one that supports the cease-fire led by Mustafa Hamza, and another, led by Rifa'i Taha Musa, that calls for a return to armed operations. In early 2001 Taha Musa published a book in which he attempted to justify terrorist attacks that would cause mass casualties. Musa disappeared several months thereafter, and there are conflicting reports as to his current whereabouts. In March 2002 members of the group's historic leadership in Egypt declared the use of violence misguided and renounced its future use, prompting denunciations by much of the leadership abroad. For members still dedicated to violent *jihad*, the primary goal is to overthrow the Egyptian Government and replace it with an **Islamic state**. Disaffected members, inspired by Taha Musa or Sheikh Abd ar-Rahman, may, however, also be interested in carrying out attacks against US and Israeli interests, although the Gama'a has never specifically attacked a US citizen or facility but has threatened US interests. The size of its membership at present is unknown. At its peak, it probably comprised several thousand committed members and a similar number of sympathizers. The 1999 cease-fire and security crackdowns following the attack in Luxor in 1997 and, more recently, security efforts following 11 September 2001, probably have resulted in a substantial decrease in the group's numbers. In Egypt it operates mainly in the Al-Minya, Asyut, Qina, and Sohaj governorates of upper (southern) Egypt. It also appears to have support in **Cairo, Alexandria** and other urban locations, particularly among unemployed graduates and students. It has a world-wide presence, including in the United Kingdom, Afghanistan, Yemen, and various locations in Europe. The Egyptian Government believes that Iran, Osama bin Laden and Afghan militant groups support the organization. It may also obtain some funding through various Islamic NGOs.

Islamic Iran Participation Front

Iranian political grouping.

Islamic Jihad (Egypt) – *see* Al-Jihad

Islamic Jihad (Lebanon)

Al-Jihad al-Islami

Pro-Iranian fundamentalist guerrilla group in Lebanon, widely believed to be the linked to the **Islamic Resistance**, used by **Hezbollah** for attacking Western interests. The name first appeared in claims of responsibility for the bombing of the US embassy in **Beirut** in April 1983, followed by the suicide bombing of the Israeli military headquarters in Tyre in October 1985, and the kidnapping of Westerners, mainly US citizens, in March 1984. Imaad Moughniyeh reportedly controlled the organization. Although there has been no news of Islamic Jihad since 1988, some reports indicate that Moughniyeh is still active and in charge of Hezbollah's overseas security apparatus (which handles intelligence and conducts overseas terrorist acts).

Islamic Jihad (Palestine)

Al-Jihad al-Islami

The Islamic Jihad movement in Palestine was initially a relatively small group of militant **Sunni** factions such as the Brigades of Islamic Jihad (Saraya al-Jihad al-Islami) and the **Izz ad-Din al-Qassam Brigades**. Born in the slums and refugee camps of **Gaza**, Islamic Jihad followed the teachings of Ayatollah **Khomeini** and Egypt's **Tanzim al-Jihad** in its use of violence and readiness for **martyrdom** to achieve an Islamic order. With the support of the **Palestine Liberation Organization**, it escalated guerrilla attacks on Israeli targets in 1986, thereby helping to initiate the *intifada*. Israel responded in the spring of 1988 by expelling its spiritual guide, Abd al-'Aziz 'Awda, to Lebanon and arresting scores of his followers. Islamic Jihad has gained increasing support over the last decade or so and is now operational in the **Occupied Territories** of the **West Bank** and Gaza Strip, especially in the latter. Islamic Jihad claimed responsibility for a suicide bombing in May 2003 in which two people were killed in Afula, north of **Jenin**. Some witnesses suggested that the bomber was a woman. Another Islamist group—the **Al-Aqsa Martyrs' Brigade**—also claimed responsibility for the attack.

Islamic jurisprudence

Islamic jurisprudence, (*fiqh* in **Arabic**), is made up of the rulings of Islamic scholars for the direction of the lives of Muslims. There are four schools (*madhhab*) of fiqh. The four schools of **Sunni Islam** are each named after a classical jurist. The Sunni schools are the **Shafi'i** (Malaysia), **Hanafi** (Indian subcontinent, West Africa, Egypt), **Maliki** (North Africa and West Africa), and **Hanbali** (Arabia). These four schools share most of their rulings but differ on the particular **Hadiths** they accept as authentically given by the **Prophet Muhammad** and the weight they give to analogy or reason (qiyas, *ijtihad*) in making decisions on difficulties. The Jaferi school (Iran and Iraq) is more associated with **Shi'a** Islam. The *fatwas* are taken rather more seriously in this school, due to the more hierarchical structure of **Shi'a** Islam, which is ruled by imams. However, they are also more flexible, in that the Imams have considerable power to consider the context of a decision, which has been lacking in Sunni Islam historically.

Early **Shari'a** had a much more flexible character, and many modern Muslim scholars believe that it should be renewed, and the classical jurists should lose their special status. This would require formulating a new *fiqh* suitable for the modern world, e.g. as proposed by advocates of the Islamization of knowledge, and would deal with the modern context. This modernization is opposed by most *ulema* who spend much time memorizing the traditional schools of classical jurists, and who typically lack the power or infrastructure to research or to reliably enforce rulings that go beyond the traditional norms. They often accuse those who seek to reform *fiqh* of seeking simply to replace Islam with a more secular form of **democracy** and law.

Islamic Law (Shari'a)

In **Arabic** Shari'a means 'way' or 'road'. Islamic Law is held by Muslims to be a complete legal system that governs every aspect of individual and social life and is derived directly from the traditions and sayings of the **Prophet Muhammad**, as directed in the **Koran**, the Sunna, older Arabic law systems, parallel traditions and the work of Muslim scholars over the first two centuries of **Islam**. There are traces of many non-Muslim juridical systems in the Shari'a, such as Old Arab **Bedouin** law, commercial law from **Mecca**, agrarian law from **Medina**, law from the conquered countries, Roman law and Jewish law. Calling the Shari'a the 'law' can be misleading, as it extends beyond the law. Shari'a is the totality of religious, political, social, domestic and private life. Shari'a is primarily meant for all Muslims, but applies to a certain extent to all people living in a Muslim society. Muslims are not totally bound by the Shari'a when they live or travel outside the Muslim world.

Islamic League for Call and Jihad

Ligue islamique de la da'awa et du djihad (LIDD)

Algerian Islamist opposition group. Led by Sheikh Ali Benhadjar. Part of the LIDD joined the cease-fire announced by the **AIS—Armée islamique du salut** (Islamic Salvation Army) in October 1997 and dissolved itself after the 1999 amnesty. A dissident splinter group of the LIDD continued fighting in eastern Algeria. Little is known about the LIDD other than that the splinter group has issued dire statements prophesizing that more blood will be shed and accusing the Algerian regime of tyranny.

Islamic Martyrs' Movement

Libyan opposition movement. Its spokesman is Abdallah Ahmad.

Islamic Movement

Al-Haraka al-Islamiya

The Islamic Movement, which has almost 200 members, is a seemingly independent, semi-clandestine group based in the **Beka'a Valley** in Lebanon, and headed by Sadiq al-Musawi, a cousin of **Islamic Amal**'s Husayn al-Musawi. It has been inspired by Ayatollah **Khomeini** but is independent of **Hezbollah** and enjoys direct access to Iranian militants. Its militia, Army of the Truth (Jund al-Haqq), has ties with **Shi'i** minorities in the **Arabian Peninsula**; in the mid-1980s it targeted Saudi diplomats in retaliation for Saudi Arabia's execution of Shi'i activists. Though apparently inactive since 1989, the movement may have gone underground. In 1993 Sadiq al-Musawi accused Hezbollah of having deviated from Khomeini's teachings and called for an Islamic republic in Lebanon.

Islamic Movement of Kurdistan

Iraqi political organization formed by the amalgamation of **Kurdish Hezbollah**, the Kurdish Mujahidin and the Kurdish **Ansar al-Islam** in 1991.

Islamic Movement of Uzbekistan (IMU)

The IMU, also known as the Islamic Party of Turkestan, was formed in 1998, by those dissatisfied with the moderation of the **Islamic Renaissance Party** and determined to overthrow the government of **Islam Karimov** in Uzbekistan. Its leaders were Tohir Abdouhalilovitch and **Juma Namangiani**. The IMU, which had a network spreading across several Central Asian republics, declared *jihad* against the Uzbek government. It was supported by a combination of external funding and self-finance. In 1999, for example, it received US $25m. from foreign sponsors—mainly Turkish, but also from Saudi Arabia and the **Taliban**. Under the military leadership of Namangiani, the IMU launched guerrilla attacks from bases in Tajikistan and Afghanistan in 1999–2001. The key target of these attacks was the **Fergana Valley**, divided between the three states of Uzbekistan, Kyrgyzstan and Tajikistan. Each of these countries thus faced a direct military threat, as well as political opposition, and military spending has increased significantly over the last few years. So too has the influence of foreign advisers and experts, from Russia, China and the USA, which are competing to secure a foothold in the region. Increased repression in the Central Asian states has served only to increase the number of those sympathizing with, actively supporting and fighting for the Islamist cause. The result is that the IMU is growing. Dissidents from all over the region, as well as Chechens and Dagestanis from the Caucasus, and Uighurs from China's extreme north-western province of **Xinjiang**, are joining the movement. Support flows in from across the region, and funding comes from as far away as Saudi Arabia—as well as from the narcotics and weapons trade out of Afghanistan. Namangiani's networks in Tajikistan and **Central Asia** were used to smuggle **opium** from Afghanistan; it was partly due to his contacts in **Chechnya** that **heroin** reached Europe. According to Interpol, about 60% of Afghan narcotics exported in 2002 passed through Central Asia. The IMU controlled 70% of the opium and heroin that moved through this area, and set up heroin laboratories in the territories under its control. The armed groups' stronghold is the Tavildara Valley, in Tajikistan. Since 1999 it has fought to gain control of the Fergana Valley as well. The US attack on Afghanistan hit the IMU hard; even before the bombing began on 7 Octobe 2001, the IMU had maintained military bases in Afghanistan, fought alongside the Taliban and received support from **Osama bin Laden**. As the IMU fought with the Taliban in northern Afghanistan, hundreds of IMU members were killed by US bombing, particularly during the capture of **Mazar-i-Sharif** and Kunduz by the **Northern Alliance**. There were reports that Juma Namangani, the IMU military commander, had been killed near Mazar-i-Sharif in a US bombing raid. Hundreds more IMU fighters escaped to eastern Afghanistan, where some were caught up in the subsequent US operations in Tora Bora and Gardez, while others fled across the borders to Iran and Pakistan. Without doubt, the IMU has suffered the loss of its bases, its sources of funding from **al-Qa'ida**, and the ability to use Afghanistan as a recruitment base. However, its extensive underground network in Central Asia, particularly in Tajikistan and the Fergana Valley, remains intact. Furthermore, although the USA has declared Juma Namangiani to be dead, senior officials from Uzbekistan, Tajikistan and Russia believe that he is still alive, in hiding in either Pakistan or Tajikistan, awaiting a US withdrawal so that he can rally his supporters. Certainly, **Tohir Yuldeshev**, the political leader of the IMU, is widely suspected by the intelligence agencies of Central Asian republics to be in hiding in Pakistan, where hundreds of Taliban and al-Qa'ida fighters have also taken refuge. Although the IMU's primary goal remains to overthrow Karimov and establish an **Islamic state** in Uzbekistan, Yuldeshev is working to rebuild the organization and appears to have widened the IMU's targets to include all those he perceives as fighting **Islam**. The IMU generally has been unable to operate in Uzbekistan and thus has been more active in Kyrgyzstan and Tajikistan. The IMU primarily targeted Uzbekistani interests before October 2001 and is believed to have been responsible for five car bombs detonated in Tashkent in February 1999. Militants also took foreigners hostage in 1999 and 2000. Even though the IMU's rhetoric and ultimate goals may have been focused on Uzbekistan, it was generally more active in Kyrgyzstan and Tajikistan. In Operation Enduring Freedom, the counter-**terrorism** coalition captured, killed, and dispersed many of the IMU's militants who were fighting with the Taliban in Afghanistan and severely degraded the movement's ability to attack Uzbekistani or coalition interests in the near term. IMU military leader Juma Namangiani was reportedly killed during an air strike **in** Afghanistan in November 2001; Yuldeshev remains at large.

Islamic Party of Turkestan – *see* Islamic Movement of Uzbekistan

Islamic Renaissance Party (IRP)

The first populist manifestation of **Islamic fundamentalism** in **Central Asia**.

Formed in the Soviet Union as an Islamic political party that would have an independent branch in each Central Asian state. It was never able to register as a legal party in Uzbekistan and formed the core of the **United Tajik Opposition** in the **Tajik civil war**.

Islamic Republic(an) Party (IRP, Iran)

Established in February 1979 by Ayatollah Mohammed-Ali Beheshti, Hojatoleslam **Hashemi Rafsanjani** and Hojatoleslam Ali **Khamenei**. The Party regards Ayatollah **Khomeini** as its main source of inspiration, deriving its legitimacy from its close association with him. Beheshti, regarded as the second most powerful cleric after Khomeini, head of the IRP and chief justice of the Supreme Court, died, at the age of 52, in an explosion in **Tehran** in June 1981, which killed most of the Party's leadership. He was succeeded as leader of the Party in September 1981, after a short interlude, by Ali Khamenei, who became President of Iran in October of the same year, following the assassination of President **Muhammad Ali Rajai**. The IRP managed to institutionalize the revolution and assure its own survival by creating organizations which parallel government agencies and hold real power. It is, in effect, the governing party of Iran; its main supporters are to be found among the urban poor and support is organized mainly through mass public prayer meetings held throughout the country on Fridays. In the early years these included the **Revolutionary Guards** (*pasdaran*) and other groups of zealots, including **Islamic associations** (*anjoman-e eslami*), the Party of God (**Hezbollah**), **Islamic Revolutionry** *komitehs* (committees), and revolutionary courts.

Islamic Resistance

Al-Muqawama al-Islamiya

The Lebanese Islamic Resistance has almost 5,000 members. It was established after the Israeli invasion of 1982, when it fought a guerrilla war against Israeli forces and those commanded by Gen. Lahud's forces. It originally consisted of both **Shi'i** and **Sunni** fighters, who represented virtually all Islamic militant groups, but Shi'i fighters played a growing combat role over time. In 1985 the Islamic Resistance became the combat arm of **Hezbollah**.

Islamic Revolution – *see* Iranian Revolution

Islamic revolutionary *komitehs*

Hundreds of revolutionary committees were established throughout Iran in the early revolutionary period and became *de facto* local governments, acting as tribunals and police. This was widely resented, and in April 1986 the **Majlis** moved to reduce the autonomy of the *komitehs* by placing them under the control of the Ministry of the Interior. As the police force was gradually reconstructed, the *komitehs* yielded a degree of power, but they continue to monitor activities and behaviour they consider to be counter-revolutionary and unIslamic, as do the **Islamic associations**.

Islamic Salvation Army – *see* AIS—Armée islamique du salut

Islamic Salvation Front – *see* FIS—Front islamique du salut

Islamic state

The Islamic state is a state in which **Islamic Law**—the **Shari'a**—provides the basis for law and politics. Many Islamist groups in the region are struggling to bring about the overthrow of the current regimes, which they regard as illegitimate, and their replacement by Islamic regimes that will provide the appropriate God-given framework for public and private life.

The Islamic Struggle Movement

Al-Haraka al-Islamiyya al-Mujahid, Lebanon

The Movement has almost 100 members. It first appeared in 1987 under the direction of Sheikh Abdullah al-Hallaq, a **Sunni** cleric influenced by **Hezbollah** and the Lebanese **Islamic Resistance**. The movement aims to recruit Sunni and Palestinian fighters in the Sidon area to attack Israel. It failed, however, to organize a Sunni resistance in the south similar to that of the **Shi'a** Hezbollah.

Islamic taxation – *see zakat*

Islamic Tendency Movement

Under the leadership of **Habib Bourguiba**, who held power in 1956–87, and backed by Western governments, Tunisia's post-independence Government pursued an aggressive programme of secularization and modernization. The Government abolished the **Shari'a** courts, closed the Zaytouna (a renowned centre of Muslim learning), banned the **headscarf** for women, and debilitated the *ulema.* These events led to the formation in 1979 of the Islamic Tendency Movement (MTI, or Renaissance Party), led by Rashid Ghannoushi. Though initially apolitical, it sought a humanitarian restructuring of society and the economy based on Islamic principles, together with participation in the democratic political process, rejecting violence as a means of change.

The group's status changed in January 1978 when Bourguiba used the **military** to suppress protesters associated with the group. This event, in combination with the success of the **Islamic Revolution** in Iran, convinced Ghannoushi and the movement of the need to move beyond broad ideological statements and to relate **Islam** directly and specifically to the real, everyday political, economic, and social problems of the people. Ghannoushi was arrested in 1981, and sentenced to 11 years' imprisonment, but was released in 1984. Rearrested in 1987, he was released following **Ben Ali**'s ouster of Bourguiba. When Ben Ali replaced Bourguiba, the former also refused to allow the MTI to participate in public life. Instead, he voiced a 'firm belief in the need not to mix religion and politics, as experience has shown that anarchy emerges and the rule of law and institutions is undermined when such a mixing takes place'. Yet, the MTI's actual agenda did not represent an attempt to establish a militant **Islamic state**. Instead, it included a reassertion of Tunisia's Islamic-Arabic way of life and values, the restriction of Tunisia's Westernized (Francophile) profile, and the promotion of **democracy**, political pluralism, and economic and social justice. Due to its Islamist affiliations, however, secular leaders automatically classified the party with pro-Iranian groups such as **Islamic Jihad** and **Hezbollah.** As a result, MTI was banned from formal political participation despite its widespread legitimacy among the Tunisian people and its relatively progressive nationalist agenda. In 1988 Ghannouchi restyled the organization as the **an-Nahda (Renaissance) Movement**.

Islamic Transitional Government of Afghanistan (ITGA)

Afghanistan is governed by the ITGA, a government that followed the **Afghan Interim Authority**. (See **Afghanistan**.)

Islamic Union

Iraqi political group.

Islamic Unity (Unification) Movement

Harakat at-Tawshid al-Islami, Lebanon

A **Sunni** militia and political movement, with around 1,000 members, that originated in the port town of Tripoli in 1982. It was very much the creation of Sheikh
Sa'id Sha'ban, previously a leader of the **Islamic Association**. Islamic Unity serves
as an institutional extension of Sha'ban's personal power base, as one of the Islamist
movement's few charismatic leaders in Lebanon. It consolidated its control over
Tripoli in 1983–84 by defeating a number of rivals and then, at the height of its
power in 1985, splintered, as Khalil 'Akkawi and Kan'an Naji left to organize their
own associations. In the autumn of 1985 the Syrian army entered Tripoli and
crushed Islamic Unity's militia, though it permitted Sha'ban to maintain leadership
of his now unarmed movement. This defeat did not prevent the militia's subsequent
re-emergence in **Beirut**, Sidon, and south Lebanon. In 1988 the Tawshid forces
joined the **Islamic Resistance** to fight the South Lebanese Army and the Israeli
forces in Israel's 'security zone' in south Lebanon. Sha'ban's ideology derives from
the radical wing of the **Muslim Brotherhood**. Curiously, Sha'ban is said to have
been born into a **Shi'i** family of Batroun in north Lebanon and only later became a
Sunni. He forged close political ties to Iran during visits to **Tehran** and through
Hezbollah, which considers Sha'ban to be, doctrinally, a follower of Ayatollah
Khomeini. While accepting the validity of the **Iranian Revolution** and emphasizing that the path started by Khomeini should be followed by all Muslims, Sha'ban
does not call for an Iranian-style order in Lebanon, knowing that this would alienate
his Sunni followers. He seeks ways to unite Sunnis and Shi'a, for example by
suggesting that the **Koran** and the **Prophet Muhammad**'s biography provide
foundations on which all Muslim groups and sects can unite. Instead of arguing
about sectarian representation in the parliament, he suggests that Muslims call for
Islamic rule based on the **Shari'a**, without which no government can be legitimate.
Sha'ban rejects nationalism, sectarianism and democratic pluralism in favor of
Islamic rule that 'absorbs and dissolves all social differences and unites them in one
crucible'. He regrets the Syrian intervention in Lebanon of 1976 to help the
Maronites who, he asserts, would have otherwise fled to Cyprus or Latin
America. Aside from such rare instances of mild criticism, he is careful not to
antagonize the Syrian authorities; indeed, he speaks favourably of the Syrian
military presence in Lebanon as a framework for unified, armed action against
Israel.

Islamism – *see* political Islam

Islamophobia

A fear of **Islam** and Muslims; it is directed against so-called '**Islamic fundamentalism**', based on the belief that most Muslims are hostile and intolerant towards

other societies and that through their religion they can undermine the traditional integrity of Western cultures and civilization.

Ismail, Abdul Fattah

President of the **People's Democratic Republic of Yemen** from 1978 until 1980, when he resigned.

Ismail Khan

Powerful warlord in western Afghanistan and Governor of **Herat**. Maintains close relations with Iran. In March 2003 he visited **Tehran** to discuss Iranian **aid** to Afghanistan, in particular the Herat region. Iran has as a result pledged US $560m. over five years to help rebuild Afghanistan's infrastructure.

Ismailis

The Ismailis are an Islamic sect who seceded from the mainstream on the question of the succession of the sixth Imam. They were the founders of the Karmat states and the brilliant Fatimid dynasty in the 10th century in Egypt, as well as of the 'sect of the assassins' founded in the fortress of Alamut at the end of the 11th century, and of the **Druze** doctrine. Today, the **Aga Khan** is the leader of the main Ismaili community, which is scattered across Iran, Afghanistan, Pakistan, India, and east Africa.

Israel, State of
Medinat Yisra'el

Israel lies along the eastern **Mediterranean** coast between Egypt (to the south) and Lebanon (to the north). It also borders Syria (to the north-east), Jordan and the **Occupied Territories** which **Palestinians** anticipate will be the future state of Palestine (to the east). The area of Israel is 20,770 sq km (of which 440 sq km is **water**), but it also occupies territory in the **West Bank** and **Gaza Strip**. In February 2002 it was estimated that there were 242 Israeli **settlements** and civilian land use sites in the West Bank, 42 in the Israeli-occupied **Golan Heights**, 25 in the Gaza Strip, and 29 in **East Jerusalem**; the Sea of **Galilee** is an important freshwater source. **Jerusalem** is regarded by **Israelis** as the capital of Israel, but its status as such is not internationally recognized. The future status of Jerusalem remains to be determined. Most countries locate their embassies in **Tel-Aviv**. The main administrative regions or districts (*mehoz*, plural *mehozot*) are Central, **Haifa**, Jerusalem, Northern District, Southern District and Tel-Aviv. At July 2002 the population was estimated at 6,029,529, of which Jews constituted the majority (79%), Arabs 20% and 'others' 1%. This figure, according to estimates made in February 2003, includes about 187,000 Israeli settlers in the West Bank, about 20,000 in the

Israeli-occupied Golan Heights, more than 5,000 in the Gaza Strip, and fewer than 177,000 in East Jerusalem. With regard to religion, Jews constitute the majority of the population (82%), Muslims (mostly **Sunni**) 14%, Christians (2%), and **Druze** and other religious groups 3%. Languages in use are **Hebrew** (official) and **Arabic** (used officially for the Arab **minority**).

Political profile

Israel has no formal constitution. Some of the functions of a constitution are filled by the Declaration of Establishment (1948), the Basic Laws of the parliament (**Knesset**), and the Israeli citizenship law. Israeli is a parliamentary **democracy**. The head of state is the President (Moshe Katsav since 31 July 2000) and the head of government is the Prime Minister (**Ariel Sharon** since 7 March 2001). The Cabinet is selected by the Prime Minister and approved by the Knesset. The President is elected by the Knesset for a seven-year term of office. The most recent presidential election was held in July 2000 and the next is scheduled to be held in 2007. Following legislative elections, the President assigns a Knesset member—traditionally the leader of the largest party—the task of forming a governing coalition. The most recent legislative elections were held in January 2003 and the next are scheduled to be held in 2007. The legislature is the unicameral Knesset, which has 120 seats. Its members are elected by popular vote to serve four-year terms of office. The legal system is a mixture of English common law, British Mandate regulations, and, in personal matters, Jewish, Christian, and Muslim legal systems. In the Supreme Court, justices are appointed for life by the President. In December 1985 Israel informed the UN Secretariat that it would no longer accept compulsory International Court of Justice jurisdiction. There are numerous political parties and groups and most governments are formed from multiple coalitions. There is, consequently, rarely a unified opposition. The **military** is heavily involved in political affairs and the media. Officers of high and middle rank have considerable influence in most aspects of Israeli society and political culture. Officers who have left the army have always been considered qualified for any civilian leadership position. Hence, the military is directly and indirectly a partner in almost any major decision-making process. Under Sharon's regime, the **Likud** has formed a coalition government with **Shinui** under Tommy Lapid, the **National Religious Party**, led by Itzhak Levy, and the **National Union** (including Tekuma and **Moledet**, led by Benyamin Elon. Other parties and groupings include: The **Centre Party**; **Democratic Front for Peace and Equality** (**Hadash**); **the Democratic Movement**; **Gesher**; **Herut**; the **Israel Labour Party**; **Likud**; **Meimad**; **Meretz**; the **National Democratic Alliance** (**Balad**); **One Israel**; **One People** (**Nation**); **Shas**; the **United Arab List**; **United Torah Judaism**; **Yisra'el Ba'Aliya**; and **Yisra'el Beiteinu**. There are also social movements, such as Peace Now, which supports territorial concessions in the West Bank and Gaza Strip, Yesha Council, which promotes settler interests and opposes territorial compromise, B'Tselem which monitors human rights abuses, and the **International Solidarity Movement**.

Media

Israeli media are under increasing pressure to conform to the government's and the army's line on the issue of the occupation. The Israeli media are disproportionately right-wing.

Foreign journalists are subject to harassment. In 2003 the government officially stated that the British Broadcasting Corporation (BBC) would 'find it difficult' to work there after the BBC reported on Israel's stock of **weapons of mass destruction**. There are 34 daily newspapers, the leading ones being *Ha'aretz* and the English-language *Jerusalem Post*. There are two television stations, one state-owned and one independent. There are two state-owned radio services and many independent radio stations. In 2000 there were 21 internet service providers and in 2001 there were 1.94m. internet users.

History

Following the Second World War Britain withdrew from the Mandate of Palestine, and the UN partitioned the area into Arab and Jewish states, an arrangement rejected by Arab states. Subsequently, Israel defeated Arab forces in a series of wars without ending the deep tensions between the two sides.   On 25 April 1982 Israel withdrew from the Sinai pursuant to the 1979 Israel-Egypt Peace Treaty.

Outstanding territorial and other disputes with Jordan were resolved in the 26 October 1994 Israel-Jordan Treaty of Peace. In addition, on 25 May 2000, Israel withdrew from southern Lebanon, which it had occupied since 1982. In keeping with the framework established at the **Madrid Peace Conference** in October 1991, bilateral negotiations were conducted between Israel and Palestinian representatives (from the Israeli-occupied West Bank and Gaza Strip) and Syria with the aim of reaching a permanent settlement. However, progress toward a permanent status agreement was undermined by the hegemonic peace, an Oslo process that gave close to nothing to the Palestinians, and the outbreak of Palestinian–Israeli violence since September 2000.

International relations

The West Bank and Gaza Strip are occupied by Israel, as are the Syrian Golan Heights. (Lebanon claims the Shab'a Farms area of the Golan Heights.) There is increasing concern within Israel over cocaine and **heroin** abuse. **Drugs** arrive in the country from Lebanon.

Israel, economy

Israel is the fourth largest economy in the **Middle East** (after Saudi Arabia, Turkey and Iran) with a gross national product of US $108,300m. Israel has a technologically advanced market economy with substantial government participation. It depends on imports of crude **oil**, grains, raw materials, and military equipment.

Despite limited natural resources, Israel has intensively developed its agricultural and industrial sectors over the past 20 years. Israel is largely self-sufficient in food production except for grains. Cut diamonds, high-technology equipment, and agricultural products (fruits and vegetables) are the leading exports. Israel usually records sizeable current account deficits, which are covered by large transfer payments from abroad and by foreign loans. Roughly one-half of the government's external **debt** is owed to the USA, which is its major source of economic and military **aid**. However, the bitter Israeli-Palestinian conflict, increasingly the declines in the high-technology and tourist sectors, and fiscal austerity measures in the face of growing inflation led to declines in gross domestic product in 2001 and 2002.

Strengths

Modern infrastructure and educated population. Israel uses occupied territories as a cheap source of labour. There is considerable potential for **agriculture**, manufacturing and high-technology **industry**. The banking sector is vibrant.

Weaknesses

Israel is politically instable owing to the continuing occupation of Palestine and the Palestinian *intifada* is having an adverse effect on **trade**, **tourism** and investment. There is a huge defence budget. The financial burden of absorbing immigrants and subsidizing **settlements** is considerable. Israeli engages in little trade with its Arab neighbours. There is **corruption** and rising unemployment.

Israel Communist Party
Miflaga Kommunistit Yisraelit (Maki)

Originally established in 1922, the Communist Party was for a long time the only Israeli political party which united Arabs and Jews. It underwent numerous splits. The last was in 1965. Anti-Zionist in a Zionist state, pro-Soviet in a predominantly anti-Soviet state, advocates of a Palestinian state, Israeli communists have yet to win 5% of the vote. The splinter group, the New Communist List (Reshima Kommunistit HaDasha—**Rakah**) was pro-Moscow, strongly anti-Zionist and primarily Arab in membership. In the 1981 elections the Rakah-led **Hadash**, or **Democratic Front for Peace and Equality**, won four seats in the **Knesset**. Two other members from the extreme left wing were elected in 1984 as part of the **Progressive List for Peace**, the heir of Meir Pail's **Sheli**, Uri Avnery's Haolam Hazeh and Moked. This called for the total withdrawal of Israel from the **Occupied Territories**, equal rights for the Arab community, the establishment of a democratic, socialist, secular state in Palestine, peace with the surrounding Arab states, and a non-aligned foreign policy. **Shulamit Aloni**'s **Citizens' Rights Movement** made great strides between 1981, when it had only one seat in the Knesset, and 1984, when its representation totalled three seats, and 1988, when it held five seats.

Electorally marginal, these leftist groups were able to contribute to the expression of a powerful pacifist movement formed by Shalom Achsav (Peace Now), the Committee Against the War in Lebanon and the soldiers' organization, Yesh Gvul (There is a Limit).

Israel Labour Party
Mifleget HaAvodah HaYisraelit

Created in 1968 from the merger (or Alignment) of three parties: **Mapai**, **Achdut HaAvoda** and **Rafi**. The Labour Party is a centre-left, Zionist, democratic socialist party with strong links to the trade union movement and the **Histadrut**. Often considered more broadly sympathetic towards the Palestinian 'cause' than, for example, the **Likud**, the Labour Party has been difficult to distinguish in this regard, in reality, from its main political rivals. It was very successful in the 1969 elections, when the Alignment was joined by **Mapam**, winning 46% per cent of the vote and 56 seats in the **Knesset**. It was again successful in the 1973 elections, when it obtained 40% of the vote and 51 parliamentary seats, becoming the largest party in the Knesset. In 1977, however, lacklustre leadership, **corruption** scandals and the founding of the Democratic Movement for Change made way for a Likud victory, with the Labour Party winning only one-quarter of the vote and 23 seats. It performed better in 1981, but still failed to move ahead of Likud, which secured 48 parliamentary seats compared with the Labour Party's 47. In 1984 the Alignment emerged as the largest party in the Knesset and **Shimon Peres** was given the mandate to form a new government. He formed a government of national unity in which he himself served initially as Prime Minister.

Israel-Palestine Liberation Organization 15 January 1997 Protocol

This Protocol concerned redeployment in **Hebron**.

Israel-Palestine Liberation Organization 23 October 1998 Wye River Memorandum

This Memorandum concerned redeployment in various parts of the occupied **West Bank**.

Israeli Arabs

The largest **minority** group in Israel. The Israeli government refuses to refer to as **Palestinians** those Arabs living inside Israel proper, preferring to use the term Israeli Arabs. Approximately 20% (1.2m. individuals) of the Israeli population is so designated. Human rights groups claim that Israeli Arabs are treated as second-class citizens, even though they have virtually the same civil rights as any other Israeli citizen. However, they are not liable for compulsory military service and usually reside in the poorer areas of the north. Israeli Arabs tend to define themselves as Palestinians or **Israeli Palestinians**.

Israeli Defence Force

The Israeli **armed forces**, which came into existence in 1948 after the establishment of the State of Israel. Based on existing paramilitary groups.

Israeli-Palestinian Interim Agreement

The Israeli-Palestinian Interim Agreement on the **West Bank** and the **Gaza Strip** was signed by the chairman of the **Palestine Liberation Organization**, **Yasser Arafat**, and the Israeli Minister of Foreign Affairs, **Shimon Peres**, in Washington, DC, USA on 28 September 1995. The agreement was witnessed by representatives of the USA, Russia, Egypt, Jordan, Norway and the **European Union**. The Interim Agreement was formulated within the framework of the **Middle East** peace process initiated at Madrid, Spain, in October 1991 and in the context of the **Declaration of Principles on Palestinian Self-Rule** signed in Washington, DC, in September 1993 and the agreed minutes thereto (referred to as the DoP). It dealt first with the establishment of a Palestinian Council, then with Redeployment and Security, then with legal affairs and co-operation. There was progress made in many respects on the basis of this Interim Agreement, but three years later it was felt by all concerned that progress was slow and inadequate in various different respects and a meeting was convened under the auspices of US President **Bill Clinton** in Maryland, USA, which resulted in the **Wye River Memorandum**.

Israeli Palestinians

This is how many Arabs inside Israel proper define themselves. The Israeli government defines them as **Israeli Arabs**.

Israeli peace initiative

In May 1989 the Israeli Government approved a four-point peace initiative for a resolution of the **Middle East** conflict, the details of which had first been announced during a meeting between US President **Bush** and Israeli Prime Minister **Itzhak Shamir** in Washington, DC, in April. Based largely on proposals made by the Israeli defence minister **Itzhak Rabin** in January 1989, the new plan followed increased international diplomatic pressure on Israel to respond to the uprising (*intifada*) in the **Occupied Territories** with constructive proposals to end the conflict. In July 1989 four amendments (involving essentially stricter conditions) were approved by the central committee of the **Likud**, but at the end of the month the Israeli Government once again endorsed the original initiative. In September 1989 President **Mubarak** of Egypt sought assurances on 10 points from the Israeli Government and offered to host talks between Palestinian and Israeli delegations. This invitation was rejected by the 'inner Cabinet' of the Israeli Government in October. In the same month US Secretary of State, James Baker, put forward a series of unofficial proposals aimed to give new impetus to the Israeli initiative (now referred to as the Shamir Plan) and the subsequent clarifications requested by President Mubarak. The USA sought (through the so-called Baker Plan) assurances that Egypt could not and would not substitute itself for the **Palestinians** in any future discussions and that both Palestinians and Israel would take part in any future dialogue on the basis of the Shamir Plan. Very little was achieved by this initiative.

Israeli War of Independence

Name given by **Israelis** to the first **Arab–Israeli War** between the newly established State of Israel and various Arab states in 1948.

Israelis

Citizens of Israel. These include Jews, who constitute the majority, and Arabs (both Christian and Muslim). **Israeli Arabs** have most of the formal civil rights enjoyed by Jewish Israelis, but are widely regarded as second-class citizens. All Jews have the 'right to return' to Israel and become Israeli citizens.

Istanbul

Largest city in Turkey, with a population of some 8.3m. Lying across the Bosphorous, with one part in Europe and the other (known as Scutari) in Asia. Major city, industrial and commercial centre.

Istiqlal (Morocco)

Original independence party established in Morocco in 1944 and led by **Allal al-Fassi** until his death in 1974. A split in 1959 led to the establishment of the Union des forces populaires, led by **Mehdi Ben Barka**. It remains a major political force. Istiqlal stresses the Moroccan right to the **Western Sahara**. On the domestic front, it aims to raise living standards and to secure greater equality. The party's secretary-general is Abbas al-Fassi.

IT – *see* Information technology

Italy

As part of the **Coalition (in Iraq)**, Italy has troops in Iraq. In April 2004 Italian hostages were taken and one was killed by his Iraqi captors.

ITGA – *see* **Islamic Transitional Government of Afghanistan**

Izz ad-Din al-Qassam Brigades

The military wing of **Hamas**, led by Salah Shehadeh.

Izzedin Salim

Leader of the **Islamic Da'awa Movement**. Izzedin Salim's real name was Abdul Zahra Othman Mohammed, but he adopted a pseudonym in order to protect his family. He was killed by a suicide bomber in **Baghdad** while he was acting president of the US-appointed **Iraqi Provisional Governing Council**. Born in **Basra**, Iraq, he was an intellectual, a writer and a moderate **Shi'a** Muslim. In 1961 he joined the **ad-Da'awa** party, the leading religious party in the Shi'a community. He graduated from the teacher training institute in Basra in 1964 and devoted much of his spare time to politics and writing. In 1969 he produced a study of Fatima, the daughter of the **Prophet Muhammad**. Four years later he became the ad-Da'awa party's leader in Basra and was imprisoned by the regime of **Saddam Hussain** in the following year. Released after a few months, he fled to Kuwait where he worked as a teacher for five years before moving to Iran, where he spent the next two decades, in **Tehran**. He was close to the leaders of the **Iranian Revolution** and broke from the **Islamic Da'awa Party** in order to co-found the **Islamic Da'awa Movement**. He also established a centre of Islamic political studies. In 1983 he joined the **Supreme Council for the Islamic Revolution in Iraq** (SCIRI), the largest Iranian-based Iraqi group. He edited its weekly newspaper for 12 years until 1995. In 2001 he became more critical of SCIRI. He was nominated to represent the group at the 2002 conference of Iraqi exiles in London, but was increasingly concerned to raise the profile of the Islamic Da'awa Movement. It was in his capacity as leader of this movement that he was selected by the USA to sit on the Governing Council that it established in July 2003. He argued for wider representation of different **minority** groups on the Council and for the greater involvement of **women**. He was an advocate of a larger role for the United Nations in Iraq's transition to independence.

J

Ja'afari Code

The **Shi'a** Islamic tradition emanating from the 8th century Imam Ja'afar, who is said to have adopted a 'quietist' as opposed to an 'activist' approach—more in the manner of Hassan than of Hussein. Differences between the four legal Codes of **Sunni Islam** (**Hanbali**, **Hanafi**, **Maliki** and **Shafi'i**) and the Ja'afari Code are not very great. There are small differences in the ritual of prayer. Most significant are differences in the laws of inheritance, **women**'s rights and marriage.

Al-Jabha al-Islamiyya li-Inqadh – *see* FIS—Front islamique du salut

Jabha ye Nejat e Milli ye Afghanistan
Afghan National Liberation Front

Led by Sibghatullah Mojaddedi, whose authority derives in part from his association with a well-known religious family. Mojaddedi had support in the Kohistan and Kohedaman regions, and parts of Paktia.

Jabotinsky, Vladimir

Vladimir Zeev: 1880–1940. Jabotinsky settled in Palestine after the First World War and is regarded by many as the leading Zionist figure after **Theodor Herzl**. Founder of the Revisionist Movement, which advocated militant ultra-nationalistic action as the means to achieve Jewish statehood. It called for the creation of a Jewish state in 'Greater Israel' (all of Palestine and Jordan), rapid mass immigration of Jews into Palestine, the formation of a free-enterprise economy, rapid industrialization, increase in employment opportunities, a ban on strikes and a strong army. The Revisionists formed the New Zionist organization in 1935, but Betar, the Revisionist youth movement had been established by Jabotinsky in 1920 (it continues as the youth wing of **Herut** in Israel today). They also formed two paramilitary groups: **Irgun Zvai Leumi** (Etzel), founded in 1937, and the even more radical **Lechi** (**Stern Gang**), founded in 1939–40. The Irgun was commanded by **Menachem Begin** after 1943.

Jadidism

In **Arabic** *jadid* means 'new'. An Islamic cultural reform movement, which arose in **Central Asia** towards the end of the 19th century. The movement sought to interpret the Muslim heritage in the context of Russian conquest. The Jadids attributed the 'decline' and 'degeneration' of their community to its departure from the true path of 'pure' **Islam**. Corruption of the faith was perceived as contributing to a decline in culture and innovation. It was also regarded as a major factor in the Islamic world's political and military decline. The solution was a return to an Islam based on a rationalist interpretation of the scriptural texts. However, the prerequisite for this—and for 'progress'—was mastery of 'contemporary' or modern knowledge. The early work of leading Jadidists (e.g. Hamza Hakimzoda, Abdurauf Fitrat, and Abdulhamid Cho'lpon) reveals their fascination with progress and technology, as much as their concern with the path of 'pure' Islam. Increasingly, the Jadids regarded Islam itself as a self-contained system of knowledge, separable from the rest of life. Jadidism was clearly a movement for change from within Islam, but one that emphasized the links between knowledge and progress. The Jadids faced vigorous opposition from within their society, but the very existence of the debate points to the dynamic nature of Islamic identities. When the Bolshevik revolution replaced the Tsarist state it advocated far-reaching social and cultural transformation, in which religion was generally considered an impediment to social progress in the Marxist sense of the term. The Jadids' own trajectory led them to favour a radical agenda of secular social and cultural change. The reformist, modernist view of Islam articulated by the Jadids survived the Soviet period among the small group of clerics officially recognized by the regime. For most Muslims in Central Asia, however, 'pure' Islam today often means the rejection of those aspects of modern life that fascinated the Jadids. This takes the form of a rigorous excision from daily life of many customs and habits that entered Central Asian life during the Soviet period. Those adopting this position are usually referred to as 'Wahhabis'.

Jaffa

Old Palestinian town.

Jaffari, Ibrahim

A member of the **Iraqi Provisional Governing Council**, a spokesman for the **Shi'ite Islamic Da'awa Party**. A medical doctor, he joined the **Islamic Da'awa Movement** in 1966. The group, the oldest Islamist movement in Iraq, was founded in 1957–58 and is based on the ideology of reforming Islamic thought and modernizing religious institutions. The party was banned in 1980, when Jaffari fled the country. In April 2004 Jaffari worked hard as an intermediary between **Paul Bremer**, the US administrator-in-chief in Iraq, and Ayatollah **Ali Sistani**, with a view to managing the conflict between the **coalition** forces and the supporters and militia of **Moqtada as-Sadr**.

Jahiliyya

This term can mean 'ignorance', 'unbelief', or even 'barbarism' in **Arabic**. It referred originally to the state people lived in before the advent of **Islam**. This was a time of lawlessness and idolatry, as contrasted with the period of time under Islamic rule, characterized by morality, enlightenment and divine law. The concept of *jahiliyya* has been adopted to modern times by some Islamist thinkers/ideologues, especially the Pakistani **Maududi** and the Egyptian **Sayyid Qutb**. In the modern context, the concept of *jahiliyya* serves as the boundary marker between believers (Muslims) and 'the ignorant'. Sayyid Qutb has written, in *Milestones*, that the world is now steeped in *jahiliyya*. Qutb has argued that Muslims should form an **Ummah** as a guide for other people (unbelievers) and undertake a *jihad* or holy struggle to eliminate *jahiliyya*. This led to the formation of Islamist groups in Egypt and elsewhere that interpreted Qutb very literally.

Jaish al-Mahdi

The army of the Mahdi, the militia loyal to **Moqtada as-Sadr**, radical Iraqi **Shi'a** cleric. During **Ashura**—a major annual holy festival in memory of the martyrdom of Imam Hussein—which took place in March–April in 2004, the supporters of as-Sadr rose up against the **coalition (in Iraq)** forces and extended their control over much of central southern Iraq, notably in **Najaf**, the holy city where the shrine of the Imam Ali is situated. The Jaish al-Mahdi are heavily armed with automatic weapons, machine guns, rocket-propelled grenade launchers and hand grenades.

Al-Jama'a al-Islamiyya (Egypt) – *see also* Gama'a Islamiyah

An Egyptian Islamist political grouping founded following the imposition of a ban on the **Muslim Brotherhood**. Involved in armed struggle. Declared a cease-fire in March 1999. Its spiritual leader is Sheikh **Omar Abd ar-Rahman**, the chairman of the Shura Council is Moustafa Hamzah and its military commander is Ala Abd ar-Raqil.

Al-Jama'a al-Islamiyya (Iraq)

Sunni Islamic political grouping in Iraq.

Al-Jama'a al-Islamiyya (Lebanon)

Led by Fathi Yakan, this organization represents the **Sunni Muslim Brotherhood** within Lebanon. Its activities peaked during the wars of Lebanon against Israel and the **Maronites** in the 1970s and early 1980s.

Jamahiriya

In **Arabic**: a 'state of the masses', or 'republic'. The type of government found in Libya. In theory *Jamahiriya* is government by the populace through local councils.

Jamiat-i Islami (Afghanistan)

Led by Prof. **Burhanuddin Rabbani**, originally associated with the **Muslim Brotherhood**. Fled Afghanistan after the suppression of the Muslim Brotherhood by President Daoud in the mid-1970s. Draws support mainly from the **Tajiks** of north-eastern Afghanistan, the Shomali region north of **Kabul** and in the **Panjshir Valley**, where some of the fiercest resistance fighting occurred.

Jamiat al-Mashari' al-Khayriya al-Islamiya – *see* Al-Ahbash

Jam'iyat-e Isargaran

Society of Self-sacrificing Devotees

Iranian political organization established in the late 1990s after the election of President **Khatami**.

Jam'iyyat at-Takfir wa'l-Hijra

Society of Excommunication and Emigration, Morocco

Radical Moroccan Islamic group associated with a series of murders and preaching holy war. Some members of the group who have been arrested had spent time in **Osama bin Laden**'s training camps in Afghanistan and had fought with the **Taliban**.

Jam'iyyat-e Rouhaniyate Mobarez

Militant Clergy Association (MCA), Iran

This is perhaps the oldest political clerical group since the 1979 victory of the **Islamic Revolution** in Iran. The MCA leads the 'conservatives' and 'conservative' groups and co-ordinates their political behaviour and policies with the views and decisions of the Association. Mohammad Reza Mahdavi Kani is the secretary-general of the MCA and Akbar Hashemi **Rafsanjani**, Ali Akbar Nateq Nouri, Hassan Rowhani, Mohammad Emami Kashani (former member of the **Council of**

Guardians and substitute leader of **Tehran** Friday prayers), Mohammad Yazdi (former head of the Judiciary), Seyed Reza Taqavi (head of the Islamic Guidance Commission of the fifth **Majlis** and MCA spokesman), Ahmad Jannati (substitute leader of Tehran Friday prayers), and Qorbanali Dorri Najafabadi (former information/intelligence minister) are among prominent members of this group. Unlike other Iranian groups and parties, the MCA does not publish any newspaper or magazine and has not obtained a permit from the interior minister for political activities. The MCA was among major supporters of Ali Akbar Nateq Nouri (**Khatami**'s main rival) in the presidential election held on 23 May 1997. During the impeachment of former Islamic culture and guidance minister Ayatollah Mohajerani, and former interior minister Abdullah Nouri, MCA advocates were among the main opponents (of Mohajerani and Nouri).

Janusian

A London-based security firm, operating in Iraq. According to David Claridge, Janusian's managing director, contracts in Iraq have boosted British security companies' revenues from *c*. US $320m. before the war to more than $1,000m., making security by far the most lucrative British export to Iraq.

Japan

Japan committed 550 troops to the US-led coalition for 'peace-keeping' purposes in the aftermath of the **Iraq War (2003)**. In April three members of the Japanese force were taken hostage and threatened with death if Japan did not withdraw its troops from the southern Iraqi town of Samawa.

Al-Jazeera

Independent satellite news channel, broadcasting in **Arabic**, from Qatar. Launched in 1996, it started as a project in Saudi Arabia with the help of the British Broadcasting Corporation. It was considered too critical by the Saudi authorities and relocated to Qatar. Regarded by many as 'the critical voice of the **Arab World**', it is highly controversial, both in the **Middle East** and elsewhere, for its liberal and critical approach to radio journalism and its ability to gain exclusive 'scoops' because of its distinctive contacts and networks. It came to prominence after 11 September 2001 for its reporting of **al-Qa'ida**'s activities and for broadcasting videotapes of **Osama bin Laden**, as well as its coverage of the bombing of Afghanistan and of developments before and during the **Iraq War (2003)**, when it provided exceptionally well-informed on-the-spot reports and analysis of the war and of Middle Eastern politics more generally. In the weeks following 11 September 2001, **Colin Powell** visited Emir **ath-Thani**, ruler of Qatar and financier of al-Jazeera, to request that he bring the media under control. The Emir spoke in public of the visit. During the war in Afghanistan the offices of al-Jazeera in **Kabul** were bombed by US forces. One al-Jazeera cameraman (Sami al-Haj), seized in Afghanistan, remains in detention in Guantanamo Bay, Cuba. Al-Jazeera encountered problems with the authorities in Saudi Arabia, Iraq and Bahrain, and in August 2002 its office in **Amman** was closed by the Jordanian government for 'provoking sedition' by broadcasting views critical of the late King **Hussein** and his grandfather King **Abdullah** I, whom he succeeded, for being pro-Israeli. Some 20 al-Jazeera journalists were arrested by US forces in Iraq in 2003–04 and one (Tariq Ayoub) was killed in April 2003 when a US tank fired a shell at the al-Jazeera offices in **Baghdad**'s Palestine Hotel. In November 2003 an al-Jazeera cameraman (Salah Hassan) was arrested in Iraq, held incommunicado in a small cell and forced to stand hooded, bound and naked for up to 11 hours at a time. He was beaten by US soldiers, who would address him only as 'al-Jazeera' or 'bitch'. Finally, after a month's incarceration, he was dumped on a road just outside Baghdad. Despite continuing harassment, al-Jazeera continues to maintain its tradition of clear and well-informed reporting, pluralism and even-handedness. Israeli Cabinet minister Gideon Ezra famously told *The Jerusalem Post*: 'I wish all Arab media were like al-Jazeera'.

Jebbeh-ye Masharekat-e Iran-e Islami

Islamic Iran Participation Front

Iranian political organization established in the late 1990s after the election of President **Khatami**.

Jenin

A town in the occupied **West Bank**, home to some 13,000 Palestinian **refugees**. On 3 April 2002 dozens of Israeli tanks entered Jenin and surrounded the adjacent refugee camp. This was the seventh raid on Jenin since the start of the **al-Aqsa intifada** in September 2000 and was expected to be the most violent. In fact, the fighting in Jenin turned out to be the fiercest during **Operation Defensive Shield**. Helicopters and tanks fired machine guns at **Palestinians**, who threw grenades and fired on the Israeli troops with assault rifles. Initially, Israeli commandos moved from house to house but they encountered stiff resistance from Palestinian fighters. Several Israeli soldiers were killed and 13 army reservists died in a booby-trapped building in the refugee camp. It was eventually reported that 23 Israeli soldiers had died in Jenin. Many of the camp's inhabitants fled during the fighting, especially those whose homes were in the centre, which came under the heaviest attack. Nevertheless, there were civilian casualties as well as casualties among the Palestinian fighters. The fighting ended on 11 April. Two days earlier, Palestinian medical workers estimated that at least 124 Palestinians had been killed and it was expected that this total would rise when a proper investigation could take place. The area was, however, declared a 'closed military zone'—journalists and even medical personnel were not allowed to enter. The Association for Civil Rights in Israel complained to the Minister of Defence that the **military** had committed serious human rights violations in the camp, including the demolition of homes with the residents still inside. Jenin became, for many months, a symbol of Palestinian resistance and of Israeli brutality. There were appeals for UN intervention and for the UN Human Rights Commission to condemn the human rights violations and 'mass killings'—which it did, by 40 votes to 5. The Israeli justification for the intervention was that several suicide bombers who had carried out attacks in Israel had come from the camp and that they had encountered heavy resistance.

Jericho

Ancient town in the **West Bank**. One of the earliest areas to come under the auspices of the **Palestinian National Authority**.

Jerusalem

Al-Quds

Otherwise known as Bait al-Maqdis—The Holy Place. The disputed capital of Israel with 650,000 inhabitants (2003 estimate). A divided city, **West Jerusalem** is within Israeli territory; **East Jerusalem**, with a population of about 300,000, is internationally recognized as Palestinian territory, but remains under Israeli rule. Jerusalem lies about 55 km to the east of the **Mediterranean** coast and 25 km from the Dead Sea. It is divided into an old city, a new city and satellite towns or suburbs scattered around it on all sides. On the eastern side the towns have been built on land expropriated from its Palestinian owners, and filled with Jewish families, with the aim of making the return of East Jerusalem to Arab control as difficult as possible. Jerusalem has had a Jewish majority since the late 19th century. Jews represent the majority in some parts of the old city, but prior to 1948 were the largest group in the entire old city. Today, the **Palestinians** make up the majority in the old city. Jerusalem's economy is unusually limited for such a large city in the **Middle East**, with practically no **industry**. The lack of modern industry is to a large degree a political issue: the Israeli state has decided in favour of protecting the uniqueness of the city. It is a major tourist attraction as the historic centre of three great religions, being the most holy city in **Christianity** and **Judaism**, and the third holiest in **Islam** (after **Mecca** and **Medina**). Some of the holy sites and buildings occupy virtually the same places, and the status of Jerusalem is one of the most difficult issues in the Israeli–Arab Conflict. Jerusalem's importance for Islam derives from the tradition that the **Prophet Muhammad** began a celestial 'night journey' from the place where the ruins of the Jewish temples were and where the Islamic shrine, the **Dome of the Rock**, was later erected. However, Muslims also revere Jerusalem because Islam recognizes both the Jewish and the Christian sites as part of the history of Islam. Today, the old city is divided into four zones, one

Muslim (the largest), one Jewish and two Christian. All holy places and religious communities are administered through the Ministry of Religious Affairs. There are special desks for every major group. The Chief Rabbinate of Israel has its head-quarters in the synagogue at Hekhal Shelomo. Muslims administer their affairs through the Council of Waqf and Muslim Affairs (**Sunni** orientation) created in 1967. In 2000 the leader of the **Likud** party, **Ariel Sharon**, visited the area of Muslim sanctuaries, in what was seen by Palestinians and Muslims as a deliberate provocation. Violence erupted and the second **(al-Aqsa)** *intifada* began.

The Jerusalem Bill

Controversial proposal, made in July 1980, that **Jerusalem** should be for ever the undivided Israeli capital and seat of government, parliament and judiciary. Condemned by successive UN General Assembly resolutions and UN Security Council Resolution 478 of 20 August 1980.

Jew

A member of the Jewish faith.

The Jewish Agency

In May 1947 the Jewish Agency proposed the creation of a Jewish state covering more than 80% of Palestine—approximately the area occupied by Israel today without the **Occupied Territories**, which it handed to **UNSCOP**.

Jewish fundamentalism

Interpretations of **Judaism** which require literal interpretation of the Torah and holy scriptures.

Jewish nationalism

The belief that Jews constitute not only the members of a religious community by virtue of their religious beliefs and practices, but also a people and a nation, with rights to a homeland and a self-governing state.

Al-Jibhat al-Inqath – *see* FIS—Front islamique du salut

Jibril, Ahmed

Leader of the **Popular Front for the Liberation of Palestine-General Command** (PFLP-GC). Since the 1960s Jibril had succeeded in selling his services to the major sponsors of armed Palestinian groups. For more than a decade he was the USSR's unofficial representative in the **Middle East**, having direct relations with the KGB, acting as a mediator between the USSR and Syria, brokering Soviet arms and other services, and promoting the role of **Bulgaria** in the region. He broke with **George Habash** and the PFLP because he considered them to be too focused on exporting the Palestinian cause to Europe. He was committed to maintaining a state of permanent military confrontation between Israel and the Arabs and was opposed to diplomatic efforts to orchestrate a peaceful settlement. He was supported by those Arab states that were also committed to the armed struggle against Israel. Libya paid the salaries of the members, supplied arms and financed several operations. Training facilities and housing were also supplied. In exchange, Jibril carried out attacks and supplied Libya with his own fighters for the war in Chad. In the summer of 1988, however, Libya suspended its annual payment of US $25m. and Jibril was unclear how to support his 400–600 fighters.

Jiddah

Major port and city in Saudi Arabia.

Jihad

Literally holy struggle. It can refer to a personal moral struggle to become a better Muslim and be of service to society (also known as the Greater *Jihad*). Can also be a call to holy war against non-Muslims (also known as the Lesser *Jihad*).

Al-Jihad (Egyptian Islamic Jihad also known as Islamic Jihad, Jihad Group)

Egyptian Islamic extremist group active since the late 1970s. Merged with **Osama bin Laden**'s **al-Qa'ida** organization in June 2001, but retains a capability to conduct independent operations. Its primary goals are to overthrow the Egyptian Government and replace it with an **Islamic state**, and to attack US and Israeli interests in Egypt and abroad. Historically it has specialized in armed attacks against high-level Egyptian government personnel, including Cabinet ministers, and car bombings against official US and Egyptian facilities. The original Jihad was responsible for the assassination in 1981 of Egyptian President **Anwar Sadat**. It also claimed responsibility for the attempted assassinations of interior minister Hassan al-Alfi in August 1993 and Prime Minister Atef Sedky in November 1993. It has not conducted an attack inside Egypt since 1993 and has never targeted foreign tourists there. It was responsible for bombing the Egyptian embassy in Islamabad in 1995; in 1998 an attack against the US embassy in Albania was thwarted. Historically it has operated in the **Cairo** area, but most of its network is outside Egypt, in Yemen, Afghanistan, Pakistan, Lebanon, and the United Kingdom, among other locations, and its activities have been conducted outside of Egypt for several years. The Egyptian Government claims that Iran supports the Jihad. Its merger with al-Qa'ida also boosted bin Laden's support for the group. It may also obtain some of its funding through various Islamic non-governmental organizations, cover businesses, and criminal acts.

Jordan, Hashemite Kingdom of

Al-Mamlakah al-Urduniyah al-Hashimiyah

Situated to the north-west of Saudi Arabia, bordering Iraq to the west, Israel and Palestine to the east and Syria to the north. Jordan has 26 km of maritime coastline on the **Gulf of Aqaba**. The country's total area is 91,971 sq km. The capital is **Amman**. For administrative purposes Jordan is divided into 12 governorates (*muhafazah*, plural *muhafazat*): Ajlun, Al-Aqabah, Al-Balqa', Al-Karak, Al-Mafraq, 'Amman, At-Tafilah, Az-Zarqa', Irbid, Jarash, Ma'an, Madaba.

In July 2002 the population was estimated at 5,307,470, of which 98% were Arab, 1% **Circassian** and 1% **Armenian**. About one-half of the population are of Palestinian origin. The official religion is **Islam**, with the majority (92%) **Sunni** Muslim, 6% Christian (mainly Greek Orthodox, with some Greek and Roman Catholic, Syrian Orthodox, **Coptic** Orthodox, Armenian Orthodox, and Protestant denominations) and 'other' (several small **Shi'a** Muslim and **Druze** populations) 2%. The official language is **Arabic**; English is widely understood among the upper and middle classes.

Political profile

The Hashemite Kingdom of Jordan is an independent, indivisible sovereign state. Its governmental form is monarchical, with a parliament. The revised Constitution was approved by King Talal bin Abdullah al-Hashemi (King **Talal** I) on 1 January 1952. Executive power rests with the king, who exercises it through ministers. The king appoints, dismisses, or accepts the resignation of the Prime Minister; and on his recommendation other ministers are appointed or dismissed, or their resignation accepted. The king also appoints the members and president of the Senate—the upper house of parliament. The Cabinet manages all state affairs. If the parliament's lower chamber—the House of Representatives—withdraws its confidence from the Cabinet or any minister, the latter must resign. The king is the supreme commander of the **armed forces**. The head of state is King Abdullah ibn al-Hussein (**Abdullah II**, since 7 February 1999); the head of government is Prime Minister Ali Abu ar-Ragheb (since 19 June 2000). The Cabinet is appointed by the Prime Minister in consultation with the monarch. The legislature consists of the bicameral National Assembly, or **Majlis** al-'Umma, which consists of the Senate, also called the House of Notables (Majlis al-Aayan), a 40-member body appointed by the monarch from designated categories of public figures; members serve four-year terms; and the House of Representatives, also called the House of Deputies (Majlis an-Nuwaab), an 80-member body (to be increased to 104 from the next general election) elected by popular vote on the basis of proportional representation to serve four-year terms. Suffrage is universal for Jordanian citizens over the age of 20. The legal system is based on **Islamic Law** and French codes; judicial review of legislative acts is by a specially provided High Tribunal; there is a Court of Cassation and a Supreme Court (court of final appeal). Jordan has not accepted compulsory International Court of Justice jurisdiction.

Political parties were banned before the elections of July 1963. In September 1971 King **Hussein** announced the formation of the Jordanian National Union, which was the only legal political organization. In March 1972 it was renamed the Arab National Union. In April 1974 King Hussein dissolved the executive committee and accepted the resignation of the secretary-general. In February 1976 the Union was abolished. In January King Hussein approved the National Charter, which legitimized political parties, and in July 1992 the House of Representatives formally permitted the establishment of political parties. Organizations that achieved representation in the general election of November 1993 included: the **Islamic Action Front**, **al-Mustaqbal** (Future), the Jordanian **(Arab) Ba'ath(ist) Socialist Party**, **al-Yakatha** (Reawakening), **Jordan National Alliance**, the **Jordan People's Democratic (Hashd) Party**, the Jordan Social Democratic Party, and the Jordanian Arab Democratic Party. In May 1997 nine centre parties, including **al-Ahd** and the Jordan National Alliance, united to form the **National Constitution Party** (NCP), which became Jordan's largest political grouping. The formation of the NCP, together with the establishment in 1996 of the **Unionist Arab Democratic Party** (a coalition of three leftist parties), reduced the total number of political parties from 24 to 14. In July 1997 a new party was formed, the **Popular Democratic Pan-Arab Party**. In May 1999 the **Popular Participation Bloc** was established to contest forthcoming municipal elections. This was a new grouping of 13 leftist, Ba'athist and pan-Arab parties. The formation of two new political parties was announced in late 1999—the **New Generation Party** and the **Jordanian Arab New Dawn Party**. In September 2000 a new political grouping, the **Arab Democratic Front**, was established. In July 2001 the **Muslim Centrist Party** was formed by dissidents from the **Muslim Brotherhood**; and two further political organizations were granted licences in late 2001—the **Jordanian People's Committee Movement** and the **Jordan Rafah (Welfare)** party. Other parties include: al-Umma ('Nation'); the Arab Land Party; the **Arab Democratic Front**, the **Communist Party**, the Constitutional Front, the Jordanian Democratic Popular Unity Party, the Jordanian Progressive Party and the National Action **(Haqq)** Party. Political pressure groups and unofficial opposition groups include: the Jordanian Press Association; the Muslim Brotherhood; the Anti-Normalization Committee; and the Jordanian Bar Association.

Media

A restrictive press and publications law was enacted in 1998. Radio and television are controlled by the state. Newspapers include *Ad-Dustour*, *Al-Akhbar*, *Al-Hadath*, *Assabeel*, *The Star*, *Jordan Times*, *Ar-Ra'i*, *Arab Daily*, *Al-Aswaq*, *Al-Mitheq*, *Sawt ash-Shaab*, *Al-Ahali*, *Akhbar al-Usbou*, *Al-Liwa'*, *Al-Majd*, *As-Sabah*, and *Shihan*.

Televison stations include the state-controlled Jordan Television and Radio and JRTV International News. In 2000 there were five internet service providers. In 2002 there were 212,000 internet users.

History

Jordan did not develop as an independent state until the 20th century. Previously it was seldom more than a rugged and backward appendage to more powerful kingdoms and empires, and never existed alone. However, following the disintegration of the **Ottoman Empire** in 1918, Abdullah ibn Hussein al-Hashem and his army entered the British-mandated area east of the **Jordan river** called **Transjordan** and established a government in Amman in 1921. Britain agreed to recognize Abdullah's rule if he accepted Britain's mandate over Transjordan and Palestine, which he did. In 1923 Transjordan became a semi-autonomous emirate, which agreed to formulate a common foreign policy with Britain and allow British troops to be stationed on its soil.

When Transjordan became independent in May 1946, Abdullah assumed the title of king and renamed the Emirate of Transjordan the Hashemite Kingdom of Jordan. The 1923 treaty was replaced by a new one in 1948, which limited British influence to military and defence matters. With the withdrawal of British troops from Palestine and the proclamation of the State of Israel, war (1948–49) in Palestine broke out. Arab armies entered the former Palestinian territory from all sides. However, only those from Transjordan played a significant part in the fighting, and by the time that major hostilities ceased in July they had succeeded in occupying a considerable area of Palestine; the **West Bank**, as well as **East Jerusalem** and the **al-Aqsa mosque**. Suspicion arose among the Arab states that King Abdullah was prepared to accept a *fait accompli* and to negotiate with the Israeli authorities for a formal recognition of the existing military boundaries. The other Arab states refused to accept any move that implied recognition of the status quo—such as the resettlement of **refugees**. Transjordan followed a different line in an attempt to formally annex new territory. In stark opposition to the wishes of the **Arab League**, helped by the armistice signed with Israel, Jordan formally annexed the West Bank after the general election in April. On 24 April 1950 the East Bank and West Bank united in the Hashemite Kingdom of Jordan. Jordan's relationship with the **Arab World**, however, had worsened. The war profoundly altered the contours of the state. The population, barely 500,000 at the beginning of the war, was tripled within a few months by the arrival of 500,000 refugees and 500,000 West Bank **Palestinians**. This influx of Palestinians would later prove to be a destabilizing element in Jordanian domestic and international politics. Inhabitants of the West Bank were given full Jordanian citizenship and the same parliamentary representation as the citizens of the East Bank. Following the assassination of King Abdullah by a Palestinian at the al-Aqsa mosque in Jerusalem on 20 July 1952, his son **Talal** ibn Abdullah al-Hashemi succeeded him. Owing to mental illness he abdicated in the following year in favour of his son, **Hussein** ibn Talal. Both King Talal and King

Hussein sought to improve Jordan's relationship with the rest of the Arab World. One sign of this was Jordan's signing the Arab Collective Security pact—which it had failed to join in the summer of 1950—and the establishment of closer financial and economic ties with Syria. However poll-rigging in the 1954 general election was met by massive protest. With the growth of **Arab nationalism** and the emergence of the iconic **Gamal Abdel Nasser**, Hussein chose the Western camp. This helped him to survive the Suez Crisis of 1956–57 and the crisis of 1965–66, which brought him into opposition with the **Palestine Liberation Organization** (PLO) as their guerrilla attacks into Israel from Jordanian territory made it difficult for Hussein to regularize relations with Israel. Following a free and fair election in 1956 a national-leftist government under Suleiman Nablusi came to power. It abrogated the 1948 treaty with Great Britain and King Hussein acquiesced. However, after he had crushed an incipient coup by his newly appointed chief-of-staff in 1957, he dismissed the Nablusi Government and dissolved parliament and all political parties. Though parliament was revived in 1963, political parties remained banned.

In September 1963 the creation of a unified 'Palestinian entity' was approved by the Council of the Arab League, despite opposition from the Jordanian government, which regarded the proposal as a threat to Jordan's sovereignty over the West Bank. Shortly afterwards the PLO was created by Palestinian Arab groups to be 'the only legitimate spokesman for all matters concerning the Palestinian people'. The PLO was financed by the Arab League and was to recruit military units from refugees, to constitute a **Palestine Liberation Army** (PLA). From the outset, King Hussein refused to allow the PLA to train forces in Jordan or the PLO to levy taxes from Palestinian refugees in Jordan.

During 1965–66 the principal guerrilla organization to emerge from the PLO, **Fatah** (the Palestine National Liberation Movement), unleashed a series of attacks against Israel. This was usually done across the Jordanian border, provoking violent retaliatory attacks by Israeli forces, and made regularized relations with Israel difficult. Thus, in 1966 Jordan suspended its support for the PLO. In response, the PLO and Syria appealed to Jordanians to revolt against King Hussein. Relations with the **United Arab Republic** deteriorated, but in the charged atmosphere during the build-up to the **Six-Day War** (June 1967), Jordan joined the Egyptian-Syrian defence treaty. During the war the Jordanian army took part in the fighting, which resulted in the loss of the territories it had conquered in 1948–49.

After losing the West Bank to Israel, Jordan had to absorb 250,000 Palestinian refugees from the territory, who presented the government with serious social, political and economic problems. The main factor in Jordan's domestic politics between June 1967 and 1971 was the rivalry between the government and the Palestinian guerrilla organizations, principally Fatah. These organizations gradually assumed effective control of the refugee camps and commanded widespread support among the Palestinian majority of Jordan's population. In addition, they received armaments and training from other Arab countries, particularly Syria and the **Gulf States**. The *Fedayeen* movement virtually became a state within a state. Its leaders stated that they had '. . . no wish to interfere in the internal affairs of Jordan provided it does not place any obstacles in the way of our struggle to liberate Palestine'. The *fedayeen*'s popularity and influence, combined with guerrilla attacks into Israel and Israeli reprisals, seriously challenged the authority of King Hussein and the prospects of normalizing relations with Israel. Confrontation between the Palestinians and the Jordanian government seemed inevitable.

After a series of smaller confrontations, the events of **Black September** took place. Bitter fighting between government and the *fedayeen* broke out at the end of August 1970. This escalated into full civil war in the latter half of September, causing thousands of deaths and injuries and the liquidation of the Palestinian armed presence. After the events of Black September, the Palestinian fighters moved to Lebanon. Jordan's suppression of the Palestinians provoked strong reactions from other Arab governments; Iraq and Syria closed their borders with Jordan, Algeria suspended diplomatic relations, and Egypt, Libya, Sudan and both of the Yemeni states voiced strong public criticism. Jordan managed not to become involved in the **Arab–Israeli War (1973)**, dispatching troops to the **Golan Heights** only, where little fighting took place.

When the Arab League summit in October–November 1974 recognized the PLO as the sole legitimate representative of the Palestinian people, Jordan reluctantly accepted the resolution. Dismissing the West Bank half of the House of Representatives, King Hussein suspended it. Jordan refused to join the peace process initiated with the **Camp David Accords** in 1978. It sided with Iraq in the **Iran–Iraq War**, thus accelerating its economic integration with that country. In 1984 King Hussein revived the House of Representatives. His agreement with PLO chairman **Yasser Arafat** in 1985 on a joint approach to a **Middle East** peace process was rejected by the **Palestine National Council** two years later. On 31 July 1988 King Hussein, in an historic speech, withdrew all demands regarding the West Bank and acknowledged Palestinian sovereignty. A free and fair election in 1989 resulted in a House of Representatives with 40% Islamist membership.

Plagued by serious economic problems since the mid-1980s, Jordan received increased economic **aid** from the USA in 1990. During the Gulf crisis that followed Iraq's invasion of Kuwait in August 1990, Jordan attempted to find an Arab solution. The outbreak, in 1991, of the (second) **Gulf War** led to the cancellation of US aid to Jordan owing to King Hussein's support of Iraq (Jordan's major source of **oil**). Jordan also suffered a loss of aid from Saudi Arabia and Kuwait during the war. The country endured further economic hardship when approximately 700,000 Jordanian workers and refugees returned to Jordan as a result of the fighting in the **Persian (Arabian) Gulf**, causing housing and employment shortages. Not until 2001 did an accord again permit Jordanians to work in Kuwait. Later Jordan attempted to repair the damage done to its standing in the West by distancing itself from Iraq. Before the Middle East peace conference in Madrid in October 1991, Jordan agreed to a joint Jordanian-Palestinian delegation. In 1994 a peace agreement between Jordan and Israel ended the official state of war between the two nations, Jordan being the second Arab country to sign a peace treaty with Israel. Hussein went on to encourage peace negotiations between other Arab states and Israel. The country's economy continued to decline, however, and the government became less tolerant of dissent. Laws restricting freedom of the press were instituted in 1997, and in that year Islamic parties boycotted the legislative elections, claiming that they were unfair. Hussein died in 1999 and was succeeded by his son, Abdullah, who pledged to work toward a more open government and to ease restrictions on public expression. Although there has been some progress in terms of economic development, the country remains dependent on **tourism**, which has been damaged by Jordan's location between Israel and Iraq. Political liberalization has been slow in coming.

Jordan, economy

Jordan is a small country with inadequate supplies of **water** and other natural resources, such as **oil**. About 70% of its gross domestic product is derived from the services sector, with manufacturing generating about one-third. Jordan's main exports are **phosphates**, fertilizers, potash, agricultural and livestock products (wheat, barley, citrus fruits, tomatoes, melons, olives, sheepmeat, goatmeat and poultry), manufactures and pharmaceuticals. **Debt**, poverty, unemployment and an increasing **trade** deficit are fundamental problems. Since assuming the throne in 1999 King **Abdullah** has undertaken economic reforms. **Amman** in the past three years has worked closely with the **International Monetary Fund** (IMF), practised stringent monetary policy, and embarked on a programme of privatization. The government also has liberalized the trade regime sufficiently to secure Jordan's membership of the **World Trade Organization** (2000), an association agreement with the **European Union** (2000), and a free-trade accord with USA (2000). These measures have helped improve productivity, and Jordanian officials hope that they will attract foreign investment. The substantial trade deficit is covered by **tourism** receipts, workers' **remittances** and foreign assistance. Ongoing challenges include the further adoption of IMF conditionalities in respect of fiscal policies, attracting investment and employment creation. Jordan is a major exporter of phosphates. It has a skilled workforce. The tourist industry has recovered since the **Gulf War (1991)**. The port of Aqaba is a special economic zone. The country is reliant on imports of **energy**, has a poor balance of imports to exports ratio, and unemployment has been exacerbated by the influx of **refugees** from Kuwait after the 1991 Gulf War.

Jordan National Alliance

Political party. In May 1997 it joined with others to form the National Constitution Party, Jordan's largest political alliance.

Jordan People's Democratic Party

Political party led by Taysir az-Zabri. Its secretary-general is Salem Nahhas.

Jordan Rafah

Welfare Party

Jordanian political party, formed in late 2001. Its leader is Muhammad Rijal Shumali.

Jordan river

The Jordan river flows through the Jordan Rift Valley into the Dead Sea. Its section north of Lake Kinneret is within the boundaries of Israel. South of the lake, it forms the border between Jordan (to the east) and Israel (to the west). Further south, it forms the border between Jordan and the **West Bank**/Palestine.

Jordanian Arab New Dawn Party

Political party formed in late 1999.

Jordanian Arab Socialist Ba'ath Party

Political party. Tayseer Salameh al-Homsi is its secretary-general.

Jordanian-Israeli Peace Treaty

Peace Treaty signed in 1994.

The Jordanian Option

The proposal made by Israel in 1977 to divide the **West Bank** between Israel and Jordan. The Jordanian Option, as the proposal was called, was later adopted by the US Reagan Administration as its own peace plan. When **Likud** came to power in Israel, the 'option' was abandoned, but it was revived for a while by the Israeli national unity government of 1984–87.

Jordanian-Palestinian Accord

An agreement concluded in February 1985, 'emanating from the spirit of the Fez Summit resolutions' and from UN resolutions relating to the Palestinian question. The Jordanian government and the **Palestine Liberation Organization** (PLO) agreed to work towards a peaceful and just settlement based on the following principles: the total withdrawal by Israel from the territories occupied in 1967; the right of self-determination for the Palestinian people; the resolution of the problem of Palestinian **refugees**; the resolution of the Palestine question in all its aspects. On the above basis, peace negotiations were to be conducted under the auspices of an international conference in which the five permanent members of the Security Council and all of the parties to the conflict would participate, including the PLO, the sole legitimate representative of the Palestinian people, within a joint Jordanian-Palestinian delegation.

Jordanian Peoples' Committee Movement

Moderate Jordanian political group, formed in late 2001. Its secretary-general is Khalid Shubaki.

Judaism

The religion of the Jews. Refers to the Land of Judah. See also **Judea and Samaria**.

Judea and Samaria

Ancient names for two areas of the occupied **West Bank**, referred to in the **Bible** and used by Revisionist Jews to identify that area as part of the **Holy Land** and therefore part of an ancient entity not to be divided into two states.

Juhul

Arabic term, taken from the **Koran**, meaning 'ignorant', but having the implication of being unIslamic. Hence *jahiliyya*—a state of ignorance or refusal of **Islam**. Used by the **Shi'ite** Ayatollah **Khomeini** of the predominantly **Sunni Taliban** in Afghanistan.

Jumbesh

National Islamic Movement, Afghanistan

A largely Uzbek party under the leadership of Gen. **Dostum**. Dostum had been a communist supporter until he changed sides and helped bring down President Najibullah in 1992. By the mid-1990s he had become the key player in the Mazar area. After 1998, however, with the **Taliban** in power in **Mazar-i-Sharif**, he went into exile in Turkey. He remained there until after the US bombing campaign started in late 2001. It is thought that he was supported by the USA, but his party had control of trade with Turkmenistan and of local **gas** and oilfields. It also had a share in the fertilizer factory in Mazar, and thus commanded considerable regional resources.

Jund al-Imam

The Imam's Soldiers, Iraq

A radical off-shoot of an Iranian-backed Islamist group based in **Halabja**. After its formation, Jund seized Tawela and Biyara and declared *jihad* against the secular

Kurdish authorities and the **Patriotic Union of Kurdistan** (PUK). There were, almost immediately, clashes with the PUK—in September 2001 Jund militants 'speaking **Arabic** and Persian' slit the throats of and mutilated more than 20 PUK *peshmerga*. They also attempted to assassinate Barham Salih, the PUK's Prime Minister. In the winter of 2002–03 they merged with another small group called Islah ('reform') to form **Ansar al-Islam**.

Jund al-Islam

A militant Islamic faction of the Islamic Unity Movement of Kurdistan. Founded in 2001 and led by Abu Abdullah ash-Shafti.

June War – *see* Arab–Israeli War (1967)

Justice and Development Party (AKP, Turkey)

Founded in 2001, the AKP came to power in Turkey in November 2002, winning almost two-thirds of the seats in an emphatic electoral victory. It changed the Constitution to enable its chairman, **Recep Tayyip Erdoğan**, to stand for election in the eastern province of Siirt (60 miles from the border with Iraq) and win with about 85% of the vote, thereby allowing him to take a seat in parliament and end the power-sharing regime in which he held power without office. Erdoğan had been barred from standing (prior to the change in the Constitution) because of a previous conviction for inciting religious hatred. The AKP is a strongly Islamist party, built out of two previously banned Islamist groups. However, it has learned the lesson of the past, when **Necmettin Erbakan**, the virtual founder of **political Islam** in Turkey, leader of the **Welfare Party** (which was banned in 1998) and mentor of Erdoğan, was removed from power by the army, which considered him to have overstepped the mark as Prime Minister in 1997. 'We did not establish our party as a party based on religion; politicians can be religious but religion should not establish the basis of politics,' Erdoğan is quoted as having said. Unlike Erbakan, who made visits to Iran and Libya almost as soon as he entered office, Erdoğan and the AKP have turned more towards the West. Erdogan toured **European Union** (EU) capitals in the first weeks after the AKP's electoral victory. In December he travelled to Washington, DC, where he attempted to persuade US President **Bush** to pressure the EU into agreeing to talks in 2003 regarding Turkish entry into the EU. The EU would prefer a 2005 date, provided a 2004 review of human rights in Turkey proves satisfactory.

Justice Party

Conservative party in Turkey. **Süleyman Demirel** was elected leader in 1964 of the then recently formed party.

K

Kabul

Capital of Afghanistan. Ancient city and traditional capital of Afghanistan. Modern commercial centre.

Kach

Also known as Thus. Israeli political party of the extreme right, led by **Meir Kahane**, an American-born rabbi who founded the Jewish Defence League in the USA and emigrated to Israel in 1971. It supported the expulsion of all Arabs from Israel and the **Occupied Territories** to ensure that Israel is a wholly Jewish state.

KADEK

Successor to the **Patriotic Union of Kurdistan**. Dissolved itself at its most recent congress in November 2003, but plans to re-form in the near future.

Kahane, Meir

Rabbi and political leader of the **Kach** movement, whose aim was the expulsion of the Palestinian Arabs from Greater Israel. Member of the **Knesset** from 1984 until 1988, when the Supreme Court banned his candidature.

Kahane Chai

Kahane Lives, Israel

Formed originally in 1977 as **Kach** ('Thus'). A right-wing religious nationalist party, it advocates the creation of a Torah state, the expulsion of all Arabs from Israel, and the annexation of the **Occupied Territories**. Named after the leader of its predecessor, Kach, **Meir Kahane**, who was assassinated for his extreme beliefs.

Kandahar

Major town in Afghanistan. A former stronghold of the **Taliban**.

Karbala (Kerbala)

Shi'ite holy city of pilgrimage in central southern Iraq. Site of the shrine of the 7th-century martyr, Hussein bin 'Ali, a grandson of the **Prophet Muhammad**. For Shi'ites, Karbala rivals **Mecca** as a place of pilgrimage and is more highly regarded than the Mashad 'Ali in **Najaf**. Under **Saddam Hussain**'s largely **Sunni** Muslim regime, Shi'ites, who comprise a majority of the Iraqi population, experienced severe oppression and were prohibited from visiting the shrine by the **Ba'ath Party**. The first pilgrimage since 1977 took place shortly after the **coalition** invasion of 2003, with more than 1m. people participating in it. Several bombing incidents took place there during 2003–04, and in April 2004 Polish and Hungarian troops (part of the coalition forces) were attacked near the city hall.

Karimov, Islam

President of Uzbekistan since 1990. Born on 30 January 1938 in the southern city of Samarkand to a **Tajik** mother and an **Uzbek** father, Karimov lost both his parents at a young age and grew up in an orphanage. After studying engineering, he began his career in a factory in Tashkent, then worked for five years at the Chkalov aviation factory in the city. In 1966 he joined the Uzbek State Planning Agency, of which he became deputy chairman. His great leap forward came in 1983, when he became Uzbek finance minister. In 1986 he became deputy chairman of the Council of Ministers and chairman of the State Planning Agency. From 1989 until 1991 he was first secretary of the Uzbek Central Committee, the top political job in the republic, answering only to the USSR. In 1990 he was elected to the Soviet politburo. Following the invention of the post of President in the late Soviet period (March 1990), Karimov followed suit in the same month, being chosen as president of the Uzbek Soviet Socialist Republic by the Uzbek Supreme Soviet (he was the only candidate). From September 1991 his country was renamed the Uzbek Republic in the wake of the failed coup in Moscow. In December 1991 he stood for election as President in a national poll and won 86% of the vote—the only other candidate was hindered at every turn and the election results were manipulated. He took his oath of office with one hand on the **Koran** and the other on the Constitution although he subsequently paid little attention to either. For Karimov, who had espoused Moscow's line and spoke Russian far better than Uzbek, championing Uzbekistan's independence represented an about-face. However, he managed that smoothly, with the help of some language coaching in Uzbek. Karimov has headed the People's Democratic Party of Uzbekistan since it was established in November 1991 when the local communists were seeking a new identity.

Parties that emerged at the end of the Soviet period have all been banned. Unity, founded in May 1989, and Freedom, founded in April 1990, were deregistered in 1993 when all parties were required to undergo re-registration in the wake of the adoption of the new Constitution. The Uzbek branch of the **Islamic Renaissance Party** was banned in 1992 (not long before its leader, Abdulla Utaev, disappeared in

December 1992), and the People's Movement of Turkestan has been denied registration. The Homeland Progress Party was set up as a 'loyal opposition party' in June 1992. Three other parties have been established by the government since the December 1994–January 1995 parliamentary elections: the Social Democratic Party, the National Rebirth Democratic Party, and the National Unity Social Movement.

To avoid having to stand again for election, Karimov staged a referendum in March 1995, when electors dutifully voted to prolong his rule without new elections until 2000. According to the December 1992 Uzbek Constitution, a President may serve a maximum of two terms. Parliament declared in August 1995 that the March 1995 referendum extending Karimov's term meant he was still serving his first term, not beginning his second. Karimov's ambition to become the strongman of **Central Asia** and the regional policeman received some support in the mid-1990s from the USA once it had abandoned its 'Russia First' policy. However, Karimov's authoritarian rule and indifference to world opinion has dissolved any such backing.

Karimov's latest offensive has been against religious activists of all faiths. Although he has cause to fear Islamic radicals, Karimov has enacted draconian laws that have affected moderate Muslims and religious **minorities**. In the past few years thousands of Muslims of all opinions have 'disappeared'. Addressing parliament in May 2004 to urge deputies to support the harsh new law on religion, he declared his hatred of the Wahhabis, a fundamentalist strand of **Islam**, as he dubs all Muslims who oppose him. 'Such people must be shot in the head. If necessary, I'll shoot them myself, if you lack the resolve,' he told the assembled deputies, although this sentiment was excised from the official reports of the speech.

Karzai, Hamid

Born in **Kandahar**, interim leader of Afghanistan since 2001. Karzai was elected as President after a landslide electoral victory during June's *loya jirga*, or grand council, of 1,500 delegates. He had led an interim Afghan government since 5 December 2001. He assembled a Cabinet, selecting representatives from Afghanistan's many ethnic groups. Karzai's enormous popularity in the West led to a flow of both financial assistance and troops to the war-ravaged country. However, his grasp on power within the country remained somewhat tenuous, with warlords maintaining tight regional control. Indeed, he survived an assassination attempt in September 2002, which threatened the stability of an already volatile government. In addition to the support he receives from the West, Karzai has also been embraced by a broad spectrum of factions in Afghanistan, where ethnic and tribal identity dominates politics. An ethnic **Pashtun** from the city of Kandahar, Karzai is leader of the powerful 500,000-strong Populzai clan, which has supplied Afghanistan's kings since 1747. Karzai is also a close ally of the former king, **Mohammed Zahir Shah**. Even many **Taliban** supporters, most of whom were ethnic Pashtuns from Kandahar, found Karzai preferable to **Northern Alliance** leaders who were ethnic **Tajiks** or **Uzbeks**. During the fight against the Soviet invasion of the 1980s, Karzai provided money and arms to the ***mujahidin***. He then served as deputy foreign minister in the post-Soviet government of **Burhanuddin Rabbani**, which was overthrown by the Taliban in 1996. At first a Taliban supporter, Karzai gradually came to oppose their rigid policies and to distrust their connections to Pakistani intelligence and Arab Islamic radicals. When the Taliban asked Karzai to serve as ambassador to the United Nations, he refused. During the US-led campaign against the Taliban in the autumn of 2001, Karzai was instrumental in convincing a number of Pashtun tribes to end their support for the Taliban.

Kassem, Abdul Karim (1914–63)

Iraqi general and politician. A graduate (1934) of the Iraqi military academy, he attended the army staff college. His outstanding bravery, displayed in campaigns against the **Kurds** and in the Palestinian war of 1948, won him many military decorations. He organized the **military** coup in July 1958 which overthrew the Iraqi **monarchy** and established Kassem as premier of the new republic. An Arab nationalist, he quelled a pro-Communist uprising in 1959. After this, Kassem's power and influence steadily declined. He was overthrown and executed by military and civilian members of the **Ba'ath Party** in February 1963.

Kata'ib Party

Also known as Phalange Libanais. Christian Lebanese political party, founded in 1936 by **Pierre Gemayel**. National, reformist, social-democratic party. The largest **Maronite** party with some 100,000 members. In 1976 **Bashir Gemayel** founded the **Lebanese Force**, a coalition of the Kata'ib Party, the National Party, the Tanzim and the Guardians of the Cedar. In May 1979 a merger of the party with the **National Liberal Party** was announced. Mounir el-Hajj is president of the Kata'ib Party.

Katibat el Ahoual (Algeria)

This group appears to be a recent splinter group from the **GIA—Groupe islamique armé** (Armed Islamic Group) and is reportedly one of the most active and dangerous armed groups in the centre-west of the country. Within this area it is said to operate mainly in El Ourenis in the east, Remka and Relizane in the west, and Chlef in the north.

Kazakhs

A Turkic-speaking people, the second largest Muslim group of **Central Asia**. In the past they were perhaps the most influential of the various Central Asian ethnic groups. There are now more than 10m. Kazakhs (Cossacks) in the world; 7.9m. live in Kazakhstan, where they constitute 48.3% of the population, 1.2m. live in the

People's Republic of China, 808,000 in Uzbekistan, 636,000 in Russia, and there are smaller communities in Mongolia, Turkmenistan, Tajikistan, Ukraine, Iran, Afghanistan and Turkey.

Kazakhstan, Republic of

Qazaqstan Respublikasy

The largest and most northerly of the southern Central Asian states of the former Soviet Union. Located to the north-west of the People's Republic of China, with Russia to the north, and Turkmenistan, Uzbekistan and Kyrgyzstan to the south, it has a total area of 2,669,800 sq km, with 2,964 km of maritime coastline on the Caspian and Aral Seas. The capital is now Astana—the seat of government was transferred from Almaty in the far south to Astana in December 1998. The country is divided into 14 provinces (*oblys*, plural *oblystar*) and three municipalities (*qalasy*, plural *qala*): Almaty Oblysy, Almaty Qalasy, Aqmola Oblysy (Astana), Aqtobe Oblysy, Astana Qalasy, Atyrau Oblysy, Batys Qazaqstan Oblysy (Oral), Bayqongyr Qalasy, Mangghystau Oblysy (Aqtau), Ongtustik Qazaqstan Oblysy (Shymkent), Pavlodar Oblysy, Qaraghandy Oblysy, Qostanay Oblysy, Qyzylorda Oblysy, Shyghys Qazaqstan Oblysy (Oskemen), Soltustik Qazaqstan Oblysy (Petropavlovsk), Zhambyl Oblysy (Taraz). Kazakhastan's population was estimated at 16,741,519 in July 2002, of which the majority (53.4%) is of Kazakh (Qazaq) ethnic origin. There are several **minority** groups: Russians (30%), Ukrainians (3.7%), **Uzbeks** (2.5%), Germans (2.4%), Uighurs (1.4%) and 'others' (6.6%), according to the 1999 census. The two main religious groups are Muslims (47%) and Russian Orthodox (44%), with 'others' comprising 7% (Protestants 2%) of the population. The official state language is Kazakh (Qazaq), spoken by 64.4% of the population, while Russian, which is widely used in everyday business, is designated the 'language of interethnic communication' and was spoken by an estimated 95% of the population in 2001.

Political profile

The Republic of Kazakhstan is a sovereign, democratic, secular, law-based, unitary state with a presidential system of rule. State power belongs to the people, which exercises it directly through referendums and free elections, and also delegate the exercise of their power to state bodies. State power is divided into legislative, executive and judicial spheres—interacting with a system of checks and balances. Ideological and political diversity are recognized. State and private property have equal protection. The President is elected for a seven-year term by secret ballot on the basis of general, equal and direct suffrage. The most recent election was held on 10 January 1999, one year before it was scheduled; the next election is due to be held in 2006. President **Nazarbayev**'s previous term had been extended to 2000 by a nation-wide referendum held on 30 April 1995. He, with the consent of parliament, appoints the Prime Minister and Deputy Prime Minister, and may relieve him of office. On the Prime Minister's recommendation, the President determines the structure of government and appoints members of the Cabinet. In addition, the President appoints seven members of the Senate—the upper house of the parliament. The present head of state is President Nursultan Äbishuly Nazarbayev (chairman of the Supreme Soviet from 22 February 1990, elected as President on 1 December 1991, re-elected on 10 January 1999). The head of government is Prime Minister Imangali Tasmagambetov (since 28 January 2002). The legislature is a bicameral parliament, consisting of the Senate (upper chamber), a 39-member body with seven senators appointed by the President, and the remaining 32 members popularly elected, two from each of the 14 oblasts, the capital of Astana and the city of Almaty, to serve six-year terms. The **Majlis** (the assembly or lower chamber) is a 77-member body. Ten of the 77 members are elected from the winning party's lists, and the remainder are popularly elected from single-mandate constituencies to serve five-year terms. Elections are based on secret ballot on the basis of general, equal and direct suffrage and 10 party lists. Senate elections were last held on 17 September 1999 (the next are scheduled to be held in December 2005); Majlis elections were last held on 10 and 24 October and 26 December 1999 (the next are scheduled to be held in 2004).

The legal system is based on a civil law system. The Supreme Court has 44 members and the Constitutional Council seven members. The Constitutional Council decides whether to hold presidential or parliamentary elections, or a republican referendum. The President has a veto over the decision of the Constitutional Council.

While there are formal democratic freedoms in Kazakhstan, the President has almost complete political power. The 1995 Constitution strengthened presidential powers, giving Nazarbayev a veto over the decisions of the Constitutional Council. As the Constitutional Council decides whether to hold presidential or parliamentary elections, or a republican referendum, Nazarbayev can now effectively veto new elections. There have been allegations of electoral fraud, **corruption** and domestic and international criticism of President Nazarbayev's attempts to secure more presidential powers. Only he can initiate constitutional amendments, appoint and dismiss the government, dissolve parliament, hold referendums at his discretion, and appoint administrative heads of regions and cities. In 2002 opposition parties were effectively pacified by reform of the party registration process. In early 2001 nine political parties were officially registered with the authorities. Several other parties, as well as some 300 social movements/NGOs also exist.

- Agrarian Party of Kazakhstan; Leader Romin Madinov
- Alash; Leader Sabet-Kazy Akatay
- Aul (Village) Peasant and Social Democratic Party; Leader Gani Kaliyev
- AZAMAT (Citizen) Democratic Party of Kazakhstan; Co-chairmen Petr Svoik, Murat Auezov, Galym Abilseitov
- Civic Party of Kazakhstan; First Sec. Azat Peruashev

- Communist Party of Kazakhstan; First Sec. Serikbolsyn Abdildin
- Forum of Democratic Forces (a union of opposition parties, movements, and NGOs which includes Communists, RNPK, Orleu 'Development' Movement, Pokoleniye 'Generation' Pensioners' Movement, Labour Movement, Association of Independent Mass Media of Central Asia, and the Tabighat 'Nature' Ecological Movement
- Justice Party of Kazakhstan; Leader Talagat Zhanabayev
- Labour and Workers' Movement; Chair. Madel Ismailov
- National Co-operative Party; Leader Umzirak Sarsenov
- Orleu 'Development' Movement; Leader Seidakhmet Kuttykadam
- Otan 'Fatherland'; Chair. Sergei Tereschenko
- Party of Patriots of Kazakhstan; Leader Gani Kasymov
- Pensioners' Movement (or Pokoleniye); Chair. Irina Savostina
- People's Congress Party of Kazakhstan; Chair. Olzhas Suleimenov
- People's Co-operative Party of Kazakhstan; Leader Umirzak Sarsenov
- People's Front Movement; Leader Madel Ismailov
- People's Unity Party; Leader Nursultan A. Nazarbayev
- Renaissance Party of Kazakhstan; Leader Dzaghanova Altynshash
- Republican Party-Azat; Leader Kamal Ormantayev
- Republican People's Party of Kazakhstan; Leader Akezhan Kazhegeldin
- Republican Political Labour Party; Leader Bakhytzhan Zhumagulov
- Socialist Party of Kazakhstan; Leader Anatoli Antonov
- United Democratic Party
- Adil-Soz; Leader Tamara Kaleyeva
- Democratic Choice of Kazakhstan; Co-founders Galymzhan Zhakiyanov, Uraz Zhandosov, Nurzhan Subkhanberdin, Mukhtar Ablyazov, Zhanat Yertlesova, Bulat Abilov
- Kazakhstan International Bureau on Human Rights; Exec. Dir Yevgeniy Zhovtis

Media

Independent and private media—independent publications, private television and radio channels, and internet service providers with their own international channels—flourished in Kazakhstan in the decade after independence, operating relatively independently alongside state-owned media. The 1995 Constitution guarantees the freedom of ideas and expression and explicitly bans censorship. However, opposition newspapers are banned and outright censorship has been exercised, usually on the pretext of 'security reasons'. It is forbidden by law to criticize the President or members of the President's family—a law that is strictly enforced. In addition, the recent amendments (2001) to the Media Law have strengthened state control over broadcast outlets and internet sites, and have created more grounds for libel charges against editors and owners. These measures have restricted the independent media and have also greatly reduced the number of media outlets.

In 1999 there were an estimated 689 newspapers and 161 periodical titles published in the country. This has now fallen to some 400 newspapers, including: *Almat Asia Times*, *Almaty Herald*, *Ekspress-K*, *Kazhakstanskaya Pravda*, *Khalyk Kenesi*, *Vecherniy Almaty* and *Yegemen Kazakhstan*.

The electronic media remain under state control. Many private production companies exist, but access to television and radio is still controlled by the State Television and Radio Broadcasting Corpn. Television stations include: Kazakh State Television and Broadcasting Corpn, Khabar Agency, Kazakh Commercial Television and NTK. In 2001 there were 10 internet service providers (with their own international channels and (in 2002) 100,000 internet users.

History

Kazakhstan became a Soviet Republic in 1936. During the 1950s and 1960s, as part of the agricultural 'Virgin Lands' programme, Soviet citizens were encouraged to help cultivate Kazakhstan's northern pastures. This influx of immigrants (mostly Russians, but also some other deported nationalities) altered the ethnic balance, with Russians becoming an influential group. With the collapse of the Soviet Union, the republic of Kazakhstan declared its independence on 16 December 1991. It immediately joined the **Commonwealth of Independent States**.

In 1989 the Communist Party (CP) appointed Nursultan Nazarbayev to the party leadership. He managed to retain office immediately after independence, and subsequently disbanded the CP and formed his own Unity Party. Kazakhstan has, like its Central Asian neighbours, become increasingly authoritarian and corrupt. Nazarbayev's Unity Party has won all presidential and parliamentary elections, assisted by Nazarbayev's daughter's control of 80% of the country's media. In order to retain power the élite resorts to state pressure, electoral fraud, the suppression of opposition parties and the harassment of opposition parties and newspapers. In June 2000 Nazarbayev manoeuvred parliament into enacting legislation that conferred lifelong political and legal rights to him and his entire family, thus effectively establishing a family dynasty.

The government remained wary of the nationalist sentiment that was widespread during the *glasnost/perestroika* period. Ethnic relations is the most pressing political problem facing the republic, with Kazakhs constituting the majority of the population by only a small margin. Ethnic tensions are high, and the Russian population of the north regularly threatens to secede. However, Nazarbayev has managed to maintain balance between the Russian and the Kazakh factions, and has been lauded as a stabilizing force in the country.

Of the Central Asian Republics, Kazakhstan has been the most effective in attracting foreign investment and **aid**. This is due to its vast natural resources—especially **oil**—and also to the fact that Kazakhstan still held 104 Soviet-era SS19 ballistic missiles with more than 1,000 nuclear warheads after independence.

Nazarbayev managed to extract significant economic aid from the USA and NATO countries in exchange for dismantling the missiles.

The influx of foreign investment, the transition to a market economy and swift privatization have made corruption and nepotism a serious problem. Foreign companies' desire to obtain lucrative contracts has fostered corruption at all levels of the bureaucracy and well-placed government officials have managed to exploit the privatization of state assets for their personal enrichment. As a result inequality is increasing; a small class of 'entrepreneurs' are super-rich, while living standards for the majority of the population remain desperately low. Little of Kazakhstan's new wealth has reached its people. Combined with political and religious repression, the economic disparity is fuelling political unrest and driving more and more people to radical, especially Islamist, movements.

A significant number of young Kazakhs and Uzbeks are believed to have joined the ranks of Islamic parties such as the **Islamic Movement of Uzbekistan** (IMU) and the **Hizb ut-Tahrir**. The government of Kazakhstan regards this as a serious problem and doubled its military budget in 2001 so that the army would be ready to fight possible incursions from the IMU.

International relations/Transnational issues

There is significant illicit cultivation of **cannabis** for CIS markets, as well as limited cultivation of **opium** poppy and ephedra (from which the drug ephedrine is derived); there has been limited government eradication of illicit crops; Kazakhstan is a transit point for south-west Asian narcotics bound for Russia and the rest of Europe. Kazakhstan is working rapidly with the People's Republic of China and Russia to delimit its large open borders in order to control population migration, illegal activities and **trade**; it has signed a bilateral agreement with Russia delimiting the Caspian Sea seabed, but littoral states are far from any multilateral agreement on dividing the waters and seabed regimes—Iran insists on the division of the Caspian Sea into five equal sectors, while Azerbaijan, Kazakhstan, Russia and Turkmenistan have generally agreed upon equidistant seabed boundaries; Kazakhstan's border with Uzbekistan has been largely delimited, but an unresolved dispute remains over the sovereignty of two border villages, Bagys and Turkestan, and around the Arnasay dam; Kazakhstan, Tajikistan, Turkmenistan and Uzbekistan are engaged in a difficult struggle to share limited **water** resources and to combat regional environmental degradation caused by the shrinking of the Aral Sea; Kazakhstan is involved in disputes with Kyrgyzstan over that country's supply of water and hydropower to Kazakhstan

Kazakhstan, economy

Kazakhstan possesses enormous fossil fuel reserves—it is believed to be the largest unexplored **oil**-bearing region in the world—as well as plentiful supplies of other **minerals** and metals. It also is a large agricultural—livestock and grain—producer.

Kazakhstan's industrial sector is based on the extraction and processing of these natural resources and also on a growing machine-building sector that specializes in construction equipment, tractors, agricultural machinery, and some defence items.

The disintegration of the USSR in December 1991 and the collapse in demand for Kazakhstan's traditional heavy **industry** products resulted in a short-term contraction of the economy, with the steepest annual decline occurring in 1994. Kazakhstan also suffered major economic difficulties in 1997 as its terms of **trade** worsened due to a fall in world prices for its principal exports. As the President concentrated on market reforms in 1995–97, the pace of the government programme of economic reform and privatization quickened, resulting in a substantial transfer of assets into the private sector. This has helped Kazakhstan to attract more foreign investment—Kazakhstan has drawn by far the largest share of foreign direct investment in **Central Asia**—and gained it the good-will of **IFIs**, but has also led to increasing inequality and rampant **corruption**.

In 2000–01 Kazakhstan enjoyed economic growth in excess of 10%, thanks largely to its booming **energy** sector, but also to good harvests and foreign investment. The opening of the Caspian Consortium pipeline in 2001, from western Kazakhstan's Tengiz oilfield to the Black Sea, substantially raised export capacity. The government has embarked on an industrial policy designed to diversify the economy away from over-dependence on the oil sector by developing light industry.

However, Russia has been obstructive, insisting that Kazakhstan uses the Russian pipeline system to export oil to Europe, thereby making it dependent on Russia for exports. In addition, Russia demands a stake in every joint venture Kazakhstan enters into with Western oil companies. Kazakhstan is continually trying to become independent from Russian markets and pipeline infrastructure.

Economic performance has generally been good but the statistics that quantify it must be viewed with caution.

Strengths

Mineral resources, notably oil and **gas**, and bismuth and cadmium (used in electronics industry). Reputation as an investor-friendly country.

Weaknesses

Collapse of former Soviet economic and trading system. Reliance on imported consumer goods. Rapid introduction of the Tenge in 1993 increased instability and led to high inflation. Inefficient industrial plants. Poor infrastructure (independent from Russia). Corruption. Rising inequality is causing instability in some areas.

KDP – *see* **Kurdistan Democratic Party**

Kellogg, Brown & Root

The **Halliburton** subsidiary operating the Mina al-Bakra **oil** terminal (MABOT) which is exporting some US $60m.-worth of crude oil a day, and is currently projected to export oil worth $21,000m. annually.

Kemal, Mustafa – *see* Atatürk, Kemal

Keshet Demokratit Mizrahit – *see also* Mizrahi Democratic Rainbow

Secular, leftist Israeli political party, predominantly Mizrahi membership and support. A two-year-old movement of Mizrahi intellectuals with a stated claim of staying out of party politics. Keshet stands for a vision of social equality that includes not only **Mizrahim** and their civic rights but also equal rights for **women** and for **Palestinians**. Keshet defends the right to difference as a universal right and sees itself as the only real left movement in Israel at the present time. Its stated concern is not to gain political power but to work for a broader, more inclusive vision of Israeli society.

KFAED – *see* Kuwait Fund for Arab Economic Development

Khafji

Saudi Arabian town eight miles south of the Kuwaiti border. It was the site of the only major Iraqi offensive in the **Gulf War (1991)** when, on 29 January 1991, Iraqi tanks and mechanized infantry in eastern and southern Kuwait attacked US Marine Forces, Central Command and Arab Joint Forces Command-East units at several points along the Kuwaiti-Saudi Arabian border. The Iraqi offensive lasted a little more than four days, continuing until 2 February. Known collectively as the Battle of Khafji, the series of engagements between Iraqi forces and the US-led anti-Iraq coalition represented the first significant ground action of the Gulf War. At the time it was fought, the Battle of Khafji was viewed as a small and relatively inconsequential attack on an abandoned Saudi border town. In fact, Khafji was a very significant engagement, since described in one highly regarded study as the 'defining moment' of **Operation Desert Storm**. Apart from Scud missile attacks, Khafji was the only major Iraqi offensive of the war and its outcome demonstrated the impotence of the Iraqi army in the face of Coalition (primarily US) airpower.

Khalid, Sheikh Mohammed

Key organizer of the 11 September 2001 bomb attacks and head of **al- Qa'ida**'s military committee. Involved in al-Qa'ida operations in the Philippines, Khalid had strong connections to the Abu Sayaff group and helped to organize an unsuccessful attempt to assassinate Pope John Paul II in Manila in 1999. He was also involved in an attack on a Philippines airliner bound for Japan in December 1994. He was indicted for the first attack on the **World Trade Center** in 1993. He was arrested in Rawalpindi, Pakistan, on 1 March as a result of US electronic surveillance and bribes made to alleged al-Qa'ida members. Pakistan's **Inter-Services Intelligence** made the arrest and was involved, together with the US Federal Bureau of Investigation, in his interrogation as the 'mastermind' of the 11 September 2001 attacks.

Al-Khalifa family

A branch of the Bani Utbah tribe which has ruled Bahrain since 1783.

Al-Khalifa, Emir Hamad ibn Isa

Ruler of Bahrain from March 1999 to present. Son of **Isa ibn Salman al-Khalifa**.

Al-Khalifa, Emir Isa ibn Salman

Ruler of Bahrain from 1961 until March 1999.

Khalkhali, Sadiq

Iranian politician, said to be responsible for the execution of hundreds of Kurdish **women**, men and children in the occupied region of East Kurdistan. When Ayatollah **Khomeini** came to power, he appointed Sheikh Sadeq Khalkhali as the 'first judge' of the revolutionary court. He was known as 'the hanging judge' by the **Kurds**.

Khamenei, Hojatoleslam Sayed Ali Hossein

Born in 1939 in **Mashad**, he received a religious education first in Mashad and then for two years in **Najaf** (in Iraq). From 1958 until 1964 he studied in **Qum** under Ayatollah **Khomeini**. In 1962 he joined other religious leaders in disseminating the revolutionary ideas of Khomeini. He then returned to Mashad, where he continued to study and teach. He helped establish the Mujahidin Ulama League as a precursor to the **Islamic Republic(an) Party**, which became the ruling party after the **Iranian Revolution** of 1979. He was one of Khomeini's first appointees to the Islamic Revolutionary Council, and in the elections for the first **Majlis** of the Islamic Republic in the spring of 1980 he received more votes than any other clerical candidate. He was Khomeini's representative at the Supreme Council of Defence and became leader of Friday prayers in **Tehran**. He was elected as President of the Islamic Republic of Iran in October 1981 (following **Muhammad Ali Rajai**), and served in this position until 1989, when he was succeeded by **Hojatoleslam Ali**

Akbar Hashemi Rafsanjani. After Khomeini's death in 1989, he was appointed as Chief Guardian (the supreme religious authority) of the Islamic Republic.

Khatami, Dr Sayed Muhammad

President of the Islamic Republic of Iran following the elections of May 1997 and, again, after those held in June 2001. During his early period in office, Iran's relations with the outside world, notably with the **European Union** (EU), improved significantly. In November 2000 an EU-Iran working group on **trade** and investment met for the first time.

Khider, Mohamed

One of the nine 'historic chiefs' who founded the Algerian **Front de libération nationale**, Khider was head of the party after independence until he broke with **Ahmed Ben Bella** in April 1963. In opposition thereafter, and a member of the Islamist association, **al-Qiyam** ('Values'), a precursor of the later radical Islamist movement in Algeria, he was assassinated in Madrid, Spain, in January 1967.

Al-Khoei, Abdul Majid

Iraqi **Shi'a** leader, murdered in the holy shrine at **Najaf**, together with his aide, by a mob as tensions between different factions within the Shi'a community increased in the aftermath of the **Gulf War (2003)**.

Khomeini, Ruhollah Mousavi (1902–89)

Iranian **Shi'ite** fundamentalist cleric and spiritual leader of the 1979 **Iranian Revolution** that overthrew **Mohammed Reza Pahlavi**, the Shah of Iran. He is considered to be the founder of the modern Shi'ite state. He was born in the town of Khomein as Ruhollah Mousavi in 1902. Khomeini was named an **ayatollah** in the 1950s. In 1964 he was exiled from Iran for his constant criticism of the government. He fled to Iraq, where he remained until forced to leave in 1978, after which he went to France. He became a symbol and leader of the Iranian opposition and managed to build and maintain a powerful religiously-oriented revolutionary alliance. He returned to Iran on 1 February 1979, invited by a revolution already in progress against the Shah, and seized power on 11 February (it was later claimed by his supporters that more than 98% of the population were in favour of him taking power, though independent observers question the number). An Islamic republic was established in which presidential elections are held every four years. Only candidates approved by the ayatollahs may contest the presidency. Shortly after taking power, Khomeini began calling for similar Islamic revolutions across the **Middle East**. Fearful of the threat of the spread of Khomeini's militant brand of Shi'ism, Iraq, led by **Saddam Hussain** and spurred on by the USA, invaded Iran, effectively starting what would become the decade-long **Iran–Iraq War**. In 1989

Khomeini provoked international controversy by issuing a *fatwa* that ordered the killing of the British author **Salman Rushdie** for having allegedly committed apostasy in *The Satanic Verses*.

Khomeinism

Religious-political doctrine/ideology espoused by **Ruhollah Mousavi Khomeini** and his regime. There is some debate regarding whether it is first and foremost a religious doctrine, or whether it is primarily socio-political. Khomeinism has been influenced by **Islam**, **liberation theology** and **Marxism.**

Al-Khuri, Bishara

President of Lebanon from 1943 until 1952.

Khuzistan

The Mesopotamian province of Khuzistan (formerly Arabistan) in the south-western corner of Iran that lies adjacent to the Iraqi border and close to the southern oilfields.

Al-Kifah

Al-Kifah refugee centre. Located on Atlantic Avenue in Brooklyn, New York. Described by some as 'the New York City headquarters of Islamist terror'.

King-Crane Commission

The Commission was set up by US President Wilson to determine which power should receive the Mandate for Palestine to ensure the 'well-being and development' of its peoples. Its recommendations were made public in August 1919. While expressing itself sympathetic to the Jewish cause, it ruled out the proposals of the Zionists that Palestine become a distinctly and exclusively Jewish commonwealth. The Mandate for Palestine was eventually allocated to Great Britain by the League of Nations.

Kirkuk

Town in northern Iraq, in an **oil**-rich area of territory under Kurdish control. The Turkomans of north-eastern Iraq regard Kirkuk as their capital.

Knesset

Israeli National Assembly. The supreme authority in the State of Israel, the Knesset is a single-chamber elected body of 120 members. Its functions include legislation—draft legislation is usually presented by the Cabinet, having been drawn up by ministerial committee, and then sent to the appropriate committee of the Knesset for consideration, before being passed or rejected by a simple majority of votes in the Knesset. Members of the Knesset may also initiate private bills. The Knesset also participates in the formulation of national policy, approves budgets and taxation, generally supervises the activities of the administration, and elects the President.

Komala

Kurdish Iranian Marxist-Leninist party, founded in 1969. Its first secretary is Ibrahim Alizadeh.

Koran

The holy book of **Islam**. Believed by Muslims to be literally the words of God/ Allah spoken to the **Prophet Muhammad**.

Korea

Having previously had little involvement in the **Middle East**, the government of the Republic of Korea (South Korea) sent 600 mainly technical personnel (engineers and medical specialists) to join the coalition forces in Iraq in 2003–04. A fact-finding team was dispatched to Iraq in mid-April 2004 to explore the possibility of deploying 3,000 additional troops in the provinces of Irbil and Sulaimaniya. Shortly before seven South Korean missionaries had been seized by gunmen while travelling from **Amman**, Jordan, to **Baghdad** and held for five hours before being freed after they proved that they were not soldiers.

Koruturk, Fahri

President of Turkey from 1973 until September 1980, when he was overthrown by a **military** coup, led by **Gen. Kenan Evren**.

Krekar, Mulla

Former leader of **Ansar al-Islam**, an Islamist group operating in the Kurdish area of northern Iraq. He reputedly has links to **al-Qa'ida** (although this has been denied by al-Qa'ida's leadership) and with the former Iraqi regime (unconfirmed) of **Saddam Hussain**. Krekar studied **Islamic jurisprudence** in Pakistan in the 1980s under the Palestinian ideologue, **Abdullah Azzam**, the founder of al-Qa'ida and mentor of **Osama bin Laden**. His links with al-Qa'ida as such go back to the war in Afghanistan against the Soviet forces. It seems that at least some of his followers were also involved in the war in Afghanistan. He enjoys asylum status in Oslo, Norway, where he now lives with his wife and four children, but remains in contact with the group.

Kufr

Unbelief (as a basis for war)

The **Arabic** word *kufr* (plural *kafirun*) is typically translated into English as 'unbelief'. However, it literally means 'ingratitude'. The characteristic position of human beings, according to the **Koran**, is not their ignorance of the existence of God, but their failure to be grateful for His kindness and blessings, which should prompt people to turn to Him in worship and give generous charity to the poor, orphans and widows. The Koran contrasts the believers, who are grateful (*shakirun*), with the unbelievers, who are ungrateful (*kafirun*).

Kurdish autonomy (Iraq)

The Kurds in Iraq have struggled for greater autonomy for many years. Limited autonomy was granted in 1970 with the creation of a unified autonomous area, comprising As-Sulaimaniya, D'hok, Irbil and the Kurdish sector of the city of **Kirkuk**, and the establishment of a 50-member Kurdish Legislative Council. Since 1991, when the US-led coalition defeated the forces of **Saddam Hussain**, imposed 'no-fly zones' in the north and south of Iraq and established the Kurdish northern areas of Iraq as 'safe havens', Iraqi **Kurdistan** has been practically semi-autonomous, with its own parliament and administration. In January 2004 an agreement to preserve Kurdish autonomy was reached in the Kurdish city of **Irbil** when the US administrator in Iraq, **Paul Bremer**, and his British deputy, Sir Jeremy Greenstock, met **Jalal Talabani**, the leader of the **Patriotic Union of Kurdistan** (PUK), and **Masoud Barzani**, head of the **Kurdish Democratic Party** (KDP). The latter group is determined to extend its control beyond what were once the 'safe havens' to the whole of the predominantly Kurdish north, including Kirkuk. A spokesman for the PUK stated that the USA and the United Kingdom had agreed that the existing safe havens would remain after 30 June 2004—the date when Iraq is supposed to become independent. The borders of the 'Kurdish' region have not yet been agreed, and will have to await a proper census and decisions to be taken by the independent Iraqi government. At the Irbil meeting it was also agreed that up to 200,000 **Kurds** expelled from the Kirkuk region under Saddam Hussain would be allowed to return. Apparently, Bremer favours the establishment of a federal system in Iraq in which the largest devolved entities would become Iraq's 18 governorates. Some fear that the agreement threatens not only the future integrity of Iraq, but also the future of the estimated 2m. Turkomans who live mainly in north-east Iraq. The Kurds became increasingly exasperated during 2004 at their failure to gain support within the **Iraqi Provisional Governing Council** for a federal system with Kurdish autonomy in the north, and at mounting pressure from the Turkish government to forestall Kurdish autonomy. Popular opinion has become more nationalist with calls for secession becoming increasingly loud. The devastation wrought in Irbil at the beginning of February 2004 by suicide bombers targeting both the PUK and the KDP—attacks that claimed the lives of more than 100 people, including some of the KDP leadership—have resulted in a hardening of popular opinion regarding autonomy.

Kurdish (Kurdistan) Democratic Party (KDP)

Iraqi Kurdish party, established in the mid-1950s to fight against the **Ba'ath Party** regime in Iraq, the KDP was led by Mullah **Mustafa Barzani**, of the Barzan tribe in northern Iraqi **Kurdistan**. It remained the main political vehicle of the Kurdish movement in Iraq until 1975, when the unified movement collapsed after the **Algiers Accord** between the Shah of Iran and **Saddam Hussain** (then Prime Minister of Iraq). In 1975 the movement split when **Jalal Talabani**, of the Talabani **tribe**, founded the **Patriotic Union of Kurdistan** (PUK), and 'civil war' broke out between the PUK and the KDP. This war has only recently come to an end. Currently, Mustafa Barzani's son, **Masoud Barzani**, leads the KDP, which controls the northern part of Iraqi Kurdistan. Until recently the KDP had the support of the Turkish government, but relations have deteriorated as Turkey has armed and supported the Turkmen minority in Iraqi Kurdistan, which constitutes a threat to the KDP's authority.

Kurdish Hezbollah

Founded in 1985, Kurdish Hezbollah is a breakaway group from the **Kurdish Democratic Party** and a member of the **Supreme Council for the Islamic Revolution in Iraq**.

Kurdistan

Kurdistan is an area in the **Middle East**, inhabited mainly by the **Kurds**. It consists of about 518,000 sq km of territory. It resembles an inverted letter V, with the joint pointing in the direction of the Caucasus and the arms toward the **Mediterranean** Sea and the **Persian (Arabian) Gulf**. In the absence of an independent state, Kurdistan is defined as the areas in which Kurds constitute an ethnic majority. Thus, Kurdistan covers parts of Turkey, Iraq, Iran, Georgia and Syria. The borders of Kurdistan are hard to define, as none of the states in question acknowledge Kurdistan as a demographical or geographical region. For more than a century Kurds have been campaigning to make Kurdistan an independent state. However, despite promises of the creation of such a state made in the early 20th century, all of the region's governments are opposed to it.

In Turkey, Iran and Iraq Kurdish guerrilla groups fight against the government and have some control over Kurdish local politics. In Iraq the **Patriotic Union of Kurdistan** and **Kurdistan Democratic Party** control most of the IraqiKurdish areas. In Turkey, the **Kurdistan Workers Party** has been most active, leading an armed struggle during the 1980s and 1990s, but engaging in more political dialogue in the late 1990s and early 2000, having transformed itself into the Kurdistan Freedom and Democracy Congress **(KADEK)**.

Kurdistan Iraqi Front

An alliance of the **Kurdish Democratic Party**, the **Patriotic Union of Kurdistan**, the SPK, the **Kurdistan People's Democratic Party** and other, smaller Kurdish groups. Founded in 1988, but subsequently disintegrated.

Kurdistan Liberation Brigades

Guerrilla units of the **Kurdistan Workers Party** (PKK) operating in Turkey from across the border in Iraq and Syria and attacking police posts and army units in south-eastern Turkey during the mid-1980s.

Kurdistan People's Democratic Party

Iraqi Kurdish political party, led by Sami Abd ar-Rahman.

Kurdistan Revolutionary Party

Founded in 1972 as successor to the **Democratic Kurdistan Party**. It was admitted to the **National Progressive Front** in 1974. Its secretary-general is Abd as-Sattar Taher Sharef.

Kurdistan Toilers Party (KTP)

Iraqi Kurdish political party, a breakaway faction of the SPK, founded in 1985, and led by Qadir Aziz.

Kurdistan Unity Party (KUP)

In September 1992 the **Kurdistan People's Democratic Party**, the SPK and the Kurdish Democratic Independence Party were reported to have merged to form the KUP.

Kurdistan Workers Party

Partiya Karkeren Kurdistan (PKK—see also KADEK)

Founded in 1978 by **Abdullah Öcalan** and others at **Ankara** University, Turkey. The group's goal was to establish an independent, democratic Kurdish state in southern Turkey and northern Iraq. It arose from a radical youth movement in Turkey during the 1970s that proclaimed itself a revolutionary socialist national liberation movement following a Marxist-Leninist doctrine. Since 1978 the PKK has been led by Abdullah Öcalan. It clashed with other Kurdish groups in 1979 and gradually established itself as one of the leading Kurdish nationalist groups. After the **military** coup of 1980, the army bombed the Kurdish opposition in the rural areas and Öcalan and his supporters retreated to Syria, where they established a guerrilla training camp. The group remained in exile during 1980–84, developing links with Iraqi Kurdish groups. In the summer of 1984 the PKK announced the formation of the **Kurdistan Liberation Brigades** and began to attack army units and police posts in south-eastern Turkey. In 1985 they emerged as the Front for the National Liberation of Kurdistan and began to operate on a relatively large scale. For the remainder of the decade the south-east of Turkey came under a form of martial law introduced by Prime Minister **Turgut Özal**. By 1990 support for the PKK had increased considerably, and other Kurdish armed groups had emerged, including **Turkish Hezbollah**. In the early 1990s the PKK moved beyond rural-based insurgent activities to include urban **terrorism**. In an attempt to damage Turkey's tourist industry, the PKK bombed tourist sites and hotels and kidnapped foreign tourists in the early and mid-1990s. A number of legal Kurdish parties also emerged, however, during the early 1990s, including the People's Labour Party, the Democratic Party (DEP) and the People's Democratic Party. However, they were harassed by the state security forces and their leadership was constantly under threat of assassination. In September 1993 Mehmet Sincar, a DEP deputy for Mardin province, was killed in the street, despite having an official police escort. In all there were over 500 assassinations during 1993 alone. All of the legal Kurdish parties were subsequently banned. The PKK has received modest support from Syria, Iraq and Iran, all of which have also provided 'safe havens' on occasion. It receives substantial support from **Kurds** in Turkey and Europe. It has approximately 4,000–5,000 members, most of whom are currently located in northern Iraq. The Turkish authorities captured PKK leader Abdullah Öcalan in Kenya in early 1999 and the Turkish State Security Court subsequently sentenced him to death. In August 1999 Öcalan announced a 'peace initiative', ordering PKK members to refrain from violence and requesting dialogue with the Turkish authorities on Kurdish issues. At a PKK congress in January 2000, members supported Öcalan's initiative and claimed that the group would henceforth use only political means to achieve its new goal of improved rights for Kurds in Turkey. In April 2002, at its 8th party congress, the PKK changed its name to the Kurdistan Freedom and Democracy Congress (**KADEK**) and proclaimed a commitment to non-violent activities in support of Kurdish rights. A PKK/KADEK spokesman stated that its armed wing, the People's Defence Force, would not disband or surrender its weapons for reasons of self-defence. This statement by the PKK/KADEK confirms that the organization is prepared to maintain its capability to carry out terrorist operations. It periodically threatens to resume violence if the conditions of its imprisoned leader are not improved, and it continues its military training and planning. In 2002 the government of Turkey accepted certain conditions for entry into the **European Union** (EU), including abolition of the death penalty (which means Abdullah Öcalan will no longer face a death sentence) and changes to official government policy on basic human rights for its Kurdish population.

Kurds

The Kurds are a distinct people, whose predominantly mountain territory lies across four Middle Eastern states—Turkey, Syria, Iran and Iraq. The Turkish Kurds number about 15m. (out of Turkey's total population of some 65m.). They have struggled for independence for many decades, but it was in the 1980s that the separatist struggle became most intense. The separatists are led by the **Kurdistan Workers Party**. The leader of the militant Kurds, **Abdullah Öcalan**, a Marxist activist, initially based in Syria, first made demands for an independent **Kurdistan**, which would be formed by the Kurdish areas of Turkey, Syria and Iran, in 1984, when he launched his movement. More than 30,000 were people were killed in conflict that ensued. A cease-fire was agreed in 1993 and most Kurdish activists and civilians accepted that, rather than seek separation and independence, they would press for rights within Turkey. However, progress in this direction has been slow and human rights violations in the Kurdish areas continued over the next decade.

Kut

Major **Shi'a**-dominated town south of **Baghdad** in Iraq. Came under the control of the Shi'a militia loyal to the radical cleric **Moqtada as-Sadr** in early April 2004, as the Ukrainian 'peace-keeping' force was pushed out, but was retaken by US troops later in the month.

Kuwait, State of

Dawlat al-Kuwayt

Bordering the **Persian (Arabian) Gulf**, between Iraq and Saudi Arabia, Kuwait is at a strategic location at the head of the Gulf. It has an area of 17,820 sq km. The capital is Kuwait City and the administrative regions are five governorates (*muhafazah*, plural *muhafazat*): Al-Ahmadi, Al-Farwaniyah, Al-'Asimah, Al-Jahra' and Hawalli. Its population is 2,111,561, of which Kuwaiti nationals account for 45%, other Arabs for 35%, South Asians 9%, Iranians 4%, and 'others' 7%. Native Kuwaitis are outnumbered by resident foreign nationals—estimated at 1,159,913 in July 2002. Religious composition: Muslims 85% (**Sunni** 70%, **Shi'a** 30%) and Christians, Hindus, Parsis and 'others' 15%. **Arabic** is the official language and English is also widely spoken.

Political profile

Kuwait is nominally a constitutional **monarchy**. The head of state is **Amir Jabir al-Ahmad al-Jabir as-Sabah** (since 31 December 1977). The head of government is Prime Minister and Crown Prince **Saad al-Abdallah as-Salim as-Sabah** (since 8 February 1978). The first deputy Prime Minister is Sabah al-Ahmad al-Jabir as-Sabah (since 17 October 1992); the deputy Prime Ministers are Jabir Mubarak al-Hamud as-Sabah and Muhammad Khalid al-Hamed as-Sabah. The Council of

Ministers is appointed by the Prime Minister and approved by the Amir. There are no elections in Kuwait as the monarch is hereditary; the Prime Minister and deputy Prime Ministers are appointed by the monarch. The legislative branch is the unicameral **Majlis** al-Umma (National Assembly); its 50 members are elected by popular vote to serve four-year terms. Elections were held in July 1999, and again in 2003. Suffrage is only for males. Although the Amir has decreed female enfranchisement, it has been repeatedly blocked by the National Assembly. The legal system is based on a civil law system; **Islamic Law** is significant in personal matters. There is a High Court of Appeal. Kuwait has not accepted compulsory International Court of Justice jurisdiction. Formal political parties are illegal in Kuwait. However, several groupings act as *de facto* parties, lobbying on behalf of specific social interest groups.

Media

While, in theory, there is a free press, radio and television are state-controlled. However, satellite television is freely available. There are seven daily newspapers, the most important of which are *Al-Qabas* and *As-Seyassah*. In 2000 there were three internet service providers. In 2002 the number of internet users was 200,000.

History

Britain oversaw foreign relations and defence for the ruling Kuwaiti as-Sabah dynasty from 1899 until independence in 1961.

In August 1990 Iraq invaded Kuwait, claiming it as its 19th province. Following several weeks of aerial bombardment, a US-led UN coalition began a ground assault on 23 February 1991 that completely liberated Kuwait within four days, expelled Iraqi forces and restored the rule of the as-Sabah dynasty. Kuwait spent more than US \$5,000m. on the repair of **oil** infrastructure damaged in 1990–91. Even after the war, politics remained dominated by the as-Sabah family. However, the Amir restored the National Assembly and long-promised elections were eventually held in October 1992. **Women** were not given the vote and the franchise remained limited, covering only 81,000 of the total population. With a turn-out of 85% of those eligible to vote, more than 30 of the 50 assembly seats were won by critics of the government or by independent candidates, including 18 Islamists—the Islamic Tendency won nine seats, the **Shi'ite** Islamists three seats, the Salafi Islamists three seats and the **Muslim Brotherhood** three seats. It was, in effect, a vote of 'no confidence' in the post-war Government led by Crown Prince Sheikh Saad. There was then a government of 'national unity' until the 1999 elections, when the Amir's Islamist and liberal opponents were strengthened.

International relations

In November 1994 Iraq formally accepted the UN-demarcated border with Kuwait as stipulated by UN Security Council Resolutions 687 (1991), 773 (1993) and 883

(1993). This formally ended earlier Iraqi claims to Kuwait and to Bubiyan and Warbah islands.

Kuwait, economy

Kuwait is a small, rich, relatively open economy with proven crude **oil** reserves of 94,000m. barrels—10% of world reserves. Petroleum accounts for nearly one-half of the country's gross domestic product, 90% of export revenue, and 75% of government **income**. Kuwait's climate limits agricultural development. Consequently, with the exception of fish, it depends almost wholly on food imports. About 75% of potable **water** must be distilled or imported. Higher oil prices put the budget for the fiscal year 1999/2000 into a US $2,000m.-surplus. The budget for the fiscal year 2000/01 covered only nine months because of a change in the fiscal year. The budget for the fiscal year 2001/02 provided for higher expenditure on salaries, construction and other general categories. Kuwait is involved in discussions with foreign oil companies regarding the development of oilfields in the northern part of the country.

Strengths

Oil and **gas**; large overseas investments; stable banking system.

Weaknesses

Over-reliance on oil and gas. Dependence on imported skilled labour, food and raw materials. Unproductive spending. Exploitation of migrant labour.

Kuwait Democratic Forum

A quasi-political grouping represented in the Kuwaiti **Majlis**. Founded in 1991 and representing a secular, liberal position.

Kuwait Fund for Arab Economic Development

Established in 1961, this Fund, complementing **World Bank** policies, can be used for extending loans for development projects ranging from railroads and fertilizer plants to sewage and **water**-supply systems to livestock and crop production. One of the region's attempts to use capital as an instrument of economic integration within the wider Islamic world.

Kuwait, invasion of

In August 1990 Iraq invaded Kuwait. **Saddam Hussain** had previously warned Kuwait that its unilateral decision to increase **oil** production and, thus, to tend to reduce oil prices was, in effect, 'an act of war', given the commitment of the **Organization of Petroleum Exporting Countries** to maintaining quotas and oil prices. He had reason to believe that the rest of the world would not intervene while the invasion took place, even if it condemned it. Iraq quickly occupied Kuwait, subdued all resistance and introduced an Iraqi provisional administration. Reactions were strong and while debates and negotiations took place, the USA orchestrated a campaign and constructed a coalition of forces to remove Iraqi forces from Kuwait and to protect Saudi Arabia.

Kuwait Investment Authority (KIA)

The KIA is one of the largest institutional investors in the **Middle East**, with estimated assets of at least US $100,000m.

Kyrgyzstan (Kyrgyz Republic)

Kyrgyz Respublikasy

Kyrgyzstan is located in **Central Asia**, to the west of the People's Republic of China. It borders Uzbekistan to the east, Kazakhstan to the north and Tajikistan to the south. Kyrgyzstan is landlocked and entirely mountainous. The country's area is 198,500 sq km. The capital is Bishkek. For administrative purposes the country is divided into seven provinces (*oblasty*, plural *oblastlar*) and one city (*shaar*): Batken Oblasty, Bishkek Shaary, Chuy Oblasty (Bishkek), Jalal-Abad Oblasty, Naryn Oblasty, Osh Oblasty, Talas Oblasty, Ysyk-Kol Oblasty (Karakol). In July 2002 the population was estimated at 4,822,166, of which Kyrgyz constituted 52.4%, Russians 18%, **Uzbeks** 12.9%, Ukrainians 2.5%, Germans 2.4%, **Tatars** 2% and 'others' 9.8%. The religious composition is: Muslim 75%, Russian Orthodox 20% and 'other' 5%. The official languages are Kyrgyz and Russian.

Political profile

President **Akayev**'s administration has become increasingly autocratic and corrupt. In the presidential and legislative elections of 2000, Akayev was accused of electoral fraud. He was elected for an unconstitutional third term of office and has also been accused of fostering a personality cult. In addition, the government has been accused of intimidating the opposition through the arrest of its leaders and candidates for the presidency and the Supreme Council. The Kyrgyz Republic is a sovereign, unitary, democratic republic founded on the principle of lawful, secular government. All state power belongs to the people, who exercise it through the state bodies on the basis of the Constitution and the laws of the republic. Matters of legislation and other issues pertaining to the state may be decided by the people by referendum. The President of the Republic, the deputies of the Zhogorku Kenesh (Supreme Council) and representatives of local administrative bodies are all elected directly by the people. Elections are held on the basis of universal, equal and direct suffrage by secret ballot. All citizens of 18 years of age and over are eligible to vote. The head of state is Askar Akayev (since 28 October 1990, re-elected on 29 October 2000). The head of government is Prime Minister Nikolay Tanayev (since 22 May

2002). A Cabinet is appointed by the President on the recommendation of the Prime Minister. The President is directly elected by the people for five-year terms for a maximum of two consecutive terms. The President appoints or dismisses the Prime Minister, subject to approval by the legislature. The bicameral Zhogorku Kenesh (Supreme Council) consists of the 35-member Legislative Assembly (upper chamber), which is a permanent chamber, and the 70-member Assembly of People's Representatives (lower chamber), which sits twice yearly and represents regional interests. Members of both chambers are elected for a term of five years on the basis of direct, universal and equal suffrage by secret ballot. Fifteen members of the Zhogorku Kenesh are elected by party lists, with the remaining 90 members being elected in single-mandate constituency seats. There is a Supreme Court whose judges are appointed for 10-year terms by the Supreme Council on the recommendation of the President). There is also a Constitutional Court and a Higher Court of Arbitration. The legal system is based on civil law.

Political Parties and Groups

Since the mid-1990s it has become increasingly difficult for political groups and social organizations with a critical stance towards the government to gain legal recognition.

- Adilettuuluk (*Justice*); Leader Marat Sultanov; campaigns for the rights of national minorities
- Agrarian Labour Party of Kyrgyzstan; Leader Uson S. Sydykov
- Agrarian Party of Kyrgyzstan; Arkin Aliyev; represents farmers' interests
- Ar-Nayms (*Dignity*) Party; Leader Feliks Kulov; moderate opposition party
- Asaba (*Banner*) Party of National Revival; Leader Ch. Bazarbayev; nationalist party
- Ashar (*Solidarity*); Leader Zhumagazy Usup-Chonaiu; socio-political movement concerned with the development of a parliamentary state and the revival of national architecture
- Ata-Meken (*Fatherland*) Socialist Party; Leader Omurbek Tekevayev; nationalist party
- Birimdik Party; Leader Karypbek Alymkulov; seeks to unite people within a democratic movement
- Communist Party of Kyrgyzstan; Leader Klara Ajibekova; split from the Party of Communists of Kyrgyzstan
- Democratic Movement of Kyrgyzstan; Leader Jypar Jeksheyev; campaigns for civil liberties
- Democratic Party of Economic Unity; Leader A. D. Tashtanbekov
- Democratic Women's Party of Kyrgyzstan; Leader T. A. Shailiyeva; encourages the participation of **women** in politics
- El (Beibecharalai) Partiyasy; Leader Danyar Usenov
- Emgekchil el Partiyasy; supports the Democratic Movement and private ownership

- Erkin Kyrgyzstan Progressive and Democratic Party; Leader Bakir Uulu Tursunbay; key social-democratic party opposition party
- Erkindik
- Islamic Democratic Party; Leader Narkas Mulladzhanov
- Movement for the People's Salvation; Leader Jumgalbek Amambayev
- Mutual Help Movement or Ashar; Leader Jumagazy Usupov
- My Country of Action; Leader Almazbek Ismankulov
- National Unity Democratic Movement; Leader Yury Razgulyayev
- Party of Communists of Kyrgyzstan; Leader Absamat M. Masaliyev
- Party of the Veterans of the War in Afghanistan
- Peasant Party
- People's Party; Leader Melis Eshimkanov
- Republican Popular Party of Kyrgyzstan; Leader J. Sharshenaliyev
- Social Democratic Party; Leader J. Ibramov
- Union of Democratic Forces (composed of Social Democratic Party, Economic Revival Party, and Birimdik Party)
- Ar-Namys Party; Leader Emil Aliyev
- Council of Free Trade Unions
- Kyrgyz Committee on Human Rights; Leader Ramazan Dyryldayev
- National Unity Democratic Movement
- Union of Entrepreneurs
- People's Patriotic Movement (PPM); formed by nine political parties to oppose Akayev's centralization of power and to defend **democracy** and the human and constitutional rights of the population of the country. The PPM consists of the Agrarian Labour Party, Ar-Nayms, Ata Meken, the Communist Party of Kyrgyzstan, the Party of Communists of Kyrgyzstan, Erkindik Party, Kairian-El, People's Party and the Republican Party
- Coalition of NGOs (for democracy and civil society); an independent, non-partisan association of 55 NGOs and 300 citizens; works in poverty alleviation and monitoring the government.
- **Islamic Movement of Uzbekistan**; military incursions
- **Hizb ut-Tahrir**; has gained a foothold in southern Kyrgyzstan

Media

In Kyrgyzstan more than 300 mass media are registered, of which 111 are state-controlled, 40 are private and 75 are independent television and radio companies. Although the Constitution states that mass media shall be free, the Kyrgyz press has, since the mid-1990s, faced increasing pressure from the Government and the élite to silence opposition views and journalistic criticism. In 1996 there were 146 non-daily newspapers. Currently there are four daily newspapers. The four most popular newspapers are *Slovo Kyrgyzstana* (daily organ of the government), *Kyrgyz Tuusu* (daily organ of the government), *Vecherniy Bishkek* (daily independent), *Asaba* (weekly independent, publication resumed in October 2001 after a seven-month suspension) and *Delo No* (tabloid-style, most popular daily newspaper. Kyrgyz Television (National Television and Radio Broadcasting Company) is a state-owned service. In addition, Russian Public Television broadcasts for six hours daily in some regions of Kyrgyzstan, and relays from Kazakhstan, Turkey and Uzbekistan are also broadcast. Kyrgyz Radio (National Television and Radio Broadcasting Company) is a state-owned service. There are several private radio stations operating in Kyrgyzstan, such as Dom Radio, Radio Pyramid and Sodruzhestvo. There are no internet service providers. In 2001 there were 51,600 internet users.

History

Kyrgyzstan was annexed by Russia in 1864 and became part of the Turkestan Autonomous Soviet Socialist Republic in 1918 after considerable opposition from **Basmachi** groups and nationalists. During the Soviet period Kyrgyzstan shared the experiences of its Central Asian neighbours: land reform, collectivization and the attempt to settle the nomadic population—leading to thousands of deaths. Native Kyrgyz were mostly ignored and the majority positions of power were given to ethnic Russians. At independence this meant that few Kyrgyz had any technological or administrative expertise. Stalin's arbitrary map-making has led to acute ethnic problems in Kyrgyzstan with a substantial Russian population in the cities in the north and a large **Uzbek** population in Osh and the south.

Kyrgyzstan's nationalist movement found its voice during the *glastnost/perestroika* period. By 1989 signs of popular resistance had begun to appear; the media cautiously adopted a critical tone towards the government and a number of informal political groups emerged. A particular focus for dissent was the acute housing crisis and homeless people, mainly Kyrgyz, began to seize land and squat houses. In the south this led to intercommunal fighting between Kyrgyz and Uzbeks and order was restored only two months later. Ethnic tension has led to a 'brain drain' as ethnic Russians, Germans and Slavs have left the country in fear of discrimination; and has caused some Uzbeks to advocate union with neighbouring Uzbekistan.

In February 1990 elections were held to the Supreme Soviet, but these were largely manipulated by the Communist Party in order to exclude any opposition parties from power. Absamat Masaliyev was elected to the post of chairman of the Supreme Soviet, but he came under attack immediately by groups supporting various other candidates. Various factions united in the Kyrgyzstan Democratic Movement and in the October elections the neutral candidate of Askar Akayev was elected as chairman. With the dissolution of the Soviet Union Kyrgyzstan was made independent and Akayev reinforced his position, being elected, unopposed, in direct popular elections.

Initially Akayev put great emphasis on independent Kyrgyzstan's need to develop a liberal democracy, based upon a strong civil society and a market economy. The first year of independence witnessed the growth of civil society with a thriving and critical media. At the same time Kyrgyzstan had plunged into the worst economic crisis suffered by a Central Asian state after independence, and hence financial aid and subsidies from the Soviet Union were required. Inflation rose as high as 1,200% in 1993. Akayev's announcements and the severe economic crisis precipitated a flow of much-needed financial **aid** from the **International Monetary Fund** and some Western countries, though not without conditionalities. In 1993 Kyrgyzstan adopted austerity measures and privatized state-owned businesses and land. In 1998 Kyrgyzstan became the first Central Asian state to join the **World Trade Organization**. However, the country remained economically weak, with widespread poverty, unemployment and decreasing living standards. In 1999 Kyrgyzstan had a crippling **debt** of US \$1,270m. and began to default on its repayments.

As Kyrgyzstan's economic situation worsened, political opposition grew. Nationalist, communist and liberal critics accused Akayev of having no genuine commitment to democratization and of replacing the dominance of Russia with that of the **IFIs**. As political opposition grew, Akayev followed the line of other Central Asian leaders and became more authoritarian. In 1995 Kyrgyzstan held free, multi-party elections—it is the only Central Asian state to have done so—that ensured a thriving opposition in parliament. However, after 1996 parliament and the President were locked in a continuous struggle for power. After winning the presidential elections in 1995, Akayev organized a constitutional referendum to increase his formal powers. The populace voted in favour of Akayev's proposals. After the 1996 referendum Akayev began to harass hostile journalists and to imprison political opponents. In the 2000 presidential elections rival candidates were harassed and the candidature of Akayev's only effective challenger, Feliks Kulov, was barred. Kulov was later arrested. Akayev won the elections amid allegations of fraud. Civil unrest has flared up and protests and strikes are commonplace.

Of growing political and social importance from the late 1990s onwards was the issue of religion and, in particular, the threat of Islamic fundamentalist groups. The advances of the **Taliban** in Afghanistan and the increasing popularity of the **Islamic Movement of Uzbekistan** (IMU) and Hizb ut-Tahrir (HT) in Uzbekistan increased these fears. In addition, the Chinese authorities have put pressure on the government to control the actions of the Muslim Uighur population, which China has accused of instigating unrest amongst Chinese Uighurs in **Xinjiang** and of creating the organization For a Free Eastern Turkestan/Committee for Eastern Turkistan that seeks to create an **Islamic state** in the Uighur Autonomous Region in Xinjang. The consequence has been that the government has begun to monitor all Muslim communities within the country, arresting some of their members.

In 1999 several IMU militants crossed into Kyrgyzstan and captured 20 hostages, including four Japanese geologists. The militants were seeking passage to the **Fergana Valley** where they planned to set up bases from which to oppose Uzbekistan's President **Karimov**. After a military stand-off, the militants withdrew only to return in the following year. The HT has attracted a growing following from the marginal class of unemployed young people created by the country's economic and social problems.

International relations/Transnational issues

There is a territorial dispute with Tajikistan regarding the south-western boundary in the Isfara Valley area. There is also a dispute over access to Sokh and other Uzbek enclaves in Kyrgyzstan that mars progress on boundary delimitation. Further disputes exist over the provision of **water** and hydroelectric power to Kazakhstan. Kyrgyzstan is the periodic target of Islamic insurgents from Uzbekistan, Tajikistan, and Afghanistan.

There is limited illicit cultivation of **cannabis** and **opium** poppy for markets in the former Soviet Union. The government has made some attempt to eradicate illicit crops. Kyrgyzstan is a transit point for south-west Asian narcotics bound for Russia and the rest of Europe.

Kyrgyzstan, economy

Kyrgyzstan is a small, poor, mountainous country with a predominantly agricultural economy. Cotton, wool, and meat are the main agricultural products and exports. Industrial exports include **gold**, mercury, uranium and electricity. Kyrgyzstan has been one of the most aggressive countries of the former Soviet Union in adopting market reforms. An embryonic free market has been created, but one in which **corruption** is chronic, and one that has, for the most part, only benefited a small class of private entrepreneurs. For the majority of the population the economic situation has worsened, and social provisioning in **health** and **education** has deteriorated drastically.

At the macroeconomic level there has been improvement since the latter part of the 1990s, with inflation having been reduced to 7% in 2001 and growth rates of 5% having been achieved in 2000 and 2001. However, inflation still fluctuates from year to year, and critics have argued that the growth was largely due to expenditure in the war against Islamist groups. Productivity has reportedly improved and exports have increased.

Although the government has defaulted on some of its **debt** repayments, it managed to secure a US $93m. Poverty Reduction and Growth Facility in November 2001, with financing assurance from the 'Paris Club'.

Although Kyrgyzstan has seemingly managed to effect a fragile stabilization of its economy, it has been unsuccessful in securing improvements in the standard of living of its people.

Strengths

Agricultural self-sufficiency. Gold and mercury exports. Hydropower potential.

Weaknesses

Sharp economic decline since the disintegration of the Soviet Union, on which Kyrgyzstan depended for **trade** and supplies. Chronic inflation.

L

Labour Alignment (Israel)

Israeli political bloc—formed by the merger of **Mapai, Achdut HaAvoda** and **Rafi** in 1968, with the addition of **Mapam** in 1969. See also **Labour-Mapam Alignment**.

Labour force

The 10 countries (or territories) in the world with the highest proportion of males in the labour force are: Algeria (87.8%), **West Bank** and **Gaza Strip** (86.7%), Pakistan (84.4%), Bahrain (82.6%), Syria (79.7%), Egypt (79.0%), Guatemala (77.4%), Turkey (73.4%), Malta (70.8%) and Nicaragua (69.2%). Those with the lowest percentage of the total population in the labour force are: the West Bank and Gaza Strip (20.8%), Algeria (27.0%), Pakistan (29.0%), Togo (29.6%), Egypt (29.6%), Puerto Rico (30.4%), the Republic of the Congo (32.3%), Syria (32.6%), Turkey (32.9%) and Suriname (34.6%). Those with the highest rates of unemployment include: Algeria (25%, the sixth highest rate in the world), Morocco (19%, ninth), Tunisia (15.4%, 17th), the West Bank and Gaza Strip (14.1%, 22nd), Jordan (13.2%, 27th) and Israel (9.3%, 40th).

Labour-Mapam Alignment

The **Israel Labour Party** (Mifleget HaAvoda HaYisraelit), formed from the merger in 1968 of **Mapai, Achdut HaAvoda** and **Rafi**, formed an Alignment with **Mapam** in 1969. This resulted in the Alignment gaining 46% of the vote and 56 seats in the **Knesset** in elections held in that year. The Alignment also performed well in the 1973 elections, gaining 40% of the vote and 51 Knesset seats. Mapam ended its alliance with Labour in September 1984 over the issue of the formation of a government of national unity with the **Likud** party, and veteran politician Victor Shemtov retired as party leader.

Labour Zionism and Zionists

There was always a close association between **Zionism** (and the Zionists) and the **Israel Labour Party**. The early settlers had a clear vision of a homeland built from their own labours and epitomized by the *kibbutz*, or collective farm **settlement**.

Lahoud, Emile

Born in 1936. Lebanese military leader and politician. President of Lebanon from 1998 to the present. Despite great expectations from Christians and nationalists, Lahoud is regarded as a weak leader, defined as a Syrian marionette. He was elected by the National Assembly in a vote that was almost unanimous—Walid Jumblatt and his supporters boycotted the election. Gen. **Michel Aoun**, who was President between 1988 and 1990, also protested against the appointment. Lahoud replaced **Elias Hrawi** and assumed powers that had been stripped from the presidency by the **Ta'if Agreement** of 1989. Prime Minister **Rafiq al-Hariri** refused to form a new government. Lahoud introduced compulsory military service, but he also allowed Syrian influence to the extent that Syria was able to overrule the decisions of the highest officials in the Lebanese army. In 1999, on the order of Lahoud, security forces stormed university campuses where students were protesting against the Syrian presence in Lebanon. The elections of 2000 greatly strengthened the positions of both al-Hariri and Jumblatt and Hariri returned to office as Prime Minister. Lahoud's popularity is low and it is possible that he will not be re-elected as President in 2004 unless Syria forces the Lebanese parliament to vote against its interests.

Laiklik

A term meaning 'secularism' in Turkish. One of the pillars of the Kemalist state and the Kemalist political tradition in Turkey.

Land of Israel – *see* Eretz Israel

Landmines

Landmines have been used to devastating effect in many of the conflicts that have affected the region over the years. Nowhere is the issue more prominent than in Afghanistan, which is one of the most heavily mined countries in the world. There landmines kill or maim an estimated 100 people every month, more than half of them children. In the Herat region alone some 20 victims a month were reported in October 2003. A UN Report issued in September indicated that 17,000 deaths and injuries could be avoided if demining were accelerated. Shortfalls in international funding and worsening security in the south, where the **Taliban** were laying new mines, hindered progress in demining.

Lavon Affair – *see* **Lavon, Pinhas**

Lavon, Pinhas

Born in Poland and educated at Lvov University, Pinhas Lavon was among the early pioneers to Palestine. He started his career as a militant member of **Mapai** Youth Movement of which he eventually became leader. Before independence he was secretary-general of the **Histadrut**, the Jewish Labour Federation. He was Minister of Agriculture in 1950–51, and then, from 1951, Minister of Defence under the premiership of Moshe Sharett. He made considerable use of the secret services, including **Mossad** and **Shin Beth**, in operations against Egypt during the early 1950s, against the wishes of **Moshe Dayan**, then army chief of staff. In 1954 a special operation was planned, involving the bombing of British and US offices in **Cairo**, with the aim of implicating Egypt in an apparent plot against Britain and the USA. The raids were to be carried out by a special group (Unit 131) of Israeli secret agents comprised entirely of Egyptian Jews. The operation proved a total catastrophe—some bombs were planted but failed to explode, while the rest of the plan was never carried out, the entire network associated with the operation was apprehended, of whom two were hanged and eight jailed, while a key agent, Max Bennett, was arrested, tortured and committed suicide. The operation became known as the Lavon Affair. When it became public, it created a tremendous political dispute, dividing the government (with Lavon and his supporters on one side and Moshe Dayan, **Shimon Peres** and others on the other) and the Israeli people. Lavon insisted he had not given the order for the operation to be put into effect. Eventually, in February 1955, Lavon resigned and **Ben-Gurion** took over the defence portfolio. In 1960 Lavon persuaded Prime Minister Ben-Gurion to conduct an inquiry, which at the end of the year suggested that Lavon had not given the original order and that sabotage action had been implemented without his knowledge or authorization. The Cabinet accepted the report, but Ben-Gurion and Dayan withheld their endorsement of its findings. Ben-Gurion resigned shortly afterwards.

Law of return (1950)

This law made it possible for any Jew to 'return' to Israel, as a matter of right, from any other country in the world.

Lawrence, T. E.

Thomas Edward Lawrence was recruited in 1914 in **Cairo**, Egypt, into the British intelligence service in order to organize an uprising against the Turks (and the **Ottoman Empire**) by the Arabs under the **Hashemite** King Hussein. In 1915 Hussein agreed to that objective and Lawrence worked closely with his sons, particularly the youngest son, Faisal (later **Faisal I**). As Faisal's liaison officer, Lawrence took part in the mobilization of the **Bedouin** in battles against the Turks, and in the capture of important towns, such as Aqaba in July 1917. The Arab troops backed Gen. Allenby's offensive in Palestine and Syria, and made a major contribution to the defeat of Turks and the eventual allied victory. Promises made to the Arabs of an Arab state were not kept, however. Hussein was obliged to accept only the **Hejaz**, which **Ibn Saud** was later to seize from him, while Faisal, after having been named king in Syria, was driven from that country by France and eventually placed on the throne of Iraq by Britain. **Abdullah**, another of Hussein's sons was made king in the newly created **Transjordan**. Lawrence felt that the Arabs, with whom he had come to identify, had been betrayed and in July 1922 he resigned from the Office of Colonial Affairs. He subsequently wrote *The Seven Pillars of Wisdom*—an extraordinary personal account of the **Arab Revolt**. He was eventually killed in a motorcycle accident in May 1935.

Lawrence of Arabia – *see* Lawrence, T. E.

League of Arab States – *see* Arab League

League of the Followers (Lebanon) – *see* Asbat al-Ansar

League of the Sons of Yemen

Rabitat Abnaa al-Yaman

Yemeni opposition party.

Lebanese Broadcasting Company

This **Arabic**-language broadcasting company has become one of the new 'breed' of radio and television stations operating in the **Middle East**. It is committed to good coverage and accurate reporting and analysis of Middle Eastern affairs.

Lebanese civil war (1975–76)

The second Lebanese civil war erupted in April 1975, when a bus in which **Palestinians** and Lebanese were returning from Sabra refugee camp was fired on by Phalangists as it crossed the Ain ar-Rummaneh zone controlled by the Phalangists. Twenty-seven passengers were killed. Reprisals and counter-reprisals led to fighting across the country for more than one year. The war ended officially in September 1976, but the conflict in Lebanon did not. The Lebanese civil war of 1975–76 was a decisive turning point in Lebanon's relationship with Israel. Israel subsequently established close links with the Christian villages of the frontier zone and from 1976 began to practise a 'good fences' policy (opening the Israeli border to 'good' Lebanese). It intervened directly alongside the Christian forces that had emerged from the disbandment of the army, commanded by Maj. Saad Haddad.

Lebanese Communist Party – *see* Communist Party of Lebanon

Lebanese Democratic Movement (LDM)

The LDM's president is Jacques Tamer, its secretary-general Naji Hatab.

Lebanese Force

In 1976 **Bashir Gemayel** founded the Lebanese Force, a coalition of the **Kata'ib Party**, the National Party, the Tanzim and the Guardians of the Cedar.

Lebanese Islamic Resistance Front (LIRF)

Jabhat al-Muqawama al-Islamiya al-Lubnaniya

The LIRF has almost 500 members. It was founded by Sheikh 'Abd al-Hafiz Qassim in the wake of the 1982 Israeli invasion of Lebanon. A militia made up of an alliance of the **Sunni** Muslims and Palestinian guerrillas, it claimed responsibility in 1982–83 for attacks against Israeli troops inside West **Beirut**. It embraced Arab unity tentatively in 1964, when members of an older organization established the **Islamic Association** in Tripoli. Following the Arab defeat in 1967 and the decline of **Nasserism**, the **Islamic Association** and other Islamist groups throughout the **Arab World** gained strength. During the civil war, its militia, called the *Mujahidin*, fought with the **Lebanese National Movement** against Christian **Maronite** forces; in 1982–83 it participated in fighting against Israeli forces.

Lebanese National Movement (LNM)

Al-Haraka al-Wataniyya

A loose association of political organizations and armed militias in opposition to the Christian **Maronite** Phalange or **Kata'ib Party**. The LNM aimed to transform Lebanon into a pure Arab state without the European heritage of the Christian groups. Established in principle in 1969, but active only from 1973–74, the LNM consisted of the Progressive Socialist Party (**Druze**); the **Ba'ath(ist) Socialist Party** (Syria), Lebanese branch; the Ba'ath(ist) Socialist Party (Iraq), Lebanese branch; the **Communist Party of Lebanon**; the Communist Action organization; the October 24 Movement (Tripoli—*Harakat Arba-wa-ishrin Tishrin*), the **Syrian Socialist Nationalist Party**; the Shi'ite Movement of the Deprived (*Harakat al-Mahrumin*); the **Independent Nasserite Movement** (*Murabitun* or *Harakat al-Nasiriyyin al-Mustaqillin*); the Popular Nasserist Organization (*At-Tanzim ash-Shabi an-Nasiri*); the Nasserist Organization-Union of Popular Labour Forces

(*At-Tanzim an-Nasiri-Ittahad Qiwa ash-Shab al-Amil*); the **Nasserist Corrective Party** (*At-Tanzim an-Nasiri-al Haraka at-Tashiyya*); and the **Arab Socialist Union** (*Al-Ittihad al-Ishtiraki al-Arabi*).

Lebanese Popular Congress

Lebanese political grouping. Its president is Kamal Shatila.

Lebanon, Republic of

Lebanon's western border is the **Mediterranean** Sea; to the north and east is Syria, to the south, Israel. Lebanon covers an area of 10,400 sq km (of which 170 sq km is **water**). The capital is **Beirut**. For administrative purposes Lebanon is divided into six governorates (*mohafazah*, plural *mohafazat*): Beyrouth, Beqaa, Liban-Nord, Liban-Sud, Mont-Liban and Nabatiye.

In July 2002 the population was estimated at 3,677,780, of which Arabs accounted for 95%, Armenians 4% and 'others' 1%. The religious composition of the country is Muslim 70% (including **Shi'a**, **Sunni**, **Druze**, Isma'ilite and **Alawite** or Nusayri), Christian 30% (including Orthodox Christian, Catholic, Protestant), and small number of Jewish Lebanese. **Arabic** is the official language. French, English and Armenian are also spoken.

Political profile

The Constitution of 23 May 1926 has been amended a number of times, most recently by the Charter of Lebanese National Reconciliation (**Ta'if Agreement**) of October 1989. The head of state is President **Emile Lahoud** (since 24 November 1998). The head of government is Prime Minister **Rafiq al-Hariri** (since 23 October 2000). The Deputy Prime Minister is Issam Fares (since 23 October 2000). The Cabinet is chosen by the Prime Minister in consultation with the President and members of the National Assembly. The President is elected by the National Assembly (**Majlis** an-Nuwab) for a six-year term. The most recent presidential election was held on 15 October 1998 and the next is scheduled to be held in 2004. The Prime Minister and Deputy Prime Minister are appointed by the President in consultation with the National Assembly. By custom the president is a **Maronite** Christian, the Prime Minister is a Sunni Muslim, and the speaker of the legislature is a Shi'a Muslim. The 128 members of the single-chamber National Assembly are elected by popular vote on the basis of sectarian proportional representation to serve four-year terms. Legislative elections were most recently held in August–September 2000. The next legislative elections are scheduled to be held in 2004.

The legal system is based on a mixture of Ottoman law, canon law, Napoleonic code, and civil law. There is no judicial review of legislative acts. Lebanon has not accepted compulsory International Court of Justice jurisdiction. It has four Courts of Cassation—three courts for civil and commercial cases and one court for criminal cases. A Constitutional Council, provided for by the Ta'if Agreement—rules on the constitutionality of laws. There is a Supreme Council which hears charges against the President and Prime Minister as needed.

Political party activity is organized along largely sectarian lines. Numerous political groupings exist, consisting of individual political figures and followers motivated by religious, clan, and economic considerations. Major lists include: Resistance and Development List; Dignity; Baalbek-Hermel List; National Struggle List; Mount Lebanon Unity.

Media

There are five television services—one state-controlled and four independent stations. There is a single, state-controlled radio service. In the late 1990s the government banned news and political programmes on private satellite television channels. In 2002 the local MTV station was also banned. There were 22 internet service providers in 2000 and 300,000 internet users in 2001. There are approximately 40 daily newspapers, of which the most important include *Al-Anwar*, *An-Nahar*, *L'Orient-Le Jour* and the *Morning Star*.

Lebanon has made progress towards rebuilding its political institutions since 1991 and the end of the devastating 16-year civil war. Under the Ta'if Agreement— the blueprint for national reconciliation—Lebanon has established a more equitable political system, particularly by giving Muslims greater influence in the political process while institutionalizing sectarian divisions in the government. Since the end of the war, Lebanon has conducted several successful elections, most of the militias have been weakened or disbanded, and the Lebanese **armed forces** have extended central government authority over about two-thirds of the country. **Hezbollah**, the radical Shi'a party, retains its weapons. Syria, which has deployed troops in Lebanon since October 1976, maintains about 20,000 troops there today, based mainly in Beirut, North Lebanon, and the **Beka'a Valley**. Syria's troop deployment was legitimized by the **Arab League** during Lebanon's civil war and in the Ta'if Agreement. Syria itself justifies its continued military presence in Lebanon by citing the Lebanese government's requests and the failure of that government to implement all of the constitutional reforms in the Ta'if Agreement. Israel's withdrawal from its security zone in southern Lebanon in May 2000, however, has emboldened some Lebanese Christians and Druze to demand that Syria withdraw its forces as well. The Lebanese government claims the Shab'a Farms area of the Israeli-occupied **Golan Heights**.

Lebanon, economy

The 1975–91 civil war seriously damaged Lebanon's economic infrastructure, reduced national output by half, and all but ended Lebanon's position as a Middle Eastern banking hub. Peace enabled the central government to restore control in **Beirut**, begin collecting taxes, and regain access to key port and government facilities. Economic recovery was helped by a financially sound banking system and resilient small- and medium-scale manufacturers. Family **remittances**, banking services, manufactured and farm exports, and international **aid** provided the main sources of foreign exchange. Lebanon's economy made impressive gains immediately after the launch in 1993 of 'Horizon 2000', the government's US $20,000m. reconstruction programme. In fact, in 1991–2001 Lebanon's gross domestic product (GDP) increased by an annual average of 6.6%, the sixth highest growth rate in the world. However, the rate of increase has been declining. Real GDP growth was 8% in 1994 and 7% in 1995 but it slowed to 4% in 1996 and 1997, and then declined to 2% in 1998. In 1999 there was a recession of - 1%, and another, of -0.5%, in 2000. Growth recovered slightly in 2001, to 1%. Annual inflation, however, fell during the 1990s from more than 100% to almost zero and Lebanon has rebuilt much of its war-torn physical and financial infrastructure. The government none the less faces serious challenges in economic affairs. It has funded reconstruction by borrowing heavily—mostly from domestic banks. In order to reduce the growing national **debt**, the reinstalled **Hariri** Government initiated an economic austerity programme to rein in public expenditure, increase revenue collection, and privatize state enterprises. The Hariri Government met with international donors at the Paris II conference in November 2002 in order to seek bilateral assistance to restructure its higher interest rate-bearing domestic debt obligations at lower rates. While privatization of state-owned enterprises had not occurred by the end of 2002, the Government had successfully avoided a currency devaluation and debt default in 2002. The construction boom that has occurred in the post-civil war years is likely to become an economic liability in the future owing to the high level of foreign debt incurred as a result of it.

Lasting peace is a prerequisite for Lebanon's successful economic development. It is not clear that Lebanon will be able to regain its position as the Arab centre for banking and services, given developments in the **Gulf** over the last 20 years. As far as industrial development is concerned, the economy remains dependent on imported **oil** and **gas**. Agricultural output has still not recovered to its pre-war level, but Lebanon is potentially a major producer of wine and fruit. **Cannabis** cultivation, previously of major significance, particularly in the **Beka'a Valley**, was dramatically reduced to 2,500 ha in 2002; **opium** poppy cultivation is minimal. Small amounts of Latin American cocaine and south-west Asian **heroin** transit the country *en route* to US and European markets.

Lebanon hostage crisis

In the mid-1980s US hostages held captive in **Beirut** were released only after the USA had turned to Iran to act as mediator with **Islamic Jihad**, the armed group that held the hostages. Following an agreement between the two governments, the US **Central Intelligence Agency** (CIA) shipped US $12m. of Defense Department weapons to Iran via Israel in January–September 1986. The profit made by the CIA on the deal was transferred into a Swiss account nominated by Oliver North and controlled by the '*contras*' (see **Iran-*Contra* affair**).

Lebanon War (1982)

In one sense this was the fifth Arab–Israeli war, but it was more of a conflict between the **Palestinians** in Lebanon and Israel. The invasion of Lebanon in June 1982 was launched by the Israeli Government of **Menachem Begin** after clashes between the **Palestine Liberation Organization** (PLO) and the **Israeli Defence Force** in southern Lebanon had resulted in a cease-fire negotiated between the two parties by the USA. The cease-fire was observed by the PLO, but the Israeli forces took the opportunity to move northwards, initially to secure a 40 km strip as a 'fire-break', but eventually advancing (at the end of June) to **Beirut**. The siege of Beirut then began, in which the Palestinians and the **Lebanese National Movement** fought side by side against the Israeli forces, while the Phalangists gave support—but did not participate in the fighting—to the Israeli forces, who received substantial air support. At the end of the first week of August, the American mediator, Philip Habib, declared an American-Lebanese-Palestinian agreement to allow the departure of the PLO militia, under the protection of an international contingent. At the end of August, the last of the PLO troops left Beirut, to establish a base in **Tunis**. Two weeks later, on the day after the assassination of **Bashir Gemayel**, Israeli forces under Gen. **Ariel Sharon** entered the city. During the next two days the Phalangists were allowed to massacre hundreds of men, **women** and children in the Palestinian refugee camps of **Sabra and Chatila**. Israeli forces withdrew from Beirut, but remained, effectively, in occupation of south Lebanon for a further three years until the cost of the occupation became too great and the area was abandoned to Israel's Lebanese collaborators, the South Lebanese Army, under Gen. Lahad.

Lechi

A Jewish paramilitary organization which carried out operations against both the Arabs and the British in Palestine. Its full name was Lohamei Herut Israel, but it was referred to by the British as the **Stern Gang**. The Gang was responsible, among other actions, for the assassination of the unpopular anti-Semitic Lord Moyne, who had been colonial secretary in the British Churchill Government, after Lord Lloyd, and then resident minister in **Cairo**, Egypt.

Lesser Tunb Island – *see* Tunb Islands

Levant

The Levant (literally 'the land of the rising sun') is a geographical term referring to an area roughly bounded by the **Mediterranean** Sea in the west and the Zagros Mountains in the east. It includes the countries of Palestine, Israel, Jordan and the western parts of Lebanon and Syria.

Lewis, Bernard

Influential right-wing American orientalist historian and academic 'expert' on the **Middle East**. He is the author of *Islam and the West*, which has been reprinted on numerous occasions since it was first published in the 1950s. More recently he was the author of the highly contentious *What Went Wrong?*

Liberal Party

Ahrar, Lebanon

A Christian party of the **Chamoun** family.

Liberal Party

HaMiflagah HaLiberalit, Israel

The origins of the Israeli Liberal Party can be traced to those who wanted to unite Zionists, without regard to socialist, revisionist or religious feelings, around an economic programme that privileged private enterprise and industrial development. The group split into two wings in 1935, but merged again in 1946 to form the General Zionist Party. In 1948 this party split, when one group formed the Progressive Party, and merged again in 1961 as the Liberal Party. It won 17 seats in the 1961 elections. In 1965 it formed an alliance with **Herut**, called **Gahal**. Seven of the Liberal deputies in the **Knesset** refused to join Gahal and instead established the **Independent Liberal Party**. In 1973 Gen. (retd) **Ariel Sharon**, then a member of the Liberal Party within Gahal, advocated a wider union of parties that could present a genuine alternative to the **Labour Alignment**. Sharon successfully encouraged the Free Centre Party, the **State List**, and the **Land of Israel** movement (a non-party group advocating immediate Israeli **settlement** and development of the **Occupied Territories**) to join the Herut-Liberal alliance, to form **Likud**.

Liberal Socialist Party (LSP)

Egyptian political party, founded in 1976. It advocates the expansion of 'open door' economic policies and greater freedom for private enterprise and the press. The position of leader is currently vacant.

Liberation Movement of Iran

Nahzat-i Azadi-ye Iran

The Liberation Movement of Iran was the only legal opposition movement in the early years of the Islamic Republic. It was founded in 1957 by **Mehdi Bazargan**, Ayatollah Mahmud Taleqani and other French-educated technocrats. They hoped that the party, influenced by **Shi'a Islam** and European **socialism**, would show Islam's relevance to modern politics in a way that the traditional *ulema* could not. Bazargan, who had long opposed the Shah, was named Prime Minister in the first revolutionary government, serving from February to November 1979. He was dismissed after the 'hostage crisis' but his party won five seats in the 1980 elections. It boycotted the 1984 elections, but Bazargan attempted to contest the presidency in 1985. He was disqualified, however, by the **Council of Guardians**. He favoured an Islamic Republic, but wished to see reforms introduced as a result of persuasion and public protest, not violent action. In a visit to the Federal Republic of Germany in October 1985, he told Iranian exiles that 'you cannot solve the problems of Iran by complaining from abroad'.

Liberation Rally

A mass party established in Egypt after the **military** coup of 1952. It lasted until the political union with Syria in 1958, when it was replaced by the **National Union Movement**.

Liberation theology

More widely found in regions that are predominantly Catholic Christian, in the **Middle East** liberation theology was especially popular in Iran at the time of the **Iranian Revolution**. It shares many similarities with the Christian liberation theology with its focus on political activism and social justice. It is considered to be a left-leaning form of **Islam**. Its main proponent has perhaps been **Ali Shari'ati**. Contemporary liberation theologists include Hasan Hanafi.

Libya (Great Socialist People's Libyan Arab Jamahiriyah)

Al-Jumahiriyah al-Arabiyah al-Libiyah ash-Shabiyah al-Ishtirakiyah al-Uzma

Libya is located in North Africa, bordering the **Mediterranean** Sea, between Egypt and Algeria. It borders Tunisia to the east, Niger and Chad to the south and Sudan to the south-west. More than 90% of the country is desert or semi-desert. Its total area is 1,759,540 sq km. The capital is **Tripoli**. For administrative purposes Libya was formerly divided into 25 municipalities (*baladiyah*, plural *baladiyat*): Ajdabiya, Al-'Aziziyah, Al-Fatih, Al-Jabal al-Akhdar, Al-Jufrah, Al-Khums, Al-Kufrah, An-Nuqat al-Khams, Ash-Shati', Awbari, Az-Zawiyah, Banghazi, Darnah, Ghadamis,

Gharyan, Misratah, Murzuq, Sabha, Sawfajjin, Surt, Tarabulus, Tarhunah, Tubruq, Yafran and Zlitan. These have now been replaced by 13 regions.

The population is 5,368,585, of which **Berbers** and Arabs constitute 97%. The total includes 662,669 non-nationals, of which, in July 2002, an estimated 500,000 or more were north Africans living in Libya. The religious composition of the country is Muslim (official, mainly **Sunni**) 97% and 'other' 3%. The official language is **Arabic**. Italian and English are widely understood in the major cities.

Political profile

Libya is a republic (*Jamahiriya*—a 'state of the masses'), governed, in theory, by the populace through local councils. In practice, ultimate control rests with Col **Muammar Abu Minyar al-Qaddafi** and his close associates. The head of state since 1 September 1969 has been Revolutionary Leader Col al-Qaddafi. Qaddafi holds no official title, but is *de facto* head of state. The head of government is the Secretary of the General People's Committee (Premier), Mubarak ash-Shamekh (since 2 March 2000).

The General People's Committee is established by the General People's Congress. National elections are held indirectly, through a hierarchy of about 2000 people's committees; the head of government is elected by the General People's Congress—the most recent election was held on 2 March 2000. The legislature is the unicameral General People's Congress whose members are elected indirectly through a hierarchy of people's committees.

The legal system is based on the Italian civil law system and **Islamic Law**. There is no constitutional provision for judicial review of legislative acts. There is a Supreme Court and separate religious courts. Libya has not accepted compulsory International Court of Justice jurisdiction. Political parties were banned in 1971. Various opposition groups with almost negligible memberships function clandestinely, or from exile in Egypt and Sudan. Political dissidents, including Islamist militants, have been heavily suppressed. Some Libyan dissidents abroad have also been murdered.

Media

The Libyan media are under the control of the regime and are its mouthpiece. There is one state-controlled television station. Satellite television and the internet are widely available, but are heavily censored. There are two radio services, one state-controlled and one independent.

There are four daily newspapers, including *Al-Fajr al-Jadid*. In 2002 there was one internet service provider. In 2001 there were 20,000 internet users.

History

Since he took power in a 1969 **military** coup, Col Qaddafi has imposed his own political system—a combination of **socialism** and **Islam**—which he calls the **Third International Theory**. Regarding himself as a revolutionary leader, in the 1970s and 1980s he used **oil** funds to promote his ideology outside Libya, even supporting subversives and terrorists abroad to hasten the end of **Marxism** and capitalism. Libyan military adventures failed: the prolonged foray of Libyan troops into the Aouzou Strip in northern Chad, for example, was finally repulsed in 1987. Libyan support for **terrorism** decreased after UN sanctions were imposed in 1992. Those sanctions were suspended in April 1999. Since then Libya has been drawn gradually back into diplmatic and economic relations with the international community.

International relations

Chadian rebels from the Aouzou region reside in Libya. Libya claims about 19,400 sq km in Niger as well as part of south-eastern Algeria in currently dormant disputes.

Libya, economy

Libya's command-economy depends primarily upon revenues from the **oil** sector, which contributes practically all export earnings and about one-quarter of the country's gross domestic product (GDP). These oil revenues and a small population give Libya one of the highest per caput levels of GDP in Africa, but little of this income flows down to the lower orders of society. Import restrictions and inefficient resource allocations have led to periodic shortages of basic goods and foodstuffs. The non-oil manufacturing and construction sectors, which account for about 20% of GDP, have expanded from processing mostly agricultural products to include the production of petrochemicals, iron, steel and aluminum. Climatic conditions and poor soils severely limit agricultural output, and Libya imports about 75% of its food. Higher oil prices in 1999 and 2000 led to an increase in export revenues, which improved macroeconomic balances and helped to stimulate the economy. The suspension of UN sanctions in 1999 also boosted growth. In January 2002 a 51% devaluation of the official exchange rate of the dinar was a positive fiscal move, although it will lead to higher inflation.

Strengths

Oil and **gas** production. High investment in downstream industries such as petro-chemicals, refineries, fertilizers and aluminium smelting.

Weaknesses

Over-reliance on oil. Most food is imported. Reliance on foreign labour. Lack of **water**. Unreliable reputation internationally.

Libyan Ba'athist Party – *see* Ba'athist Party (Libya)

Libyan Change and Reform Movement

Libyan opposition party. Breakaway group from the **National Front for the Salvation of Libya**.

Libyan Conservatives Party

Libyan opposition party, founded in 1996.

Libyan Constitutional Grouping

Libyan opposition group.

Libyan Democratic Authority

Libyan opposition party, founded in 1993.

Libyan Democratic Conference

Libyan opposition party, founded in 1992.

Libyan Democratic Movement

Libyan opposition party, founded in 1977. An external group.

Libyan Islamic Fighting Group

Al-Jama'a al-Islamiyyah al-Muqatilah bi-Libya

Emerged in 1995 among Libyans who had fought against Soviet forces in Afghanistan. It declared the Government of Libyan leader Col **Qaddafi** to be un-Islamic and pledged to overthrow it. Some members maintain a strictly anti-Qaddafi focus and organize against Libyan Government interests, but others are aligned with **Osama bin Laden**'s **al-Qa'ida** organization or are active in the international *mujahidin* network. The group was designated for asset freezing under E. O. 13224 and UN Security Council Resolution 1333 in September 2001. It claimed responsibility for an unsuccessful attempt to assassinate Col Qaddafi in 1996 and engaged Libyan security forces in armed clashes in the mid- and late 1990s. It continues to target Libyan interests and may engage in sporadic clashes with Libyan security forces. It probably maintains a clandestine presence in Libya, but since the late 1990s many of its members have fled to various Middle Eastern and European countries.

Libyan Movement for Change and Reform

Libyan opposition movement, founded in 1994 and based in the United Kingdom.

Libyan National Alliance

Libyan opposition movement, founded in 1980, based in **Cairo**, Egypt.

Libyan National Democratic Rally

Libyan opposition grouping.

Likud

In **Hebrew**: 'unity' or 'consolidation'. Israeli political alliance formed in 1973. It crystallized at the time of the 1977 elections. It consisted of the **Gahal** alliance (**Herut** and the **Liberal Party** of Israel), the La'am (For the Nation) alliance (the **State List** and the Free Centre), **Achdut** (a one-man faction in the **Knesset**) and Shlomozion, **Ariel Sharon**'s former party. Likud came to power in 1977, ousting the Labour government for the first time since Israel became independent. Although it retained its government position after the 1981 elections, its majority in the Knesset seldom exceeded two or three votes. La'am, founded in 1976, left the coalition before the 1984 election and its leader, Yigael Hurwitz, formed his own party, Ometz. In 1984 Likud lost its majority and joined with the **Labour Alignment** to form a government of national unity in which it shared power and ministerial position. **TAMI**, formed in 1981, which represents the interests of Sephardic Jews, joined Likud in June 1987. In 1988 Herut and the Liberal Party formally merged to form the Likud-National Liberal Movement. Likud is centre-right, strongly nationalistic and assertive in foreign policy. Members tend to share a strong belief that the territories occupied by Israel in the **Six-Day War** of 1967—Sinai, the **Gaza Strip**, the **West Bank**, and the **Golan Heights**—should be incorporated into the State of Israel, and in 2002 it voted against the acceptance of a Palestinian state regardless of the conditions. In elections to the Knesset held in May 1999 Likud received 14% of the vote and obtained 19 seats, becoming the second largest bloc after **One Israel**. It is currently led by Ariel Sharon and dominates the government.

Literacy

Literacy rates are low relative to average per caput incomes in much of the region, but there have been significant improvements in some countries in the last 50 years. In Iran the literacy rate rose from 51% to 77% in 1980–2000. **Women**'s literacy rates remain strikingly low and reflect severe gender inequality throughout the region, although here too there have been important gains.

Lmrabet, Ali

Prominent Moroccan newspaper editor, jailed for three years after an appeal in June 2003, on charges of insulting the king, **Mohammed VI**, 'undermining the

monarchy' and 'threatening the integrity of the national territory' on the basis of several articles, cartoons and a photomontage that had appeared in his newspapers. The articles included extracts from an interview, already published in a Spanish newspaper, with a former political prisoner advocating the right of self-determination for the **Sahrawis** in the **Western Sahara** and a cartoon commenting on the parliamentary approval of the budget for the royal household. He was also fined 20,000 dirhams and a ban was imposed on his newspapers. He was pardoned in January 2004 by royal decree after spending more than seven months in prison. He was freed on 'humanitarian grounds'. Around 25 other political prisoners were also pardoned at the same time, including prisoners of conscience.

Lockerbie

On 21 December 1988 Pan-Am flight 103 to New York exploded in mid-air over Lockerbie, a small town in Scotland. All 259 people on board died in the crash. Libya was accused of involvement and, after numerous delays, eventually, in 1999, surrendered two suspects for trial. In 2001 a Scottish court convicted one of the Libyan accused and sentenced him to life imprisonment. The evidence and the responsibility for the crash remain disputed. There is some evidence to suggest that the Palestinian group, the **Popular Front for the Liberation of Palestine-General Command**, might have been involved. Libya, however, agreed in August 2003 to pay US $4m. to the families of each of those killed. The UN Security Council immediately commenced the removal of the sanctions that had been applied against Libya. However, the families of the victims were not able to receive the full amount of compensation from Libya until the USA lifted its unilateral sanctions, which it was still not prepared to do. The USA did not block the Security Council vote, but retained its own sanctions because of Libya's alleged human rights violations, its role in perpetuating regional conflicts and its pursuit of **weapons of mass destruction**. US sanctions have been applied since 1986, when the USA, under President Reagan, bombed **Tripoli** in retaliation against alleged Libyan **terrorism**. More sanctions were imposed in 1996 when the D'Amato Act targeted Libya and Iran for their alleged support of terrorism and efforts to acquire weapons of mass destruction. In 2001 the Act was renewed until 2006. If the USA were to lift sanctions on Libya, the Lockerbie relatives would receive a further $4m. If Libya is removed from the US Department of State's list of sponsors of terrorism, they would receive an additional $2m. and compensation would thus total $10m. in all. If the USA does not lift sanctions before May 2004, the families will receive only $1m. more—$5m. in total. Although the Government of Libya formally accepted responsibility for the Lockerbie explosion in return for being allowed to rejoin the international community after a decade of isolation, there are some (including Libya's Prime Minister, Shukri Ghanem) who have indicated that Libya was not actually responsible.

Ould Louly, Lt-Col Mohammed Mahmoud

Head of state of Mauritania from June 1979 until January 1980, when he was overthrown by **Lt-Col Khouna Ould Haidalla**.

Loya Jirga (Afghanistan)

A traditional Afghan Grand Council; a forum unique to Afghanistan in which, traditionally, tribal elders—**Pashtuns**, **Tajiks**, **Hazaras** and **Uzbeks**—have come together to settle inter-tribal disputes. Similar in conception to the Persian *majlis* or Arab '*shura*', i.e. a consultative assembly. A Loya Jirga was called, following the **Bonn Agreement** of December 2001, to assist in the establishment of a transitional government for Afghanistan. It met on 13 June 2003 in **Kabul** and elected **Hamid Karzai** to head the Transitional Government. About 1,500 delegates from all over Afghanistan took part; more than 1,000 were elected in a two-stage process. Each district elected 20 people, who then held a secret vote to select one person to represent the whole district. Each of the country's 362 districts had at least one seat, with further seats allotted for every 22,000 people. No group was excluded from the assembly, but anyone alleged to have committed acts of **terrorism** or suspected of involvement in **drugs**, human rights abuses, war crimes, plunder or the theft of public property was barred from attending. Of the remainder of the seats, a total of 160 were allocated to **women**. Nomads, **refugees**, academics, cultural institutions, social organizations and religious scholars were also represented. The **Taliban** movement was not represented, but groups which shared their political, social and cultural views sent representatives. Even among the carefully-screened delegates to the *loya jirga* there was considerable criticism of the anti-democratic character of procedures, their manipulation by foreign observers, and the oppressive presence of regional warlords and undercover intelligence officials. On 17 June more than one-half of the delegates abandoned the assembly, frustrated at the lack of substance in the discussion, critical of 'foreign influence' and angry over threats and intimidation. At the close of business on 19 June no agreement had been reached on the format of a parliament, the means for establishing it, or even the composition of a group delegated to make a decision as to whether a parliament would have legislative powers or be advisory only. On this, as on other matters, considerable powers were left in the hands of Karzai, who has been accused of being an American puppet (having spent some years in the USA), dependent on the political and economic support of the major powers. Finally, late on 19 June, as he was being sworn in as transitional head of state, Karzai made his much-awaited announcement. It was little more than a token gesture—14 of approximately 25 ministers as well as three vice-presidents and the country's chief justice were presented to the *loya jirga* for approval. There was no debate or formal vote.

Loya Jirga (December 2003)

The Grand Council of Afghanistan met in December 2003 to approve a new constitution for Afghanistan. Of the 500 delegates, one-fifth were **women**. The draft constitution favours a centralized presidential system, but **Hamid Karzai**, President of the Transitional Government, made it clear that he would not contest elections scheduled to be held in the following year if the *Loya Jirga* preferred a parliamentary system. Presidential elections were planned for 2004 and parliamentary elections for 2005. A lack of funds, however, delayed preparations for voter registration, which was supposed to begin in October 2003 and continue until March 2004. Voter registraton required US $80m., but the response from those states helping to reconstruct Afghanistan after two decades of war was slow. Another issue was what kind of legal code would be adopted. The 1964 Constitution called for laws 'in keeping with the principles of **Islam**'; the new draft refers to 'laws in keeping with Islam'.

Luristan

Area of Iran largely inhabited by the **Lurs**.

Lurs

A tribal ethnic and linguistic **minority** group in Iran, **Shi'a** for the most part, numbering 500,000–800,000.

M

Maarach

The Alignment, Israel

A Labour alignment resulting from an alliance of the **Israel Labour Party** and **Mapam**, formed in 1969.

MABOT—Mina al-Bakr Oil Terminal

Iraqi **oil** terminal currently exporting some US $60m.-worth of crude oil daily under the direction of US **Halliburton** subsidiary, **Kellogg, Brown & Root**. Currently projected to export $21,000m.-worth of oil annually, MABOT will double production over the next year. MABOT is Iraq's main source of foreign exchange for reconstruction. MABOT draws oil from a pumping station outside the town of al-Faw, that in turn feeds from the Zubayr and Rumaylah oil fields.

McMahon, Sir Henry

Replaced Kitchener as British High Commissioner of Egypt in 1914. He embarked on a secret exchange of letters with Sherif Hussein of **Mecca**—known as the Hussein-**MacMahon Correspondence**—on the future independence of the Arabs in the **Ottoman Empire**.

McMahon Correspondence

Ten letters passed between Sir Henry McMahon, British High Commissioner in **Cairo**, Egypt, and Sherif Hussein of **Mecca** in July 1915–March 1916. Hussein offered Arab help in the war against the **Ottoman Empire** if Britain would support the principle of an independent Arab state. In his letter of 24 October 1915, McMahon appears clearly to assure Hussein that, excluding certain areas (the two districts of Mersina and Alexandretta and portions of Syria lying to the west of the districts of **Damascus**, Homs, **Hamah** and **Aleppo**) but as far as concerns 'those regions lying within those frontiers wherein Great Britain is free to act without detriment to the interest of her ally, France', Great Britain was 'prepared to recognise and support the independence of the Arabs in all the regions within the limits demanded by the Sherif of Mecca'. Furthermore, Great Britain would 'guarantee the Holy Places against all external aggression and will recognise their inviolability'. He ended the letter by stating that he was 'convinced that this declaration will assure you beyond all possible doubt of the sympathy of Great Britain towards the aspirations of her friends the Arabs and will result in a firm and lasting alliance, the immediate results of which will be the expulsion of the Turks from the Arab countries and the freeing of the Arab peoples from the Turkish yoke. . .'.

Madani, Abbasi

Referred to widely in the foreign language press as Madani, as though this were his surname, in fact Madani is his given name and Abbasi his family name. Madani was a founder member of the **Front de libération nationale** (National Liberation Front) in 1954 and spent most of the Algerian war of independence in prison. He became a university teacher after independence and subsequently obtained a doctorate from the Institute of Education at the University of London in the mid-1970s. Married to an Englishwoman, he personifies the middle-class, middle-aged and pragmatic element within the **FIS—Front islamique du salut** (Islamic Salvation Front). In the late 1970s helped found Islamic welfare organizations in the slums to meet the growing needs of the impoverished. He became politically active and organized protests against the Algerian government for which he was jailed for two years in 1982. In 1989 he assumed the leadership of the FIS, an umbrella group of some six organizations seeking Islamic social, political and economic reform. The FIS achieved victories in local elections and was on the verge of winning national legislative elections in 1992 when the **military** took power and aborted the electoral process. The FIS was banned and Madani was arrested together with other Islamic leaders. The Algerian civil war erupted as a result with radicalized Islamic groups, especially the **GIA—Groupe islamique armé** (Armed Islamic Group), resorting to violence. Madani was released in 1997 and is now under house arrest.

Madrasas

Although *madrasa* in contemporary Arabic simply means 'school', the term has come to imply religious (or Koranic) schools. Many tend to provide an ideological as well as a theological introduction to **Islam** and other subjects, and encourage the adoption of an essentially **political Islam**. This was the case along the Afghan–Pakistan border and in the Afghan refugee camps from which the **Taliban** is thought to have sprung.

Madrid Peace Conference

Official 'peace talks' between Israel and Jordanian-Palestinian representatives held in Madrid, Spain, in 1991.

Madrid process

The Madrid process of 1991, which took place at the **Madrid Peace Conference** while secret talks were under way in Oslo, Norway, was the result of a US initiative in the aftermath of the **Gulf War (1991)**. It involved high-level discussions between an Israeli delegation and another comprising representatives of Jordan and the **Palestine Liberation Organization**. The **Palestinians** were attracted by an Israeli promise, enshrined in Article 5, Clause 3 of the **Oslo Agreements**, that after five years of catering for Israeli security needs, the main Palestinian demands would be subject to negotiation in preparation for a final agreement. Meanwhile the Palestinians were offered the opportunity to form the **Palestinian National Authority**.

Mafdal

Founded in 1956, the **National Religious Party** in Israel is also known as Miflaqa Datit-leumit, hence Mafdal. It has played a part in most government coalitions in Israel. A splinter group, under the name of **Meimad**, developed within it in 1988, reacting against what it considered to be a move to the right. Increased its representation in the **Knesset** in 1988 from five seats to six.

MAFTA

Mediterranean Arab Free Trade Area, proposed at a meeting in Morocco in May 2001, by Egypt, Jordan, Morocco, and Tunisia—all members of the **Euro-Mediterranean Partnership**—as a cornerstone of a future, larger Arab-Mediterranean Free Trade Area.

Maghreb

In **Arabic**: 'the West'. Arabic term for the north-west of Africa. It is generally applied to all of Morocco, Algeria, and Tunisia, but, strictly, only refers to the area of the three countries between the high ranges of the Atlas Mountains and the **Mediterranean** Sea. Isolated from the rest of the continent by the Atlas Mountains and the Sahara, the Maghreb is more closely related in terms of climate, landforms, population, economy, and history to northern Mediterranean areas than to the rest of Africa. Thus the Arab North African states have formed the **Arab Maghreb Union**.

Mahdi

A holy man or prophet, whose coming is often foretold in the scriptures. A title adopted by those who wish to claim religious authority.

Mahdi's Army – *see* Jaish al-Mahdi

Mahmoud, Abed Hamid

Saddam Hussain's personal secretary and former bodyguard. Reputedly one of the most important members of Saddam's inner circle, he was captured by **coalition** forces in June 2003.

Al-Majid, Ali Hassan

A cousin of **Saddam Hussain**, known as 'Chemical Ali' for his role in poison gas attacks on Kurdish villages in 1988, and fifth on the US 'most wanted' list of supporters of Saddam Hussain's regime. He was captured by **coalition** forces in August 2003.

Majlis

Arabic (and Persian) word meaning 'council'.

Majlis ad-Dawlah

Council of State of Oman, established in December 1997, in accordance with the basic statute of the state. An advisory body, comprising 41 members appointed by the Sultan. Its function is to liaise between the government and the people of Oman.

Majlis-e Khobregan

Council of Experts, Iran

Iranian institution which selects the Wali Faqih (Senior Cleric). Elections were first held in December 1982 to elect a Council of Experts which was eventually to choose a successor to Ayatollah **Khomeini** after his death. The Constitution provides for a three- or five-man body to assume the leadership of the country if there is no recognized successor on the death of the Wali Faqih. The Council comprises 86 clerics. Elections to a third term were held in October 1998. The Speaker of the Council is Ayatollah Ali Meshkini and the Deputy Speaker **Hojatoleslam Ali Akbar Hashemi Rafsanjani**.

Majlis ash-Shura (Jordan, Algeria, Saudi Arabia)

In **Arabic** *majlis* means 'council' or 'parliament'; *shura* means 'consultation'. Generally, a Consultative Assembly or Council. In some countries within the region it operates very like a National Assembly, having the powers of a legislature and consisting of directly elected representatives of the people; in others, notably in the **Gulf states**, it is largely advisory or consultative, and may consist largely or entirely of nominees and appointees, or of individuals representing the population only indirectly.

Majlis-e-Shora-ye Eslami
Islamic Consultative Assembly, Iran

The Iranian parliament, originally established in 1906–07. It is the oldest elected legislative body in the **Middle East**. The 24th **Majlis** (1975–79) was the last to be elected under the Shah. The Majlis is now the Consultative Assembly of the Islamic Republic of Iran. Re-established in 1980 with 270 members, each elected for four-year terms, the Majlis is empowered to make laws and approve international agreements. It is also authorized to conduct investigations into all of the affairs of the country. It is by no means a 'rubber stamp' for the government; there is often spirited debate and on occasion the Majlis has refused to confirm some of the Prime Minister's choices for Cabinet posts. The Assembly normally holds open sessions. Elections to the sixth Majlis were held in 2000. The successful candidates were generally associated either with Iran's 'conservative' tendency or with the 'reformists'. The sixth Majlis was one in which, for the first time, so-called 'reformists' were estimated to have achieved a working majority. In the 2004 elections for the seventh Majlis, however, many 'reformist' candidates were blocked and prevented from standing. The 'conservatives', therefore, were able to maintain a majority. The divisions within the Majlis reflect a growing tension between the two tendencies in wider Iranian society.

Al-Majlis al'Ala li'l-Thawra al-Islamiyya fi'l-Iraq – *see* Supreme Council for the Islamic Revolution in Iraq

Majma'-e Niruha-ye Khat-e Imam
Assembly of the Followers of the Imam's List

Iranian political organization established in the late 1990s after the election of President **Khatami**.

MAK – *see* Afghan Service Bureau

Maki – *see* Israel Communist Party

Makkawi, Mohamed (also known as Said al-Adel)

Makkawi was a colonel in the Egyptian army's special forces before joining **al-Qa'ida**. He is believed to have trained and fought with the Somali forces in Mogadishu in 1993, when 18 US army rangers were killed, and he helped to plan the 1998 attacks on US embassies in Dar es Salaam, Tanzania and in Nairobi, Kenya. He was also the key planner in the attack on USS *Cole* in **Aden** harbour.

Maktab al-Khidmat lil Mujahiddin al-Arab – *see* Afghan Service Bureau

al-Maktum, Sheikh Maktum ibn Rashid

Sheikh Maktum is ruler of Dubai, United Arab Emirates, having acceded in 1990.

Maliki Code

One of the four legal codes of **Sunni Islam**. The Malikis are found mainly in North Africa, in Upper Egypt and Sudan, in the **Maghreb** and the Sahelian countries, and in Nigeria.

MAN – *see* Movement of Arab Nationalists

Manama

Capital of Bahrain, with a population of 153,395 in 2001.

Mandate for Palestine

On 24 July 1922 the Council of the League of Nations agreed to entrust to a Mandatory, selected by the Principal Allied Powers, the administration of the territory of Palestine, which had formerly been part of the Turkish (Ottoman) Empire. Britain was selected as the Mandatory power and accepted the Mandate in respect of Palestine. Recognition was given to the historical connection of the Jewish people with Palestine and to the grounds for reconstituting their national home in that country. It was agreed that the Mandatory power should have full powers of legislation and of administration, save as they might be limited by the terms of the Mandate.

Mapai—Mifleget Poalei Yisrael

Mapai, the Labour Party of **Eretz Israel** or the Israeli Workers' Party, originated with the union in 1930 of two smaller parties which had established the trade union federation, the **Histadrut**, in 1920. Reformist, advocating alliance with Britain and the Zionist right, it increased its share of the vote from 42% in 1931 to 59% in 1944. Mapai came to control the Histadrut as well as the National Assembly. Many notable Israeli political figures were associated with Mapai in its early years—including **David Ben-Gurion**, **Moshe Sharett** (Shertok), **Golda Meir** (Myerson) and **Moshe Dayan**. It merged with **Achdut HaAvoda**, originally the party of Ben-Gurion in the 1920s, between 1930 and 1944, after which the two split, largely over Mapai's gradualist policies and general exclusion of more radical elements. The two parties joined up again in 1965. After Israel was established in 1948, Mapai consistently won the largest number of votes in elections to the **Knesset**. It was the leading member of all government coalitions and ordinarily filled the key portfolios of defence, foreign affairs and finance, as well as the position of Prime Minister. However, support for Mapai gradually declined, from a high point of 53% in 1949. Ben-Gurion, Moshe Dayan and **Shimon Peres** left the party in 1965, partly owing to dissatisfaction with the leadership of **Levi Eshkol** and to more strategic differences, to form **Rafi**. Rafi stood alone for only one election (in 1965) before it merged again with Mapai in 1968, to form the **Israel Labour Party.** Support for Mapai had fallen to 26% by 1977, but recovered to 37% in 1981. In 1988 it stabilized at 30%.

Mapam—Mifleget HaPoalim HaMeuhedet

Mapam, or the **United Workers' Party**, was established in 1948 when HaShomar HaTzair (Young Guard) and Poalei Zion Smole (Left-wing Workers of Zion) merged with radical elements from **Achdut HaAvoda**. From the outset Mapam was more Marxist than **Mapai**. The former Achdut HaAvoda members left Mapam in 1954 because of the latter's pro-Soviet stance, support for a binational state and acceptance of Arabs as members. Its share in the vote in national elections (6.6% and eight seats in the **Knesset** in 1965) declined steadily before it joined the **Israel Labour Party** in the **Alignment** for the 1969 elections (although it had entered government in 1967). It ended its alliance with Labour in September 1984 over the issue of the formation by **Shimon Peres** of a government of national unity with **Likud**. It paid dearly for this rupture, with the number of its members in the Knesset falling from six in 1984 to three in 1988.

Maraboutism

A term derived from the French word for the cult of saints or holy men (*marabtin*) widespread throughout the rural areas of the **Maghreb** and parts of French West Africa (e.g. Senegal) in particular.

March 23 (23 Mars)

Moroccan left-wing political group. Established in 1970 following a split in the **UNFP**, March 23 was led by Mohamed Ben Said. In 1978 and 1979 it split over attitudes towards the **Union socialiste des forces populaires** (USFP) and the **Western Sahara** issue. One faction joined the USFP; other factions remained outlawed, and some of their members were jailed for their beliefs. The March 23 group is active and influential within the UNEM.

Mardom

Loyal opposition party created by the Shah of Iran in 1957 as part of a two-party system that he established to suggest the existence of a significant degree of political debate. The pro-government party was **Mellioun**, which was replaced in 1963 by **Iran-e Novin**. Both pro-government and opposition parties were led by trusted friends of the Shah. There were also a few smaller parties of lesser importance, such as the Pan-Iranists, but serious opposition was outlawed.

Maronite Catholic Church

The church of the Maronite Christians in Lebanon and Syria.

Maronites

Community of Christian Arabs in Lebanon and Syria. The Maronites have been a distinct community since the 7th century. In the 19th century massacres of Maronites by the **Druze** gave rise to French intervention, which marked the beginning of France's continuing influence in Lebanon and Syria. Elements of the Maronite community formed the fascist **Phalange** in Lebanon, and fought in the **Lebanese civil war**.

Marrakesh

Major historic city in the south of Morocco at the foot of the High Atlas mountains. Capital of the Almoravid dynasty in the 11th century, the Almohad dynasty in the 12th century and the Sa'adian dynasty in the 16th century, Marrakesh has always been an important link between Morocco and the 'south'—the Sahara and sub-Saharan Africa.

Marsh Arabs (Iraq)

A distinctive population living in marshlands formed by the **Tigris** and **Euphrates** rivers in south-eastern Iraq. With their way of life—believed to have changed relatively little over the preceding 5,000 years—increasingly threatened by the draining of the marshes for agricultural purposes during the 1960s and 1970s and by political repression during the 1980s and 1990s, this predominantly **Shi'a** Muslim population has been declining in recent decades. It is estimated that some 500,000 Marsh Arabs once inhabited a freshwater marshland region covering at least 20,000 sq km. Until 15 years ago a community of 250,000 Marsh Arabs remained. The marsh terrain was relatively inaccessible to security forces, provided shelter to political opponents of the Iraqi regime and army deserters and was the location of some of Iraq's richest **oil** deposits. Consequently the regime of **Saddam Hussain** systematically bombarded villages and carried out widespread arbitrary arrests, acts of torture, abductions and summary executions. Many of the region's inhabitants were forced to emigrate and many have become **refugees**, living in camps further to the east across the border in Iran. This has reduced the Marsh Arabs' number to as few as 40,000 in their original home. In addition, large-scale government drainage projects have virtually destroyed the Marsh Arab economy. It is believed that there are at least 100,000 internally displaced Marsh Arabs and another 40,000 living in Iran as refugees. The area once constituted the largest wetlands ecosystem in the **Middle East**, (the UN has called its destruction one of the world's greatest environmental disasters). Since the US-led **coalition**'s occupation of Iraq, some of the Marsh Arab refugees have returned to try to re-establish their livelihoods in the wetlands.

Martyrdom

There is a long tradition in **Islam**, particularly in **Shi'a** Islam, dating back to Hussein and Ali, of martyrdom. Those who die in the context of a religious act—in *jihad*, for example—may become martyrs. In recent years the use of 'suicide bombers' to launch attacks on buildings and people has been justified in terms of the 'tradition of jihad' and martyrdom. In 2001 the association of Palestinian religious scholars granted its sanction to martyrdom. They declared suicide attacks to be part of a just war, because they 'destroy the enemy and put fear in the hearts of the enemy, provoke the enemy, shake the foundations of its establishment and make it think of leaving Palestine . . . [They] will reduce the number of Jewish immigrants to Palestine, and will make [the Israelis] suffer financially'. According to Dr **Ayman az-Zawahiri**, the leader of Egyptian **Islamic Jihad**, 'the method of martyrdom operation [is] the most successful way of inflicting damage against the opponent and the least costly to the *mujahidin* in terms of casualties'. This appalling cost-benefit analysis can be applied to the attacks of 11 September 2001 in the USA to show that a budget of US $500,000 and 19 hijackers willing to give their lives for the cause were sufficient to kill some 3,000 people and inflict a permanent scar on the American psyche. It has, however, also been responsible for the launch of an international 'war against terror', regarded by many as a 'clash of civilizations', with undoubtedly far-reaching but as yet unpredictable implications.

Marxism

The influence of Marxism in the region has been significant largely in the ideological and political formation of small left-wing groups and movements. Relatively few states have adopted classical Marxist-Leninist ideology and principles, the possible exception being the **People's Democratic Republic of Yemen**. The establishment of Communist Party branches took place in most of the colonial territories from the 1920s onwards, but in most cases they remained very much minority parties. **Arab nationalism** remained a dominant ideological and political force throughout the period from the 1920s to the 1960s and most regimes or dominant parties adopted versions of Arab nationalism, which tended to espouse an authoritarian **populism** or 'national **socialism**', rather than the classic Marxist-Leninist 'socialism' as a transitional phase in a process of transformation leading to communism. Communist parties were often marginalized by such dominant movements and proscribed or banned when they came to power. **Military** governments, like the various civilian populist 'Arab socialist' governments, have also tended to emphasize national unity and to identify class-based politics as 'divisive'. During the 1970s and 1980s the rise of **political Islam** and Islamism sometimes generated efforts to reconcile Marxism and Islam—interesting examples of such efforts are to be seen in the writings of **Ali Shari'ati** in Iran and of several Egyptian intellectuals, such as Adel Hussein.

Marxist Leninist Communist Party (MLCP)

Illegal opposition party in Turkey. *Atilim* is a Turkish newspaper sympathetic to the MLCP.

Masada

The site of a heroic struggle by Jews in Roman times.

Mashad – *see* Meshed

Mashreq

The eastern region of the **Arab World**. It includes Egypt, Jordan, Palestine, Lebanon, Syria and Iraq.

Masoud, Ahmed Shah

Legendary **Tajik** military leader who controlled the strip of northern Afghanistan that bordered Turkmenistan, Uzbekistan and Tajikistan. He was the major figure in the **Northern Alliance** and the **United Front** until he was assassinated by suicide bombers posing as journalists two days before the attacks on the **World Trade Center** and the Pentagon in 2001. His main base was in the **Panjsher Valley**, north of **Kabul**, where he fought first against Soviet forces and then those of the **Taliban** for more than two decades.

Maududi, Maulana

Pakistani Islamic thinker. He expanded the concept of *jahiliyya* and was highly influential on the Indian subcontinent. His theories were influential in the thinking of **Sayyid Qutb** and **Osama bin Laden**.

Mauritania, Islamic Republic of

Al-Jumhuriyah al-Islamiyah al-Muritaniyah

Mauritania is bordered to the north by the **Western Sahara** and Algeria, to the east and south-east by Mali, to the south by Senegal, and to the west by 754 km of Atlantic coastline, stretching from the Senegal river to the peninsula of Nouadhibou and Guera. The northern three-quarters of this vast country (with an area of 1.03m. sq km) consists largely of the Sahara (desert) while the southern quarter is essentially Sahelian (semi-desert). Most of the population is concentrated in the cities of **Nouakchott** (the capital) and Nouadhibou, and along the Senegal river in the southern part of the country. The country is divided into 12 administrative regions and the capital district: Adrar, Assaba, Brakna, Dakhlet Nouadhibou, Gorgol, Guidimaka, Hodh Ech Chargui, Hodh El Gharbi, Inchiri, Nouakchott (capital district), Tagant, Tiris Zemmour and Trarza. In July 2002 the population was estimated at 2,828,858, of which 40% are mixed Moors and Black Africans (*harratin*), 30% are so-called 'white' Moors (*beidane*) and 30% are Blacks. With regard to religion, the entire population is **Sunni** Muslim. The official languages are Hassaniya **Arabic** and Wolof. Pulaar, Soninke and French are also spoken.

Political profile

Mauritania is a republic. The head of state is President **Maaouiya Ould Sidi Ahmed Taya**, who first came to power in December 1984 through a *coup d'état*, but was elected as President in the first multiparty elections, held in January 1992. The President is elected by popular vote for a six-year term of office. Presidential elections were held in December 1997 and December 2003, and Ould Taya was re-elected on both occasions. The Prime Minister is appointed by the President. The current Prime Minister is Cheikh El Avia Ould Mohamed Khouna (since 17 November 1998). There is a Council of Ministers. The legislature consists of the Assembly of Sheikhs (**Majlis** ash-Shuyukh) comprising 56 seats, to some of which elections are held every two years; members are elected by municipal leaders to serve six-year terms) and the National Assembly (Majlis al-Watani)—comprising 81 seats; members are elected by popular vote to serve five-year terms. Elections for the Assembly of Sheikhs were last held in April 2002 (the next are scheduled to be held in April 2004), and those for the National Assembly were last held in October 2001 (the next being scheduled for 2006). The judiciary consists of the Supreme Court and Courts of Appeal. The legal system is a combination of **Shari'a** and French civil law. Political parties were legalized by the Constitution that was ratified in July 1991, although politics remains strongly tribally-based.

Political organizations

- Action for Change; Leader **Messoud Ould Boulkheir**
- Alliance for Justice and Democracy; Leader Kebe Abdoulaye
- Democratic and Social Republican Party (ruling party); President **Maaouiya Ould Sidi Ahmed Taya**
- Mauritanian Party for Renewal and Concord; Leader Molaye El Hassen Ould Jiyid
- Movement of Democratic Forces; Leader Mohamed Jemil Mansour
- National Union for Democracy and Development; Leader Tidjane Koita

- Party for Liberty, Equality and Justice; Leader Daouda M'bagniga
- Popular Front; Leader Ch'bih Ould Cheikh Malainine
- Popular Progress Alliance; Leader Mohamed El Hafed Ould Ismael
- Popular Social and Democratic Union; Leader Mohamed Mahmoud Ould Mah
- Progress Force Union or UFP; Leader Mohamed Ould Maouloud
- Rally of Democratic Forces; Leader Ahmed Ould Daddah
- Rally for Democracy and Unity; Leader Ahmed Ould Sidi Baba
- Union for Democracy and Progress; Leader Naha Mint Mouknass
- The Action for Change party was banned in January 2002. The leader of the Movement of Democratic Forces, Mohamed Jemil Mansour, was arrested in May 2003 and charged with treason, 'using places of worship for subversive propaganda and of having connection with foreign networks'. Mansour's arrest was one of a number that took place in the aftermath of bomb attacks in Saudi Arabia and Morocco.

Other political organizations include:

- General Confederation of Mauritanian Workers; Sec.-Gen. Abdallahi Ould Mohamed
- Independent Confederation of Mauritanian Workers; Leader Samory Ould Beye
- Mauritanian Workers' Union; Sec.-Gen. Mohamed Ely Ould Brahim

Media

The press is heavily censored. The broadcast media are state-owned. There are three daily newspapers, of which the state-owned *Chaab* is the most widely read. There is one state-owned television service and one state-owned radio station. In 2001 there were five internet service providers and 7,500 internet users.

History

In 1891 France and Spain agreed a boundary between their respective possessions in north-west Africa and in 1898 two major Moorish groups accepted French arbitration in a local 'civil war', increasing French influence north of the Senegal river and paving the way for French penetration between 1902 and 1904 of the Trarza and the Brakna regions, in the south-west of what is now Mauritania. It was not until 1934, however, that the entire territory was pacified. During the colonial period, St Louis on the Senegal river was the capital for the French administration of Mauritania, which constituted an 'economic appendix' to Senegal. For much of the colonial period, Mauritania remained a transition zone between the two major regions of French **colonialism** in north-west Africa: the **Maghreb** (Morocco, Algeria and Tunisia) and French West Africa (Senegal and other territories). At the time of independence (1960) virtually no modern infrastructure had been established by the French, not even a capital city.

The first political reform of French colonial policy in Mauritania began after the Second World War, when the territory was allowed to elect a representative to the French National Assembly. The second political reform was the election of territorial assemblies in the French West African colonial territories. One of those elected in March 1957 was **Mokhtar Ould Daddah**, one of Mauritania's first university graduates, who was nominated as Vice-President of the first Council of the Government in May 1957. In May 1958, his political party, the UPM, merged with elements of the Entente Mauritanienne to become the Mauritanian Regroupment Party (Parti de regroupement mauritanien—PRM). It took power on independence in 1960, with Ould Daddah as President.

By the late 1950s the black ethnic minorities had grown from virtually nothing to constitute some 20% per cent of the total population, and already ethnic divisions were beginning to affect Mauritanian politics. In 1958 the Association of Mauritanian Youth (Rabitat ash-Shabab al-Muritany), which had been established in 1955, founded the Mauritanian National Renaissance Party (Hizb an-Nahda al-Wataniya al-Muritaniya), inspired by **Arab nationalism**. The party opposed integration within French West Africa and many of its members sought a federation with Morocco, claiming that Mauritania was a part of 'Greater Morocco'. Ould Daddah, then Prime Minister, declared in 1958 that if there were to be a choice between a federation with the Maghreb or a federation with French West Africa, our (*sic*) preferences go to the Maghreb'. On the other hand, the Union of Natives of the South (Union des originaires du sud), created in Dakar, Senegal, and the Democratic Bloc of Gorgol (Bloc démocratique du Gorgol), founded in 1957, sought a federation within the framework of French West Africa.

There was to be no federation, either way, until 30 years later (and the establishment of the **Arab Maghreb Union**), although Mauritania was declared an Islamic republic on independence. It was a founder member of the Organisation of African Unity when it was established in 1963, and only joined the **Arab League** a decade later, in 1973. In 1964 the PRM changed its name to the Party of the Mauritanian People (PPM). Mauritania now became, in effect, a one-party state. Gradually, as a result of efforts to break free from the neocolonial ties that had been maintained with France (and French capital in the mining sector) after independence, there emerged a compromise between a genuine Mauritanian nationalism and a form of authoritarian **populism**, comparable in many ways to regimes that had emerged elsewhere in Africa and the **Middle East**. The regime adopted an increasingly radical position on international issues, supporting African national liberation movements and developing closer relations with the People's Republic of China. It left the West African Monetary Union and French army personnel were withdrawn.

At home, the regime remained strongly opposed to the growth of political opposition movements (notably the clandestine Democratic Movement, which began as a leftist student movement but grew to become a significant political force) and to trade unions. In September 1970 it was announced that 'no trade union or group of any kind in Mauritania has the right to express political ideas which contradict those of the party'. The Mauritanian Workers' Union was brought under the control of the PPM and the government in 1973, and in 1975 the PPM adopted a 'party charter' and declared that the political system was to be 'Islamic, national, centrist, and socialist'.

Towards the end of 1975 the Mauritanian government signed a tripartite agreement with Morocco and Spain that ended Spanish occupation of the Western Sahara (then the Spanish Sahara) and transferred the territory to Morocco and Mauritania. This was opposed by the **POLISARIO Front**, the main vehicle of the **Sahrawi** nationalist movement, established in 1973, which sought self-determination and independence for the Western Sahara. The case was referred to the World Court at The Hague, Netherlands, which ruled in favour of Sahrawi self-determination. Morocco launched a blitzkrieg against the POLISARIO forces, and Mauritania was dragged into the war that followed. Participation in the conflict cost Mauritania dearly; its adverse effect on the economy was made worse by drought. Opposition to Mauritania's involvement in the war and dissatisfaction with government policy and the Ould Daddah regime more generally led to the overthrow of the President (and the banning of the PPM) in July 1978 by a group of army officers, who established a Military Committee for National Salvation (CMSN). The 10 July Movement—a faction within the CMSN, which took its name from the date of the coup—had three declared aims: withdrawal from the war and neutrality with regard to the conflict, economic recovery and the restoration of **democracy**.

Between 1978 and 1980 there were three different military heads of state and frequent changes of personnel within the CMSN. Lt-Col Ould Haidalla took over as head of State in January 1980, having negotiated an effective cease-fire with the POLISARIO, and in December a civilian Prime Minister was appointed to head a transitional government and a constitution was drafted, which provided for a multi-party state with a presidential system of government. Ould Haidalla's position was not, however, unchallenged. The main opposition came from the Alliance for a Democratic Mauritania (AMD), established by the supporters of Ould Daddah and members of the banned PPM and based in Paris, France, but also receiving support from Senegal and Morocco. The AMD sponsored a failed coup attempt against Ould Haidalla in March 1981. The move towards political liberalization was halted: the Constitution was suspended, army officers returned to key government posts as members of the CMSN, and known members of the AMD within Mauritania were arrested and either jailed or executed. Angered by the support given by Morocco to the attempted coup, Ould Haidalla signed a peace agreement with the POLISARIO Front and a friendship treaty with Algeria, the Front's main backer. However, Ould Haidalla faced continuing opposition at home, with one former military head of state and a former Prime Minister involved in plots to remove him from power. In 1982 the Democratic Movement called for the formation of a united national front with the participation of all political groupings. This appeal was rejected by the CMSN, which supported the development of the official mass movements established in 1978 (and maintained as the basis for 'mass mobilization' by Ould Haidalla in 1980), known as the Structures for the Education of the Masses.

Successive droughts marked the early 1980s and the economic crisis deepened; in 1983, the government declared the whole country a disaster area and requested **aid** from the international community. In December 1984 Ould Haidalla was replaced as chairman of the CMSN and head of state, following a coup led by Col Maaouiya Ould Sid'Ahmed Taya. Ould Taya stated that his government would respect human rights, free political prisoners and 'end the use of cruel, inhuman and degrading punishment'; he did not, however, announce any plan for the restoration of the Constitution or for a return to civilian government. Administrative decentralization was initiated and elections were held for mayors in the capital, Nouakchott, and the 12 regional capitals in 1986, but political parties remained proscribed and strict rules on forms of association were maintained. Ould Taya's Government recognized the **Sahrawi Arab Democratic Republic** and brought the war with the POLISARIO Front officially to an end. It also embarked on a programme for economic and financial adjustment for the period 1985–88, which coincided with a period of economic recovery and growth.

Opposition parties were legalized and a new constitution was approved in 1991. Two multi-party presidential elections held subsequently which elected Ould Taya were widely regarded as flawed, but legislative and municipal elections held in October 2001 were generally free and open. Mauritania remains, in reality, a one-party state. The country continues to experience ethnic tensions between its black **minority** population and the dominant Maur (Arab-Berber) populace.

International relations

The establishment of full diplomatic relations between Mauritania and Israel in 1999 precipitated intense diplomatic activity in the Middle East. Mauritania recalled its ambassador to Iraq, after the Iraqi Government criticized the upgrading of relations as harmful to the interests of the Arab nation. There has also been criticism from opposition figures in Mauritania itself, as well as from the Iranian Government. Libya has had talks on the decision—which it described as a dangerous violation—with the other three members of the Arab Maghreb Union, as well as with Egypt and Sudan. Previously, Egypt and Jordan were the only Arab states to have full diplomatic relations with Israel.

Since September 2001 the government has on several occasions reiterated its determination to combat **international terrorism**. In June 2003 an attempted coup against the government of Maaouiya Ould Taya by elements of the army was effectively put down within days. In the month prior to the attempted coup 36 alleged Islamic militants had been arraigned for allegedly having plotted against the constitutional order, and nine politicians from the Ba'ath movement had been sentenced to terms of imprisonment (suspended) of three months for the creation of an unauthorized association and the reorganization of a dissolved political party.

The state remains wary of all opposition movements considered to be a threat to the regime and is clearly intent on maintaining tight control on domestic politics while adopting a pragmatic strategy in foreign relations.

Mauritania, economy

One-half of Mauritania's population still depends on **agriculture** and livestock for a livelihood, even though most of the nomads and many subsistence farmers were forced into the cities by recurrent droughts in the 1970s and 1980s. Mauritania has extensive deposits of iron ore, which account for 50% of total exports. The decline in world demand for this ore, however, has led to cutbacks in production. Mauritania's coastal waters are among the richest fishing areas in the world, but over-exploitation by foreign fleets threatens this key source of revenue. The country's first deepwater port opened near **Nouakchott** in 1986. In the past drought and economic mismanagement resulted in an accumulation of foreign **debt**. In February 2000 Mauritania qualified for debt relief under the Heavily Indebted Poor Countries (HIPC) initiative and in December 2001 received strong support from donor and lending countries at a triennial Consultative Group review. Mauritania withdrew from the Economic Community of West African States (ECOWAS) in 2000 and subsequently increased commercial ties with **Arab Maghreb Union** members Morocco and Tunisia, most notably in telecommunications. In 2001 exploratory **oil** wells sunk 80 km off shore indicated potential viable extraction at the then prevailing international price of oil. However, the refinery in Nouadhibou historically has not exceeded 20% of its distillation capacity and handled no crude at all in 2000. A new Investment Code approved in December 2001 improved the opportunities for direct foreign investment.

Strengths

Iron. Largest gypsum deposits in the world. Copper, yet to be exploited. Offshore fishing among the best in Africa. Significant debt cancellations in 2002.

Weaknesses

Poor land. Drought. Locust attacks. Vulnerability to fluctuating commodity prices.

May 15 Organization

Formed in 1979 from remnants of **Wadi Haddad**'s **Popular Front for the Liberation of Palestine-General Command**. Led by Muhammad al-Umari, who is known in Palestinian circles as 'Abu Ibrahim' or the 'bomb man'. The May 15 Organization was never part of the **Palestine Liberation Organization**. It was reportedly disbanded in the mid-1980s when several key members joined Col Hawari's Special Operations Group of **al-Fatah**. It claimed credit for several bombings in the early and mid–1980s, including a hotel bombing in London (1980), and attacks on **El Al**'s Rome and **Istanbul** offices (1981) and Israeli embassies in Athens and Vienna (1981). Anti-US attacks include an attempted bombing of a Pan Am airliner in Rio de Janeiro, Brazil, and a bombing on board a Pan Am flight *en route* from Tokyo to Honolulu in August 1982. Until 1985 May 15 Organization's location/area of Operation was **Baghdad**. It probably received logistic and financial support from Iraq until 1984.

Mazar-i-Sharif

Major town in the north-west of Afghanistan in Balkh Province. From the 1930s the town was the most important commercial centre for northern Afghanistan, exporting local products south-east to **Kabul** and, from 1979 onwards, north to the Soviet Union, and subsequently to the ex-Soviet states of south **Central Asia**. It is also an industrial town, producing fertilizer, rugs and textiles. With the Soviet invasion in 1979 Mazar became a major stronghold of the Kabul regime in the north. With the withdrawal of the Soviet army in 1988, until to the fall of President Najibullah in 1992, it was a stronghold of various groups that were to become members of the Coalition Forces that, in one alliance or another, were to hold Kabul from 1992 until it was taken by the **Taliban** in 1996. The Taliban made their first assault on Mazar in 1997. They captured the city but were unable to secure it and suffered an estimated 4,000 deaths when an uprising took place. They retook the city one year later, however, and exacted harsh revenge, mainly on the **Hazaras**. Tension remained high for the next four years and some of the fiercest fighting after 11 September 2001 was in and around Mazar. After the US-led assault on the Taliban, the anti-Taliban forces had managed to reassert themselves by the early part of 2002.

Mazen, Abu – *see* Mahmoud Abbas

MDA – *see* Movement for Democracy in Algeria (Mouvement pour la démocratie en Algérie)

Mecca (Makkah)

Together with Medina, also in the province of **Hejaz**, the city to which the **Prophet Muhammad** fled, Mecca is one of the two most important holy places in Saudi Arabia. It is the location of the annual Muslim ceremony that completes the *hajj* or pilgrimage. The ancient Ka'aba Sharifa, in the direction of which all Muslims pray and around which Muslim pilgrims undertaking the *hajj* walk during their stay in Mecca, is located at the centre of the city. It stands in the centre of the vast courtyard of the Great Mosque.

Medina

Medina, synonymous, in **Arabic**, with the word for a town, is the second most holy city of **Islam** and, like **Mecca**, is situated in the province of **Hejaz** in Saudi Arabia.

It was the location of the first Muslim community or ***ummah***. The **Prophet Muhammad** is buried there in the Mosque of the Prophet. Close to his tomb are those of his companions, Abu Bakr and 'Umar, and, a little further away, that of his daughter, Fatima. The mosque building was extensively renovated by the Saudi government in 1955.

Mediterranean

The Mediterranean usually refers to those countries bordering (and islands in) the Mediterranean Sea and their associated cultures. Historically the area within which successive ancient civilizations flourished, today the area is generally considered to include Algeria, Cyprus, Egypt, Israel, Jordan, Lebanon, Libya, Malta, Morocco, Syria, Tunisia and Turkey. The **EU-Mediterranean Partnership**, established in the mid-1990s, is designed to create a set of economic, social and political relations between Meditteranean countries and the **European Union**, leading eventually to a **Mediterranean Free Trade Area**.

Mediterranean Free Trade Area

The long-term objective of the **EU-Mediterranean Partnership** established in the mid-1990s and involving the **European Union** with a number of Mediterranean countries, initially Tunisia and Morocco.

MEFTA – *see* Mediterranean Free Trade Area and Middle East Free Trade Area (US)

Meimad

'Moderate' Israeli political grouping. A splinter group within **Mafdal**, which emerged in 1988. It is currently led by Rabbi Michael Melchior.

Meir (Meyerson), Golda

Prime Minister of Israel from 1969 until 1974.

Mellioun

Pro-government Iranian political party—led by trusted friends of the Shah—established in 1957 by the Shah himself to provide an impression of significant multi-party political debate in Iran.

MENA

Abbreviation for the **Middle East** and North Africa. Often used by the **World Bank** and other international agencies for the purposes of global comparisons by region.

Mauritania, **Western Sahara** and Sudan in North Africa are sometimes included, sometimes omitted. Greece is occasionally included, but more usually omitted. Malta and Cyprus are sometimes included and sometimes omitted. Afghanistan is sometimes included and sometimes omitted. The Central Asian states are usually not included—although they are in this dictionary. One recent definition (in *Globalization and the Politics of Development in the Middle East* (2001) by Clement Henry and Robert Springborg) regards MENA as 'extending from Morocco to Turkey along the southern and eastern shores of the **Mediterranean** and as far east as Iran and south to the Sudan, Saudi Arabia and Yemen. It is the non-European parts of the old **Ottoman Empire**, plus its respective western, southern and eastern peripheries in Morocco, Arabia and Iran'.

Mercenaries – *see* Security companies

Meretz

A left-wing Israeli political grouping, whose name means 'vitality' in **Hebrew**, currently led by Yossi Sarid. Meretz-Democratic Israel won 10 seats in the **Knesset** in the May 1999 elections, with 8% of the vote. An alliance of **Ratz**, **Shinui** and the **United Workers' Party**, it stands for civil rights, electoral reform, welfarism, Palestinian self-determination, separation of religion from the state and a halt to **settlement** in the **Occupied Territories**.

Mernissi, Fatima

Influential Moroccan feminist writer, sociologist and political activist. Her book *Beyond the Veil* in particular has been widely cited and deployed by activists in other parts of the **Middle East**.

Meshed

The second largest city in Iran, with a population of around 2m. Major religious centre in north-east Iran, famous for the shrine of Imam 'Ali ar-Rida/Riza, the eighth imam of the **Twelver Shi'is** (the main Shi'a grouping or sect), which attracts some 100,000 pilgrims each year.

Mesopotamia

The name, meaning 'between rivers' in Greek, of an ancient country of Asia, located on the alluvial plain between the **Tigris** and **Euphrates** rivers that now lies within modern Iraq. The region extends from the **Persian (Arabian) Gulf** north to the mountains of Armenia and from the Zagros and Kurdish mountains in the east to the Syrian Desert. From the mountainous north, Mesopotamia slopes down through grassy steppes to a central alluvial plain, which was once rendered exceedingly fertile by a network of waterways. It was home to, or conquered by, numerous ancient civilizations, including those of Sumeria, Babylonia, Assyria, Akkad, Egypt, the Hittites, and Elam. It has been home for many centuries to the **Marsh Arabs**.

MGK (National Security Council, Turkey)

The **military** authorities, responsible for the coup in Turkey in 1980, established the MGK as the command centre of the country's government. This comprised the coup leaders, the heads of the services, the paramilitary gendarmerie and Gen. **Evren**. Later, following partial democratization in the early 1980s, civilians were introduced into the MGK. With the gradual relaxation of military rule, civilians assumed greater authority. The President chaired the more contemporary MGK, with the leaders of the elected government counterbalanced by military figures. The balance of power remained in favour of the military, with the MGK secretary-general a military official. In 1997 it was from the MGK that the military authorities launched the 'soft coup' that eventually led to the resignation of the pro-Islamist government. Subsequently the MGK was once again dominated by the military, while its permanent secretariat comprised mainly staff officers. In recent years, however, the influence of the army seems to have waned, as the state of the economy and membership of the **European Union** have become more important than security issues. Even during the approach to the **Iraq War (2003)**, the military authorities had little to say publicly regarding Turkey's involvement. In theory, under new legislation, the MGK will have a purely advisory function, but the Government of **Recip Tayyip Erdoğan** has adopted a gradualist approach—in August 2003 a military figure was once again appointed as the MGK's secretary-general. The role of the military has diminished since the 1980s, but it remains an important force in Turkish politics and one which civilian politicians must handle with care.

Middle East

Generally replacing the older term, the **Near East** (which comprised Turkey and the Balkans, the **Levant** and Egypt), the Middle East roughly describes the region to the immediate south and south-east of Europe. The heartlands of the region are predominantly **Arabic**-speaking and are often referred to as the **Arab World**. The northern tier of non-Arabic-speaking countries—Turkey, Iran and Afghanistan—are usually also included in the Middle East. Often the region, loosely defined, includes North Africa (as part of the Arab World), with the countries of the Arab **Maghreb** (west)—usually Libya, Tunisia, Morocco (and sometimes **Western Sahara** and Mauritania)—distinguished from those of the Arab **Mashreq** (east)—Egypt, Jordan, Palestine (Israel), Lebanon, Syria and Iraq. Sometimes, North Africa includes Sudan, and even the Sahelian countries south of the Sahara (Mali, Niger, Chad), many of whose northern populations speak Arabic. In recent years, after the disintegration of the Soviet Union, the Central Asian states to the north of Afghanistan—especially Uzbekistan, Tajikistan and Turkmenistan—have become increasingly closely involved in the economics and politics of the Middle East and may rightly be included in a broad definition of the region. Israel, although undoubtedly an anomaly in some respects within the region, is also a key player in regional economics and politics.

Middle East Airlines

The national Lebanese airline.

Middle East Free Trade Area (US)

An old idea that has received new attention as a result of US President **George W. Bush**'s wish to see a US-Middle East Free Trade Area as part of the **Road Map to peace**. In May 2003 President Bush announced a sweeping proposal to create a US-Middle East Free Trade Area. It was formally unveiled in June at a summit in Jordan by US Trade Representative, Robert Zoellnick. It would create a US-Middle East Common Market within 10 years, embracing the countries of the **Maghreb**, the **Mashreq**, the **Gulf**, Israel, Turkey and, possibly, Iran. At present the USA has free-trade agreements with Israel and Jordan in the region. It is currently negotiating with Egypt, Morocco and Bahrain. It relies heavily, however, on a number of major political assumptions regarding the future of Iraq, Palestine-Israel and Iran. Other obstacles include the fact that a customs union agreement with the **European Union** creates a barrier to the creation of a US Free Trade Area.

Middle East and North Africa – *see* MENA

Middle East Partnership Initiative (MEPI)

The US MEPI, announced in December 2002, provides a framework and funding for the USA to work together with governments and people in the **Arab World** to expand economic, political and educational opportunity. With US $29m. in seed funding, the US Department of State and its inter-agency collaborators have engaged in consultations with Arab governments, non-governmental organizations and the private sector to inaugurate pilot projects in a number of Arab states. The pilot projects encompass all three MEPI pillars, with special attention to the needs of **women** and youth. The Department is seeking $145m. in funding for fiscal year 2004, in addition to emergency supplementary funding for the current fiscal year.

Middle East Peace Conference

On 30 October 1991 the first, symbolic session of a Middle East Peace Conference, sponsored by the USA and the USSR and attended by Israeli, Syrian, Egyptian, Lebanese, and joint Jordanian/Palestinian delegations, and by representatives of the

European Community, the **Gulf Co-operation Council** and the UN, commenced in Madrid, Spain. Direct bilateral negotiations were to begin four days after the opening of the conference.

Migration

Historically a region through which populations have continually moved, the **Middle East** is today an important centre of migration. There are significant diasporas of Middle Eastern populations in other parts of the world, notably of Jews, **Palestinians** and Lebanese, but including also groups from most parts of the region. Although there had been Jewish immigration into Palestine over many decades, from the late 19th century onwards there was a dramatic increase of immigration into the region after the establishment of the State of Israel in 1948, as Jews from across the Middle East and North Africa, and from other parts of the world also, sought to emigrate to Israel. The creation of Israel led to a substantial exodus of Arabs from Palestine, mainly into the neighbouring countries, but also further afield. After the **Arab–Israeli War (1967)** there was a further mass emigration of Palestinians. As the discovery of **oil** led to a massive expansion of the economies of the oil-rich states of the **Gulf** (and Libya), a new regional pattern of migration from the poorer countries of the region in search of employment in the oil-rich states, became established.

Milestones (or *Signposts Along the Road*)—*M'alim fil Tariq*

The title of a book, published in 1964, that provides a short account of the vision of the author, **Sayyid Qutb**, of an Islamic society. Banned by the Egyptian Government, *Milestones* is believed to have inspired some of the more extreme expressions of Islamic revivalism, and to have acted as the inspiration for contemporary Muslim political activism.

Militarism

Militarism refers to the tendency of a society and/or state to assign a disproportionate importance to military organization, to the **armed forces** and to preparation for and/or involvement in war. It is usually associated with very strong nationalism. The disproportionate role of the armed forces and of military expenditure in political and economic affairs is causally related to militarism. Many states in the **Middle East**, including Algeria, Egypt, Jordan, Iraq, Syria, Turkey and Israel, could be termed militaristic, given the pervasive social and political significance of the armed forces and the scale of military expenditure there.

Military

The role of the military in Middle Eastern politics has always been of major importance. The size and scale of the armed forces of individual countries, and of state expenditure on military hardware and technology, weapons and equipment, have been substantial in comparison with other regions of the developing world. (See **military expenditure**.)

Military Committee for National Salvation

Comité militaire de salut national

Executive committee and effective government of Mauritania after the coup by **Ould Taya** in 1984.

Military expenditure

The states of the region generally have high levels of military expenditure. Indeed, the region as a whole displays the highest levels of military expenditure in relation to national output in the developing world. The averages are increased by the level of spending of the **oil**-rich states of the **Gulf** (and Libya) and of Israel, Yemen, Jordan and Syria. Most show a reduction in military expenditure as a percentage of gross domestic product from the 1970s until the 1990s, with some exceptions—e.g. Saudi Arabia, Kuwait, the United Arab Emirates, Iraq and Syria. Levels ranged between 20%–40% and were below 20% in only Algeria, Egypt (after 1980), Lebanon, Morocco, Tunisia, Bahrain and Kuwait before the **Gulf War (1991)**. Arms imports by **Arab** countries climbed from more than US \$12,000m. in 1980 to nearly \$20,000m. by the end of the 1980s. This figure was boosted by the arms imports of Egypt, Iraq, Libya, Saudi Arabia and Syria, which together with India absorbed nearly 50% of all the world's arms imports.

Mineral(s) and mineral production

Within the region the major producers of valuable minerals are Kazakhstan, Uzbekistan and Morocco. Kazakhstan is the 10th largest producer of copper in the world and the seventh largest producer of zinc. Uzbekistan is the world's ninth largest producer of **gold** and Kazakhstan the ninthth largest producer of silver. Morocco is the eighth largest producer of lead and one of the world's largest producers and exporters of **phosphates**. **Western Sahara** has substantial phosphate deposits, which are being currently exploited, illegally, by Morocco as the occupying power.

Minority/minorities (religious, ethnic, linguistic)

Despite the tendency to regard the majority of the populations of the **Middle East** as **Arabic**-speaking and of Arab origin, the region contains a very large number of religious, ethnic and linguistic minorities. Few states in the region are without minorities and in most cases these minorities play a significant role in the social, cultural, political and economic life of the country concerned. Although, with regard to religion, the majority of the population of the Middle East is Muslim, there are also significant populations of Christians and Jews as well as many other smaller populations that adhere to distinctive religions, with distinctive associated customs and cultures. In addition to religious minorities within the region, there are also important ethnic and linguistic minorities, with their own distinctive identities.

MINURSO

The United Nations Mission for the Referendum in **Western Sahara** was established in April 1991 to verify a cease-fire in the disputed territory of Western Sahara, which came into effect in September 1991, to implement a settlement plan, involving the repatriation of **Sahrawi refugees**, the release of all political prisoners on both sides of the conflict (with Morocco) and to organize a referendum on the future of the territory. Originally scheduled for January 1992, the referendum has been continually deferred and has not yet taken place. There were serious disagreements between the **POLISARIO Front**, representing the Sahrawi people, and the Moroccan government with regard to who was eligible to vote in a referendum and this—together with other difficulties—has resulted in a stalemate, in which little progress towards the referendum has been made in a decade. The identification and registration process was eventually formally started in August 1994, but in December 1995 the UN Secretary-General reported that the identification of voters had stalled, owing to persistent obstructions on both sides. In early 1997 the new UN Secretary-General, Kofi Annan, attempted to revive the possibility of an imminent resolution of the dispute amidst increasing concerns that the cease-fire would collapse and be followed by a resumption of hostilities. In October 1997 the mission was strengthened, to enable it to supervise nine voter identification centres. By early September 1998 the initial identification process had been completed, with a total of 147,350 voters identified. Debates continued, however, regarding three particular tribal groups. A new timetable envisaged the referendum being held in July 2000. In December 1999 the UN Security Council acknowledged that persisting disagreements obstructing the implementation of the settlement plan precluded any possibility of conducting the planned referendum before 2002. In June 2001 the personal envoy of the UN Secretary-General elaborated a new draft Framework Agreement which envisaged the disputed area remaining part of Morocco but with substantial devolution of authority. Any referendum would be postponed. The Security Council agreed to extend MINURSO's mandate until November 2001 and then again until February 2002. In January the new special representative visited the region and the mandate of MINURSO has been extended several times.

MIRA—Movement for Islamic Reform in Arabia

The founders of MIRA have all been key figures in the reform movement in **Arabia** since the **Gulf War (1991)**. They were the main authors of the famous Letter of Demands and the Advice Memorandum presented to the Saudi regime.

Mirror of the Jihad

A gruesome video, available since January 2002 in several mosques in London, United Kingdom, showing **Taliban** forces decapitating members of the **Northern Alliance** in Afghanistan with knives. The video was distributed by an Islamist organization based in Paddington, central London. The money raised from sales of the video was used to fund armed Islamist organizations.

Misr el-Fatah

Young Egypt Party

Egyptian political party, founded in 1990. Its chairman is Gamal Rabie.

Mizrachi

The Committee for the Defence of Legitimate Rights—an Israeli political organization

Mizrahi

The Oriental Jewish-Zionist grouping, founded in 1902. Gave birth to the **Mafdal** (National Religious Party).

Mizrahi Democratic Rainbow

Keshet Demokratit Mizrahit, Israel

Political organization of 'oriental' Jews (Arab Jews).

Mizrahim

'Oriental'Jews (Arab Jews).

Moderation and Development Party

Political grouping in Iran.

Mohammed V, King (Sultan)

Initially, during the colonial **French** (and Spanish) **Protectorate of Morocco** period (1912–56), Sultan, then, after independence, King of Morocco from March 1956 until 1961. As legitimate Sultan of Morocco, Mohammed V maintained this status and title even when exiled to Madagascar for his role in supporting the emerging Moroccan nationalist movement. Mohammed V established contact with the nationalists as early as 1934. In many ways, his distinctive role as the Commander of the Faithful as well as that of a political figurehead gave him additional authority as a symbol of Moroccan tradition. Many of the early founders of the **Istiqlal** (Independence) party—such as **Allal al-Fassi**—were themselves traditionalists, deriving their principles of **democracy** and egalitarianism from Islamic values. He returned from exile in 1956 to take up the throne and become Morocco's head of state. Having accepted the status of a constitutional monarch, he managed to maintain the balance between the conservative and the more progressive forces in Moroccan politics during the first four years of independence. In international affairs he was progressive, a founder member of the Casablanca Group and a supporter of various pan-African and pan-Arab initiatives. On his death, in 1961, he was succeeded by his son, **Hassan II.**

Mohammed VI, King

Grandson of **Mohammed V** and son of **Hassan II**, kings of Morocco, Mohammed VI succeeded his father as King of Morocco and head of state in July 1999. The king in Morocco is also a religious leader, known to his people as Commander of the Faithful (Emir al-Mouminin). Expected to make some significant political and social changes, Mohammed VI has proved extremely cautious, but has made efforts to introduce social reforms, particularly with regard to **women**'s rights in Morocco. He initially made gestures which led some to believe that he would initiate changes affecting human rights (a subject of criticism by international human rights agencies during his father's reign), but has remained obdurate on the issue of the **Western Sahara**.

Moked – *see* **Israel Communist Party**

Moledet

Homeland/Fatherland, Israel

Moledet is a right-wing nationalist political grouping. Formed in 1988, it merged in 1994 with the **Tehiya Party** to become Moledet, the Eretz Israel Faithful and the Tehiya. Its aims include the transfer (expulsion) of the **Palestinians** in the **Occupied Territories**. It is led by Rabbi Binyamin (Benny) Elon.

Monarchy/monarchies

The **Middle East** is the region with the greatest number of ruling monarchs and royal dynasties in the world. Monarchy in the Middle East is a form of political regime which effectively claims legitimacy for the ruler by virtue of the links between contemporary rulers and much earlier rulers and, in many cases, through links supposedly traceable back to the **Prophet Muhammad**. Most Middle Eastern monarchs claim to be spiritual and social as well as political leaders and to combine these different kinds of authority and legitimacy in a distinctive fashion. This is notably the claim of the Moroccan **Alawite** dynasty, the latest descendant of which is **King Mohammed VI**. The House of Saud would also claim religious as well as political legitimacy by virtue of its association with the religious leaders of **Wahhabism**. Other monarchs have more secular and more recent claims to rule, such as the '**Hashemites**' of Jordan. Titles such as sultan, emir, imam and sheikh were formerly used to indicate a combination of religious and political legitimacy, although the title king has become more popular in recent times.

Money-laundering – *see also* **Hawala**

The international transfer of money by informal means is widespread in the region. The *hawala* system is most commonly used for informal transfer, which evades normal international currency regulations and taxation systems. It lends itself to forms of money transfer, in which the precise paths whereby funds are transferred are secret or obscured. This is known as money-laundering, which may also involve normal but highly confidential banking channels, with numerous transfers being made in order to make it difficult, if not impossible, to trace the origins and final destinations of the sums involved. It may also involve secret and illegal money transfers through informal channels. It may even involve the movement of cash or bullion or other goods illegally, through smuggling, across borders.

Morasha

Heritage, Israel

Created by a religious nationalist splinter group from the **National Religious Party** that joined with **Poale Agudat Israel** to contest the 1984 Israeli elections. The party advocated more Jewish settlements in the **West Bank** and claimed the support of **Gush Emunim**.

Moroccan Communist Party (MCP)

Parti communiste marocain (PCM)

The first MCP cells were established in **Casablanca** at the time of the reforms of the Popular Front in France. In 1944 the MCP condemned the **Istiqlal** independence manifesto, but reversed its position in the following year when its French leader was replaced by the Moroccan communist, Ali Yata. Operating under the French initially in semi-clandestine fashion, the MCP was banned in 1952 and effectively went underground during the last years of the struggle for independence, some of its members joining the Black Cross, an urban terrorist group. The Party's secretary-general, Ali Yata, was sent into exile, attempting, unsuccessfully, to return twice in 1955 and twice in 1957. The status of the MCP was unclear immediately after independence, although it was able to circulate a newssheet in French and **Arabic** without official opposition. In the summer of 1958, when other parties were suppressed, the MCP-oriented *La Nation* was able to publish, and several book-stores selling inexpensive communist literature were opened.

Attracting support mainly among organized labour and students, the MCP probably had some 10,000–15,000 sympathizers, but only about 1,000 party cadres and full members in 1958. Its major concerns prior to independence were: the abrogation of the Treaty of Fez, the evacuation of French troops and the abolition of US bases. Its priorities were nationalist and anti-imperialist. It favoured some nationalization of land and **mineral** resources and, generally, 'liberation from capitalist grips'. However, its domestic policies for economic and social reform were moderate. Even so, it was officially dissolved in September 1959 by the **UNFP** (Union nationale des forces populaires) government, under severe pressure from the **monarchy** and other conservative forces.

It was judged, by the Minister of Justice, that the party's statutes violated an article of the 1958 decree regulating rights of association. In other words, the MCP had objectives that were designed to undermine the government and the monarchy. The matter went to court and the case of the MCP was upheld on the grounds that the state had failed to provide adequate evidence of the party's intentions. The King himself made a speech (in November 1959) in which he roundly condemned 'materialist doctrines' and at the Court of Appeals the state prosecutor based his case squarely on the King's words which, he claimed, had the force of law. The prosecutor's case was upheld, but the MCP appealed to the Supreme Court, which, finally, in May 1964, rejected the Party's appeal, arguing that when neither party presents adequate evidence, the judges are fully justified in relying on the legal pronouncements of the king.

Since 1964–65 revolutionary communists in Morocco have been obliged, effectively, to remain underground, although a number of groups have managed to maintain a degree of operational activity. In 1968 the Party of Liberation and Socialism (Parti de libération et du socialisme—PLS) was founded, but it was banned in 1969. In 1970 **Forward** (Ilal Amam) was founded by former members of the PLS; the party was never legal. Also founded in 1970, by former members of the UNFP, was **March 23** (23 Mars); this grouping also remains outlawed. The Party of Progress and Socialism (**Parti du progrès et du socialisme**—PPS) was permitted to constitute itself legally in 1974. Representing a moderate brand of pro-Moscow communist doctrine and avoiding any criticism of the monarchy or the government's position on the **Western Sahara**, the PPS has been led by Ali Yata, former secretary-general of the MCP.

Moroccan Islamic Combatant Group (GICM)

The goals of the GICM reportedly include the establishment of an **Islamic state** in Morocco and support for **al-Qa'ida**'s *jihad* against the West. The Group appears to have emerged in the late 1990s and comprises Moroccan recruits who were trained in Afghanistan. GICM members interact with other North African extremists, particularly in Europe. On 22 November 2002 the USA designated the GICM for 'asset freeze' under E. O. 13224. This followed the submission of the GICM to the UN Security Council Resolution 1267 sanctions committee. GICM members, working with other North African extremists, engage in trafficking falsified documents and, possibly, arms. The group in the past has issued communiqués and statements against the Moroccan government.

Morocco, Kingdom of

Al-Mamlakah al-Maghribiyah

The Kingdom of Morocco is situated in north Africa, bordering the North Atlantic Ocean and the **Mediterranean** Sea, between Algeria to the east and **Western Sahara** to the south. Morocco is in a strategic location opposite Spain and the Straits of Gibraltar. The country's total area is 446,550 sq km (of which 250 sq km is **water**). The capital is **Rabat**. For administrative purposes the country is divided into 37 provinces and two *wilayas*: Agadir, Al-Hoceima, Azilal, Beni Mellal, Ben Slimane, Boulemane, Casablanca (*wilayat*), Chaouen, El Jadida, El Kelaa des Sraghna, Er Rachidia, Essaouira, Fes (Fez), Figuig, Guelmim, Ifrane, Kenitra, Khemisset, Khenifra, Khouribga, Laayoune, Larache, Marrakech, Meknes, Nador, Ouarzazate, Oujda, Rabat-Sale (*wilayat*), Safi, Settat, Sidi Kacem, Tanger, Tan-Tan, Taounate, Taroudannt, Tata, Taza, Tetouan and Tiznit.

The three additional provinces of Ad Dakhla (Oued Eddahab), Boujdour, and Es-Smara, as well as parts of Tan-Tan and Laayoune, fall within Moroccan-claimed Western Sahara.

In July 2002 the population was estimated at 31,167,783, comprising Arabs (70%), **Berbers** (29%), 'others' 0.8% and Jews (0.2%). The religious composition of the country is: Muslims (mostly **Sunni**) 98.7%, Christians 1.1%, Jews 0.2%. **Arabic** is the official language. Berber dialects are also spoken and French is often used in business, government and diplomacy.

Political profile

Morocco is a constitutional **monarchy**. The head of state is King **Mohammed VI** (since 23 July 1999). The head of government is Prime Minister Driss Jettou (since 9 October 2002). A Council of Ministers is appointed by the monarch. The monarchy is hereditary and the Prime Minister is appointed by the monarch following legislative elections. Gradual political reforms in the 1990s resulted in the establishment of a bicameral legislature in 1997.

Legislative elections held in 1997 resulted in a tripartite division of the parliament. The eventual formation of a socialist-led government was regarded as a clear expression of the increasing role of the party system. The bicameral parliament consists of a Chamber of Counsellors (upper house) and a Chamber of Representatives (lower house). The Chamber of Counsellors has 270 seats. Members of the Chamber are elected indirectly by local councils, professional organizations and labour syndicates for nine-year terms. One-third of the members are renewed every three years. The Chamber of Representatives has 325 seats and members are elected by popular vote for five-year terms. The most recent elections to the Chamber of Counsellors were held on 15 September 2000. The most recent elections to the Chamber of Representatives were held on 27 September 2002. The next elections to the Chamber of Representatives will be held in 2007.

There is a Supreme Court, to which judges are appointed on the recommendation of the Supreme Council of the Judiciary, which is presided by the monarch. The legal system is based on **Islamic Law** and on the French and Spanish systems of civil law. Judicial review of legislative acts takes place in the Constitutional Chamber of the Supreme Court.

Political Parties and Groups

With Mohammed VI's succession to the throne the Islamists have been tolerated. In 2000 the leader of the banned Islamic movement 'Justice and Good Deeds' was released after 10 years' imprisonment without trial.

- Action Party; Leader Muhammad El Idrissi
- Alliance of Liberties; Leader Ali Beljaj
- Annahj Addimocrati; Leader Abdellah El Harif
- Avant Garde Social Democratic Party; Leader Ahmed Benjelloun
- Citizen Forces; Leader Abderrahman Lahjouji
- Citizens' Initiatives for Development; Leader Mohamed Benjamou
- Constitutional Union; Leader Mohamed Abied
- Democratic and Independence Party; Leader Abdelwahed Maach
- Democratic and Social Movement; Leader Mahmoud Archane
- Democratic Socialist Party; Leader Aissa Ouardighi
- Democratic Union; Leader Bouazza Ikken
- Environment and Development Party; Leader Ahmed El Alami
- Front of Democratic Forces; Leader Thami El Khyari
- **Istiqlal** Party (Independence Party); Leader **Abbas El Fassi**
- Justice and Development Party (formerly the Party of Justice and Development); Leader Abdelkrim El Khatib
- Moroccan Liberal Party; Leader Mohamed Ziane
- National Democratic Party; Leader Abdallah Kadiri
- National Ittihadi Congress Party; Leader Abdelmajid Bouzoubaa
- National Popular Movement; Leader Mahjoubi Aherdane
- National Rally of Independents; Leader Ahmed Osman
- National Union of Popular Forces; Leader Abdellah Ibrahim
- Parti Al Ahd (Al Ahd); Chair. Najib El Ouazzani
- Party of Progress and Socialism; Leader Ismail Alaoui
- Party of Renewment and Equity; Leader Chakir Achabar
- Party of the Unified Socialist Left; Leader Mohamed Ben Said Ait Idder

- Popular Movement; Leader Mohamed Laenser
- Reform and Development Party; Leader Abderrahmane El Kouhen
- Social Centre Party; Leader Lahcen Madih
- Socialist Union of Popular Forces; Leader Abderrahman El-Youssoufi

Political groups and trade unions

- Democratic Confederation of Labour; Leader Noubir Amaoui
- General Union of Moroccan Workers; Leader Abderrazzak Afilal
- Moroccan Employers' Association
- National Labour Union of Morocco; Leader Abdelslam Maati
- Union of Moroccan Workers; Leader Mahjoub Benseddik

Media

The media remain under strict control, although the succession of Mohammed VI has created a more liberal climate. The issue of Western Sahara is subject to particular censorship. In 2000 the French-language weekly *Demain* was banned. Morocco can receive Spanish television and radio broadcasts. There are 22 daily newspapers, of which the most important are *Le Matin du Sahara et du Maghreb*, *Rissalat al-Oumma*, *al-Alam* and *L'Opinion*. There are two television services, one state-owned and one independent. There are three radio services, one state-owned and two independent. In 2000 there were eight internet service providers, and in 2002 there were 400,000 internet users.

History

As an **Alawite**, the King of Morocco, Mohammed VI, claims descent from the **Prophet Muhammad** through the 17th-century Sultan Moulay Ismail and the Filali dynasty. Morocco was never incorporated into the **Ottoman Empire** and, although divided in the time of the colonial protectorate regime into a French zone (the majority of the country) and a Spanish zone (in the north and to the south), it maintained its monarchy throughout the colonial period.

The nationalist movement, established during the early 1930s, maintained good relations with the palace. In 1936–37 efforts were made to extend the nationalist movement from a small nucleus into a mass movement. Riots that broke out in Meknes in 1937 increased French repression of the movement and for the next decade all nationalist activity had to be undertaken semi-clandestinely. **Allal al-Fassi** was in exile from 1937 until 1945. Pressure for independence from France increased, however, during the Second World War, and US President Roosevelt, meeting privately with the Sultan in January 1943 in **Casablanca** (at the time of his meeting there with Winston Churchill and Charles de Gaulle) led him to believe that he would promote Moroccan independence after the war. In January 1944 the National Party announced the establishment of a new party, the Istiqlal (Independence) Party. Over the next five years the Sultan identified himself ever more closely with the ambitions for independence expressed by the Istiqlal. In

August 1953, as a result of his uncompromising position, the Sultan was exiled to Madagascar. However, after the end of the Second World War, Allal al-Fassi returned to Morocco, the nationalist leadership regrouped and the membership of the Istiqlal grew from 10,000 in 1947 to around 100,000 by 1951.

For many years, during the 1930s and 1940s, and even the 1950s, the nationalists were dominated by an urban élite, which allied itself with and gave unconditional support to the Sultan. Allal al-Fassi epitomized this conservative bourgeois nationalist leadership, which combined a sense of nationalism with a full sense of Morocco's religious and political history as a sultanate. Referred to as Sheikh Allal (an honorific title suggesting a religious status), Allal al-Fassi was increasingly associated, as the Istiqlal party began to split between the conservatives and the radicals, with 'the old turbans' as the former were known (the latter became known as 'the young Turks' and included the leftist ideologue, **Mehdi Ben Barka**).

Morocco's long struggle for independence from France ended in 1956. The internationalized city of Tangier was transferred to the new country in the same year. Morocco virtually annexed Western Sahara during the late 1970s, but no final resolution has been achieved with regard to the status of the territory.

Morocco claims and administers the Western Sahara, but sovereignty remains unresolved. Off the coast of Morocco Spain controls the islands of Penon de Alhucemas, Penon de Velez de la Gomera, the Islas Chafarinas and two autonomous communities on the coast of Morocco—Ceuta and Melilla. Morocco rejected Spain's unilateral designation of a median line from the Canary Islands in 2002 to explore undersea resources and to interdict illegal **refugees** from Africa. Hashish is produced illicitly. Trafficking of the drug is increasing for both domestic and international (mainly western European) drug markets. Morocco is a transit point for cocaine from South America destined for western Europe.

Morocco, economy

Morocco faces the problems typical of developing countries—restraining government spending, reducing constraints on private activity and foreign **trade**, and achieving sustainable economic growth. Following structural adjustment programmes supported by the **International Monetary Fund**, the **World Bank**, and the Paris Club, the dirham is now fully convertible for current account transactions, and reforms of the financial sector have been implemented. Droughts depressed activity in the key agricultural sector and contributed to the stagnation of the economy in 1999 and 2000. Favourable rainfall in 2001 led to economic growth of 5%. Formidable long-term challenges include: servicing the external **debt**; preparing the economy for freer trade with the **European Union**; and improving **education** and attracting foreign investment to boost living standards and job prospects for the country's youth.

Strengths

Attracts substantial foreign investment. Morocco has recently reported large foreign exchange inflows from the sale of a mobile telephone licence and the partial privatization of the state-owned telecommunications company. Abundant labour. Low inflation. Great potential for the already important tourist industry. **Phosphates** and **agriculture**.

Weaknesses

High unemployment and population growth. Droughts.

Mossad

One of the branches of the Israeli secret service. The Mossad Le Aliyah Beth (Institution for Intelligence and Special Services) was founded by the **Haganah** in 1937 as a secret organization, mainly for carrying out the large-scale illegal immigration known in **Hebrew** as Ha'apala. Gradually its activities came to include espionage, especially overseas, the procurement of arms and counter-espionage. It became the foreign intelligence wing of the Haganah. It was supported by Shai—the 'information service' established by the Haganah in 1940. After the creation of the State of Israel, Mossad became one of the three key branches of the Israeli secret intelligence services dealing essentially with international intelligence, and it has been compared with the US **Central Intelligence Agency** and the British MI6. The two other major branches are **Shin Beth** and **AMAN** (Agaf Modiin or Information Bureau). Having run a very successful operation for three decades, Mossad was less effective during the 1980s and 1990s. After several attempts to restructure the organization, in September 2002 Meir Dagan was appointed to reinvigorate Mossad. A sign that the reforms have been successful is **Ariel Sharon**'s decision to charge Mossad with leading efforts to combat Iran's nuclear programme—one of Israel's current major concerns. Dagan is close to Sharon, under whom he served in the early 1970s. Sharon envisages a return to the 'glory days' of the 1970s for Mossad, when for more than a decade Mossad tracked and killed all but one of **Black September**'s operatives involved in the 1972 Munich Olympics terrorist attack.

Mossadegh, Muhammad – *see* Mussadegh, Muhammad

Mosul

Predominantly Kurdish '**oil**' town in northern Iraq.

el Motassadeq, Mounir

Convicted in Germany in 2003 for facilitating the 11 September 2001 bomb attacks in the USA and for being a member of a terrorist organization, he was sentenced to a

15-year term of imprisonment. He remained in prison despite new evidence that freed a fellow Moroccan tried on the same charges. He has appealed against his conviction.

Motherland Party (MP)

Conservative/right-wing Turkish political party. It was in power from 1983 onwards for most of the remainder of the 1980s, led by Prime Minister **Turgut Özal**. It initially accommodated the rising power and influence of the Islamists in the party and provided an alternative to the Islamist **Welfare Party.**

Moulsabbat, Abdelhaq

Allegedly organized the suicide bombings in which 43 people in five different locations in **Casablanca**, Morocco, died in May 2003. A cleric from the city of Fez, whose poorer districts are reputed to be Islamist strongholds, he was arrested in that city and died shortly thereafter in police custody, as a result, according to an announcement made on Moroccan state television, of 'heart and liver problems'. Other suspects were also arrested and appeared before the public prosecutor. It is not clear whether these persons had any links with the group known as Al-Assirat al-Moustaqim (The Righteous Path), which is based in the slum areas of Casablanca.

Mount Lebanon

A term first used during the Ottoman era to designate the central part of the Lebanon Mountains inhabited mostly by **Maronites** and **Druze**. After 1864 the area was administered as a separate entity and Christians prospered. Most of the region surrounding Mount Lebanon (often called simply 'the Mountain') was considered part of **Greater Syria**, an area that encompassed present-day Syria, Lebanon, Israel, and Jordan. In 1920, while under the French Mandate, parts of Greater Syria were annexed to Mount Lebanon to create Greater Lebanon. This newly established territory eventually became the present-day state of Lebanon.

Mousavi, Mir Hossein

Iranian politican, born in 1941. He was a co-founder of the **Islamic Republic(an) Party**. Mousavi was appointed Prime Minister in October 1981, but an amendment to the Constitution in 1989 abolished the premiership. Although he was appointed by **Rafsanjani** in 1989 as an adviser, his position lacked power.

Moussaoui, Zacharias

A French national involved in the 11 September 2001 bomb attacks, with links to Islamist groups in France, who took flying lessons in Minnesota, USA. He was arrested in August 2001 after the US Federal Bureau of Investigation (FBI) learned that he was training to hijack a an aircraft in the USA. Identified by the FBI in Minnesota as a terrorist threat, higher authorities within the FBI nevertheless refused a request to search his possessions, which would have revealed links to the other hijackers.

Mouvement algérien pour la justice et le développement (MAJD)

Algerian political group established in 1990. A leftist reformist party supporting the policies of former President **Boumedienne**. The MAJD is led by Moulay Habib.

Mouvement pour la démocratie en Algérie

Movement for Democracy in Algeria—MDI

Algerian political party, founded in 1985 by exiled **Front de libération nationale** leader, the former President, **Ahmed Ben Bella**.

Mouvement pour la démocratie et la citoyenneté

Algerian political group, formed in 1997 by dissident members of the **Front des forces socialistes**. It is based in Tizi Ouzou and led by Said Khelil.

Mouvement démocratique et social

Algerian political party, formed in 1998 by former members of Ettahadi. A left-wing party with about 4,000 members. Its secretary-general is Hachemi Cherif.

Mouvement démocratique et sociale

Moroccan political party, founded in 1996 as the Mouvement national démocratique et social after splitting from the Mouvement national populaire. Adopted its current name in November 1996. Its leader is Mahmoud Archane.

Mouvement pour la liberté

Algerian political party, established in 1999 in opposition to President **Bouteflika**. It is led by **Mouloud Hamrouche.**

Mouvement de la Nahda islamique – *see* Mouvement de la renaissance islamique

Mouvement national populaire

Moroccan political party of the centre, founded in 1991. Its leader is Mahjoub Aherdane.

Mouvement populaire (MP)

Moroccan political party, formally established in February 1959. Initiated by Mahjoub Aherdane (b. 1921), then governor of Rabat province, at a press conference in November 1957, the new party had no finances, no programme and was not even legal. It was more than one year before it was formally recognized. A Provisional Committee of Direction was established to draw up a programme and secure financial support. It held its constituent Congress in November 1959. The party drew on rural support, particularly in areas where the Liberation Army had been active, such as the Rif, and proposed to challenge the dominance of the **Istiqlal**. In some ways it presented itself as a rural/**Berber** party as opposed to the urban/Arab Istiqlal, although the distinction was rarely explicit. It gave loyal support to the King, and joined the Front pour la défense des institutions constitutionnelles in the 1960s. It was allocated four ministerial posts after the 1977 elections. In elections held in 1984 it obtained 47 seats in the Chamber of Representatives, helping relegate the Istiqlal party into fourth place. Today it is a less powerful force than in the past. Its secretary-general is Mohand Laenser.

Mouvement populaire pour la démocratie

Moroccan political party, led by M. el-Khatib.

Mouvement de la réforme nationale

Algerian political group, formed in 1998 but based on the earlier **Mouvement de la renaissance islamique**. Its leader is Sheikh Abdullah Djaballah.

Mouvement de la renaissance islamique (MRI)—Harakat an-Nahda al-Islamiyya

Movement of the Islamic Renaissance, Algeria

Algerian Islamist political grouping. The MRI received official legal approval in December 1990, although its leader, Sheikh Abdullah Djaballah, claimed that it had existed clandestinely since 1974. Sheikh Djaballah—a man in his mid-40s—was a lawyer by training. Like **Hamas**, the MRI was close in spirit and outlook to the **Muslim Brotherhood**, although not organizationally linked to it (any more than Hamas in Algeria appeared to be). Unlike the **FIS—Front Islamique du Salut** (Islamic Salvation Front) and Hamas, the MRI opposed the Algerian government's economic reform measures, defending the public sector against further privatization. It has therefore appeared to be trying to establish a distinctive position for itself on the left wing of the Islamist movement. In the early 1990s it was argued that the MRI did not appear to have much of a popular constituency, but it was reported to have a substantial following among intellectuals, particularly in Constantine, the cultural capital of eastern Algeria, where Sheikh Djaballah was based, and to be more coherent intellectually than the FIS. Sheikh Djaballah called for people to vote for the FIS in June 1990, but the MRI was expected to contest elections to the National Assembly in 1991. The MRI was banned in 1992.

Mouvement de la société pour la paix (MSP)—Harakat Moudjtamaa as-Silm, formerly HAMAS

Movement of a Peaceful Society, Algeria

This Algerian Islamist party was formerly known by its **Arabic** acronym— HAMAS. The name was changed in April 1997 in order to comply with the law that banned political parties based on religious or ethnic issues. It is now considered to be a moderate Islamic party. Led by Mahfoud Nahnah, it condemns violence and intolerance in the name of religion. It promotes respect for human rights, including **women**'s rights in the workplace.

Mouvement de la tendance islamique (MTI)

Islamic Tendency Movement, Tunisia

Islamist movement and party. Originated by a group of young sheikhs meeting in **Tunis** in the late 1960s under the leadership of Rached el-Ghannouchi (who had just returned from Syria) and publishing the Islamic review, *El Maarifa* (*Conscience*). It was a response to the wide-ranging assault on the traditional **Islam** of the *ulema* and the attempt to build a modernist, alternative Islam by the state during the late 1950s and the 1960s as part of a broader programme for the modernization of Tunisia on the basis of Destourian principles (see **Destour Party** and **Neo-Destour Party**). It became the **An-Nahda (Renaissance) Party**, and was banned by the government.

Movement for the Advancement of the Zionist Idea

Israeli political group, formed in 1990 as a breakaway group of **Likud**. Led by Itzhak Modai.

Movement of Arab Nationalists (MAN)

Movement founded by **Palestinians Wadi Haddad** and **George Habash** together with others, including Kuwait-born Ahmad al-Khalil. In 1968 the MAN was transformed into the **Popular Front for the Liberation of Palestine**. The leaders disagreed with the strategy of **al-Fatah**, which concentrated on striking strategic targets inside Israel, and wished to widen the struggle. The **El Al hijacking** in July 1968 was one of the MAN's first major initiatives.

Movement for the Deprived – *see* Harakat Amal

Movement for Fidelity and Justice – *see* WAFA—Wafa wa al-Adl

Movement for Guidance and Reform – *see* al-Irshad wa'l-Islah

Movement for Islamic Reform in Arabia

Saudi Arabian opposition group, dedicated to the overthrow of the Saudi regime, based in London, United Kingdom. Headed by Dr Saad al-Fagih, who has been granted political asylum in the United Kingdom. Al-Fagih also has links with **al-Qa'ida** and purchased a satellite telephone which was used for two years to link al-Qa'ida operatives in Afghanistan, Yemen, Sudan, Iran, Saudi Arabia, Pakistan and Baku through London.

Movement for an Islamic Society—al-Haraka li-Mujtama' Islam/ Harakat al-Muqawama al-Islamiyya – *see* Hamas

Movement of Patriotic Libyans

Libyan opposition movement, founded in 1997.

Movement for the Struggle of the Jordanian Islamic Resistance

The Movement for the Struggle of the Jordanian Islamic Resistance Movement and the Ahmad al-Daqamisah Group have both claimed responsibility for the attempted assassination, in **Amman**, of the Israeli Vice-Consul.

Mu'alla, Sheikh Rashid ibn Ahmad

Ruler of **Umm al-Qaiwain** (United Arab Emirates); acceded in 1981.

Mubarak, Hosni Muhammad Said (1928–)

Current President of the Arab Republic of Egypt. He was born into an upper middle-class family. He underwent a military education—at the National Military Academy and the Air Force Academy in Egypt, and at the Frunze General Staff Academy in the Soviet Union. In 1964 Mubarak headed the Egyptian military delegation to the USSR and was appointed as Commander of the Western Air Force Base, at **Cairo** West Airfield. In 1967–72 he was appointed as director of the Air Force Academy and as Chief of Staff of the Egyptian Air Force, remaining in the latter post until 1972, when he became Commander of the Air Force and Deputy Minister for Military Affairs. In October 1973 he was promoted to the rank of Air Marshall. In April 1975 Mubarak was named the Vice-President of Egypt and in 1978 he was appointed as vice-chairman of the **National Democratic Party**. In 1981, one week after President **Sadat** had been assassinated, Mubarak declared on his inauguration that he would continue the policies of Sadat, which had been to seek reconciliation with the West, and peace with Israel inside internationally recognized borders. Since 1981 his programme has been one of economic reform, greater political freedom, allowing the **Muslim Brotherhood** to enter parliament and granting a greater degree of press freedom. Internationally, he has focused on neutrality between the great powers and sought to improve relations with other Arab states. He was re-elected by majority votes in 1987, 1993 and 1999, unopposed. Mubarak supported the UN sanctions against Iraq, after its occupation of Kuwait in 1990. Egypt participated in the **Gulf War (1991)**, contributing 38,500 troops, and has been part of the post-war efforts to stabilize the **Gulf** region. Mubarak's Government advised the **Palestinians** during the talks in Norway in 1993 that led to the **Oslo Agreement**. Since Mubarak came to power in 1981 he has received considerable military and economic **aid** from the USA, the OECD countries and the **World Bank**. A political moderate, Mubarak has taken a hard line with extremist groups in Egypt. As a result, he has been the target of several assassination plots. In June 1995 gunmen fired on his motorcade as he arrived in Addis Ababa, Ethiopia, for a meeting of the Organisation of African Unity. He escaped uninjured. Three Egyptian militants were later sentenced to death for the attack.

Al-Muhajiroun

Radical Islamist movement founded, while he was living in Saudi Arabia, by the Syrian cleric Sheikh Omar Bakri Mohammed. After being deported in 1985, Omar Bakri transferred his organization to the United Kingdom. Al-Muhajiroun has been a vocal organization, building support and membership at the grassroots level and organizing a number of dramatic events. In 2000 it invited **Osama bin Laden** to address a meeting (subsequently cancelled) in London via satellite. The organization has a well-designed website and international links.

Muhammad, the Prophet

Born *c.* 570 in the city of **Mecca** in present-day Saudi Arabia, he was the founder of **Islam**, one of the world's greatest monotheistic religions. Today, 14 centuries after his death, his influence is still powerful and pervasive. In Islam, Muhammad is the final prophet, the messenger of Allah. While he is not considered divine, he is set apart as the final messenger, the 'seal of the prophets'. The son of an Arab merchant named Abdullah (and, thus, sometimes referred to as Muhammad ibn Abdullah), he was born into the Quraysh tribe, began receiving the revelations that form the **Koran** in about 610 and died in 632.

Muhammad, Ali Nasser

President of the **People's Democratic Republic of Yemen** from 1980 until 1986.

Mujahidin

Arabic term meaning 'fighters' (*mu-jihad-in*).

Mujahidin (Iran)

The *mujahidin* emerged in Iran at around the same time as the ***Fedayeen***, in the mid-1960s. However, whereas the latter had their origins in the **Tudeh Party**, the roots of the *mujahidin* were in the religious wing of the National Front, particularly the **Liberation Movement of Iran** (Nehzat-e Azadi-ye Iran). The *mujahidin* sought inspiration in the writings and lectures of **Ali Shari'ati**, often considered the ideologist of the **Iranian Revolution**. Formed in 1966, the *mujahidin* initiated its military operations in August 1971; over the next five years they robbed banks, bombed airline offices, assassinated several US military officials working in Iran and attempted to hijack an Iran Air jet and to interrupt the Shah's celebrations of 2,500 years of history at Persepolis. In May 1975 the *mujahidin* split into two groups: the smaller (Marxist-inspired) became known as the Battle Organization (**Sazman-e Paykar Baraye Azadi-ye Kargar**), but decided to abandon the armed struggle in favour of political work; the larger (Islamist-inspired) continued as the *mujahidin*. The latter voted in favour of the Islamic Republic in March 1979, but not for the new Constitution. After two years of uneasy co-operation with the **Khomeini** regime, the *mujahidin* broke decisively with the government in June 1981 after the authorities had fired on a huge demonstration that the *mujahidin* had organized to protest at the dismissal of President **Bani Sadr**. The group went underground, and over the next six months, in response to a wave of bombings, the government arrested and executed thousands of suspected *mujahidin*. Their leader, **Massoud Rajavi** (who had unsuccessfully contested the presidency in January 1980), went into exile (in Paris, France) in June 1981 and some of the remaining leadership were killed in a shoot-out with government forces in February 1982; after that, the group's activities were significantly reduced. Rajavi remained in exile in Paris until expelled by the French authorities in 1986 and placed the *mujahidin* within the framework of the **National Council of Resistance**.

Mujahidin-e Khalq Organization (MEK or MKO)

Holy Warriors of the People, Iran

An organization consisting of a number of groups: the National Liberation Army of Iran (NLA, the militant wing of the MEK/MKO); the **People's Mujahidin of Iran**; the **National Council of Resistance**; and the Muslim Iranian Students' Society (a front organization used to raise financial support). The MEK's philosophy combines **Marxism** and **Islam**. Formed in the 1960s, the Organization was expelled from Iran after the **Islamic Revolution** in 1979, and its primary support then came from the Iraqi regime. In its world-wide campaign against the Iranian government it stresses propaganda and occasionally resorts to terrorist violence. During the 1970s the

MEK assassinated US military personnel and US civilians working on defence projects in **Tehran** and supported the occupation, in 1979, of the US embassy there. In 1981 the MEK detonated bombs in the head office of the **Islamic Republic(an) Party** and the Premier's office, killing some 70 high-ranking Iranian officials, including chief Justice Ayatollah Mohammad Beheshti, President **Muhammad Ali Rajai**, and Premier Mohammad-Javad Bahonar himself. In the 1980s the MEK's leaders were forced by Iranian security forces to flee to France. After resettling in Iraq in 1987, almost all of its armed units were stationed in fortified bases near the border with Iran. Some members of its leadership (**Massoud Rajavi** and Maryam Rajavi) were based in **Baghdad** from 1986 onwards. Most of its fighters were organized in the MEK's NLA. Some NLA units possessed tanks, armoured vehicles and heavy artillery. The MEK also had an overseas support structure. Towards the end of the war with Iran, Iraq armed the MEK with military equipment and sent it into action against Iranian forces; by the 1990s the MEK had claimed responsibility for a number of operations in Iran. In 1991 it assisted the Iraqi regime in suppressing the **Shi'a** rebellion in southern Iraq and the Kurdish uprisings in the north, and then continued to perform internal security services for the Iraqi Government. In April 1992 the MEK conducted near-simultaneous attacks on Iranian embassies and installations in 13 countries, underlining its ability to mount large-scale operations overseas. In recent years the MEK has targeted key military officers and, in April 1999, assassinated the deputy chief of the Iranian **armed forces** general staff. In April 2000 the MEK attempted to assassinate the commander of the Nasr Headquarters—the inter-agency board responsible for co-ordinating policies on Iraq. The normal pace of anti-Iranian operations increased during the 'Operation Great Bahman' in February 2000, when the group launched a dozen attacks against Iran, including a mortar attack against the leadership complex in Tehran that houses the offices of the Supreme Leader and the President. During 2000 and 2001 the MEK was regularly involved in mortar attacks and hit-and-run raids on Iranian military and law-enforcement units and on government buildings near the Iran-Iraq border, although its activities have declined since 2001. Many of its members (an estimated 3,800) are now held in Iraq by US forces in a camp north-east of Baghdad. The idea of promoting the MKO, possibly under a new name, to destabilize the Iranian regime, was proposed—to 'horrified reactions' from the US Department of State and UK foreign ministry—in May 2003 by US Undersecretary of Defense, Douglas Feith.

Mujtahid

A **Shi'ite** authority. A *mujtahid* is someone qualified to exercise *ijtihad*. A *mujtahid mutlaq*—absolute *mujtahid*—is someone who has attained the rank of the Four Imams (Abu Hanifa, Malik, ash-Shafi'i, and Ahmad) in knowledge of **Arabic**, qualification to apply legal reasoning, draw analogies and infer rulings from evidence, independently of the methodology and findings of the **Sunni** Schools, through his own linguistic and juridical perspicuity and extensive knowledge of texts.

Mujtama ar-Risali

In **Arabic**: 'a prophetic society'. A term used by Islamists in Algeria to describe the kind of society for which they are struggling. It also means an Islamic society generally, for **Muhammad**, the major human 'source' of **Islam**, was 'the Prophet' (*ar-Rasullah*).

Mukhabarat

Arabic term for 'the secret service', widely used in Jordan and Iraq.

Al-Muqawma al-Mu'mina – *see* Faithful Resistance

Murabitun

Plural of the **Arabic** *mrabet*—a holy man or marabout.

Murabitun

Lebanese **Sunni** Muslim militia, also known as the **Independent Nasserite Movement**.

Musandam Peninsula

Territory claimed by both Oman and two of the United Arab Emirates—Ras al-Khaima and Sharjah.

Al-Musawi, 'Abbas (1952–92)

Lebanese **Shi'ite** Muslim cleric and secretary-general (1991–92) of the militant **Hezbollah** (Party of God) movement. Musawi studied at a Shi'ite *madrasa* (religious college) in **Najaf**, Iraq, where he was strongly influenced by the teachings of Iranian cleric Ayatollah **Khomeini**. In 1992 he was assassinated by the **Israeli Defence Force**.

Muslim Arab Youth Association

An organization based in Los Angeles, USA, one of whose activities has involved raising funds for **Hamas**.

The Muslim Brotherhood

Founded in Al-Ismailiyyah, Egypt, in 1928 by **Hassan al-Banna**, the Muslim Brotherhood developed into an influential movement not only in Egypt, but also elsewhere in the **Middle East**. The classic account of the early phase of the movement is *The Muslim Brethren* by Ishaq Musa al-Husayni. The movement later inspired more militant and radical offshoots that would take its message to other countries. The Brotherhood sought to establish a modern international political movement with **Islam** as its ideological foundation. It sought the application of **Islamic Law**, and to resist the penetration of Western laws, in all so-called Muslim societies, mainly in North Africa and the Middle East. The essentially corporatist vision of society developed by the Brotherhood, especially during the 1940s and 1950s, owed something to European traditions of **national socialism**, but also much to medieval Muslim thought.

The Muslim Brotherhood (Egypt)

Strong particularly among the **Sunni** commercial bourgeoisie in Egypt, the relationship of the Muslim Brotherhood with the populist and statist tendency, epitomized by the **military** coup of the **Free Officers**' in 1952, was severed in 1954 when it was declared illegal. The struggle between the regime of **Gamal Abdel Nasser** and the Muslim Brotherhood was bitter, despite certain similarities in political thought between the two. After the death of Nasser, the attitude of the regime, under President **Sadat**, towards the Brotherhood relaxed somewhat and by 1975 Sadat had released hundreds of members of the Brotherhood who had been jailed after the assassination attempt on Nasser in 1954 and an attempted coup in 1965. During the 1970s, however, many within the Brotherhood became radicalized and new Islamist groups began to emerge. An attack in April 1974 on the **Cairo** Military Engineering College by the Islamic Liberation Organization was intended to preface an assassination attempt on Sadat himself. The attack was put down and most of the leaders executed. One of those seized and then released in the ensuing crackdown was Mustafa Shukri, previously a member of the Muslim Brotherhood. He went on to form a militant group called **at-Takfir wa al-Hijra** (Repentance and Flight/Migration), which in July 1977 kidnapped and killed a former minister. Within weeks Shukri and the members of his group had been captured and executed. In 1981, however, after the regime had apprehended and jailed some 1,500 persons considered to constitute a serious opposition to the government (most but not all of whom were religious personalities), at-Takfir and another group, **al-Jihad** (Holy War/Religious Struggle), assassinated President Sadat. Incoming President **Mubarak** sought to crush the radical Islamist movements, but maintained a more cautious position with respect to the Muslim Brotherhood, which increasingly came to represent the 'moderate' face of **Islam** in Egypt. In the mid-1980s, although it remained proscribed as a political organization in its own right, the Muslim Brotherhood was able to ally itself opportunistically with the (New) **Wafd Party**, which in elections held in May 1984 won 15% of the vote and 12 seats. Three years later, in 1987, it allied itself with the Alliance of Labour, enabling it to win 17% of the vote and 56 seats, while the Wafd won only 11% of the vote and 35 seats.

The Muslim Brotherhood (Jordan)

Elections held in Jordan in November 1989, in response to growing economic and political tension revealed by the '**bread riots**' earlier in the year, allowed 'independent elements', including members of the Muslim Brotherhood, to stand as candidates. The political liberalization enabled a wide range of parties to be represented and to gain seats. Startlingly—although its success was perhaps foreshadowed by its performance in the supplementary elections of 1984—the Muslim Brotherhood won 22 seats, while other Islamist candidates won 12 seats. The speaker of parliament was a member of the Muslim Brotherhood, which, in January 1991, was granted five Cabinet posts (from some of which it was, however, later excluded). Further liberalization measures followed the national elections. The Islamists also performed well in local elections, but they were unable to sustain their success. The crisis in the **Gulf** in 1990–91 revealed yet again the close relationship between Jordan's international vulnerability and need for internal 'security' as a paramount feature of Jordanian domestic politics. The fact that the Muslim Brotherhood formed the largest bloc and the real opposition in parliament—their allies controlled more than one-third of the legislative body—and disagreed with the Government on a number of important policies was perhaps less important than their increasing success in permeating a range of 'civil society' and professional organizations. The 1993 elections reduced the number of Islamists in parliament although the 16 'organized' and 10 'independent' Islamists returned still represented almost one-quarter of all the deputies.

The Muslim Brotherhood (Lebanon)

In elections held in Lebanon in 1992 11 Islamists of various orientations, including members of the Muslim Brotherhood, plus three others elected on the 'Islamic list', were returned to the parliament.

The Muslim Brotherhood (Mauritania)

The smallest Arab nationalist faction in Mauritanian politics. A somewhat conservative force, the Mauritanian Muslim Brotherhood is composed largely of middle-aged businessmen. It favours the strict application of **Shari'a** law.

The Muslim Brotherhood (Syria)

In Syria, the **Hamah** revolt of February 1982 revealed genuine opposition to both the Government's economic programmes and to the regime itself. The Muslim Brotherhood was very much involved in the revolt, providing overall ideological guidance to political action, and indicating its potential longer-term threat to the **Ba'ath** regime. A degree of political liberalization was entertained in May 1990, when Syrian voters were invited to elect a new People's Assembly (**Majlis** ash-Shaab). The number of seats was expanded from 195 to 250 in order to encourage 'independent' candidates, for whom about one-third of all seats was now reserved (the remaining two-thirds were for the Ba'ath Party and its allies in the **National Progressive Front**). The Majlis is a consultative, quasi-corporatist body, but even so the incorporation of even some independent businessmen and figures associated with the Muslim Brotherhood is revealing as an attempt to preclude the wider growth of an Islamist opposition.

Muslim Centrist Party

Moderate Islamic political party in Jordan, established in July 2001 by dissidents of the **Muslim Brotherhood** and the **Islamic Action Front**.

Muslims

Followers of the Islamic faith. 'Muslim' literally means one who believes in **Islam**/ has Islam in his/her heart. Islam literally means 'peace' or 'submission'.

Mussadegh, Muhammad

Iranian political leader and Prime Minister of Iran in 1951–53. Born in 1880, he held a variety of government posts in 1914–25, but retired to private life in protest against the Shah's assumption of dictatorial powers in 1925. He returned to government in 1944 as a member of parliament and quickly established himself as an opponent of foreign interference in Iranian affairs. He successfully fought Soviet attempts to exploit the oilfields of northern Iran and led the movement to nationalize the British-owned Anglo-Iranian Oil Co. He became immensely popular, and after parliament passed his **oil** nationalization act in 1951, the Shah was forced to appoint him Prime Minister. Mussadegh's refusal to negotiate a settlement with Britain alienated the Shah and members of Iran's ruling class. A political crisis developed, and in August 1953 the US **Central Intelligence Agency**, at Britain's instigation, removed him in a *coup d'état* which restored the Shah's absolute powers. Subsequently tried for treason, he was jailed for three years and barred from public life. After his release he was kept under house arrest until his death in 1967.

Mustapha Kemal – *see* Atatürk, Kemal

Al-Mustaqbal

Future

Jordanian political party, whose secretary-general is Suleiman Arar. It won representation for the first time in the general election held in November 1993.

Mutawa

Religious police in Saudi Arabia. It consists of 5,000 police-officers who enforce the *Salat*—five times daily prayers—during which businesses must close. During **Ramadan** the Mutawa are especially diligent.

N

Nablus

A Palestinian town in the **West Bank**.

An-Nahayan, Sheikh Zayed ibn Sultan

Ruler of Abu Dhabi since 1966. Head of state of the United Arab Emirates since December 1971.

An-Nahda (Renaissance) Movement

Algerian Islamist political grouping, led by Lahbib Adami. Suppressed after the declaration of a state of emergency in March 1992.

An-Nahda (Renaissance) Party

Outlawed Tunisian Islamic fundamentalist party. Its membership are, for the most part, in jail, in hiding or in exile. Led by Rachid Ghannouchi, the an-Nahda party was originally established in the 1960s as the **Islamic Tendency Movement**, a peaceful Islamic movement dedicated to creating an Islamic society in Tunisia. It has been illegal ever since, despite widespread support in the country, and has regularly been brutally suppressed.

Najaf

Holy city of Iraq, about 160 km south of **Baghdad**, with a population of 585,600 in 2003. It is the capital of an-Najaf province. Najaf is a great centre of **Shi'a** pilgrimage from throughout the Islamic world. Most important in this respect is the shrine where the imam 'Ali bin Abi Talib, fourth caliph, the cousin and son-in-law of the **Prophet Muhammad**, is buried. Nearby is the Wadi-us-Salaam (Valley of Peace), the world's second largest cemetery, which contains the tombs of several other prophets, including Ibrahim and Ishaq. At the end of the **Gulf War (1991)** there was a large uprising in southern Iraq, including Najaf, against the regime of **Saddam Hussain**. It was put down by the Iraqi **military** with considerable brutality and damage to the city. It proved to be the centre of Shi'a opposition to the US-led

coalition and of demands for full representation of Shi'a interests in the post-war political reconstruction in the aftermath of the **Gulf War (2003)**. Militia loyal to the radical cleric **Moqtada as-Sadr** took control of the city in March–April 2004.

Najd

Central region of Saudi Arabia, which was the centre of **Wahhabism**.

An-Najjade

The Helpers

A small Lebanese Arab socialist unionist party, founded in 1936. It now has some 3,000 members. Its founder and president is Adnane Moustafa al-Hakim.

An-Nakhba

In **Arabic** means 'catacalysm', 'calamity', 'catastrophe'. The term is often used by Arabs to describe the outcome of the 1948 war in Palestine (Arab–Israeli War). During the course of the war about 700,000 **Palestinians** fled from villages and cities in the area which eventually became the State of Israel. They have so far never been allowed to return, and their land was seized by the Israeli government and given to Jewish immigrants.

Namangiani, Juma

Military leader of the **Islamic Movement of Uzbekistan** and of the rebellion of 1998. Strongly influenced by **Wahhabism**, his stated goal was to substitute the corrupt and undemocratic Uzbek government with a political entity covering much of the territory of the newly independent states of Uzbekistan, Tajikistan and Kyrgyzstan, reminiscent of the 15th century Uzbek Khanate. He was reported to have been killed near **Mazar-i-Sharif** in northern Afghanistan, where he is believed to have commanded the **Taliban** forces against the **Northern Alliance** and US troops. However, other reports have suggested that he is still alive in Pakistan or Tajikistan, waiting for the USA to withdraw from Afghanistan.

Nasrallah, Sayyed Hassan

Secretary-general of Lebanese **Hezbollah**.

Nasser, Gamal Abdel

Egyptian Prime Minister in 1954–56 and President in 1956–70. A pragmatic populist regarded as the pioneer of **Arab socialism** and the leader of the Arabs in one of the most critical periods in their history, Nasser was born on 15 January 1918 in the poor Alexandrian suburb of Bacos to southern Egyptian parents. Nasser was able to attend the Royal Military Academy in **Cairo** after the signature of the 1936 pact which, for the first time, allowed the lower class youth to join it. He graduated in July 1938 and joined the Egyptian army. He fought in the first **Arab–Israeli War** in 1948, which increased his awareness of the Palestinian problem and of the contemporary Arabic case. Dissatisfied with the continuing British occupation and the **corruption** of the regime of King **Farouk**, he formed a semi-underground organization, the **Free Officers** (el-Dhobatt el-Ahrar), which ousted Farouk in 1952, forcing him to leave Egypt. The son of King Farouk, Ahmad **Fuad**, was declared king, although only a child. In 1953 the Free Officers deposed Fuad and declared Egypt a republic, with **Muhammad Neguib** as its first President. The remaining British troops were requested to evacuate the country and, by 1954, had done so. Neguib was himself deposed in 1954 by Nasser, who became Prime Minister. In 1956 he announced the nationalization of the **Suez Canal**—a move that was followed by the Suez Crisis and military intervention by Israel, Britain and France in a short-lived attempt to reverse the move. US pressure ended the efforts of the former colonial powers to intervene directly. Nasser was elected President for a six-year term. He was re-elected twice and remained President until his death in 1970. In the **Middle East** Nasser was highly praised for his nationalization of the Suez Canal, his subsequent agrarian reforms and his radical **populism**, and he achieved unprecedented popularity throughout the **Arab World**. He was admired for his support of **Arab nationalism**, and his domestic economic and social reforms that sought to modernize Egypt in the name of the Egyptian masses. He became recognized as a major international power-broker in the politics of the developing world. He was a founding leader of the **Non-aligned Movement**, together with India's Nehru and Indonesia's Sukarno. The defeat of the Arab armies in the **Arab–Israeli War (1967)** virtually destroyed Nasser and he resigned, retracting his resignation after demonstrations of popular support. In November 1967 he accepted **UN Security Council Resolution 242**, which called for the peaceful coexistence of Israel and Arab states in return for Israel's evacuation of the occupied Arab territories. Nasser remained a figure of major importance in Arab politics, acting as the elder statesman of the progressive Arab World, mediating between the **Palestine Liberation Organization** (PLO) and Lebanon to achieve the **Cairo Agreement** of 1969, and again between the PLO and the Jordanian army in 1970. He died of a heart attack in 1970.

Nasserism

An ideology or socio-political doctrine based on the thoughts and actions of **Gamal Abdel Nasser**. It emerged as a series of practical responses to the problems—domestic and foreign—that were encountered by Egypt following the **Free Officers'** coup. A form of populist authoritarianism, it emphasizes the role of the one-party state in economic and social progress at home and a radical anti-imperialist, Third World nationalist stance in foreign affairs. It remains an important current in the political life in Egypt. (See also **Arab socialism**.)

Nasserist Corrective Party

Hizb at-Tas-hih an-Nassir

Yemeni opposition party.

Nasserist Party

Egyptian political party, founded in 1991. Its chairman is Diaa ed-Din Daoud.

Nasserite Popular Organization

Lebanese political grouping that merged with the **Arab Socialist Union** in January 1987. Its secretary-general is Mustafa Saad.

National Action Party

Extreme right-wing 'neo-fascist' party in Turkey, led by Alparslan Turkes. It initially dismissed **Islam** as Arab and therefore inimical to Turkish culture and politics, but later proposed a Turkish-Islamic synthesis. Turkes himself, a life-long pan-Turkist and Turkish nationalist, made the pilgrimage to **Mecca** and returned a *haji* (holy man).

National Bloc (Syria)

Formed in 1927 by a large group of Syrian landowners who represented most of the country's political leadership. After witnessing the defeat of the Great Revolt, they decided that it was necessary to co-operate with the French authorities in order to win greater autonomy. The membership of the Bloc was drawn mostly from the commercial and absentee landowning classes. Its leaders held sway in Syrian politics until new groups began to challenge their authority and legitimacy in the 1940s. Among the most prominent politicians during the period of the Mandate were Abd ar-Rahman Shahbandar, Shukri al-Quwwatli and Jamil Mardam.

National Charter (Iraqi National Accord, INA)

Established in 1990 to achieve a democratic pluralist regime in Iraq that respects human rights and lives peacefully with its citizens, neighbours and the whole world. INA advocated the removal of **Saddam Hussain**'s regime and the promotion of a democratic 'post-Saddam' Iraq.

National Charter (Jordan)

A 60-member royal commission was appointed by King **Hussein** in April 1990 with the aim of drafting guide-lines for the conduct of party political activity in Jordan. The commission comprised members representing all of the political groups in the country, and it produced a written consensus in the form of the National Charter. The Charter was adopted in June 1991 at a national conference of 2,000 leading Jordanians. The National Charter outlines general guide-lines for constructive dialogue between the executive and legislative organs, as well as between decision-makers and political and intellectual élites, concerning questions of authority, rights and responsibility. It enunciated the terms under which political parties could operate—namely, within the framework of the Constitution and free of foreign funding—and also emphasized broad agreement on the need for the reflection in politics of Jordan's cultural pluralism.

National Charter (Yemen)

The National Charter of 1982 is the backbone of the current Yemeni President's **General People's Congress** (GPC) party. It was the result of a committee of more than 50 politicians and intellectuals representing various trends and opinions. The Charter sets out the principles for a democratic republican system in Yemen. It was reissued in 1993 as part of the GPC's electoral programme.

National Commercial Bank

In 1999 the Saudi Arabian government discovered that Khalid bin Mahfouz, son of the founder and now head of the National Commercial Bank (who had received unsecured loans well in excess of his 20% shareholding in the **Bank of Credit and Commerce International**), had used the Bank to transfer US $3m. to charitable organizations that were, in fact, working on behalf of **Osama bin Laden**'s network. Among them were Islamic Relief and **Blessed Relief**. Part of the funds transferred was sent to the International Islamic Relief organization in the Philippines, a Saudi charity established in the early 1990s by Mohammed Jamal Khalifa, bin Laden's brother-in-law. Allegedly, donations were used to finance the Abu Sayyef Islamic group. In 2000, as a result of mounting pressure from the USA, the Saudi government purchased 50% of the National Commercial Bank, thereby reducing Mahfouz's participation to that of a minority shareholder.

National Congress for Popular Forces

Egyptian political coalition.

National Constitution Party

Jordan's largest political coalition, formed in May 1997 from nine centre parties, including **al-Ahd** and the **Jordan National Alliance**. Its secretary-general is Abd al-Hadi al-Majali.

National Consultative Assembly – *see* **Majlis**

National Council of Resistance (NCR)

The Iranian NCR was founded in Paris, France, in July 1981, when former Iranian President **Bani Sadr** and former leader of the **Mujahidin-e Khalq**, **Massoud Rajavi**, found themselves exiled there. It was a coalition of four main groups— the *Mujahidin*, the **National Democratic Front**, the **Kurdish Democratic Party** (KDP) and a group around Bani Sadr—and a number of other groups (15 in all, according to the NCR). The NCR was committed to the idea of a democratic Islamic republic based on a nation-wide system of locally elected councils, to the implementation of radical land reforms, the nationalization of foreign **trade**, a non-aligned foreign policy, to the guaranteed rights of **women**, **minorities**, trade unions and other professional organizations and to the freedom of the press and of political association. Bani Sadr and Rajavi split in March 1984 over the latter's links with Iraq. The KDP split with Rajavi in 1985. The French government asked Rajavi to leave Paris in June 1986 and he moved to **Baghdad**. In June 1987 Rajavi announced the formation of a National Liberation Army as the military wing of the **Mujahidin-e Khalq**. There is also a National Movement of Iranian Resistance based in Paris.

National Council of Revolutionary Command (NCRC—Iraq)

A junta led by **Ahmad Hassan Bakr** and **Abul Salam Arif**, which overthrew **Brig.–Gen. Abdel Karim Kassem** in February 1963. Bakr subsequently became President and Arif Prime Minister until the NCRC was in turn overthrown and Arif took power and became head of state.

National Democratic Alliance

Israeli political grouping, otherwise known as **Balad**. It is currently led by Azmi Bishara.

National Democratic Front

An illegal opposition movement, which existed in the early 1980s in **North Yemen**, supported by the **People's Democratic Republic of Yemen**. It was involved in a number of terrorist actions.

National Democratic Front

Iranian political grouping, founded in 1979. Its leader, Ayatollah Matine-Daftari, has resided in Paris, France, since January 1982.

National Democratic Party (NDP)

Hizb al-Dimuqratti al-Wattaniyya

Originally the Egyptian Arab Socialist Party, the Party was renamed in August 1978. Thereafter President **Sadat** himself took a considerable interest in the NDP, which was closely identified with the regime. With the resignation of Prime Minister Salem in 1978 from the Misr Party, more than 250 members of the People's Assembly joined the NDP and after 1979 it became the dominant political party in Egypt, winning sweeping majorities in elections that year, and consequently achieving an overwhelming majority in the People's Assembly. Following the assassination of Sadat in 1981, **Hosni Mubarak** took over as President of the Republic and became chairman of the NDP as well as the Party's general secretary. For 20 years it dominated Egyptian politics, making Egypt in effect a one-party state. In parliamentary elections held in 2000, however, the NDP won only 388 of the 442 seats in the People's Assembly (compared with 410 in the previous election), which was considered a relatively poor performance. Following these elections, the NDP initiated an internal reform process in order to develop both its structures and principles.

National Democratic Rally

A quasi-political grouping in the Kuwaiti **Majlis**. Founded in 1997, it represents a secular, liberal position. Its secretary-general is Dr Ahmad Bishara.

National Entente Movement

Algerian political grouping, led by Ali Boukhazna

National Front (Iran)

Jebhe-ye Melli

A coalition of nationalists, led by Dr Mohammed Mossadeq, which was strongly opposed to the regime of the Shah and forced him briefly into exile in August 1953. Its ideology was leftist and secular. Its long-term policy has been to call for a restoration of the Constitution of 1906, nationalization of major industries and the creation of a distinctively Iranian form of society that would be 'neither capitalist nor communist'. When Mossadeq presided over the nationalization of the **oil** industry this provoked a confrontation with Britain, leading to his overthrow (with assistance from the US **Central Intelligence Agency**) and the return of the Shah.

Most National Front leaders were arrested after the fall of Mossadeq's Government in 1953 and the movement was reconstituted as the National Resistance Movement. This, in turn, was banned by the government in 1956. During a period of revival, from 1960 to 1963, a religious faction, led by Mehdi Bazargan emerged—the **Liberation Movement of Iran**. During the second half of the 1970s, however, this Islamic faction was overshadowed by more prominent secular and socialist parties—the **Iran Nationalist Party**, the **Iranian Party** and the Society of Iranian Students—which constituted the Union of National Front Forces. In 1978 there was a rift between two of the leaders of the party, Karim Sanjabi and **Shahpur Bakhtiar**. Sanjabi concluded a pact with **Khomeini**—then in exile in Paris—to work for the overthrow of the Shah. He subsequently became foreign minister in Khomeini's first government, although he resigned in April 1979. Bakhtiar, who did not oppose the idea of a constitutional **monarchy**, severely criticized Khomeini and served as the last Prime Minister under the Shah. He was expelled from the party as a traitor and he left Iran in February 1979 after trying to prevent the return of Khomeini.

National Front for the Opposition

Opposition party in Yemen.

National Front for the Salvation of Libya (NFSL)

Libyan opposition group, founded in 1981 in Khartoum, Sudan. It aims to replace the existing regime in Libya by a democratically elected government. The Front's leader is Muhammad Megarief. In May 1984 Libyan intelligence uncovered a plot by the NFSL to assassinate Col **Qaddafi**. The plotters' hideout was attacked and a fierce gun battle ensued. **'Abu Nidal'** was visiting Libya at the time and was staying in a nearby villa, waiting to leave for the airport.

National Guard (Saudi Arabia)

The most prominent internal Saudi Arabian security force, subordinated directly to the king with an approximate strength of 75,000, of which 20,000 serve in the capacity of a reserve militia. The training of the Saudi Arabian National Guard became the responsibility of the Vinnell Corpn of the USA in 1975. About 1,000 US Vietnam veterans were initially recruited to serve in the long-term training programme, designed to convert the Guard into a mobile and hard-hitting counter-insurgency force that could also reinforce the regular army if necessary. The National Guard was swiftly deployed to the border area after Iraq's invasion of Kuwait in 1990 and was actively engaged in the war.

National Homeland Security, Department of

Established in the USA after 11 September 2001 in order to improve the co-ordination of intelligence in 'the war against **terrorism**'.

National Iranian Resistance Movement

This was the first Iranian group to establish itself in exile in Paris, France, after the **Iranian Revolution**. It sought to establish a social-democratic government in Iran and was well funded. Its leader was **Shahpur Bakhtiar**, born in 1917, who had long opposed the Shah, although not so vehemently as to prevent him from being appointed as the Shah's last Prime Minister. He maintained some considerable influence inside Iran, despite being in exile, during the early years of the Islamic Republic, encouraging **Tehran** residents to stage mass protests by means of traffic jams in August 1983 and May 1985. He remained sufficiently close to the monarchists—his willingness to contemplate a constitutional **monarchy** in Iran was known—to prevent many from joining his group.

National Islamic Coalition

A quasi-political grouping in the Kuwaiti **Majlis** that represents **Shi'a** Muslims.

National Islamic Front of Afghanistan

Mahaz e Mill ye Islami ye Afghanistan

Led by Sayyid Ahmad Gailani, whose authority derived in part from his association with a well-known religious family. It has support in **Kandahar** and from the powerful Mangal tribe of Paktia province.

National Lebanese Front

Lebanese political grouping founded in 1999. Its president is Ernest Karam.

National Liberal Party (PNL)

Al-Wataniyin al-Ahrar

Lebanese political grouping founded in 1958. The PNL is a reformist secular party, although it has traditionally had a predominantly **Maronite** Christian membership. Its president is Dory Chamoun.

National Liberation Front (Yemen)

In October 1963 young men from the various British Protectorates of South Arabia, inspired by the ideals of **Arab nationalism** and **socialism**, and supported by Egypt, formed the National Liberation Front (NLF). They provoked a tribal revolt in Radfan, which was heavily put down by British **armed forces** in the name of the **Federation of South Arabia**. The NLF spearheaded a three-year campaign across the territory, but particularly in **Aden** itself, in which 60 people were killed and 350 were injured in Aden alone, one-third of the casualties being British. A state of emergency was declared and the NLF was banned. The Supreme Council of the

Federation of South Arabia, however, which had come into existence in 1959, failed to deal with the uprising and Abd al-Qawi Makkawi, appointed chief minister of Aden in March 1965, appeared more anxious to appease the terrorists than to collaborate with the British. He went into exile and, with Egyptian support, formed an alliance with the NLF, called the **Front for the Liberation of Occupied South Yemen** (FLOSY). As the militants of the NLF became more radical they began to break with the more 'moderate' leaders of the old Federation and to free themselves from financial dependence on Egypt by various means. Assisted by fellow tribesmen in the police force and the federal armed forces, and under the leadership of Qahtan ash-Shaabi (who had emerged as their leader at their first Congress in 1965), they fought the British through 1966 and 1967 and effectively wrested control of the nationalist liberation movement from FLOSY. In December 1966 the NLF declared itself the sole representative of the people of South Arabia. Throughout the early part of the following year it began to take control of state after state in the interior, and by September had forced the High Commissioner to declare openly that the federal government had ceased to exist. The British then supported the NLF (in effect against the pro-**Nasser** FLOSY) to take over formal control. The handover to the NLF was formalized at a meeting in Geneva, Switzerland, where Qahtan ash-Shaabi proclaimed himself President, Prime Minister and commander-in-chief. He at once declared **South Yemen** a unitary state.

National Order Party (NOP)

Efforts by the National Unity Council, the **military** junta that took power in Turkey in May 1960, to detach **Islam** from reactionary political movements emerging during the late 1950s and early 1960s, provided unsuccessful, and by the late 1960s there was a significant increase in political support for the right-wing Islamist party—the NOP—led by Prof. **Necmettin Erbakan**. There was an increasing tendency among conservative politicians to make use of the reactionary elements within the Islamic canon, while, at the same time, they warned of the danger of 'communists'. The Kemalists and those on the left were identified as opponents of 'traditional' Turkish values, while the supporters of big business were labelled 'Masons' or 'Zionists'. The NOP was disbanded by the military regime that took power in 1971. It re-emerged in 1973, however, as the **National Salvation Party**, again led by Necmettin Erbakan.

National Pact (Lebanon)

Al-Mithaq al-Watani

An unwritten agreement that established the political foundations of modern Lebanon, allocating political power according to an essentially confessional system based on the 1932 census. Until 1990 seats in the Lebanese parliament were divided according to a 6-to-5 ratio of Christians to Muslims. After 1990 they were allocated in equal proportions. Positions in the government bureaucracy are allocated on a similar basis. Indeed, gaining political office in Lebanon is virtually impossible without the firm backing of a particular religious or confessional group. The Pact also allocated public offices along religious lines, with the top three positions in the ruling 'troika' distributed as follows: the presidency is reserved for a **Maronite** Christian; the premiership for a **Sunni** Muslim; and the presidency of the National Assembly for a **Shi'a** Muslim. Efforts to alter or abolish the confessional system have been at the centre of Lebanese politics for decades. Those religious groups most favoured by the 1943 formula sought to preserve it, while those who regarded themselves as thereby disadvantaged sought to either revise it after updating key demographic data or to abolish it entirely. None the less, many of the provisions of the National Pact were codified in the 1989 **Ta'if Agreement**, perpetuating sectarianism as a key element of Lebanese political life.

National Pact (Tunisia)

On 7 November 1988 President **Ben Ali** invited Tunisia's seven political parties to join with representatives of the business community, the trade unions, the human rights community, the farmers' association, national **women**'s organizations and the lawyers' guild in co-writing the National Pact, a major consensus-based document establishing the rules of political engagement in a republican **democracy**, as well as the basic economic and foreign policy orientations of the country.

National Progressive Front (Iraq)

In July 1973, in order to broaden its base, the **Ba'ath** regime in Iraq formed a **National Progressive Front** (NPF) that included the **Communist Party of Iraq** (CPI). In 1975 representatives of the **Kurds**—the Democratic Kurdistan Party (later the **Kurdistan Revolutionary Party**)—joined the NPF. The Front was to be directed by the High Council, controlled by the Ba'ath, of which three members were to be communists, three Kurds and two others were to represent pre-Ba'ath liberal parties, such as the National Democratic Party and the Independence Party. Eight members, including the NPF secretary-general, were to be Ba'ath. The NPF, which did not have official Kurdish support, was fairly ineffectual throughout its existence. It effectively ceased to have any significance after the suppression of the CPI in mid-1979.

National Progressive Unionist Group or National Union Progressive Party (Egypt)

Hizb at-Tagamaa al-Watani at-Taqaddam al-Wahdawi

The Egyptian Tagammu party was founded in 1976 as a party of the left in the tradition of the **Arab Socialist Union**. It was originally known as the National

Progressive Unionist Organization and was led by Khalid Mohi ad-Din (Muhiyyidin), one of the few **Free Officers** from July 1952 still prominent in politics, and a Marxist. The party regards itself as a coalition of leftist forces and has historically included Nasserists, Marxists and Arab nationalists. It was critical of the 1978 **Camp David Accords** and Egypt's March 1979 peace treaty with Israel. It supports a more radical foreign policy and opposes the **National Democratic Party**'s privatization agenda, favouring instead a return to a national command economy. It made some attempts to break away from its élitist core and reach out to the grassroots, but it lacks a strong popular base, partly because government controls on labour organization and unions restrict its ability to mobilize its natural constituency among the Egyptian working class. It was only able to gain about 4% of the vote in the 1984 elections. The party has moved noticeably to the centre in recent years, dropping the word 'socialist' from its title in 1995 and voting to abstain from rather than to oppose **Mubarak**'s re-election referendum in 1999. Khalid Mohi ad-Din remains its leader, while Tagammu's secretary is Dr Rifa'at es-Said. It has a membership of about 160,000.

National Reform Movement

Algerian political grouping, led by Abdullah Djaballah

National Renewal Party

Algerian political grouping.

National Religious Party (NRP—Israel)

Miflaqa Datit-Leumit, Mafdal

Founded in 1956, the NRP was a merger of **Mizrachi** (short for 'spiritual centre'), formally established in 1918, and HaPoel HaMizrachi (Mizrachi Worker), founded in 1922. The movement of orthodox religious Zionists that this party represented from the outset (it was well represented in the Twelfth Zionist Conference in 1921) has been of very considerable influence. The NRP served in every government after the establishment of Israel, except for a brief period from 1958 to 1959, when it left the coalition over the issue of who should be considered a Jew for purposes of immigration. The party is overseen by a World Centre, a council elected by the world conference of the party (which is nevertheless overwhelmingly an Israeli political movement), which also supervises the party's youth and **women**'s organizations. It is strongly focused on religious issues, and since 1967 has regarded the capture and occupation of ancient Israeli towns and territory as fulfilment of the covenant between God and the Jewish people. Some of the youth groups have close relations with the **Gush Emunim** (Bloc of the Faithful), the leading movement of **West Bank** settlers. In fact, in some respects, the Youth Faction of the NRP considers itself the political representative of the Gush Emunim. Most of the support for the NRP comes from Orthodox Jews, and mainly from the **Ashkenazim** (so-called **Oriental** Jews). The NRP has seats in the **Knesset**.

National Resistance Council (Iran) – *see* National Council of Resistance

National Salvation Party (NSP—Turkey)

Formed in 1973, the NSP was the major Islamist party in Turkey during the 1970s. Based on elements of an earlier **National Order Party**, led by **Necmettin Erbakan** until it was disbanded by the **military** regime in 1971, it emerged as the third party in the elections of 1973 after winning nearly 12% of the vote. Four years later its share of the vote fell to 8.6%, while that of the essentially secular **Republican People's Party** (RPP) rose from 33% to 41.4%. The 'Save **Jerusalem**' rally of 6 September 1980 in Konya, organized by the NSP and led by the Party's leader, Erbakan, stirred the fears of the secularists in Turkey that the country might be deeply affected by the **Iranian Revolution** and the emergence of the Islamic Republic of Iran. At the rally, demonstrators marched in green robes and the fez cap associated with the long-defunct Ottoman **Caliphate** (abolished in March 1924), calling for the restoration of an **Islamic state**. Six days later the armed forces seized power. Political parties were disbanded, their assets seized and their leaders banned from political activity. Erbakan was arrested and tried for attempting to subvert the state. Lack of evidence meant that the prosecution failed. The junta drew up a new constitution in 1982, and political parties were allowed to operate again in the spring of 1983. General elections were held later in that year. For a while, the **Motherland Party**, which came to power in 1983, and which pursued deeply conservative policies, was able to contain the Islamist tendencies, largely by patronage. By 1987, however, the Islamists had gained even greater strength. In January 1987 a major rally was organized by the supporters of Erbakan at Beyazit Square in **Istanbul** following prayers at the Sultan's Mosque. Congregations throughout the city had been prepared for the demonstration. Some imams were said to have gone so far as to denounce the 1982 Constitution as being in violation of the **Koran**. The Islamists were showing their strength—having infiltrated the schools and universities, the bureaucracy and administration, and even the armed services. Now, however, the party which represented their interests was the **Welfare Party**, which had emerged in 1983 when new political parties were allowed to register once more.

National socialism

A term used loosely here to designate a strongly nationalist political ideology committed to the establishment of a unified, corporate state in which class and sectarian divisions are minimized by the implementation of legislation repressing the institutional expression of such divisions (through trades unions, a plurality of political parties, etc.). State control of the 'commanding heights' of the economy, various forms of collective ownership and control, an emphasis on public and collective social and cultural forms, and a strong apparatus of coercion and repression are characteristics of such a system or regime. (See also **Arab socialism**.)

National Union of Algerian Students

Independent national student movement's organizational vehicle. It was dissolved by decree in January 1971.

National Union Movement

The official party of the Egyptian and Syrian regions of the **United Arab Republic** from 1958 until 1961, when it was replaced by the **Arab Socialist Union**.

National Union Party

Israeli political party supportive of Jewish **settlements** in the **Occupied Territories** of the **West Bank** and **Gaza Strip**. It claimed that the Israeli delegation negotiating the **Geneva Accord** was in contravention of Israeli law that prevents the unauthorized negotiation of territorial concessions.

National Unity

Right-wing Israeli political grouping, comprising **Moledet**, Tekuma and **Herut**.

National Unity Committee (NUC)

In May 1960 a **military** coup replaced the **Democratic Party** in Turkey and established the NUC, a junta which espoused Kemalist traditions, but maintained a relatively liberal regime. It established a new Constitution in 1961. It recognized the importance of **Islam** to the Turkish people and seemed to be trying to return to the Kemalist policy of the 1920s, when Islam was regarded as an instrument of state policy, out of reach of sectarian politics. However, the country was returned to civilian control after only a brief period of military rule, and multi-party politics resumed, until the next coup in 1971.

National Unity Front

Political grouping in Qatar.

Nationalism, Arab – *see* **Arab nationalism**

Nationalist Front

Right-wing coalitions that governed Turkey in 1975–78.

Nationalist Labour Party

Reconstituted Turkish neo-fascist party.

Natural gas

Many of the major **oil**-producing countries in the region are also producers and exporters of natural gas. Algeria is the largest, ranking fifth in the world with an output of 78,200m. cu m. Iran is also a major producer (ranking eighth in the world), as is Saudi Arabia (10th). In recent years Qatar has developed a world-class gas industry by tapping capital markets and structured financing to underwrite the rapid development of its 900,000,000m. cu ft of North Field gas reserves. Iran and Saudi Arabia are also major consumers of natural gas (respectively the eighth and 10th largest in the world).

Nazarbayev, Nursultan (1940–)

Chairman of the Kazakh Supreme Soviet (1989–90), a member of the Soviet politburo (1990), and President of the Kazakh SSR (1990–91), he became independent Kazakhstan's first President in 1991.

Nazareth

Town on the **West Bank**.

Near East

A term coined by Western geographers to designate a region distinct from the **Middle East** and the Far East. The Near East (in French, Proche Orient) virtually coincided with the **Ottoman Empire**. The term Middle East (Moyen Orient) is now more commonly used and roughly incorporates both the Near and earlier Middle East.

Neguib, Muhammad (1901–84)

Muhammad Neguib was born in Khartoum, Sudan, in 1901. He was educated at the **Cairo** Military Academy and during the Second World War he joined the **Free Officers' Movement**. The failed 1948 Palestine campaign reinforced Neguib's view that the Government of **Farouk I** was inefficient and corrupt. In July 1952 Gen. Neguib, Col **Gamal Abdel Nasser**, Abdul al-Hakim and the Free Officers forced Farouk to abdicate through a *putsch*. After the Egyptian Revolution Neguib became commander-in-chief, Prime Minister and President of the republic while

Nasser held the post of Minister of the Interior. The young officers considered Neguib to be too moderate and in November 1954 he resigned as President and retired from public life, to be replaced by Nasser.

Nehzat-e Azadi-ye Iran

Liberation Movement of Iran

Movement founded in 1961. It emphasizes human rights as defined in **Islam**. The Movement's general secretary is Dr Ibrahim Yazdi.

Neo-colonialism

A term used to refer to the system of economic, political and cultural links, which continue to tie a formally independent state to a former colonial power, thereby reducing its real autonomy and independence.

Neo-Destour Party (Tunisia)

Established in the 1930s by **Habib Bourguiba** and his colleagues (including Mahmoud Materi, Taher Safer and Bahri Guiga) to replace the **Destour Party**—which had been the first political organization to challenge French colonial rule in Tunisia—as the vehicle for the nationalist movement in Tunisia. The Neo-Destour leadership had little in common with the traditional élites that dominated the Destour Party. They were, for the most part, members of a new intelligentsia of modest social origins with their roots in the provinces, educated in Franco-Arab schools, especially Sadiki College, in Tunisia and at university in France. The group who founded the Neo-Destour originally participated in the Destour, but decided early on that an effective nationalist movement would require a larger popular base. The new party included some members of the traditional élite, but reached beyond the privileged minority to involve ordinary urban and rural Tunisians. The Neo-Destour regarded itself as leading a mass nationalist movement whose objective, after independence, was modernization under the tutelage of intellectuals. It stressed the unified, corporate nature of Tunisian society and the ability of the party to represent the interests of this society as a whole. In fact, however, despite this strong political ideology, the Neo-Destour relied heavily on funding from the large rural landowners and merchants, and on the mobilization of the rural masses, for its success in displacing the Destour as the main vehicle for the nationalist movement.

Netanyahu, Binyamin

Israeli Prime Minister and leader of a **Likud** government from 1996 until 1999.

Neve Shalom

Synagogue in **Istanbul**. It was bombed by the organization of **'Abu Nidal'** in 1986, an attack in which 22 people were killed. In November 2000 it was bombed again, together with the Beth Israel synagogue. Responsibility for the 2003 bombing was claimed by both the **Abu Hafs al-Masri Brigade** and the **Great Eastern Islamic Raiders' Front**, a small fundamentalist group.

New Generation Party

A centrist, Green political party in Jordan, formed in late 1999. It is led by Zahi Karim.

New Great Game

The Great Game originally referred to the colonial enterprise in South Asia, and in particular to Afghanistan, where Russia and Great Britain struggled for control. The so-called New Great Game is about Central Asian **oil** and **gas**. The players this time are Russia, China, the USA, and other states in the region (e.g. Iran, Turkey and Saudi Arabia).

New Liberal Party

Israeli political party, formed in 1987 by a merger of three groups: **Shinui-Movement for Change** (formed in 1974 and restored in 1978 when the Democratic Movement for Change split into two parties), the Centre Liberal Party (formed in 1986 by members of the **Liberal Party** of Israel) and the **Independent Liberal Party** (formed in 1965 by seven Liberal Party of Israel **Knesset** members, after the formation of the **Herut-Liberal Party** bloc). It has around 20,000 members.

New Wafd Party

Hizb al-Wafd al-Jadid

The Egyptian New Wafd Party, founded in February 1978, disbanded in June 1978 and reformed in 1983, gains some strength from its association with the old **Wafd Party**, which was founded in 1919 and enjoyed great popularity for its strenuous resistance to British interference in Egyptian affairs, but was banned in 1952. On the other hand, the party has not been helped by the fact that its leader, Fuad Seraq ad-Din, was associated with the party's prior history of **corruption**. The New Wafd has tried to place itself at the ideological 'centre' between the main historic traditions in Egypt of **Arab socialism** and private capitalism. It has been critical of the government's encouragement of foreign private investment and advocated a more balanced approach to the relationship between private and public sectors. It is led now by Nu'man Jum'ah, with Ibrahim Farag as secretary-general.

401

Nile river

The longest river in Africa, rising in Uganda, passing through Sudan and Egypt and disgorging into the **Mediterranean**. It is a crucial source of **water** for irrigation in both Sudan and Egypt and subject of a long history of negotiations and disputes regarding access to and control of its waters.

9/11 Commission

A 10-member bipartisan independent Commission established to investigate the background to the events of 11 September 2001, under the chairmanship of Thomas Kean, former Republican governor of New Jersey, appointed by the US **Bush** Administration. The full report was released in July 2004. Preliminary findings suggested that there were many indications, from as far back as 1995 and certainly during 2001, that a terrorist attack on US targets, probably using hijacked aircraft, was being planned.

Niyazov, Saparmyrat (1940–)

On 13 January 1990 Saparmyrat Niyazov became Chairman of the Supreme Soviet, the supreme legislative body in the Turkmen Soviet Socialist Republic. On 27 October he was elected as the first President of the Republic of Turkmenistan. On 22 October 1993 he renamed himself Turkmenbashi, 'Leader/Father of all Turkmens'. On 29 December 1999 he was proclaimed President for Life. Niyazov is an authoritarian leader, well known for the personality cult he has established. After an alleged assassination attempt against him on 25 November 2002, the Turkmen authorities conducted a campaign of arresting suspected conspirators and members of their families on a massive scale.

Non-aligned Movement (NAM)

The NAM is an international organization of states which consider themselves not formally aligned with or against any major power bloc. It was formed in 1961 on the initiative of Josip Broz Tito, then President of Yugoslavia. The first conference of non-aligned heads of state, at which 25 countries were represented, was convened at Belgrade in September 1961, largely through the initiative of Tito, who had expressed concern that an accelerating arms race might result in war between the Soviet Union and the USA.

Subsequent conferences involved ever-increasing participation by developing countries. The 1964 conference in **Cairo**, at which 47 countries were represented, featured widespread condemnation of Western **colonialism** and the retention of foreign military installations. Thereafter, the focus shifted away from essentially political issues to the advocacy of solutions to global economic and other problems.

Northern Alliance (Afghanistan)

Anti-**Taliban** Afghan military coalition consisting of warlords from the fight against the Soviet Union and the subsequent civil war.

Northern Tier

Term used to refer to the non-Arab countries of the **Middle East** in the north of the region—notably Turkey, Iran and Afghanistan. Also included are the Central Asian states of the former Soviet Union—Kazakhstan, Kyrgyzstan, Turkmenistan, Tajikistan and Uzbekistan.

North Yemen

The division of 'Yemen' into two parts originates in the division of South Arabia between the Ottoman Turks and the British in the latter part of the 19th century. In 1911, after several uprisings in the north, Imam **Yahya** concluded the Treaty of Da'an, which conceded nominal control of 'foreign affairs' to the Turks and gave the local ruler effective control of 'the north'. The British had already concluded a series of treaties with the numerous sheikhdoms and **tribes** of the 'south'. In the period after the First World War, Yahya was able to bring the major areas (Zaidi and Shafai) of 'the north' under either his control or that of friendly local chiefs. In 1934 Imam Yahya tacitly accepted the boundaries agreed between Britain and the Turks, and was recognized as 'king' in return. Yahya made his son, Ahmad, crown prince, and provoked a struggle over the succession. In February 1948, Yahya was assassinated, in the first post-war coup in the **Arab World**. His son managed to rally the tribes, despite his unpopularity in some quarters, and survived a failed **military** coup and several assassination attempts. He ended the country's isolation and maintained a claim to rule the whole of South Arabia. Autocratic and traditionalist though he was 'at home', he was hostile to the continuing British presence in **Aden** and in 1953, with the support of other Arab states, raised the issue at the UN. In order to acquire external support and arms, he signed a treaty in 1955 with Saudi Arabia and Egypt and later made similar agreements with a number of Eastern European governments. He also joined with Egypt and Syria in the **United Arab States**, which implied backing **Nasser**, champion of radical **Arab nationalism**. After another assassination attempt, Imam Ahmad gradually handed over power to Badr. When he died in September 1962, Badr assumed the throne. Almost immediately, there was an attempted coup by Yemeni army officers assisted by the Egyptian army. A senior Yemeni army officer, **Col Abdullah as-Sallal**, was proclaimed President of a new **Yemen Arab Republic**. Badr was reported dead and his uncle, Hassan, rallied the royalists, taking the title of imam. After two months of fighting, in which Egypt and Saudi Arabia were both involved (on opposite sides), Badr reappeared and resumed the imamate. The USA recognized the new republic; Britain did not. The Yemen Arab Republic was admitted to the United Nations.

North Yemen civil war

After the ruler of **North Yemen**, Imam **Ahmad ben Yahya**, was overthrown by a republican *coup d'état*, civil war ensued, lasting until 1970. The republicans were supported by Egyptian forces and the monarchists by the army of Saudi Arabia. These external interventions prolonged the civil war.

Nouakchott

Capital of Mauritania. Port and centre of commerce. Nouakchott lies between the southern Sahelian regions and northern Saharan regions of the country.

Nuri, Abdullah

Former Iranian Minister of the Interior, one of Iran's leading reformers.

Nusayri/Nusayriyyah

The Nusayri are a **Shi'ite** group which traces its origins to the eleventh Shi'a imam al-Hasan al-Askari (d. 873) and his pupil Abu Shu'ayb Mohammed Ibn Nusayr (d. 868). They are also known as **Alawites**. The Nusayri doctrine is a mixture of Islamic, Gnostic and Christian beliefs, some of which have led them to be treated as heretics by **Sunni** Muslims. Nusayris have their own distinct religious leaders, called sheikhs, believed to be endowed with divine authority. Nusayris are born into the sect; an initiation ceremony serves to confirm their membership. Historically, the Nusayris lived mainly in the mountains of Syria. At the end of the 13th century many Shi'as were massacred by Sunni Muslims who objected to Shi'a support for the Christian crusaders. From then on the Nusayris and other Shi'ite branches were required to conform to the practices of Sunni **Islam**. In the 20th century Nusayris/ Alawites have enjoyed a degree of political influence disproportionate to their numbers. It is estimated that there are about 600,000 Nusayris in Syria, where they have located their headquarters in **Damascus**. After the First World War France made an unsuccessful attempt to establish a separate Nusayri/Alawite state. Since 1970, following the coup of the Nusayri/Alawite air force chief, **Hafiz al-Assad**, the Nusayris/Alawites have dominated Syrian political and military life. Attempts to discredit President Assad politically because of his heterodox religious beliefs were unsuccessful.

O

OAPEC – *see* **Organization of Arab Petroleum Exporting Countries**

Öcalan, Abdullah

Leader of the **Kurdistan Workers' Party**. Captured and tried in 1999, he was sentenced to death. However, international protest prevented his execution. He remains imprisoned.

Occupied Territories

The Occupied Territories refer usually to the **West Bank** (of the Jordan river) and the **Gaza Strip**, which were occupied by Israel during the **Arab–Israeli War (1967)** and which remained illegally occupied, under Israeli military rule for the most part, until the mid-1990s, when the **Palestinian National Authority** acquired limited authority over certain functions and activities. The peace process which resulted in a peace agreement between Egypt and Israel following the 1978 **Camp David Accords** that restored Sinai to Egypt, brought about the withdrawal of Israeli forces of occupation there. Negotiated agreement between Israel and Syria resulted in the withdrawal of Israeli forces from most of the **Golan Heights**, also occupied during the 1967 war. The Gaza Strip, however, which was once Egyptian territory, remains under Israeli occupation although there has been a partial withdrawal of Israeli forces and of Jewish **settlements** in recent years. The West Bank, however, remains for the most part under Israeli occupation, with the number of Jewish settlements there having continued to increase over the past two-and-a-half decades, despite the agreements regarding Jewish settlement in the Occupied Territories at Camp David in 1978. There have been two uprisings (*intifada*) in the Occupied Territories—the first in 1987–93 and the second (known as the **al-Aqsa** *intifada*) from 2000 onwards.

October War – *see* Arab–Israeli War (1973)

Office of the Iraq Programme

UN Office established in October 1997 to assume responsibility for the implementation of UN Security Council Resolution 986, adopted in April 1995 to provide for the limited sale of Iraqi petroleum to enable the purchase of humanitarian supplies and the provision of contributions to the UN Compensation Committee, which had been established to settle claims against Iraq resulting from the **Gulf War (1991)**. In February 1998 the UN Security Council approved a resolution expanding the **Oil for Food** programme; it was extended again in October 1999. In December 1999 the Security Council adopted a resolution that established a new policy towards Iraq. This provided for an unlimited 'ceiling' on petroleum exports under the agreed humanitarian programme and for a suspension of sanctions, dependent on Iraq's co-operation with a new arms inspection body, the UN Monitoring, Verification and Inspection Committee (**UNMOVIC**), that was to replace the UN Special Commission (**UNSCOM**) established in 1991 to monitor the disposal of weapons. At the end of March 2000 the Security Council doubled the maximum permitted revenue from the sale of **oil** and enlarged the range of possible purchases. The existing oil-for-food regime was extended in early July 2001 and a further extension was granted in November. By the end of May 2002 assistance totalling US \$22,000m. had arrived in Iraq under the programme.

Office of Services – *see* Afghan Service Bureau

OIC – *see* Organization of the Islamic Conference

Oil

The discovery of oil in the **Middle East** during the period between the 1930s and 1950s began to transform the economies of those countries in which it was found and gave a new economic impetus to the region as a whole. Several of the **Gulf states** in particular are major oil producers—notably Saudi Arabia (the world's largest oil-producing country, with output of some 9,000m. barrels per day), the United Arab Emirates and Kuwait (respectively the world's 11th and 14th largest producers). Other major producers include Iran (which ranks fourth in the world), Iraq (which ranks 12th) and Algeria (15th). Libya, Egypt and several other countries also produce significant amounts of oil. Saudi Arabia is also a major consumer of oil, as a major industrial economy, ranking 15th in the world.

Oil exploration (Western Sahara)

In recent years the Moroccan authorities in occupied **Western Sahara** have allowed foreign companies to explore for **oil**, even though the status of the territory remains in dispute, with a UN 'peace process' under way (albeit long delayed) that requires a referendum to determine its final status. US companies (e.g. Kerr-McGee) and French companies (e.g. Total) are involved in these exploration activities.

Oil for Food

The UN policy which enabled Iraq after the **Gulf War (1991)** to sell limited amounts of **oil** on the international market in return for which it was able to import specified food and medical supplies. The policy was followed throughout the 1990s.

Oil prices

Oil prices have fluctuated significantly, both in nominal and real terms, in recent decades. The rapid expansion of oil production in the 1950s and generally low prices throughout the 1960s and into the early 1970s helped promote the post-war economic recovery and boom. This boom was already faltering and running into crisis by the late 1960s and early 1970s, but the dramatic increase in oil prices engineered by the **Organization of Petroleum Exporting Countries** (OPEC) in the mid-1970s and, again, in the late 1970s undoubtedly further accelerated the onset of global recession in the late 1970s and early 1980s. Price rises enabled the oil-rich states of the **Middle East** to dramatically increase their export earnings and revenues and to reinvest in their economies and welfare provision. For states deficient in the resource, the increase in **energy** costs that was a consequence of higher oil prices increased their debts, often to intolerable levels. The pressure for economic reform and liberalization, which led to austerity measures that included cuts in subsidies, and to sharp rises in the cost of basic goods and growing unemployment, derived in large part from changes in oil prices. World-wide responses to OPEC's strategy—including the increasing levels of output and export from non-Middle Eastern oilfields during the 1980s—contributed to a relative decline in oil prices and, thus, to declining oil revenues for the Middle Eastern members of the **Organization of Arab Petroeleum Exporting Countries** from the latter part of the 1980s into and throughout the 1990s. Even states with substantial oil reserves, such as Iraq, became desperate to maintain prices, particularly when they had major expenditure commitments (such as the war with Iran) to fund. Arguably, Kuwait's evident willingness to increase production levels and allow prices to slip was a crucial factor behind Iraq's invasion of that country in 1990. In the aftermath of the **Gulf War (1991)**, however, Iran and Saudi Arabia were able to make up the lost production with little effect on consumer prices. As oil production expanded in the 1990s, the relative contribution of the Middle East declined; by 1998 it contributed only 34% of total world crude oil production. Total revenues declined from US \$250,000m. in 1981 to about \$110,000m. in 1998. It was not until 1999–2000, when relations between Iran and Saudi Arabia improved, that OPEC was able to cut production and drive oil prices and revenues upwards once again.

Oil production and reserves

Saudi Arabia is the world's largest **oil** producer, with output of more than 262,000m. barrels in 2002. Iraq is the second largest producer, with output of more than 110,000m. barrels, followed by the United Arab Emirates (100,000m. barrels), Kuwait (slightly less than 100,000m. barrels), Iran (about 90,000m. barrels) and Venezuela (slightly more than 75,000m. barrels). All of these countries have reserves that will last 75–100 years at current rates of production. Oil producers with an annual output of 25,000m. barrels and more include Russia (about 60,000m. barrels) and the USA (about 30,000m. barrels), with reserves sufficient, respectively, for 22 years and 11 years of production at current levels, and Libya (about 30,000m. barrels), with reserves sufficient for another 59 years. Other significant oil producers in the region include Qatar, Algeria, Oman and Egypt. Modern exploration techniques are very sophisticated, but never allow a precise assessment of oil reserves. Saudi Arabia is considered to have the largest known oil reserves in the world, but many other countries in the **Arabian Peninsula**, such as Kuwait, Qatar and some of the United Arab Emirates, also have substantial reserves. Large reserves are known to exist in Iraq and Iran. Egypt has significant although smaller oil reserves, as do Libya, Algeria and Tunisia.

Oman, Sultanate of

Saltanat Uman

Oman borders the Arabian Sea, the Gulf of Oman, and the **Persian (Arabian) Gulf**, lying between Yemen and the United Arab Emirates, with Saudi Arabia to the west. Its strategic location on Musandam Peninsula, adjacent to the Straits of Hormuz, makes it a vital transit point for world crude **oil**. Its total area is 212,460 sq km. Muscat is its capital. There are six regions (*mintaqah*, plural *mintaqat*) and two governorates (*muhafazah*, plural *muhafazat*): Ad-Dakhiliyah, Al-Batinah, Al-Wusta, Ash-Sharqiyah, Az-Zahirah, Masqat, Musandam (governorate), and Zufar (governorate). The total population is 2,713,462, of which the majority are indigenous and local Arabs, but a significant **minority** are **Baluchis** and South Asian (Indian, Pakistani, Sri Lankan, Bangladeshi). There is also a smaller minority of Africans. At July 2002 the estimated population included 527,078 non-nationals. Most (75%) of the indigenous population are Ibadhi Muslims, but there are also **Sunni** and **Shi'a** Muslims, Hindus and others. **Arabic** is the official language, but English, Baluchi, Urdu and various Indian dialects are spoken. There is no formal constitution, but on 6 November 1996 the ruling monarch, **Sultan Qaboos ibn Said as-Said,** issued a royal decree promulgating a new basic law which, among other things, clarifies the royal succession, provides for a Prime Minister, bars ministers from holding interests in companies doing business with the government, establishes a bicameral legislature, and guarantees basic civil liberties for Omani citizens. The head of state and Prime Minister is Sultan Qaboos (since 23 July 1970). The

Cabinet is appointed by the monarch. The **monarchy** is hereditary. The bicameral **Majlis** of Oman consists of an upper chamber, or Majlis ad-Dawla (which has 48 members, all appointed by the monarch and with advisory powers only), and a lower chamber, or Majlis ash-Shura. The lower chamber has 83 members who are elected by limited suffrage for three-year terms. The monarch makes the final selections, however, and can negate election results. The Majlis ash-Shura has limited power to propose legislation, but otherwise acts in an advisory capacity only. Elections were last held in September 2000 and were next due to be held in September 2003. The legal system is based on English common law and **Islamic Law**, with ultimate appeal to the monarch. Oman has not accepted compulsory International Court of Justice jurisdiction. There are no recognized political parties.

Media

Despite a 1984 law allowing for 'freedom of opinion', nothing critical of the government may be published. There are five daily newspapers, of which *al-Watan* and the *Oman Daily Newspaper* are widely read. There is one state-controlled television service and two state-controlled radio services. In 2000 there was one internet service provider, and in 2002 there were 120,000 internet users.

History

Qaboos ibn Said as-Said ousted his father in 1970 and has ruled as sultan ever since. His extensive modernization programme has opened the country to the outside world and has preserved a long-standing political and military relationship with the United Kingdom. Oman's moderate, independent foreign policy has sought to maintain good relations with all Middle Eastern countries. Sultan Qaboos is an authoritarian but paternalistic monarch. Members of his family hold key political positions. The regime faces no serious opposition, though religious fundamentalists are feared.

International relations

As regards international relations, Oman signed a boundary treaty with the United Arab Emirates in 1999, but the completed boundary agreement was not ratified until the end of 2002; undefined segments of the Oman-UAE boundary remain with Ra's al-Khaymah and ash-Shariqah (Sharjah) emirates, including the Musandam Peninsula, where an administrative boundary substitutes for an international boundary.

Oman, economy

Oman's economic performance improved significantly in 2000, due largely to the upturn in **oil** prices. The government is proceeding with the privatization of utilities, the development of a body of commercial law to facilitate foreign investment, and increased budgetary outlays. Oman continues to liberalize its markets and joined the

World Trade Organization in November 2000. The rate of growth of the country's gross domestic product improved in 2001 despite the global slowdown.

Strengths

Oman has been able to exploit its non-membership of the **Organization of Petroleum Exporting Countries**. It has the potential to develop a sizeable fishing industry.

Weaknesses

Over-dependence on oil, which contributes 90% of gross national product. Proven reserves of oil are sufficient to last only another 20 years at current levels of production. The services sector is undeveloped. All sectors of the economy are dependent on immigrant labour.

Omar, Mullah Mohammad

The spiritual leader of the **Taliban**. He remained at large at the end of 2003.

OMETZ – *see* Political Zionist Opposition

Omnium Nord Africain (ONA)

A Moroccan holding company founded in 1934. In 1980 the Moroccan *makhzen* (the king's royal household) acquired a major interest in the company—an industrial conglomerate whose gross revenues accounted for more than 5% of Morocco's gross domestic product. King **Hassan II** appointed his son-in-law to administer the company. ONA subsequently acquired major stakes in Morocco's leading commercial banks, giving the *makhzen* a strategic position in private-sector **industry** and finance at a time when many public-sector enterprises were being privatized.

One Israel

Israel Ahat

Major Israeli political grouping, comprising the **Israel Labour Party**, **Gesher** and **Meimad.** It is currently led by Ra'anan Cohen. In elections to the **Knesset** held in May 1999 it obtained 20% of the vote and 26 of the 120 seats.

One People (Nation)

Israeli leftist political party. It is currently led by Amir Peretz.

OPEC – *see* Organization of Petroleum Exporting Countries

OPEC Development Fund

The OPEC Fund for International Development is a multilateral development finance institution. It was established in January 1976 by the member countries of the **Organization of Petroleum Exporting Countries** following a decision taken in March 1975 by the sovereigns and heads of state of the members of that organization, meeting in **Algiers**, Algeria. Its aim is to promote co-operation between OPEC members and other developing countries as an expression of south-south solidarity, and, in particular, to help the poorer, low-**income** countries in pursuit of their social and economic advancement. The Fund does this by providing loans, grants, consultancy to developing countries in the areas of humanitarian **aid** and development projects, balance-of-payments support, etc. The Fund's resources derive from voluntary contributions made by OPEC member countries and loan repayments, as well as from income accruing from the Fund's investments and loans. All developing countries, with the exception of OPEC member countries, are in principle eligible for Fund assistance. The least developed countries are accorded higher priority. In addition, the Fund has co-operated with multilateral, bilateral, national, non-governmental and other organizations worldwide.

Operation Avalanche

Operation Avalanche, undertaken in the southern part of Afghanistan during the final weeks of 2003 against **Taliban** forces, was the largest military operation launched by the US-led forces after the collapse of the Taliban and establishment of the new interim government of Afghanistan. Major targets were Gazni and Paktia.

Operation Defensive Shield

In March 2002, after a wave of suicide bombings had taken a severe toll of Israeli lives, **Ariel Sharon** authorized a major assault on areas of the **West Bank** controlled by the **Palestinian National Authority**, in particular Ramallah, where Israeli forces took control of **Yasser Arafat**'s presidential compound. The city was placed under a strict curfew while Israeli troops carried out searches and arrested more than 700 people. Sharon appeared on television to announce that Israel was at war and that the **Israeli Defence Force** (IDF) was embarking on Operation Defensive Shield, a campaign of indefinite length designed to 'vanquish the Palestinian terrorist infrastructure'. Arafat was declared an enemy to be isolated. In the following days, and with overwhelming Israeli support, the IDF overran Qalqilya, Tulkarm and **Bethlehem**, causing widespread destruction and loss of life. It then turned its attention to **Nablus** and **Jenin**. Serious fighting took place in both towns before the IDF was able to gain the upper hand. Much of the central area of Jenin refugee camp was destroyed in the Israeli assault and Palestinian sources claimed that a massacre had taken place. This was strenuously denied by Israel, which nevertheless denied independent observers access to the area.

Operation Desert Fox

Operation undertaken by US and British allied forces in December 1998 in order to enforce the 'no-fly zones' over Iraq. It involved substantial bombing of ground targets in the area of **Baghdad** over a period of four days. Operation Desert Fox was undertaken in response to continued efforts by **Saddam Hussain** to test and threaten the **containment** policy being applied by the UN and the coalition in the aftermath of the **Gulf War (1991)**, in accordance with **UN Security Council Resolution 687.**

Operation Desert Shield

The initial mobilization (during September–November 1990) of US-led coalition forces after Iraq's **invasion of Kuwait** in August 1990, in order to defend Saudi Arabia. Operation Desert Shield was followed by the war with Iraq—**Operation Desert Storm**—led by the USA.

Operation Desert Storm

The military intervention which followed **Operation Desert Shield** in mid-January 1991, when the deadline stipulated by the US Administration for Iraqi withdrawal from occupied Kuwait had been passed. An initial aerial bombardment of **Baghdad** and other targets was followed 39 days and 91,000 air missions later by a deployment of ground forces, on 23 February 1991. The ground war lasted less than five days. Iraqi troops defending Kuwait's border were overwhelmed within hours. A massive flanking movement by the coalition ground forces cut the main **Basra** to Baghdad road, isolating the Iraqi troops in Kuwait. Iraqi forces generally abandoned their positions, their vehicles and their equipment. Troops retreating along the main Baghdad road were strafed mercilessly and hundreds of thousands were estimated to have been killed or injured. On the evening of 27 February US President **George Bush** announced that Kuwait had been liberated and Iraq's army defeated. The military objectives had been met. It was, President Bush stressed, a victory for the United Nations and for the rule of law.

Operation Determined Path

In late June 2002, after two suicide bombings in **Jerusalem** had killed at least 26 **Israelis**, the Israeli army began to reoccupy large sections of the **West Bank**. The operation—codenamed **Operation Determined Path**—met with minimal Palestinian resistance and limited international criticism. Israeli troops moved steadily into the Palestinian areas, confining at least 600,000 **Palestinians** to effective house arrest through round-the-clock curfews in six Palestinian cities and towns—**Bethlehem**, **Nablus**, **Jenin**, Tulkarm, Qalqilya and Ramallah—and banning the media from covering their advance. As Israeli forces moved into the West Bank, Prime Minister **Ariel Sharon** pledged to extend his military offensive to the **Gaza Strip**. Six Palestinians (including at least one senior **Hamas** leader) were killed shortly afterwards in an Israeli missile attack at Rafah refugee camp in Gaza.

Operation Enduring Freedom

The security operation undertaken by the US-led coalition in Afghanistan as part of the immediate post-war intervention. Taking place mainly in the southern and eastern part of the country, the coalition troops (mainly US soldiers together with the Afghan army and some additional support) have encountered greater-than-anticipated resistance from the **Taliban** and other forces opposed to the interim government and to foreign occupation.

Operation Grapes of Wrath

In April 1996, with talks between Israel and Syria on the issue of the **Golan Heights** deadlocked and the proxy war in Lebanon intensifying, **Shimon Peres** authorized the intensification of aerial and artillery attacks, not only against suspected **Hezbollah** targets, but also against power stations near **Beirut** and the main north-south arterial highway in Operation Grapes of Wrath. Continued rocket attacks on northern Israel by Hezbollah forces showed that their operational abilities remained largely unaffected by the Israeli onslaught, while some reports suggested that 'hundreds of Lebanese youth' were volunteering to join the Islamist militia. Peres' sense of unease at the failure of Operation Grapes of Wrath was magnified by strong criticism from abroad. This criticism became more forceful after Israeli shells landed on a UNIFIL base at Qana in southern Lebanon, killing 105 civilian **refugees** and wounding Fijian soldiers serving with the UN peace-keeping force.

Operation Iraqi (Enduring) Freedom – *see* Gulf War (2003)

Operation Peace for Galilee

Israeli operation which led to military intervention in Lebanon, supposedly in retaliation for guerrilla attacks by the **Palestine Liberation Organization** (PLO) based in Lebanon and in defence of **Galilee**. Launched in June 1982, it was originally intended as a brief and limited campaign. By the end of the month, however, Israeli forces had advanced across Lebanon and surrounded West **Beirut**, where 6,000 PLO and large numbers of Syrian fighters had become trapped. The evacuation of the trapped forces was achieved after much diplomatic activity during the latter part of August. Israeli forces remained in effective control of Beirut, although under the terms of the evacuation agreement an international peace-keeping force was stationed in various parts of the city. Despite US protests, Israeli forces moved into West Beirut again in September 1982, taking up positions around Palestinian refugee camps. On 17 September reports began to emerge of a massacre in the **Sabra and Chatila** refugee camps by armed Christian forces ostensibly seeking PLO guerrillas. At the end of the month the Israeli government ordered an inquiry and the report which was released in February 1983 placed the direct responsibility for the massacre with the Lebanese Phalangists, but concluded that Israel's political and military leaders bore an indirect responsibility for the massacre. Prime Minister **Menachem Begin** was censured and **Ariel Sharon**, then Minister of Defence, resigned his ministerial post, as recommended by the inquiry. Direct talks between Israel and Lebanon for the withdrawal of foreign forces began at the end of December 1982. Progress was slow, but an agreement was finally signed in May 1983. On the same day, however, Israel signed a secret agreement with the USA which recognized Israel's right, despite the accord with Lebanon, to retaliate against terrorist attacks in Lebanon and to delay its withdrawal beyond the date stipulated in the agreement with Lebanon (three months from the date of signing) if Syrian and PLO forces remained there. Eventually, in September, Israel redeployed its forces south of Beirut along the Awali river, producing a *de facto* partition of the country. It was not until January 1985 that the Israeli government voted to withdraw from Lebanon. The first phase of the withdrawal—from Sidon to the Litani river area around Nabatiyah—took place in February, but the final phase did not take place until some nine months later. The cost of the withdrawal was estimated at US $100m. and that of Operation Peace for Galilee in total at $3,500m.

Operation Rainbow

Operation Rainbow involved a massive crackdown on the Rafah (Palestinian) refugee camp by Israeli forces in May 2004. Israeli troops killed at least 20 people, including children, at the beginning of Operation Rainbow as they occupied the Tel as-Sultan district on the margins of the camp in preparation for an expected assault on the heart of Rafah. The Israeli operation followed a number of 'successful' attacks by **Hamas** and **Islamic Jihad** on Israeli troops in previous weeks, inflicting some of the worst casualties of the **al-Aqsa** *intifada* on Israeli soldiers in **Gaza**. With more than 100 tanks and armoured vehicles and thousands of troops mobilized for Operation Rainbow, the Israeli press likened it to the army's 2002 assault on the **West Bank**. (**Operation Defensive Shield** resulted in widespread destruction and death in **Jenin**, **Nablus** and other cities.) The assault on Rafah was supposed to target terrorist groups, weapons stockpiles and entry routes across the border from Egypt. However, Israeli security sources indicated that the army intended to eradicate Palestinian resistance and prevent Gaza from becoming 'Hamasland' at all costs. As a result, large numbers of buildings were bulldozed, some of which contained several homes (the UN figures suggest 133 buildings destroyed, housing 304 families or 1,639 people, while B'Tselem reported at least 183 homes destroyed), and 54–61 people (including an estimated 6–10 children) were killed.

Operation Rockingham – *see* Rockingham cell

Opium

Opium production takes place in a number of countries in the region, but the major producer is Afghanistan. Most (90%) locally produced opium remains in the region, but much of it is trafficked abroad. Nintey-five per cent of British **heroin**, for example, derives from Afghan opium. Iran is also a major producer. Both countries have a large number of opium and heroin addicts—Iran an estimated 2m. and Afghanistan perhaps 1m., mainly among the **refugees** who have returned from Iran and Pakistan during the two years since the fall of the **Taliban**. Opium production increased dramatically after the fall of the Taliban regime, which had managed to control it to a considerable extent. Opium and, particularly, heroin addiction is on the increase in Afghanistan.

Oppressed of the Earth Organization
Munazzamat al-Mustadafin fi'l-Ard

Linked to the **Revolutionary Justice Organization** (Munazzamat al-'Adala ath-Thawriya). Both organizations served as covers for **Hezbollah**'s militant activities in the 1980s. The former claimed responsibility in December 1986 for the kidnap-ping of four university professors whom it described as spies; the latter claimed responsibility for kidnapping two US citizens and four French television crewmen. Both organizations have been inactive since 1988.

Organization for Combating Tyrants in Algeria

Algerian political grouping.

Organization for Economic Co-operation and Development (OECD)

OECD is an international organization established in 1961. It superseded the Organization for European Economic Co-operation, which had been founded in 1948 to co-ordinate the Marshall Plan for European economic recovery following the Second World War. Later its membership was extended to non-European states. Its charter pledges member states to work together to promote their economies, to extend **aid** to underdeveloped nations, and to contribute to the expansion of world **trade**. The OECD has 29 full members: Australia, Austria, Belgium, Canada, the Czech Republic, Denmark, Finland, France, Germany, Greece, Hungary, Iceland, Ireland, Italy, Japan, Korea, Luxembourg, Mexico, the Netherlands, New Zealand, Norway, Poland, Portugal, Spain, Sweden, Switzerland, Turkey, the United Kingdom and the USA.

Organization of Arab Petroleum Exporting Countries (OAPEC)

Established 9 January 1968. Its aim is to promote co-operation in the **petroleum** industry. Its member states are Algeria, Bahrain, Egypt, Iraq, Kuwait, Libya, Qatar, Saudi Arabia, Syria and the United Arab Emirates.

Organization of Democratic and Popular Action

Organisation de l'action démocratique et populaire (OADP)

A Moroccan political party, established in 1983. The OADP was, in effect, a recreation of the **March 23** movement. Its secretary-general is Muhammad ben Said ait Idder. It was unable to put forward candidates for the 1983 local elections, as its registration came 11 days too late. It gained one seat in the national elections.

Organization of Iranian People's *Fedayeen* (Majority)—OIPFM

The first meeting of the People's *Fedayeen* Movement was organized in 1963 by Bijan Jazani and his colleagues. They had reached the conclusion that the powerful US influence in Iran and the repression of liberal dissidents there had made peaceful activism entirely ineffective. Armed struggle was therefore viewed as the only effective way to liberation. In 1971–79 *Fedayeen* came under an intense attack from the Shah's regime: nearly 300 *Fedayeen* members were murdered by the regime. In this period the majority of the Organization's leaders were captured and murdered. *Fedayeen* played an effective and active role in the revolution of 1979, which was predominantly led by the supporters of Ayatollah **Khomeini**. Disagreements over armed struggle led to a split within the Organization in May 1981, when the term 'Guerrilla' was deleted from the name of the Organization and the term 'Majority' added to it.

Organization of Islamic Action (Munazzamat al-Amal al-Islami) – *see* Amal

Organization of the Islamic Conference (OIC)

Established in 1969, OIC aims to promote Islamic solidarity in economic, social, cultural, and political affairs. Its member states are Afghanistan, Albania, Algeria, Azerbaijan, Bahrain, Bangladesh, Benin, Brunei, Burkina Faso, Cameroon, Chad, Comoros, Côte d'Ivoire, Djibouti, Egypt, Gabon, The Gambia, Guinea, Guinea-Bissau, Guyana, Indonesia, Iran, Iraq, Jordan, Kazakhstan, Kuwait, Kyrgyzstan, Lebanon, Libya, Malaysia, Maldives, Mali, Mauritania, Morocco, Mozambique, Niger, Nigeria, Oman, Pakistan, Qatar, Saudi Arabia, Senegal, Sierra Leone, Somalia, Sudan, Suriname, Syria, Tajikistan, Togo, Tunisia, Turkey, Turkmenistan, Uganda, the United Arab Emirates, Uzbekistan, Yemen and the

Palestine Liberation Organization. In addition, Bosnia and Herzegovina, Central African Republic and Thailand have observer status.

Organization of Petroleum Exporting Countries (OPEC)

Established in 1960, OPEC aims to co-ordinate **petroleum** policies. Its members are Algeria, Indonesia, Iran, Iraq, Kuwait, Libya, Nigeria, Qatar, Saudi Arabia, the United Arab Emirates and Venezuela.

Oriental Jews

A term used to refer to Jews who had lived in the **Middle East** and North Africa for generations.

Orientalism

Orientalism originally referred to the study of Eastern societies and cultures, generally by Westerners. However, its contemporary meaning comes from the Palestinian academic **Edward Said**, who argued in *Orientalism* that past and current accounts of the **Middle East**, India, China, and elsewhere reflect long-held Western biases and the view that 'the Orient' consists of seductive **women** and dangerous men living in a static society with a glorious but distant past. Thus, Orientalism as part of an effort to justify **colonialism** through the concept of the 'white man's burden'.

Oslo Agreements

Agreements reached in 1993 after secret negotiations between representatives of the Israeli government and of the **Palestine Liberation Organization** in Oslo, Norway. They provided the foundation for further negotiations, which eventually resulted in the establishment of the **Palestinian National Authority** and the withdrawal of Israeli forces from limited areas of the **Occupied Territories**.

Othman, Abdul Zahra

Former head of the US-appointed **Iraqi Provisional Governing Council**—he was killed by a suicide bomber in May 2004. Described as 'a moderate **Shi'a**' and one who stood for 'a civilized **Islam**', Othman spent nearly 25 years in exile in Iran until 2003. He was head of the **Basra**-based **Islamic Da'awa Movement**. He took over (under the system of rotation) as president of the Governing Council only a few weeks before his death. He was the second, and highest ranking, of the Council's members to be killed since its establishment.

Ottoman Empire

The Ottoman Empire was established in the early 14th century by Osman I (in **Arabic** Uthman, hence the 'Ottoman' Empire), leader of the Turkish tribe of Sogut in western Anatolia. Mehmed II conquered **Constantinople (Istanbul)** in 1453. The Empire reached its apex under Suleiman the Magnificent in the 16th century, when it stretched from the **Persian (Arabian) Gulf** in the east to Hungary to the north west, in Europe, and Tunisia to the west in North Africa; and from Egypt and the borders of **Arabia** to the south to the Caucasus to the north east. Ottoman armies even reached the gates of Vienna at the height of the Empire. In the 17th century the Ottoman Empire began a long decline, linked to the rise of Europe. By the second half of the 19th century European intervention in the Empire's affairs and territories was beginning to have profound cultural, ideological, political, social and economic effects. One of these was an emerging **Arab nationalism**. During the First World War this movement was channelled by Britain and France into a sense of dissatisfaction with Ottoman rule, which fuelled, among other things, the **Arab Revolt** in the **Middle East**. After the First World War the Empire effectively lost many of its provinces to Britain and France which, through the **Sykes-Picot Agreement**, divided up the Middle East between them. The Ottoman Empire was officially ended by the Treaty of Lausanne in 1923, four years after its defeat by the allied forces in the First World War I, giving rise to the new state of Turkey.

Oufkir, Mohammed

A **Berber** member of the Moroccan élite, Oufkir was a general in the army and subsequently Minister of the Interior in the 1960s and 1970s. He is believed to have been responsible for the kidnapping, torture and killing of **Mehdi Ben Barka**.

Oujda clan

So called because it consisted of those former staff officers of the Algerian National Liberation Army (Armée de libération nationale) who had served at its Moroccan headquarters in Oujda. These were Kaid Ahmed, Ahmed Medeghri, **Abdelaziz Bouteflika**, Cherif Belkacem and Mohamed Tayebi Larbi Belhadj. They had formed the nucleus of the Algerian regime since 1965, but the political 'change of direction' adopted in 1971 by **Houari Boumedienne** led to divisions within the regime and to the break-up of the Oujda clan over the next four years.

Özal, Turgut

Leader of the Turkish **Motherland Party** in the 1980s, Özal came from a provincial background and was once active in the **National Salvation Party** (NSP), standing as an NSP candidate in Izmir in elections held in 1977, but receiving only 1.6% of the vote. While recognizing the importance of **Islam** in Turkish politics (and more generally in Turkish culture and society), he and his circle regarded themselves rather as technocrats and modernizers. Unlike the Kemalists and the **Republican People's Party**, however, he and his party espoused a vision of Turkish development through the promotion of private capitalism. He was elected as President of Turkey in October 1989, replacing Gen. **Kenan Evren** who had been head of state since the **military** coup of September 1980, which he had led. Özal remained President until April 1993, when he was replaced by **Süleyman Demirel**.

P

Pachachi, Adnan

Former Iraqi foreign minister, **Sunni** elder, currently adviser to the United Arab Emirates government, who has the backing of the USA to play a future role in a new Iraqi government. He is viewed as acceptable by Saudi Arabia and other **Gulf states**. He has no party affiliation or power base. He was proposed by the USA for the position of President, but did not accept it.

Pahlavi, Mohammed Reza Shah (1919–80)

Mohammed ascended the throne to become Shah of Iran (Persia) in 1941 after his father, Reza Shah Pahlavi, was suspected of collaboration with Germany and was deposed by the British and Soviet governments. He narrowly escaped assassination in 1949 by a member of the leftist **Tudeh Party**, and in 1953 briefly fled the country after a clash with the supporters of **Muhammad Mussadegh**. In the early 1960s the Shah, with US assistance, launched a reform programme called the 'White Revolution', which included land redistribution among citizens, extensive construction, the promotion of **literacy**, and the emancipation of **women**. However, in the process the grassroots population became increasingly isolated as wealth, emanating from the **oil** industry, was increasingly unequally distributed. The Shah faced further criticism from the clerics, who opposed his pro-Western and modernization policies. As popular discontent grew, particularly in the early 1970s, the regime became more repressive, with the secret police crushing any opposition. Exiled religious leader Ayatollah **Ruhollah Khomeini** began to have an increasing influence as popular discontent grew towards the end of the 1970s. Discontent turned to open revolt and in January 1979 Mohammed Reza Shah fled the country, eventually finding refuge in Egypt. Ayatollah Khomeini returned to Iran and began a process of taking power into the hands of the clerics. The former Shah died in Egypt in 1980.

Pakhtun

A member of a distinctive ethnic/tribal and linguistic group located for the most part in the hill and mountain areas of central and south-eastern Afghanistan and of western Pakistan.

Pakhtunistan

Area inhabited by **Pakhtuns** in central and south-eastern Afghanistan and western Pakistan.

Palestine

Literally 'the land of the Filistins' who struggled with the Israelites in Biblical times.

Palestine was part of the **Ottoman Empire** during the 19th century and up until the end of the First World War. Jewish immigration into this area had taken place since the 1870s, but increased after the creation of the Zionist movement and the **Zionist Organization** in the 1880s. In 1917 the British foreign secretary, Lord Balfour, declared (the **Balfour Declaration**) that Palestine could in future provide a homeland for European Jews. In 1922 Palestine was established as Mandated Territory of the League of Nations, entrusted to Britain. Jewish immigration increased. Increasingly, through the 1920s and 1930s, there was conflict, both between the indigenous Arabs and the immigrant Jews, and between both of these populations and Britain. After several proposals for the future of Palestine, including partition, by various parties (notably the Jews, the Arabs, Britain, the USA and the UN), the British decided to depart from Palestine. The Arab states intervened and the Jews fought for an independent state. The State of Israel was established in 1948. **Palestinians** left the new Jewish State of Israel in their hundreds of thousands, to become **refugees**, mainly in the adjacent territories of Egypt, Jordan, Lebanon and Syria. After the **Arab–Israeli War (1967)**, Israel occupied the **West Bank** (of the Jordan river) and the **Gaza Strip** and remained in control there for the next 40 years. The **Palestine Liberation Organization** (PLO) increasingly expressed the wish of the Palestinian Arabs for self-determination, autonomy and independence, through its armed struggle against Israel.

For many Palestinians, 'Palestine' comprises not only the **Occupied Territories** but also the lost lands that are now within the borders of Israel. For them, the territory now under the nominal control of the **Palestinian National Authority** (PNA) is a very small part of Palestine. Thus, in the most radical version, Palestine is the entirety of the territory previously under the British Mandate. In another version, the so-called two-state solution to the Palestinian issue, Palestine would be the totality (or majority) of the territory of the West Bank and Gaza occupied by Israel in 1967. The most limited interpretation, favoured by the Israeli Government of **Ariel Sharon**, is that Palestine would be that territory within the West Bank and Gaza Strip under the jurisdiction of the PNA, as distinct from the land that will remain under Israeli occupation and settlement in the West Bank and that of the State of Israel itself.

The West Bank (5,860 sq km, of which lakes and inland seas account for 220 sq km) lies between Jordan and Israel, with Syria to the north. In July 2002 its total population was estimated at 163,667. There are 242 Israeli **settlements** and civilian land use sites in the West Bank, and a total of about 187,000 Israeli settlers. The Gaza Strip (*Qita Ghazzah*) is a narrow strip of land (360 sq km in area) bordering the **Mediterranean** Sea, between Egypt and Israel. Highly urbanized and the location of several major refugee camps, the Strip's population was estimated in July 2002 at 1,225,911. There are approximately 25 major Israeli settlements and civilian land use sites in the Israeli-occupied Gaza Strip, and a total of some 5,000 Israeli settlers. The capital of Palestine (defined as the territory under the jurisdiction of the PNA) is **East Jerusalem**. In February 2002, when there were 29 Israeli settlements, the population of East Jerusalem was estimated at about 177,000. In all, Palestinian Arabs and others account for 99.4% of the population in Gaza (the Jewish population thus represents 0.6% of the total) and for 83% in the West Bank (the Jewish population accordingly accounting for 17%). The vast majority (98.7%) of the population living in Gaza are Muslim (predominantly **Sunni**), with a small minority of Christians (0.7%) and Jews (0.6%). In the West Bank the majority (75%) are Muslim, with Jews accounting for a significant **minority** (17%), and Christians and others for about 8%. Languages spoken include **Arabic**, **Hebrew** (spoken by Israeli settlers and many Palestinians) and English (widely understood).

In its narrow definition, contemporary Palestine is the area falling under the jurisdiction of the PNA. The head of state and President is **Yasser Arafat** and the Prime Minister is **Ahmed Qurei**. The legislature is the **Palestine National Council**. There are numerous political groupings and parties associated with the Palestinian movement: the **Communist Party (Palestine)**, the **Democratic Front for the Liberation of Palestine**, **al-Fatah (Palestinian National Liberation Movement)**, **al Fatah/al-'Asifa**, **Hamas—Harakat al-Muqawama al-Islamiyya)**, **International Solidarity Movement**, the **Palestine Liberation Organization**, **Palestinian Islamic Jihad**, **Islamic Jihad Organization**, **al-Jihad**, Jihad Organization (Tanzim al-Jihad), **Movement for an Islamic Society (al-Haraka li-Mujtama' Islam)**, the **Popular Front for the Liberation of Palestine**, the Brigades of Islamic Jihad (Saraya al-Jihad al-Islami), Tanzimat Hawari Group/Fatah Special Operations Group/Martyrs of Tal az-Za'atar/Amn Araissi, **Popular Front for the Liberation of Palestine-General Command**, **Popular Front for the Liberation of Palestine-Special Command**, **Unified National Leadership of the Uprising**.

Media

In 2000 there were eight internet service providers. In 2001 there were 60,000 internet users.

History

The **Israel-PLO Declaration of Principles on Palestinian Self-Rule** (DoP), signed in Washington, DC, USA on 13 September 1993, provided for a transitional period not exceeding five years of Palestinian interim self-government in the Gaza Strip and the West Bank. Under the DoP, Israel agreed to transfer certain powers and responsibilities to the PNA, which includes the Palestinian Legislative Council elected in January 1996, as part of the interim self-governing arrangements in the West Bank and Gaza Strip. A transfer of powers and responsibilities for the Gaza Strip and **Jericho** took place pursuant to the Israel-PLO 4 May 1994 **Cairo Agreement on the Gaza Strip and Jericho** and in additional areas of the West Bank pursuant to the **Israeli-Palestinian Interim Agreement of** 28 September 1995, the **Israel-PLO 15 January 1997 Protocol** concerning Redeployment in Hebron, the **Israel-PLO 23 October 1998 Wye River Memorandum**, and the 4 September 1999 **Sharm esh-Sheikh Agreement**. The DoP provides that Israel will retain responsibility during the transitional period for external security and for the internal security and public order of settlements and Israeli citizens. Direct negotiations to determine the permanent status of Gaza and West Bank began in September 1999 after a three-year hiatus, but were derailed by a second *intifada* that broke out in September 2000. The resulting widespread violence in the West Bank and Gaza Strip, Israel's military response, and instability within the PNA continue to undermine progress toward a permanent agreement.

The West Bank and Gaza Strip are occupied by Israel with current status subject to the Israeli-Palestinian Interim Agreement. Permanent status is to be determined through further negotiation

Palestine, economy

The **Palestine Liberation Organization** (PLO) itself has, over the years, built up a substantial economy of its own. In the 1980s the **Arab Bank**, which acts in effect as the central bank of Palestine, had assets of more than US $10,000m. in investments and bank holdings across the world. It is able to provide support for the economic and social infrastructure of the territories under the jurisdiction of the **Palestinian National Authority** (PNA). Even before the establishment of the PNA it was able to transfer substantial resources into the **Occupied Territories**. According to a report published by the PLO's Occupied Homeland Department, from 1979 until the end of February 1987 almost $500m. was spent in the Occupied Territories, including almost $110m. on **education** and culture, and $100m. on **transport**.

Palestine Communist Party (PCP) – *see* Communist Party (Palestine)

Palestine Democratic Alliance

Pro-**Arafat** alliance.

Palestine Liberation Army (PLA)

Armed forces of the **Palestine Liberation Organization**.

Palestine Liberation Front (PLF)

Established in April 1977, having split from the **Popular Front for the Liberation of Palestine-General Command** (PFLP-GC), which was itself a splinter group of the PFLP, founded in 1967. The PLF split into two factions at the end of 1983, both retaining the name PLF. One faction, whose leader was Muhammad or Mahmoud Zaidan, known as 'Abu Abbas', was initially based in **Tunis** and remained nominally loyal to **Yasser Arafat**, within the framework of the **Palestine Democratic Alliance**. The other faction, led by Talaat Yaqoub, belonged to the anti-Arafat **Palestine National Alliance** and, from March 1985, to the **Palestinian National Salvation Front**, established under Syrian auspices as a radical alternative to Arafat's wing of the **Palestine Liberation Organization** (PLO). The 'Abu Abbas' faction of the PLF became known for its aerial attacks against Israel. In October 1985 it hijacked an Italian cruise ship, the *Achille Lauro*, and an elderly disabled American passenger, Leon Klinghoffer, was killed. A warrant for the arrest of 'Abu Abbas' is outstanding in Italy. A third faction of the PLF, more inclined towards Libya, was reputedly formed in 1986 by followers of the PLF central committee secretary, Abd al-Fattah Ghanim. A programme for the reunification of the PLF was announced in April 1987 at the 18th session of the **Palestine National Council**, with Talaat Yaqoub as secretary-general and 'Abu Abbas' appointed to the PLO Executive Committee. The merger took place in June 1987, with 'Abu Abbas' becoming secretary-general of the party and remaining on the PLO Executive Committee. The PLF became virtually inactive as such for more than a decade after 1987, becoming reconciled to its role within the PLO through its participation in the Central Council of the **Palestine Resistance Movement** and its representation on the PLO Executive Committee. The PLF has become more active again since the start of the **al-Aqsa** *intifada*, and several PLF members have been arrested by Israeli authorities for planning attacks in Israel and the **West Bank**. Based in Iraq after 1990, it also maintained a presence in Lebanon and the West Bank.

Palestine Liberation Organization (PLO)

Founded in 1964 by the **Arab League**, the PLO gradually achieved considerable independence, as a Palestinian nationalist organization dedicated to the establishment of an independent Palestinian state, from the Arab regimes. The major factions within the PLO were **al-Fatah**, the largest group, led by **Yasser Arafat**, the **Popular Front for the Liberation of Palestine** (PFLP), the **Democratic Front for the Liberation of Palestine** (DFLP) and the **Communist Party (Palestine)**. After the **Arab–Israeli War (1967)**, the PLO remained the umbrella organization for the **Palestinians**, although for many purposes (particularly those associated with the armed struggle) control devolved to the leadership of the various *fedayeen* militia groups, the most prominent of which was Arafat's al-Fatah. Arafat's election in 1968 as chairman of the PLO's Executive Committee (a position he still holds) represented an important milestone in the Palestinian struggle for self-determination. The PLO has played a central role in the process of politicization and the consolidation of a collective Palestinian identity.

In the early 1970s several groups affiliated with the PLO carried out numerous international terrorist attacks. Several terrorist attacks were also carried out later by groups affiliated with the PLO/Fatah, including the Hawari Group, the **Palestine Liberation Front** and **Force 17**, against targets inside and outside Israel. By the mid-1970s, however, under international pressure, the PLO claimed it would restrict attacks to Israel and the **Occupied Territories**. By 1974 not only the Arab states, but also the international community as a whole agreed that the PLO, as the legitimate government—state in exile—of the Palestinians, could speak for the Palestinians and represent them in international bodies and forums, including those of the UN and its related organizations. The Israeli government, however, still refused to talk to what it viewed as a terrorist group, or to recognize the Palestinians' existence and right to self-determination. The PLO maintained officially recognized embassies in many Arab capitals, and Arab governments in the **Gulf** deducted PLO taxes from Palestinian workers' wages and salaries.

When Egyptian President **Anwar Sadat** announced that he would travel to Israel to talk peace directly with the Israeli government, this move was condemned by the Arab states and by the PLO as a betrayal of the struggle for a just and lasting settlement of the Palestinian question. The **Camp David Agreement** of 1978 and subsequent **Egyptian-Israeli Peace Treaty** of 1979, which provided not only for a phased withdrawal of Israeli troops from Sinai and full diplomatic relations between Egypt and Israel, but also for ongoing negotiations about the status of Palestinians under Israeli occupation, were denounced by the PLO as illegitimate and as ignoring its status as the legitimate negotiating party in any such matter.

Despite its condemnation of the Camp David Accords, the PLO began during the late 1970s to signal its increasing readiness for a political settlement and to moderate its public rhetoric. Israel ignored this and tension increased within the Occupied Territories. Regarding much of the local Palestinian opposition as the work of the PLO, operating from Lebanon, Israel attempted in 1978 to destroy the PLO's headquarters and bases in that country. It failed, but in June 1982 launched an invasion of Lebanon (for the second time), encircling and bombing **Beirut** in an attempt to force the evacuation of the PLO. Indeed, the bombing stopped only after the completion of the PLO's evacuation in late August. After the expulsion of its leadership from Beirut in 1982 and its subsequent establishment in **Tunis**, the PLO became increasingly fragmented, partly as a result of internal dissension and partly as a result of the different perspectives and positions of the various Arab states supporting the various factions of the PLO. The continued occupation by Israel eventually (in 1987) resulted in an internal uprising (*intifada*) in the **West Bank** and **Gaza**, which was only partly directed by the PLO from outside and which developed a strong local dynamic of its own. In November 1988 Yasser Arafat, as leader of the PLO, formally and publicly endorsed the two-state solution and proclaimed the independent State of Palestine in the West Bank and Gaza Strip. Any progressive momentum was, however, compromised by the impact of the **Gulf War (1991)**. Although the official Palestinian position throughout the crisis was to denounce the Iraqi invasion and occupation of Kuwait and oppose a military solution, many sections of Palestinian society openly sympathized not only with the Iraqi people but also with **Saddam Hussain**'s unwillingness to surrender in the face of US and Western intervention. The sight of Yasser Arafat embracing Saddam Hussain 'as a brother' confirmed, for some (including most **Israelis** and many Americans), the 'threat to peace' posed by the PLO. Chairman Arafat publicly renounced **terrorism** in December 1988 on behalf of the PLO. The USA considers that all PLO groups, including al-Fatah, Force 17, the Hawari Group, the PLF and the PFLP, are bound by Arafat's renunciation of terrorism. However, the USA also recalls that members of the PLO have in the past advocated, carried out, or accepted responsibility for acts of terrorism. The US-PLO dialogue that had opened up in the late 1980s was suspended after the PLO failed to condemn the 30 May 1990 PLF attack on Israeli beaches. PLF head 'Abu Abbas' left the PLO Executive Committee in September 1991; his seat was filled by another PLF member. External contributions from the **Gulf states** to the PLO and to Palestinian institutions, such as hospitals, school and universities, and social welfare organizations, were cancelled almost immediately, and many Palestinians who worked in the Gulf were sent home.

In the aftermath of the Gulf War the **Arab–Israeli Conflict** was back on the agenda and in October 1991, after months of intensive and shuttle diplomacy, an international peace conference was convened in Madrid, Spain, under the joint sponsorship of the Soviet Union and the USA. The Israeli government refused to accept an independent Palestinian delegation led by the PLO, so the Palestinians were represented by a joint Jordanian-Palestinian delegation. These peace talks continued throughout 1992 and the first half of 1993 in Washington, DC, and elsewhere. By mid-1993 negotiations were at a standstill, although by now Israeli and Palestinian officials were participating in face-to-face discussions. In late August 1993 it was revealed that secret negotiations between Israeli government officials and official representatives of the PLO had been conducted in Oslo, Norway, for many months. The two parties had even signed a joint **Declaration of Principles on Palestinian Self-Rule** (DoP) after the **Oslo Agreement**. Shortly afterwards, on 13 September 1993, Yasser Arafat and Israeli Prime Minister **Itzhak Rabin** shook hands at the conclusion of a ceremony marking the signing of the DoP at the White House in Washington, DC. On 9 September 1993, in letters to Israeli Prime Minister Rabin and Norwegian foreign minister Holst, Arafat committed the PLO to cease all violence and terrorism. There is no evidence that any PLO element under Arafat's control was involved in terrorism from that time until the end of 1995. (There were two incidents in 1993 in which the responsible individuals apparently acted independently.) One group under the PLO umbrella, the PFLP, suspended its participation in the PLO in protest against the agreement and continues its sporadic campaign of violence. The US government continues closely to monitor the PLO's compliance with its commitment to abandon terrorism and violence.

In May 1994, following the conclusion of the **Cairo Agreement on the Gaza Strip and Jericho** that was designed to ratify the DoP, the Israeli military began its redeployment and the PLO the transferral of its headquarters from Tunis to the Gaza Strip and, subsequently, to Ramallah and Qalqilya in the West Bank. In July 1994, after 27 years in exile, Arafat set foot on Palestinian soil. Soon afterwards, the **Palestinian National Authority** was formed and the first democratic Palestinian elections were held in January 1996. Palestinian police began to move into the 'newly autonomous areas'.

Palestine Martyrs Work Society – *see* **Samed**

Palestine National Alliance

Anti-**Arafat** grouping of Palestinian parties and organizations.

Palestine National Charter

Otherwise known as the **Palestine Liberation Organization** (PLO) Covenant, the Charter of July 1968 sets out, in 33 articles, the basic position of the **Palestine National Council** on Palestine, **Palestinian identity**, the Palestinian community, Arab unity, the liberation of Palestine and the rights of the Palestinian people. In September 1993 **Yasser Arafat** declared those articles that deny Israel's right to exist, or that are inconsistent with the PLO's commitments to Israel under the terms of subsequent accords, to be invalid. Revision of those articles (viii, ix, x, xv, xix, xx, xxii, and xxiii) was to be undertaken as part of the ongoing peace process.

Palestine National Council (PNC)

Prior to the establishment of the **Palestinian National Authority** (PNA), the PNC was the central decision-making body of the **Palestine Liberation Organization**. Since the establishment of the PNA the PNC has been the equivalent of a house of representatives.

Palestine National Front (PNF)

Political movement that swept to power in the **West Bank** local elections of 1976.

Palestine National Liberation Army – *see* **Palestine Liberation Army**

Palestine Resistance Movement

The Palestine Resistance Movement in western Europe played a similar role during the 1970s and 1980s to that played by Cuba in Latin America. The Soviet Union provided arms, ammunition, technical expertise and military and strategic training; the **Palestinians** brokered these to various European armed groups.

Palestinian Central Council

The equivalent to the Cabinet of the **Palestinian National Authority**.

Palestinian identity

Generally, the Arabs who inhabited Palestine in Ottoman times considered themselves to be like Arabs in other provinces of the **Ottoman Empire**, in contrast to the ruling Ottomans or Turks. The Arabs in Palestine tended not to identify themselves as **Palestinians** until after the establishment of Israel. The creation of Palestinian identity in its contemporary sense was formed essentially during the 1960s with the creation of the **Palestine Liberation Organization** (PLO). This effectively became the legitimate representative of the 'Palestinian people' and their government ('in exile') until the establishment of the **Palestinian National Authority** in the 1990s. The PLO maintained officially recognized embassies in many Arab capitals, and Arab governments in the **Gulf** deducted PLO taxes from Palestinian workers' earnings. Along with regular elections to the **Palestinian (National) Council**, these tax payments, large infusions of Arab foreign **aid**, and the many informal institutions of Palestinian society encouraged the development of a distinctive Palestinian identity, despite the absence of a Palestinian territorial state. However, the existence of a population with a recognizably similar name ('the Philistines') in Biblical times suggests a degree of continuity over a long historical period (much as 'the Israelites' of the **Bible** suggest a long historical continuity in the same region).

Palestinian Islamic Jihad (PIJ)

PIJ originated among militant **Palestinians** in the **Gaza Strip** during the 1970s. Its leader, Fathi Shkaki, was assassinated by **Mossad** operatives in Malta in October 1995. PIJ is committed to the creation of an Islamic Palestinian state and to the destruction of Israel through holy war. It also opposes moderate Arab governments that it believes have been tainted by Western secularism. PIJ activists have carried out many attacks, including large-scale suicide bombings against Israeli civilian and military targets. The group intensified its operations in 2002, claiming responsibility for numerous attacks against Israeli interests. The group has not yet targeted US interests and continues to confine its attacks to Israeli targets inside Israel and the **Occupied Territories**, although US citizens have died in attacks mounted by the PIJ. The group's leaders reside primarily in Israel, the **West Bank**, and **Gaza Strip**, but also in other parts of the **Middle East**, including Lebanon and Syria. The PIJ-Shkaki faction, currently led by Ramadan Shallah in **Damascus**, is the most active.

Palestinian National Authority (PNA)

The **West Bank** and **Gaza Strip** are now administered to varying extents by Israel and the PNA. Pursuant to the May 1994 Gaza-**Jericho** agreement and the September 1995 Interim Agreement, Israel transferred most responsibilities for civil government in the Gaza Strip and parts of the West Bank to the PNA. In January 1996 **Palestinians** chose their first popularly elected government in democratic elections, which were generally well conducted. The 88-member Council and the Chairman of the Executive Authority were elected. The PNA also has a Cabinet of 20 appointed ministers who oversee 23 ministries. PNA chairman **Yasser Arafat** continues to dominate the affairs of government and to make major decisions. Most senior government positions in the PNA are held by individuals who are members of, or loyal to, Arafat's **al-Fatah** faction of the **Palestine Liberation Organization** (PLO). The PNA was established in 1995, shortly after the withdrawal of Israeli forces from 'the newly autonomous areas' in the West Bank and Gaza and the return of Yasser Arafat to Palestine for the first time in 27 years. The first democratic elections were held in January 1996. The PNA has formal jurisdiction over some 6.6% of the territory of historical Palestine (27% of the **Occupied Territories**—3% of the West Bank and 60% of the Gaza Strip). In the West Bank the PNA has only civil and police powers, and Israel remains responsible for 'internal security', the meaning of which is open to interpretation. Israel also remains in command of the road network linking the Palestinian villages and towns in 'the autonomous areas'—so that all movement of goods and persons into and out of these enclaves, as well as between them, can be stopped—and of the areas surrounding the numerous Israeli **settlements** in these areas. Under the PNA, the Palestinians have achieved a limited form of self-rule, held general elections, and begun to establish social and political institutions, such as security and welfare services, a legal system, a Palestinian supreme court, and a house of representatives, the **Palestinian (National) Council**.

Palestinian (National) Council

The Palestinian house of representatives (parliament).

Palestinian National Fund (PNF)

The PNF was established in 1964 in order to raise funds to finance the activities of the **Palestine Liberation Organization** (PLO). In the early days most of these funds came from the Arab states that supported the Palestinian struggle for self-determination. Increasingly, over time, the PLO was able to secure access to resources of its own, in various ways. During the period when it established itself in the **Beka'a Valley** in Lebanon, it was able to take advantage of the production and sale and smuggling of **cannabis** and hashish to generate income through various forms of 'taxation' on the particular set of activities associated with **drugs**. Over time, however, an astute policy of long-term investment, combined with a wide range of fund-raising activities and methods, and close control of expenditure, created a very substantial asset base. By the late 1980s the PNF was independently wealthy and managed a portfolio with an estimated value of US $6,000m. The Steadfast Fund was associated with funds coming from supportive Arab states, mainly the **oil**-rich **Gulf states**; and a wide range of organizations inside the **Occupied Territories** of the **West Bank** and **Gaza Strip** benefited from funds through the Palestinian Welfare Association—established in 1983 by a group of wealthy **Palestinians**—which collected donations from the Palestinian diaspora and sympathizers world-wide. In addition to the overt budget of the PNF, there was the Secret Chairman's Budget (SCB), which was part of the Chairman's Secret Fund, controlled exclusively by Chairman **Arafat**. Details of the revenues and portfolio of the SCB have always remained 'unknown', but it was estimated that by the end of the 1980s the SCB controlled an estimated $2,000m. in assets. Sources of revenue for the SCB included illegal and terrorist activities, which were in turn funded through the SCB, as were the Chairman's security and exceptional expenditures (such as the cost of relocation from **Beirut** to **Tunis** in 1982–83). By 1990, according to the US **Central Intelligence Agency**, the wealth of the PLO totalled $8,000m.–$14,000m.

Palestinian National Liberation Movement

Al-Fatah

Founded in 1957, the largest single Palestinian movement embraces a coalition of political forces. Its leader is **Yasser Arafat**, its secretary-general Farouk Kaddoumi. Al-Fatah's central committee is elected by the organization's 530-member congress.

Palestinian National Salvation Front (PNSF)

An anti-**Arafat** coalition organized in **Damascus**, Syria. It was established by a group of dissidents from within **al-Fatah** in March 1985. In June and July 1988, with the support of the **Ba'ath Party**, the PNSF took control of the Palestinian refugee camps at Chatila and Burj Barajneh, in **Beirut**, Lebanon. The dissidents, together with the Saiqa and the **Popular Front for the Liberation of Palestine-General Command**, refused to participate in the various **Palestine National Councils**. They condemned the decisions taken by the **Palestine Liberation Organization** at the Palestine National Council in November 1988.

Palestinian Popular Struggle Front (PPSF)

Palestinian political group founded in 1967. Its secretary-general is Dr Samir Ghousha.

Palestinians – *see also* Palestinian identity

The Arab inhabitants—Muslim, Christian and **Druze**—of Palestine. The number of Palestinians world-wide is estimated at more than 5m. They are usually divided into those who live within the pre-1967 borders of Israel and have Israeli citizenship (also called **Israeli Arabs**), those who live in the **West Bank** and **Gaza Strip**, territories illegally occupied by Israel since the 1967 war, and those who live in the diaspora, elsewhere in the **Middle East** and beyond.

Palmach

Palmach was the paramilitary striking arm of **Haganah**, the Jewish defence organization, developed before the creation of the State of Israel. Palyam was its maritime branch.

Pan-Arabism

The idea of a political alliance or union of all the Arab nations. (See also **Arab nationalism** and **Ba'ath Party**.)

Pan-Iranist Party

Extreme right-wing party that calls for a Greater Persia. It is led by Dr Mohsen Pezeshkpour.

Pan-Islamism

The idea of a universal, transnational Islamic community.

Panjshir Valley

Situated in Badakshan, Afghanistan. Valley of the River Panjshir, which rises in the Panjshir range to the north of **Kabul**, eastern Afghanistan. It was the chief centre of the *mujahidin* resistance against the Soviet occupation.

Pan-Turanism

Political ideology that emphasizes the common identity of all Turkic-speaking peoples and envisages some form of political grouping for all countries where Turkic-speaking peoples dominate. It is closely linked to Pan-Turkish political ideology.

PAPP – *see* **Programme of Assistance to the Palestinian People**

Parliaments

While the majority of states in the region have some form of elected national assembly, several of the more conservative states have advisory councils (***majlis ash-shura***) with limited powers and consisting largely of appointed members.

Parti de l'action

Moroccan political party, founded in 1974. It advocates democracy and progress. Its general-secretary is Mohammed el-Idrissi

Parti al-Ahd

Moroccan political party. Its president is Najib el Ouazzani

Parti de l'avant-garde démocratique socialiste

Moroccan political party, legalized in April 1992. An offshoot of the **Union socialiste des forces populaires**. Its secretary-general is Ahmad Benjelloune

Parti du congrès national unioniste

Moroccan political party, founded in 2001 by dissident members of the **Union socialiste des forces populaires**. Its secretary-general is Abdelmajid Bouzoubaa.

Parti démocratique et de l'indépendance

Moroccan political party, founded in 1946. Its secretary-general is Abdelwahed Maach.

Parti démocratique progressif

Algerian political party, established in 1990. It is led by Saci Mabrouk.

Parti de l'environnement et du développement

Moroccan political party, founded in 2002. Its secretary-general is Ahmad al-Alami.

Parti des forces citoyennes

Moroccan political party, founded in 2001. Its secretary-general is Abderrahman Lahjouji.

Parti de la gauche socialiste unifiée

Moroccan political party, founded in 2001. A left-wing coalition that includes the **Organization of Democratic and Popular Action**, the **Mouvement populaire pour la démocratie**, the Activistes de gauche, and the Démocrats indépendants. Its president is Muhammad Ben Said Aït Idder.

Parti de la justice et du développement (PJD)

Moroccan political party, founded in 1967 as the Mouvement populaire constitutionnel et démocratique. A breakaway party from the **Mouvement populaire**. In June 1996 it formally absorbed members of the Islamic Association, al-Islah wa'l Attajdid. The PJD adopted its current name in October 1998. Its secretary-general is Abdelkrim Khatib.

Parti marocain libéral (PML)

Moroccan political party, founded in 2002. The PML's national co-ordinator is Muhammad Ziane.

Parti national démocrate

Moroccan political party, founded in 1981 by a split within the **Rassemblement national des indépendants**. Its leader is Abdellah Kadiri.

Parti national libéral

Al-Wataniyin al-Ahrar

Lebanese political party, founded in 1958. Liberal reformist secular party with traditionally a predominance of support from **Maronite** Christians.

Parti national pour la solidarité et le développement

Algerian political party founded in 1989 as the Parti social démocrate. It is led by Mohammed Cherif Taleb.

Parti du progrès et du socialisme (PPS—Morocco)

A moderate pro-Moscow communist party, the PPS was established in Morocco in 1974 after previous communist parties (the Moroccan Communist Party and the Party of Liberation and Socialism) had been banned. Ali Yata, who was secretary-general of the earlier (banned) communist parties, also led the PPS. A small, tightly knit organization, headed by a central committee and a politburo, the PPS is essentially an urban-based party, drawing most of its support from the organized working class and the trade unions belonging to the Moroccan Union of Labour (Union marocaine du travail) and from students, teachers and other intellectuals.

The party is represented in the leadership of the National Union of Moroccan Students (Union nationale des étudiants marocains). The PPS faithfully adopted the same position as the Soviet Union on major international issues, with the exception of the **Western Sahara** question, on which the Soviet Union supported **Saharawi** self-determination, while the PPS defended Morocco's invasion and annexation of part of the territory and supported the government's position on the future of the territory. It adheres to the classic two-stage theory of revolution, in which there must first be a 'national democratic revolution' to achieve land reform, democratization and an end to imperialist domination, before a socialist revolution is possible. The overall position of the PPS in Moroccan domestic politics is not generally regarded as problematic for the **monarchy** or for the government. The Party's daily newspaper, *Al Bayane* (published in French and **Arabic**), was banned for four weeks after the June 1981 riots, but generally the party is tolerated as an integral part of the 'multiparty regime'.

Parti de la réforme et du développement

Moroccan political party, founded in 2001 by former members of the **Rassemblement national des indépendants**. Its leader is Abd ar-Rahmane Kohen.

Parti du renouveau algérien

Algerian political party. Its secretary-general is Yacine Terkmane and its leader Noureddine Boukrouh.

Parti républicain progressif

Algerian political party, founded in 1990. Its secretary-general is Slimane Cherif.

Parti social démocrate – *see* Parti national pour la solidarité et le développement

Parti socialiste démocratique

Moroccan political party, founded in 1996 after splitting from the **Organization of Democratic and Popular Action**. Its leader is Issa Ouardighi.

Parti socialiste nationaliste syrien

Lebanese political party, founded in1932 and banned between 1962 and 1969. It advocates a **Greater Syria** composed of Syria, Lebanon, Iraq, Jordan, Palestine and Cyprus. Its leader is Jibran Araiji.

Parti socialiste progressiste—At-Takadumi al-Ishterak
Progressive Socialist Party

Lebanese political party, founded in 1949. A progressive party that advocates the constitutional road to **democracy** and **socialism**. It has more than 25,000 members, mainly **Druze**. Its president is Walid Joumblatt, its secretary-general Sharif Fayad.

Parti des travailleurs

Algerian workers' party, led by Louisa Hanoune, who contested the 2004 presidential election.

Partisans of Islam – *see* Ansar al-Islam

Partition (of Palestine)

Various proposals for the partition of Palestine were made during the years immediately before the establishment of the State of Israel. The United Nations Partition Plan of November 1947 was one of the most influential.

Pasdaran – *see* Revolutionary Guards

Pashtuns/Pashto

The largest ethnic group in Afghanistan and along the Pakistan-Afghanistan border (especially in North West Frontier Province). Throughout Afghan history Pashtuns have generally held power in Afghanistan.

Pashtunistan

Pashtunistan is the Pashtun-dominated area of eastern Afghanistan and western Pakistan (Chitral and Sibi). Some **Pashtuns** aspire to form an independent Pashtunistan.

Patriotic Union of Kurdistan (PUK)

One of two Kurdish groups controlling northern Iraq after the war in Iraq in 2003. Its leader, **Jalal Talabani**, is the head of the **Iraqi Provisional Governing Council**. In November 2003 the PUK's headquarters in **Kirkuk** were the target of a suicide bomb attack in which at least five people were killed and about 40 injured. The bombing was believed by PUK members to be the work of **Ansar al-Islam**, a group which, until the war, had controlled a mountain stronghold near the Iranian border and is reported to have links with **al-Qa'ida**.

Peace process

Term widely, but misleadingly, used to refer to ongoing negotiations regarding the resolution of conflict (usually with reference to the future of Israeli-Palestinian relations). Usually, more specifically, the process initiated at the **Madrid peace conference** in 1991.

Peace Treaty between Egypt and Israel (1979)

A peace treaty between Egypt and Israel was signed, by **Menachem Begin** and **Anwar Sadat** on behalf of the governments of Israel and Egypt respectively, on 26 March 1979 in Washington, DC, under the auspices of US President **Jimmy Carter**. An historic event, it resulted in the immediate expulsion of Egypt from the **Arab League**.

Peel Commission

The Commission under Lord Peel was appointed in 1936. It concluded that there was no possibility of solving the Palestinian problem under the existing Mandate, or even under a scheme of cantonization. It therefore recommended the termination of the Mandate on the basis of **partition** and put forward a definite scheme which it considered to be practicable, honourable and just. It proposed that the Mandate be replaced by a Treaty System in accordance with the precedent set in Iraq and Syria. Under treaties to be negotiated by the Mandatory with the government of **Transjordan** and representatives of the Arabs of Palestine on the one hand, and with the **Zionist Organization** on the other, it would be declared that two sovereign independent states would shortly be established: one an Arab state consisting of Transjordan united with that part of Palestine allotted to the Arabs; the other a Jewish state consisting of that part of Palestine allotted to the Jews. The treaties would include strict guarantees for the protection of **minorities**. A new Mandate should be instituted to execute the trust of maintaining the sanctity of **Jerusalem** and **Bethlehem** and ensuring free and safe access to them for all the world. An enclave should be demarcated to which this Mandate should apply, extending from a point north of Jerusalem to a point south of Bethlehem, and access to the sea should be provided by a corridor extending from Jerusalem to **Jaffa**. The policy of the **Balfour Declaration** would not apply to the Mandated area. The Jewish state should pay a subvention to the Arab state. A Finance Commission should be appointed to advise as to its amount and as to the division of the public debt of Palestine and other financial questions. In view of the backwardness of Transjordan, Parliament should be asked to make a grant of £2m. to the Arab state.

People's Democratic Republic of Yemen

The People's Democratic Republic of Yemen (PDRY) was formally established in 1970 when the new Constitution professed a commitment to **socialism**, a tolerance of **Islam**, stressed the rights of **women** and vested all power in the Presidential Council of the **National Liberation Front** (NLF), which had originally taken control in **South Yemen** in 1967. Qahtan ash-Shaabi had emerged as the leader of the NLF in 1965, had led the delegation to the Geneva talks and in November 1967 had proclaimed himself President, Prime Minister and commander-in-chief of the new South Yemen. He had declared South Yemen a unitary state, abolished the old sheikhdoms and demanded the end of all tribal blood-feuds. Other parties were banned, the press controlled, a state security supreme court created and political authority established. An extreme leftist group under Abd al-Fattah Ismail and Ali Salim al-Baid was initially suppressed and then brought into government. In June 1969 ash-Shaabi was deposed, and replaced by a five-man presidential council, chaircd by Salim Rubai Ali and including Abd al-Fattah Ismail. There was a period of harsh repression at home and calls for a revolution in 'the occupied **Gulf**' abroad. In 1970 the PDRY was declared, with Ismail as secretary-general of the ruling NLF. Chairman Ali visited the People's Republic of China and returned inspired by Maoism. In the mean time the PDRY received foreign **aid** from the Soviet Union. There was fighting with the **Yemen Arab Republic** (YAR) to the north, but a cease-fire was eventually mediated by an **Arab League** mission and in October 1972 an agreement was reached by the PDRY and YAR for a single unified state. A Treaty of Union was signed in November 1972, but progress towards union was slow over the next five years as both the YAR and the PDRY experienced their own internal divisions and the assassinations of major political leaders. In the PDRY Ali was executed in July 1978 and replaced as chairman of the presidential council by Ali Nasser Muhammad. Ismail changed the NLF into a 'vanguard party', the **Yemen Socialist Party** (YSP), and in December became head of state. In February 1979 the PDRY launched an attack on the YAR in an attempt to bring about unity by force. Other Arab states intervened, however, and the two Presidents signed an agreement to unite that was almost identical to that signed nearly seven years before. In April 1980, after a visit to the Soviet Union, Ismail resigned on grounds of ill health and went into exile in the USSR; Muhammad resumed the presidency. The PDRY continued to support the leftist **National Democratic Front** against the government in the YAR and adopted a different stance from that of the YAR in the **Iran–Iraq War**, but there was a gradual increase in co-operation and co-ordination between the two in the early 1980s. Ismail returned from exile in 1985 and there were growing divisions within the presidential council. Muhammad attempted a coup, Ismail disappeared (his body was never found) and a brief but bitter civil war ensued in which at least 2,000 (including 55 senior party figures) were killed. The Prime Minister, Haidar abu Bakr al-Attas, assumed the post of President and secretary-general of the YSP and gradually brought the country under control. In 1986 Muhammad and 93 others were tried *in absentia* on charges of treason and **terrorism** and 35 (including Muhammad) were sentenced to death. Only five were actually executed, however, and even Muhammad was offered a retrial in 1988 if he returned voluntarily. Gradually, there was reform at home and in foreign policy. In

December 1989 the YSP ended its monopoly; in January 1990 the ban on foreign publications was lifted and a range of independent newspapers and journals was allowed. The PDRY began to develop better relations with other states in the Gulf, the Horn of Africa and the **Middle East** more generally, and progress towards unification accelerated to the point where, in May 1990, unification was eventually achieved and the Republic of **Yemen** created.

People's Front for the Liberation of the Sahara and the Río de Oro – *see* POLISARIO Front

People's Mujahidin of Iran (PMI)

An Iranian opposition movement whose headquarters are in Paris, France. Banned as a terrorist organization in the United Kingdom, it claims that its aims are to promote **democracy** and human rights in Iran. It is supported by a number of British parliamentarians. It functions as a member of a coalition group, the **National Council of Resistance** of Iran, whose press spokesman in London has described the PMI as a 'tolerant Islamic group'. Detractors claim that the PMI was sheltered by **Saddam Hussain** during the **Iran–Iraq War** (1980–88), when an armed element of the group fought Iranians to 'liberate the homeland'.

Perejil

In July 2002 relations between the **European Union** and Morocco were strained when the Moroccan Government briefly deployed a contingent of troops on, and reiterated a territorial claim to, the small Spanish-held **Mediterranean** island of Perejil. The European Commission urged bilateral dialogue between Morocco and Spain, and shortly afterwards an agreement was reached to maintain the status quo existing prior to the incident.

Peres, Shimon

Born in 1923, Peres was once an ally of **David Ben-Gurion** and **Moshe Dayan** in **Rafi**. A leading Israeli political figure for many decades, he was associated with the centre-left and the **Israel Labour Party**, which he led from 1968. In 1974–77 he served in the Government of **Itzhak Rabin**. Peres was acting Prime Minister in 1977, after Itzhak Rabin and before **Menachem Begin**. In 1984 he became Prime Minister in a government of national unity and remained in that post until 1986, when he was replaced by **Itzhak Shamir**. He was Prime Minister again in 1995–96, before being replaced by **Binyamin Netanyahu** of the **Likud** party.

Persia

The historical name for modern day Iran. Always to the east of the **Arab World** and home to a succession of major empires and dynasties over several centuries: the Sassanians (AD 224–642), the period of the Arab conquest (AD 642–1037), the Seljuks (AD 1037–1220), the Mongol period (AD 122–1380), the Timurids (AD 1380–1500) and the Safavids (AD 1500–1736). A turbulent period known as 'the interregnum' (1736–87) led to the last of the great Persian dynasties, the Qajars (1787–1925). The constitutional revolution of 1905 virtually swept away the last of the Qajars, while the final end came with the transfer of power to a military officer, **Reza Khan**, in 1922. Reza Khan established a new dynasty, the Pahlavi dynasty, when he named himself Shah, but under his regime (1925–41) Persia was to give way to modern Iran.

Persian (Arabian) Gulf

Waterway leading from the **Shatt al-Arab**, at the confluence of the **Tigris** and **Euphrates** rivers, south-eastwards to the Indian Ocean. The name the 'Persian Gulf' and the implied control over the waterways and reserves of **oil** and **natural gas** under the sea have been hotly contested by all of the bordering states. The Persian (Arabian) Gulf is the main waterway for the export of oil from southern Iran, and from Iraq, Kuwait, Saudi Arabia, the United Arab Emirates, Bahrain and Qatar.

Peshmerga

A Kurdish word, meaning 'one who is ready to die'. It refers to Kurdish 'freedom fighters'—the forces deployed in support of the struggle for greater Kurdish political recognition, autonomy or independence, whether in Syria, Iraq, Iran or Turkey.

Petroleum – *see* oil

PFLP – *see* Popular Front for the Liberation of Palestine

PFLP-GC – *see* Popular Front for the Liberation of Palestine-General Command

Phalange Libanais

Also known as **Kata'ib Party**

Phosphate(s)

Minerals used mainly for the production of (phosphate-based) fertilizers. Morocco is one of the world's largest phosphate exporters and a major producer. The sector is dominated by the state-owned Office chérifien des phosphates. The disputed territory of **Western Sahara** also has significant deposits, which were first extracted by Spain during the 1960s and early 1970s, mainly from the Bou Craa mines in territory now illegally occupied by Morocco. One of Morocco's incentives for attempting to ensure the effective integration of Western Sahara under its government, the existence of known phosphate deposits is an issue of contention between Morocco and the **Sahrawis**, still struggling for self-determination.

PKK – *see* **Kurdish (Kurdistan) Workers' Party** and **KADEK**

Plan Dalet

On 10 March 1948 the Jewish leadership adopted Plan Dalet, which resulted in the 'ethnic cleansing' of the areas regarded as the future Jewish state in Palestine. The issue of the extent to which the mass exodus of **Palestinians** as **refugees** from the area which became the State of Israel was planned has been hotly debated. Revisionist Israeli historians, such as Benny Morris, author of *The Origins of the Palestinian Problem*, have tended to argue that it was not planned as such, even if the effect was as if it had been a clear and coherent plan. The existence of the Plan Dalet and other contemporary evidence makes this view difficult to sustain.

Plan of Joint Action (1984)

After a series of negotiations which began in January 1984, establishing a platform for joint action, King **Hussein** of Jordan and **Yasser Arafat**, chairman of the **Palestine Liberation Organization** (PLO), announced in **Amman** on 23 February 1984 their proposals for a **Middle East** peace settlement and a plan of joint action. The failure of these proposals to further the **peace process** was acknowledged by King Hussein in February 1986, when he abandoned Jordan's political collaboration with the PLO. The PLO did not formally abrogate the Amman agreement until the 18th session of the **Palestine National Council** in **Algiers** in April 1987.

PLO – *see* **Palestine Liberation Organization**

PNA – *see* **Palestinian National Authority**

PNC – *see* **Palestine National Council**

Pnina Rosenblum

Israeli political party.

Poale Agudat Israel

Workers of the Community of Israel

A right-wing grouping, with largely Orthodox Jewish working-class membership. Founded in 1924, it is currently led by Dr Kalman Kahane.

Poale Zion

The **Workers of Zion**, a political group formed in the late 19th century in eastern Europe. Inside Russia the party was truly revolutionary; in other parts of Europe it gathered information on the enemies of the Jews and through its defence units gave what protection it could to Jewish citizens. Later, defence units were created in Palestine by Poale Zion to give support to Jewish immigrants from Europe as well as to native Jews.

Poland

Poland dispatched 2,400 troops to Iraq to participate in the 'peace-keeping force' in the aftermath of the **Iraq War (2003)** and commanded some 9,500 soldiers from 23 countries, including Spain, in the south-central sector of Iraq. The troops were sent, in part, in exchange for US reconstruction contracts, but also to show solidarity with the **coalition**. They were deployed in 2004, together with a small Bulgarian contingent, near the city of **Karbala (Kerbala)**, in order to protect pilgrims to the holy city during one of the most important weeks in the **Shi'a** calendar. They were rendered helpless by the take-over of the city during March 2004 by the so-called Mahdi Army, the militia loyal to **Moqtada as-Sadr**, a radical Shi'a cleric. In April 2004 Poland's Prime Minister, Leszek Miller, stated that he was considering a withdrawal of Polish troops, although after the bomb attacks in Madrid, Spain, that took place in March he had pledged that Poland would maintain its mission in Iraq and the foreign minister insisted that Poland would keep its troops at the same level throughout the year, gradually reducing its commitment over the following year, on the assumption that an Iraqi government would by then be in place.

POLISARIO Front

Frente Popular para la Liberación de Saguia el-Hamra y Río de Oro

Sahrawi nationalist political movement, founded in 1973 to pursue self-determination and independence for the Sahrawi people of **Western Sahara** (then **Spanish Sahara**). It declared the independent **Sahrawi Arab Democratic Republic** (SADR) in 1976, although the majority of the population was by then resident in refugee camps in south-west Algeria (near Tindouf). It continued to struggle for Sahrawi independence against Morocco and Mauritania from 1976 and then against Morocco alone from 1978. The Front signed a peace treaty with Mauritania in 1979. The secretary-general of the POLISARIO Front and the President of the SADR is Muhammad Abd al-Aziz.

Political freedom

According to the 'political freedom' index, developed by the UN Development Programme together with other international agencies, the Arab countries of the **Middle East** had the lowest score of seven world regions in the late 1990s, significantly lower than that of sub-Saharan Africa, the next poorly ranked. This is confirmed by a set of indicators of 'voice and accountability' (including various aspects of the political process, civil liberties, political rights and independence of the media) derived from an international database which, again, places the Arab countries well below those of sub-Saharan Africa. (See also **Democracy**.)

Political Islam

Political Islam is a term for the radical intellectual, cultural, social, and political movement that has emerged throughout the Islamic world over the last three decades. The movement is often referred to as the Islamic Resurgence or Islamic Revival, and political Islam is only one component of a greater resurgence and revival of Islamic ideas, practices, and rhetoric. It refers to the increasing prominence and politicization of Islamic ideologies and symbols in Muslim societies and in the public life of Muslims as individuals. It falls into two main groupings, the first of which calls for direct political action and advocates the use of democratic and electoral means—political organization, mobilization, and participation—to bring about a non-violent transfer of power in a nation. The reform of both state and society is at the heart of this political agenda. The **Muslim Brotherhood** has traditionally been a reformist group. The second grouping includes militant hard-liners who wish to transfer power quickly by any means, political or military. It is the last group that often is associated with **Islamic fundamentalism.**

Political Zionist Opposition (OMETZ)

Founded in 1982 as a one-man party—Yigael Hurwitz.

Pollution

Environmental pollution is a serious problem in the region. The high demand for scarce **water** resources and mismanagement are both sources of severe water pollution and degradation. Many countries are responsible for high CO^2 emissions: Qatar is by far the worst offender at 91.5 tons per person, followed by the United Arab Emirates (31.3 tons), Bahrain (29.4 tons) and Kuwait (24.9 tons)—all ahead of the USA (19.7 tons). Saudi Arabia (11.7 tons), Israel (10.0 tons) and Oman (8.5 tons) are also major culprits. Sulphur dioxide emissions are worst in Kuwait (which produces 7,120 tons per populated sq km), Egypt (4,090 tons), Israel (3,310 tons), Libya (3,220 tons) and Jordan (2,710 tons).

Polytheism

In Greek: 'many gods'. Polytheism is the belief in, or worship of, multiple gods or divinities. Ancient religions were mostly polytheistic, adhering to pantheons of traditional deities. Present-day polytheistic religions include Hinduism and Shinto. Some Buddhist sects are also polytheistic, although this view of the religion is rejected by most of its adherents. Some Jewish and Islamic scholars regard the Christian doctrine of the Trinity as bordering on polytheism.

Popular Bloc

Political grouping in Bahrain.

Popular Committees

A relatively new phenomenon found (mainly) in Egypt. They refer to extra parliamentary groups such as the Egyptian Popular Committee for the Solidarity with the Palestinian *Intifada*, the Anti-Globalization Groups Egypt (AGEG). They were also found in Jordan during the **Gulf War (1991)**.

Popular Democratic Pan-Arab Party

Jordanian political party, formed in July 1997.

Popular Democratic Party

Political grouping in Saudi Arabia.

Popular Front for the Liberation of Palestine (PFLP)

Marxist-Leninist group founded in 1967 by **George Habash**—as a member of the **Palestinian Liberation Organization**—when it broke away from the **Arab Nationalist Movement**. The PFLP views the Palestinian struggle as a legitimate struggle against illegal occupation. It is opposed to negotiations with Israel. The PFLP carried out numerous international terrorist attacks during the 1970s. Since 1978 it has conducted attacks against Israeli or moderate Arab targets, including killing a settler and her son in December 1996. In 1994 the PFLP announced the formation of the Democratic National Action Front which it described as an open, popular political forum , an extension of the PFLP. The PFLP has intensified its operational activities since the start of the current *intifada*, as shown by its assassination of the Israeli **tourism** minister in October 2001 in revenge for

Israel's killing of the PFLP secretary-general earlier that year. The PFLP's areas of operation are mainly Syria, Lebanon, Israel, the **West Bank** and **Gaza**.

Popular Front for the Liberation of Palestine-General Command (PFLP-GC)

The PFLP-GC split from the **Popular Front for the Liberation of Palestine** (led by **George Habash**) in 1968, claiming that it wished to focus more on fighting and less on politics. Like the PFLP it was critical of **Arafat**'s leadership and the direction of the **Palestine Liberation Organization**. Led by Ahmed Jibril, a former captain in the Syrian army, the PFLP-GC carried out dozens of attacks in Europe and the **Middle East** during the 1970s and 1980s. It became known for cross-border terrorist attacks into Israel using unusual means, such as hot-air balloons and motorized hang gliders. It enjoyed close relations with the Soviet Union during the 1970s and 1980s and received support from various Arab states, notably Syria and Libya. In the summer of 1988, however, Libya suspended its annual funding of US \$25m. and Jibril and his 400–600 fighters were unsure how to maintain themselves. When in July the USS *Vincennes* accidentally shot down an Iranian plane with 290 people on board, Jibril contacted the Iranian authorities and offered, at a price, to carry out a retaliatory attack on a US target—he suggested a US plane, possibly a Boeing 747. Iran agreed and as a sign of goodwill deposited \$2m. in PFLP-GC accounts. In September 1988, however, one of Jibril's key aides, Hafeth el-Dalkamuni abu Mohammed, was arrested in West Germany and a cache of bombs and explosives were discovered. A second hide-out in the suburbs of Frankfurt was never found. There is some evidence to suggest that it was from this second base that the operation was launched which led to the explosion in mid-air over **Lockerbie** in Scotland. Two days after the Lockerbie disaster, Iran transferred the balance of its payment to the PFLP-GC accounts. Jibril's son, Jihad, was killed by a car bomb in May 2002. The PFLP-GC is now mainly involved in guerrilla operations in southern Lebanon and small-scale attacks in Israel, the **West Bank** and **Gaza Strip**.

Popular Front for the Liberation of Palestine-Special Command (PFLP-SC)

A Marxist-Leninist group formed by 'Abu Salim' in 1979 after breaking away from the now defunct PFLP-Special Operations Group. It claimed responsibility for several notorious international terrorist attacks in western Europe, including the bombing of a restaurant frequented by US servicemen in Torrejon, Spain, in April 1985, in which 18 Spanish civilians were killed.

Popular Liberation Army

Lebanese **Sunni** Muslim faction, active in the south of Lebanon. Its leader is Mustafa Saad.

Popular Movement – *see* **Mouvement populaire (Morocco)**

Popular Participation Bloc

Jordanian political coalition formed in May 1999 to contest the municipal elections held in July. A grouping of 13 leftist, Ba'athist and pan-Arab parties.

Popular Struggle Front (PSF)

Radical Palestinian terrorist group once closely involved in the Syrian-dominated **Palestinian National Salvation Front**. The PSF is led by Dr Samir Ghosheh. It rejoined the **Palestine Liberation Organization** in September 1991. The group is internally divided over the **Declaration of Principles on Palestinian Self-Rule** signed in 1993.

Populism

A political ideology and/or form of political regime which emphasizes the interests of 'the people' over and above any specific sectional interest.

Post-colonial states

States which have inherited many of the characteristics of the colonial state, and which maintain strong links with the former colonial power, despite formal political independence. (See also **neo-colonialism**.)

Powell, Colin

US Secretary of State under the Administration of **George W. Bush**.

Programme of Assistance to the Palestinian People

This UN Programme, established in 1978, is committed to strengthening newly created institutions, creating employment opportunities and stimulating private and public investments to enhance **trade** and export potential in the **Occupied Territories** and Palestinian autonomous areas of the **West Bank** and **Gaza**.

Progressive List for Peace

Israeli political grouping, founded in 1984. With Jewish-Arab membership, it advocates recognition of the **Palestine Liberation Organization** and the establishment of a Palestinian state in the **West Bank** and **Gaza Strip**. It is led by Muhammed Mi'ari.

Progressive Republican Party

Algerian political grouping, led by Khadir Driss.

Provincial Reconstruction Teams (PRTs)

Clusters of lightly armed troops meant to assist the international development agencies and other organizations in reconstruction work throughout Afghanistan. PRTs are not **ISAF**, but draw on ISAF experience; they are not part of the coalition force, **Operation Enduring Freedom**, but receive air support from the coalition. The USA has already established several PRTs, as have the United Kingdom, New Zealand and Germany. The UK PRT (72 men) in **Mazar-i-Sharif** is responsible for an area the size of Scotland. Eventually some one dozen such units may be deployed in Afghanistan.

Q

Qabil – *see also* **Berber(s)** and **tribe(s)**

In **Arabic** the word means 'tribe'. A term used widely in the **Gulf states** and in the **Arabian Peninsula** more generally to refer to local tribes. In the **Maghreb**, however, the term Kabyle is used to refer specifically to the **Berber** tribes of the region known as Kabylia.

Qaboos ibn Said – *see* **as-Said, Qabus (Qaboos) ibn Said**

al-Qaddafi, Col Muammar Abu Minyar (1942–)

Revolutionary leader of Libya since 1969, Muammar al-Qaddafi became an army officer in 1965. In 1969, together with a group of fellow officers, he formed a secret revolutionary committee and in 1969 led a successful coup against **King Idris I** (a leading member of the Sanussi religious brotherhood). Qaddafi established himself as Libya's commander-in-chief and chairman of the Revolutionary Command Council. Blending **Arab nationalism**, revolutionary **socialism**, and Islamic ortho-doxy, Qaddafi pursued a strongly anti-Western foreign policy, while experimenting with various forms of government at home. Foreign military bases were closed and assets in Western and Jewish hands were nationalized. All **petroleum** assets were nationalized in 1973. A fervent Arab nationalist, Qaddafi sought to unify Libya with other Arab countries, including Egypt and Tunisia, while bitterly opposing Israel. His *Green Book* (2 vols, 1976–80) is a treatise on Islamic socialism which he calls the **Third International Theory**. In 1979 he officially declared himself leader of the Revolution and supreme commander of the **armed forces**. Since Qaddafi took power the Libyan government has undoubtedly supported various terrorist organi-zations, including the Irish Republican Army, the **Palestine Liberation Organization** (PLO) and various leftist Palestinian groups. In 1986 the USA sought to quell Libya's alleged terrorist activities by bombing several targets in the country. Qaddafi survived, but several of his children were wounded or killed. In 1999, following the surrender of the suspects in the **Lockerbie** bombing, Qaddafi sought improved relations with western European nations and issued a denunciation of **terrorism**. In 2004 Qaddafi's willingness to accept UN inspection of his nuclear weapons facilities and a visit by UK Prime Minister Tony Blair marked another step towards Libya's international rehabilitation.

Al-Qa'ida

In **Arabic** means 'the base'. Established initially as a base for the **Afghan Arabs** fighting in Afghanistan, and as an organization providing support and services to these fighters (**Afghan Service Bureau**), al-Qa'ida subsequently developed, particularly after the end of the war in Afghanistan—**Afghan–Soviet War (1979–89)**—and the subsequent dispersal of the Afghan Arabs, into a loosely-knit but ideologically coherent international Islamist network (see **al-Qa'ida network**) supposedly under the leadership of **Osama bin Laden**. A report by the International Institute of Strategic Studies in May 2004 suggested that the US-led assault on the **Taliban** and on alleged al-Qa'ida training camps in 2001–02, followed by the occupation of parts of Afghanistan by US-led forces during 2003, compelled al-Qa'ida to disperse and become even more decentralized, 'virtual' and invisible.

As of the end of 2003, scores, perhaps hundreds, of fugitive al-Qa'ida operatives were believed to be 'in custody' in Iran. It was thought they included several leading figures, notably al-Qa'ida's chiefs of military planning, finance and public relations (Saif al-Adel and Abu Mohammed al-Masri), as well as **Osama bin Laden**'s son, Saad bin Laden. Jordan, Egypt and Saudi Arabia have pressed Iran to surrender all of their nationals suspected of **terrorism**. In 2002 Iran handed over dozens of low-level al-Qa'ida operatives and Afghan Arabs to Saudi Arabia and Egypt. Jordan and Egypt's leaders met Iranian President **Khatami** towards the end of 2003, their first meetings with an Iranian head of state since 1979. President Khatami stated that he would be willing to hand over some 130 al-Qa'ida suspects to their countries of origin. A report by the International Institute of Strategic Studies in May 2004 suggested that al-Qa'ida is now established in more than 60 countries. Despite the death or capture of half of its 30 senior leaders, as well as some 2,000 rank-and-file supporters, a rump of leadership reportedly remained intact.

Al-Qa'ida network

Al-Qa'ida 'associated' consists of a more or less coherent 'core' network and numerous disparate and widely diffused local and national groups. A report by the International Institute of Strategic Studies in May 2004 suggested that al-Qa'ida has tended to delegate more responsibility to 'local talent', while maintaining loose links and communications. Tracing all of these links, many of which have been over-emphasized or even imagined by the international media and commentators, is extremely difficult—although the intelligence agencies of most countries now have a vested interest in doing so. An indication of the scope of this global network is provided by a list of the organizations and groups with varying links to al-Qa'ida, but this provides only an indication and cannot nearly be definitive. Older groups split and change; new groups are formed. The precise nature and intensity of links between the different cells and groupings that now constitute the al-Qa'ida network is unknown. Some of the better known groups with links to al-Qa'ida include: **al-Gama'a al-Islamiyya**; Jihad Organization of Jordan; Pakistani al-Hadith Group; Lebanese Partisans League; Bayt al-Imam Group of Jordan; **Asbat al-Ansar** (Lebanon); Harakat al-Ansar/*Mujahidin*; Al-Badr; Talaa al-Fath (**Vanguards of Conquest**); Groupe Roubaix (Canada/France); Harakat ul Jihad (Pakistan); Jaysh-e Mohammed; **Jamiat-e Ulema-e Islam**; **Hezbollah** (Lebanon); Hezb ul-Mujahidin (Pakistan); **Islamic Movement of Uzbekistan**; Jihad Group of Bangladesh; Jihad Group of Yemen; Lashkar-e-Tayyiba; Moro Islamic Liberation Front (Philippines); the Partisans Movement (Kashmir); Abu Sayyaf (Philippines); Al-Ittihad (Somalia); **Ulema Union** (Afghanistan); Takfir wa-l Hijra (Egypt, Algeria).

Qairawan

City in Tunisia regarded as a holy place by Muslims. Seven pilgrimages to the Great Mosque of Sidi 'Uqbah bin Nafi' (founder of Qairawan) is considered as the equivalent of one pilgrimage to **Mecca**. Qairawan is the site of a famous university and library.

Qajar dynasty

The last dynasty of Persia. Muzaffar ad-Din (1896–1907), Muhammad Ali (1907–09) and Ahmad (1909–24) were the last three rulers of this dynasty. In 1924 Ahmad was replaced by **Reza Khan**, a military officer, who made himself Shah of Persia.

Qashqai

Significant ethnic and linguistic **minority** tribal group in southern Iran. They number about 400,000 and are **Shi'a**. The government of the Islamic Republic of Iran rejected any idea of ethnic/tribal political autonomy and was relatively suspicious of the political leadership of these groups. Armed clashes took place between government forces and supporters of ethnic/tribal autonomy after 1979. In June 1980 a leader of the Qashqai, Khosrow Qashqai, was elected to the **Majlis**, but was not permitted to take his seat. He was executed in the autumn of 1982.

Qasimi, Sheikh Saqr ibn Muhammad

Ruler of Ras al-Khaimah, one of the United Arab Emirates, who acceded to power in 1948.

Qasimi, Sheikh Sultan ibn Muhammad

Ruler of Sharjah, one of the United Arab Emirates, who acceded to power in 1972.

Qassam, Izz ad-Din

Palestinian fighting group.

Qatar, State of

Dawlat Qatar

Small independent state (*c*. 11,500 sq km in area) located on a small peninsula that protrudes from the main **Arabian Peninsula** into the **Persian (Arabian) Gulf**. The capital is **Doha**. For administrative purposes Qatar is divided into nine municipalities (*baladiyah*, plural *baladiyat*): Ad-Dawhah, Al-Ghuwayriyah, Al-Jumayliyah, Al-Khawr, Al-Wakrah, Ar-Rayyan, Jarayan al-Batinah, Madinat ash-Shamal and Umm Salal. In July 2002 the population was estimated at 793,341, of which Arabs constituted 40%, Pakistanis 18%, Indians 18%, Iranians 10% and 'others' 14%. With regard to religion, Muslims (Wahhabi **Sunni**) account for 95% of the population and Christians and 'others' 5%. **Arabic** is the official language. English is commonly used as a second language.

Qatar is a hereditary **monarchy**. Emir **Hamad ibn Khalifa ath-Thani** has been the ruler and head of state since 27 June 1995 when, as crown prince, he ousted his father, Emir Khalifa ibn Hamad ath-Thani, in a bloodless coup. Emir Hamad is also Minister of Defence and commander-in-chief of the **armed forces**. Crown Prince Jassim bin Hamad ibn Khalifa ath-Thani, the third son of the monarch, was selected as crown prince by his father on 22 October 1996. The head of the government since 30 October 1996 has been Prime Minister Abdallah bin Khalifa ath-Thani, brother of the monarch; since 20 January 1998 the Deputy Prime Minister has been Muhammad bin Khalifa ath-Thani, brother of the monarch. A Council of Ministers is appointed by the monarch. The unicameral **Majlis** ash-Shura (Advisory Council) is a 35-member body to which members are appointed. The Constitution sets forth that elections should be held for part of this consultative body, but none have taken place since those, partial, of 1970. Council members have since had their terms of office extended every four years. A directly elected parliament was to be established in 2003.

There are no recognized political parties or groupings. In March 1999 Qatar held nation-wide elections for a 29-member Central Municipal Council, which has consultative powers aimed at improving the provision of municipal services. The legal system is based on a discretionary system of law controlled by the Emir, although civil codes are being implemented. **Islamic Law** dominates family and personal matters. There is a Court of Appeal.

Media

There is one state-controlled radio service. Of the two television services, one is independent and one is state-controlled. Qatari television is the most independent in the region. The independent television station **al-Jazeera**, based in Qatar, offers an international Arabic-language perspective. There are six daily newspapers, of which *Ar-Rayah*, *Gulf Times*, *al-Arab* and *ash-Sharq* are the most widely read. In 2000 there was one internet service provider. In 2001 there were 75,000 internet users.

History

Ruled by the ath-Thani family since the mid-1800s, Qatar was transformed in the mid-20th century from a poor British protectorate noted mainly for pearl fishing into an independent state with significant **oil** and **natural gas** revenues. During the late 1980s and early 1990s, the Qatari economy was crippled by the continuous appropriation of petroleum revenues by the Emir, who had ruled the country since 1972. He was overthrown by his son, the current Emir Hamad ibn Khalifa ath-Thani, in a bloodless coup in 1995. In 2001 Qatar resolved its long-standing border disputes with both Bahrain and Saudi Arabia. Oil and natural gas revenues enable Qatar to maintain a per caput level of **income** that is not far below those of the leading industrial countries of western Europe.

Qatar, economy

The people of Qatar enjoy the highest living standards in the **Middle East**: gross domestic product (GDP) per head, at US $28,620, is the eighth highest in the world. **Oil** accounts for more than 30% of GDP, roughly 80% of export earnings, and 58% of government revenues. Proven oil reserves of 3,700m. barrels are suffcent for another 23 years of production at current levels. In 2000 Qatar recorded its highest **trade** surplus ever—$7,000m.—owing, mainly, to high oil prices and increased **natural gas** exports, and managed to maintain the surplus in 2001. Qatar's proven reserves of natural gas exceed 7,000,000m. cu m, constituting the third largest natural gas resource in the world and more than 5% of the world total. The production and export of natural gas are becoming increasingly important. Long-term economic objectives emphasize the development of offshore natural gas reserves. The economy has diversified into oil-related and other industries. It has a modern infrastructure. Qatar is highly dependent on immigrant labour, all raw materials are imported and virtually all **water** has to be desalinated.

Al-Qiyam

An Islamist association established in **Algiers**, Algeria, in the early 1960s. It became prominent in 1964 at a time of growing political divisions within the ruling **Front de libération nationale** (National Liberation Front) government and within Algeria as a whole. Its leaders included Malek Bennabi and **Mohamed Khider**, the latter having been one of the nine 'historic chiefs' who founded the FLN and became its head after independence. It can be regarded as a precursor of the later Algerian Islamist movement. In 1965, in its journal *Humanisme Musulman*, it stated that 'all political parties, all regimes and all leaders which do not base themselves on **Islam** are decreed illegal and dangerous'. Al-Qiyam was dissolved by prefectoral decree in the governorate of Algiers (where it had its principal presence) in September 1966 and formally banned throughout the country in March 1970. Mohamed Khider was assassinated in Madrid, Spain, in January 1967.

Qualified Industrial Zones (Jordan)

Roughly equivalent to export and processing Zones.

Al-Quds

The Palestinian name for **Jerusalem**. The status of Al-Quds/Jerusalem is one of the final status items for negotiation between Israel and the **Palestinian National Authority**. Israel has illegally settled a large part of Jerusalem and does not want to partition it. (See also **Jerusalem**.)

Al-Quds Committee

Established in 1975 as a standing committee of the **Organization of the Islamic Conference**, to implement the resolutions of the Islamic Conference on the status of **Jerusalem** (**al-Quds**). It meets at the level of foreign ministers, maintains the al-Quds Fund and is currently chaired by King **Abdullah II** of Jordan.

Al-Qudsi, Nazim

President of Syria from 1961 until 1963, when he was replaced by Gen. **Amin al-Hafiz**.

Qum (Qom)

Holy city in central Iran. Venerated as the location of the tomb of Fatima, sister of Imam ar-Rida/Riza (see **Meshed**), and those of hundreds of saints and kings, including the Imams 'Ali bin Ja'far and Ibrahim, and the Shahs Safi and 'Abbas II. Following the **Iranian Revolution** in 1979 it became the centre favoured by Ayatollah **Khomeini**.

Qur'anic Literacy Institute

A Chicago-based charity whose founder, Mohammad Salah, was an agent for **Hamas**, to which the organization channels funds. Yasin al-Qadi, a Saudi magnate, helped transfer millions of dollars to various Middle Eastern organizations, including Hamas, both through the Qur'anic Literacy Institute and through another charity, **Blessed Relief**. After 11 September 2001 his assets and investments in several countries were 'frozen'.

Qurei, Ahmed

Prime Minister of the **Palestinian National Authority**. He replaced **Mahmoud Abbas ('Abu Mazen')** in September 2003. Born in 1938, the former speaker of the Palestinian house was also one of those closely involved in the **Oslo Agreements** of 1993. His *nom de guerre* was 'Abu Ala'a'. A wealthy exile who returned to Palestine after decades abroad, his unremarkable public statements have done little to give him political legitimacy, but his pro-**Arafat** stance has made him seem less of a US stooge. He initially wished to avoid public discussion of the Palestinian leadership, but was eventually called on to replace 'Abu Mazen'. Nominated as Palestinian Prime Minister after the resignation of Mahmoud Abbas in September 2003, he is closer to Arafat than Abbas ever was. Only the second Palestinian Prime Minister, he has a difficult job. In December 2003 he stated that he would not meet **Ariel Sharon** as long as Israel continued to construct a security wall in the **West Bank**.

Qutb, Sayyid (1906–66)

Egyptian religious leader (member of the **Muslim Brotherhood**) and writer who was executed by President **Gamal Abdel Nasser**. He was born into a family of rural notables who had fallen on hard times. His most famous book, *Milestones* [or Signposts] *Along the Road*—which has been extremely influential in the evolution of radical Islamist thought since his death harshly criticized Nasser's rule and any secularized society where **Islam** was the majority religion. Qutb, who provided a comprehensive account of *jahiliyya*, which he defined explicitly as 'opposition to God's rule', argued that the entire world was today living in a state of *jahiliyya*. For him, 'the degradation of man in general in the collectivist regimes, the injustice suffered by individuals and peoples dominated by capitalism and **colonialism**, are the consequences of this opposition to the rule of God'. He advocated the formation of a vanguard of Muslim youth to fight the new *jahiliyya*, just as the **Prophet Muhammad** had fought the original one. His ideas set the agenda for Islamic radicals, not only in Egypt but throughout the **Middle East** and North Africa, and beyond. Many former leftist intellectuals and activists were persuaded by this vision, as were increasing numbers of ordinary Muslims—**Sunni** and **Shi'ite**. After the Muslim Brotherhood tried to assassinate Nasser in 1954, Qutb was among those arrested and imprisoned (1954–64). Rearrested in 1966, he was accused of conspiracy, convicted of treason, and executed.

Al-Quwatli, Shukri

President of Syria from 1946 until March 1949, when he was overthrown in a bloodless coup and replaced by **Husni az-Zaim**.

R

Ra'am

Israeli political grouping, comprising the Islamic Movement, the National Unity Front and the Arab Democratic Party.

Rabat

Capital of Morocco. Major city on the western coast, north of **Casablanca**.

Rabat Resolution

The Seventh Arab Summit Conference in **Rabat** resolved in October 1974: to affirm the right of the Palestinian people to self-determination and to return to their homeland; to affirm the right of the Palestinian people to establish an independent national authority under the command of the **Palestine Liberation Organization** (PLO), the sole legitimate representative of the Palestinian people in any Palestinian territory that is liberated . . .; to support the PLO in the exercise of its responsibility at the national and international levels within the framework of Arab commitment; to call on the **Hashemite** Kingdom of Jordan, the Syrian Arab Republic, the Arab Republic of Egypt and the PLO to devise a formula for the regulation of relations between them in the light of these decisions so as to ensure their implementation; that all the Arab states undertake to defend Palestinian national unity and not to interfere in the internal affairs of Palestinian action.

Rabbani, Burhanuddin

A former professor of **Islamic Law** at **Kabul** University, he became president of a *mujahidin*-led Afghan government in 1992 but was ousted by the **Taliban** in 1996.

Rabin, Itzhak

Born in 1922, Rabin was Israeli chief of staff during the **Arab–Israeli War (1967)**. He was the main rival of **Shimon Peres** for the leadership of the **Israel Labour Party** and the **Alignment Bloc**. He was Prime Minister of Israel from 1974 until 1977, served as Minister of Defence in the government of national unity created in

1984, with Shimon Peres as Prime Minister, and was Prime Minister again from 1992 until 1995, when he was assassinated.

Rafah

Refugee camp in the **Gaza Strip**. It was one of the targets of **Operation Rainbow** in May 2004—a military operation that resulted in numerous civilian deaths and the destruction of large numbers of buildings and homes.

Rafi

Israeli political party which emerged in 1965 when **David Ben-Gurion** and his protégés, **Moshe Dayan** and **Shimon Peres**, left **Mapai** over several policy issues as well as out of dissatisfaction with the leadership of **Levi Eshkol**. Rafi stood alone for only one election (1965) and gained 10 seats in the **Knesset** with about 8% of the vote. It merged in 1968 with **Achdut HaAvoda** and Mapai to form the **Israel Labour Party**.

Rafsanjani, Hojatoleslam Ali Akbar Hashemi

Iranian religious and political leader, President of Iran (1989–97). A **Shi'ite** cleric, supporter and half-brother of Ayotallah **Khomeini**, Rafsanjani was imprisoned several times during the 1960s and 1970s for his political activities. After the ouster of the Shah (see **Muhammad Reza Shah Pahlavi**), he was appointed Minister of the Interior in July 1979 and from July 1980 served for nine years as speaker of the **Majlis**, a position which helped him build a substantial political power base. From relatively early on, although he openly supported **Ayatollah** Montazeri as Khomeini's successor, he sought greater power and influence. In trips abroad he often acted as head of state. From 1988 until 1989 he was also acting commander-in-chief of the **armed forces**. In 1989 Rafsanjani was elected as President, receiving some 95% of the vote. He sought to revive Iran's failing economy on free-market principles and moved to improve relations with the West, re-establish Iran as a regional power, and gradually reopen his country to foreign investment. He was re-elected in 1993 with about two-thirds of the vote, but was barred from seeking a third presidential term in the 1997 elections. His influence remains strong, particularly among those now considered 'conservatives', but he has not been central to Iranian politics for five years. He is still, however, active, and in April 2004 preached a sermon in which he praised the so-called **Mahdi Army** of **Moqtar as-Sadr** in Iraq as 'enthusiastic, heroic young people'.

Ar-Rahman Battalion (Algeria)

Established shortly after the declaration of the state of emergency in Algeria, the Rahman Battalion was led by Mustapha Kertali. It joined the cease-fire announced by the **AIS—Armée islamique du salut** (Islamic Salvation Army) in October 1997 and has been dissolved.

Rahman, Sheikh Omar Abdul

Islamist religious leader of the Egyptian **Islamic Group** origin, known also as the 'Blind Sheikh'.

Rajai, Muhammad Ali

President of Iran from September 1980 until October 1981. He succeeded **Abol Hassan Bani Sadr**, and was succeeded in turn by **Sayed Ali Khamenei**.

Rajavi, Massoud

Leader of the Iranian *Mujahidin*. Born in 1948, he joined the *Mujahidin* shortly after its establishment in the mid-1960s. He fought for the **Palestinians** in Jordan in September 1970. He was imprisoned by the Shah from 1971 until 1978 and sentenced to death, but the sentence was commuted to life imprisonment after his trial attracted international attention. In 1975, when the movement split into two factions, he continued actively to support the Islamist tendency, from prison. Released from prison after the downfall of the Shah, he attempted to contest the presidency in January 1980 on the grounds that he and his movement opposed the new Constitution. He escaped from Iran with former President **Bani Sadr** in July 1981 and lived in exile in Paris, France, until expelled by the French government in June 1986. He married Bani Sadr's daughter Firuzeh in 1982, but when Bani Sadr and he severed their political ties in March 1984, largely over Rajavi's links with the Iraqi leadership, he divorced her at the same time. He placed the *Mujahidin* within the framework of the **National Council of Resistance** and tried to moderate the image of the *Mujahidin* as 'Islamist Marxist fighters'. Many former *Mujahidin* emigrated to Europe or the USA and the number active in Iran—in June 1980, at the height of their popularity, the *Mujahidin* were able to attract 150,000 supporters and sympathizers to a rally in **Tehran**—declined to about 1,000. In 1985 the US Department of State protested at *Mujahidin* fund-raising and public-relations work in the USA, arguing that it was a terrorist organization. It is probable, however, that funds were raised mainly through links with Iraq, given Rajavi's own inclinations at that time.

Rakah

New Communist Party of Israel, formed in 1965. (See **Hadash**.)

Rakhmonov, Imamali

President of Tajikistan since 1992. Rakhmonov has become increasingly authoritarian and has alienated his government partners in the **United Tajik Opposition/ Islamic Renaissance Party**.

Ramadan

The ninth month in the Islamic calendar, the fasting month.

Ramadan, Taha Yassin

Vice-President of Iraq under the regime of **Saddam Hussain**. He was born in 1936. A **Ba'ath Party** veteran, he was captured by Kurdish forces in August 2003.

Rand Corporation

In 2002 an analyst from the Rand Corpn urged the USA to target Saudi oilfields and overseas assets if the kingdom refused to stop funding Islamism and **terrorism** abroad. The briefing, given at the Pentagon in July, identified Saudi Arabia as an emerging enemy of the USA and suggested that 'the Saudis are active at every level of the terror chain from planner to financier, from cadre to foot soldier, from ideologist to cheerleader'.

Rantissi, Abdul Aziz

Leader of **Hamas** who was assassinated by Israeli forces in April 2004.

Ras al-Khaimah

One of the United Arab Emirates (UAE), with a population in 1995 of 144,430. Its area is 1,680 sq km. Ras al-Khaimah is a free-trade zone. Previously affiliated with Sharjah, Ras al-Khaimah became a separate sheikhdom under British protection in 1921. **Oil** production began in 1969. After some hesitation, the Emirate joined the UAE in 1972.

Rassemblement pour la concorde nationale

Algerian political grouping, founded in 2001 to support the policies of President **Bouteflika**. Its chairman is Sid Ahmed Abachi.

Rassemblement pour la culture et la démocratie

Algerian political grouping, established in 1989. A secular party which advocates the inclusion of **Berber** traditions into the Algerian identity. Supported by many Berbers. Its president is Said Saadi.

Rassemblement national démocratique

Algerian political grouping, founded in 1997. A party of the centre. Its secretary-general is Ahmed Ouyahia.

Rassemblement national des indépendants

Moroccan political party, founded in 1978 from the pro-government independents who formed the majority in the Chamber of Representatives. Its leader is Ahmad Ousman.

Rastakiz Party (Iran)

Rastakiz-e Iran

Official political party created in 1975 by the Shah of Iran, intended to mobilize the people behind the government. It replaced the previous system of an official pro-government party (**Mellioun**, 1957–63—subsequently **Iran-e Novin**), an official loyal opposition party (**Mardom**) and several smaller parties. This was the only legal party in Iran until shortly before the overthrow of the Shah in 1979.

Ratz

Civil Rights and Peace Movement. Formed 1973, Ratz is concerned with human and civil rights, opposes discrimination on the basis of religion, gender or **ethnicity**, and advocates a peace settlement with the Arab states and the **Palestinians**. It is led by **Shulamit Aloni**.

RCC – *see* Revolutionary Command Council (Iraq)

Reagan Plan

After the Israeli invasion of Lebanon in June 1982, and the consequent evacuation of the **Palestine Liberation Organization** from **Beirut**, the US government made strenuous efforts to continue the **Camp David** peace process and to fund a permanent solution to the **Arab–Israeli Conflict**. A plan for a peace settlement in the **Middle East**, involving **Israelis** and **Palestinians**, was developed by the Reagan Administration and put forward in a speech by President Reagan at the beginning of September 1982. The central question posed was how best to reconcile Israel's legitimate security concerns with the legitimate rights of the Palestinians. The answer, it was suggested, would come from negotiations based on the **Camp David Agreement**. It foresaw a five-year period of transition, after free elections for a self-governing Palestinian authority, during which time the Palestinian inhabitants of the **West Bank** and **Gaza** would have full autonomy over their affairs and demonstrate that such Palestinian autonomy posed no threat to Israel's security. The

USA would not support any extension of Israeli **settlements** in the **Occupied Territories**. The USA would not support an independent Palestinian State in the West Bank and Gaza. Nor would it support annexation of permanent control by Israel. It was the view of the USA that self-government by the Palestinians in association with Jordan offered the best chance for a durable, just and lasting peace. Negotiations should involve an exchange of territory for peace; an exchange enshrined in **UN Security Council Resolution 242**, which, in turn, is incorporated in all its parts into the Camp David Agreement. The USA felt that **Jerusalem** should remain undivided, but that its final status should be decided by negotiation.

Refai, Ahmed Taha

A leader of the Egyptian **Islamic Group**, Taha signed the 1998 '*fatwa*' and has been sentenced to death in Egypt in the 'returnees from Afghanistan' case. His name is linked with the assassination of President **Anwar Sadat**.

Refugees

The number of those who have been displaced and forced to flee from countries in the region is very considerable. The series of **wars** and conflicts in Afghanistan has resulted in large numbers of refugees from that country—an estimated 3.8m. in 2001—seeking safety in Pakistan, Iran and elsewhere in the region and beyond. Afghans constitute the largest single group of asylum seekers in the developed countries (nearly 53,000). The second largest group is of **Palestinians**, whose diaspora involves some 3.7m. in the region, living in Jordan (1.5m.), in the **Occupied Territories** (1.4m.), and in Lebanon, Syria and other countries. The UN enshrined the right of Palestinian refugees to return to their homes in **UN General Assembly Resolution 194** (III) of December 1948 (Article 11). Since then, it has been the policy of the **Palestine Liberation Organization** to maintain the status of Palestinians living outside Israel as that of refugees. The **West Bank** and **Gaza Strip** are home to nearly 350,000 refugees. Palestinians and Yemenis were the two groups that suffered most from forced repatriation after the invasion of Kuwait by Iraq in 1990 and in the aftermath of the **Gulf War (1991)**, although other groups were also affected. The repression of the Iraqi population under **Saddam Hussain** resulted in large numbers of refugees—an estimated 530,000 in 2001— and of asylum seekers (50,000). Iran is host to large numbers of refugees (around 1.8m.), mainly from Afghanistan during the war against the Soviet Union (1979–89) and subsequently (1990–2004), while the earlier overthrow of the Shah and subsequent Islamic Revolution in Iran in 1979–80 also resulted in large numbers of Iranians seeking refuge abroad, including nearly 16,000 asylum seekers in the West. Repression by four states—Iraq, Turkey, Syria and Iran—has resulted in a substantial Kurdish diaspora, with **Kurds** seeking safety outside their homelands in significant numbers, while Turkish asylum seekers number around 32,000. Saudi Arabia is host to some 245,000 refugees, while Algeria has nearly 170,000.

Regional Bureau for Arab States

UNDP regional bureau.

Regional Business Council

The Regional Business Council linking Jordan, Palestine and Israel collapsed as a result of the recent **al-Aqsa** *intifada*.

Religious minorities

Although the majority of the population of the **Middle East** is Muslim, there are many other active religious groups within the region. Muslims themselves are by no means homogeneous. The main distinction is between **Sunnis** and **Shi'ites** (Shi'a), but each of these has its own divisions, with smaller sects and 'ways' emphasizing their distinctiveness. There are also significant populations of Christians, and these too are divided into many 'churches' and sects. The third major religious group is that of the Jews, and here again there are sub-divisions of significance. In addition to these three 'great' religions there are others with relatively small numbers of adherents—**Druzes**, **Zoroastrians**, etc.—some of which are closer to one of the 'great' religions than to the others, some of which claim to be syncretic, idiosyncratic and unique.

Remittances

Many Middle Eastern economies rely heavily on remittances from migrant workers employed or in business overseas. Arguably, remittances are a larger and more reliable source of foreign exchange earnings for these countries than foreign aid. The biggest recipients are Egypt (whose remittances have averaged US $3,000m.–$4,000m. annually since the mid-1980s, Turkey (with a total rising towards $5,500m. by the end of the 1990s) and probably Algeria (where a significant proportion of the money remitted passes through informal channels). Egypt's **income** from remittances increased dramatically after the country's participation in the coalition against Iraq, largely because of new contracts with employers in Saudi Arabia—to reach $6,000m. However, they subsequently declined to somewhat below their pre-**Gulf War (1991)** level. Besides the above-mentioned countries, Morocco, Tunisia, Lebanon, Jordan, the **West Bank** and **Gaza Strip**, and Yemen all continue to rely heavily on remittance income, having weathered the temporary repatriation of foreigners from Kuwait and Saudi Arabia during the Gulf War (1991).

Rentier state

A term that is often applied to those states that are regarded as living off 'rent' derived from the sale of assets which they possess simply by virtue of their geological or geographical location—usually natural resources extracted from beneath the surface of the earth or the sea, as in the case of those states which are rich in **minerals**, **oil** or **natural gas**. Rentier states are also frequently such by virtue of their ability to take advantage of their strategic location (positional advantage) to offer port, base or other facilities. Usually the term implies a contrast with 'productive' states, which are obliged to develop more complex economic infrastructures for the production of goods and services, and which will usually have 'more developed' social structures as a consequence.

Republic of Yemen – *see* Yemen

Republican Guard (Iraq)

The élite force of the Iraqi **military** under **Saddam Hussain**. Members of the Republican Guard were better trained, disciplined, equipped and paid than ordinary Iraqi soldiers. They were reported to have been some of the most effective forces in the **Iran–Iraq War**. Republican Guard troops were volunteers rather than conscripts, and received bonuses and subsidized housing. Their main task was to protect the government and Saddam Hussain and his family. The Republican Guard was effectively destroyed/disbanded after the **Gulf War (2003)**. However, the US and UK governments claim that remnants of the Guard, together with what is left of the *Fedayeen* **Saddam**, are responsible for guerrilla attacks on US/UK occupation personnel.

Republican People's Party (RPP)

Strongly secular Turkish nationalist party founded by **Kemal Atatürk**. In effect, the only party in Turkey until 1945. Its political programme declared Turkey a secular state as early as 1931, although it was not confirmed as a secular state until 1937, when a specific clause was added to the 1924 Constitution. In the 1930s, after an ineffective opposition party, the Free Republican Party, took a religious form and was rapidly dissolved in the year it was created (1930), the RPP moved away from secular liberalism towards a more aggressive, militant nationalism. The **Koran** was translated into Turkish and the *ezan*—the call to prayer in Turkish—was introduced, becoming mandatory thus, in the vernacular, in 1940. The influence of European **national socialism** and of **'socialism'** in the Soviet Union influenced the attitude of the RPP towards religion in general and **Islam** in particular during the 1930s. After party politics were restored in 1945, and a setback was experienced by the ruling RPP in the 1946 general elections, the RPP government began again to adopt a more liberal approach towards Islam. Its concessions to Muslim sentiment did not bring the expected dividends and the opposition **Democrat Party** won an emphatic victory in the next election.

Research and development

Economic performance depends, in the case of industrial and service-based econo-mies, to a significant degree on research and development. Only Israel, of the countries in the region, ranks highly (sixth in the world, equal with the USA) in terms of expenditure on research and development. Turkey is next, in regional terms, ranking 38th in the world, equal with with Chile and Hong Kong. Israel ranks 20th in the world for the number of patents granted to residents in 2000—433, compared with world leader Japan's total of 123,978.

Revolutionary Command Council (RCC, Iraq)

The RCC was established as the ruling organ of the **Ba'ath Party** in Iraq after the coup in July 1968 which overthrew **Abdul Salam Arif** and brought to power a group of Ba'athists, including **Ahmad Hassan al-Bakr** and **Saddam Hussain**. Successive purges of the RCC brought al-Bakr and Saddam Hussain almost complete control of the Iraqi state. President of Iraq for a decade from July 1968 onwards, al-Bakr resigned in July 1979 for reasons of health and Saddam Hussain took full control of the Party, purged the **armed forces** and reshuffled the RCC, five of whose members were tried and executed for their alleged involvement in a Syrian Ba'athist plot. The RCC remained formally the top decision-making body of the state, with legislative and executive powers. Technically, it shared legislative powers with the National Assembly, which was a body of members elected by secret ballot under universal suffrage. In practice, however, the National Assembly was subordinate to the RCC and to the head of state. Individual members of the RCC were answerable only to the Council of Ministers, appointed by the head of state. The President of the Republic (after 1979, Saddam Hussain) was the head of state and chairman of the RCC. Saddam Hussain was to remain President until his overthrow during the **Gulf War (2003)** and subsequent capture by US forces.

Revolutionary Committees (*komitehs*)

Revolutionary Committees (*komitehs*) sprang up throughout Iran during the early period of the **Iranian Revolution** and became in most regions *de facto* local governments, acting also as tribunals and assuming police functions. As the police forces were reconstructed, they lost some of their formal powers but continued to monitor activities considered to be 'counter-revolutionary'. In April 1986 the autonomy of the Revolutionary Committees was brought to an end when the **Majlis** placed them under the jurisdiction of the Ministry of the Interior. Their major role was to enforce 'Islamic morality' and to supervise and assist in the distribution of welfare goods and services and rationed supplies.

Revolutionary Council (Iran)

A secret committee, formed in January 1979, with 14 members appointed by Ayatollah **Khomeini**, this was for a time the most important decision-making body in Iran. It was dissolved in September 1980, after the installation of the Government of President **Rajai**.

Revolutionary Cultural Society of the East

The first legal Kurdish organization, the Revolutionary Cultural Society of the East was a left-wing organization which was only legal because it did not refer to the **Kurds** or to **Kurdistan** but simply to 'the East'. It produced publications, which outlined the economic, social and political problems of the 'Easterners', the feudal oppression of villagers by landlords and tribal leaders, and the brutal behaviour of the Turkish army stationed in the rural areas of 'the East'. Eventually it split and lost momentum, but not before it was banned in March 1971, following a coup in Turkey.

Revolutionary Guards

The Revolutionary Guards (*pasdaran*) were a militia of zealous young Muslims, who strongly supported the new government of the Islamic Republic of Iran. The militia was intended to counterbalance the army, police and gendarmes, which were regarded as possibly loyal to the Shah; to combat the leftist groups (and in particular the *Mujahidin*); and to uphold the political and religious ideology of the Islamic Revolution. It was also used to combat Kurdish dissidents and to fight alongside the army against Iraq during the **Iran–Iraq War**; and to ensure internal security and to enforce morality. It was also sometimes used to enforce decisions made by the **Revolutionary Committees**.

Revolutionary Justice Organization

Munazzamat al-'Adala ath-Thawriya

Linked to the **Oppressed of the Earth Organization** (Munazzamat al-Mustadafin fi'l-Ard), each with around 100 members. Both served as covers for **Hezbollah**'s militant activities in the 1980s. The former claimed responsibility in December 1986 for the kidnapping of four university professors whom it described as spies; the latter claimed responsibility for kidnapping two US citizens and four French television crewmen. Both organizations have been inactive since 1988.

Revolutionary *Komitehs* (Iran) – *see* Revolutionary Committees

Revolutionary Organization of Socialist Muslims – *see* ANO

Revolutionary People's Liberation Front

Originally formed in 1978 as **Devrimci Sol** (or **Dev Sol**), the Turkish Revolutionary People's Liberation Front was a splinter faction of the Turkish People's Liberation Party or Front. Renamed in 1994, after factional infighting, it espouses a Marxist ideology and is strongly anti-imperialist, anti-US and anti-NATO. The group finances its activities mainly through armed robberies and extortion.

Reza Khan, Shah

Army officer who replaced the last of the old Qajar dynasty, Ahmad, to make himself head of state and Shah of Persia. He established the **Pahlavi** dynasty.

Riyadh

Capital of Saudi Arabia. Three suicide attacks on expatriate compounds in the city took place in May 2003, in which 25 people died, nine of them Americans. Among those who have been arrested since the attacks is Ali Abd ar-Rahman al-Faqasi al-Ghamdii, described by US officials as one of the most senior **al-Qa'ida** members in Saudi Arabia, who fought with **Osama bin Laden** at Tora Bora. During June and July Saudi police and security services made numerous arrests (at least 125 alleged militants were arrested and others were killed in gun battles) in connection with the May bomb attacks and tightened security. Officials reported that 'a number of cells' had been uncovered, and that they were looking for more. On 22 July 2003 the Saudi authorities reported that they had captured 16 members of a cell operating in Riyadh and in al-Qasim, north of Riyadh, together with a cache of weapons and explosives.

Road Map to peace

The full name of the so-called Road Map to peace in the **Middle East** is the 'Performance-Based Road Map to a Permanent Two-State Solution to the Israeli-Palestinian Conflict'. A meeting held on 18 September 2002 between the USA, Russia, the **European Union** (EU) and the UN endorsed the proposal of the EU, which provided for a three-phase plan to end the Middle East conflict by the end of 2005. The first phase of the plan (lasting until mid-2003) included a comprehensive security reform, the withdrawal of Israeli forces to the positions they held prior to 28 September 2000, and the **Palestinians**' organization of free, fair and credible elections. In the second phase (lasting until the end of 2003) a Palestinian state with provisional borders was to be established. A new constitution forms the basis for the desired 'permanent status settlement'. In the third phase (2004–05) negotiations would take place between representatives of Israel and the Palestinians, leading to a permanent status solution in 2005. The Road Map was formulated by the USA, together with the UN Secretariat, Russia and the EU (the so-called 'Quartet'). With the UN as a whole effectively sidelined in the so-called **peace process**, this Quartet, established in mid-2002, provided a substitute. The Road Map was ready to be publicly released by November 2002, but **Ariel Sharon** opposed this, stating that it would interfere with forthcoming Israeli elections. Only under pressure from UK Prime Minister Tony Blair, as a precondition for his alliance on the eve of the **Iraq War (2003)** did US President **George W. Bush** announce the Road Map in March 2003—after the Israeli parliamentary elections, the formation of a new Israeli government, the appointment of **Mahmoud Abbas** as **Palestinian National Authority** (PNA) Prime Minister and the approval of Abbas' Cabinet by the Palestinian legislature. In addition, international involvement in Afghanistan and in Iraq has prevented a concerted effort to push it forwards. The Palestinians and Israelblame each other for the failure of the Road Map, but many on both sides of the conflict regard the Road Map as inadequate in any case, and as no substitute for wider UN involvement. The Quartet eventually agreed on a document that was clearly more in line with Israeli and US priorities than were the many UN resolutions passed on the conflict. The wording of the Road Map document is sharp in tone with regard to Israel—employing words and phrases such as 'occupation', 'freezing of **settlement** activity', 'dismantling of settlements' and 'Palestinian state' (terms banned in the Oslo peace process)—but it capitulates to the Israeli priority of 'security before diplomacy' with its demands for unilateral Palestinian cessation of resistance to the occupation before further 'progress' can be made. The Road Map as adopted by the Israeli government contains Israeli objections and reservations, which severely mitigate, and sometimes reject, the document's key provisions. Among these reservations is a demand that the PNA give up the right of return for Palestinians made **refugees** in 1948. Similarly, Sharon refused to endorse the establishment of 'an independent, viable and sovereign Palestinian state' as required by the initiative. Rather, he expressed 'understanding' for Palestinian 'territorial contiguity in the **West Bank**'. The Road Map runs the same risk as its many predecessors of obstructing rather than facilitating progress towards genuine peace; indeed, there is a real danger that it will, like Oslo, leave an even more destructive conflict in its wake.

Rockingham cell

A unit set up by defence intelligence staff within the British Ministry of Defence in 1991. It was a clearing house for intelligence from Iraq, drawing on information from Iraqi defectors, and concerned among other things with the question of the continuing existence of **weapons of mass destruction** (WMD) in Iraq. Referred to by David Kelly in his evidence to the Prime Minister's intelligence and security committee in closed session on 16 July 2003, it was also referred to by Brig. Richard Holmes when he gave evidence to the defence select committee in 1998. He linked it to **UNSCOM** inspections, but it was clear that Rockingham staff included military officers and intelligence services representatives, together with civilian Ministry of Defence personnel. Within British intelligence, it had a central though covert role in seeking to identify an active Iraqi WMD programme.

Rogers Plan

The Rogers Peace Plan (named after US Secretary of State William Rogers) was devised in 1969 to halt the war of attrition and set up indirect talks to bring Egypt and Israel to a peace settlement based on **UN Security Council Resolution 242**. **Nasser** accepted the Rogers Peace Plan, but effectively sabotaged it by moving missiles to positions near the **Suez Canal**. The Plan collapsed in 1971 as both Israel and the Arab states refused to make the necessary concessions.

Rubayyi'ali, Salim

President of the **People's Democratic Republic of Yemen** from 1969 until 1978, when he was executed.

Rushdie, Salman

Indian author of *The Satanic Verses*, which many Muslims regarded as blasphemous. Iranian leader Ayatollah **Khomeini** issued a *fatwa* that called for Rushdie's death.

Russia

Russian involvement in the **Middle East** has been significantly less interventionist since the break up of the Soviet Union because of Russian concern not to undermine its generally more positive relations with the USA. Actively involved during the approach to the **Gulf War (1991)** in diplomatic endeavours to prevent a conflict, it developed its own relations with Iraq during the 1990s. When the US-led coalition began to consider further intervention in Iraq after 2001, Russia expressed concern, refused to join the **coalition** and allied itself with Germany and France in opposing intervention. In the aftermath of the **Gulf War (2003)**, however, it sent technicians to assist in the reconstruction effort, mainly in the **energy** sector. In April 2004, following the kidnapping of three Russians and five Ukrainians, Russia began the evacuation of some 800 technicians and other Russians from Iraq, although those kidnapped were later released. It was stressed that this did not mean that Russia was withdrawing from Iraq, where it has substantial energy interests. The largest Russian company in Iraq, Tekhnopromexport, whose 370 employees were rebuilding a power plant in Jusifa, had decided to evacuate even before the kidnappings, for security reasons. Another Russian company, Interenergoservis, however, whose employees were kidnapped, said that most of its staff would remain in Iraq—only 25 of the total workforce of 365 were to leave. Another company, Power Machines, had yet to decide whether it would evacuate its workers.

S

As-Sabah family

The as-Sabah dynasty has dominated the political life of Kuwait since 1756. The **monarchy** is a hereditary emirate and succession is decided by the selection of a recognized tribal leader from the descendants of the seventh ruler of Kuwait, Sheikh **Mubarak as-Sabah as-Sabah**. The dynasty rests upon a network of relationships that link the royal family, the pre-eminent tribal leaders, the *ulema*, the military establishment and the main commercial families. The powers of the reigning emir are dictated by the **Shari'a** and he is approved by a majority of the delegates in the national assembly. In 1962, one year after Kuwait gained its formal independence from Britain, a new constitution, drafted by a constituent assembly, was promulgated by the Emir. It declared that Kuwait was a sovereign, independent state within the larger **Arab World**. Freedom of expression was permitted within the confines of the legal system and it was planned to institute an independent judiciary, an elected national assembly and a responsible Cabinet of ministers. The first, 50-member assembly was elected in 1963. The next in line to the throne from the as-Sabah family was appointed as Prime Minister. Government posts were shared by members of the dynasty with commoners, usually from wealthy merchant families, but 11 of the 14 members of the Cabinet were of the royal family. The as-Sabah dynasty was supportive of the Palestinian cause and significant numbers of **Palestinians** were employed in Kuwait. By 1975 the Palestinian population had reached nearly 300,000 and had gained significant political influence in the national assembly, particularly among opponents of the regime. In 1976 the Emir closed the parliament in order to prevent further erosion of the authority of the as-Sabah dynasty and of the government. It was not reopened until 1980, after new elections had been held. By this time the dynasty had re-established its control over the tribal leaders, restricted the activities of the political opposition and restored the tradition of rule by 'tribal consensus', which effectively offset the influence of non-Kuwaitis, who had become a majority in the country. The as-Sabah family retained its supremacy and its authority in part through its control of **oil** revenues, which have been used not only to provide far-reaching welfare services for Kuwaiti nationals but also as 'retainers' for its loyal supporters. Kuwait was the only state in the **Arabian Peninsula** with an established, modern legal system. Moves towards a more open system of government were brought to an abrupt halt by the invasion by Iraq in 1990 and the subsequent **Gulf War (1991)**. The as-Sabah family remain the dominant political authority.

As-Sabah, Jabir III al-Ahmad I al-Jabir II as-Sabah

Emir of Kuwait since 31 December1977.

As-Sabah, Saad al-Abdullah

Crown prince of Kuwait.

As-Sabah, Sheikh Abdullah III

Emir of Kuwait from 1950 until 1965.

As-Sabah, Sheikh Mubarak

The seventh ruler of Kuwait from whom all recent and contemporary rulers trace their descent.

As-Sabah, Sheikh Sabah ibn Salim

Emir of Kuwait from 1965 until 1977.

Sabra and Chatila

Palestinian refugee camps in Lebanon. Site of the massacre of Palestinian **refugees** by the Christian militia, the **Phalange Libanais**, with the full complicity of Israeli defence minister, **Ariel Sharon**, in 1982.

El-Sadaawi, Nawal

Influential Egyptian Islamic feminist, writer and political activist. Nawal el-Sadaawi trained as a doctor.

Es-Sadat, Anwar

President of Egypt in 1970–81. Born in 1918, Sadat entered the Abbasia Military Academy in 1936, where he became friendly with **Gamal Abdel Nasser** and other fellow cadets committed to Egyptian nationalism. A German agent during the Second World War, he was imprisoned by the British authorities in 1942, but escaped after two years in jail. He was jailed again in 1946–49 for his involvement in terrorist acts against pro-British Egyptian officials. Sadat took part in the *coup d'état* by the **Free Officers** in 1952 that deposed King **Farouk**. Between 1952 and 1968 he held a variety of government positions, including director of army public relations; secretary-general of the **National Union Movement**, Egypt's only political party; and president of the national assembly. In 1969 he was appointed as Vice-President by Nasser, on whose death in 1970 he succeeded to the presidency. Less charismatic than his predecessor, Sadat was nevertheless able to establish himself as Egypt's 'strongman' and a leader of the **Arab World**. He assumed the premiership in 1973 and in October of that same year led Egypt into war with Israel. He became an Arab hero when Egyptian troops recaptured a small part of the Sinai Peninsula, taken by Israel in 1967. A pragmatist, Sadat indicated his willingness to consider a negotiated settlement with Israel and shared the 1978 Nobel Peace Prize with **Menachem Begin** as a result of the **Camp David Accords**. Together with the launching of the *infitah* laws, he transferred Egypt's allegiance from the Soviet Union to the West during the Cold War. He was assassinated by Muslim extremists during a military parade in 1981.

SADR – *see* **Sahrawi Arab Democratic Republic**

As-Sadr, Hussein

Iraqi **Shi'a** leader, son of Muhammad Baqir.

As-Sadr, Ayatollah Mohammed Sadiq

Iraqi **Shi'a** leader in the 1990s, who established extensive mosque-based welfare systems for the poor in the largely Shi'a areas of **Baghdad**. He admired the clerics of the Islamic Republic of Iran for leading their country's government. He was killed in 1999. His son, **Moqtada as-Sadr**, is the charismatic young Shi'a leader who raised the so-called **Mahdi Army** in 2004 to defend the interests of the Shi'ites in central and southern Iraq.

As-Sadr, Moqtada

Son of **Ayatollah Mohammed Sadiq as-Sadr**. A radical **Shi'a** leader of a substantial militia (he referred to it as 'the army of al-Mahdi'—the so-called 'hidden imam' who disappeared in AD 874 and is expected to return one day to save the world) of some 10,000 fighters, opposed to the US-led occupation of Iraq and based in the city of **Najaf**. During April 2004, his forces took control of the city.

As-Sadr, Musa

Lebanese politician who, on the eve of the civil war, created the Movement of the Disinherited which was succeeded by the Lebanese **Amal** (Hope) Organization. After the Phalangist Party, it was the first organization able to circumvent the authority of the great families, without, however, rejecting confessionalism. Musa came to Lebanon from Iran in 1960 and settled in Tyre, where he succeeded the community's spiritual leader. After 1967 he broadened his activities to include politics and managed to persuade the state to form a **Shi'ite** Supreme Council, of which he became president, with the title of imam. He presented a programme aimed at mobilizing Shi'ites of all social classes, gaining rights of access for them to the most important state positions, defence of religion and **aid** for the economic development of the south of the country. He opposed both the traditional leaders and the left-wing parties. He disappeared in Libya in 1978, creating a lasting antagonism between the Lebanese Shi'ites and the Libyan regime.

Safari Club

The name given, by Egyptian writer Muhammad Haykal (after finding in the imperial archives in **Tehran** the original version of an agreement signed in September 1976), to a secret organization of heads of counter-espionage agencies of several countries—including the USA, France, Morocco, Egypt, Saudi Arabia and Iran—established to carry out anti-communist operations in Africa and the Third World more generally on behalf of the West. Its headquarters were in **Cairo** in a building donated by President **Anwar Sadat**. One of its first operations was to support the Somali dictator, Siad Barre in his war against Ethiopia, which was receiving Soviet **aid**. This support was stopped not long afterwards.

Saharan Republic

In the 1970s Libyan leader Col **Qaddafi** planned to establish a Saharan Republic which would have included Libya, Tunisia, Algeria, the **Western Sahara**, Mauritania, Niger and Chad, under Libyan leadership. In 1973 he took advantage of the civil war in Chad to further his expansionist designs. Offering its support to military leader Goukouni Oueddai against Hussein Habre, Libya occupied the Aouzou Strip in the north of Chad, a region rich in manganese and uranium. There was an immediate reaction from France, which dispatched 3,500 troops to support Habre, who succeeded in defeating Oueddai. The war continued for many years and cost Libya dearly. Libya eventually withdrew from Aouzou and the idea of a Saharan Republic was abandoned.

Sahrawi Arab Democratic Republic (SADR)

Declared by the **POLISARIO Front** in 1976, the SADR is recognized by 76 states. It fought for effective independence from 1976 onwards against Morocco and Mauritania, and then, from 1979 onwards, after signing a peace treaty with Mauritania, against Morocco alone. The SADR was admitted, despite strong Moroccan opposition, as the 51st member of the Organisation of African Unity in February 1982. It agreed a cease-fire in 1991, after UN intervention to initiate a 'peace process'. The SADR has consistently tried to move towards the referendum planned by the UN and **MINURSO**, but this has been stalled by Moroccan objections and filibustering. The SADR is a state in exile, with much of its territory under Moroccan occupation since 1976. Its main organs are a 33-member National Secretariat, a 101-member Sahrawi National Assembly and a 13-member government. The head of state and President of the SADR is **Muhammad Abdel Aziz.**

Sahrawis

The people of the **Western Sahara** (former **Spanish Sahara**). A significant majority of the population has been living in refugee camps in south-west Algeria, near Tindouf, since the Moroccan invasion of the former Spanish Sahara in late 1975; a smaller number have been living under Moroccan occupation in the western coastal regions of the territory. Sahrawi opposition to Spanish colonial rule led to the establishment in 1973 of the **POLISARIO Front** and, in 1976, to the declaration of an independent state—the **Sahrawi Arab Democratic Republic**.

As-Said dynasty

The as-Said family have ruled the Sultanate of Oman for more than a century.

As-Said, Faisal ibn Turki

Ruler of the Sultanate of Oman from 1888 until 1913. He was succeeded by his son, **Tamir as-Said**.

As-Said, Nuri (Nouri)

Strongly pro-British Prime Minister of Iraq under King **Faisal II** during the post-war period. When **Nasser** came to power, King Faisal and Nuri Said took on the leadership of the pro-Western Arab coalition. In 1955 Iraq joined the **Baghdad Pact** and in 1958 formed a coalition with Jordan to counter that of the **United Arab Republic**. In July 1958 a group of young officers, led by Gen. **Kassem**, overthrew the **monarchy** and the government of Nuri Said and established a new republic. Said himself was killed during the fighting.

As-Said, Qabus (Qaboos) ibn Said

Sultan of Oman since 1970, when he came to power by ousting his father, **Said ibn Tamir**. He took advantage of Oman's **oil** resources to consolidate his regime and to undertake the economic and infrastructural development of Oman. In 1981 an Advisory Council was created, but otherwise there has been little sign of political development.

As-Said, Said ibn Tamir

Ruler of the Sultanate of Oman from 1932 until 1970. He was succeeded by his son, the present sultan, **Qabus (Qaboos) ibn Said as-Said**.

As-Said, Tamir ibn Faisal

Ruler of the Sultanate of Oman from 1913 until 1932. He was succeeded by his son, **Said ibn Tamir as-Said**.

Said, Edward

Born in West **Jerusalem** and christened Edward after the British Prince of Wales in 1935, Said was brought up in **Cairo** and educated in the USA. He inherited an American passport from his father's service with the US army in the First World War. A Palestinian scholar of English literature, political writer and activist, he was also Professor of English and Comparative Literature at Columbia University. His book *Orientalism*—a critique of Western perspectives on the **Middle East** and 'the Orient' more generally—has continued to provoke debate since its publication in 1978. 'It is the role of the Arab intellectual', he wrote, 'to articulate and defend the principles of liberation and **democracy** at all costs'. After *Orientalism* Said published *The Question of Palestine* (1979), *Covering Islam* (1981) and *After the Last Sky* (1986)—the last of these a meditation on **Palestinian identity**. He also edited writings on the Israeli–Palestinian struggle collected under the title *Blaming the Victims*. In the 1980s Said was a member of the **Palestine National Council** and was influential in urging **Yasser Arafat** towards the 'two-state solution' in which Palestine and Israel could co-exist. In the early 1990s he was critical of the Oslo process and agreements made in 1993, which, he argued, meant certain disaster for the **Palestinians**. His book *Culture and Imperialism* (1993) re-engaged with the themes of *Orientalism*; this was followed by a collection of political essays, *Peace and its Discontents* (1995), a memoir, *Out of Place* (1999), and a collection of writings on the aftermath of the **Oslo Agreement**, *The End of the Peace Process* (2000).

Salafeen

The Islamic Popular Movement. A quasi-political grouping represented in the Kuwaiti **Majlis**, or National Assembly.

Salafism, salafists

Salafism is an Islamic tendency, the precise significance of which varies considerably from place to place and period to period, but which implies a return to basic Islamic tenets. Today almost always associated with radical Islamist theory and practice, it was a reformist movement in the late 19th and early 20th century. There are salafists in virtually every Middle Eastern country.

Salafism (Morocco)

The Moroccan nationalist movement had its origins in a revival of Islamic orthodoxy best understood as yet another example of a classical historical pattern—a puritanical movement appealing to a threatened people during a period of breakdown. Known as Salafism, this Islamic reformism called for a return to the tradition of the founders of **Islam**, the pious ancestors (*as-salaf as-salih*). The main figures associated with this movement were Jamal ad-Din al-Afghani, Mohamed 'Abduh and, later, Rashid Rida, and it was through contact with these men and their writings that their ideas began to circulate in North Africa. The first Moroccan Salafists ('Abdulah ben Driss Senoussi and Boucha'ib ad-Doukkali) were not preoccupied with nationalism, although their cause became inextricably caught up after the First World War with nationalist objectives. The link between the original Salafist movement and the first nationalist groups was Moulay al'Arabi al'Alawi, student of ad-Doukkali and tutor of **Allal al-Fassi**. The funeral of ad-Doukkali in 1928 was the occasion for some of the first guarded criticism of the Protectorate.

Salafist Group for Call and Combat (Algeria) – *see* GSPC— Groupe salafiste pour la prédication et le combat

Salafist Jihad

On 16 May 2003 13 suicide bombers killed themselves and 28 other people in a co-ordinated attack on five tourist and Jewish targets in **Casablanca**, Morocco. The worst of these struck the Casa de España, a popular private club; the other targets were the Israeli Alliance Club, a major business hotel, the Hotel Safir, the Belgian consulate and a Jewish cemetery. A 14th suicide bomber, who escaped from the attack on the hotel, was subsequently detained and helped identify eight colleagues, some of them Moroccans living abroad. According to Morocco's justice minister, he gave information on his criminal accomplices and helped identify those involved. There were some indications that linked them with a group calling itself Assirat al-Moustaquim (Righteous Path). This group, several of whose members have recently been jailed, is believed to be a splinter group of Salafist Jihad. One of the Salafist Jihad's main spiritual leaders, Ould Mohamed Abdelwahab Raqiqi, alias 'Abu Hafs', was jailed earlier in the year for inciting violence against westerners.

Salafiyya movement – *see* Salafism

As-Salahi, Naguib

Former divisional commander of **Saddam Hussain**'s **Republican Guard** who defected from Iraq in 1995. He heads the Iraqi **Free Officers' Movement** and has close links with the Iraqi army. He also has close relations with the US **Central Intelligence Agency** and the US Department of State.

As-Sallal, Brig.-Gen. Abdullah

The leader of a **military** coup in **North Yemen** in 1962 in which he came to power, replacing Muhammad al-Badr and Imam Ahmad Ben **Yahya**. He remained head of state in North Yemen until 1967.

Salameh, Ali Hassan

Operational chief of **Black September** and later head of **Force 17**.

Salat

Prayer, one of the **Five Pillars of Islam**. Muslims are enjoined to pray five times a day: in the morning (*al-fajr*); at midday (*ad dh hur*); midway between midday and sunset (*al-'asr*); at sunset (*al-maghrib*); and one hour after sunset (*al-'isha*).

Ould Mohammed Salek, Lt-Col Mustapha

Head of state of Mauritania from July 1978, after the coup which overthrew **Mokhtar Ould Daddah**. Forced to resign in June 1979, he was succeeded by Lt-Col **Mohammed Mahmoud Ould Louly**.

Salih (Saleh), Ali Abdullah

President of Yemen from 1978 until 1990. President of the united Republic of **Yemen** from 1990 onwards.

SAMA – *see* Saudi Arabian Monetary Agency

Samaria

One of the two territories into which Israel and **Israelis** conventionally divide the occupied territory of the **West Bank**. The other is **Judea.**

Samed

Samed, otherwise known as the Palestine Martyrs Work Society, was originally established by the **Palestine Liberation Organization** (PLO) in 1970 to provide vocational training to Palestinian orphans. After the PLO was ousted from Jordan and relocated in Lebanon, however, Samed was reorganized. It actively participated in the creation of a Palestinian state inside Lebanon. In particular, it assisted in the resettlement of Palestinian **refugees** and channelled the workforce of the Palestinian refugee camps towards the creation of a solid social and industrial infrastructure—

its ultimate goal was to make the **Palestinians** self-sufficient and the PLO independent of donations from the Arab regimes. In 1973 Samed became independent of the PLO's Social Affairs Department and was reorganized into four main divisions: industrial, agricultural, commercial and information. It had a dual function: to train and fund employment for individuals; and to provide products at accessible prices to the Palestinian population. It transformed itself from a social welfare institution into the core of a new Palestinian economy. In 1981 it exported 100,000 shirts and 50,000 pairs of trousers to the Soviet Union. Only 35% of all sales at that time came from the PLO. Of the remainder, Lebanon accounted for 8%, other Arab countries for 30%, and other world markets for 27%. By 1982 Samed controlled 46 factories in Lebanon and five in Syria, and owned several businesses abroad, exporting regularly to East European and Arab countries; its turnover was estimated at US $45m. It was by now largely self-financed, but could apply for interest-free loans from the PLO when they were needed. It also received funds from abroad. The Israeli invasion of Lebanon in 1982 was a blow to Samed, generating losses of $17m., but it quickly regenerated. In 1986 its gross revenues were $39m., only $6m. less than in 1982, and by 1989 they had rebounded to $70m. Samed's ability to survive was the result of its sectoral and geographical diversification. It held investments and had branches in more than 30 countries in the **Middle East**, Africa, Eastern Europe and Latin America; and employed 12,000 people. Its investments in those regions were estimated at $50m.

San'a

Capital of united Republic of **Yemen**. Previously capital of the **People's Democratic Republic of Yemen**.

Saraya al-Mujahidin

Mujahidin Brigades

A previously unknown Iraqi group which 'emerged' in April 2004 when it captured three Japanese hostages and threatened to execute them unless Japan withdrew its troops from Iraq.

Sarkis, Elias

President of Lebanon from 1976 until 1982.

As-Saud, Abdul Aziz ibn Abdul Rahman – *see* Ibn Saud

As-Saud, Fahd ibn Abdul Aziz

Crown Prince Fahd succeeded his brother Khalid in 1982, after Khalid's death, as king of Saudi Arabia. His mother was Hassa bint Ahmad as-Sudairi; the Sudairi line is perhaps the most notable of the branches of the family. Together with his six brothers, Fahd represented the most numerous branch.

As-Saud, Faisal ibn Abdul Aziz

In the mid-1960s Faisal replaced his brother, **Saud ibn Saud**, as king of Saudi Arabia. It was during his reign (1964–75) that Saudi Arabia became an **oil**-rich state and the country began to play an increasingly important role in the **Arab World** and in Middle Eastern affairs. Faisal was assassinated by an estranged member of his extended family. He was succeeded by his brother, Khalid.

As-Saud, Khalid ibn Abdul Aziz

Khalid succeeded his assassinated brother Faisal in 1975, but was quickly identified as a figurehead, real authority resting with other members of the family, notably Crown Prince Fahd. Khalid intervened little in the affairs of state during his reign (1975–82) and his death in June 1982 caused little public concern. Fahd assumed the throne within hours of Khalid's death.

As-Saud, Saud ibn Abdul Aziz

Son of Abdul Aziz, and ruler of Saudi Arabia from 1953 until 1964.

Saudi Arabia, Kingdom of

Al-Mamlakah al-Arabiyah as-Saudiyah

Saudi Arabia dominates the **Arabian Peninsula**, bordering the **Persian (Arabian) Gulf** and the Red Sea, north of Yemen. It also has borders with the United Arab Emirates (UAE), Qatar, Oman, Iraq and Jordan. Saudi Arabia has extensive coastlines on the Persian (Arabian) Gulf to the east and on the Red Sea, to the west, that provide ports for shipping (especially crude **oil**) through the Gulf and the **Suez Canal**. It is a large country, with an area of some 1,960,582 sq km. The capital is **Riyadh**—**Jiddah** is the administrative capital. The administrative regions consist of 13 provinces (*mintaqah*, plural *mintaqat*): Al-Bahah, Al-Hudud ash-Shamaliyah, Al-Jawf, Al-Madinah, Al-Qasim, Ar-Riyad, Ash-Sharqiyah (Eastern Province), 'Asir, Ha'il, Jizan, Makkah, Najran and Tabuk. The population numbers 23,513,330, of which 90% are Arab and 10% 'other'. At July 2002 the population included 5,360,526 non-nationals. The majority of Saudi Arabian nationals are Muslims, 85% **Sunni** and 15% **Shi'a**. The official language is **Arabic**.

Saudi Arabia is governed according to **Shari'a**. The Basic Law that articulates the government's rights and responsibilities was introduced in 1993. The form of government is that of a hereditary **monarchy**. The head of state and of government since 13 June 1982 has been King **Fahd ibn Abdul Aziz as-Saud**, who is also Prime Minister. In fact, the Crown Prince and First Deputy Prime Minister,

Abdallah ibn Abdul Aziz as-Saud, half-brother of the monarch, heir to the throne since 13 June 1982 and regent in 1 January–22 February 1996, takes on much of the business of the monarchy. The Council of Ministers is appointed by the monarch and includes mainly royal family members. A **Majlis ash-Shura** (Consultative Council), consisting of 90 members and a chairman, all of whom are appointed by the monarch for four-year terms, provides advice. It was introduced for the first time in 1993, after the trauma of the **Gulf War (1991)** and local petitions against arbitrary government. The legal system is based on the Shari'a—several secular codes have been introduced—and depends on the Supreme Council of Justice. Commercial disputes are handled by special committees. Saudi Arabia has not accepted compulsory International Court of Justice jurisdiction. Political parties and groups are not allowed in Saudi Arabia. Opposition groups do exist, however, some with leaders abroad. Islamists operate in clandestine cells. **Al-Qa'ida** has operated in the country.

Media

The government imposes total press censorship and insists on strict morality. In 1994 the regime banned satellite television receivers for private citizens, though this is not strictly enforced. There is censorship/blocking of internet sites concerned with the state and religion. There are 13 daily newspapers in Arabic and English. The most widely read are *Ar-Riyadh*, *Sharq al-Awsat*, *Al-Jazirah* and *Riyadh Daily*. There are two state-owned television stations/services. There are two radio stations/services—one state-owned, the other owned by a private oil company. In 2001 there were 42 internet service providers and 570,000 internet users.

History

The Saud dynasty developed during the 18th century in the **Najd** highland of the Arabian interior. Mohamed ibn Saud led his tribal army in a successful campaign that conquered a large part of the Arabian Peninsula. After the death of Mohamed in 1765, his son, Abdul Aziz, undertook even more extensive conquests and in 1787 established the hereditary succession of the **House of Saud**. The Saudis expanded their territorial control throughout the Pensinsula and north into Iraq during the early part of the 19th century. They were forced, however, by Ottoman forces led by Mohammed Ali, the Sultan's commanding general in Egypt, to give up many of their gains and to retreat into the Arabian interior.

In 1902 **Abd al-Aziz Ibn Saud** captured Riyadh and set out on a 30-year campaign to unify the Arabian Peninsula. In the 1930s the discovery of oil transformed the country. Following Iraq's invasion of Kuwait in 1990 Saudi Arabia gave refuge to the Kuwaiti royal family and 400,000 **refugees**, while allowing the deployment of Western and Arab troops on its soil for the liberation of Kuwait in the following year. A burgeoning population, aquifer depletion, and an economy largely dependent on petroleum output and prices are all major governmental concerns.

The royal family rules by carefully manipulating appointments in all sectors of government. Frequent changes of personnel in the **armed forces** ensure that officers do not build personal followings. All influential Cabinet positions, except the portfolios of oil and religious affairs, are held by members of the royal family. Thus, the rule is absolute. There is no legitimate arena for domestic politics. The royal family's legitimacy rests on its adherence to Wahhabi **Islam**, and on the support of the *ulema*.

After the Gulf War (1991) civil rights campaigners began to challenge the legitimacy of the royal family and to question its rule, in particular its adherence to Islam. The movement objected to the presence of US troops in the country. The royal family quickly suppressed this group, but it continues to operate in exile.

Saudi Arabia has a 5,000-strong **Mutawa**.

International relations/Transnational issues

The demarcation of the boundary with Yemen involves nomadic tribal affiliations. Because the details of treaties concluded in 1974 and 1977 have not been made public, the exact location of the Saudi Arabia-UAE boundary is unknown and its status is considered to be *de facto*.

Saudi Arabia, economy

This is an **oil**-based economy in which the government exercises strong control over the major activities. Saudi Arabia has the largest reserves of petroleum in the world (26% of the proven world total), ranks as the world's largest exporter of petroleum, and plays a leading role in the **Organization of Petroleum Exporting Countries**. It has an estimated gross domestic product (GDP) of some US \$186,000m., making it the 23rd largest economy in the world. The petroleum sector accounts for roughly 75% of budget revenues, 45% of GDP, and 90% of export earnings. About 25% of GDP comes from the private sector. Approximately 4m. foreign workers play an important role in the Saudi economy, for example, in the oil and service sectors. Saudi Arabia expected to record a budget deficit in 2002, in part because of increased spending for **education** and other social programmes. In 1999 the government announced plans to begin privatizing the national electricity companies, following the (ongoing) privatization of the national telecommunications company. The government is expected to continue to call for private-sector growth to lessen the kingdom's dependence on oil and increase employment opportunities for the growing Saudi population. Shortages of **water** and rapid population growth will constrain government efforts to increase self-sufficiency in agricultural products.

Strengths

Vast oil and **gas** reserves and world-leading associated industries. Accumulated surpluses and steady current **income**. Large income from the *c*. 2m. pilgrims who visit **Mecca** each year.

Weaknesses

Lack of local skilled labour. Food production is heavily subsidized. Most consumer items and industrial raw materials are imported. The rate of youth unemployment is more than 20%. There is a large national **debt**. Most wealth is concentrated in the royal family. There is unproductive spending and patronage by the royal family.

Saudi Arabian Monetary Agency

Agency responsible for Saudi Arabia's financial and monetary policy.

Saudi ARAMCO

The 'heir' of **ARAMCO**, now under Saudi control, but in which foreign technical advisers still play a leading role.

Saum

Saum (the Fast) is the fourth of the **Five Pillars of Islam** and involves fasting during **Ramadan**.

SAVAK—Sazman-e Ettelaatva Amniyat-e Keshvar

The secret police of the Shah of Iran.

Sayerat Matkal

Israeli General Staff Reconnaissance Unit. Israel's equivalent to the British Special Air Service.

Sayyaf, Abdul Rasul

The head of Islamic Unity, the only opposition party in Afghanistan, whose membership is largely **Pashtun**. Sixty per cent of Afghanistan's population of 21m.—and most of the approximately 30,000 **Taliban** fighters—are Pashtuns. Sayyaf and the Taliban have shared similar views. Like **Osama bin Laden**, the Taliban's guest and prime suspect in the 11 September 2001 terror attacks on US targets, Sayyaf has loudly protested against the presence of US troops in Saudi Arabia, the location of **Islam**'s holiest shrines. He has even offered to wage war to remove the US forces. During the nine-year Soviet occupation of Afghanistan, Sayyaf's party received massive financial support from Saudi Arabia, but funding was severed owing to his support for **Saddam Hussain** in the **Gulf War (1991)**. It was Sayyaf's party that attracted most of the so-called **Afghan Arabs**—Middle Eastern Muslims who fought the Soviet forces in Afghanistan. After the Taliban took over, Sayyaf remained loyal to **Rabbani**. Most of the Afghan Arabs became the backbone of bin Laden's **al-Qa'ida** group, supporting the Taliban, but even though they are now at war with his **Northern Alliance**, Sayyaf has never denounced them. During the Soviet occupation, bin Laden and many other Afghan Arabs joined an Islamic party led by Younus Khalis, who is now pro-Taliban.

Sazman-e Peykar dar Rahe Azadieh Tabaq-e Kargar

Organization Struggling for the Freedom of the Working Class

An Iranian Marxist-Leninist political grouping.

Schwarzkopf, Gen. Norman

US Commander of Allied Forces in the **Gulf War (1991)**.

SCIRI – *see* Supreme Council for the Islamic Revolution in Iraq

Security companies

Security companies—or private military companies (PMCs)—have become a major business opportunity for British mercenaries in post-war Iraq. They provide more manpower and personnel in total than most of the members of the **coalition** in Iraq. The British companies are particularly popular—although there are PMCs from other countries and many are of mixed nationality—because of the reputation of the Special Air Service regiment whose former employees are in charge of many of them. Among the better known operating in Iraq are: **Janusian**, Global Risk Strategies, Control Risks, Erinys and ArmorGroup. **Paul Bremer**, the US adminstorator in Iraq, is protected by Blackwater, a US company.

Sephardim

A term that is generally used to refer to Jews from the **Middle East** and North Africa.

Servants of Construction Party

Political grouping in Iran.

Settlement(s)

Generally used to refer to Jewish settlements in the **Occupied Territories** of the **West Bank** and **Gaza Strip**. Since 1967 Israel has constructed numerous Jewish urban settlements in the West Bank and Gaza Strip. The settlements have been declared illegal under international law by many parties, including the US and European governments and the UN. Since the **Oslo Agreement** of 1993, the number of settlers in the West Bank and Gaza (excluding **East Jerusalem**) has almost doubled, having risen from 115,000 to 200,000. As of November 2000 slightly fewer than 400,000 **Israelis** lived in settlements on the West Bank, Gaza, East Jerusalem and the **Golan Heights** (all occupied territories), according to Israeli government statistics. Altogether, about 42% of the area of the West Bank (a total of some 2,400 sq km) is effectively controlled by Israeli settlers. Of that, about 4% is built-up, the remainder having been assigned by Israel to Settlement Councils. The 'rural' settlements are connected by roads that are accessible to Israelis only. Palestinian property, including houses and agricultural land, such as olive groves, has been altered, claimed, or destroyed when these roads have been built. Finally, in many cases, travel by these roads is controlled through special checkpoints, which are controlled by the **Israeli Defence Force**. This practice separates communities and is a source of continuing humiliation and anger among ordinary **Palestinians**. Palestinians sometimes prefer to use the word 'colonies' for these Israeli enclaves. Israel regards that term is inappropriate; unlike the traditional concept of overseas colonies, the settlements are in most cases only several miles away from Israeli cities.

There have been dozens of **UN Security Council** resolutions and other attempts to sanction Israel with respect to the growth of settlements in the Occupied Territories. Most of these were nearly unanimous, with the exception of those vetoed by the USA or subject to US abstention. Many Israelis hold that most of these sanctions are motivated by anti-**Zionism** and anti-Semitism, as similar actions by many other UN members states have never been the object of a single UN Security Council sanction. Given this perceived bias, many Israelis believe that the UN resolutions have no legal or moral authority. Often, the Fourth Geneva Convention, which forbids an occupying country from moving its citizens into the occupied territory, has been claimed by the Palestinians as a legal defence. Israel, in return, argues that the West Bank and Gaza do not constitute occupied territories in any sense of the word, and denies the applicability of the Geneva Convention. The USA, the United Kingdom, the **European Union** and the United Nations, however, have stated that they consider the Fourth Geneva Convention to be fully applicable. The settlements have been declared to be illegal by **UN Security Council Resolution 446**, and Israel is required by that resolution to cease further settlement activity. Resolution 465 (1980) declared that Israel's policy and practice of settling parts of its population and new immigrants in territories occupied since 1967, including **Jerusalem**, constitutes a flagrant violation of the Fourth Geneva Convention. However, since Resolutions 446 and 465 were not made under Chapter VI or VII of the UN Charter, Israel argues that they are purely advisory. The issue of the legal status of resolutions of the UN Security Council not made under Chapters VI or VII of the Charter is controversial in international law—some accept Israel's argument, others reject it and consider the resolution to be legally binding on Israel. Israel argues that armistice agreements in effect at the time of the 1967 **Six-Day War** were violated by the Arab states when they declared war, rendering the existing cease-fire lines meaningless. Thus there is no effective border between

Israel and the former Jordanian, Egyptian, and Syrian territories within the former Palestine Mandate. The settlements are therefore not within an occupied territory. The current international consensus is that there should be new borders, defined by multilateral negotiations (*see* **UN Security Council Resolution 242**); this supports Israel's viewpoint. The territories in question, it is argued, were never legally a part of Jordan and Egypt, these countries' control over them after the **Arab–Israeli War (1948)** having been declared illegal internationally. Moreover, these territories are no longer even claimed by these countries—both have withdrawn their claims as parts of their peace agreements with Israel. Therefore, Israel holds that it is impossible to define these lands as 'occupied', and denies the *de jure* applicability of the Geneva Conventions to them. Palestinians reason that Jordan withdrew its claims so that a Palestinian Arab state could be established there—not Israeli settlements. To that, Israel replies that the stance of both Jordan and Egypt on this issue was that it was to be resolved bilaterally by Israel and the Palestinians. Israel further observes that in the Oslo Agreement, the Palestinians accepted at least the temporary presence of Israeli settlements. Palestinians argue that Israel has violated the Oslo Agreement by continuing to expand the settlements after signing it. Israel argues that it has not constructed new settlements, but rather made improvements to or expanded settlements that already existed, in order to accommodate 'natural growth'. Palestinians claim that such 'natural growth' settlements often are established well away from any previously existing settlements, and have far exceeded the actual natural growth of those settlements.

Palestinians and other Arab states also accuse Israel of attacking refugee camps and villages in an attempt to drive Palestinians away and claim the land as its own. Israel previously also had settlements in the Sinai, but these were withdrawn as a result of the peace agreement with Egypt.

Most proposals for achieving a final settlement of the **Middle East** conflict involve Israel dismantling a large number of settlements in the West Bank and Gaza Strip. A poll conducted by **Peace Now** in July 2002 indicated that as many as two-thirds of the settler population would agree to evacuate, provided that evacuation takes place as the result of a democratically-made and accepted decision of the Israeli government. The other one-third, however, would refuse to leave peacefully. Most Israeli and US proposals for final settlement have also involved Israel being allowed to retain settlements near Israel proper and in East Jerusalem (the majority of the settler population is near the 'Green Line'), with Israel annexing the land on which the settlements are located. This would result in a transfer of roughly 5% of the West Bank to Israel, with the Palestinians being compensated by the transfer of a similar share of Israeli territory (i.e. territory behind the 'Green Line') to the Palestinian state. Palestinians complain that the land offered in exchange is situated in the Judean desert, while the areas that Israel seeks to retain are considered to be among the West Bank's most fertile areas; to this Israel replies that if the current 'Green Line' is fully retained, Israel would have at some points no more than 17 km from the border to the sea, which is widely considered an immense security risk.

The settlements have on several occasions been a source of tension between Israel and the USA. In 1991 there was a clash between the **Bush** Administration and Israel as a result of which the USA delayed payment of a subsidized loan in an attempt to persuade Israel not to proceed with the establishment of settlements in, for example, the Jerusalem-**Bethlehem** corridor. Former US President **Carter** has stated that he considered the settlements to consitute a major obstacle to peace. The current US Bush Administration, while it generally supports Israel, has said that settlements are 'unhelpful' to the **peace process**. Generally, these US efforts have at most temporarily delayed the further expansion of Israeli settlements. US public opinion is divided, with many strongly supporting the Israeli position, while public opinion outside the USA and Israel often strongly opposes the settlements. In April 2004 US President **George W. Bush** stated that, in the light of new realities on the ground, 'including already existing major Israeli population centres', it was 'unrealistic' to expect the outcome of any future talks to mark 'a full and complete return to the armistice lines of 1949'. This was a reversal of former US policy and a recognition of the *fait accompli* by the Israeli programme of settlement construction and development. **Palestinian National Authority** leader **Yasser Arafat** expressed outrage and Prime Minister **Ahmed Qurei** pointed out that President Bush was the first US President to have, in effect, legitimized Israel's settlements in the Occupied Territories, and that this was unacceptable.

Seveners – *see also* Ismailis

A distinctive sect of **Shi'ism**, the Seveners are generally called **Ismailis**. They claim allegiance to Ismail—the eldest son of the Imam Ja'afar (the source of the **Ja'afari** Shi'a legal Code)—whom they believe should have been the seventh imam. The **Twelvers**, or Imamis, deny this.

Ash-Sha'abi, Qahtan Muhammad

President of the **People's Democratic Republic of Yemen** from 1967 until 1969, when he was overthrown.

Sha'b

Arabic word meaning 'people', 'masses'.

Shabak – *see* Shin Beth and General Security Service

Ash-Shabiba al-Islamiyya

Islamist Youth/People

An illegal Moroccan Islamist political grouping. Some 70 members of this group were arrested in 1983 and charged with plotting to overthrow the **monarchy**. The accused had been distributing leaflets, displaying anti-monarchist posters and taking part in demonstrations. Their subsequent convictions were based on confessions signed under torture during months of secret detention. The trial took place in 1984 and 13 of those convicted were sentenced to death (11 *in absentia*). The others were sentenced to terms of imprisonment ranging from four to 20 years. Those who remained in jail in 1994 were released in an amnesty, apart from those originally sentenced to death, whose sentences were commuted to life imprisonment in 1994. Four at least remained in prison until 1996.

Shafi'i Code

One of the four legal Codes of **Sunni Islam**. The Shafi'i Code has the widest range of adherents in geographical terms, with followers in Egypt, Palestine, Syria, southern Arabia and south-east Asia.

Shah, Mohammed Reza Pahlavi – *see* Pahlavi, Mohammed Reza Shah

Shah, Reza – *see* Reza Khan, Shah

Shahaddah

The profession of faith in **Islam** that every Muslim must recite every day: '*Ashhadu an la ilaha illa Llah, wa ashhadu ana Muhammad rasulu Llah*' ('I testify that there is no God but Allah, and I testify that Muhammad is his prophet'). One of the **Five Pillars of Islam**.

Shahar

Dawn

An Israeli political movement, founded in 2002, which seeks to guarantee 'the Jewish and democratic existence of Israel, based on peace and social justice'. Founded and led by **Yossi Beilin**.

Shalom Achsav (Peace Now) – *see* Israel Communist Party

Shamir, Itzhak (1915–)

Zionist activist and Israeli politician, Prime Minister of Israel in 1983–84, 1986–90 and 1990–92. Born Itzhak Yertinski in Poland in 1915, Shamir emigrated to Palestine in 1935. He was a follower of **Vladimir Jabotinsky** (the founder of the revisionist movement, a Zionist faction), a man at once radical and yet fascinated by

Mussolini, dedicated to the cult of force, and committed to the Judaization of Palestine on both banks of the Jordan river. Shamir was twice arrested by the British for participating in a militant Jewish organization (the Fighters for the Freedom of Israel, whose initials in Hebrew were LEHI), which he had founded in 1940. In 1946 he was arrested and deported. He returned to Israel only after independence. A group of which he was leader was implicated in, amongst other things, the assassination of the UN mediator, Swedish Count Folke Bernadotte, in September 1948. He served in the secret service of Israel from 1948 until 1965. He helped to found the conservative **Likud** party, becoming its leader and Prime Minister upon the retirement of **Menachem Begin** in 1983 and serving as such from September 1983 to July 1984. In 1984 and 1988, Likud and Labour formed governments of national unity in which Shamir served, respectively, as foreign minister (1984–86) and Prime Minister (1986–90). The deadlock created by the elections of November 1988 allowed him, once again, to lead the Israeli government. From 1990 until 1992 Shamir was Prime Minister of a Likud-led right-wing government.

Sharett, Moshe

Prime Minister of Israel from 1953 until 1955.

Shari'a

In **Arabic** means 'way' or 'road'. **Islamic Law** consisting of divine revelation in the form of the **Koran** and prophetic practice, Sunna (as recorded in the **Hadith**), the Shari'a governs the individual and the social life of the believer. The Shari'a is the basis for judging acts as good or evil. The Koran provides the principles and the Hadith the details of their application. As the Koran and the Hadith do not cover all aspects of life, Islamic jurists later included *ijma* (consensus) and *ijtihad* as components of the Shari'a.

Shari'ati, Ali

Born in 1933, Iranian Islamic thinker and liberation theologist. He is often considered to have been the ideologist of the **Iranian Revolution**. He combined a Western education and concern for anti-colonial struggles with a strong consciousness of his identity as a **Shi'a** Muslim. He believed that the true Shi'a faith was a revolutionary ideology which called for political activism to end oppression and injustice. His goal was to create a just and classless society. He believed that the intelligentsia, not the conservative *ulema*, should lead the revolution. His writings and speeches found a ready audience in the early 1970s, and even more so after his death in 1977 and the Iranian Revolution.

Sharjah, Emirate of

Sheikhdom with a population of 400,339 in 1995. In area it totals some 2,590 sq km. Sharjah is part of the federation of seven United Arab Emirates (UAE), in south-eastern Arabia, on the **Persian (Arabian) Gulf** and the Gulf of Oman. The modernized town of Sharjah, on the Persian (Arabian) Gulf, is, after Abu Dhabi, the largest town in the federation. **Oil** has been produced in Sharjah since 1961. Formerly a British protectorate, Sharjah was the site of a British base until 1971, when Britain withdrew from the Gulf and Sharjah joined the UAE. Its Gulf port has long been important both strategically and commercially.

Sharm esh-Sheikh Agreement (Memorandum)

The implementation of the **Wye River Memorandum** having stalled under the Israeli Government of **Binyamin Netanyahu**, the new Israeli Prime Minister, **Ehud Barak**, and the **Palestinian National Authority** President, **Yasser Arafat**, met at Sharm esh-Sheikh to discuss the possible reactivation of the Memorandum. A revised Wye Memorandum (Wye Two) was signed by Arafat and Barak in Sharm esh-Sheikh in Egypt on 4 September 1999, in the presence of US Secretary of State Madeleine Albright, President **Mubarak** of Egypt and King **Abdullah** of Jordan. Wye Two was ratified by the Israeli Cabinet and the **Knesset** in September. There was some progress towards implementation during that month, but in mid-November, despite three days of talks, the programme stalled.

Sharm esh-Sheikh Fact-Finding Committee Report

Otherwise known as the Mitchell Report, produced by the Fact-Finding Committee chaired by former US Senator George Mitchell in May 2001. The decision to undertake the fact-finding mission was made at a summit meeting at Sharm esh-Sheikh which brought together delegations led by Israeli Prime Minister **Ehud Barak** and **Palestinian National Authority** President **Yasser Arafat**, with the mediation of US President **Bill Clinton**. In November 2000 a commission was appointed by Clinton to investigate the factors responsible for the violence which had erupted in September, following a visit by the leader of Israel's **Likud** party, **Ariel Sharon**, to the site of the Temple Mount or Haram ash-Sharif in **East Jerusalem**, and to make recommendations. Its recommendations were to end the violence, rebuild confidence and resume negotiations. It concluded that 'the parties are at a crossroads'.

Sharon, Ariel

With a long history as a **military** commander and major figure on the right of Israeli politics, Ariel Sharon has been a well-known personality for many years. His involvement in the massacres of Palestinians in the Lebanese refugee camps of **Sabra and Chatila** led many even in Israel to deplore his views and his methods.

However, he remained a popular figure on the right and became chairman of the **Likud** party in May 1999 after the resignation of **Binyamin Netanyahu** who had been defeated in the prime-ministerial election by **Ehud Barak**. Many **Palestinians** regard Sharon as the source of the violence which erupted in late September 2000 after he visited the site of the Temple Mount or the Haram ash-Sharif in **East Jerusalem** and which developed into what is widely referred to as the **al-Aqsa** *intifada* or uprising (the **al-Aqsa mosque** is located at the Haram ash-Sharif). Despite (or, perhaps, because of) this, he was regarded as an aggressive defender of Israeli rights and became Israel's new Prime Minister following the election of February 2001. He had campaigned on a platform of a **Jerusalem** united under Israeli sovereignty and it was clear from his political past that his national unity government would not be willing to grant many concessions to the Palestinians, with regard to Jerusalem or anything else. A series of suicide bombings during 2001 led to a government proposal to build a **wall** (or fence) between Jerusalem and the main Palestinian population centres of the **West Bank**. The wall was constructed and the Sharon Government's position on 'Palestinian violence' hardened. He approved a policy of assassination directed at the leadership of **Hamas**, the main Islamist group involved in suicide bombings, which led to the killing of Sheikh **Ahmed Yassin** and **Abdul Aziz Rantissi**, respectively the spiritual and the political leader of Hamas, in March and April 2004. Towards the end of April 2004 Sharon informed US President **Bush** that he was no longer prepared to exempt **Yasser Arafat** from physical harm.

Ash-Sharqi, Sheikh Hamad ibn Muhammad

Ruler of **Fujairah**, one of the United Arab Emirates. He acceded to power in 1974.

Shas

Israeli right-wing ultra-orthodox religious political party. It was formed in 1984 by splinter groups from **Agudat Israel**. Shas draws mainly on lower class Mizrahi (Oriental Jewish) voters and supports a grassroots, alternative Mizrahi educational system that extends from day-care centres to Yeshivas. The Yemenis formed **Yahad Shivtei Yisrael** from this in 1988. In 1988 Shas increased its representation in the **Knesset** from six to eight seats. In elections to the Knesset held in May 1999 it received 13% of the vote and secured 17 seats. Having won 10 seats in the Knesset in the most recent legislative elections, Shas joined the **Likud**-led coalition. Its current leader is Eliyahu Yishai, its spiritual leader Rabbi Ovadia Yosef.

Shatt al-Arab

The narrow waterway at the head of the **Persian (Arabian) Gulf** giving Iran and Iraq access to the Gulf and beyond. Of critical geopolitical significance for the two oil-producing countries which make use of it, and thus for international relations within the region.

Shawkat, Ahmad

Born in 1951 in **Mosul**, Ahmad Shawkat was a Kurdish writer and journalist, who was murdered in his home town in October 2003, reportedly by Islamists. He entered the University of Mosul in 1968, the year in which the **Ba'ath Party** came to power in Iraq, and although he graduated with a degree in biology and became a lecturer at the university's prestigious medical school, he was better known for his poetry and political sermons in the guise of literary criticism. In the mid-1990s he was arrested and tortured for the fourth time for having written a collection of stories that lampooned **Saddam Hussain**. His family ransomed him from jail, but he was forced to burn in public all the copies of his book. Shawkat fled to **Irbil**, in the Kurdish autonomous region, in 1997. In the summer following the fall of Saddam Hussain's regime Shawkat commenced publishing a weekly journal, *Bela Etajah* (*No Directions*), and had written a series of scathing editorials on the subject of Islamist **terrorism** when he was assassinated while making a telephone call on the roof of his office in Mosul.

Sheikh (Shaikh)

Leader, chief, spiritual guide. A title usually given by popular acclaim to a respected figure.

Sheikh Bakr Group

An armed Islamist group active in Yemen.

Shelli—Shalom LeYisrael

Peace for Israel

After the split with the New Communist List in 1965, **Maki** became more moderate in its opposition to government policies and its membership became more Jewish. In 1975 it merged with Moked (Focus), a socialist party, and in 1977 Moked united with other leftist non-communist groups to form Shelli. The new party was founded by Arye Eliav, a former secretary-general of the **Israel Labour Party**. The party called for the withdrawal of Israel to its pre-1967 borders, political negotiations with the **Palestine Liberation Organization** on the basis of mutual recognition, and the establishment of an Arab Palestinian state. Shelli gained two seats in the 1977 elections but was unsuccessful in securing representation in 1981.

Shi'a or Shi'ite Muslims

The Legitimist Shi'a or Shi'ites pay allegiance to Ali, the **Prophet Muhammad**'s cousin and son-in-law, regarding him as the only legitimate successor of Muhammad. The largest Shi'a school is that of the **Twelvers** (Ithna'ashriya) who acknowledge a succession of 12 imams. From 1502 Shi'ism became the established school of **Islam** in Iran under the Safavid ruler Sultan Shah Ismail. Another group of Shi'a, the **Ismailis**, or **Seveners**, do not recognize Musa al-Kazim, son of Ja'far as-Sadiq, as the seventh imam, believing that the last imam visible on earth was Ismail, the other son of Ja'far as-Sadiq. The Seveners are divided into several groups on the basis of their beliefs as to the succession from Ismail; one of these groups is that of the Nizari Ismailis, of whom the **Aga Khan** is the spiritual head.

Shi'ism—Shi'a Islam

One of the two great religious divisions of Islam that regards Ali, the son-in-law of the **Prophet Muhammad**, as the legitimate successor of Muhammad, and dis-regards the three caliphs who succeeded him. Shi'a Islam is the second largest division of Islam, constituting about 10%-15% of all Muslims. They reside in all parts of the world, but some countries have particularly high concentrations of Shi'a. Iran, for instance, is almost entirely Shi'a, and some two-thirds of the Muslims who make up 95% of the Iraqi population are Shi'a.

Shin Beth

A branch of the Israeli secret service, whose full name is Shabak. It has traditionally been regarded as less capable than **Mossad**, but, nevertheless, has been very effective in recent years. (See also **General Security Services**.)

Shinui

Change

Israeli political party, formed in 1974 as a new liberal party. In 1976 it joined with others to form the Democratic Movement for Change (DMC) which won 15 seats in the **Knesset** in the 1977 elections. The DMC dissolved itself just before the 1981 elections and Shinui again emerged as an independent grouping that won two seats in the Knesset. In the legislative elections held in 1984 Shinui won three seats and joined the the government of national unity. It combines a secular vision of Israeli politics with a free-market economic philosophy. Its leaders are Joseph (Tommy) Lapid and Avraham Poraz.

Shiraz

Town in southern Iran that was the birthplace of the poet Hafez.

Shishakli, Col Adib

Head of state of Syria from December 1949 until February 1954, when he was overthrown and replaced by Sabri al-Asali.

Shuhada

Arabic term for 'martyrs'. It is widely used by Islamists to refer to 'suicide bombers'. There is a strong tradition of martyrdom, particularly in **Shi'ism**, which traces its origin to the 'martyrdom' of Ali (the seventh imam) and Hussein.

Shultz Plan

At the beginning of February 1988 the US government announced a new plan for the resolution of the Palestinian issue, which became known as the Shultz Plan. At the end of February US Secretary of State, George Shultz, embarked on a tour of Middle Eastern capitals in an attempt to elicit support for a new peace initiative. The Shultz Plan proposed a six-month period of negotiations between Israel and a joint Jordanian/Palestinian delegation to determine the details of transitional autonomy arrangements for the **West Bank** and **Gaza Strip**, which would last for three years; during the transitional period a permanent settlement would be negotiated; both sets of negotiations were to take place concurrently with and, if necessary, with reference to an international peace conference involving all parties to the **Arab–Israeli Conflict** and the five permanent members of the UN Security Council, with the **Palestinians** represented in a joint Jordanian/Palestinian delegation, excluding the **Palestine Liberation Organization** (PLO). By the time that Shultz returned to the USA at the beginning of March, however, his plan already appeared unworkable. Although **Shimon Peres** generally endorsed the proposals (albeit reluctantly), **Itzhak Shamir** declared that there was 'no prospect of implementation'. The Arab states were unprepared to accept the exclusion of the PLO.

Shura (Afghanistan)

Council.

Shura (Central Asia)

Religious (Islamic) or political council. It usually consist of the notables and/or elders of a community.

Sista-Ahoti

Israeli political grouping representing the interests of (**Mizrahim**) in Israel.

Sistani, Grand Ayatollah Ali

Widely considered to be the supreme or leading **Shi'a** cleric in Iraq. Sistani is based in **Najaf** where the Hawza—the order that gives authority to the **ayatollahs**—is also centred. Towards the end of 2003 Sistani began to articulate a concern that proper elections should be held before the proposed US withdrawal from Iraq and the transfer of power by the **Coalition Provisional Authority** (CPA) to an **Iraqi Provisional Governing Council** by 30 June 2004. The CPA, under the direction of **Paul Bremer**, preferred a system of caucuses of 'the great and the good' in 18 provinces to select a transitional government. The views of the Grand Ayatollah command considerable support, particularly among Shi'as. Tens of thousands have taken to the streets of Iraq's main cities to express their support for the Ayatollah's proposal for direct elections. By adopting this position Sistani has mobilized secular and religious Shi'ite tendencies under the banner of democratic rights. This places considerable pressure on the CPA.

Six-Day War

The Six-Day War—**Arab–Israeli War (1967)**—marked a turning point in Middle Eastern politics that was associated with the rise of radical or **political Islam** and the beginning of the decline of secular **Arab nationalism**. It also marked the occupation by Israeli forces of territories previously belonging to Egypt (the **Gaza Strip**) and Jordan (the **West Bank**) and the real beginning of the Palestinian nationalist movement.

Social Justice Party

An Egyptian political party, founded in 1993. Its chairman is Muhammad Abd al-Aal.

Social Liberal Party

Algerian political grouping, led by Ahmed Khelil.

Socialism

There are several different socialist traditions in the **Middle East**—those that derive from an essentially liberal, social-democratic tradition of socialism, those that derive from an essentially Marxist tradition, those that derive from a corporatist, nationalist tradition, and those which attempt to combine **Islam** with socialism. The first is associated with a number of left-of-centre political parties, often closely linked to the labour movement; the second with the numerous small communist and 'socialist workers' parties and other left-wing revolutionary socialist groupings; the third, which is probably the mainstream tradition in the region, is associated not only with many political parties, but also with several governments, past and present—particularly those which have laid claim to represent some form of **Arab socialism** (including the **Ba'ath** parties). The fourth tradition, which is often close in important respects to the third, draws on the Islamic conception of the 'community of believers' to emphasize the importance of unity, solidarity and cohesion. Only the first tradition is intrinsically tolerant and pluralistic; the others tend to be characterized by various forms of 'democratic centralism' and a tendency towards authoritarianism.

Socialist Labour Party

Founded in 1978. The official opposition party. Pro-Islamist, its leader is Ibrahim Shukri.

Socialist Labour Party (Egypt)

Hizb al-Amal al-Ishtiraki

The Socialist Labour Party, like the **New Wafd Party**, has pre-1952 origins. It has historical links with a proto-fascist movement, the Green Shirts or Egyptian Youth (Misr al-Fatat). Under the leadership of Ibrahim Shukri, it generally supported the liberalization policies of President **Sadat**, but criticized the peace treaty with Israel. Until the 1984 presidential elections, it was designated the official opposition party by the regime. It has links with the higher echelons of the labour movement, but little to do with the rank and file. It is less of a socialist party in the European sense than a party of **national socialism** in the corporatist or fascist tradition.

Socialist Liberal Party (Egypt)

Hizb al-Ahrar al-Ishtiraki

The Egyptian Socialist Liberal Party, which represents the interests of liberal capitalism, is led by Hilmi Murad. The party was mildly critical of Egypt's peace treaty with Israel, but broadly supportive of the economic policies of Presidents **Sadat** and **Mubarak**. It is very much a party that emerged as a result of reforms made in the mid- and late 1970s. It has limited political support, and received only 7% of the vote in elections held in 1984.

Socialist Nationalist Syrian Party

Lebanese political party, founded in 1932. It was banned between 1962 and 1969. It advocates a **Greater Syria** comprising Lebanon, Syria, Iraq, Jordan, Palestine and Cyprus. Its leader is Jibran Araiji.

Socialist Party of Kurdistan

An Iraqi political group, founded in 1975 and led by Rassoul Marmand.

Socialist Union of Popular Forces (Morocco)

Union socialiste des forces populaires (USFP)

The USFP, a Moroccan left-wing political party, emerged after splitting from the **UNFP** in 1972. One faction of the UNFP, led by Abderrahim Bouabid (b. 1920), was briefly banned in 1973 and 1974, but was relegalized as a result of political liberalization initiated by the king in 1974. It changed its name to the USFP in the same year. It remained in opposition to the government throughout the rest of the decade, accusing it of election rigging in 1977. It was severely repressed after the riots in **Casablanca** in June 1981; its newspapers were banned for about one year and some 200 leading cadres, including Bouabid and two other members of the party's politburo, as well as leading members of the allied Democratic Labour Confederation (Confédération démocratique du travail—CDT) were arrested and jailed. Some of these were pardoned in May 1983, and the USFP decided to participate, for the first time, in local and national elections. In November 1983 Bouabid was included in the government as a minister of state. After the '**bread riots**' of January 1984 large numbers of USFP militants were arrested and detained for their involvement in the protests. Generally, the USFP gains its support mainly in the urban areas among the organized working class and the trade unions (particularly those affiliated to the CDT, which it controls) and among students, teachers and other intellectuals. It is, in effect, the heir of the UNFP, with the main thrust of the party being towards social **democracy**, while a more radical wing might be termed democratic socialist. It has a youth wing, known as the United Youth. It has also contained a minority revolutionary socialist tendency, known by the name of its clandestine newspaper, *Revolutionary Option* (*Al-Ikhtier al-Haouri*), inspired by one of the UNFP's historical leaders, Mohammed Basri, who remained in exile in Paris, France, from the early 1960s onwards. It has always maintained a nationalistic position, supporting the government with regard to the **Western Sahara** and, like the communist **Parti du progrès et du socialisme**, has tended to criticize the government for alleged weakness in prosecuting the war effort.

The Socialist Vanguard Party

Parti de l'avant-garde socialiste (PAGS)

The PAGS rallied to the support of the **Front de libération nationale** (National Liberation Front) Government of Algeria in 1971 in respect of its 'anti-imperialist' policies during its 'left turn' in the so-called 'socialist revolution' of the early 1970s under **Boumedienne**.

Society of Self-Sacrificing Devotees

Political grouping in Iran.

Software

In world terms, the region ranks lowly in statistics on **research and development**, on information and communications technology development and use, and on patents. It ranks highly, however, in statistics on business software piracy. Lebanon ranks 'highest' in this respect within the region (seventh in the world), with 79% of software that is pirated. Qatar follows (with 78%), then Bahrain and Oman (77%), Kuwait (76%), Jordan (67%) and Morocco (61%).

South Korea – *see* Korea

South Yemen

South Yemen came into existence in November 1967. President, Prime Minister and commander-in-chief was Qahtan ash-Shaabi, leader of the **National Liberation Front** which had fought the British for independence in South Arabia since 1963. Ash-Shaabi declared that 'the aim of our Revolution has been since the beginning to unite both parts of Yemen. We are all one people'. He appointed one of the most influential of NLF leaders, Abd al-Fattah Ismail, as Minister of Yemeni Unity Affairs; a similar ministry was set up in **San'a**. Ash-Shaabi was a radical populist, but other members of the NLF were socialists in the Marxist-Leninist tradition. The economy of South Yemen was in a desperate state as a result of the ending of British subsidies and the departure of the large, free-spending expatriate community which coincided with the closure of the **Suez Canal**, which had been Aden's only other real source of **income**. As the leftists called for the introduction of 'scientific **socialism**', with rural soviets, collectivization of the land, nationalization of the banks and foreign **trade**, and the export of the revolution throughout the Peninsula, ash-Shaabi was himself forced to the left. In 1969 ash-Shaabi and his cousin, now Prime Minister, were deposed in a bloodless coup. They were replaced by a five-man presidential council, which immediately adopted a more aggressive radical policy, both at home and abroad. In 1970 a new constitution was adopted and South Yemen became the **People's Democratic Republic of Yemen**.

Spanish Morocco

Also known as the Spanish Protectorate of Morocco, which lasted from 1912 until 1956. Located along the **Mediterranean** coastline in the north of the country, it included the Rif mountains and the two Spanish presidiums, Ceuta and Melilla. Formally reunited with the main part of Morocco, which had been under the **French Protectorate of Morocco** since 1912, at independence in 1956, it was effectively reunited with the rest of Morocco after 1958.

Spanish Sahara

Large desert territory to the south of Morocco, occupied by Spain until 1975/76, when it withdrew, leaving Morocco and Mauritania to invade and occupy most of the territory, against the declared wish of the local inhabitants, the **Sahrawis**, for self-determination and independence. Former name of **Western Sahara**.

The State List

Founded in 1968 by **David Ben-Gurion**, Israel's first Prime Minister, when he and several followers refused to join the new **Israel Labour Party**. The State List won four seats in the **Knesset** in 1969 when it could still be considered a party of the left. In 1973 sizeable remnants of the party joined the **Likud** alliance, eventually merging with other groups to form La'am.

Stern, Avraham (Yair)

A scholar and a poet (he was the author of *Anonymous Soldiers*, the battle hymn of **Irgun Zvai Leumi**) as well as the leader of the **Stern Gang** or Lechi, a Jewish paramilitary group in Palestine. In the summer of 1941 he set in motion a plan for making a deal with Hitler to turn Nazi anti-Semitism to the advantage of the Jews. The plan was for Germany to send a fleet of ships containing tens of thousands of Jews into the **Mediterranean**, to break the British blockade, upset the Royal Navy's dispositions and land the Jews in Palestine. The plan never materialized: Stern was hunted down by the British, and finally located in a flat in **Tel-Aviv** where he was reportedly 'shot while trying to escape'.

Stern Gang/Group—Lechi

Paramilitary Jewish nationalist group, Lohamei Herut Israel (Lechi), led by **Avraham Stern** (hence the 'Stern Gang'), operational in the 1930s and 1940s in Palestine. It was in effect a splinter group from **Irgun Zvai Leumi**, led by David Raziel. It carried out the assassination of the anti-semitic British Colonial Secretary, Lord Moyne, in 1943.

Stockmarkets

Several countries in the region have been promoting the development of stock-markets in recent years as a means of encouraging private investment and capital accumulation. In terms of market capitalization, the Saudi Arabian stockmarket is the largest in the region at around US $73,200m., closely followed by that of Israel at $70,300m.. Turkey ranks third with $47,000m., followed by Iran with $44,000m. The Egyptian stockmarket is capitalized at $24,000m., while those of Morocco ($9,000m.), the United Arab Emirates ($7,800m.) and Bahrain ($6,600m.) are considerably smaller. The highest growth in market capitalization in 1996–2001 was registered by Iran (an increase of 158%), Qatar (99%), Israel (96%), Egypt (72%) and Saudi Arabia (60%). The highest growth in value traded (in terms of US dollars) in the same period was registered in Kazakhstan (an increase of 15,900%). After this, the most significant increases were registered in Israel (270%), Qatar (251%), Saudi Arabia (228%), Jordan (214%), the **West Bank** and **Gaza Strip** (200%), Morocco (125%), Turkey (112%) and Iran (89%). The highest growth in the number of listed companies was in Kazakhstan (933%). Egypt, Jordan, Iran, Turkey, Lebanon, Kuwait, the West Bank and Gaza Strip, Uzbekistan and Qatar all registered significant increases, ranging from 71% (Egypt) to 22% (Qatar).

Strict Nationalists

Nationalistes étroits, Mauritania

This group of Black Mauritanians advocated greater freedom for Blacks and a more secular state. They were opposed to the annexation of the **Western Sahara**.

Suez Canal

The Suez Canal forms a 163 km ship canal in Egypt between Port Said on the **Mediterranean** and Suez on the Red Sea. The canal allows water **transport** from Europe to Asia without circumnavigating Africa. Before its construction some transport was conducted by offloading ships and carrying the goods overland between the Mediterranean and the Red Sea. It was built between 1859 and 1869 by a French company led by Ferdinand de Lesseps and the Canal was owned by the Egyptian government and France. External debts forced Egypt to sell its share in the Canal to Great Britain, and British troops moved in to protect it in 1882.

   In 1956 **Gamal Abdel Nasser** and the Egyptian state nationalized the Canal which caused Britain, France and Israel to invade in the week-long Suez War.

Sufism

Term derived from the **Arabic** word for wool, with reference to the woollen capes worn by early Sufis. Sufism generally refers to the esoteric or mystical path within **Islam**. Two central Sufi concepts are *tawakkul*, total reliance on God, and *dhikr*, perpetual remembrance of God. Sufi orders (*tariq*, plural *turuq*), which assimilated aspects of native religious traditions more readily than more dogmatic versions of Islam, played a major role in the expansion of Islam into sub-Saharan Africa and central, southern and south-east Asia. The oldest extant order is probably the Qadiriyya, founded by Abd al-Qadir al-Jilani (d. 1166) in **Baghdad**. Other important orders include the Ahmadiyya, Naqshbandiyya, Nimatullahiyya, Rifaiyya Shadhiliyya, Suhrawardiyya, Chishtiyya, and Tijaniyya. Although Sufism has made significant contributions to the spread of Islam and the development of various aspects of Islamic civilization (e.g. literature and calligraphy), many conservative Muslims disagree with many popular Sufi practices, particularly saint worship, the visiting of tombs, and the incorporation of non-Islamic customs. Consequently, in recent centuries Sufism has been a target for Islamic reformist, fundamentalist and modernist movements.

Sunay, Cevdet

President of Turkey from 1966 until 1973.

Sunni Leadership Council (Iraq)

In January 2004 **Sunni** elders from across Iraq established a leadership council or *shura* to increase their influence on the post-war political process from which they felt marginalized. The Council includes representatives from all major Sunni religious groups, the Salafis, the **Muslim Brotherhood**, **al-Jama'a al-Islamiyya**, as well as **Kurds** and Turkmens. However, raids by US troops on the Ibn Taymiyah mosque in **Baghdad** led to 34 arrests, including those of several leading members of the *shura*, before a meeting of the body.

Sunnis and Sunnism

The great majority (probably more than 80%) of Muslims are followers of the Sunna (the way, course, rule or manner of conduct) of the **Prophet Muhammad**. The remainder are mainly followers of the **Shi'a** tradition. The Sunnis recognize the first four caliphs as *rashidun* (following the right way). They base their Sunna on the **Koran** and six books of Traditions, and are organized into four orthodox schools or rites—**Hanafi**, **Hanbali**, **Shafi'i** and **Maliki**—each with their specific religious/legal Code. Thirty years after the death of the Prophet, the Islamic community was plunged into a civil war that gave rise to three sects. One proximal cause of this first civil war was that the Muslims of Iraq and Egypt resented the power of the third caliph and his governors; another cause was business rivalries between factions of the mercantile aristocracy. After the caliph was murdered, war broke out in full force between different groups. The war ended with a new dynasty of caliphs, which ruled from **Damascus**. The Sunnis recognized the authority of the fourth and the succeeding caliphs. Two smaller groups emerged as a result of this schism. The Shi'ites believed that the only legitimate leadership rested with the lineage of Muhammad's cousin and son-in-law, Ali. A third group maintained that leadership should be based on Islamic scholarship and the will of the people, and not on inherited power. This group was labelled by other Muslims as Kharijites or the Khawarij (seceders).

Sunnis and Shi'ites in Iraq

Although Iraq's **Shi'a** community constitutes about one-half of the country's population, Iraq's government has traditionally been dominated by the country's **Sunni** minority, concentrated mainly in the central region. This is the reverse of the situation in Syria. While there are Shi'a in other parts of Iraq, much of the country's Shi'a population lives in the south, including the marshland regions near the Iranian border—which the **Marsh Arabs** historically inhabited.

Sunnis and Shi'ites in Syria

In Syria the majority of the population are **Sunni** Muslims, but the ruling élite are predominantly **Shi'ite** Alavis or Alevis. This is the reverse of the situation in Iraq.

Supporters of Islam – *see* **Ansar al-Islam**

Supporters of the Islamic League (Lebanon)

Ansar al-'Usba al-Islamiyya

The Supporters of the Islamic League has almost 200 members. It is headed by Ahmad as-Sa'di (known as Abu Muhjin), formerly of the **Islamic Association**. The League declares its aim to be the liberation of Palestine and the Muslim community. The League first appeared in August 1995 with the assassination of Nizar al-Halabi, president of **al-Ahbash**. Despite evidence of Abu Muhjin's involvement in the assassination, the Lebanese authorities have not been able to locate him.

Supreme Council for the Islamic Revolution in Iraq (SCIRI)

SCIRI, a **Shi'ite** resistance group, was formed in Iran in 1982 in order to provide an opposition to Iraqi aggression against Iran. Following the **Iran–Iraq War**, from 1986 onwards, the organization continued to operate with the aim of toppling the regime of **Saddam Hussain**. SCIRI has about 4,000–8,000 fighters, composed of Iraqi Shi'ite exiles and prisoners of war, operating against the Iraqi military in southern Iraq. Although SCIRI has distanced itself from Iran to some extent, Iran's **Revolutionary Guards** reportedly continue to provide it with weapons and training. SCIRI was headed by Ayatollah **Muhammad Baqir al-Hakim**, the son of the late Grand Ayatollah Mushin al-Hakim, who was the spiritual leader for the Shi'a in the world in 1955–70. SCIRI consisted of a general assembly of 70 members who represented various Islamic movements and scholars. Its military wing was known as the **Badr Brigade** or Badr Corps. The Badr Corps consist of thousands of former Iraqi officers and soldiers who defected from the Iraqi army, Iraqi **refugees** and prisoners of war. A mutual agreement was signed by SCIRI with the **Patriotic Union of Kurdistan**, headed by **Jalal Talabani**, to work against Saddam Hussain's regime. A similar agreement was signed with the **Kurdish Democratic Party**, headed by **Masoud Barzani**, several years ago. At the conclusion of **Operation Desert Storm**, Iraqi **Kurds** in the north of Iraq and the Iraqi Shi'a in the south launched an armed revolt against the regime of Saddam Hussain. Iraqi government troops attempted to crush the movement, reportedly razing mosques and other

Shi'ite shrines and executing thousands. Amid allegations that the Iraqi army used chemical and biological weapons in their efforts, the Shi'a revolt was suppressed while the Kurdish revolt ended in the granting of political autonomy to the Kurds. However, the resistance continued, and tens of thousands of rebels and Shi'ite civilians fled into the southern marshlands between the **Tigris** and **Euphrates** rivers. There are now approximately 300,000 such refugees in the southern marshes or over the borders in Iran and Saudi Arabia. In 1992 the **Gulf War (1991)** allies imposed 'no-fly zones' over both northern and southern Iraq. The zones deterred aerial attacks on the marsh dwellers in southern Iraq and residents of northern Iraq, but they did not prevent artillery attacks on villages in either area, nor the military's large-scale burning operations in the southern marshes. In 1997 Iraqi armed forces conducted deliberate artillery attacks against Shi'a civilians in the southern marshes and against **minority** groups in northern Iraq. The Iraqi Government also continued its **water**-diversion and other projects in the south, accelerating the process of large-scale environmental destruction. The Government claimed that the drainage was part of a land reclamation plan to increase the acreage of arable land, spur agricultural production, and reduce salt **pollution** in the Tigris and Euphrates rivers. However, the evidence of large-scale human and ecological destruction appears to belie this claim, and other credible reports confirmed the ongoing destruction of the marshes. SCIRI claimed to have obtained government documents describing its long-term plans to drain the marshes completely. The army continued to construct canals, causeways, and earthern *berms* to divert water from the wetlands. Hundreds of square kilometers have been burned in military operations. Moreover, the regime's diversion of supplies in the south limited the population's access to food, medicine, drinking water and transportation. A political movement, bringing together various Shi'a groups, in post-conflict Iraq, SCIRI condemned the attack in **Najaf** in which **Ayatollah** Muhammad Baqir al-Hakim, religious leader and senior cleric, died in August 2003. The party continues to maintain close relations with Iran.

Sykes-Picot Agreement

The Sykes-Picot Agreement of April–May 1916 was an understanding between the governments of Britain and France (named after Mark Sykes and Georges Picot, those countries' respective foreign ministers) defining their respective areas of post-First World War control in the **Middle East**. Broadly, Britain was allocated control of Palestine (including modern Jordan) and Iraq, while France was to receive Syria (including present-day Lebanon). While the Agreement refers to the willingness of Britain and France to recognize and protect an independent Arab state or a Confederation of Arab states, it is viewed to this day among Arab nationalists as a gross betrayal of Britain's undertakings to support Arab independence in the McMahon letters and during the **Arab Revolt**. The document was unknown to

Sherif Hussein until its publication by the new Bolshevik Government of Russia in 1917.

Syria (Syrian Arab Republic)
Al-Jumhuriyah al-Arabiyah as-Suriyah

Bordering the **Mediterranean** Sea to the west, and Turkey to the north, Syria also has borders with Iraq to the east and Jordan, Israel and Lebanon to the south. There are still Israeli **settlements** and civilian land use sites in the Israeli-occupied **Golan Heights**, which are claimed by Syria. The country's total area is 185,180 sq km (of which 1,295 sq km is Israeli-occupied and 1,130 sq km is **water**). The capital is **Damascus** and the main administrative regions are the 14 provinces (*muhafazah*, plural *muhafazat*) of Al-Hasakah, Al-Ladhiqiyah, Al-Qunaytirah, Ar-Raqqah, As-Suwayda', Dar'a, Dayr az-Zawr, Dimashq, Halab, Hamah, Hims, Idlib, Rif Dimashq and Tartus. In July 2002 the population was estimated at 17,155,814, of which Arabs constituted 90.3%, and **Kurds**, **Armenians** and 'others' 9.7%. In addition, about 40,000 people live in the Israeli-occupied Golan Heights—20,000 Arabs (18,000 **Druze** and 2,000 **Alawites**) and about 20,000 Israeli settlers, according to estimates made in February 2003. With regard to the country's religious composition, **Sunni** Muslims account for 74%, Alawites, Druzes and other Muslim sects for 16% and Christians (various sects) for 10% of the population. There are very small Jewish communities in Damascus, Al-Qamishli and **Aleppo**. The official language is **Arabic**. Kurdish, Armenian, Aramaic and Circassian are widely understood, French and English less so.

Political profile
Syria has been a republic since the coup of March 1963. The head of state since 17 July 2000 has been President **Bashar al-Assad**. Abd al-Halim ibn Said Khaddam and Muhammad Zuhayr Mashariqa have been the country's Vice-Presidents since 11 March 1984. Prime Minister Muhammad Mustafa Miru has been the head of government since 13 March 2000. Lt-Gen. Mustafa Talas (since 11 March 1984), Farouk ash-Shara (since 13 December 2001) and Dr Muhammad al-Husayn (since 13 December 2001) are the country's Deputy Prime Ministers. The Council of Ministers is appointed by the President. The President is elected by popular vote for a seven-year term. **Hafiz al-Assad**, father of the current President, died on 10 June 2000. On 20 June the **Baa'th Party** nominated Bashar al-Assad as his successor, presenting his name to the People's Council on 25 June. A presidential referendum/election was last held in July 2000, following the death of President Hafiz al-Assad. The next election is to be held in 2007. Vice-Presidents, the Prime Minister and Deputy Prime Ministers are all appointed by the President. The legislature is the unicameral, 250-seat **Majlis** ash-Shaab (People's Council). Its members are elected by popular vote to serve four-year terms. Elections were last held on 30 November–1 December 1998. The legal system is based on **Islamic Law** and a civil law

system. There are special religious courts. The Supreme Constitutional Court justices are appointed for four-year terms by the President. There is also a High Judicial Council, a Court of Cassation and State Security Courts. Syria has not accepted compulsory International Court of Justice jurisdiction. Syria is in effect a single party state, with the **(Arab) Ba'ath Socialist Party** under Bashar al-Assad and its support parties in the **National Progressive Front**—which includes the Arab Socialist Party, the Arab Socialist Union, the Syrian Social National Party, the Socialist Unionist Democratic Party and the **Communist Party**—in full control of parliament and the government. The non-Baa'th parties have little effective political influence. Bashar al-Assad allowed discussion clubs after assuming the presidency, but these were later curtailed. Real political opposition comes from conservative religious leaders and the **Muslim Brotherhood** that operates from exile in Jordan and Yemen.

Media

Since Bashar al-Assad became President the media has been given more freedom, though it is still heavily censored. Satellite television is widely watched and internet use is encouraged, but censored. There is one state-controlled television service and one state-controlled radio service. Independent music radio stations were permitted in 2002. Independent publications appeared for the first time in 2001. There are 10 daily newspapers, of which *Al-Ba'ath*, *ath-Thawra* and *Tishrin* have the widest circulations. In 2000 there was one internet service provider, and in 2002 there were 60,000 internet users.

History

Following the disintegration of the **Ottoman Empire** during the First World War, Syria was administered by France until independence in 1946. Martial law has been in place since the **military** coup of 1963. In the **Arab–Israeli War (1967)**, Syria lost the **Golan Heights** to Israel, which remains in occupation. In recent years, Syria and Israel have held occasional negotiations on the return of the Golan Heights. Since October 1976 Syrian troops have been deployed in Lebanon, ostensibly in a peace-keeping capacity. Syria is in dispute with Turkey over Turkish **water** development plans upstream on the **Tigris** and **Euphrates** rivers. Syria claims Hatay province in Turkey. Syria is a transit point for opiates and hashish bound for regional and Western markets.

Syria, economy

Syria's strongly state-controlled economy has been growing at a rate less than the country's annual 2.5% population growth rate, causing a persistent decline in per caput gross domestic product. President **Bashar al-Assad** appears willing to permit a gradual strengthening of the private sector. Significant in this respect was the enactment of legislation that allows private banks to operate in Syria, although a private banking sector will require several years and further government co-operation in order to develop. Assad's recent Cabinet reshuffle may improve his chances of implementing further growth-oriented policies, although external factors, such as the international war on **terrorism**, the Israeli–Palestinian conflict and any decline in the international price of **oil**, could reduce the foreign investment and government revenues that Syria needs in order to flourish. A long-term economic constraint is the pressure on **water** supplies caused by rapid population growth, industrial expansion, and increased water **pollution**. Syria produces some crude oil, and has a growing manufacturing base and a reasonably successful agricultural sector. Inflation is low. High defence spending, however, is a major drain on the country's resources. There is a large black market. Many state-run companies are inefficient. Population and unemployment growth are both high.

T

Tai'f Agreement

The Tai'f Agreement, supported by the Arab Summit Conference in **Casablanca**, Morocco, and brokered in October 1989 by the Higher Arab Committee (comprising the Kings of Saudi Arabia and Morocco and the President of Algeria), was launched with the endorsement of the **Arab League** and the United Nations in the hope of restoring peace in Lebanon following the Lebanese civil war. The agreement introduced 31 important constitutional amendments, which were approved by the Lebanese parliament on 21 August 1990, and signed into law by President **Elias Hrawi** on 21 September. Lebanon's new Government of national unity adopted the Tai'f Agreement, now called the Document of National Accord, and it became an integral part of the Lebanese Constitution. The agreement promoted

- Constitutional reforms
- A gradual withdrawal of Syrian forces from Lebanon
- Extension of the Lebanese government's sovereignty over all of its national territory through its own forces
- Liberation of southern Lebanon and the western Beka'a from Israeli occupation

Tajammu' al-Ulama' al-Muslimin – *see* **Association of Muslim Clergy**

Tajik civil war

In May 1992 the Tajik opposition seized power from the Tajik Supreme Soviet, precipitating a civil war in which some 60,000 lives were lost. At one point 560,000 **Tajiks**, more than 11% of the total population of Tajikistan, became **refugees** in adjoining states. The opposition was defeated in December 1992 and the current Tajik Government assumed control. The defeated opposition comprised a coalition of self-declared democratic and Islamic groups and Islamic fundamentalists, a plurality of whom originate from the Garm-Kartogin region of the country; and Pamiris, who were traditionally under-represented in the ruling coalitions during

Soviet and pre-Soviet rule. Since early 1993 the ongoing armed insurgency of the opposition forces, in particular from across the Tajik-Afghan border, has continued to destabilize the country. Russian, **Commonwealth of Independent States** and Uzbek forces supported the winning coalition. The Supreme Soviet (parliament) elected **Imamali Rakhmonov**, Kulyab regional executive chairman, as its chairman and head of state. Much of Rakhmonov's support came from the victorious People's Front forces, which originated in Kulyab and Kurgan-Tube, the Uzbek-dominated Hissar region that gave assistance in the battle of Dushanbe, and from members of the traditional northern economic élite of Leninabad. The process of national reconciliation in this impoverished Central Asian country was set in motion by a June 1997 UN-mediated settlement between Tajikistan's Moscow-backed government and the Islamic-led **United Tajik Opposition**. However, the country missed almost every deadline set in the power-sharing agreement that ended the bloody five-year civil war, and some armed clashes involving renegade forces still take place.

Tajikistan, Republic of

Jumhurii Tojikiston

Lying to the west of China in southern central Asia, Tajikistan borders Uzbekistan to the west and north, Kyrgyzstan to the north and Afghanistan to the south. Landlocked and mountainous, only 6% of its 143,100 sq km is arable. The capital is Dushanbe and the country is divided administratively into two provinces (*viloyat*, plural *viloyatho*) and one autonomous province (*viloyati mukhtor*): Kuhistoni Badakhshon (autonomous province, centre: Khorugh), Khatlon (Qurghonteppa) and Sughd (Khujand). In July 2002 the population was estimated at 6,719,567, of which **Tajiks** accounted for 64.9%, **Uzbeks** for 25%, Russians (whose numbers are declining through emigration) for 3.5% and 'others' for 6.6%. With regard to religion, **Sunni** Muslims account for 80% of the population, **Shi'a** Muslims for 5% and 'others' for 15%. The official language is Tajik. Russian is used for business and administrative purposes.

According to the Constitution of 6 November 1994, the Republic of Tajikistan is a sovereign, democratic, law-governed, secular and unitary state. Recognition, observance and protection of human and civil rights and freedoms are the obligations of the state. The people of Tajikistan are the expression of sovereignty and the sole source of power of the state, which they express through their elected representatives. No ideology, including religious ideology, can be granted the status of state ideology. Religious organizations are separate from the state and may not interfere in state affairs. Agitation and actions aimed at disunity of the state are prohibited. The head of state and chairman of the Supreme Assembly since November 1992 has been President **Imamali Rakhmonov** (elected 6 November 1994, re-elected 6 November 1999). Since 20 January 1999 Oqil Oqilov has been Prime Minister. The Council of Ministers is appointed by the President and approved by the Supreme Assembly. The President is elected by popular vote for a seven-year term. The most recent election was held in November 1999 and the next is scheduled to be held in 2006. The Prime Minister is appointed by the President. The legislature comprises the 96-member bicameral Majlisi Oli (Supreme Assembly). This body consists of the 63-member Majlisi Namoyandagon (Assembly of Representatives—lower chamber) and the 33-member Majlisi Milliy (National Assembly—upper chamber). Members of the Assembly of Representatives are elected for five-year terms by popular vote—22 members are elected by proportional representation and 41 in single-mandate constituencies. The members of the National Assembly are indirectly elected for five-year terms—25 are selected by local deputies and eight are appointed by the President. Supreme Court judges are appointed by the President. The legal system is based on civil law. There is no judicial review of legislative acts.

Registered political parties

- Adaltkoh (Justice); Leader Abdurakhmon Karimov; campaigns for the establishment of social justice; banned in August 2001.
- Communist Party of Tajikistan (CPT); Leader Tuygun Bagirov
- Democratic Party (Almaty Platform); Chair. Mahmadruzi Isakndarov
- Islamic Rebirth Party of Tajikistan (IRP—formerly known as **Islamic Renaissance Party**); Leader Said Abdullo Nuri
- Socialist Party of Tajikistan; Leader Sherali Kenjayev
- People's Democratic Party of Tajikistan (PDPT); Leader Imamali Rakhmonov

Parties not recognized by the government or the Supreme Court before the 2000 legislative elections:

- Agrarian Party; Leader K. Nasriddinov
- Social Democratic Party; Leader Rahmatullo Zoirov
- Justice and Development Party
- Party of the National Movement of Tajikistan
- Party of National Unity; Leader Hikmatuko Saidov
- Democratic Party of Tajikistan (**Tehran** Platform)
- Equality and Development Party
- Justice and Development Party
- Renaissance of Tajikistan

Other groups:

- Progressive Party; Leader Suton Quvvatov
- **United Tajik Opposition**; dominated by the IRP
- National Movement Party; Leader Hakim Muhabbatov
- Party of Correction; Islamist party established by Uzbek fundamentalists seeking an **Islamic state** in **Central Asia**
- **Hizb ut-Tahrir** (HT); Central Asian Islamist Party

- **Islamic Movement of Uzbekistan** (IMU); members frequently cross Tajik territory into Kyrgyzstan and Uzbekistan; a destabilizing force)

Media

The state owns and the government has close to complete control of the broadcast media, after a decree of February 1994 that placed the State Television-Radio Broadcasting Co of Tajikistan under the supervision of the chairman of the Supreme Assembly. The government tries to block television and radio signals broadcast from other countries. In 1996 there were 73 non-daily newspapers. There are currently three daily newspapers: *Djavononi Todjikiston* (organ of the Union of Youth of Tajikistan), *Tochikiston Ovozi* (organ of the Central Committee of the Communist Party of Tajikistan) and *Jumhuriyat* (organ of the President of the Republic). Television stations include the State Television-Radio Broadcasting Co of Tajikistan; Internews Tajikistan (an NGO to promote free and independent media); and Samaniyan, an Iranian-funded station which began broadcasting a selection of local and Iranian programmes in 1996. Radio stations include the State Television-Radio Broadcasting Co of Tajikistan and Tajik Radio. The rebel opposition group Voice of Free Tajikistan began broadcasting in 1993. In 2002 there were four internet service providers and 5,000 internet users.

History

In 1918 the Bolsheviks formally incorporated northern Tajikistan into the Turkestan Autonomous Soviet Socialist Republic (ASSR) within the Russian Federation. However, real control of the region was difficult to establish, in part due to the **Basmachi**, a resistance movement of local guerrillas who continually opposed the imposition of Soviet rule and the Red Army. In the early 1920s the consolidation of Soviet rule in Central Asia led to the creation of Tajikistan as a republic within the Soviet Union. This new entity had little ethnic or geographical rationale, and was deliberately established to pacify potential nationalisms by sowing strife between Tajiks and Uzbeks. The historically Tajik cities of Samarkand and Bukhara were given to Uzbekistan, and a substantial Tajik population was left in Afghanistan. Conversely, the western parts of Tajikistan have a considerable Uzbek population. While the northern part of Tajikistan and the city of Khujand in particular were developed as an industrial centre (becoming the recruiting base of Communist Party members), the remaining regions were mostly left undeveloped and relatively poor. In addition, Soviet rule led to the collectivization of **agriculture**, the instalment of ethnic Russians in the main positions of power and the suppression of **Islam**. All of these factors would later contribute to the start of the **Tajik civil war**. In the early 1980s, after the Soviet invasion of Afghanistan in 1979, there were repeated reports of growing Islamist and anti-Russian sentiment, which translated into a crypto-nationalism and discussion of the country's Iranian and Islamic heritage during the *glasnost/perestroika* period. This resulted in Tajik becoming the primary language of communication in state and **education**. However, at independence the people of Tajikistan still had almost no sense of nationhood.

Independence was a volatile political and economic experience for Tajikistan. The loss of subsidies, foodstuffs and **aid** created an immediate crisis and frequent rioting in Dushanbe. Politically the Communist Party of Tajikistan did not manage to consolidate power or to create a sense of common belonging among the people. The leadership in Tajikistan changed three times between 1990 and 1992, but remained unrepresentative for the majority of the people. The main opposition came from the IRP, and powerful clan-based parties and militias that threatened to create their own states. The IRP and several democratic and nationalist groups managed to form a coalition government, but were bloodily overthrown when neo-Communist forces from the provinces of Khujand and Khulab invaded the capital and installed Imamali Rakhmonov as President. Rakhmonov quickly began to assert authority by detaining his opponents in an attempt to gain control of the areas of the country dominated by them. This coup was the 'official' start of the Tajik civil war that lasted for five years (1992–97), led to more than 50,000 casualties, created 250,000 **refugees** and made almost 500,000 homeless.

During the civil war the IRP formed a broad-based alliance called the United Tajik Opposition (UTO)—led by Sayed Abdullo Nuri of the IRP—that operated as a guerrilla group from the Pamir Mountains in Afghanistan. Neighbouring states were concerned that the civil war might destabilize their regimes, especially the Central Asian countries with Islamist opposition, and pressed the sides in the civil war to initiate peace talks. In April 1994 the Rakhmonov regime and the UTO commenced negotiations that lasted for three years while the fighting continued.

With the **Taliban**'s move north in Afghanistan in 1996, containing it became a vital security concern for Russia and the Central Asian states, and pressure was placed on Rakhmonov to sign a peace accord with Nuri. The rival factions did eventually sign such an agreement in 1997—it was finally implemented in 2000. The accord envisaged the legalization of political opposition parties, the creation of a National Reconciliation Council (of which Nuri was elected chairman), the granting of 30% of government posts to the opposition, elections to be held in 1998, the exchange of prisoners and the integration of UTO forces into the national army.

The UTO and Rakhmonov's PDPT formed a coalition government, accommodating most opposition parties. However, this administration was weakened by continual civil unrest, the slow implementation of the peace accords, economic hardship and resistance from local warlords and IRP elements. In 1998 the legislature banned all religious parties from operating in the country, a serious violation of the peace accord that forced Rakhmonov to veto the decision for fear of upsetting the fragile peace.

In 1999 a constitutional amendment referendum approved the formation of a new bicameral parliament and the extension of the presidential term of office. However, problems continued with the presidential elections in the same year as the Central

Election Commission barred three of the challengers to Rakhmonov, and then at the last moment gave the IRP candidate, Davlat Usmanov, permission to contest them. Usmanov refused to campaign under such conditions and Rakhmonov was elected with 97% of the vote of the 99% of the electorate that participated.

For the parliamentary elections in the following year six parties were formally registered to participate, including Rakhmonov's PDPT, the IRP and the CPT. The election campaign was marred by violence, kidnappings and assassinations, and international observers reported many abuses of the electoral process. The PDPT won 64.5% of the seats, the CPT 20.6% and the IRP 7.8%. These elections formally implemented the peace accord, but it did not resolve the tensions in Tajik society and elements from both sides of the civil war have remained distrustful of each other, their suspicions increased by Rakhmonov's increasingly authoritarian policies. In 2002 Rakhmonov used the country's new alliance with the USA as an excuse to expel several Islamist ministers from the government.

Violence has persisted, armed groups have *de facto* control over some parts of the country and in 2000–01 the problem of insecurity was exacerbated by the presence of guerrillas from the IMU in the **Fergana Valley**. Tajik authorities have been unable prevent IMU guerrillas from using their territory to launch attacks into Kyrgyzstan and Uzbekistan, which has damaged Tajikistan's relations with those countries. Regional governments have also expressed concern at the influence of the HT on young people in the Fergana Valley area. The Tajik authorities have begun imprisoning alleged HT members. In June 2001 there were four days of violent clashes between Tajikistan's armed forces and Islamist fighters.

After the start of US air strikes on Afghanistan, the Tajik government offered the USA use of its air space and military facilities. This has reportedly strengthened the IMU and HT. Attention by the international community, in particular by the USA in the wake of the war in Afghanistan, has brought increased economic development assistance, which could create jobs and increase stability in the long term.

International relations/Transnational issues

Uzbekistan has mined much of its undemarcated southern and eastern border with Tajikistan. Border demarcation negotiations continuing with Kyrgyzstan in respect of the Isfara Valley area. Kazakhstan, Tajikistan, Turkmenistan, Kyrgyzstan and Uzbekistan are forced to share **water** resources and attempt to contain environmental degradation that has been caused by the shrinking of the Aral Sea.

Illicit drugs

Tajikistan is a major transit country for Afghan narcotics bound for Russian and, to a lesser extent, Western European markets. There is limited illicit cultivation of **opium** poppy for domestic consumption. Tajikistan seizes roughly 80% of all **drugs** intercepted in Central Asia and stands third world-wide in terms of seizures of opiates (**heroin** and raw opium).

Tajikistan, economy

Tajikistan has the lowest per caput gross domestic product among the 15 former Soviet republics, its economy having been shattered by the civil war. The economic infrastructure was severely damaged and industrial and agricultural production plummeted. While economic recovery has begun, it has only been marginal and most of the population lives in poverty.

The formal economy is precarious and much depends on barter. Only 6% of the land is arable—cotton is the most important crop. **Mineral** resources—varied but limited in quantity—include silver, **gold**, tungsten and uranium (14% of the world's known reserves). **Industry** consists only of a large aluminium plant, but there is potential for the development of hydroelectric power. There are small factories, mainly for light industry and food processing, and carpet production. During and after the negotiations that culminated in the peace accords, the **International Monetary Fund** (IMF), the **World Bank** and other **IFIs** were willing to become involved in Tajikistan's economic recovery. In 1996 Tajikistan was offered a structural adjustment programme of US $50m., involving mass privatization and reform of the financial sector. A further loan of $40m. was granted by the IMF in 1999 in order to support Tajikistan's balance of payments and improve prospects for economic growth. In 2000 the *somenei* was introduced to replace the Tajik *rouble*. There is now little central planning. Privatization of medium and large state-owned enterprises has been pursued with rigour, and the Tajik government has managed to keep inflation under control. Tajikistan's economic situation, however, remains fragile due to the uneven implementation of structural reforms, weak governance, and the growing **debt** burden. Servicing of the debt, owed principally to Russia and Uzbekistan, could require as much as 50% of government revenues in 2002, thus limiting the country's ability to meet pressing development needs. There is an exodus of skilled labour (mainly Russians). Production in all sectors is in decline.

Tajiks

Ethnic group found in **Central Asia**, particularly in Tajikistan and Afghanistan.

Et-Takaful

Solidarity

Egyptian political party, established in 1995. It advocates the imposition of a solidarity tax on the rich in order to provide for the needs of the poor. Its chairman is Dr Usama Muhammad Shaltout.

Takfir wa-l Hijra

An international Islamist group whose name is variously translated as 'Penance and Flight' or 'Penance and Exodus'. It operates mainly in Egypt, but there are other groups with the same name and some links to groups in Jordan and Algeria.

Takfir wa-l Hijra (Jordan)

Penance and Exodus

In early 2002 riots broke out in the town of Maan, in southern Jordan, after a student was killed in police custody. The riots were apparently instigated by the banned Islamist group, Takfir wa-l Hijra, whose leader, Mohammed Ahmad ach-Chalabi, remained at large for 11 months, until November, when another outbreak of violence occurred. On this occasion demonstrations were held in protest at the killing of a US development worker, Laurence Foley, in **Amman** in October. Army units and riot police apprehended suspects in mid- November after four people, including a police sergeant, died and two dozen were injured in clashes throughout the city. The focus of the Maan operation was believed to be the Islamist group Takfir wa-l Hijra, although an official statement referred to the arrest of 'a gang of outlaws' (15 Jordanians and 10 foreigners, believed to be Iraqis and Egyptians), who were accused of smuggling arms and **drugs**, killings, assaults and robberies, challenging the government and burning female students' dormitories and vehicles belonging to university professors.

Et-Takaful

Solidarity

Egyptian political party, established in 1995. It advocates the imposition of a solidarity tax on the rich in order to provide for the needs of the poor. Its chairman is Dr Usama Muhammad Shaltout.

Talaa al-Fath – *see* Vanguards of Conquest

Talabani

A Kurdish tribal group influential mainly in the Iraqi province of Sulaimaniya, the southern, more urbanized and culturally developed part of Iraqi **Kurdistan**, historically home to many famous Kurdish intellectuals, artists, poets and politicians.

Talabani, Jalal

Member of the central committee of the **Kurdish Democratic Party** (KDP) until 1975. After the collapse of the unified Kurdish movement, Talabani founded and led the **Patriotic Union of Kurdistan** (PUK), which was then involved, for almost 25 years (with some interruptions), in a 'civil war' with the KDP. The 'war' has recently ended. The PUK controls some 25,000 fighters in the eastern part of Iraqi **Kurdistan** from Sulaimaniya.

Talal, King of Jordan

Talal ibn Abdullah succeeded his father **Abdullah**, King of Jordan, when the latter was assassinated in 1951. After a short reign, during which time he maintained an essentially anti-British policy, he was forced to abdicate on the grounds of insanity, and his son **Hussein** was crowned king when he came of age in May 1953.

Taliban Islamic Movement of Afghanistan

The term describes what originated as a political movement in the late 1980s and early 1990s and eventually became the effective government of much of Afghanistan during the second half of the 1990s. The movement took its name from the plural of the Pashto (and **Arabic**) word for student (*talib*) as it initially included many of those who had attended the numerous small religious schools and institutions (*madrasas*) established in the Afghan refugee camps in Pakistan, often with Saudi support, for those who had fled their country during the conflict between the *mujahidin* and the Soviet and Soviet-supported government troops. The Taliban ideology was a mixture of Afghan nationalism and religious fervour, and major influences on the latter were the mullahs (or religious teachers) inspired by the strict Wahhabist tradition imported from Saudi Arabia and the fundamentalist thinking of the Pakistani **Jamiat-e-Ulema-e-Islami**. The movement developed in the refugee camps and in the southern province of Kandahar in Afghanistan. It advocated an Islamic revolution in Afghanistan and drew in a combination of war veterans and younger men from predominantly humble village backgrounds.

The movement emerged as a political and **military** force in 1994 when members of the Taliban Islamic Movement of Afghanistan materialized under the leadership of a village-level religious leader, **Mullah Mohammad Omar**, who had been a commander in the local *mujahidin* near Kandahar during the war (and was blind in one eye from a war wound). The Taliban swept through Kandahar province and captured the city of **Kandahar**. Their base secure, they then attacked the Helmand Valley—a major centre of **opium** poppy production—to the west. Over a relatively short period they had gained considerable ground, incorporating many of the local *mujahidin* and their commanders as they went, often without a shot being fired. Increasingly they gained real military power as well as political and religious legitimacy. They were initially supported by the USA. The Soviet threat had been removed and a unified, peaceful Afghanistan under local government seemed a possibility. The Pakistani army and Intelligence Services—with their own links to the Taliban—also viewed them as a potent force to be supported and cultivated. The majority of the Taliban were from the south of Afghanistan and shared ethnic and other ties with many Pakistanis. The rise of the Taliban might well serve Pakistani interests.

By September 1996 the Taliban had gained control of several major cities in the west and east of the country and at the end of that month they captured **Kabul**, ousting the government and establishing themselves as the new regime. By mid-1997 they effectively controlled two-thirds of Afghanistan; only in the north was there sustained and organized opposition from the so-called **Northern Alliance** of war-lords and military leaders, many of whom were traditional enemies of the southern **Pashtuns** on whom the Taliban had built their movement. In October 1997 the Taliban changed the name of Afghanistan to the Islamic Emirate of Afghanistan and Mullah Omar, who had previously adopted a religious title (Emir of the Faithful) became head of state. Formally, a six-member Council ruled from Kabul, but ultimate authority rested with the Taliban's inner *shura* (council), located in Kandahar, and with Mullah Omar. The regime was recognized by only a few governments, and many of those states which had initially supported the Taliban as a basis for reunification and stability in Afghanistan now regarded them as reactionary and repressive. The Taliban established a very strict interpretation of the **Shari'a** and constructed a form of religious-political authoritarianism very alien to Afghanistan's own indigenous Islamic and tribal traditions. They provided a refuge for **Osama bin Laden** and his organization (**al-Qai'da**) when he was forced to leave Sudan and enabled training camps to be established. It was this willingness to support the emerging international network of radical Islamism that led to the bombing of Taliban strongholds by the USA in the aftermath of the terrorist attacks of 11 September 2001.

TAMI

TAMI (Tenuah LeMassoret Israel), or Movement for Jewish Tradition, was founded in May 1981 by Aharon Abu Hatzeira, who was Minister of Religious Affairs at the time and who split from the **National Religious Party**, accusing its leadership of 'ethnic discrimination' against Sephardic Jews.

Tanzim al-Jihad

Egyptian grouping formed after splitting from **al-Gama'a al-Islamiyya** in Egypt and then joining the somewhat dormant Jihad group in Egypt. It is barely active.

Tanzimat

In Turkish ('tän 'zemät') the word means 'reorganization'. A period of modernizing reforms instituted under the **Ottoman Empire** from 1839 until 1876. In 1839, under the rule of Sultan Abd al-Majid, the edict entitled *Hatti-i Sharif* of Gulhane laid out the fundamental principles of Tanzimat reform. Foremost among the laws was the security of honour, life, and property for all Ottoman subjects, regardless of race or religion. Other reforms, which sought to reduce theological dominance, included the lifting of monopolies, fairer taxation, secularized schools, a changed judicial system, and new rules regarding military service. Tanzimat was ended in 1876 under Abd al-Hamid II's reign, when the ideas for a Turkish constitution and parliament promoted by the vizier Midhant Pasha were rejected by the sultan.

Taqlid

In **Arabic:** the word means 'repetition', 'imitation'. The debate regarding *taqlid* and *ijtihad* is central in **Islam**'s relationship to the (modern) West. Should one imitate (*taqlid*) the West or should there be an Islamic renewal based on interpretation and reasoning (*ijtihad*)?

Tashkent

The capital of Uzbekistan. For centuries it was an important point on the trade route (the Silk Road) from Asia to Europe.

Tatars

Ethnic group of **Central Asia**.

Tawheed Islami

The Islamic Unification Movement. A **Sunni** Muslim Lebanese political organization, established in 1982.

Ould Taya, Col Maaouiya Ould Sidi Ahmed

Head of state of Mauritania from December 1984, when he overthrew his predecessor, Lt-Col **Mohamed Khouna Ould Haidalla**, until the present. He was elected as President in the first multi-party elections in Mauritania in January 1992.

Ibn Taymiyah Mosque

Mosque in **Baghdad** used by **Sunni** Muslims.

Tehran

Capital of Iran, with more than 7m. inhabitants. A major industrial and commercial centre in the north of the country.

Tehiya (Renaissance) Party

Tehiya is a party of 'true believers' focusing on the Land of Israel (**Eretz Israel**), with a religious fervour reminiscent of the early years of independence and before. It is composed of both religious and secular elements and appeals strongly to Israeli youth. It has a component from **Gush Emunim** (Bloc of the Faithful). Tehiya used to include old associates of **Menachem Begin** from the anti-British undergound, and in July 1982 it joined the ruling **Likud** coalition under Begin.

Tel-Aviv

Capital of Israel. Port and major commercial centre.

Telem

Telem was **Moshe Dayan**'s party for the 1981 Israeli elections. Dayan died in October 1980, but the party won two seats in the **Knesset**. Those two members joined the **Likud** and Telem was dissolved.

Tenuat HaHerut (Israel)

The Freedom Movement. Descended from the Revisionist Movement of **Vladimir Jabotinsky**, 1880–1940), who settled in Palestine after the First World War and is regarded by many as the leading Zionist figure, after **Theodor Herzl**, **Zionism**'s founder. Revisionism called for the creation of a Jewish state in 'Greater Israel' (all of Palestine and Jordan), the formation of a free-enterprise economy, rapid indus-trialization, an increase in employment opportunities, a ban on strikes and a strong army. The Revisionists formed the New Zionist Organization in 1935. Their rejection of the socialist and liberal Zionist leadership led them to form two paramilitary groups, **Irgun Zvai Leumi** (Etzel), founded in 1937, and the even more radical **Stern Gang** (Lechi), founded in 1939–40. Betar, the Revisionist youth movement founded by Jabotinsky in 1920, continues as the Herut youth wing today. (See also **Herut**.)

Terrorism

Terrorism could be said to involve 'the use of violence against specific or non-specific targets to create terror in order to induce a change of policy'. Like war, it is an 'extension of politics by other means'. There is a long history of the use of terror as a political tool in the region, starting during the colonial period—when it was used both by the nationalists and by the colonial regimes—and continuing until the present. Some would make a distinction between the terrorism of specific political groups, usually underground and illegal, that is used to change the policies of governments, and 'state terrorism', which is used to quell opposition and to suppress such groups. The current 'war against terrorism', declared by US President **George W. Bush**, following the attacks on Washington, DC, and New York by members of **al-Qa'ida**, is directed mainly against Islamist groups but is, in effect, an internationally orchestrated effort to suppress a wide range of groups across the world, identified as 'terrorist'.

Ath-Thani dynasty

Ruling dynasty of Qatar. **Ahmad ibn Ali (ath-Thani)** was supplanted in 1972 by his cousin (and Prime Minister) **Khalifa ibn Hamad (ath-Thani)**, who in 1977 appointed his son, **Hamad ibn Khalifa ath-Thani**, as crown prince.

Ath-Thani, Ahmad ibn Ali

Emir of Qatar from 1971 until 1972, when he was ousted by his cousin, **Khalifa ibn Hamad ath-Thani**.

Ath-Thani, Hamad ibn Khalifa ath-Thani

Emir of Qatar since June 1995.

Ath-Thani, Khalifa ibn Hamad ath-Thani

Emir of Qatar from 1972 until June 1995. He was succeeded by his son, **Hamad ibn Khalifa ath-Thani**, in 1995.

Third International Theory

Libyan leader Col **Qaddafi**'s political system as outlined in his two-volume *Green Book*.

The Third Way

Israeli political party. Formed in 1995. It is opposed to the return of the **Golan Heights** to Syria. The Third Way is led by Avigdor Kalahani.

Third World Relief Agency (TWRA)

Sudan-based, supposedly humanitarian organization that has been used as an intermediary between suppliers and fighters in Bosnia as part of the so-called **Croatian Pipeline**. TWRA had links with leading Islamists, such as Sheikh **Omar Abdul ar-Rahman** (the 'Blind Sheikh') involved in the first **World Trade Center** bombing, and **Osama bin Laden**.

Tigris

In **Arabic**: 'Dijla'. The eastern member of the pair of great rivers—the other is the **Euphrates**—that define **Mesopotamia**. The river then merges with the Euphrates in southern Iraq to form the **Shatt al-Arab**, which in turn flows into the **Persian (Arabian) Gulf**.

Tikrit

Iraqi town some 145 km north of **Baghdad** and 80 km south-west of **Kirkuk**. The birthplace of **Saddam Hussain** and home of many of his relatives—the Takriti clan. Tikrit was at the centre of an area which was remained particularly loyal to Saddam Hussain in the aftermath of the **Gulf War (2003)**, despite a statement by the new mayor of Tikrit, Wail al-Ali (a former member of the **Ba'ath Party** who resigned in 1976 but was able to carry on his career in the foreign ministry and later in the Ministry of Education), after his election by a group of 25 local leaders, that 'anyone who thinks Saddam Hussain is coming back is stupid'.

Tiqva

Hope

Israeli political party, formed in 1999. Campaigns for rights for new immigrants, particularly those from the former Soviet Union.

TISA – *see* Afghanistan, Transitional Islamic State of

Tourism

Tourism has become a major source of foreign exchange earnings for many countries in the region. Turkey has the largest overall tourist receipts of any country in the region—in 2001 they totalled some US \$5,500m. It also had the largest number of tourist arrivals (9.6m.). Saudi Arabia had the next largest number (6.3m.), followed by Egypt (5.7m.), Tunisia (5.1m.), Morocco (4.2m.) and the United Arab Emirates (3.9m.).

Trade

Despite the existence of several multilateral trading arrangements, including those governed by the **Arab Maghreb Union** and the **Gulf Co-operation Council**, etc., the volume of trade that takes place within the **Middle East** is relatively small. Most trade is with partners outside the region. In terms of integration into regional trading blocs, few economies in the region rank high in global terms. Jordan ranks highest (28th in the world), but Turkey and Israel are the only others that rank in the top 40 in the world (32nd and 40th respectively). Saudi Arabia is the largest trading economy in the Middle East. Turkey, Israel and the United Arab Emirates are also significant trading economies in terms of volume and value. Syria is one of the three most trade-dependent economies in the world, with trade accounting for 106% of the country's gross domestic product (GDP). The UAE, where trade accounts for 63% of GDP, and Bahrain, where it accounts for 60.5%, are also highly trade-dependent.

Transitional Administrative Law (Iraq)

The 25-page, 62-article document which sets out Iraq's interim Constitution. Hailed as one of the most liberal constitutions anywhere in the region, the interim Constitution was finally adopted in early March 2004 by the **Iraqi Provisional Governing Council**. Many disagreements remain between representatives of the different communities in Iraq with regard to issues covered by the document and issues that are not—including the extent and powers of the federal regions and the status of disputed territories, such as **Kirkuk**.

Transitional Islamic State of Afghanistan (TISA) – *see* Afghanistan, Transitional Islamic State of

Transjordan

In April 1921 Great Britain detached from the **Mandate for Palestine**, entrusted to it by the League of Nations, the territory to the east of the Jordan river, in order to construct the Emirate of Transjordan. At its head, in 1923, they placed **Abdullah**, brother of **Faisal** and, like him, a son of the **Hashemite** Sherif Hussein. Corresponding geographically to today's Kingdom of Jordan, Transjordan was an autonomous political subdivision of the **Middle East** carved out of the former **Ottoman Empire** after the First World War. The frontier of this new territory was recognized in 1927 by **Ibn Saud** and its constitution and a treaty sanctioning its British character were adopted in 1928. The Emirate obtained formal independence in 1946. It existed for three years thereafter. In 1950 King Abdullah annexed **Jerusalem** and the **West Bank** and renamed the Emirate the Hashemite Kingdom of Jordan. Previously a part of the territory covered by the planned League of Nations Mandate for Palestine, Transjordan was created as a separate administrative entity on 11 April 1921, in order to provide a throne of sorts (albeit one under British control) for the Hashemite **Emir** Abdullah, the elder son of Britain's war-time Arab ally Sherif Hussein of **Mecca**. The move also excluded the land east of the Jordan from Britain's war-time undertaking in the **Balfour Declaration** (2 November 1917) to support the creation in Palestine of a Jewish national home. Britain recognized Transjordan as a state on 15 May 1923. On 25 May 1946 the parliament of Transjordan proclaimed the Emir king, establishing the independent Hashemite Kingdom of Transjordan, later the Hashemite Kingdom of Jordan.

Transport

The volume of goods and persons moving both within a country and internationally provides an indication of the dynamism of an economy and society. Good transport networks are increasingly crucial. Throughout the 20th century traffic through the **Suez Canal** has been a major source of revenue to Egypt. Increasingly, international air traffic from 'West' to 'East' and vice versa passes through the **Gulf**, which has become an important regional hub for the movement of freight and passengers. Both Saudi Arabia and the United Arab Emirates figure significantly in the statistics on passenger km per year; but no other countries within the region do so. The busiest airports continue to be in North America, Western Europe and South-East Asia. Air transport and air travel within the region remains limited. Several countries (Turkey, Iran, Saudi Arabia and Algeria) have substantial road networks, but mainly as a function of their large geographical area and long distances between centres, rather than as an indicator of heavy traffic. The same may apply in the case of railways: Kazakhstan, which has the longest railway network in the region (followed by Turkey, Iran and Egypt) also ranks fourth in the world for the number of km travelled by rail passengers, while Egypt ranks 16th. On the other hand, a good deal of freight travels on Kazakhstan's railways, which carry the seventh largest volume of freight in world terms annually. Bahrain has one of the densest road networks (ranking third in the world in this respect, with 5.2 km of road per sq km of land area); only Israel (ranked 38th with 0.8 km of road per sq km of land area) also figures in the world top 40. Lebanon has the highest rate of car ownership in the world, and, not surprisingly therefore, the most crowded roads in the region are in Lebanon, which ranks fourth in the world in terms of vehicles per km of road network—191. Kuwait, Qatar, Israel and Bahrain all have more than 60 vehicles per km of road network and Jordan and Tunisia more than 40. Israel has one of the most used road networks, ranking fifth in the world in terms of vehicle km per km of road network, with Bahrain and Tunisia not far behind.

Treaty of Friendship and Co-operation

Treaty signed in April 1972 between Iraq and the Soviet Union. It was supplemented in 1978 by a further agreement between the two countries. By these agreements Iraq received arms and technical assistance in return for allowing the Iraqi Communist Party to participate in a National Front.

Treaty of London

The Treaty of London, signed in 1915 by Britain, Russia, France and Italy, made concessions to Italy as the price for entering the First World War on the Allied side. Libya was formally transferred to Italy from the Ottoman Sultan, the Dodecanese Islands off the Turkish coast, occupied by Italy since 1912, were recognized as Italian possessions and the Italian interest in the eastern **Mediterranean** was to be confirmed after the war by a zone of influence along the southern coast in the Antalya area.

Tribe(s)

Many of the countries in the region (e.g. Afghanistan and Iran) include significant ethnic and linguistic **minorities**, often still organized to some extent along tribal lines. Others (e.g. Jordan, Saudi Arabia and Libya) include rural **Arabic**-speaking groups (**Bedouin** or *beduin*) that are still to some extent attached to their historical tribal, social and political structures and way of life. The Arabic term (*qabil,* plural *qabayl*) is often used to refer to these groups and populations. In the **Maghreb** ethnic and linguistic minorities speaking different variants of Tamasheq/Tamazight are referred to widely as **Berbers**, the best known of which are the Kabyles of central-eastern Algeria. Tribal groups normally define their affiliation in terms of a common ancestor from whom they trace their descent, and more broadly in terms of common kinship; they may or may not share a common leader, overlord or sheikh. Some tribal groups might more properly be referred to as a people or even a nation.

Tripoli

Capital of Libya. Port and major commercial centre.

Trucial states

The Trucial States were the British colonies Abu Dhabi (the largest), Dubai, Sharjah, Ajman, Fujairah, Ras al-Khaimah and Umm al-Qaiwain that joined to form the United Arab Emirates.

True Path Party

Right-wing Turkish political party led by **Süleyman Demirel** after 1987, when Turkey's ban on pre-1980s politicians was lifted.

Tsomet/Tzomet

Crossroads

A Zionist revivalist right-wing grouping in Israeli politics, formed in 1988 as a breakaway group from the **Tehiya Party**. It is led by Rafael Eitan.

Tudeh Party—The Party of the Masses

Hezb-e Tudeh

The Communist Party of Iran. Established in 1941, the Tudeh Party is one of the oldest existing communist parties in the **Middle East**. Dr Arani, who died in prison for his Marxist beliefs, is regarded as its founder, although it was in fact founded by his followers after their release from jail. The Party was strongest in the northern areas under Soviet occupation between 1941 and 1946, particularly in Azerbaijan and the Caspian provinces of Mazandaran and Gilan. From the mid-1940s onwards the pro-Soviet faction tended to dominate the more independent wing of the Party. The Party also had support in industrial and **oil**-producing towns in the south. In the elections for the 14th parliament (1944–46), the Party won eight out of 136 seats.

Three Tudeh Party members were briefly in the Cabinet of 1946. The Party declined after 1946 and was banned in 1949, when an assassination attempt on the Shah was blamed on one of its members. It operated freely during the **Mussadegh** period (1951–53) and the Western powers feared that Mussadegh was influenced by its strongly pro-Soviet inclinations. The Party did little to prevent the return of the Shah in August 1953. It was heavily repressed by him and its leaders fled to eastern Europe and the Soviet Union. It established a radio station, Iran Courier (Peik-e Iran), which began broadcasting from Baku in 1959 and then, in the 1960s, was transferred to Sofia, Bulgaria. It experienced a revival in the early 1960s during a more liberal period, but failed to mobilize significant support until the development of the widespread movement that led to the overthrow of the Shah in the late 1970s, when it enjoyed a rebirth, coming into the open after many decades. The long-time secretary-general, Iraj Eskandari, was replaced in January 1979 by his deputy, Nureddin Kianuri, under whom the Tudeh Party called for a United Front of all parties opposed to the Shah's regime, thereby in effect supporting Ayatollah **Khomeini**. This initiative was spurned by Khomeini, and by Karim Sanjabi, leader of the National Front. Its failure to provide a clear alternative to the leadership of the clerics and the **Islamic Republic(an) Party** (IRP) discredited the Tudeh Party in the eyes of many on the left. Its existence under the new Islamic regime was at first tolerated, although it was kept out of mainstream politics. Its membership was periodically purged during the first three years of the new regime, and in May 1983, although it was a faithful supporter of the IRP, the Tudeh Party was finally banned. During the 1980s an 'unaffiliated' radio station, the National Voice of Iran, which supported the Tudeh Party and Soviet objectives in Iran, and criticized the harassment of communists within Iran as well as the policies of the Iranian government more generally at home and abroad, began to broadcast in Persian and Azeri from Baku once again. Inside Iran the leadership was imprisoned, in some instances for many years. The first secretary of the central committee is Ali Khavari.

The Tunb Islands

The United Arab Emirates (UAE) currently seeks **Arab League** and other international support for its opposition to Iran's occupation of the Tunb Islands—greater Tunb Island (called Tunb al-Kubra in **Arabic** by the UAE and Jazireh-ye Tonb-e Bozorg in **Persian** by Iran) and Lesser Tunb Island (called Tunb as-Sughra in Arabic by the UAE and Jazireh-ye Tonb-e Kuchek in Persian by Iran)—and its attempts to occupy a jointly administered island in the **Persian (Arabian) Gulf** (called **Abu Musa** in Arabic by the UAE and Jazireh-ye Abu Musa in Persian by Iran).

Tunis

Capital of Tunisia. Port and major industrial and commercial centre on the **Mediterranean** coast.

Tunisia, Republic of

Al Jumhuriyah at-Tunisiyah

Tunisia is situated in North Africa, bordering the **Mediterranean** Sea, between Algeria and Libya. The capital is **Tunis** and, for administrative purposes, the country is divided into 23 governorates: Ariana (Aryanah), Beja (Bajah), Ben Arous (Bin 'Arus), Bizerte (Banzart), El-Kef (Al-Kaf), Gabes (Qabis), Gafsa (Qafsah), Jendouba (Jundubah), Kairouan (Al-Qayrawan), Kasserine (Al-Qasrayn), Kebili (Qibili), Mahdia (Al-Mahdiyah), Medenine (Madanin), Monastir (Al-Munastir), Nabeul (Nabul), Sfax (Safaqis), Sidi Bou Zid (Sidi Bu Zayd), Siliana (Silyanah), Sousse (Susah), Tataouine (Tatawin), Tozeur (Tawzar), Tunis and Zaghouan (Zaghwan). At July 2002 the population was estimated at 9,815,644, of which Arabs and **Berbers** together comprised 98%, Europeans 1% and Jews and 'others' a further 1%. The state religion is **Islam**. Ninety-eight per cent of the population are Muslims and 1% Christians. Jews and 'others' account for the remaining 1%. **Arabic** and French are the two official languages.

Political profile

The Constitution of the Republic of Tunisia was promulgated on 1 June 1959 and amended on 12 July 1988. Both the National Assembly and the President of the Republic are elected every five years by universal suffrage. Every citizen who has had Tunisian nationality for at least five years and who has attained 20 years of age has the right to vote. The head of state and President of the Republic is **Zine al-Abidine Ben Ali** (took office on 7 November 1987; re-elected 2 April 1989, 20 March 1994 and 24 October 1999). The head of government and Prime Minister is Muhammad Ghannouchi. The Council of Ministers is appointed by the President. The legislative branch is the unicameral Chamber of Deputies or **Majlis** an-Nuwaab (182 seats). The most recent legislative elections, in which the Rassemblement constitutionnel démocratique (RCD) received 92% of the vote, were held on 24 October 1999. In the resulting Majlis the RCD occupied 148 seats, the Movement of Democratic Socialists (MDS) 13, the Union démocratique unioniste (UDU) seven, the Parti de l'unité populaire (PUP) seven, At-Tajdid five and the Parti social libéral (PSL) two. Reforms enabled opposition parties to win up to 20% of the total number of seats, and the number they occupied rose, accordingly, from 19 to 34. The next legislative elections are scheduled to be held in 2004. The legal system is based on the French civil law system and **Islamic Law**. There is some judicial review of legislative acts in the Supreme Court in joint session. There is also a Court of Cassation (Cour de Cassation).

Tunisia became a multi-party **democracy** in 1988. In order to gain legal recognition, political parties must uphold the aims of and work within the Constitution, and are not permitted to pursue purely religious, racial, regional or linguistic objectives. Political parties can only be formed with the approval of the Minister of the Interior.

Political organizations include: At-Tajdid/Ettajdid Movement (Renewal), Leader Adel Chaouch; the RCD (the official ruling party), Leader President Zine al-Abidine Ben Ali; ; the PSL, Leader Mounir Beji; the MDS, Leader Khamis Chammari; the PUP, Leader Muhammed Bouchiha; the UDU, Leader Abderrahmane Tlili; and the Parti démocratique progressiste, Leader Nejib Chebbi. Illegal parties include **An-Nahda** (Parti de la renaissance—Renaissance Party); the Parti des ouvriers communistes tunisiens, Leader Hamma Hammani; and the Rassemblement national arabe, Leader Bashir Assad.

Media

Reforms since the late 1980s have in theory increased press freedom in Tunisia. However, in practice government restrictions remain and today press freedom is almost non-existent. Several newspapers are owned by the ruling RCD, and the single radio-station and all television channels are state-controlled. While there are several privately owned and independently managed newspapers, they are under close scrutiny by the regime and are often censored or in some cases even barred from publication. The government's 'no-go areas' for the media are **corruption** and human-rights issues (including any discussion of banned Islamic movements). The foreign press is also occasionally banned, but the arrival of satellite television broadcasts from Europe has enabled Tunisians to receive a wide range of programmes. Qatar-based **al-Jazeera** and Dubai Television attract viewers for their news coverage. Recently the Tunisian government commenced heavy censorship of the internet. Newspapers include *Al-Amal* (Action), organ of the RCD; *La Presse de Tunisie*; *Le Renouveau*, organ of the RCD; and *As-Sabah*. In 2002 there was one internet service provider and 400,000 internet users.

History

In the 19th century the heavy debts that the *beys* had contracted provided the European powers with a pretext for intervention in Tunisia. France, Great Britain, and Italy took control of Tunisia's finances in 1869. In 1881 France dispatched 30,000 troops to Tunisia on the pretext of countering border raids into French-occupied Algeria. They quickly occupied Tunis and forced the ruling *bey* to sign over his power to France, through the treaties of Bardo (1881) and Mersa (1883), which provided for the discreet transformation of Tunisia into a protectorate under a French resident general.

A nationalist movement developed relatively quickly in Tunisia. In 1920 the **Destour Party** (Constitutional Party) was organized. In 1934 a more radical faction, led by **Habib Bourguiba**, formed the **Neo-Destour Party**. During the Second World War Tunisia came under Vichy rule after the fall of France (June 1940), and Tunisian nationalists took advantage of this to intensify their campaign for independence. After the war nationalist agitation intensified further, and Bourguiba set about bringing Tunisia's position to international attention. By the early 1950s France was ready to make concessions and granted Tunisia a large degree of autonomy. The French settler (*colon*) population, however, opposed further reforms and negotiations quickly broke down. Bourguiba was arrested in 1952 and his subsequent imprisonment precipitated a wave of civil unrest and violence.

In 1954 Bourguiba was released in order to negotiate the agreement that led, in 1955, to Tunisian internal self-government and, in 1956, to full independence. Habib Bourguiba became Prime Minister. The country became a republic in 1957 when the *bey*, Sidi Lamine, was deposed by a vote of the constituent assembly, which then made Bourguiba President. He instituted sweeping political and social changes. He established Tunisia as a strict one-party state and implemented rights for **women** that were unmatched by any other Arab nation. Regarding **Islam** as a force that was holding the country back, Bourguiba set about reducing its role in society by removing religious leaders from their traditional areas of influence, especially in areas such as **education** and law. The **Shari'a** courts were also abolished, and lands that had financed mosques and religious institutions were confiscated.

Bourguiba followed a generally pro-Western foreign policy, but relations with France were strained over Algerian independence, which Tunisia supported, and the evacuation of French troops from Tunisia. The French naval installations at Bizerte were the scene of violent confrontation in 1961; France finally agreed to evacuate them in 1963. Relations between Tunisia and Algeria deteriorated after the latter gained its independence from France in 1962, and border disputes between the two countries were not settled until 1970. Bourguiba's support for a negotiated settlement with Israel in the **Arab–Israeli Conflict** caused strains in its relations with other Arab countries. Domestically, Bourguiba's policies emphasized modernization and planned economic growth. An agrarian reform plan, involving the formation of co-operatives, was begun in 1962, but it was halted in 1969 owing to harsh implementation and corruption. In the 1970s there was increasing conflict within the ruling Destour Party between liberals and conservatives, as well as public demonstrations ('**bread riots**') against the government. In 1981 Bourguiba authorized the legal formation of opposition political parties, indicating a possible shift in the direction of **democracy**, and multi-party legislative elections were held for the first time in 1981. By 1986 six opposition parties had legal status. None the less the 1980s were largely characterized by popular unrest and labour difficulties, as well as by the search for a successor to the aged Bourguiba.

In 1987 Bourguiba was ousted by Gen. Zine al-Abidine Ben Ali, who had served as Minister for the Interior. Ben Ali quickly moved to appease the Islamic opposition, making a pilgrimage to **Mecca** and ordering that the **Ramadan** fast be observed. Since he took power the domination of the government by the RCD has held fast. The new regime restored diplomatic relations with Libya and signed a treaty of economic co-operation with Libya, Algeria, Mauritania and Morocco. Ben Ali initially moved towards liberal reforms, but after elections in 1989 in which Islamic activists performed strongly, he instituted repressive measures against them. During the 1994 election campaign the government arrested political dissidents and barred the Islamic party An-Nahda from participating. Running uncontested and endorsed by all of the legal opposition parties, Ben Ali received almost 100% of the vote. In 1999 Ben Ali was again re-elected, once more with almost 100% of the vote, although on this occasion he had faced a token challenge from two opposition candidates. Bourguiba's death in April 2000 inspired widespread and open dissent against Ben Ali's regime, and there are continuing signs of unrest.

International relations

Tunisia is attempting to strengthen its contacts with the West, relations with which have generally been good owing to Tunisia's liberal economic and social policies and its suppression of **Islamic fundamentalism**. Tunisia was host to the **Palestine Liberation Organization** after it was expelled from Lebanon. Relations with other Arab states, particularly those with Kuwait and Saudi Arabia, deteriorated as a result of Tunisia's support for Iraq during the **Gulf War (1991)**. The government regards the political impact of Islamic fundamentalism (in the form of the **Groupe islamique armé**) in neighbouring Algeria with concern. Relations with Libya are improving, not least owing to the fact that the government ignores the activities on its territory of those seeking to circumvent sanctions in force against Libya.

Tunisia, economy

Tunisia has a diverse economy, with important agricultural, mining, **energy**, **tourism**, and manufacturing sectors. Governmental control of economic affairs, while still substantial, has gradually lessened over the past decade with increasing privatization, simplification of the tax structure, and a prudent approach to **debt**. Real growth averaged 5.4% in the past five years, and inflation is slowing. Growth in tourism and increased **trade** have been key elements in this steady growth, although tourism revenues have slowed since 11 September 2001 and may take another year or longer to fully recover. Tunisia's association agreement with the **European Union** (EU) entered into force on 1 March 1998, the first such accord between the EU and a **Mediterranean** country. Under the agreement Tunisia will gradually remove barriers to trade with the EU over the next decade. Broader privatization, further liberalization of the investment code to increase foreign investment, and improvements in government efficiency are among the challenges for the future. Tunisia was ranked as the most competitive African economy in the World Economic Forum's 2000–2001 report.

Strengths

Well-diversified economy despite limited resources. Tourism. **Oil** and **gas** exports, also agricultural exports: olive oil, olives, fruits, in particular citrus fruits, dates. Expanding manufacturing sector, whose output increased by an annual average of 5.4% in 1990–98; important sectors are textiles, construction materials, machinery and chemicals. European investment.

Weaknesses

Dependence on drought-prone agricultural sector. Growing domestic energy demand on oil and gas resources. Trade deficit, fluctuating tourism. Low social provisions (performs poorly with regard to **literacy**, etc.).

Tunisian Combatant Group (TCG)

Also referred to as the Tunisian Islamic Fighting Group, the TCG's goals reportedly include establishing an **Islamic government** in Tunisia and targeting Tunisian and Western interests. Founded probably in 2000 by Tarek Maaroufi and Saifallah Ben Hassine, the group has come to be associated with **al-Qa'ida** and other North African Islamic extremists in Europe who have been implicated in anti-US terrorist plots there during 2001. In December the Belgian authorities arrested Maaroufi and charged him with providing stolen passports and fraudulent visas for those involved in the assassination of Ahmed Shah Massood, according to press reports. Tunisians associated with the TCG are part of the support network of the international Salafist movement. According to the Italian authorities, TCG members engage in false document trafficking and recruitment for Afghan training camps. Some TCG associates are suspected of planning an attack against US, Algerian, and Tunisian diplomatic interests in Rome, Italy, in January. Members reportedly maintain ties to the Algerian **Groupe salafiste pour la prédication et le combat.**

Tunisians, The

A term referring, usually disparagingly, to the leadership of the **Palestine Liberation Organization.**

Turkey, Republic of

Turkiye Cumhuriyeti

Located in south-eastern Europe and south-western Asia, bordering the Black Sea, between Bulgaria and Georgia, and bordering the Aegean Sea and the **Mediterranean** Sea, between Greece and Syria. Turkey also has borders with Iraq, Iran, Armenia and Azerbaijan. The country is in a strategic location controlling the Turkish Straits (Bosporus, Sea of Marmara, Dardanelles) that link the Black and Aegean Seas. It has a total area of 780,580 sq km, of which 9,820 sq km is **water**. The capital is **Ankara**. For administrative purposes Turkey is divided into 81 provinces (*il*, plural *iller*): Adana, Adiyaman, Afyon, Agri, Aksaray, Amasya, Ankara, Antalya, Ardahan, Artvin, Aydin, Balikesir, Bartin, Batman, Bayburt, Bilecik, Bingol, Bitlis, Bolu, Burdur, Bursa, Canakkale, Cankiri, Corum, Denizli, Diyarbakir, Duzce, Edirne, Elazig, Erzincan, Erzurum, Eskisehir, Gaziantep, Giresun, Gumushane, Hakkari, Hatay, Icel, Igdir, Isparta, Istanbul, Izmir, Kahramanmaras, Karabuk, Karaman, Kars, Kastamonu, Kayseri, Kilis, Kirikkale,

Kirklareli, Kirsehir, Kocaeli, Konya, Kutahya, Malatya, Manisa, Mardin, Mugla, Mus, Nevsehir, Nigde, Ordu, Osmaniye, Rize, Sakarya, Samsun, Sanliurfa, Siirt, Sinop, Sirnak, Sivas, Tekirdag, Tokat, Trabzon, Tunceli, Usak, Van, Yalova, Yozgat and Zonguldak. At July 2002 the population was estimated at 67,308,928, of which 70% was Turkish, 20% Kurdish, 2% Arab and 8% 'others'. Muslims (mostly **Sunni**) account for 99% of the population, 'others' (mainly Christians and Jews) for the remaining 1%. Turkish is the official language. Other languages in use are Kurdish, **Arabic**, Armenian and Greek.

Political profile

Turkey is a republican parliamentary **democracy**. Since 16 May 2000 the head of state has been President Ahmet Necdet Sezer. Since 14 March 2003 the head of government has been Prime Minister **Recep Tayyip Erdoğan**. After Abdullah Gul resigned on 11 March 2003 Erdoğan received a mandate to form a government. The Council of Ministers is appointed by the President after having been nominated by the Prime Minister. The President is elected by the National Assembly for a seven-year term of office. The most recent presidential election was held on 5 May 2000, and the next is scheduled to be held in May 2007. The Prime Minister and Deputy Prime Ministers are appointed by the President. There is a National Security Council that serves as an advisory body to the President and the Council of Ministers. The legislature is formed by the unicameral, 550-seat Grand National Assembly (Büyük Millet Meclisi). Its members are elected by popular vote to serve five-year terms of office. The most recent legislative elections were held on 3 November 2002, and the next are scheduled to be held in 2007. There is a Constitutional Court whose judges are appointed by the President; and a Court of Appeal whose judges are elected by the Supreme Council of Judges and Prosecutors. The legal system is derived from various European continental legal systems. Turkey accepts compulsory International Court of Justice jurisdiction, with reservations.

Political Parties and Groups

- Democratik Sol Partisi (Democratic Left Party), Leader Bülent Ecevit
- AK Partisi (**Justice and Development Party**), Leader Recep Tayyip Erdoğan
- Anavatan Partisi (**Motherland Party**), Leader Mesut Yilmaz
- Milliyetçi Hareket Partisi (Nationalist Action Party), Leader Devlet Bahçeli
- Cumhuriyet Halk Partisi (Republican People's Party), Leader Deniz Baykal
- Saadet Partisi (Contentment Party), Leader Recai Kutan (Kutan was formerly leader of the Fazilet (Virtue) Party, which was banned by Turkey's Constitutional Court in June 2001)
- Socialist Democratic Party, Leader Sema Piskinsut
- Doğru Yol Partisi (**True Path Party**), Leader Tansu Çiller

Other organizations and associations

Confederation of Revolutionary Workers Unions, Leader Ridvan Budak; Independent Industrialists' and Businessmen's Association, Leader Erol Yarar; Moral Rights Workers' Union, Leader Salim Uslu; Turkish Industrialists' and Businessmen's Association, Leader Muharrem Kayhan; Turkish Confederation of Employers' Unions, Leader Refik Baydur; Turkish Confederation of Labour, Leader Bayram Meral; Turkish Union of Chambers of Commerce and Commodity Exchanges, Leader Fuat Miras.

Media

The Turkish press is diverse and largely privately owned. Reporting on the Kurdish issue may be subject to censorship. Media in the Kurdish language are banned. A large number of critical and independent journalists have been imprisoned. State control over internet content has been increased since 2001. Cable and satellite television are easily available. There are approximately 60 daily newspapers. Those with the widest circulations are *Cumhuriyet* and *Hurriyet*. There is one state-controlled television service with five national channels. There is one state-controlled national radio service and more than 50 local stations. In 2001 there were 50 internet service providers. In 2002 there were 2.5m. internet users.

History

Turkey was created in 1923 from the Turkish remnants of the **Ottoman Empire**. Soon thereafter the country instituted secular laws to replace traditional religious fiats. In 1945 Turkey joined the UN, and in 1952 it became a member of the North Atlantic Treaty Organization. Turkey occupied the northern portion of Cyprus in 1974 to prevent a Greek takeover of the island; relations between Turkey and Greece remain strained, but have begun to improve over the past three years. In 1984 the **Kurdish Workers' Party** (PKK), a Marxist-Leninist, separatist group, initiated an insurgency in south-east Turkey, often using terrorist tactics to try to attain its goal of an independent **Kurdistan**. The PKK—whose leader, **Abdullah Öcalan**, was captured in Kenya in February 1999—has observed a unilateral cease-fire since September 1999, although there have been occasional clashes between Turkish military units and some of the 4,000–5,000 armed PKK militants, most of whom are currently encamped in northern Iraq. The PKK changed its name to the Kurdistan Freedom and Democracy Congress (**KADEK**) in April 2002.

International relations/Transnational issues

Maritime, air, and territorial disputes exist with Greece with regard to the Aegean Sea and Cyprus. There are disputes with downstream riparian states (Syria and Iraq) over **water** development plans for the **Tigris** and **Euphrates** rivers. Syria claims Hatay province. The border with Armenia remains closed over the Nagorno–Karabakh dispute.

Turkey is a key transit route for south-west Asian **heroin** to Western Europe and, to a far lesser extent, the USA, via air, land, and sea routes. Major Turkish, Iranian, and other international **drugs**-trafficking organizations operate out of **Istanbul**. There are laboratories to convert imported morphine base into heroin in remote regions of Turkey as well as near Istanbul. The government maintains strict controls over areas of legal **opium** poppy cultivation and output of poppy straw concentrate.

Turkey, economy

After Saudi Arabia, Turkey is the largest economy in the **Middle East** with a gross national product (GNP) of US $147,700m., the 28th largest in the world. Turkey's economy is a complex mix of modern **industry** and commerce, together with a traditional agricultural sector that in 2001 still accounted for 40% of employment. It has a strong and rapidly growing private sector, yet the state still plays a major role in basic industry, banking, **transport**, and communications. The most important industry—and largest exporting sector—is textiles and clothing, which is almost entirely in private hands. In recent years the economic situation has been marked by erratic economic growth and serious imbalances. Real GNP growth has exceeded 6% in many years, but this strong expansion was interrupted by sharp declines in output in 1994, 1999 and 2001. Meanwhile the public-sector fiscal deficit has regularly exceeded 10% of gross domestic product, due in large part to the huge burden of interest payments, which in 2001 accounted for more than 50% of central government spending, while inflation has remained in the high double-digit range. Perhaps because of these problems, foreign direct investment in Turkey remains low—less than $1,000m. annually. In late 2000 and early 2001 a growing **trade** deficit and serious weaknesses in the banking sector plunged the economy into crisis, forcing the government to float the lira and pushing the country into recession. Results in 2002 were much better owing to strong financial support from the **International Monetary Fund** and tighter fiscal policy. Continued slow global growth and serious political tensions in the Middle East cast a shadow over growth prospects for 2003.

Strengths
Liberalization contributed to strong growth in the 1990s. The textiles, manufacturing and construction sectors are highly competitive. There is a strong **tourism** sector. Turkey is self-sufficient in **agriculture**. There is a skilled labour force. Turkey has been in a customs union with the **European Union** since 1995.

Weaknesses
There is persistent high inflation, due to liberalization. The banking sector underperforms. Organized crime is influential. Military budgets are high. There is political instability.

Turkish Hezbollah

Turkish Hezbollah is a Kurdish Islamic (**Sunni**) extremist organization that arose in the late 1980s in the Diyarbakir area in response to atrocities committed by the **Kurdish Workers' Party** (PKK) against Muslims in south-eastern Turkey, where (Turkish) Hezbollah is seeking to establish an independent **Islamic state**. The group comprises loosely organized factions, the largest of which are Ilim, which advocates the use of violence to achieve its goals, and Menzil, which supports a political approach. From the mid-1990s Turkish Hezbollah, which is unrelated to Lebanese Hezbollah, expanded its target base and *modus operandi* beyond the mere killing of PKK militants to include bomb attacks on liquor stores, brothels and other establishments that the organization considered 'anti-Islamic'. In January 2000 Turkish security forces killed Huseyin Velioglu, the leader of the Ilim faction, in a shoot-out at a safe house in **Istanbul**. The incident sparked a year-long series of operations against the group throughout Turkey that resulted in the detention of some 2,000 individuals, several hundred of whom were arrested on criminal charges. At the same time, the police recovered nearly 70 bodies of Turkish and Kurdish businessmen and journalists who had been tortured and murdered by Hezbollah in the mid- and late 1990s. The group began targeting official Turkish interests in January 2001, when 10–20 of its operatives participated in the assassination of the chief of police in Diyarbakir—the group's most sophisticated operation to date.

Turkish Islamic Development Bank (IDB)

In 1992 a delegation from the IDB visited Tirana, Albania, in order to prepare for economic co-operation between Turkey and Albania. Soon afterwards, Turkish trading companies dealing in fertilizers began to offer advantageous conditions to Albanian importers and exporters. They gained control of the market at the expense of the International Fertilizer Development Center (IFDC), the US advisory board formed to help agricultural **trade** through the transition to a market economy. Turkish traders aggressively took over from the IFDC, backed by Islamic banks actively involved in trade financing. This economic initiative was followed by similar initiatives by other Islamic countries in the following years.

Turkish Republic of Northern Cyprus (TRNC)

The Turkish Republic of Northern Cyprus was proclaimed in November 1983. It comprises all of Kyrenia, most of Famagusta and parts of Nicosia. Between the Turkish invasion of Cyprus in the summer of 1974 and this proclamation, the territory was known as the Turkish Federated State of Cyprus. Following Turkey's invasion of Cyprus, the United Nations General Assembly adopted a resolution, in November 1974, calling for the withdrawal of all foreign troops from Cyprus and the safe return of all **refugees** to their homes. Neither this nor any other UN resolution on Cyprus has been implemented. A UN peace-keeping force was deployed to control a buffer zone between the Turkish and the Greek Cypriot communities. Only Turkey recognized the 1983 proclamation; other states viewed the action as illegal. Despite this, a new constitution was approved, and presidential and legislative elections were held in 1985. The Constitution provides for a President, a Prime Minister and Cabinet, a legislative assembly and a separate judiciary. **Rauf Denktash** was elected President in June 1985, receiving more than 70% of the vote. The legislative assembly had 50 members, elected for five-year terms of office. Four parties gained representation: the National Unity Party/Uluk Birlik Partisi (24 seats), the Communal Liberation Party/Toplumu Kurtulus Partisi (12 seats), the Republican Turkish Party/Cumhuriyetci Türk Partisi (10 seats) and the New Dawn Party (four seats). Other parties that contested the elections failed to secure the 8% of the vote required to achieve representation in the legislature.

Turkmans

The Turkmans of north-east Iran are members of a tribal/ethnic and linguistic (Turkic) **minority**, who number about 300,000 and are predominantly **Sunni** Muslims. Violence flared in the Turkman areas of Iran in the spring of 1979 when tribesmen there complained that they were denied membership of the local revolutionary committees, which were dominated by **Shi'a**. There are also significant Turkman groups in northern and western Afghanistan. Turkmans constitute three-quarters of the population of the independent state (former Soviet republic) of Turkmenistan.

Turkmenistan, Republic of

Turkmenistan is situated in **Central Asia**, bordering the Caspian Sea, between Iran and Kazakhstan. It borders Afghanistan to the south-west and Uzbekistan to the north. The country is land-locked. The western and central low-lying, desolate portions of the country make up the great Garagum (Kara-Kum) desert, which occupies more than 80% of the country. Only 2% of land is arable. The total area of the country is 488,100 sq km. The capital is Ashgabat. For administrative purposes Turkmenistan is divided into five provinces (*welayat*, plural *welayatlar*): Ahal Welayaty (Ashgabat), Balkan Welayaty (Balkanabat), Dasoguz Welayaty, Labap Welayaty (Turkmenabat), Mary Welayaty. (Where the name of the administrative divisions is not the same as the administrative centre the name of the administrative centre follows in parentheses.) At July 2002 the population of Turkmenistan was estimated at 4,688,963, of which Turkmens accounted for 77%, **Uzbeks** for 9.2%, Russians for 6.7%, **Kazakhs** for 2% and 'others' 5.1%. With regard to the country's religious composition, 87% of the population is Muslim, 11% Eastern Orthodox and 2% 'others'. The official language is Turkmen, spoken by 72% of the population. Russian is the language of a further 12% and Uzbek that of 9%. Seven per cent of the population speak languages other than those listed.

Political profile

Turkmenistan is a democratic, secular, constitutional republic based on law and headed by a President. It is also termed a 'presidential republic', one that is 'based on the principles of the separation of powers—legislative, executive, and judicial—which operate independently, checking and balancing one another'. Since 27 October 1990 the head of state, President and chairman of the Council of Ministers has been Saparmyrat **Niyazov**, who was returned to those offices in the country's first direct presidential election. President Niyazov is, accordingly, also head of the government. The Council of Ministers is appointed by the President. The most recent presidential election (in which a President is, in theory, elected by popular vote for a five-year term of office), was held on 21 June 1992. President Niyazov was unanimously approved as President for life by the Assembly (see below) on 28 December 1999. Under the 1992 Constitution there are two parliamentary bodies: a unicameral People's Council, or Halk Maslahaty, which meets infrequently and which comprises more than 100 seats, to some of which deputies are returned by popular vote and some of which are filled by appointees; and a unicameral Assembly, or **Majlis**, comprising 50 seats to which members are elected by popular vote for five-year terms of office. All 50 elected officials are preapproved by President Niyazov and are, for the most part, members of the DPT. Elections to the Assembly were held most recently on 12 December 1999. The next elections to the Assembly are scheduled to be held in 2004. There is a Supreme Court whose judges are appointed by the President. The legal system is based on civil law. Officially Turkmenistan became a multi-party **democracy** at independence, but President Niyazov has banned the formation of new political parties. The former Communist Party of Turkmenistan has reconstituted itself as the Democratic Party of Turkmenistan (DPT) and has nearly complete control. President Niyazov has established an extreme personality cult. The 1992 Constitution establishes rights concerning freedom of religion, the separation of church and state, freedom of movement, privacy, and ownership of private property. Both the Constitution and the 1991 Law on Public Organizations guarantee the right to create political parties and other public associations that operate within the framework of the Constitution and the law. Such activity is restricted by prohibitions of parties that 'encroach on the health and morals of the people' and on the formation of ethnic or religious parties. This provision has been used by the government to ban several groups.

Political Parties and Groups

Turkmenistan is a one-party state in all areas of government of which the DPT is dominant. Formal opposition parties are outlawed. The DPT is led by Saparmyrat Niyazov. Opposition movements, such as the Movement for Democratic Reform and the Vatan (Motherland) Party, are either underground or based in other countries. A Social Democratic Party was reported to have been established in

Ashgabat in August 1996 by the merger of several small, unofficial groups. Agzybirlik (Unity) is a popular front organization that has been denied official registration except, briefly, in October 1991–January 1992. Its leader is Nurberdy Nurmamedov who was imprisoned in February–December 2000. The Party for Democratic Development, an offshoot of Agzybirlik, was outlawed in 1991. Gengesh (Conference), formed by the Party for Democratic Development and Agzyrbirlik, aimed at effecting democratic reforms in the republic. It operates from exile. A Peasants' Justice Party, formed by deputies of the agrarian faction in parliament, awaits official recognition.

Media

In 1989, according to official statistics, 66 newspaper titles were published. There were 34 periodicals. *Neytralnyi Turkmenistan* is the organ of the Assembly and the Council of Ministers. *Turkmenistan* is, likewise, an organ of the Council of Ministers. *Daynach* is published by the outlawed Agzybirlik party and is illegal. There is one state-controlled television operator, Turkmen Television (National Television and Radio Co of Turkmenistan). Television broadcasts can only be received in the cities. Turkmen Radio (National Television and Radio Co of Turkmenistan) is the only national radio operator. The transmissions of Islamic programmes by Iranian and Afghan radio stations are also popular. There are no internet service providers. In 2000 there were 2,000 internet users.

History

Annexed by Russia between 1865 and 1885, Turkmenistan became a Soviet republic in 1925. However, the consolidation of Soviet power did not occur without a struggle. Turkmen participated in the **Basmachi** revolt. The forced collectivization drive begun in 1929 forced many Turkmen nomads to settle, something which added impetus to the resistance. It was not until the 1930s that the Soviet authorities managed to gain control of the Turkmen revolt and nascent nationalism. The Soviet authorities implemented an extensive anti-religious policy from 1928 onwards, the harshest anti-Islamic policy in all of the Central Asian Republics. It was temporarily suspended during the Second World War, after which it was resumed with fervour. Of the approximately 500 mosques that were found on Turkmen territory in 1917, only four remained in 1979. **Islam** was forced to establish itself covertly, but this enabled it to thrive in the post-Second World War period. However, in order to survive, Islam in Turkmenistan became a mix of orthodox (**Sunni**) Islam, **Sufism**, and shamanistic practices. Thus, at the beginning of the 21st century few, even older Turkmen, knew how to pray.

With *glasnost* and *perestroika* in the 1980s members of the intelligentsia and some politicians began to argue in favour of independence. As Turkmenistan was one of the poorest of the Soviet republics in terms of per caput **income** and had the highest infant mortality rate and the lowest life expectancy in the Soviet Union, the nationalist movement argued that the relationship with the Soviet authorities was basically colonialist. Opposition movements appeared in the late 1980s, but they were effectively silenced by government harassment.

After the failed hardline *putsch* in Moscow, on which the Turkmen leadership remained silent, the government put the question of self-rule to a national referendum in October 1991. Ninety-four point one per cent of the electorate voted for independence. Independent Turkmenistan became a founding member of the **Commonwealth of Independent States** (CIS).

At independence Turkmenistan was in the most critical social and economic condition of all the Central Asian Republics, although it was and remains the state with the most potential. Turkmenistan is largely homogeneous ethnically (70% Turkmen) and has thus been spared the ethnic strife that the other Central Asian republics have experienced. In addition it has enormous economic potential, possessing substantial **oil** resources and the seventh largest reserves of **natural gas** in the world. Its strategic location, moreover, places it on the ideal route for exports of Central Asian gas to the east, west and south. However, since independence this potential has been wasted by the idiosyncracies of President **Niyazov**, who since 1984, first as general secretary of the Turkmen Communist Party and subsequently as post-independence leader, has run the country like a personal fiefdom.

In May 1992 Turkmenistan's parliament adopted a new constitution, the first of its kind in Central Asia. A direct presidential election was held on 21 June under the new Constitution, although Niyazov had been popularly elected in October 1990. Some 99.5% of the 99.8% of the electorate who participated cast their vote in favour of Niyazov. He has established an extreme personality cult around himself and his family and has managed to retain a firm hold on power. Thus in 1994, when Niyazov suggested to the parliament that it should nominate him as President until 2002, the parliament requested him to remain as President for life. A referendum confirmed him as President until 2002, when elections were to be held, but in December 1999 Niyazov was unanimously approved as President for life by parliament. Niyazov has stated that he intends to retire by 2010.

In his 10 years in power President Niyazov has retained absolute control over the country. No meetings of any kind—not even academic ones—are tolerated, and religious as well as political opposition leaders have been exiled. Because of this, there is little if any genuine opposition. Any nascent opposition is quickly suppressed and the Niyazov regime has pursued an aggressive policy of harassing opposition parties in exile. In addition, Niyazov consistently removes officials from power or has them transferred to new positions as a means of diminishing their power bases and their potential to rival him.

Opposition to Niyazov's regime is intensifying, albeit from opposition parties in exile. One notable opponent in exile is Boris Shikhmuradov, a former Minister of Foreign Affairs. In December 2002 Niyazov survived an assassination attempt.

International relations

Turkmenistan is a transit point for Afghan narcotics bound for Russian and, to a lesser extent, Western European markets. There is limited cultivation of **opium** poppy for domestic consumption. The government attempts to eradicate illicit crops, albeit on a small scale. Turkmenistan is also a transit point for **heroin** precursor chemicals bound for Afghanistan. Turkmenistan, Kazakhstan, Tajikistan, and Uzbekistan are forced to share limited water resources, and are confronted by regional environmental degradation caused by the shrinking of the Aral Sea. Multilaterally-accepted Caspian Sea seabed and maritime boundaries have not yet been established in the Caspian—Iran insists on the division of the Caspian Sea into five equal sectors while Azerbaijan, Kazakhstan, Russia, and Turkmenistan have generally agreed upon equidistant seabed boundaries. Azerbaijan and Turkmenistan await the decision of the International Court of Justice regarding a sovereignty dispute over oilfields in the Caspian Sea.

Turkmenistan, economy

At independence President Niyazov promised to turn Turkmenistan into 'a new Kuwait' by exploiting the country's vast reserves of oil and gas. Niyazov's 'Ten Years of Stability Programme' aimed to resolve the country's most pressing economic and social needs by 2002. This programme was also designed to acquiesce the population in the absence of political liberalization. From 1993 the population was supplied with free gas, **water**, electricity and salt. However, these populist measures were difficult to sustain as the Turkmen government failed to attract vital investment for the development of its infrastructure for gas exports. In November 1993 the Russian government restricted Turkmenistan's access to its pipeline network so that the country was forced to redirect its gas exports to CIS countries with little ability to pay for them. The net result was that living standards declined substantially in the mid-1990s, fuelling public dissatisfaction. Shortages of water, electricity and staple products led to some localized '**bread riots**', which were quickly suppressed. One decade after independence Turkmenistan is highly dependent on two export commodities: **natural gas**; and cotton, of which the country is the world's 10th largest producer. Agricultural diversification is difficult as only 2% of the country is arable, and what arable land there is is deteriorating rapidly owing to salination. Turkmenistan's economic prospects depend on improved export of its vast natural gas reserves (some 7,400,000m. cu m). Turkmenistan's **oil** and natural gas reserves remained undeveloped by the Soviet regime, hence the imperative is to build oil and gas pipelines that are independent of Russia. This requires substantial investment, and **Niyazov** has so far been unable to attract investors. Russia has insisted that Turkmen gas be exported to other parts of the **Commonwealth of Independent States** and Europe through its pipeline systems at prices well below those prevailing internationally. Iran constructed the only pipeline that has been completed—a small one, 190 km in length, running to northern Iran. Although economic growth was strong in 1999–2001, this was largely due to high gas prices. Poverty affects at least 34% of the population. In addition, the foreign **debt** is rising. From a starting point of zero at independence, the current debt stood at US $2,300m.–$5,000m. in 2001. Turkmenistan's economic statistics are state secrets, and such indicators as can be obtained for gross domestic product, etc., are subject to wide margins of error.

Strengths

Cotton and gas. The country's strategic location for gas exports.

Weaknesses

Cotton monoculture has forced rising food imports. A thriving black market threatens the value of the *manta*.

TUSIAD

The Turkish Industrialists' and Businessmen's Association.

Twelver Shi'is

Islamic sect. (See also **Shi'ism.**)

U

UAE – *see* **United Arab Emirates**

UAE Exchange Centre

Established in 1980 by a Dubai-based Indian businessman who had made a fortune from building a chain of private hospitals, the UAE Exchange Centre began life as a means of repatriating the savings of Malayali and Tamil migrants to their families in south India. Over the years, the business grew steadily in size, taking a major step forward when, in 1994, it became a member of SWIFT (an extremely secure electronic communications system through which major banks conduct business). This spurred further growth, especially when the Exchange Centre set up a secure Local Area Network, linking all of the other (more than 100) lower-level exchanges doing business in the UAE money market.

UAR – *see* **United Arab Republic**

Ukraine

Having previously had little involvement in the region, Ukraine dispatched 1,650 troops to Iraq as part of the **coalition** force. They were deployed in the town of **Kut** to the south of **Baghdad**, together with 27 soldiers from Kazakhstan. When they suffered their first casualties there in mid-April 2003, they withdrew from the town.

Ulema

Arabic word that refers to the community of legal scholars of **Islam** and the **Shari'a**. Their organization and powers vary from Muslim community to community. They are most powerful in **Shi'a** Islam where their role is institutionalized. In most countries they are usually religious scholars and sometimes local power figures.

Ulema Union

A political grouping in pre-**Taliban** Afghanistan.

Umm al-Qaiwain, Emirate of

The smallest of the United Arab Emirates (UAE). Its area is 780 sq km. In 1995 the population was estimated at 35,157. **Oil** has not yet been found there. It is one of the least developed of the UAE, of which it became part in 1971.

Umm Qasr

Port town in the south of Iraq. It was occupied in the early days of the **Gulf War (2003)** by **coalition** forces. US, UK and Australian mine warfare forces soon cleared the Khawr Ahd Allah waterway to allow military supply ships and humanitarian **aid** ships to use the port. The old section of the port was damaged by US air strikes, but the new port still had functioning cranes and container-handling facilities, which were used by the coalition forces to unload cargoes.

Umm al-Qura mosque

Originally known as the Mother of All Battles mosque, this, the largest **Sunni** mosque in **Baghdad**, was built shortly before the collapse of **Saddam Hussain**'s regime. It was the site of a rally of up to 200,000 **Sunni** and **Shi'a** opponents of the US-led **coalition**'s occupation of Iraq, particularly in the town of **Falluja**, on the first anniversary of the fall of the regime.

Umma (Nation) Party

Iraqi opposition party, founded in 1982. Its leader is Saad Saleh Jabr.

Ummah

Arabic word meaning 'community'. The term originally referred to the community of Muslims in **Medina**. It has since come to refer to the community of believers (Ummah al-Mouminin**).**

Ummah al-Hezbollah

Community of Hezbollah

Despite its name, this is not a Lebanese political party but, rather, an umbrella organization of some six radical **Shi'a** groups that are affiliated to **Hezbollah**.

UN—United Nations

The United Nations has been involved in Middle Eastern affairs from its very beginnings. One of the first peace-keeping forces deployed by the UN was to supervise the cease-fire after the **Arab–Israeli War (1948)** and patrol the borders of Israel. Among the earliest member states from the region were (in 1945): Egypt, Iran, Iraq, Lebanon, Saudi Arabia, Syria, and Turkey. Israel became a member in 1949, Jordan and Libya in 1955 and Morocco and Tunisia in 1956.

UN General Assembly Resolution 181

Resolution 181, of November 1947, recommended the partition of Palestine. It recommended adoption of the Plan of Partition with Economic Union, and called upon the United Kingdom, as the mandatory power for Palestine, all other members of the United Nations, and the inhabitants of Palestine to take such steps as should be necessary on their part to put this plan into effect, and appealed to all governments and all peoples to refrain from taking any action which might hamper or delay the implementation of these recommendations.

UN General Assembly Resolution 194

Resolution 194, of December 1948, relating to the situation in Palestine, expressed its deep appreciation of the progress achieved through the good offices of the late United Nations Mediator in promoting a peaceful adjustment of the future situation of Palestine, for which cause he sacrificed his life; extended its thanks to the Acting Mediator and his staff for their continued efforts and devotion to duty in Palestine; and established a Conciliation Commission consisting of three member states of the United Nations, with the following functions:

(a) To assume, in so far as it considers necessary in existing circumstances, the functions given to the United Nations Mediator on Palestine by resolution 186 (S-2) of the General Assembly of 14 May 1948;
(b) To carry out the specific functions and directives given to it by the present resolution and such additional functions and directives as may be given to it by the General Assembly or by the Security Council; and
(c) To undertake, upon the request of the Security Council, any of the functions now assigned to the United Nations Mediator on Palestine or to the United Nations Truce Commission by resolutions of the Security Council; upon such request to the Conciliation Commission by the Security Council with respect to all the remaining functions of the United Nations Mediator on Palestine under Security Council resolutions, the office of the Mediator shall be terminated.

The Resolution further: proposed that a Committee of the Assembly, consisting of China, France, the Soviet Union, the United Kingdom and the USA, shall present, before the end of the first part of the present session of the General Assembly, for the approval of the Assembly, a proposal concerning the names of the three States which will constitute the Conciliation Commission; requested the Commission to begin its functions at once, with a view to the establishment of contact between the parties themselves and the Commission at the earliest possible date; called upon the Governments and authorities concerned to extend the scope of the negotiations provided for in the Security Council's resolution of 16 November 1948 and to seek agreement by negotiations conducted either with the Conciliation Commission or directly, with a view to the final settlement of all questions outstanding between them; instructed the Conciliation Commission to take steps to assist the Governments and authorities concerned to achieve a final settlement of all questions outstanding between them; resolved that the Holy Places—including **Nazareth**—religious buildings and sites in Palestine should be protected and free access to them assured, in accordance with existing rights and historical practice; that arrangements to this end should be under effective United Nations supervision; that the United Nations Conciliation Commission, in presenting to the fourth regular session of the General Assembly its detailed proposals for a permanent international regime for the territory of **Jerusalem**, should include recommendations concerning the Holy Places in that territory; that with regard to the Holy Places in the rest of Palestine the Commission should call upon the political authorities of the areas concerned to give appropriate formal guarantees as to the protection of the Holy Places and access to them; and that these undertakings should be presented to the General Assembly for approval; resolved that, in view of its association with three world religions, the Jerusalem area, including the present municipality of Jerusalem plus the surrounding villages and towns, the most eastern of which shall be Abu Dis; the most southern, **Bethlehem**; the most western, Ein Karim (including also the built-up area of Motsa); and the most northern, Shu'fat, should be accorded special and separate treatment from the rest of Palestine and should be placed under effective United Nations control; requested the Security Council to take further steps to ensure the demilitarization of Jerusalem at the earliest possible date; instructed the Conciliation Commission to present to the fourth regular session of the General Assembly detailed proposals for a permanent international regime for the Jerusalem area which will provide for the maximum local autonomy for distinctive groups consistent with the special international status of the Jerusalem area; the Conciliation Commission is authorized to appoint a United Nations representative, who shall co-operate with the local authorities with respect to the interim administration of the Jerusalem area; resolved that, pending agreement on more detailed arrangements among the Governments and authorities concerned, the freest possible access to Jerusalem by road, rail or air should be accorded to all inhabitants of Palestine; instructed the Conciliation Commission to report immediately to the Security Council, for appropriate action by that organ, any attempt by any party to impede such access; instructed the Conciliation Commission to seek arrangements among the Governments and authorities concerned which will facilitate the economic development of the area, including arrangements for access to ports and airfields and the use of transportation and communication facilities; resolved that the **refugees** wishing to return to their homes and live at peace with their neighbours should be permitted to do so at the earliest practicable date, and that compensation should be paid for the property of those choosing not to return and for loss of or damage to property which, under principles of international law or in equity, should be made good by the Governments or authorities responsible; instructed the Conciliation Commission to facilitate the repatriation, resettlement and economic and social rehabilitation of the refugees and the payment of compensation, and to maintain close relations with the Director of the United Nations Relief for Palestine Refugees and, through him, with the appropriate organs and agencies of the United Nations; authorized the Conciliation Commission to appoint such subsidiary bodies and to employ such technical experts, acting under its authority, as it may find necessary for the effective discharge of its functions and responsibilities under the present resolution; the Conciliation Commission will have its official headquarters at Jerusalem. The authorities responsible for maintaining order in Jerusalem will be responsible for taking all measures necessary to ensure the security of the Commission. The Secretary-General will provide a limited number of guards to the protection of the staff and premises of the Commission; instructed the Conciliation Commission to render progress reports periodically to the Secretary-General for transmission to the Security Council and to the Members of the United Nations; called upon all Governments and authorities concerned to co-operate with the Conciliation Commission and to take all possible steps to assist in the implementation of the present resolution; requested the Secretary-General to provide the necessary staff and facilities and to make appropriate arrangements to provide the necessary funds required in carrying out the terms of the present resolution.

At the 186th plenary meeting on 11 December 1948, a committee of the Assembly consisting of the five States designated in paragraph three of the above resolution proposed that the following three states should constitute the Conciliation Commission: France, Turkey, USA.

UN General Assembly Resolution 273

Resolution 273, in May 1949, admitted Israel as a member of the UN.

UN General Assembly Resolution 2442

Resolution 2442, of December 1968, denounced the violation of human rights in the territories occupied by Israel. Similar denunciations were to follow throughout the 1970s and 1980s in numerous texts.

UN General Assembly Resolution 2535 B

Resolution 2535 B, of December 1969, evoked for the first time since 1948 the inalienable rights of the Palestinian people.

UN General Assembly Resolution 2628

Resolution 2628, of November 1970, claimed that the respect of Palestinian rights is an indispensable element in the establishment of a just and lasting peace.

UN General Assembly Resolution 2649

Resolution 2649, of November 1970, made explicit mention of the Palestinian people's right to self-determination.

UN General Assembly Resolution 2949

Resolution 2949, of December 1972, deemed as 'null and void' the changes brought about by Israel in the occupied Arab territories, a view that would be later coupled with a condemnation of both the transfers of population and the establishment of **settlements** in the **Occupied Territories**.

UN General Assembly Resolution 3161

Resolution 3161, of December 1976, called for a Peace Conference on the **Middle East** with the participation of the **Palestine Liberation Organization**.

UN General Assembly Resolution 3236

Resolution 3236, of November 1974, recognized the Palestinian people's right to national independence and sovereignty, in the presence of **Yasser Arafat**, who had just addressed the General Assembly.

UN General Assembly Resolution 3237

Resolution 3237, of November 1974, invited the **Palestine Liberation Organization** to participate in the sessions and works of the General Assembly of the UN in the capacity of observer.

UN General Assembly Resolution 3379

Resolution 3379, of November 1975, classed **Zionism** as a form of racism.

UN General Assembly Resolution 32/5

This Resolution, of October 1977, stipulated that 'all measures and decisions taken by the Israel government ... with the intention of altering the geographical status and the demographic composition in the Palestinian territories and other Arab territories occupied since 1967 have no legal validity and will constitute a serious obstruction to peace efforts'.

UN General Assembly Resolution 32/20

This Resolution, of November 1977, reaffirmed the status of the **Palestine Liberation Organization**.

UN General Assembly Resolution 32/30

This Resolution, of 25 November 1977, 'called anew' for the early convening of the Geneva **Middle East** peace conference.

UN General Assembly Resolution 33/29

This Resolution, of 7 December 1978, repeated the call for the convening of the Geneva **Middle East** peace conference. The main focus of attention, however, had now moved away from the UN as President **Sadat** of Egypt visited **Jerusalem** in November 1977 and, after protracted negotiations, President Sadat and Israeli Prime Minister **Menachem Begin** signed two agreements at **Camp David** in September 1978 and a peace treaty in Washington, DC, in March 1979.

UN General Assembly Resolution 34/65

This Resolution, of December 1979, concluded that the **Camp David Agreement** had been reached outside the framework of the United Nations and without the participation of the **Palestine Liberation Organization**, which represents the Palestinian people. It also condemned all partial and separate accords as a flagrant violation of the rights of the Palestinian people, the principles of the Charter of the United Nations and the resolutions adopted concerning the Palestinian question.

UN General Assembly Resolution on the Internationalization of Jerusalem

This Resolution, of December 1949, refers back to Resolutions 181 (II) of 29 November 1947 and 194 (III) of 11 December 1948, and restates 'the intention of the UN General Assembly that **Jerusalem** should be placed under a permanent international regime, which should envisage appropriate guarantees for the protection of the Holy Places, both within and outside Jerusalem, and to confirm specifically the following provisions of General Assembly resolution 181 (II): 1. The City of Jerusalem shall be established as a *corpus separatum* under a special international regime and shall be administered by the United Nations, 2. the Trusteeship Council shall be designated to discharge the responsibilities of the Administering Authority... and 3. The City of Jerusalem shall include the present municipality of Jerusalem plus the surrounding villages and towns, the most eastern of which shall be Abu Dis, the most southern **Bethelehem**, the most western Ein Karim (including also the built-up area of Motsa), and the most northern Shu'fat...'.

UN Security Council

The key decision-making body of the UN with respect to international security and 'peace-keeping'. It has 15 members of which five are permanent members (the USA, the United Kingdom, France, Russia and the People's Republic of China), the others being elected on a rotational basis.

UN Security Council Resolution 242

Resolution 242, of November 1967, six months after the Arab–Israeli **Six-Day War**, acknowledged the existence and security of the State of Israel but also made the withdrawal of Israeli **armed forces** from the **Occupied Territories** the condition of a lasting peace. Various UN resolutions between 1967 and October 1973 reaffirmed this key resolution. The Palestine question was still treated only as a problem of **refugees**, just as in **UN Security Council Resolution 338**. This resolution of the UN Security Council, adopted unanimously, expressing its continuing concern with the grave situation in the **Middle East**, emphasizing the inadmissibility of the acquisition of territory by war and the need to work for a just and lasting peace in which every State in the area can live in security, emphasizing further that all Member States in their acceptance of the Charter of the United Nations have undertaken a commitment to act in accordance with Article 2 of the Charter, affirmed that the fulfilment of Charter principles requires the establishment of a just and lasting peace in the Middle East which should include the application of both the following principles: (i) Withdrawal of Israeli armed forces from territories occupied in the recent conflict; (ii) Termination of all claims or states of belligerency and respect for and acknowledgment of the sovereignty, territorial integrity and political independence of every State in the area and their right to live in peace within secure and recognized boundaries free from threats or acts of force; affirmed further the necessity (a) For guaranteeing freedom of navigation through international waterways in the area; (b) For achieving a just settlement of the refugee problem; (c) For guaranteeing the territorial inviolability and political independence of every State in the area, through measures including the establishment of demilitarized zones; requested the Secretary-General to designate a Special Representative to proceed to the Middle East to establish and maintain contacts with the States concerned in order to promote agreement and assist efforts to achieve a peaceful and accepted settlement in accordance with the provisions and principles in this resolution; and requested the Secretary-General to report to the Security Council on the progress of the efforts of the Special Representative as soon as possible.

UN Security Council Resolution 252

Resolution 252, of 21 May 1968, was the first Security Council resolution to deal specifically with the issue of **Jerusalem**.

UN Security Council Resolution 298

This resolution, of 25 September 1971, recalled **UN Security Council Resolution 252** (1968) and Resolution 267 (1969) and the earlier UN General Assembly Resolutions 2253 (ES-V) and 2254 (ES-V) of July 1967, concerning measures and actions by Israel designed to change the status of the Israeli-occupied section of **Jerusalem**. It noted with concern the non-compliance of Israel with these resolutions and reaffirmed Resolutions 252 and 267, calling on Israel to meanwhile rescind all previous measures and actions and to take no further steps in the occupied section of Jerusalem which may purport to change the status of the City, or which would prejudice the rights of the inhabitants and the interests of the international community, or a just and lasting peace.

UN Security Council Resolution 338

Resolution 338, of 22 October 1973, after the **Arab–Israeli War (1973)**, called on the parties to the conflict to begin immediately, after a cease-fire, to apply **UN Security Council Resolution 242** in all its provisions.

UN Security Council Resolution 340

This resolution, of 25 October 1973, recalled the earlier **UN Security Council Resolution 338** and Resolution 339, noted the violations of the cease-fire and the fact that UN military observers had been unable to place themselves on both sides of the cease-fire line, demanded an immediate and complete cease-fire and called for the establishment of a UN emergency force to reinforce the cease-fire.

UN Security Council Resolution 425

Resolution 425, adopted in March 1978, demanded that Israel withdraw its troops from Lebanon, under UN supervision (**UNIFIL**), and respect Lebanese territorial integrity, sovereignty and independence.

UN Security Council Resolution 465

Resolution 465 of 1 March 1980, which expressed its deep concern and opposition to the continuing settlement, supported by the government of Israel, by Jews in the **Occupied Territories** of the **West Bank** and **Gaza Strip**, and called for the dismantling of **settlements**, was adopted unanimously by the 15 members of the UN Security Council. The USA subsequently repudiated its vote in favour of the resolution. President **Carter** made a statement on 3 March 1980 stating that 'the vote of the US in the Security Council of the UN does not represent a change in our position regarding the Israeli settlements in the occupied areas nor regarding the status of **Jerusalem**. While our opposition to the establishment of the Israeli settlements is long-standing and well-known, we made strenuous efforts to eliminate the language with reference to the dismantling of settlements in the resolution. This call for dismantling was neither proper nor practical. We believe that the future disposition of the existing settlements must be determined during the current autonomy negotiations'.

UN Security Council Resolution 687

Resolution 687 of 3 April 1991 stated that Iraq should unconditionally accept, under international supervision, the destruction, removal or rendering harmless of its **weapons of mass destruction**, ballistic missiles with a range of more than 150 km, and related production facilities and equipment. It also provided for the establishment of a system of ongoing monitoring and verification of Iraq's compliance with the ban on these weapons and missiles. Iraq accepted the resolution on 6 April 1991. This was the start of the policy that came to be known as '**containment**'.

UN Security Council Resolution 707

Resolution 707 of 15 August 1991 demanded that Iraq provide without delay full, final and complete disclosures of its proscribed weapons and programmes, as required by **UN Security Council Resolution 687**.

UN Security Council Resolution 715

Resolution 715, of 11 October 1991, approved the plans for ongoing monitoring and verification submitted by the Secretary-General and the Director-General of the **International Atomic Energy Agency**. Iraq responded by stating that it considered the ongoing monitoring and verification plans, adopted by Resolution 715, to be unlawful and that it was not ready to comply with Resolution 715. On 26 November 1993 Iraq eventually accepted Resolution 715.

UN Security Council Resolution 949

Resolution 949, of 15 October 1994, demanded that Iraq co-operate fully with **UNSCOM** and that it withdraw all military units deployed to southern Iraq to their original positions. Iraq complied.

UN Security Council Resolution 1051

Resolution 1051, of 27 March 1996, approved the import/export monitoring mechanism for Iraq and demanded that Iraq meet unconditionally all of its obligations under the mechanism and co-operate fully with the Special Commission and the director-general of the **International Atomic Energy Agency**.

UN Security Council Resolution 1060

Resolution 1060, of 12 June 1996, termed Iraq's actions, in denying the **UNSCOM** teams access to sites under investigation for their involvement in the concealment mechanism for proscribed items, a clear violation of the provisions of the Security Council's resolutions. It also demanded that Iraq grant immediate and unrestricted access to all sites designated for inspection by UNSCOM. Despite this, later in June 1996, Iraq again denied access to another inspection team. This was followed by a statement by the President of the Security Council in which the Council condemned the failure of Iraq to comply with Resolution 1060. Later in June UNSCOM and Iraq agreed a Joint 1996 Statement and a Joint Programme of Action, and Iraq provided both the fourth Full, Final and Complete Disclosure of its prohibited biological weapons programme, and the third Full, Final and Complete Disclosure of its prohibited chemicals weapons programme. In July Iraq provided the third Full, Final and Complete Disclosure of its prohibited missile programme. On 23 August 1996 a Statement by the President of the Security Council reported that the Council strongly reaffirmed its full support of the Commission in the conduct of its inspections and other tasks and expressed its grave concern at Iraq's failure to comply fully with Resolution 1060. The Council also stated that Iraq's failure to grant immediate unconditional and unrestricted access to sites and its attempts to impose conditions on the conduct of interviews with Iraqi officials constituted a gross violation of its obligations. The Council also reminded Iraq that only full compliance with its obligations would enable the Executive Chairman to present a full report in accordance with section C of **UN Security Council Resolution 687**.

UN Security Council Resolution 1115

Resolution 1115, of 21 June 1997, condemned Iraq's actions in blocking and interfering with the work of **UNSCOM** inspectors over previous months and demanded that Iraq allow UNSCOM's team immediate, unconditional and unrest-ricted access to any sites for inspection and officials for interview by UNSCOM. The Council also called for an additional report on Iraq's co-operation with the Commission and suspended the periodic sanctions reviews.

UN Security Council Resolution 1134

Resolution 1134, of 23 October 1997, demanded that Iraq co-operate fuly with the Special Commission, continued the suspension of periodic sanctions reviews and foreshadowed additional sanctions pending a further report on Iraq's co-operation with **UNSCOM**.

UN Security Council Resolution 1137

Resolution 1137, of 12 November 1997, condemned Iraq for its continuing violation of its obligations, including its unacceptable decision to seek to impose conditions on co-operation with **UNSCOM**. It also imposed a travel restriction on Iraqi officials responsible for or having participated in instances of non-compliance.

UN Security Council Resolution 1397

Resolution 1397, of 12 March 2002, affirmed for the first time the UN Security Council's vision of both Israeli and Palestinian states. It was the first US-sponsored resolution on the **Middle East** for some 25 years and was adopted by 14 votes to 0, with Syria abstaining. It recalled all of its previous relevant resolutions, in particular **UN Security Council Resolution 242** (1967) and **338** (1973) and affirmed a vision of two states living side by side within secure and recognized borders.

UN Security Council Resolution 1483

Resolution 1483 required all UN member states to identify, 'freeze', and immediately transfer to the Development Fund for Iraq all funds, financial assets or economic resources in their jurisdictions that were established or held by the previous government of Iraq. The **Oil for Food programme** was to be phased out over six months; and once again, the disbursement of the money in this fund, estimated at some US \$10,000m., was to be handed over to the **Coalition Provisional Authority**. The following are the highlights of the new US Draft Resolution:

The Resolution would establish a 'Development Fund for Iraq' for reconstruction and humanitarian purposes to be held by the central bank of Iraq and to be audited by independent accountants approved by an international advisory board. The board includes envoys from the United Nations, the **International Monetary Fund**, the **Arab Fund for Economic and Social Development** and the **World Bank**. All proceeds from **oil** sales would go into the Development Fund until an 'internationally recognized' Iraqi government is established. The money would be 'disbursed at the direction' of the authority (the USA and the United Kingdom), in consultation with the Iraqi interim authority. Five per cent of the oil revenues are to be deposited into a compensation fund (compared to the current 25%) for claims resulting from Iraq's 1990 invasion of Kuwait. The Resolution phases out the UN's Oil for Food programme over a period of six months. Some US \$13,000m. from Iraq's past oil revenues are now in the programme, administered by the UN. Whatever is not spent would be deposited into the new Development Fund. All money from Iraq's oil sales or in the Development Fund is immune from claims and law suits until an internationally recognized Iraqi government is established.

UN Security Council Resolution 1496

Resolution 1496 of 31 July 2003 extended **UNIFIL**'s mandate until 31 January 2004.

UNCTAD—United Nations Conference on Trade and Development

Established in 1964, UNCTAD is the principal organ of the UN General Assembly that concerns itself with **trade** and development, and is the focal point within the UN system for activities relating to trade, finance, technology, investment and sustainable development.

UNDOF—United Nations Disengagement Observer Force

UNDOF is based at Camp Faouar in Syria. It was established originally for a period of six months by a UN Security Council resolution of May 1974, following the signature in Geneva, Switzerland, of a disengagement agreement between Syria and Israel. The mandate has been extended by successive resolutions. The initial tasks of the Force were to take over territory evacuated by the Israeli troops, in accordance with the disengagement agreement; to hand over territory to Syrian troops; and to establish an area of separation on the **Golan Heights**. UNDOF continues to monitor the area of separation. The Force operates exclusively on Syrian territory. At July 2002 it comprised some 1,027 troops, assisted by approximately 80 military observers of **UNTSO**'s Observer Group Golan and supported by some 120 international and local civilian personnel. The UN General Assembly appropriated US $40.8m. to cover the cost of the operation for the period 1 July 2002–30 June 2003.

UNDP—United Nations Development Programme.

UN development programme established in 1965 by the UN General Assembly. Its central mission is to help countries eradicate poverty and achieve sustainable development. It is the world's largest source of grant-funded technical assistance for development. It has a regional bureau for the Arab states, as well as for Africa and for Asia and the Pacific. It maintains an office in every country receiving UNDP assistance. Special development initiatives undertaken within the region include socio-economic rehabilitation in Lebanon and environmental improvement in areas of resettlement in the **West Bank** and **Gaza Strip**. It also supports the **Programme of Assistance to the Palestinian People**. It is co-ordinating an Electricity Network Rehabilitation Programme in northern Iraq.

UNEA—Union nationale des étudiants algériens

The National Union of Algerian Students.

UNEF—United Nations Emergency Force

Established between Israel and Egypt in 1973, following the **Arab–Israeli War (1973).**

UNEP—United Nations Environment Programme

Established in 1972 by the UN General Assembly following the recommendations of the 1972 UN Conference on the Human Environment in Stockholm, Sweden. With its headquarters in Nairobi, Kenya, it maintains regional offices that include one for West Asia in **Manama**, Bahrain.

UNESCO

United Nations Educational, Scientific and Cultural Organization.

UNFICYP—United Nations Peace-Keeping Force in Cyprus

UNFICYP was established through Security Council Resolution 186 of 4 March 1964, with the mandate to prevent a recurrence of fighting between the Greek Cypriot and Turkish Cypriot communities and to contribute to the maintenance and restoration of law and order and a return to normal conditions. UNFICYP became operational on 27 March 1964. Following the hostilities of 1974, the Security Council adopted a number of resolutions expanding the mandate of UNFICYP to include supervising a *de facto* cease-fire, which came into effect on 16 August 1974, and maintaining a buffer zone between the lines of the Cyprus National Guard and of the Turkish and Turkish Cypriot forces. In the absence of a political settlement to the Cyprus problem, UNFICYP continues its presence on the island. The Security Council most recently extended the mandate of the Force until 15 December 2003 by Resolution 1486, adopted on 11 June 2003. The following nations have contributed personnel to UNFICYP: Argentina, Austria, Canada, Finland, Hungary, Ireland, the Republic of Korea, Slovakia and the United Kingdom.

UNFP—Union nationale des forces populaires (Morocco)

Moroccan political party, established in 1959 after a split occurred within the nationalist **Istiqlal** party. Its leadership was dominated by the charismatic **Mehdi Ben Barka**, who was murdered in France in 1965 after having been kidnapped by Moroccan secret agents, aided by France. Ben Barka claimed that, in breaking away from the Istiqlal, the founders of the UNFP had introduced to Morocco '... a more modern conception of political parties. Whereas before parties saw themselves much more as an assemblage or in relation to a leader than in relation to a programme—that is, somewhat like the **Middle East** in the 1930s—one can now say that, increasingly, clientele parties will be clearly differentiated from parties based on a programme and an ideology'. Critics would argue that the UNFP largely failed to make a decisive break from clientelist politics and that Ben Barka himself was built into a charismatic leader and began to act like a *zaim* (or grand patron).

UNFPA

United Nations Population Fund.

UNHCR—United Nations High Commission for Refugees

UNHCR is involved in providing support and assistance to **refugees** across the world. In the region, the major refugee population consists of **Palestinians**, but for them a special UN organization—**UNRWA**—was established and continues to operate. The UNHCR is still heavily involved in providing support for the **Sahrawi** refugees in camps in Algeria, where tens of thousands are currently suffering from malnutrition as a result of inadequate food supplies after cut-backs by 'donors'. In Afghanistan the UNHCR is responsible for managing food **aid**, but in 2002 one-third of emergency food aid (worth US $90m.) had failed to materialize by the end of the summer and aid officials criticized the **European Union** and Japan in particular for failing fully to meet their pledges. Indeed, many of the countries that promised millions of dollars in humanitarian assistance for Afghanistan at an international conference in Tokyo, Japan, at the start of 2002 had failed to deliver.

Unified National Leadership of the Uprising (UNLU)

The underground leadership of the (first) Palestinian *intifada*. It consisted of representatives from nearly all Palestinian factions, local communities and other organizations. The UNLU issued leaflets that provided information and direction to the people's uprising. Contact was also maintained with the **Palestine Liberation Organization** (PLO) in **Tunis**. After the **Oslo Agreement** the PLO, to a large extent, disbanded the UNLU.

UNIFIL—United Nations Interim Force in Lebanon

Following **UN Security Council Resolution 425** of March 1978, UNIFIL was established to supervise the Israeli withdrawal from southern Lebanon. The **Israeli Defence Force** undertook a partial withdrawal at the end of April 1978, but Israeli leaders insisted that they would maintain an armed presence in Lebanon until the UN force could ensure the security of northern Israel against Palestinian incursions. The **Palestine Liberation Organization** promised to co-operate with UNIFIL and Israeli forces eventually withdrew from Lebanese territory in June. They handed over their positions to their Lebanese militia allies, however, rather than to UNIFIL. UNIFIL remained in south Lebanon, and, during the Israeli invasion of Lebanon in 1982, provided civilians with humanitarian assistance. In April 1992 the Israeli government announced that it recognized UN Security Council Resolution 425, but stipulated that any withdrawal of its troops from southern Lebanon must be conditional on receiving security guarantees from the Lebanese authorities. A formal decision to this effect, adopted on 1 April 1992, was rejected by the Lebanese and Syrian governments. The withdrawal of Israeli troops began in mid-May and the final contingent was reported to have withdrawn from Lebanon on 24 May 1992. In mid-June the UN Secretary-General confirmed that the Israeli withdrawal had indeed taken place. In late June, however, UNIFIL reported several Israeli violations of the line of withdrawal, the so-called Blue Line. On 24 July the UN Secretary-General confirmed that no serious violations remained. UNIFIL continued to patrol the area vacated by the Israeli forces, to monitor the line of withdrawal, undertake demining activities and provide humanitarian assistance. UNIFIL was still there in April 1996, when one of its bases, at Qana in southern Lebanon, was struck by Israeli shells, which killed 105 civilians and wounded several Fijian peace-keepers. In August 2000 the Lebanese government eventually deployed a Joint Security Force to south Lebanon, but still declined to deploy military personnel along the border zone, on the grounds that a comprehensive peace agreement with Israel should be reached first. In January 2001 the UN Secretary-General stated that the area was relatively stable and it was agreed by the Security Council that UNIFIL should reconfigure to focus on its remaining mandate of maintaining and observing the cease-fire along the line of withdrawal. An initial reduction of the Force's strength to 4,550 troops was effected by July 2001. During the year there were several incidents involving attacks by **Hezbollah** on Israeli positions and violations of the area of withdrawal by Israeli military aircraft. In response to an increase in early 2002 of incidents, UNIFIL increased its patrols. By the end of 2002 UNIFIL was expected to have reduced further its complement to some 2,000 troops, but at July 2002 it still had 3,426 troops and its mandate was extended to 31 January 2003. It is still operational in mid-2004.

UNIIMOG—United Nations Iran-Iraq Military Observer Group

Established in 1988 to monitor the cease-fire between Iran and Iraq at the end of the **Iran–Iraq War**.

UNIKOM—United Nations Iraq-Kuwait Observation Mission

Established by a UN Security Council resolution (initially for a six-month period) in April 1991, to monitor a 200-km demilitarized zone along the border between Iraq and Kuwait. The task of the mission was to deter violations of the border, monitor the Khor Abdullah waterway between Iraq and Kuwait and prevent **military** activity in the area. In February 1993 the UN Security Council adopted a resolution to strengthen UNIKOM, following incursions into Kuwaiti territory by Iraqi personnel. The relocation of Iraqi citizens from Kuwait was completed by February 1994. UNIKOM provided support to the Iraqi-Kuwait Boundary Demarcation Commission, which was terminated in 1993, and to the International Committee of the Red Cross. A maritime operation to monitor the Khor Abdullah waterway began in February 2000. At 31 July 2002 UNIKOM comprised some 900 troops and 195 military observers, assisted by some 230 international and local civilian support staff. Two-thirds of the costs of UNIKOM are funded by voluntary contributions from Kuwait. The UN General Assembly voted US \$52.9m. for the mission for the period 1 July 2002–30 June 2003.

Unilateral Separation Plan

Plan announced towards the end of 2003 by Israeli Prime Minister **Ariel Sharon**, as part of an ultimatum to **Palestinians** to sit down and talk or accept a unilateral Israeli plan—a security step to disengage from the Palestinians. This would involve the closure of some of the illegal Israeli **settlements** in the **West Bank** and **Gaza**, but would consolidate Israel's hold on the largest remaining settlements, increase their fortification and deploy troops to secure them. The Palestinians would be left with a shrunken 'autonomous authority', within which would be heavily protected Israeli settlements. The new Plan would come into effect within three months, according to Israel's justice minister, Josef Lapid, 'if the Palestinians do not do what is necessary, including dismantling the terrorist organizations'.

Union of Arab Banks (UAB)

Established in 1972 and based in **Beirut**, Lebanon, the UAB aims to foster co-operation between Arab banks and to increase their efficiency. It prepares feasibility studies for projects and organized the 2001 Arab Banking Conference.

Union constitutionelle

Moroccan political party, founded in 1983. It has a 25-member politburo. Its leadership is currently vacant.

Union pour la démocratie et les libertés

Algerian political grouping, founded in 1997 and led by Abdelkrim Seddiki.

Union démocratique

Moroccan political party, founded in 2001. Its president is Bouazza Ikken.

Union générale tunisienne du travail

Tunisian trade union federation.

Union socialiste des forces populaires – *see* Socialist Union of Popular Forces (Morocco)

Unionist Arab Democratic Party

Jordanian political coalition, formed in 1996 from three leftist parties.

United Arab Emirates (UAE)

Al-Imarat al-Arabiyah al-Muttahidah

A grouping of seven emirates (*imarah,* plural *imarat*) bordering the Gulf of Oman and the **Persian (Arabian) Gulf**, between Oman and Saudi Arabia. The emirates are: Abu Zaby (Abu Dhabi), Ajman, Al-Fujayrah, Ash-Shariqah (Sharjah), Dubayy (Dubai), Ras al-Khaimah and Umm al-Qaywayn (Umm al-Qaiwain). Their capital is Abu Dhabi. The land area covers some 82,880 sq km in all, and the UAE has a total population of some 2.5m., of which 1,576,472 were estimated in July 2002 to be non-nationals. Fewer than 20% in all are UAE citizens: Emirati 19%, other Arab and Iranian 23%, South Asian 50%, other expatriates (including Westerners and East Asians) 8%. The population is 96% Muslim (**Shi'a** 16%), 4% Christian, Hindu and 'other'. **Arabic** is the official language, and English, **Persian**, Hindi and Urdu are all also commonly spoken.

The UAE has a federal government, with specified delegated powers; other powers are reserved to member emirates. Since 2 December 1971 the head of state has been President **Zayed** bin Sultan an-Nahyan, ruler of Abu Dhabi since 6 August 1966. Since 8 October 1990 the Vice-President has been **Maktum ibn Rashid al-Maktum**, ruler of Dubai. The Federal Supreme Council (FSC) comprises the seven emirate rulers. The FSC is the highest constitutional authority in the UAE. It establishes general policies and sanctions federal legislation. It meets four times a year. The rulers of Abu Dhabi and Dubai have effective veto power. Since 8 October 1990 the Prime Minister has been Maktum ibn Rashid al-Maktum. Sultan bin Zayed an-Nahyan has been Deputy Prime Minister since 20 November 1990. There is a Council of Ministers appointed by the President. The President and Vice-President are both elected by the FSC (a group of seven electors) for five-year terms. The most recent presidential election took place on 2 December 2001 and the next is scheduled to be held in 2006. The Prime Minister and Deputy Prime Minister are appointed by the President. The unicameral Federal National Council (**Majlis** al-Ittihad al-Watani)—a 40-member body—is appointed by the rulers of the constituent states for a term of two years. The Federal National Council reviews legislation proposed by the Council of Ministers, but it cannot change or veto it. The Union Supreme Court consists of judges appointed by the President. A federal court system was introduced in 1971, but, with the exceptions of Dubai and Ras al-Khaimah, the emirates are not fully integrated into the federal system. All emirates apply secular and Islamic legal systems for civil, criminal, and high courts. There are no formal political parties or political groupings.

Media

A wide range of publications is available—including at least 12 published in Abu Dhabi, eight in Dubai, three in Ras al-Khaimah and seven in Sharjah. Local news agencies include the Emirates News Agency and the UAE Press Service. There are eight radio and television broadcasting stations. The Emirates Telecommunications Corpn provides services throughout the UAE.

History

The **Trucial states** of the Persian (Arabian) Gulf coast granted the United Kingdom control of their defence and foreign affairs by 19th century treaties. In 1971 six of these states—Abu Zaby, 'Ajman, Al-Fujayrah, Ash-Shariqah, Dubayy and Umm al-Qaywayn—merged to form the UAE. They were joined in 1972 by Ra's al-Khaymah. The UAE's per caput gross domestic product is not far below those of leading Western European nations. Its generosity with **oil** revenues and its cautious foreign policy stance have allowed the UAE to play a significant if limited role in the affairs of the region.

International relations

Because details of the 1974 and 1977 treaties have not been made public, the exact location of the Saudi Arabia-UAE boundary is unknown and its status is considered *de facto*. Oman signed a boundary treaty with the UAE in 1999, and the UAE-Oman boundary line was formally recognized in June 2000. The UAE seeks **Arab League** and other international support for its opposition to Iran's occupation of the **Tunb Islands**—Greater Tunb Island (called Tunb al-Kubra in Arabic by the UAE and Jazireh-ye Tonb-e Bozorg in Persian by Iran) and Lesser Tunb Island (called Tunb as-Sughra in Arabic by theUAE and Jazireh-ye Tonb-e Kuchek in Persian by Iran)—and its attempts to occupy a jointly administered island in the Persian (Arabian) Gulf (called **Abu Musa** in Arabic by the UAE and Jazireh-ye Abu Musa in Persian by Iran). The UAE is a **drugs** transhipment point for traffickers owing to its proximity to south-west Asian drug-producing countries. The UAE's position as a major financial centre makes it vulnerable to '**money-laundering**'. Anti-money-laundering legislation was signed into law by the President on 25 January 2002.

United Arab Emirates, economy

The UAE together constitute the sixth largest economy in the **Middle East**, with a gross national product of US $67,600m. Its population enjoys the highest standard of living in terms of gross domestic product (GDP) per head of any state in the Middle East, after Qatar: $25,470, the 11th highest level in the world. The UAE has an open economy that records high per caput **income** and a sizeable annual **trade** surplus. Its wealth is based on **oil** and **gas** output (which account for about 33% of GDP), and the fortunes of the economy fluctuate with the prices of those commodities. Since 1973 the UAE has undergone a profound transformation from an impoverished region of small desert principalities to a modern state with a high standard of living. At present levels of production, oil and gas reserves are sufficient to last for more than 100 years. The government has increased spending on job creation and infrastructure expansion and is opening up its utilities to greater private-sector involvement.

United Arab List

Israeli political grouping, supported largely by **Israeli Arabs**. It is affiliated to the **Israel Labour Party** and led by Abd al-Malik Dahamshah.

United Arab Republic

The United Arab Republic resulted from the political union, in 1958, of Egypt and Syria. Its capital was **Cairo** and **Gamal Abdel Nasser** was President. As an initial step toward creating a pan-Arab union, the Republic abolished Syrian and Egyptian citizenship, termed its inhabitants Arabs, and called the country 'Arab territory'. It considered 'the Arab homeland' to be the entire area between the **Persian (Arabian) Gulf** and the Atlantic coast. In 1958, together with Yemen (**North Yemen**), it formed a loose federation called the **United Arab States**. In 1961 Syria withdrew from the union after a **military** coup, and Yemen soon followed, thus ending the union. Egypt continued to use the name until 1971.

United Arab States

A loose federation between Yemen (**North Yemen**) and the **United Arab Republic**. It was formed in 1958 and dissolved in 1961.

United Front, The

The United Front (also known as the **Northern Alliance)** was a loose confederation of different political leaders and groupings that broadly provided the basis for the Afghan government that was driven from power by the **Taliban** in 1996. It was recognized by the United Nations as the Afghan government until the **Afghan Interim Authority** was established. The front was a diverse and unstable group. The main **military** force represents the country's second largest ethnic group, the **Tajiks**, and was joined by militias representing smaller ethnic groups, such as the **Uzbeks** and the **Hazaras** who exist in isolated pockets of the country. The United Front opposed the Taliban's interpretation of **Islam** and was a historical rival of the Taliban's **Pashtun** ethnic community.

United Kingdom

A country with longstanding links to the **Middle East**, from the mid 19th century onwards. A major colonial power in the region from the late 19th century until well into the second half of the 20th century. A centre of Middle Eastern, Islamic and Arab studies (notably at Oxford, Cambridge, London, Durham, Leicester and Exeter universities). Probably the major centre of Middle Eastern politics, and of the **Arabic** press, outside of the Middle East itself. London, Birmingham, Leicester and other cities are centres of Islamist activity and many Islamist organizations. It has been said that the United Kingdom, with its large immigrant Muslim population and relatively liberal immigration laws, is one of the best recruiting grounds for Islamist organizations in the Western world. Sheikh Omar Bakri Mohammed, founder of **al-Muhajiroun**, an Islamist group based in London which has recruited for the *Jihad*, has claimed that mosques and university campuses in the United Kingdom recruit on average 18,000 British-born Muslims annually to take part in military activities in countries where armed Islamist groups are fighting. Undoubtedly an exaggeration, this figure nevertheless indicates a sizeable source of support. The majority of Muslims in the United Kingdom, however, are not supporters of radical **Islam**, although they are often sympathetic to many of the Islamists' concerns.

United Socialist Party of Kurdistan

A breakaway group from the **Patriotic Union of Kurdistan**, led by Mahmoud Osman.

United States Agency for International Development

The bilateral development agency of the USA.

United Tajik Opposition

The anti-government side in the **Tajik civil war**, consisting of Islamists, pro-**democracy** activists, nationalists and leftists. It largest faction was the **Islamic Renaissance Party**.

United Torah Judaism

Israeli political/religious grouping that comprises a number of minor ultra-orthodox groups: **Poale Agudat Israel**, Moria, **Agudat Israel** and **Degel Ha Torah**. Formed prior to the 1992 elections to overcome the increase in the election representation threshold from 1% to 1.5% of the vote and to help counter the rising influence of the Russian Jewish vote. It contested the 1999 elections as Degel Ha Torah and Agudat Israel. It is currently led by Meir Porush.

United Workers Party – *see* Mapam—Mifleget HaPoalim HaMeuhedet

Universal Declaration of Human Rights

Statement drawn up by the United Nations to provide guide-lines and a mandate for activities and interventions in support of human rights throughout the world.

UNMEM

United Nations Middle East Mission.

UNMOVIC—United Nations Monitoring, Verification and Inspection Commission

Operations in Iraq from 1999. Established to replace the **UNSCOM**.

UNRWA—United Nations Relief and Works Agency for Palestinian Refugees in the Near East

Established by the UN General Assembly to provide relief, **health**, **education** and welfare services for Palestinian **refugees** in the **Near East**, initially on a short-term basis. It began operations in May 1950 and, in the absence of a solution to the Palestine refugee problem, its mandate has been extended subsequently by the General Assembly up to the present. UNRWA employs an international staff of about 120 and a local staff of more than 22,500. Its three principal areas of activity are education, health and relief and social services. Education accounts for approximately 50% of the total budget, health for 20% and relief and social services for 10%. In mid-1996 the headquarters were relocated from Vienna, Austria, to **Gaza** and Jordan. It has no governing body but reports directly to the UN General Assembly. It has a 10-member advisory body comprising representatives of the governments of Egypt, Jordan, Lebanon, Syria, Turkey, Belgium, France, the United Kingdom, the USA and Japan.

UNSCO—Office of the United Nations Special Co-ordinator in the Occupied Territories

UNSCO was established in June 1994 to support the **Middle East** 'peace process', in particular the implementation of the **Declaration of Principles on Palestinian Self-Rule** (signed by the Israeli government and the **Palestine Liberation Organization** (PLO) in 1993), and to enhance the effectiveness of international donor assistance to the autonomous areas. Since September 1999 the Special Co-ordinator has also acted as the personal representative of the UN Secretary-General to the PLO and the **Palestinian National Authority**. The Co-ordinator also jointly chairs the Local Aid Co-ordination Committee.

UNSCOM—United Nations Special Commission on Monitoring

Charged with inspecting Iraq's suspected chemical, biological and nuclear weapons capabilities in the aftermath of the **Gulf War (1991)**. It began its first inspection of chemical weapons on 9 June 1991. It handed over its responsibilities to **UNMOVIC**, created to disarm Iraq of any **weapons of mass destruction** and to operate a system of ongoing monitoring and verification, in 1999.

UNSCOP—United Nations Special Committee on Palestine.

Reduced the proposed Jewish state to 55% of Palestine and turned the plan into the **UN General Assembly Resolution 181**.

UNTSO—United Nations Truce Supervision Organization

Established in 1948 to supervise the truce called by the UN Security Council in Palestine in May 1948. It has assisted in the application of the 1949 Armistice Agreements. This was the first peace-keeping operation undertaken by the UN. Its activities have evolved over the years in response to developments in the region. UNTSO observers remain in the **Middle East** today to maintain cease-fires, supervise armistice agreements, prevent isolated incidents from escalating and assist other UN peace-keeping operations in the region, including **UNDOF** and **UNIFIL**. The mission maintains offices in **Beirut**, Lebanon and **Damascus**, Syria. There are also a number of outposts in the Sinai region of Egypt where a UN presence is maintained.

Urabi movement (Egypt)

First nationalist movement in Egypt.

Urbanization

The process of urban growth or the growing influence of the towns on the countryside. Several countries in the region have a very high proportion of their population living in urban areas: Kuwait (96.1%), Qatar (92.9%), Bahrain (92.5%), Israel (91.8%), Malta (91.8%), Lebanon (90.1%), Libya (88%), the United Arab Emirates (UAE, 87.2%) and Saudi Arabia (86.7%). A few countries in the region have a very large proportion of the total population living in one city: Lebanon, **Beirut** (59.2%); Kuwait, Kuwait City (45.9%); the UAE, Dubai (34%), Israel (**Tel-Aviv** (33.1%); and Libya, **Tripoli** (32.8%).

US armed forces

US armed forces actually deployed in the **Middle East** amount to nearly 200,000 men and women. These include 140,000 service personnel in Iraq, 34,000 in

Kuwait, 10,000 in Afghanistan, and smaller numbers in other countries attached to US embassies and foreign missions.

US Iraq Survey Group

Organization charged by the US administration with a continuing search for **weapons of mass destruction** (WMD) in Iraq following the US-led intervention in and occupation of Iraq. Its leader, Dr Keay, stated in January 2004 that the Iraq Survey Group had not found WMD and that he believed that the identification of WMD in Iraq prior to the intervention 'was wrong'.

US military policy in the Middle East (historical)

The **Carter** Doctrine, which focused primarily on the **Middle East**, began with the establishment of a Rapid Deployment Force (later the Central Command), with bases on Diego Garcia and in Oman, Egypt, Somalia and Kenya. This military strategy was designed to contain the 1979 **Islamic Revolution** in Iran and the Soviet intervention in Afghanistan. Carter's strategy was intended to provide the military infrastructure and deployment necessary for an eventual rapid US intervention in the Middle East. The cornerstone of the Carter Doctrine was a US-Saudi agreement according to which Saudi Arabia would pay for the building of an elaborate system of command, naval and air facilities large enough 'to sustain US forces in intensive regional combat'. The Doctrine was reaffirmed by US President Reagan, who went even further by signing a Memorandum of Strategic Understanding with Israel that provided, among other things, for the prepositioning of US military supplies in Israel while surrogate US military bases were built and equipped in Saudi Arabia. Throughout the 1980s many landings and airborne manoeuvres were conducted by US troops in several countries in the region, including Somalia, Jordan and, particularly, Egypt, where Operation Bright Star in 1987 and 1989 effectively prepared the US forces for **Operation Desert Shield** and **Operation Desert Storm** in late 1990 and early 1991 in the **Gulf**. In 1993 serious efforts were under way to make Haifa (**Tel-Aviv**) a military base for the US Sixth Fleet at the same time as the US Secretary for Defense was recommending the closure or realignment of more than 130 US military bases in the aftermath of the dismantling of the Warsaw Pact. The focus of attention had already moved away from the containment of the threat of communism to that of the 'Arab bomb', **Islamic fundamentalism** and other 'hostile forces' in the Middle East. In so far as it had a coherent Middle East policy, the **Clinton** Administration carried on essentially where the Reagan Administration left off. During his tour of the Middle East in October 1994 President Clinton used the opportunity to urge all heads of state in the region to crack down on the Islamists, and promised US support for such an enterprise.

US policy in the Middle East (historical)

One of the major US concerns regarding the **Middle East** during much of the 20th century (specifically between 1917 and 1989/90) was its strategic significance in the long Cold War, its geographical proximity to the Soviet Union's southern borders, and the risk of Soviet influence and intervention in the region. US influence was limited in the period immediately after the First World War. In the post-war settlement the 14 Points of President Wilson, who opposed Europe's secret agreements, were scarcely taken into account. Little attention was paid to the opinion of the **King-Crane Commission**, which, in 1919, criticized the Zionist plan for the future of Palestine. Early involvement by US companies in the Middle Eastern **oil** industry provided the basis for a foothold in the region, and created a lasting set of vested interests. Starting with Iraq in 1927, and followed by Saudi Arabia in 1933 and Kuwait in 1934, US companies controlled 20% of Middle Eastern production and 50% of Middle Eastern reserves by the mid-1940s. In 1947, as the major European powers in the Middle East, France and Britain, were increasingly forced to recognize the pressure for independence in many of their colonial territories, the 'Truman Doctrine' was promulgated. Saudi Arabia was securely bound by lend-lease as early as 1943, and shortly thereafter, as the Second World War ended, Greece, Turkey and Iran were loaned the means to buy US arms and other equipment. Truman offered to help 'free peoples who are fighting against the attempts of armed **minorities** to enslave them or against external pressures' and began to try to develop a more direct form of influence in the region. The Four Point Plan of 1949 allowed funds to be poured into the Arab countries. However, US ratification of Israel's territorial expansion, the non-creation of the long-dreamed-of Arab state, and the Palestinian exile, led to growing discontent with US policy in the Middle East, among the Arab states in particular. Their rejection of both the Allied Supreme Command in the Middle East (set up in London in 1950) and the Middle East Defence Organization (MEDO) sponsored by the United Kingdom, the USA, France and Turkey in 1951 were part of a more general reaction in the **Arab World**. On the other hand, Turkey joined the North Atlantic Treaty Organization in 1951 and attempts by Mossadegh to regain for Iran control of its own oil were brought to an abrupt end by US intervention in 1953. Howver, the **Baghdad Pact**, which involved Britain, Turkey, Iraq, Iran and Pakistan, failed to attract Lebanon, Syria, Jordan or Egypt. The last of these, after the **Free Officers**' coup of July 1952 and the coming to power of **Gamal Abdel Nasser**, was seeking new alliances as a way of promoting national autonomy. Egypt's refusal to join the MEDO and the Baghdad Pact was followed in September 1955 by an arms contract with the Soviet Union. The USA wisely stayed aloof from the disastrous attempt by France and Britain, with the help of Israel, to regain control of the **Suez Canal** in 1956 after it had been nationalized by Egyptian President Nasser. However, the Eisenhower Doctrine, described on 5 January 1957 as a programme of economic and military **aid** aimed at combating the 'power policy' of the USSR, was very explicit about increasing US influence in the Middle East. Its willingness to back this strategy by direct intervention when considered appropriate was confirmed in July 1958, when, one day after the uprising in Iraq, US marines landed in **Beirut**, Lebanon, while British paratroopers flew into **Amman**, Jordan, to prevent the uprising from spreading. While US policy in the Middle East was always affected by its wider relationship with the Soviet Union, as indeed were all of its policies, globally, it has also been—and continues to be—critically affected by its concern on the one hand to maintain close and generally supportive relations with Israel, and its interest, on the other, to cultivate its relations with the Arab states, particularly those rich in oil and interested in the purchase of arms.

USS Cole

American warship attacked in **Aden** harbour in 2000, allegedly by Islamist elements in Yemen linked to **al-Qa'ida**.

Uzbekistan, Republic of

Ozbekiston Respublikasi

Situated in southern **Central Asia**, to the north of Afghanistan, bordering Kazakhstan to the north, Turkmenistan to the west and south, and Kyrgyzstan and Tajikistan to the east. Together with Liechtenstein, Uzbekistan is one of the only two doubly land-locked countries in the world. It covers an area of 447,400 sq km (of which 22,000 sq km is **water**). The capital is Tashkent. For administrative purposes the country is divided into 12 provinces (*viloyat*, plural *viloyatlar*), one autonomous republic (*respublika*), and one city (*shahar*): Andijon Viloyati, Buxoro Viloyati, Farg'ona Viloyati, Jizzax Viloyati, Namangan Viloyati, Navoiy Viloyati, Qashqadaryo Viloyati (Qarshi), Qaraqalpog'iston Respublikasi (Nukus), Samarqand Viloyati, Sirdaryo Viloyati (Guliston), Surxondaryo Viloyati (Termiz), Toshkent Shahri, Toshkent Viloyati, Xorazm Viloyati (Urganch). (Where the names of an administrative division and its administrative centre are not the same, the name of the administrative centre is included in in parentheses.) At July 2002 the total population was estimated at 25,563,441. In 1996 it was estimated that, of the total population, 80% were **Uzbek**, 5.5% Russian, 5% **Tajik**, 3% **Kazakh**, 2.5% Karakalpak, 1.5% **Tatar** and 2.5% 'others'. The population is largely (88%) **Sunni** Muslim, complemented by 9% who are Eastern Orthodox and 3% of other confessions. The official language is Uzbek (spoken by 74.3% of the population). Russian is spoken by 14.2%, Tajik by 4.4% and other languages by 7.1%.

Political profile

Uzbekistan is a republic. Authoritarian presidential rule is maintained and little power is devolved to the executive branch. The head of state is President **Islam Karimov** (elected as President by the then Supreme Soviet on 24 March 1990, and re-elected on 29 December 1991). Karimov's term of office was extended to 2000 by popular referendum on 27 March 1995 and he was re-elected on 9 January 2000. The President was previously elected by popular vote for successive five-year terms, but this was extended by constitutional amendment in 2002 to seven years. The next presidential election is scheduled to be held in 2007. Since 21 December 1995 the head of government has been Prime Minister Otkir S. Sultonov. The Prime Minister and deputy ministers are appointed by the President. There is a Cabinet appointed by the President with the approval of the Supreme Assembly (Oliy **Majlis**). Members of the single chamber Supreme Assembly are elected by popular vote to serve five-year terms. This 250-member body is to be supplemented by a second chamber—to be established via elections in 2004. Judges are nominated to the Supreme Court by the President and confirmed by the Supreme Assembly. The legal system is based on an evolved version of Soviet civil law and Uzbekistan still lacks an independent judicial system.

Political Parties and Groups

- Adolat (Justice) Social Democratic Party; First Sec. Anwar Jurabayev
- Democratic National Rebirth Party (Milly Tiklanish); Chair. Aziz Kayumov
- People's Democratic Party (formerly Communist Party); First Sec. Abdulkhafiz Jalolov; the party of President Karimov
- Self-Sacrificers' Party or Fidokorlar National Democratic Party; First Sec. Ahtam Tursunov
- Fatherland Progress Party (merged with Self-Sacrificers' Party)
- Birlik (Unity) Movement; Chair. Abdurakhim Polat
- Erk (Freedom) Democratic Party; Chair. Muhammad Solih; banned 9 December 1992
- Human Rights Society of Uzbekistan; Chair. Abdumannob Polat
- Independent Human Rights Society of Uzbekistan; Chair. Mikhail Ardzinov
- Ezgulik; Leader Vasilia Inoyatova
- **Islamic Renaissance Party**
- **Islamic Movement of Uzbekistan**
- Islamist Adolat
- **Hizb ut-Tahrir**

Media

The government of Uzbekistan enforces strict media control. In December 1993 all but the official media were denied registration. The expression of nationalist and Islamic opinion is forbidden, and general media control is manifested in direct censorship or self-censorship by journalists and editors. Independent journalists face harassment and imprisonment. Publications are encouraged to promote the personality cult and policies of President Karimov. Radio and television are controlled by the State Television and Radio Broadcasting Co of Uzbekistan

(UZTELERADIO). In 1997 495 newspapers and 113 periodicals were published. The principal newspapers are *Adolat* (organ of the Adolat party), *Biznes-vestnik Vostoka*, *Deoyoy Partner*, *Fidokor* (organ of the Fidokorlar National Democratic Party), *Golos Uzbekistana* (independent), *Hurryiet*, *Khalk Suzi* (organ of the Supreme Assembly and the Council of Ministers), *Kommercheskiy Vestnik*, *Ma'rifat*, *Menejer*, *Molodiozh Uzbekistan*, *Mulkdor*, *Na postu/Postsda*, *Narodnoye Slovo* (organ of the government), *Pravda Vostoka* (organ of the Council of Ministers), *Savdogar*, *Soliqar va Bojhona Habarlari/ Nalogovie I Tamojennie Vesti*, *Sport*, *Tashkentskaya Pravda*, *Toshkent Khakikati*, *Turkiston* (organ of the Kamolot Association of Young People of Uzbekistan), *Uzbekiston Adabiyoti va San'ati* (organ of the Union of Writers of Uzbekistan), *Uzbekiston Oviszi*. Kamalak Television is a joint venture between Uzteleradio and a US company. There is one cable rebroadcaster in Tashkent. In 2003 there were approximately 20 television stations in regional capitals. In 2000 there were 42 internet service providers, and in 2002 there were 100,000 internet users.

History

Russia conquered Uzbekistan in the late 19th century. Stiff resistance to the Red Army by **Basmachi** guerrillas after the First World War was eventually suppressed and the Uzbek Soviet Socialist Republic (SSR) was established in 1924. The Soviet Union transformed Uzbekistan into Central Asia's economic powerhouse through steady industrialization and an expansion of urban centres. In addition Uzbekistan is fairly homogeneous ethnically. Uzbek minorities in Tajikistan (23%), Kyrgyzstan (13%) and Turkmenistan (13%) have proved to be a constant threat to ethnic stability in their home countries, something that the current President Karimov has been able to exploit in order to gain influence in the region. In March 1990 the Supreme Soviet of Uzbekistan elected Islam Karimov as President of Uzbekistan. When the 1991 *putsch* of conservatives in Moscow failed, the Supreme Soviet of Uzbekistan declared the Uzbek SSR independent and renamed it the Republic of Uzbekistan. The Communist Party of Uzbekistan was renamed the People's Democratic Party of Uzbekistan (PDPU), and in December 1991 Karimov was re-elected as President by direct popular vote. After achieving popular support Karimov started a process of consolidation of his rule by becoming increasingly authoritarian. After a short period of democratic freedom Karimov began to suppress dissent, banning all political parties, exerting complete control over the media and even going so far as to kidnap political opponents from neighbouring countries. The Supreme Assembly's members are usually in Karimov's fold and it meets only a few times each year for the automatic approval of Karimov's policies. In presidential elections Karimov is usually opposed by only token candidates. The most recent presidential election in January 2000 was described as a farce by foreign observers.

Democratic opposition was crushed by 1992, thus blocking the democratic outlet for the revival of **Islam** and Islamic nationalism that swept across Central Asia in the *perestroika/glasnost* period (e.g. the Islamic Renaissance Party was never able to register as a legal party in Uzbekistan). Karimov then turned his attention to (clandestine) Islamic groups based in the **Fergana Valley**. In a series of crackdowns in 1992, 1993 and after 1997, hundreds of ordinary pious Muslims were arrested for alleged links with Islamic fundamentalists or for being Wahabbis. Mosques and *madrassas* were closed down and mullahs were imprisoned or forced into exile. In 1998 the government passed the infamous Law on Freedom of Conscience and Religious Organizations, which established new modes of repression against Muslims—other religious organizations were unaffected by the law. However, these repressive policies have generated precisely what they were intended to suppress: extremist Islamic militancy. The Islamic Movement of Uzbekistan (IMU), the most powerful militant group in Central Asia, and the Hizb ut-Tahrir (HT) both developed in Karimov's Uzbekistan.

Adding adherents to the IMU, HT and boosting the general dissatisfaction with Karimov's regime is the social and economic plight of the population—despite the country's enormous natural wealth. Poverty and unemployment are increasing, but the regime appears to do very little to combat these problems. Inflation is chronic—in 1994, after the introduction of the *som*, it rose to 1,500%—and food shortages have led to riots in the capital. Sixty per cent of the population is under 25 years of age. They are jobless, restless and hungry. Some of them have joined the ranks of what they view as the only real opposition: the IMU and the HT.

Uzbekistan has become the centre of the growing Islamic resistance and extremism in Central Asia. The IMU has undertaken a series of incursions from bases in Tajikistan and Afghanistan. However, resistance to the Karimov regime is not confined to Islamists alone. There is a general disillusionment in the populace with President Karimov's policies and his stranglehold on the country. This has reportedly also spread to some of Karimov's own advisers and aides. In 1999 a series of bomb explosions struck Tashkent. While the government blamed Islamist radicals, several observers believe that the perpetrators could just as well be dissatisfied junior leaders.

International relations/Transnational issues

Uzbekistan is a transit country for Afghan narcotics bound for Russian and, to a lesser extent, Western European markets. There is limited illicit cultivation of **cannabis** and small amounts of **opium** poppy for domestic consumption. Poppy cultivation has almost been wiped out by a government crop eradication programme. Uzbekistan is also a transit point for **heroin** precursor chemicals bound for Afghanistan. Dispute over access to Sokh and other Uzbek enclaves in Kyrgyzstan mars progress on international boundary delimitation. Kazakhstan, Tajikistan, Turkmenistan, Kyrgyzstan, and Uzbekistan are forced to share limited water resources. Kazakhstan, Turkmenistan and Uzbekistan have also to contend with the regional environmental degradation caused by the shrinking Aral Sea. The border with Kyrgyzstan and Tajikistan is mined in certain sections, continuing to cause civilian casualties.

Uzbekistan, economy

Under Soviet rule Uzbekistan was transformed into an economic powerhouse. The country is now the world's second largest exporter of cotton. However, this has been achieved at the cost of an enormous ecological disaster. Uzbekistan has abundant **mineral** resources which add to its economic strength. These include **gold** and **gas** reserves of 2,000,000m. cu m. The country is also self-sufficient in **oil**. In addition Uzbekistan is a regionally significant producer of chemicals and machinery.

Investors regard Uzbekistan as the jewel of **Central Asia** for its abundant natural resources and skilled labour. However, it is also viewed as a risky country to invest in. Nevertheless, Uzbekistan has attracted considerable amounts of foreign investment, both direct and indirect, in the gold and oil sectors.

Despite its promising natural resource base Uzbekistan has suffered a series of severe economic crises since independence. The economy is still largely state-run and so far sustained economic growth and macroeconomic stability have not been achieved. Uzbekistan has tried to pursue an independent economic policy, but acceded to an **International Monetary Fund** (IMF)-sponsored structural adjustment programme in 1995. However, in April 2001 the IMF closed its office in Tashkent, harshly criticizing the regime's failure to introduce reforms.

Uzbekistan has responded to the negative external conditions generated by the Asian and Russian financial crises by emphasizing import substitute industrialization and by tightening export and currency controls within its already largely closed economy. Economic policies that have repelled foreign investment are a major factor in the economy's stagnation. A growing **debt** burden, persistent inflation, and a poor business climate have led to disappointing growth since 2000.

Uzbek economic data should be viewed with caution as the Uzbek government claims that the economy is strong and stable, contrary to claims made by most independent observers. Growing economic difficulties have been identified and potential for a financial crisis exists.

Uzbekistan has received almost US $1,000m. in US **aid** since 1992. Annual aid contributions have averaged around $100m.. Aid increased dramatically after 11 September 2001. Uzbekistan became a key US ally in the 'war on terror' in October 2001, when the Pentagon set up the Khanabad base to aid its offensive against the **Taliban** in Afghanistan. US aid continued despite widespread recognition and condemnation of gross human rights abuses perpetrated by the Uzbek government and state apparatus. While recognizing that the use of torture by Uzbek police was 'routine', the US Department of State granted the country $80m. in 2002, about one-third of its total contribution in that year. However, growing concerns about the appalling human rights record of the Karimov Government, heightened by outspoken remarks by the British ambassador to Tashkent, Craig Murray, prior to the

Gulf War (2003), make it unlikely that the USA will 'certify' the regime as suitable to receive further US aid when certification becomes due in April 2004. In April 2004 Uzbekistan's failure to make progress on human rights and economic reform prompted the European Bank for Reconstruction and Development to announce that it will restrict its future operations in the country mainly to the private sector.

Strengths

Uzbekistan's economic strengths include its gold and its considerable unexploited deposits of oil and natural gas. Current production of natural gas makes a significant contribution to electricity generation. There is a manufacturing tradition that includes agricultural machinery and Central Asia's only aviation factory.

Weaknesses

The country's irrigation scheme for cotton production has caused massive environmental damage, but has resulted in a well-developed cotton market. Uzbekistan is is dependent on grain imports, as domestic production only meets 25% of needs. There is high inflation.

Uzbeks

A major ethnic group in **Central Asia**. Uzbeks are found in nearly every Central Asian state, but mostly in Uzbekistan and Afghanistan.

V

Vanguards of Conquest

Militant Egyptian Islamist grouping. Breakaway group from **Islamic Jihad**. Its leader is Yasir as-Sirri.

Vanunu, Mordechai

A student radical and then a technician at Israel's nuclear plant at Dimona until 1985. Vanunu was lured from the United Kingdom to Rome, Italy, by a **Mossad** agent named 'Cindy', kidnapped, drugged and transported back to Israel by Mossad. On his return he was charged with treason and espionage and sentenced to jail in 1986 for having revealed secrets about the Israeli nuclear programme, the production and stockpiling of nuclear weapons (as part of Israel's development of **weapons of mass destruction**) to *The Sunday Times* of London. He was released in April 2004, 17 years and five months after being kidnapped. He complained that one of the reasons for the very aggressive treatment he received was the fact that he was a Christian, not Jewish. On his release, the first thing he did was to visit an old Anglican church in **Jerusalem** to give thanks to God and his friends. He was bound over to stay in Israel for six months, but hoped subsequently to emigrate to the USA.

Veil

The veil is a powerful symbol of **women**'s modesty in Muslim societies. Sometimes used to refer generally to 'Islamic dress' for women, it refers usually to the covering of the head and/or face; the usual term used is the **Arabic** *hejab*. This may mean a **headscarf** or a veil. In Iran, the term *hejab* is used, but there is also the *chador* which usually refers not only to a covering for the head and/or face, but also to the whole outfit or dress worn by women observing 'the proprieties of **Islam**'. In Afghanistan, a more complete covering for women is referred to as the *burka*.

Velayat-i Faqih

In **Arabic** and **Persian** literally a regime of clerics. The term is used of the regime instituted by Ayatollah **Khomeini** for the Islamic Republic of Iran. It is often mistranslated as 'theocracy'. It is thought, by those who support this concept and political construct, to ensure exceptional religious authority and thereby confer legitimacy on the regime. In the case of Iran it is combined with various democratic forms.

Velayati, Ali Akbar

A layman from **Tehran** who studied medicine at Tehran University and pursued postgraduate studies in the USA in 1976. While in the USA he was active in the Muslim Students' Association. On his return to Iran, he served as a member of parliament for Tehran and was an aide to the speaker, **Hojatoleslam Ali Akbar Hashemi Rafsanjani**. When he was originally proposed as Prime Minister by President **Khamenei** in the autumn of 1981, the **Majlis** refused to confirm him in that office—apparently because of his lack of political involvement prior to the fall of the Shah. He was appointed as foreign minister in December 1981.

Venice Declaration

In Venice, Italy, on 13 June 1980 the European Economic Community (EEC) issued a statement recognizing the **Palestine Liberation Organization** as a valid (but not necessarily exclusive) representative of the Palestinian people. The heads of state and government and the Ministers of Foreign Affairs of the EEC held a comprehensive exchange of views on all aspects of the current situation in the **Middle East**, including the state of negotiations resulting from the agreements signed between Egypt and Israel in March 1979. They agreed that growing tensions in the Middle East constituted a serious danger and rendered a comprehensive solution to the **Arab–Israeli Conflict** more necessary and pressing than ever. The nine member states produced a joint statement, which set out their views and proposals regarding the conflict and possible avenues for its resolution. It acknowledged that all of the countries in the area were entitled to live in peace within secure, recognized and guaranteed borders. It considered that a just solution must be found to the Palestinian problem, which was not just one of **refugees**. The Palestinian people must be placed in a position, by an appropriate process defined within the framework of a comprehensive peace settlement, to exercise fully its right to self-determination. Israel was required to put an end to the territorial occupation which it had maintained since the conflict of 1967, as it had done for part of Sinai. It recognized the special importance of **Jerusalem** and stressed that no unilateral initiative designed to change the status of the city would be acceptable, and that any agreement on the status of Jerusalem should guarantee free access for everyone to the holy places. It considered the Israeli **settlements** in the **West Bank** and **Gaza Strip** to constitute a serious obstacle to the peace process, and emphasized that the settlements, as well as modifications in population and property in the occupied Arab territories, were illegal under international law. It considered that only the renunciation of violence by all parties could create the climate of confidence necessary for a comprehensive settlement of the conflict.

VEVAK

The intelligence service of the Islamic Republic of Iran. The successor of the Shah's secret intelligence service, **SAVAK**.

Visrael Ba'aliya

Israeli political party of the centre.

Visrael Beitunu

Right-wing Israeli political party.

Vizir

Title used to refer to a senior political figure, usually a minister or equivalent.

Al-Wa'ad

The Pledge

Lebanese national secular democratic party. It was established after the civil war by Elie Hobeika. It leadership is currently vacant.

WAFA—Wafa wa al-Adl

Algerian political grouping. WAFA's leader, Ahmed Taleb Ibrahimi, was a former Algerian foreign minister and, in 1999, presidential candidate. Founded in 1999, WAFA was refused government recognition as a political party in 2000 on the grounds that it contained a large number of supporters of the **Front islamique du salut**.

Wafd Party (Egypt)

In **Arabic** *wafd* means 'delegation'. The Wafd was formed in 1919 under the leadership of **Saad Zaghlul**, a lawyer. Two days after the end of the Second World War Zaghlul demanded that a delegation be permitted to travel to London, United Kingdom, to present the case for Egyptian independence. Refusal by the British High Commissioner was followed by three years of organized protests. In November 1922 Britain declared nominal independence for Egypt, while retaining various major powers for itself. This arrangement was underwritten by the Egyptian Constitution of 1923. The Wafd won the first general election and Zaghlul became Prime Minister. After his death in 1927 the Wafd was led by Mustafa Nahas Pasha. In 1931 Prime Minister Nahas Pasha was dismissed by King **Fuad** (reigned 1922–36), who also suspended the Constitution. Just before his death in 1936 the king reinstated the Constitution and the Wafd was returned to power with a large majority in elections held in April of that year. In August the **Anglo-Egyptian Treaty**, which retained key British responsibilities regarding foreign affairs, was signed. The Regency Council, headed by Nahas Pasha, ruled, however, on behalf of the 16-year-old King **Farouk**. When Farouk achieved his majority in 1938, he dismissed Nahas Pasha, resisting British pressure to retain him. Farouk's pro-Italian stance led the British ambassador, in 1942 (as German troops advanced on Egypt from Libya), to compel the king, on pain of deposition, to reappoint Nahas Pasha. The latter remained in office until October 1944 and ensured Egypt's affiliation to the **Arab League**. After the debacle of the 1948–49 Palestine War and the establishment of Israel, Farouk agreed to a reconciliation with the Wafd leadership. A general election held in January 1950 placed the Wafd firmly in power. The government now pressed Britain to withdraw its troops from Egypt. When Britain refused, in October 1951, the Egyptian government unilaterally abrogated the 1936 Anglo-Egyptian Treaty (which was valid until 1956) and demanded Britain's immediate and unconditional withdrawal from the **Suez Canal** zone. Guerrilla action against British forces by militant Wafdists ensued. Following riots in **Cairo** in 1951 the king dismissed the Wafd Government. A **military** coup by the **Free Officers** in July 1952 led to the banning of the Wafd along with other political parties. It was not until June 1977, a quarter of a century later, following the promulgation of the Law of the System of Political Parties, that Fuad Serag ad-Din, a veteran of the pre-1952 Wafd Party, obtained a licence to establish the **New Wafd Party**.

Wahhabis

The followers of the Wahhabi faith—**Wahhabism**. The Wahhabis call themselves Muwahidun (Unitarians).

Wahhabism

Wahhabism is a doctrine or set of beliefs and practices, based on the **Hanbali** school of **Islam**, developed by Muhammad ibn Abdul Wahhab (1703–87), a native of **Najd** in the **Arabian Peninsula**. The name was coined by those opposed to Abdul Wahhab; Wahhabis refer to themselves as Muwahidun or Unitarians. Abdul Wahhab condemned many of the superstitions and practices that had accumulated around the original teachings of Islam. He was especially against the cult of saints. In one sense a 'fundamentalist', he also favoured *ijtihad*—the reasoned interpretation of the **Shari'a (Islamic Law)**—and opposed the codification of the Shari'a into a comprehensive system of jurisprudence. Contrary to Hanbali practice, he made attendance at public prayer obligatory and forbade minarets in the building of mosques. In alliance with the followers of **Ibn Saud** of Dar'iya, who became ruler of Najd in 1745 and founded the **House of Saud**, the Wahhabis mounted a campaign against idolatry, **corruption** and adultery. Claiming the authority of the *hadith,* they banned music, dancing and even poetry, and prohibited the use of personal decoration and finery. Regarding themselves as the true believers, they launched a *jihad* against all others—whom they described as apostates. In 1802 they attacked and looted **Karbala**, the holy city of the **Shi'ites**. Under Saud, grandson of Muhammad ibn Saud (reigned 1803–14), Wahhabi rule spread to the far borders of Iraq and Syria, and included the **Hijaz** and its two holy cities (**Medina** fell in 1804 and **Mecca** in 1806). This led the Ottoman sultan to order the governor of Egypt,

Muhammad Ali, to quell the movement. The result was the defeat and execution of Abdullah ibn Saud (reigned 1814–18). The power of the Wahhabi House of Saud waxed and waned until 1881, when it was expelled even from the Riyadh region. In the early years of the 20th century, under Abdul Aziz ibn Abdul Rahman as-Saud, who fostered the **Ikhwan** (Brotherhood) movement to spread the creed, using military and state power, Wahhabism rose again in the Arabian Peninsula. The Wahhabis attacked polytheists, unbelievers and 'hypocrites' (who claimed to be Muslims but whose behaviour was regarded as unIslamic). They labelled any deviation from the Shari'a as unIslamic. Between the 1920s and 1930s the House of Saud eventually succeeded in unifying Saudi Arabia and in establishing its monarchical rule, largely thanks to its alliance with the Wahhabi religious leaders. The partnership between the political and religious powers became an integral part of the legitimacy of the House of Saud. During the late 1970s and 1980s, as **oil** wealth came increasingly to be associated with corruption and profligacy, the attraction of Wahhabism increased once again, and it became a basis for the criticism of the Saudi regime—and indeed the regimes of the oil-rich states of the **Gulf** as a whole. The deployment of US troops and others in the Arabian Peninsula in the early 1990s during the course of **Operation Desert Shield** and **Operation Desert Storm**, as part of the US-led war against Iraq, was anathema to many strict Muslims—who abhorred the presence of infidels in the land of the 'holy places' of Mecca and Medina. This increased the militancy of the beliefs and practices of an increasing number of Muslims, particularly Saudi Arabian Muslims. **Osama bin Laden** and his followers, many of whom espouse the precepts of Wahhabism, claim that the Saudi Arabian regime has become a pawn of the West, particularly of the USA, and has lost its religious and political legitimacy.

Wailing Wall

In **Hebrew** *Kotel Ma'aravi*. The Wailing Wall is part of the western extension of the retaining wall erected by Herod the Great (AD 37–4 BC) around the Jewish temple on top of Mount Moriah in **Jerusalem**. The only remnant now of the second temple (razed in AD 70), it is the most sacred site of **Judaism**, to which Jews come to grieve the destruction of the first and second temples, which once stood on this site, and to pray, particularly on the Fast Day of the ninth of Av.

The Wall (Cyprus)

After the Turkish invasion of northern Cyprus in July 1974 and the subsequent establishment of a *de facto* separate state in the north, a wall was constructed which traversed the centre of Nicosia, dividing the northern part of the city from the southern part. The wall became a flashpoint for clashes between the two Cypriot communities as well as a device that systematically reduced normal interaction between them. UN peace-keeping forces were deployed along the length of the wall at 'crossing points'.

The Wall (Israel)

Early in 2002 the Israeli Government of **Ariel Sharon** proposed the construction of an electronic 'fence' or wall between **Jerusalem** and the main Palestinian population centres of the **West Bank**. The barrier would extend east of the city and both the **settlement** of Ma'aleh Edomin and several Palestinian Area B villages (under the civil control of the **Palestinian National Authority** but Israeli security control) would fall inside its perimeter. The office of the Prime Minister denied that there were plans to change the legal status of the Palestinian villages, but claimed that these areas must now be considered part of the 'greater Jerusalem area'. During 2003 the Israeli authorities began to construct a wall dividing the West Bank physically from Israel. Described by the Israeli authorities as 'a defensive wall against **terrorism**', the construction rapidly reduced movement between Israel and the West Bank and between the West Bank and the **Gaza Strip**. Already by May 2004 it stretched for 20 km and effectively annexed more land on the West Bank; however, the plan calls for a wall of 100 km in total length and this, together with the E1 proposal for a 'bubble' which would include the mega-settlement of Ma'ale Adumim east of Jerusalem, would place 50% of the West Bank in Israeli hands. It has already become for **Palestinians** a symbol of Israel's aggressive strategy of 'apartheid' under the leadership of Ariel Sharon. The International Committee of the Red Cross has pronounced the wall contrary to international law.

The Wall (Morocco and Western Sahara)

After the initial success of the **armed forces** of the **POLISARIO Front** in their guerrilla war against Morocco, which had invaded the **Western Sahara** in 1976, the Moroccan army constructed a wall in the desert during the 1980s in order to protect the occupied territory of the Western Sahara from POLISARIO incursions. The wall was built in six stages from August 1980 until April 1987. It eventually enclosed the whole of the Moroccan-occupied territory, extending for 2,400 km (a greater length than that of the Great Wall of China), with 20,000 km of barbed wire, deep trenches, sand banks and walls of stones 2 m high and 1.8 m wide. It is 'defended' by 160,000 Moroccan soldiers, 240 heavy artillery batteries, more than 1,000 armoured vehicles, 10m. anti-personnel mines (banned by international conventions) and fully equipped with electronic surveillance devices and systems provided by the USA and by Westinghouse, an American electronics corporation involved in the production of military equipment.

War in Afghanistan (2001–)

At the end of 2003 fighting continued between **Taliban** forces and the troops of the US-backed Afghan interim government together with **US armed forces**. The coalition had 11,500 soldiers engaged in hunting down Taliban and **al-Qa'ida** fighters. Fighting was particularly fierce in the east and the south of the country. By the end of September 2003 some 35 US soldiers had been killed and 162 injured as a result of the hostilities.

War of attrition (1969–70)

After the Arab military defeat in the **Arab–Israeli War (1967)**, President **Nasser** of Egypt was concerned to keep the conflict alive, which he did through a programme of 'active deterrence', culminating in the so-called war of attrition between 1969 and 1970. By early 1969 Egypt, assisted by the Soviet Union, had re-equipped the Egyptian army to around its pre-June 1967 level. Israel responded with the saturation bombing of Egyptian targets and deep penetration raids into Egypt. However, with a sophisticated Soviet-built air defence system in operation by the spring of 1970, Egypt managed to curtail Israel's capacity for large-scale attacks. Against the background of this war of attrition, Egypt and Israel accepted the initiative of US Secretary of State William Rogers for a temporary, renewable cease-fire in August 1970.

War crimes

After considerable discussion, particularly following the capture of former Iraqi President **Saddam Hussain** in December 2003, regarding the establishment of a war crimes tribunal for the alleged perpetrators of atrocities under Saddam Hussain's regime, the US-appointed **Iraqi Provisional Governing Council** announced in December 2003 that it would establish a special tribunal, without UN or international involvement. Most international jurists and legal experts would prefer to see an independent tribunal, or a tribunal with a significant international membership.

War of Establishment (Israel) – *see* War of Independence and Arab–Israeli War (1948)

War of Independence (Israel) – *see also* Arab–Israeli War (1948)

In **Hebrew** *Milhemet HaKomemiyut*, the War of the Establishment (of Israel). The conflict in Palestine between the Jews and the Arabs and the supporting Arab states, which erupted after the Declaration of the Establishment of the State of Israel by the Yishuv's People's Council on 14 May 1948, was initially called the War of Establishment. Later it became known among **Israelis** as the War of Independence.

Wars

During the 20th century the **Middle East** has been affected directly by both the two so-called World Wars (in 1914–18 and 1939–45), by several major international wars, by a number of smaller but significant conflicts within the region and by a number of civil wars. In addition, there have been numerous minor conflicts, usually over borders. Apart from the two so-called World Wars, major international wars, directly involving states from outside the region in large-scale military action with substantial numbers of casualties, have included the decade-long (1979–89) **Afghan–Soviet War** (between the Soviet Union and central government forces and the *mujahidin*), and the two, much shorter **Gulf** wars involving the USA and its allies against Iraq (in 1991 and 2003). Earlier interventions by external powers (France and Britain) included the Suez War (1956). Other major international wars, giving rise to high levels of casualties, involving only states within the region include the long war between Iraq and Iran (1980–88). There has been a series of shorter wars and 'uprisings' over a long period of ongoing conflict between Israel on the one hand and the **Palestinians** and the Arab states that have supported them on the other: the Arab-Israeli Wars of 1948–49, 1956, 1967 and 1973 respectively, the war between Israel and the **Palestine Liberation Organization** in Lebanon (known as the Lebanon War) in 1982, and the two Palestinian *intifadas*—the first in 1987–93 and the second (the **al-Aqsa** *intifada*) from 2001 and effectively ongoing. Other wars between Middle Eastern and North African states include short border wars between Algeria and Morocco in the 1960s. Civil wars include those in which there was a substantial degree of external intervention, as in Lebanon (1975–76) and those that have been predominantly internal. The latter include those waged in Sudan, Yemen and Algeria. There were also wars that were provoked essentially by external intervention—as in the case of the invasion of the former **Spanish Sahara** by Morocco and Mauritania in 1976–78, and continuing from 1978 until the cease-fire in 1990, and that waged by Libya and Chad (1980–81). Finally there were conflicts that involved secessionist or nationalist movements for political independence—e.g. those involving the **Kurds**; **Western Sahara**; and Oman (1957–59, 1965–75). In many instances internal ethnic conflict exists on a continuing basis, but falls short of what might generally be termed a war—as in Mauritania in 1989, and in Iran, Iraq, Turkey.

Watan/wataniyya

In **Arabic** means 'homeland'. A term that can also mean 'nation' or 'state'.

Water

A major source of economic and, increasingly, political concern. The **Middle East** is generally a water-scarce region, with a tendency to low and irregular rainfall in many areas, high evaporation and transpiration, and increasing **pollution**. A water poverty index (based on five measures: resources, access, capacity, use and environmental impact) reveals Yemen to be the most vulnerable country in the region in this respect. Renewable fresh water is in extremely short supply in Kuwait (which has none), the United Arab Emirates, Libya, Saudi Arabia, Jordan, Yemen, Israel, Oman, Algeria and Tunisia (the quantities involved range from none in

Kuwait to 481 cu m per person in Tunisia). Morocco, Egypt and Lebanon are slightly better off, with renewable fresh water assessed at some 1,000 cu m per person. Water is likely, however, to be generally a continuing and increasing source of concern and conflict within the region. Famous for its great rivers—the **Nile**, the **Tigris** and **Euphrates**, the Oxus, etc.—and with a long history of river-based irrigation systems and civilizations (Sumeria, Babylon, **Mesopotamia**, Assyria, Egypt, etc.), the majority of rivers are subject to great inter-annual and intra-annual variation in flow and volume. The larger rivers (e.g. the Nile, the Tigris and the Euphrates) have their origins and headwaters in one country and their mouths in others. In some cases (e.g. the Nile) several countries are directly involved (Uganda, Sudan, Egypt), in others (the Tigris and the Euphrates) only one (Turkey). Such situations have given rise to considerable potential for international conflict over the control of water in the region. In other cases, the intention of one state to divert and control the waters of a river that constitutes a border affects other riparian states (in the case of the Jordan river, Israel and Jordan; in that of the Litani river, Israel and Lebanon). Increasing demand for water for **agriculture**, **industry**, processing and domestic purposes, combined with the generally lower and less reliable rainfall and greater water pollution, is leading to economic and real scarcity, and to conflict between different populations (e.g. **Israelis** and **Palestinians**) and different sectors over water.

Water for arms

In January 2004 Israel and Turkey agreed a '**water** for arms' deal whereby millions of litres of fresh water will be shipped in giant tankers across the eastern **Mediterranean** to Israeli ports.

Wazir, Khalil ('Abu Jihad')

Palestinian political-military leader. Born in 1938 in Ramla, Palestine, Wazir and his family fled during the 1948–49 Palestine War to **Gaza**, at that time under Egyptian administration. He grew up in the Bureij refugee camp in the Gaza Strip. He was selected by the Egyptian military for commando training and then further instruction in **Cairo**, where he met **Yasser Arafat**. He was commissioned as a lieutenant in the Gaza Brigade of the Egyptian army. Before the capture of Gaza by Israel in the 1956 Suez War he escaped to Cairo and became active in Palestinian student politics. After spending time in Stuttgart, Federal Republic of Germany, together with Salah Khalaf, he travelled to Kuwait in early 1959 to join Arafat. Together they established **al-Fatah**. Wazir then returned to Stuttgart to organize Palestinian students in West Germany. He was close to the Algerian **Front de libération nationale** (National Liberation Front) and in December 1962 he and other al-Fatah leaders visited **Algiers** to set up an office and training camps. He visited the People's Republic of China in 1963. He was arrested in January 1965 for sabotaging Israel's National Water Carrier from southern Lebanon. While imprisoned he acquired the *nom de guerre* 'Abu Jihad'. After his release in March Wazir and Arafat moved to Syria, from where they travelled to the Palestinian refugee camps on the **West Bank** (then part of Jordan) to recruit for al-Fatah. Wazir headed the military wing of al-Fatah, known as Assifa (Storm). In 1968 al-Fatah became the leading constituent of the **Palestine Liberation Organization** (PLO). In the 1970s, as al-Fatah and Assifa (based in **Beirut**, Lebanon, after the expulsion of the PLO from Jordan following **Black September**) became more active, Wazir emerged as Yasser Arafat's closest colleague. Wazir backed the idea of a centralized military command and unified political strategy for the PLO. After the expulsion of al-Fatah and the PLO from Lebanon in 1982, following Israeli military intervention, Wazir moved with the party headquarters to **Tunis**. With Palestinian fighters scattered across at least seven Arab countries, his task became even more difficult. Following the outbreak of the Palestinian *intifada* in December 1987, Wazir worked closely with the PLO's Occupied Homeland Directorate to give external direction to the uprising, and maintained good contact with the **Unified National Leadership of the Uprising**. He became a prime target for the Israeli authorities and was killed by a **Mossad** assassination squad in April 1988 at his home in Tunis. He was buried in **Damascus**.

Weapons of Mass Destruction (WMD, Iran)

Several other states in the region, besides Iraq, are thought to have been developing weapons systems involving so-called WMD, including Iran. Iran has made no secret of its 18-year uranium enrichment programme, but has continued to claim that its nuclear programme is entirely for peaceful purposes. Particularly after 11 September 2001, the USA suspected that Iran posed an international threat, not only because of its support for Islamist terrorist groups, particularly the **Shi'a** groups in Lebanon and Palestine, but also because of its alleged weapons development programme. Iran was subject to increasingly aggressive diplomatic pressure, by the USA in particular, but also by the **European Union** (mainly the United Kingdom, Germany and France) during the latter part of 2003, and responded with an indication of some willingness to allow closer inspection of its nuclear programme than hitherto. Towards the end of November the **International Atomic Energy Agency** passed a resolution censuring Iran over its nuclear programme, but stopped short of recommending economic sanctions. In December 2003 Iran accepted the principle of so-called 'snap' weapons inspections.

Weapons of Mass Destruction (WMD, Iraq)

A term widely used during the 1990s, after the **Gulf War (1991)**, as the United Nations and the international community became increasingly concerned with the possibility that Iraq had not only continued weapons programmes intended to develop WMD, but also planned to use them in the near future. WMD referred not only to nuclear, but also to chemical and biological weapons. UN weapons inspectors were deployed in the second half of the decade in order to discover the reality of the supposed threat of Iraqi WMD. Failure to find the anticipated 'caches' did not prevent the USA and the United Kingdom from identifying Iraq under **Saddam Hussain** as a threat to the region and, particularly after 11 September 2001, as a supporter and harbourer of terrorists. Intelligence sources indicating that Saddam Hussain's regime had programmes to develop WMD were used by the UK Government of Tony Blair and the US Administration of **George W. Bush**, to suggest that there was a clear and present danger that WMD might be used. The US Administration, supported by the UK Government, announced that Saddam Hussain's regime had not complied with the demand of the UN that it should co-operate with weapons inspectors, and that this necessitated immediate action. It was not prepared to await the 'discovery' by the UN weapons inspectors, or the possible use, of the WMD and decided to launch an attack on Iraq, under the cover of existing UN resolutions. The United Kingdom broadly supported this plan of action, although some effort was made to secure an additional UN resolution to justify the use of armed intervention, and in October 2003 a **coalition** force spearheaded by US and UK aircraft bombarded Iraqi positions and then landed ground forces to invade Iraq from the south. Saddam Hussain's **armed forces** proved no match for the invading coalition but made no use of WMD. Despite a continuing search for significant indications of WMD by weapons inspection teams under the authority of the coalition, none had been found by the end of 2003.

Weapons of Mass Destruction (Israel)

Identified some 20 years ago as one of the states with a nuclear weapons capacity, Israel is currently thought to have between 100 and 200 nuclear warheads as part of its arsenal of weapons of mass destruction. An Israeli technician at the Dimona nuclear plant, **Mordechai Vanunu**, was convicted of treason and jailed for 20 years in 1986 for having informed *The Sunday Times* of London of Israel's nuclear capability. It is highly probable that Israel also has an appreciable chemical and biological warfare capability. Israel is known to have been developing biological weapons at the biological institute in Nes Tziona.

Weapons of Mass Destruction (WMD, Libya)

Britain raised the issue of WMD with Libya in August 2002 when the foreign office minister, Mike O'Brien, met Col **Qaddafi** in Sirte, the first ministerial contact between the United Kingdom and Libya for 20 years. In December 2003, in a surprise move, the Government of Libya announced that it would halt its major weapons development programmes (including programmes to develop nuclear as well as chemical and biological weapons). Libya admitted to the **International Atomic Energy Agency** that it had been secretly importing uranium and other sophisticated equipment for the development of a nuclear weapons capability for more than a decade. Libya agreed to allow UN nuclear experts to conduct 'snap' inspections of its sites, and plans were agreed to enable inspectors to travel to Libya, before the end of the year, to begin dismantling its nuclear facilities in the first stage of a long-term regime of supervising the process.

Weapons of Mass Destruction (WMD, Syria)

Syria was placed under some pressure, particularly from the USA, but also from the **European Union** (EU), in the aftermath of the **Gulf War (2003)**, to indicate the level of its weapons systems development. The USA has not removed Syria from its list of alleged state sponsors of **terrorism**: in November 2003 the US Senate passed a bill to impose economic and diplomatic sanctions on Syria for backing anti-Israeli groups such as **Hezbollah**, **Hamas** and **Islamic Jihad**, and for maintaining a military presence in Lebanon; it has also accused Syria of developing WMD. It was announced towards the end of December 2003 that the United Kingdom and Germany had already demanded that Syria make a stronger commitment to abide by international laws on illegal weapons as the price for a closer relationship with the EU. Syria is the last of 12 Arab and **Mediterranean** states to sign an 'association agreement' with the EU under the **Euro-Mediterranean Partnership** programme. The most recent agreements have all required signatories to abide by international agreements on WMD. Syria has pursued a large chemical weapons programme that has included the development of nerve agents, and is not a signatory to the 1993 chemical weapons convention. It also has ballistic missiles but argues that these are necessary in order to counter Israel's undeclared nuclear weapons as well as Israel's superiority in conventional arms.

Weizmann, Chaim

Chaim Weizmann left his home near Pinsk in 1903 in order to study chemistry in England. A committed Zionist, he became strongly anglophile, took British nationality and assisted the Allies in the First World War, providing them the formula for a new process of making acetone, which greatly alleviated the shortage of explosives. He was a close confidant of William Stephenson, a Canadian who was at that time a personal adviser to Winston Churchill on German re-armament. Stephenson received a good deal of intelligence through Jewish scientists, many of them recruited by Weizmann. In the early 1920s, having become a member of the **Yishuv** (Zionist community in Palestine), Weizmann was made president of the **Zionist Organization**. He had always believed that Britain would eventually grant the Jews independence in Palestine, but by the mid-1930s it had become clear that they were reluctant to do so. Even so, the moderate Jewish leadership under Weizmann gave the British Royal Commission's plan for partition qualified support as a move in the right direction and when in September 1939 war was declared, Weizmann announced the support of the Jewish people in Palestine for the Allied war effort. Thirty thousand Jews volunteered to join the Allied forces. The Chamberlain Government responded with a White Paper that proposed allowing only 75,000 Jews into Palestine over the next five years, after which immigration was to cease. Chaim Weizmann was held in high regard, not only as President of the Zionist Organization, but also as a scientist of international stature and a recognized moderate in political affairs. He was made President of Israel in 1948 when Israel achieved independence and remains a major figure in the history of the country.

Weizmann-Faisal Accord

This agreement was concluded in 1919 between Dr **Chaim Weizmann**, a former British citizen and a leader of the Zionist movement who had become a member of the **Yishuv** (Zionist Community in Palestine), and **Faisal**, eldest son of the Sherif of **Mecca** and head of the **Hashemite** family. Their discussions took place at Aqaba in Palestine and in London, United Kingdom, during 1918 and related to co-operation between Arabs and Jews. In 1919, Faisal, by that time King of Syria, publicly accepted the **Balfour Declaration** and gave his approval to the continuation of Jewish immigration into Palestine, noting, however, that he would not be bound 'by a single word of the present Agreement' if Arab rights were in any way jeopardized. In return for this gesture of co-operation, Weizmann (who was to become the first President of Israel) pledged support in the economic development of the region and promised to work closely with the Arab leaders. The Accord aroused a great deal of controversy, particularly among Arabs who felt Faisal was in no position to represent them and who feared that Palestine would be separated from Syrian administration, and that a Jewish enclave would emerge in the midst of the **Arab World**.

Welfare Party (Turkey)

In 1991, the Welfare Party (RP)—which, as a successor to the **National Salvation Party**, represents Islamic revivalism in Turkey—won 16% of the parliamentary seats. In November 1992 the party won nearly one-third of the vote in local elections in **Istanbul**. In elections held in 1995 the RP emerged as Turkey's largest political party. It took power in mid-1996 as the first Islamic government since **Kemal Atatürk** inaugurated a secular republic in 1923. In 1996–97 Tansu Çiller, a secularist political leader who represented small business, formed a coalition which provided support to the RP. Ousted in 1997, however, it found itself under threat of a legal ban. The struggle between secularism—a tradition of 80 years' standing in Turkey—and Islamism appears to be intensifying. Welfare Party rhetoric reveals support for closer ties with the Islamic world and a distrust, if not a rejection, of Western traditions and **corruption**. According to recent surveys, some 70% of Turks claim to be 'devout Muslims', but only 3% per cent of the population wish to see **Shari'a** law replace the secular law in Turkey. Nevertheless, there is an increasing trend towards Islamization.

The West Bank

The territory on the West Bank of the Jordan river—Jordanian territory that has been occupied by Israel since the 1967 war, despite repeated UN resolutions that have declared the occupation illegal. It comprises 5,860 sq km, of which lakes and inland seas account for 220 sq km, and lies between Jordan and Israel, with Syria to the north. At July 2002 the population of the West Bank was estimated at 163,667, excluding Israeli settlers. There are 242 Israeli **settlements** and civilian land use sites in the West Bank, and a total of about 187,000 Israeli settlers. Numerous Israeli settlements were established in the occupied West Bank (and a much smaller number in **Gaza**) in the decade after 1967. The **Camp David Accords** of 1978 outlawed further Israeli settlements in the **Occupied Tterritories**. However, this has not prevented successive Israeli governments from allowing settlement and construction to continue, particularly in the West Bank. The West Bank and the Gaza Strip together constitute the Palestinian Occupied Territories and they are considered by many **Palestinians** to be co-extensive with a future Palestinian state, under the 'two-state solution' to the Palestinian issue. Some Palestinians (especially the Islamist and radical leftist groups) continue to claim a larger area, including the present State of Israel, for the future Palestinian state. Others doubt whether even the West Bank and Gaza will be 'available', given the limited territory recognized as falling under the jurisdiction of the **Palestinian National Authority** and the apparently inexorable process of Israeli land annexation and settlement, particularly in the West Bank.

West Beirut Massacre – *see* Sabra and Chatila

West Jerusalem

Jerusalem was divided in 1967 after the Arab–Israeli War, with **East Jerusalem** falling within the occupied **West Bank** and West Jerusalem becoming, in effect, an Israeli city.

Western Sahara – *see also* Sahrawi Arab Democratic Republic

The Western Sahara lies to the south of Morocco and to the north of Mauritania, and borders the Atlantic Ocean. It was formerly (until 1976) a Spanish colony, known as the **Spanish Sahara**. The Western Sahara covers an area of some 266,000 sq km. The main towns are in the north-west of the territory; the largest of these is El Ayoune. At July 2002 the total population was estimated as 256,177, of which the vast majority are Arabs and Muslims, speaking either Moroccan **Arabic** or Hassaniya Arabic.

The legal status of the territory and the issue of its sovereignty remain unresolved. The Western Sahara is currently a disputed territory, subject to a UN 'peace process' that has itself been extremely prolonged (it has been under way since 1991), following a long war (1976–91) between Morocco and the **POLISARIO Front** (the Popular Front for the Liberation of the Saguia el Hamra and Río de Oro)—the political movement representing the **Sahrawis**, or people of the Western Sahara. Morocco invaded the territory in 1976 as the Spanish left and effectively occupied the north-western areas, pushing the Sahrawis eastwards into Algeria, where many have remained, in refugee camps, since that time. The POLISARIO Front fought back, initiating a bitter guerrilla war, and 'liberated' the eastern and southern areas nearest, respectively, to Algeria and Mauritania. In February 1976 the Front formally proclaimed a government-in-exile of the Sahrawi Arab Democratic Republic (SADR) and elected **Muhammad Abdel** Aziz as President. The SADR was recognised by 54 nations and was eventually (in 1984) admitted to the Organisation of African Unity. Mauritania initially joined Morocco in fighting the POLISARIO Front in the south, but between 1978 and 1979 broke off its military involvement and renounced any claim to the territory. Morocco gradually extended the area under its control, building a '**wall**' in the desert to exclude the POLISARIO fighters. Guerrilla activities continued, however, until a UN-monitored cease-fire was implemented on 6 September 1991. The UN established a peace-keeping force (**MINURSO**), which was deployed in the Moroccan-occupied part of the territory to supervise a UN-sponsored referendum. More than a decade passed as the parties to the conflict failed to agree on precisely who would be eligible to vote in this referendum. The matter remained unresolved at the end of 2003, despite the fact that the right to self-determination of the Sahrawi people was recognized by the International Court of Justice as long ago as 1975.

Western Sahara, economy

The area of the Western Sahara under Moroccan occupation depends on rain-fed farming and livestock production, maritime and coastal fishing, **phosphate** mining and **trade** as the principal sources of **income** for the population. The territory generally lacks sufficient rainfall for sustainable agricultural production, and much of the food for the rapidly expanding (largely Moroccan immigrant) urban population must be imported. All trade and other economic activities are controlled by the Moroccan Government. There has been increasing interest from both Moroccan and foreign companies in the exploitation of **oil**, **gas** and **mineral** resources. Despite the efforts of the UN to resolve the continuing conflict, Moroccan administration, combined with a programme to encourage settlement by Moroccans in the territory, is establishing an effective Moroccan presence which many **Sahrawis** are concerned will create a *fait accompli* and undermine any possibility of self-determination and independence for the Sahrawi people in their own state. The 'liberated' areas in the east and south of the territory, outside the Moroccan-occupied areas, are generally inhospitable, although free movement allows the Sahrawis based in the refugee camps to undertake limited trade in livestock and other (often imported) goods with Mauritania. The Sahrawis in the refugee camps have depended heavily for nearly three decades on basic goods provided by the **UNHCR** and other agencies, including 'northern' NGOs, but have also made substantial efforts to achieve as much self-sufficiency and social independence as possible in their desert enclave. Their efforts to construct a dignified and self-reliant economy and society, within the severe constraints they face, have been much admired by sympathizers world-wide.

White Revolution (Iran)

During the 1960s in particular, the Shah of Iran made a major effort to transform the economy of Iran through a combination of agrarian reform, technological change and the extension of the **oil** economy into processing and **industry**. The 'revolution from above' that he instigated was known as the 'White Revolution' to distinguish it from the more violent form of change from below that usually accompanied major social and economic transformation.

Will of the Iranian Nation

An Iranian political organization founded in February 2001. It is led by Hakimi Pour.

Women

The position of women in the region as a whole is still very much limited to the domestic and private sphere. Gender inequality in the region is high in comparison with almost every other region in the world (except, possibly, South Asia), with most of the indicators relating to the position of women in economic, social and political life very poor. On the other hand, there are signs of significant improve-ments in some areas. The region's maternal mortality rate is double that of Latin America and the Caribbean, and four times that of East Asia. In the **Arab World** (a substantial portion of the **Middle East** region) about 65m. adults are illiterate, two-thirds of them women, and illiteracy rates are higher than in many much poorer states elsewhere. **Literacy** rates have expanded threefold since 1970; female primary and secondary school enrolment rates have more than doubled. These achievements have not, however, succeeding in countering gender-based social attitudes and norms that stress women's domestic and, in particular, reproductive role. As a consequence, more than one-half of Arab women are illiterate. Women suffer from unequal citizenship and legal entitlements, often evident in voting rights and legal codes, but more pervasive than these areas alone. In economic terms women in the Middle East suffer from inequality of opportunity, evident in employment status, wages and gender-based occupational segregation.

Women's rights (Bahrain)

In 2003 Bahrain became the first country in the **Gulf** where **women** are eligible to vote and to contest national parliamentary elections. Apart from Israel, which occupies the 22nd position, Bahrain, in 40th position, is the only Middle Eastern country that features in the world's top 40 states with reference to the gender-related development index.

Women's rights (Jordan)

In February 2003 King **Abdullah** of Jordan announced the creation of six new parliamentary seats for **women**. Fifty-four women, including teachers, business-women, lawyers and mothers, contested elections held in June, and six were elected to the national assembly. For the first time more women than men voted in the elections.

Women's rights (Morocco)

Women's rights in Morocco were boosted after King **Mohammed VI** announced a reform of the country's strict laws (*mudawana*) that govern women's and family rights. Changes in the law would make polygamy more difficult; they would also raise the legal age for marriage from 15 to 18, simplify divorce procedures for **women** and give divorced women greater protection. Women activists had feared that the reforms, first promised when King Mohammed came to the throne in 1999, would never take place, after large-scale public protests from Islamist conservatives. In 2000 some 300,000 demonstrators took to the streets of **Casablanca** to object to any change in the *mudawana*. The 'modernizers' could only muster some 100,000 for a march on the same day in **Rabat**. In 2003, however, an agreement among the political parties paved the way for the election of 35 women to the Moroccan parliament.

Women's rights (Turkmenistan)

One-quarter of the seats in the national assembly are held by **women**.

The Woodridge Fountain

A custom-built complex of buildings worth US $300,000–$500,000 in Du Page County. It was used in the early 1990s by the **Qur'anic Literacy Institute** to 'launder' money from a wealthy Saudi Arabian supporter of **Hamas**.

Workers Party (PT)

Algerian political grouping led by Louisa Hanoun, who contested the presidential election held in April 2004.

World Bank

The International Bank for Reconstruction and Development, better known as the World Bank, has played a significant role in the economies of the **Middle East**. As a major lending agency, it has been able to apply increasing pressure, from the late 1970s onwards, for economic reform and liberalization against a backdrop of growing **debt**. Conditionality (which allows loans to be made only when specified preconditions have been met) has increased the ability of the Bank to persuade and even oblige governments to adopt painful reform measures, usually involving cuts in public expenditure, reductions in subsidies and increased prices for basic goods, which have often resulted in outbursts of popular protest. Together with the **International Monetary Fund**, the Bank has been one of the most powerful and influential of the **international financial institutions** operating in the region.

World Food Programme (WFP)

The principal food agency of the United Nations. It aims to alleviate acute hunger by providing food relief. Priority is given to vulnerable groups, such as children and pregnant **women**. Examples of WFP activities in the region in recent years include programmes in Iraq, the **West Bank**, **Gaza Strip**, Jordan, Yemen and Syria, and among **refugees** from Iraq and Afghanistan.

World Islamic Front for the Jihad against the Jews and the Crusaders

The result of a merger between the Egyptian **Islamic Jihad** group and **Osama bin Laden**'s **al-Qa'ida**, the World Islamic Front for the Jihad against the Jews and Crusaders was formed in early 1998. The focus of the new group was to internationalize *jihad*. The proliferation of armed Islamist groups across the **Middle East** and outside the region during the 1980s and 1990s, made possible by the expansion of an international network of financial institutions and banking, facilitated the birth of a new phenomenon, the Islamist international.

World Trade Center

Located in New York, the World Trade Center was the subject of a major bomb attack in 1993, planned and executed by **Ramzi Yousef** in association with a number of other assailants. Six people died in the attack and hundreds of others suffered physical and psychological harm. Eight years later, on 11 September 2001, the World Trade Center was once again the subject of a major attack. This time some 3,000 people were killed and the Center itself was destroyed.

World Trade Organization (WTO)

International **trade** organization that regulates trading conditions on a global basis and promotes free trade. Within the **Middle East**, Israel, Kuwait, the United Arab Emirates, Qatar, Oman, Bahrain, Jordan, Egypt, Morocco, Tunisia and Turkey were all members by the end of the 1990s. In 2000 the membership of Algeria and Saudi Arabia was pending and Iran had applied for observer status. Lebanon apparently awaits a 'green light' from Syria before applying, and Syria, together with Iraq, Yemen and Lebanon, has not yet applied itself. With the exception of the member states of the **Gulf Co-operation Council**, most economies in the region have been involved in a variety of special trade relationships with the European Community (now the **European Union**), including the recently developed **Euro-Mediterranean Partnership**, the USA and Japan. It is in fact far from clear whether the benefits of global or even inter-regional free trade will outweigh the costs for most of the countries of the region, which have few comparative advantages outside the **oil** sector. On the other hand, considerable benefits could be realized from a greater degree of intra-regional trade.

Wye River Memorandum

The Wye River Memorandum was signed by Israeli Prime Minister **Binyamin Netanyahu** and **Palestinian (National) Authority** (PNA) President **Yasser Arafat**, and witnessed by US President **Bill Clinton**, at the Wye Plantation, Maryland, USA on 23 October 1998. The Memorandum was to enter into force 10 days after its signing. It committed Israel and the PNA to commence negotiations on the final status arrangements contained in the **Oslo Agreement**, including the future of **Jerusalem**, in November 1998. It laid out a number of steps to facilitate the implementation of the Interim Agreement on the **West Bank** and **Gaza Strip** of September 1995—the **Israeli-Palestinian Interim Agreement**—and other related agreements, including the Note for the Record of 17 January 1997, so that the Israeli and Palestinian sides could more effectively carry out their reciprocal responsibilities, including those relating to further redeployments and security respectively. Israel's assertion that the PNA was not complying with its security commitments, coupled with a **Knesset** vote in December for early prime ministerial and parliamentary elections, effectively stalled the peace process.

Xinjiang Province

Xinjiang Uighur Autonomous Region covers more than 1.6m. sq km, one-sixth of the total territory of the People's Republic of China, making it that country's largest province. Xinjiang borders Tibet, Qinghai, Gansu, Mongolia, Kazakhstan, Kyrgyzstan, Uzbekistan, Tajikistan, Afghanistan, Pakistan and India. With a population of more than 19m., Xinjiang is home to 47 ethnic groups, including the Uighur, the major ethnic group in Xinjiang.

Y

Yahad

Together

Israeli political party, founded in 1984. It advocates a peace settlement with the Arab states and the **Palestinians**. Yahad joined the **Israel Labour Party** parliamentary bloc in January 1987.

Yahad Shivtei Yisrael

A grouping of Yemenis within the Israeli political system, formed in 1988.

Yahiaoui, Col Mohamed Salah

Nominated co-ordinator of the Algerian **Front de libération nationale** (FLN, National Liberation Front) in October 1977 by **Houari Boumedienne** and tasked with preparing the party's first Congress since April 1964, with the aim of launching the FLN as an explicitly socialist vanguard party. He was expelled from the FLN in 1981 after the death of Boumedienne and the selection of Col **Chadli** as his successor.

Yahya, Imam

Absolutist ruler of **North Yemen**, which became independent after the First World War. His regime ended in 1948 when he was murdered in an attempted coup.

Yahya, Imam Ahmed Ben

Replaced Imam **Yahya** in 1948 and remained ruler of **North Yemen** until his regime was eventually brought to an end in 1962 by a republican *coup d'état* which brought **Muhammad al-Badr** briefly (for one week) to power before he too was overthrown by the **military**, led by Col **Abdullah as-Salal**, supported by Egypt. There followed a long civil war, which ended only in 1970.

Al-Yakatha

Reawakening

Jordanian political party. It first achieved representation in the election held in November 1993.

Yakiti Party

Illegal political party representing the **Kurds** in Syria.

Yamani, Sheikh Ahmed Zaki

Saudi Arabian politican and **oil** expert. He was born in **Mecca** in 1930 and studied law at **Cairo**, New York and Harvard universities. In 1958 he was appointed adviser to the Saudi Arabian Cabinet, in 1960 as a minister of state and in 1962 as Minister of Petroleum and Mineral Resources. In the mid-1960s he became chairman of the state-owned General Petroleum and Mineral Organization and a director of **ARAMCO** (Arabian American Oil Co). He served as secretary-general of the **Organization of Petroleum Exporting Countries** (OPEC) in 1968–69. He supported King **Faisal**'s strategy of using oil as a weapon during the **Arab–Israeli War (1973)**, but also supported the decision to lift the Arab oil embargo against the USA in March 1974, even though the conditions for lifting it—Israel's evacuation of the occupied Arab territories and the granting of **Palestinians**' rights—had not been met. Sheikh Yamani was one of the main targets of the operation undertaken in December 1975 by a group of commandos led by Illich Ramírez Sánchez (alias Carlos 'the Jackal'), in which OPEC oil ministers were taken hostage while meeting in Vienna, Austria. After two days' captivity he was freed in **Algiers**, Algeria, after a clandestine deal involving a payment estimated at US $5m.–$50m. had been made by Saudi Arabia.

As OPEC's secretary-general Yamani lobbied hard and successfully to maintain the Organization's share of global petroleum production. As Saudi Arabia's oil minister he also implemented a national policy, in tandem with Kuwait, which involved producing more than the countries' OPEC quotas. This strategy relied on the huge oil reserves possessed by both countries, particularly Saudi Arabia. It resulted in lower oil prices, and was unpopular with other OPEC countries with smaller reserves, which favoured maintaining higher prices by controlling output more strictly. During the **Iran–Iraq War** the high output strategy—which resulted in a decline in the price of oil of almost two-thirds in December 1985–July 1986, to US $10 per barrel—seriously affected Iran's ability to continue the war. In August 1986 Yamani ceded to pressure from other OPEC countries; the Organization's output of petroleum was reduced and the price of oil rose, accordingly, to $14–$16 per barrel. However, Yamani's refusal to countenance a fixed price of $18 per barrel led to his dismissal by King **Fahd** in October. Sheikh Yamani retired from public life and devoted himself to private business, establishing the Centre for Global

Energy Studies in London, United Kingdom. In the mid-1990s, based in **Jiddah**, he became a key figure for businessmen and religious leaders disaffected from Saudi government policy and practice.

Yassin, Sheikh Ahmed

Founder and spiritual leader of the Palestinian Islamist political grouping **Hamas**. He was assassinated by Israeli forces in March 2004. The wheelchair-bound quadriplegic (Yassin was disabled in an accident as a boy) was killed by a missile launched from an Israeli helicopter while being pushed by his bodyguards in his wheelchair after early morning prayers at a mosque in **Gaza**. He was 67. He had recognized that he was a target, but refused to go into hiding or vary his morning prayer routine at his local mosque, even after the Israeli authorities declared him as such. The Israeli army had tried and failed to kill him in September 2003. The Israeli army chief of staff, Lt-Gen. Moshe Yaalon stated that the motive for targeting the Hamas leadership was partly to prevent Hamas from seizing political control in Gaza. The killing was apparently personally approved by Israeli Prime Minister **Ariel Sharon**, who described the act as part of the war on terror, describing Sheikh Yassin as 'the first and foremost leader of the Palestinian terrorist murderers, responsible for the deaths of hundreds of Israelis'. He also referred to him as 'the mastermind of Palestinian terror' and 'a mass murderer who is among Israel's greatest enemies'. The USA blocked a draft UN Security Council resolution condemning the killing of Sheikh Yassin because it made no mention of Hamas **terrorism**. His funeral in Gaza was the largest there in nearly a decade.

Yassine, Sheikh Abdessalam

Morocco's main Islamic political leader. After being kept under house arrest for some years, he was released in May 2000 but warned to be cautious when making any public statements.

Yazidis

A religious sect with about 100,000 adherents. Yazidis are found in north-eastern Syria, northern Iraq and the trans-Caucasian states. Though they often speak a Kurdish dialect, their scriptures are in **Arabic**. The Yazidi doctrine is a unique mixture of religious elements. The principal divine figure of the Yazidis is the Peacock Angel, the supreme angel of the seven who ruled the Universe after it had been created by God. Yazidis do not believe in evil, sin or the devil. Violation of divine laws can be expiated by transmigration of the soul. They believe that their chief saint, Sheikh Adi, a Muslim mystic of the 12th century, acquired divine status through the transmigration of his soul. His tomb, north of **Mosul**, is the site of an annual pilgrimage.

Yemen – *see also* North Yemen

For two centuries Yemen was divided into two separate entities. North Yemen and South Yemen, the former under Ottoman rule and the latter under Britain. North Yemen acquired its independence after the end of the First World War and was then ruled by a traditional monarchy for some four decades. Eventually, the regime of Imam **Ahmad Ben Yahya** was overthrown by a republican coup in 1962 and the country was proclaimed a republic. There followed a civil war, in which Egyptian and Saudi forces were involved (on either side), which continued until 1970. South Yemen remained a British territory until independence was finally granted in 1967. The new government was Marxist-oriented and in 1970 established the **People's Democratic Republic of Yemen** (PDRY). The PDRY did not become a member of the Commonwealth. The two states were merged and Yemen, thus, reunited in May 1990, with **San'a** as its capital. Hopes for a more successful pattern of economic development after unification were dashed by the effects of the **Gulf War (1991)**, which resulted in large numbers of Yemenis working in the **Gulf** states (notably in Kuwait and Saudi Arabia) being sent home, thereby losing their employment and source of remittances. Ali Abdullah Salih (Saleh) is the head of state.

Yemen Arab Republic (YAR)

The Yemen Arab Republic was declared in September 1962 after a coup had ousted the successor to Imam Ahmad, former ruler of **North Yemen**. Fighting between 'republicans' and 'royalists' broke out with the heavy involvement of Egypt and Saudi Arabia. By the spring of 1963 Egyptian troops in the field amounted to about 28,000. In April the UN attempted to bring about a disengagement of Egyptian and Saudi forces by providing an observer mission (UNYOM); but this proved ineffective and was withdrawn in September 1964. Fighting continued over the next three years, but the situation was transformed by the Egyptian defeat by Israel in the **Arab–Israeli War (1967)**. The withdrawal of Egyptian troops was completed by the end of November. **Col Abdullah as-Sallal**, who had led the republicans since being proclaimed President in September 1962, was replaced while out of the country seeking support from Eastern Europe and the Soviet Union by a three-man council headed by Qadi Abd ar-Rahman al-Iryani, a pious Muslim and former adviser to Imam Ahmad. Fighting continued, but at the beginning of 1970 King **Faisal** of Saudi Arabia decided that he could tolerate the moderate republic of al-Iryani and terminated all **aid** to the royalists and 'ordered' them to cease fighting. The regime was recognized by Saudi Arabia and Britain and began a process of national reconciliation under al-Iryani. It was estimated that 200,000 Yemenis had died in the fighting (about 4% of the population) and the economy was devastated. The first (indirect) elections ever took place in April 1971 and al-Iryani was successful in building up good relations both at home and abroad through a careful strategy of balancing interests. Moves towards unity with the 'south' were hampered, however, by links with Saudi Arabia and opposition from some influential conservatives. In 1974, frustrated by checks to his policies, al-Iryani resigned and went to live in Syria.

His young successor, Lt-Col Ibrahim al-Hamadi, suspended the Constitution and the consultative council but managed to gain considerable support at home and abroad to relaunch the process of reconstruction and development. He aimed at a strong centralized state with wide political participation and encouraged the emergence of the leftist **National Democratic Front** (NDF). In October 1977 he and his brother were murdered. Al-Hamadi was succeeded by the chief of staff, Ahmad al-Ghashmi, who was in favour of wider political participation and nominated a 99-man constitutional assembly to prepare the way for eventual national elections. He was murdered in June 1978, however. A temporary presidential council was formed and one month later the new assembly elected Lt-Col Ali Abdullah Salih (Saleh) as President. After an uncertain start, Saleh proved an effective head of state, moving steadily towards increasing political representation over the next four years. He managed to defeat the NDF, which called for more radical economic development measures and less dependence on Saudi Arabia. Saleh cultivated a wide range of foreign governments, including the Soviet Union (with which he signed a treaty in 1984), but was careful to avoid too close a commitment to any particular country or bloc. In July 1985 the YAR held its first free elections, to local councils, and in July 1988 the long-postponed general election took place for 128 seats in the new 159-member consultative council. Its first act was to re-elect Saleh for a further five years. While the economy continued to depend heavily on **remittances** sent back by Yemenis working abroad (mainly in the **Gulf**) and on foreign aid, significant economic and social development did take place. The discovery of **oil** and **natural gas** in the mid-1980s improved its prospects. However, Yemen remained a very poor country. As regards unification with the 'south', Saleh met with Ali Nasser Muhammad of the **People's Democratic Republic of Yemen** at a summit in **Tripoli**, Libya, in July 1986 and embarked on a long process of discussions and negotiations which ended in May 1990 with the creation of the Republic of **Yemen** and the establishment of a five-man presidential council, headed by Saleh. In May 1991 the people of Yemen voted in a referendum on the Constitution for a unified state.

Yemen Socialist Party (YSP)

Legal opposition party in Yemen. The Yemen Socialist Party was established as a 'vanguard party' by Abd al-Fattah Ismail in 1978. It had its origins in the **National Liberation Front** (NLF), which had been formed in 1963. The YSP—which was the only party—had strict rules for admission, strong discipline, and was effectively the party of the government of the **People's Democratic Republic of Yemen**. On the other hand, there was always some tension between the government and the Party and when Haidar abu Bakr al-Attas was President (elected in October 1986 after having previously been Prime Minister), it was not clear that this post actually bestowed greater authority than that of secretary-general of the YSP, occupied by Salim al-Baid. In December 1989 the YSP ended its monopoly and the formerly outlawed Nasserite party applied for recognition, to be quickly followed by the Yemeni Unity Party (YUP), the first to have members both 'north' and 'south' of the frontier. By September 1990 it was reported that more than 30 new political parties had been formed in Yemen since unification. It was a sign of the times that the **Yemeni Islah Party (YIP)**, an Islamic party with widespread support, was regarded as the most important of the new parties. The two government parties of 'north' and 'south' had agreed to share power equally until elections in November 1992, but over the next year or two there was a major power struggle between the two, with numbers of leading activists on both sides being killed. In the mean time the YIP increased its strength and probably displaced the YSP in the 'north'. In the legislative elections of carly 1993, the 'northern' **General People's Congress** (GPC) won the majority of the vote and gained 123 of the 301 seats (mainly in the **Yemen Arab Republic**); the YIP took second place with 62 seats (again mainly in the 'north') and the YSP third, with 56 seats. Divisions between 'north' and 'south' continued to be significant and during 1994 fighting broke out on such a scale as to merit the description of 'civil war'. In the aftermath of the war, the YSP elected a new politburo, none of whose members had been involved in the declaration of the unified Republic of **Yemen**. However, the Party has gradually lost support, at the same time as the YIP has gained it. In October 1994 the YSP was excluded from the new government. In the elections of April 1997 the GPC obtained a clear majority, with the YIP coming a poor second. The YSP boycotted the elections, although some YSP members contested them independently. In March 1998 the year-long trial *in absentia* of the leadership of the 'southern separatists', including al-Attas and al-Baid, ended with five (including those two) being condemned to death, three sentenced to terms of imprisonment of 10 years and the remainder being either acquitted or receiving suspended sentences. By the end of the 1990s the YSP had become a politically marginal force, but was now increasingly subject to harassment both by the government security forces and by the more militant supporters of the YIP. This repression has continued since 2000.

Yemeni Assembly Unity Party

Hizb at-Tajamu al-Yemeni al-Wahdawi

Yemeni opposition party.

Yemeni Islah Party (YIP)

The Yemeni Islah Party was established after the unification of Yemen in 1990 and was immediately recognized as the most important of the new parties. From the outset it has called for **Shari'a** law to be the sole source of legislation in Yemen. It is thought to have considerable financial support from Saudi Arabia. In the elections of 1993 the YIP beat the **Yemen Socialist Party** into third place. After the election the YIP is reported to have threatened to boycott the new house of representatives unless it was admitted to government. In fact, the three main parties agree to form a coalition government and the YIP was allocated six posts in the Council of Ministers (as well as two seats on the five-man presidential council), although these did not include **education** or finance, for which the Party had specifically asked. During 1994 the YIP began to exert its influence and, as part of a programme of constitutional reforms, the Shari'a became the sole, rather than the principal, source of legislation and the last references to the rights of **women** were removed from the Constitution. Its strategy has been to move carefully and develop its strength at the grassroots level. Despite its minority representation in government, it was now the most influential party in the country with the best and most dynamic organization. Its officials were active in the towns and even the remote parts of the countryside; its broad-based constituency included the **tribes**, the commercial bourgeoisie and the influential **Muslim Brotherhood**. In September 1995 the YIP Congress elected members of the Muslim Brotherhood to most of its key posts. In October a new Council of Ministers was appointed, in which the YIP increased its membership from six to nine, including the key portfolios of education and justice. It has used those positions to reform significantly both spheres towards an 'Islamic' approach. Tensions between the **General People's Congress** (GPC) and the YIP inevitably increased as the Islamists gained influence and control. In what appears to have been a 'back-lash', in the 1997 elections, the GPC secured a clear majority; the YIP actually secured fewer seats (53) on this occasion than in 1993, when it won 62. Rivalry between these two major political groupings has increased since then, and the local elections of February 2001 were marred by conflict, mainly between supporters of these two parties, and by accusations by the YIP that there had been foul play. The results of the elections were never published, fuelling suspicion that the YIP had performed well. In August 2001 the YIP and six other opposition parties announced that they were suspending all dialogue with the government on amendments to the new electoral law. After September 2001 tensions between the government and the Islamists in Yemen (including the YIP) have increased significantly as evidence of links between Yemeni Islamists and international terrorists (including **al-Qa'ida**) has emerged.

Yertinsky, Itzhak – *see* Shamir, Itzhak

Yesh Gvul (There is a Limit) – *see* Israel Communist Party.

Yishuv

In **Hebrew** the word means 'settlement'. The terms refers to the early Jewish community in Palestine, starting with the first wave of immigration (see **aliya**) in

1882 and ending with the foundation of the State of Israel in May 1948. It is used in contrast to diaspora. Yishuv was regarded as the vanguard of settlement, laying the foundation for the Jewish state in Israel. Prior to the Second World War more than three-quarters of Jews in Palestine were **Ashkenazim**, Jews from north, central and eastern Europe; Sephardic Jews, largely from the **Mediterranean** countries, accounted for less than 10% of the population. The remainder were Jews from Yemen, Iran, Iraq, **Kurdistan** and **Central Asia**. After the creation of the State of Israel, immigration increased dramatically, particularly from other parts of the **Middle East**.

Yisra'el Ba'Aliya

Israeli political grouping led by Natan Sharansky.

Yisra'el Beiteinu

Israeli political grouping led by Avigdor Lieberman.

Yi'ud

Israeli political party, founded in 1994 as a breakaway group from the **Tzomet Party**.

Yom Kippur – *see also* **Arab–Israeli War (1973)**

The Day of Atonement. Observed on the 10th day of Tishri, the first month in the Jewish calendar, and falling between early September and early October, Yom Kippur is the Sabbath of Sabbaths. Rabbinical tradition describes Yom Kippur as the day on which Moses came down from Mount Sinai with the second set of tablets of the Law.

Refers also to the Arab–Israeli War that took place in 1973—the Yom Kippur War.

Yom Kippur War (1973) – *see* **Arab–Israeli War (1973)**

Young Officers (Ottoman)

Political-military grouping in the **Ottoman Empire**.

Young Turks

Informal term for the Ottoman Committee for Union and Progress (Osmanli Ittihat ve Terakki Cemiyeti), which grew out of a secret organization known as the Society of New Ottomans, formed in 1865, whose main concern was the establishment of new 'modern' institutions and constitutional reforms that would enable Ottoman society to compete with, and resist, European interventions in the region. The New Ottomans were forced to remain underground after 1876, but they reappeared in

1902 when they held their first Congress in Paris, France. They split into two groups, and one of these merged in 1906 with the Ottoman Freedom Association established in Salonika. The Committee of Union and Progress, as the combined movement was called, emerged as the 'Young Turks' in 1908. The Young Turk junta enjoyed army support, and the Sultan, Abdul Hamid, was deposed. The powers of the new Sultan, Muhammad V, named in 1909, were strictly limited and the Committee for Union and Progress assumed control over the Ottoman parliament. Their pan-Turkish ideology embraced all Turkic-speaking peoples, but as the European powers increasingly threatened to tear the **Ottoman Empire** apart (in 1911 Italy invaded Tripolitania and Greece seized the island of Crete, while the Balkan **Wars** of 1912–13 led to the loss of almost all of the Ottoman territories in eastern Europe), commitment to the Empire withered in the face of rival nationalist ideologies. The Young Turks promoted their Union and Progress Party, but factional rivalries weakened their unity. During the First World War, while the Young Turks aligned themselves with Germany, the Ottoman Empire continued to lose ground, but with the surrender of the Turkish forces in 1918, the Committee for Union and Progress also disintegrated. The allies moved their forces into **Constantinople** in violation of the Mudros Armistice Agreement and held the Sultan virtually as a prisoner. However, the Young Turks were now led by **Mustafa Kemal Atatürk**, the military hero of the Gallipoli campaign. He rallied opposition to European intervention and established a new Turkish government in **Ankara**. He declared an end to the Ottoman Empire and proclaimed a new Turkish Republic. The Young Turks under Atatürk abolished the Ottoman sultanate as well as the Islamic **caliphate**, and embarked on a process of modernization and reform founded on Turkish nationalism and ideas of revolution from above.

Yousef, Ramzi Ahmed

British-educated Islamist who masterminded the 1993 bombing of the **World Trade Center**. For a time he was considered by the US Federal Bureau of Investigation to be 'the most dangerous man in the world'. Having become the object of a world-wide manhunt, Yousef bombed a Philippines Airlines flight and an Iranian temple. He also made plans to destroy 11 US planes over the Pacific, to attack the US **Central Intelligence Agency** headquarters using a light aircraft armed with chemical weapons, and to assassinate US President **Clinton**, Pope John Paul II, and other world leaders. He was arrested in Pakistan in February 1995 while staying at one of **Osama bin Laden**'s 'guesthouses' in Peshawar. Extradited to the USA, he was convicted of conspiracy in a US federal court in November 1997 and sentenced to life imprisonment without the possibility of parole.

Yuldeshev, Tohir

Political head of the **Islamic Movement of Uzbekistan**. Believed to be hiding in Pakistan after the fall of the **Taliban** in Afghanistan.

Z

Zaghlul Saad

Zaghlul Pasha, born of peasant stock but educated. He was appointed as Egypt's Minister of Education in 1905. The leader of the Egyptian nationalists who formed a delegation (Wafd) to travel to London, United Kingdom, to negotiate Egyptian independence, he formed the first political party in Egypt, the **Wafd Party**. A form of political independence was achieved in February 1922 when Egypt was recognized as a separate sovereign state, although Britain retained significant powers. Upon independence Zaghlul emerged as undisputed leader of the Wafd Party and, following elections, became Egypt's first Prime Minister. By the end of his career he had become the living symbol of the Egyptian independence movement and its aspirations

Zahal

Hebrew acronym for Zvai Haganah LeIsrael (ZaHaL). An Israeli defence force.

Zahedi, Fazlullah (1897–1963)

Iranian Prime Minister in 1953–55.

Zahir Shah, Mohammed (1914–)

Former King of Afghanistan. Born in **Kabul** in 1914, Zahir Shah was educated in France and was only 19 when he ascended the throne in 1933 after his father was assassinated. During the early years of his reign power was actually exercised by his uncles, who ruled the country through the powerful office of Prime Minister. Throughout the Second World War and afterwards the King helped maintain the country's neutrality. In 1953 his cousin, Mohammed Daud, became Premier, but Zahir Shah forced his resignation in 1963, after which he began to assert his own power to the full. In 1964 he promulgated reforms, which provided for a parliament, elections and a free press. Members of the royal family were also banned from holding public office. Political parties, while not strictly legal, were tolerated. Social reforms included attempts to improve the status of **women**. Foreign **aid** flowed from both east and west but, apart from roads and irrigation projects, this help made little impact outside the Kabul area. In July 1973, while he was receiving medical treatment in Italy, Zahir Shah was ousted in a coup orchestrated by his cousin. He remained in exile until 2001 when, following the fall of the **Taliban** regime, he returned to Afghanistan to act as the symbolic 'father of the nation'.

Zaidis

The Zaidis are a liberal and moderate sect of the **Shi'a**, close enough to the **Sunni** to refer to themselves as that sect's 'Fifth School'. They number perhaps 3m. Their name derives from a grandson of al-Hussein bin 'Ali (second son of 'Ali) whom they recognize as the fifth imam. Zaidism is the dominant form of **Islam** in Yemen, its main centres being **San'a** and Dhamar.

Zaim system

In **Arabic** *zaim* means 'patron'. In Lebanon the term refers to the paternalistic leaders of the landed gentry, tribal and religious groups. In Morocco it is used for the system of patronage which identifies the king as the supreme *zaim*.

Zaim, Hosni

Syrian President whose proposal for peace with Israel was rejected by Israeli Prime Minister **David Ben-Gurion.**

Zakat (Zakât, Zakaat, Zakah)

The third of the **Five Pillars of Islam**. The literal meaning of the term is 'to grow (in goodness)' or 'increase', 'purifying' or 'making pure', but is commonly known as charity. It is prescribed in the **Koran**: 'And what you give in usury, so that it may increase through (other) people's wealth it does not increase with Allah, but what you give in Zakaat, seeking Allah's Pleasure, then it is those who shall gain reward manifold ...' (30:39)

Zaki, Mohammed

Elected in January 1946 as president of the state of Mahabad (**Kurdistan**) established by the Soviet Union during its occupation of north-western Iran in 1945–46. Following the Soviet withdrawal, the Iranian army reoccupied the area. Zaki Mohammed was seized, charged with treason and executed. Kurdistan was reabsorbed within greater Iran and the Kurdish national movement scattered by the Shah's forces.

az-Zarkawi, Abu Musa

An **al-Qa'ida** leader who spent some time in Iraq.

az-Zawahiri, Ayman

Leader of the Egyptian **Islamic Jihad**, also a founding member of **al-Qa'ida**. Zawahiri has reportedly had a huge impact on **Osama bin Laden**'s thinking—politically, militarily and religiously. At about this time, the terror war essentially turned into a religious war: the fundamental Islamic militants versus the world, with the USA, Saudi Arabia and Egypt being the prime targets. In essence, Zawahiri became bin Laden's political thinker, religious leader, organizer and planner. Because Zawahiri could not reverse the trend toward his main target, Egypt, he managed to convince bin Laden that the principal target for disruption was the USA because of its interference in the **Middle East**—particularly in Egypt and Saudi Arabia. Both Zawahiri and bin Laden sought to bring about a world dominated by their brand of **Islam**. The seeds were planted in Saudi Arabia, Egypt, Somalia, Yemen, Afghanistan, and, because of its geographic location and religious bent, Pakistan. Bin Laden had access to the necessary funding for the group's activities, while Zawahiri had the knowledge, experience, and organizational abilities to carry out those activities. Over the years the Egyptian Jihad groups had gained experience in secret work, cell building and organization. Their ranks were populated with well-trained scientists, engineers, medical personnel and seasoned fighters. Because of their talent and experience, these Egyptian Jihad groups took control of al-Qa'ida Egyptian Jihad. It is important to note that Zawahiri places a high premium on recruiting well-educated individuals. Those interested in joining al-Qa'ida Egyptian Jihad were subjected to a battery of tests, which were basically intelligence tests. Those who scored well were chosen and trained in special camps, while those who performed poorly were sent to more basic boot camps.

Zayed, Sheikh

President of the Federation of United Arab Emirates since its formation in December 1971 and Ruler of Abu Dhabi. Sheikh **Zayed** has been re-elected by the Supreme Council at successive five-year intervals and remains President. Born around 1918 (the date is uncertain) in Abu Dhabi, Sheikh Zayed is the youngest of the four sons of Sheikh Sultan bin Zayed an-Nahyan, Ruler of Abu Dhabi from 1922 until 1926.

Zéroual, Liamine

A former general who was brought out of retirement to serve as President of Algeria from January 1994, after the assassination of **Mohammed Boudiaf**. Zéroual was elected as President in November 1995 and remained in office until April 1999. He presided over the period of most intense conflict in Algeria since the declaration of a state of emergency in 1992. He fielded a succession of governments of varying political complexions, all of which implemented **International Monetary Fund** programmes agreed in May 1995 out of necessity, but without any vision of comprehensive reform, much less of political institutions to sustain it. While macroeconomic indicators showed improvements, the state of the real economy deteriorated and the country remained gripped by political conflict. In 1999 Zéroual was replaced by **Abdelaziz Bouteflika** after all six of his rivals in the presidential election withdrew, alleging electoral fraud.

Zion

Zion was the name of the hill south-west of the Old City of **Jerusalem**, venerated particularly for the tomb of David, acknowledged by Muslims as Abi Dawud.

Zionism

Zionism is, broadly, a set of beliefs according to which the State of Israel is the legitimate, God-given and exclusive homeland for the Jews. Zionism found its first expression in 1882, when a group of European Jews calling themselves the 'Lovers of Zion' adopted the term. The Zionist movement as such grew largely out of the labours of a Hungarian Jewish journalist, **Theodor Herzl**, who had reported the trial of Alfred Dreyfus, a French Jew wrongfully accused of passing secrets to Germany. The case revealed considerable anti-Semitism and in 1896 Herzl published a book (*The Jewish State*) that called for the establishment of a homeland for Jews that would provide a refuge from discrimination and injustice. Zionism has always been controversial, even among Jews. So strong was the opposition of German orthodox and reform rabbis to the Zionist idea, that Herzl changed the venue of the first world Zionist Congress in 1897 from Munich to Basle, Switzerland. Twenty years later, in November 1917, when Arthur Balfour, the British foreign secretary, made a commitment to establish a homeland for the Jews in Palestine, his declaration (the **Balfour Declaration**) was delayed by leading figures in the British Jewish community. Two hundred delegates attended the first Congress, established the **Zionist Organization** (later the World Zionist Organization) and drafted an action programme 'to create for the Jewish people a home in Palestine secured by public law'. Significant Jewish **migration** to 'the Holy Land' had already begun at the beginning of the 1880s, and by 1903, at the end of the first *aliyah* ('wave' reaching Zion), approximately 25,000 Jews had settled in Palestine. By the outbreak of the First World War, at the end of the second *aliyah*, the Zionist movement had begun to fulfil its objectives, with a further 40,000 Jewish immigrants in Palestine. The Jewish pioneers and settlers established characteristic 'frontier' communities (*kibbutzim*), usually on land purchased from absentee Arab landlords with money raised in Europe through donations and philanthropic contributions. During the First World War the Jewish population of Palestine declined, but the Balfour Declaration (which promised to support the idea of a homeland for Jews in Palestine), followed by the defeat of the **Ottoman Empire**, created renewed hope for further **settlement** within the Zionist movement. The third *aliyah* followed in the wake of the First World War, and between 1919 and 1923 a further 35,000 Jews settled in the region. The fourth *aliyah* (1930 and 1931) added another 82,000, while the fifth *aliyah* (1932–38), provoked by the persecution of Jews in Germany under the National Socialists, increased the Jewish population of Palestine by 217,000. By 1938 the total Jewish population of Palestine was around 413,000. While not all of the Jews who migrated to Palestine were formally members of the Zionist movement, still less of the Zionist Organization, the vast majority were Zionists, in that they believed a homeland for the Jews in Palestine to be in some sense 'God-given', and not simply the consequence of social and political events and structures. What was different about Zionism from most indigenous nationalist ideologies and movements in the **Middle East** was, first, that the territory identified as the homeland (Zion) was a distant land requiring migration and settlement, and, second, that it was already inhabited. In that sense, it more closely resembles the nationalism of the Afrikaaners in South Africa or of the early pioneers in America. Indeed, the combination of pioneering, settlement, 'establishing' a nation and confronting an increasingly hostile indigenous population is shared by all three of these examples of European settlement. Similarities can also be identified in the history of the settlement of Canada, Australia, Rhodesia and other 'colonial' territories.

Zionist Congress

The first Zionist congress was convened in Basle, Switzerland, in 1897 by **Theodor Herzl** (1860–1904). It established the **Zionist Organization**, later called the World Zionist Organisation. The Congress adopted a statement setting out the aims of **Zionism** and a programme for the realization of those aims.

Zionist Labour Alliance (ZLA)

One of several Zionist organizations in the USA which lobby on behalf of Israel. The ZLA has particular strength among the labour unions.

Zionist Labour Federation – *see* Histadrut

Zionist Organization

Established by Zionists at the First **Zionist Congress** in 1897. Later, with a growing Jewish diaspora across the world, its name was changed to the World Zionist Organization.

Zionist Organization of America

The Zionist Organization of America is a branch of the World Zionist Organization, which has its headquarters in Israel. Other Zionist organizations in the USA include the Zionist Labour Alliance and the America Jewish Women's Organization, or Hadassah.

Ziraat Bankasi

Turkish public-sector agricultural bank that holds one-quarter of Turkey's commercial bank deposits. Ziraat is also the government's principal patronage vehicle for rallying votes from the countryside.

Zoroaster or Zarathustra

A religious teacher believed to have lived in Persia some time between 700 and 550 BC. **Zoroastrianism** was later adopted as the official religion of the Persian Empire and remained the predominant religion until the coming of **Islam**. Zoroaster remained a symbolic spiritual and religious figure for those who did not convert to Islam after AD 637 when the Persian Sassanids were defeated by the Arabs at the battle of Qadissiyya. Many adherents of Zoroastrianism were forced by persecution to emigrate and the main centre of the faith is now Mumbai in India, where its followers are known as Parsees (Persians).

Zoroastrianism

A gnostic religious tradition. Technically a monotheistic faith, it also retains some elements of earlier **polytheism** and later became associated with fire-worship. Its adherents—mainly in Iran and India—follow the teachings of **Zoroaster**.

Zoroastrians

Followers of the Zoroastrian religion. A significant **minority** group—there are perhaps some 28,000—in Iran. Their ancient centre was in Yazd, which contains five fire temples and remains a centre for this faith. The main centre of the faith is now Mumbai in India, where its adherents are known as Parsees (Persians).

Abu Zubayda

An **al-Qa'ida** leader. Chief of external operations and one of the most senior organizers. He was arrested in Faisalabad by the Pakistani **Inter-Services Intelligence**, acting on information received from the US Federal Bureau of Investigation in March 2002. He was succeeded within al-Qa'ida by Sheikh Mohammed Khalid.

Selected References

The Middle East and North Africa. London, Europa Publications, annually.

Rashid, Ahmed. *Taliban: militant Islam, oil and fundamentalism in central Asia*. New Haven, CT, Yale University Press, 2000.

Richards, A., and Waterbury, J. *A Political Economy of the Middle East*. Boulder, CO, Westview Press, 2nd edition, 1996.

Arab Human Development Report, 2000. New York, Regional Bureau for Arab States, United Nations Development Programme and Arab Fund for Economic and Social Development, 2002.